BURTON F. PORTER

DREXEL UNIVERSITY

Reasons for Living

A Basic Ethics

MACMILLAN PUBLISHING COMPANY

NEW YORK

Note on the Author

In addition to the present work, Burton F. Porter has written or edited several books, mainly in the field of ethics. His publications include The Good Life, Alternatives in Ethics *(New York: Macmillan Publishing Co., 1980),* Personal Philosophy, Perspectives on Living *(New York: Harcourt Brace Jovanovich, 1976),* Philosophy, A Literary and Conceptual Approach *(New York: Harcourt Brace Jovanovich, 1974, rev. 1980), and* Deity and Morality, With Regard to the Naturalistic Fallacy *(London: George Allen and Unwin, Ltd., and New York: Humanities Press, 1968). Dr. Porter received his graduate education at St. Andrews University, Scotland, and Oxford University, England, and is currently Professor of Philosophy and Head of the Department of Humanities and Communications at Drexel University in Philadelphia.*

Copyright © 1988, Macmillan Publishing Company,
a division of Macmillan, Inc.

PRINTED IN THE UNITED STATES OF AMERICA

Macmillan Publishing Company
866 Third Avenue, New York, New York 10022

Collier Macmillan Canada, Inc.

LIBRARY OF CONGRESS CATALOGING-IN-PUBLICATION DATA

Porter, Burton Frederick.
  Reasons for living.

  Includes bibliographies and index.
  1. Ethics. 2. Life. I. Title.
BJ1012.P68 1988   170   87-12230
ISBN 0-02-396050-7

Printing: 4 5 6 7   Year: 1 2 3 4

ISBN 0-02-396050-7

for my son Mark Graham
to enhance his life
through clarity and awareness

*To know the chief rival attitudes toward life
as the history of thinking has developed them,
and to have heard some of the reasons they can give
for themselves ought to be considered an essential
part of liberal education.*

William James

Preface

Reasons for Living is not intended as an antidote to suicide except insofar as having an ideal in life can justify existence. Rather, it is a critical survey of the various ethical theories as to what constitutes a worthwhile life.

The book is meant to explore the major systems of normative ethics, the principal ideals that have been proposed and elaborated throughout philosophic history as to the summum bonum, the highest good and ultimate end of living. For people have always felt the need to find some reason for being, a raison d'etre that can be affirmed as the underlying purpose of their existence. Just being alive is not enough. We do not want to drift aimlessly, experiencing a disconnected series of sensations; rather, we want to use our time meaningfully, to live in terms of some concept of a valuable life. No matter how caught up we are with daily activities, there are moments when we pause and reflect upon the overall purpose behind all that we do. We ask What for?—and with that question enter into the realm of philosophic reflection on the goal in living.

This book is intended to help in answering that fundamental question by presenting the major theories offered by philosophers in their systems of ethics. Each theory is described and elaborated, with excerpts from the principal thinkers who originated them, then carefully analyzed as a possible life ideal.

The goal of maximizing pleasure or happiness is discussed in the views of the Cyrenaics and the Epicureans, respectively; the first endorsing an uninhibited hedonism, the second a more intellectual mode of enjoyment. The altruistic theories of the English Utilitarians are then examined, the "greatest happiness for the greatest number" philosophies of Jeremy Bentham and John Stuart Mill. Next, the doctrine of self-realization is presented in terms of actualizing one's individual potential and, in the Aristotelian version, of developing one's humanness. Following that, an exposition of naturalism is given, ranging from the "back to nature" movement to the evolutionary ethic of Social Darwinism. The championing of the rational life is investigated in the Stoic notion of mental fortitude and in Platonic reasonableness, and subsequently the very formalistic ethic of Immanuel Kant and Christianity is studied. Finally, the humanistic ideal of promoting the good of mankind is examined, both in the form of scientific humanism and in its existential expression.

As a preliminary step, in Part I, a critical analysis is made of three claims that undermine the credibility of any of these ethical theories: relativism, the view that no genuine knowledge is possible because every judgment is merely a reflection of one's culture and personal attitudes; egoism, that everyone always acts in terms of his own advantage; and determinism, that no free choices can ever be made since one's decisions are the necessary result of prior factors and wholly beyond one's control. Each of these claims is criticized in order to clear the ground for the discussion of the various theories of a good life that constitute the heart of the book.

We are involved, then, in an exploration of ideals in living, a study that falls within the philosophic field of ethics. It is not the whole of ethics but a traditional part that is receiving increased attention today. More precisely, we are concerned with questions of the good rather than the right in ethics, and that distinction needs to be explained.

The *good* means a worthwhile goal in living of the kind just described. Whatever a person regards as being of fundamental importance in his life, the pivotal value around which he ranges his activities constitutes his idea of the good. However, the ethicist will not simply accept an assertion that a particular goal is worthwhile; he insists upon solid justification for the claim. For the good is not just that to which we do aspire but that to which we should aspire. It is the truly important end of living and not just a life-style that reflects the current trends and by definition will one day be out of fashion. Therefore what a person considers supremely valuable must be supported with very good reasons.

The *right*, by contrast, refers to actions or conduct that is ethically correct. For example, a philosopher might defend the rightness of honoring commitments or respecting human life and argue against taking someone else's property or violating trust by telling a lie. He might endorse principles such as paying one's debts or treating others fairly and condemn adultery or deceit or exploitation of people's ignorance. Whatever judgment is made, it is acts that are referred to as right or wrong; goals inhabit a separate category and can only be judged good or bad. The same care must be taken in assessing the validity of claims but, in the case of the right, human behavior is involved not overall ideals of life.

Having made this distinction and located our study within the branch of philosophy called *ethics*, a further point needs to be made. Whether we are dealing with the right or the good, ethical questions differ from other kinds of questions in significant ways. For they are about merit and worth, what is valuable and deserving of praise and emulation. Aesthetic value can mean the attractiveness of a work of art, economic value the market price of a product, but ethical value means the moral desirability of a mode of conduct or way of life.

In ethics one uses terms such as *praiseworthy* and *blameworthy*, *fair* and *unfair*, *excusable* and *inexcusable*, *virtues* and *vices*, *worthwhile* and *worthless*, *noble* and *base*, *commendable* and *deplorable*. One asks when someone has lived well and when badly, what ought we to do and what should we avoid, what is cause for shame and, in the end, how are we to judge. This is the vocabulary of ethics and it revolves around the notion of moral worth. (It should be added that frequent reference is made to a valuable life for *man* or *mankind*, for the individual in *his* personal existence. These are obviously not intended as gender terms but refer to the entire human race.)

Finally, in the process of evaluation we are not concerned with the psychological motives that might impel someone to accept a principle or ideal but only with the justification for what is chosen. For example, one person might want to adopt an ethic of duty, another a goal of pleasure, in each case because it satisfies some emotional need. However, the only philosophical question is whether the theory is worthwhile, not satisfying or persuasive but sound and defensible.

In this book therefore we will not just be looking for what would constitute a good reason for living but for good reasons for deciding the question. We want to examine the numerous definitions of an ideal existence that have been proposed, to weigh the arguments given for their acceptance, and finally to reach some conclusions with regard to our own lives. For this is not just a disinterested study but something important to us, practically and concretely. As Plato remarked in *The Republic*, "no light matter is at stake; the question concerns the very manner in which human life is to be lived."

B.F.P.

Contents

PART I

Preliminary Problems

CHAPTER 1

Relativism

Knowledge: Thinking Makes It So

In setting out to discuss and evaluate the various reasons for living, an initial stumbling block must be cleared away. This takes the form of a philosophic position known as *relativism* which maintains that genuine knowledge is impossible, that no one can judge which ideas are actually true any more than we can know which actions are really right or which values are genuinely worth holding. It is an individual or societal matter, the relativist maintains, varying enormously among cultures and wholly dependent upon one's perspective. What is true to one person is false to another, what is valuable to the European may not matter to the African, and what people died for in the Middle Ages may be irrelevant today. All standards and judgments, it is thought, relate to a particular context and have no general validity outside that sphere. Therefore, to deliberate about which beliefs are actually worthwhile is a futile and meaningless exercise. It is all relative to the time, and place, and the person.

The relativist will point out, for example, that the Eskimos practice euthanasia, pushing their old people under the ice if they cannot keep up with the hunting party, whereas in Japan the old are supremely venerated; even after death one's ancestors continue to command a respect bordering on worship. The obvious lesson is that honoring thy father and mother is not a universal value but a relative one, depending upon the society that does the judging. The same point can be made by considering marriage customs. In various cultures it is wrong for men to have only one wife, for unmarried women to have their faces unveiled, for blood relations not to marry one another, for women to enter marriage as virgins, or for wives not to throw themselves on their husband's funeral pyre.

To take an example from science, between 140 A.D. and 1543 A.D. the Ptolemaic theory was the prevalent position in astronomy. The heavenly bodies were thought to be geocentric, with the sun revolving around the earth.[1] However, after the sixteenth century, the Copernican theory became the dominant scientific view. The heavens were then thought to be heliocentric, with the earth revolving around the sun along with all the other planets. Again the conclusion must be that knowledge is relative. What was thought correct at one period of history was considered ignorant at another, and if we can say that something used to be true then truth is a function of the time and nothing is true for all times.

Perhaps the most obvious example of relativism occurs in the field of art. Picasso's *Guernica*, for instance, is a protest against war and more specifically a memorial to those who died in the Spanish Civil War. However, it is severely fragmented in style, depicting tortured, broken figures in a modern abstract composition. To some people the painting is moving and forceful, to others it is a bad joke, and anyone living prior to this century would regard it as grotesque or incomprehensible. Who is right? Everyone is right, the relativist says, because art is just a matter of taste and beauty is in the eye of the beholder.

Whether we are dealing with moral values, scientific theories, or aesthetic judgments the same message emerges: It's all relative. In everyday life we repeat this belief to each other continually when we say "That may be good to you but it's not good to me; it's all a matter of opinion" or "What gives you the right to judge?" or "Who is to say?" This sentiment is echoed by Shakespeare in *Hamlet* when he wrote "There is nothing either good or bad, but thinking makes it so," by Pontius Pilate when he asked rhetorically What is truth? and by the Romans in the succinct saying *de gustibus non est disputandum* ("there is no disputing about tastes"). The implication in all these statements is that whatever people believe to be true is true for them, and that is the end of the matter. No one can say differently because there is no external authority to which an objective appeal can be made.

Sources for Relativism

This view is extremely prevalent today and it appears to have originated from at least four sources. First, there is our desire to practice *tolerance*, to take a liberal, open-minded approach toward other people's ideas—including those that are different. Everyone has a right to his own opinion we say. In making that claim we mean that one person's opinion is as valuable as another's, and in a democratic society every citizen has a right to be heard. We refuse to maintain that our own beliefs are correct and other people are wrong because such an attitude smacks of smugness and pronouncements ex cathedra. We are wary of individuals who are sure they are right because inquisitions, pogroms, and purges emanate from that kind of arrogance.

A second source of relativism lies in the desire to maximize our *freedom of choice*. If there are objective truths and correct moral principles, then we are obliged to acknowledge them whether we like it or not. This places enormous limits on our autonomy, whereas if there is no external reality that could be known to us, if we could judge right and wrong in purely personal terms, then our range of choices would be considerably wider. All decisions would then be based on personal preferences not objective facts, and we would have a great deal more latitude in choosing our beliefs and the lives we want to lead.

A third basis for relativism consists in the *intellectual uncertainty* we feel today in saying that any statement is really true. This is partly due to the scientific approach to knowledge—a method that in our century has all but eclipsed every other way of gaining understanding. According to the scientific attitude we should constantly analyze and criticize our assumptions because knowledge is only probable at best and never absolute. Our most cherished beliefs today could be proven wrong by new evidence tomorrow, so that the proper stance toward any idea should be one of hesitation and skepticism.

This readiness to doubt has carried over to all the ideals, values, and presuppositions of our society, placing them under continual examination and suspicion. Added to this scientific caution is the specific theory of relativity advanced by Einstein, which assumes space and time to be relative not absolute phenomena. Whatever implications Einstein's theory holds for physics, many academics took it as scientific evidence for the relativity of all knowledge, especially moral knowledge. The effect was to reinforce the notion that everything depends upon a person's point of view.

Our *awareness of diversity* is a fourth and final source of relativism. We are acutely aware of the multiplicity of societies in the world, each with its own set of beliefs, and these diverse systems of thought make us extremely doubtful about the correctness of our own ideas. In addition, we are highly conscious of the number of ideas that have proven false in human history, whether scientific theories, political doctrines, or religious beliefs, so that at this point in time we are very chary about making any truth-claims whatsoever.

In the light of such understanding, it seems presumptuous to state any opinion with deep confidence and whatever we do maintain is hedged about with a dozen qualifications. The sense of being positive about what we say has now been lost and a general tentativeness prevails because we are so conscious that every statement is potentially false. Revolutions in thought and values have occurred far too often for us to be self-satisfied about any of the ideas we hold and we are aware of the many societies that hold beliefs very different from our own. History and geography have taught us a lesson in humility. We feel that the only honest approach is to be relativistic and say "This seems right to people at this time and place or to me here and now." Anything else seems dogmatic and egotistical.

All of these factors, then, feed into the relativist position and make it a contemporary and attractive view to hold: the desire to be tolerant and to maximize our freedom of choice, and our intellectual uncertainty and awareness of cultural diversity.

Values: When in Rome . . .

When the general relativist position is applied solely to the field of ethics it takes the form of claiming that all value judgments are a reflection of personal and societal attitudes. From a relativist standpoint someone who judges stealing to be wrong is only expressing a personal distaste for stealing or reporting the fact that his society disapproves of it. He is not telling us anything about the nature of stealing or recognizing any inherent wrongdoing in taking someone else's property. The same is said to be true of a person who praises courage, loyalty, justice, patriotism, or compassion. Some of these values are more widespread than others but none is universal and each varies according to the society's perspective. To the relativist all moral evaluations are considered to be arbitrary preferences, depending entirely upon the individual, the situation, the culture, and the times. Conflicting ethical positions could be equally valid.

Within this ethical realm, a distinction may be made between relativism and subjectivism. When this is done, *subjectivism* refers to the theory that all ethical evaluations merely reflect the preferences of the person. They do not necessarily describe social attitudes and they certainly do not identify any qualities intrinsic to an act; they merely express the feelings of the individual. If those feelings were different, then the values would also be different. For example, to state that keeping promises is important means nothing more than that the person likes promise-keeping and perhaps that he wishes everyone else did also.[2] It may give him a sense of security, the positive self-image that says he is someone to be trusted, and the confident feeling that he can depend upon other people when they give their word. Whatever the motivation may be, the moral judgment is nothing more than an autobiographical statement; it tells us something about the psychology of the speaker but nothing about the nature of the act.

Subjectivism differs from relativism then by emphasizing the personal nature of ethical evaluations. In other words, the subjectivist interprets a value judgment to mean "*X* suits my taste, it appeals to me," whereas the relativist views it as a report that "our society approves of *X*."

In contrast to both theories ethical *objectivism* maintains that certain actions really are right and others are wrong, that some goals in living are inherently worth seeking and others are worthless. That is, the objectivist maintains that ethical standards do exist and that judgments can legitimately be made about human conduct. These standards are thought to be transcultural, objective, and unchanging and for that reason authoritative in settling disagreements about right and wrong, good and bad.

For example, the judgment Women should not be treated as inferior to men could be assumed to be an objectively true proposition. Or Slavery is unjust could be taken as an accurate evaluation of the institution of slavery. In neither case, according to the objectivist, are we simply describing our society's attitudes or evincing our personal dislikes; we are making judgments about the offensiveness of these practices. An objectivist might also assert the intrinsic worth of generosity, pity, or trust and the intrinsic wrongness of deceit, theft, or torture. Such evaluations could also be considered insights into the nature of these actions.

The objectivist does not maintain that he has certain knowledge of the objective standards but only that there are such standards to be known. He will admit that a perfect understanding of moral principles is impossible but he takes this as his ideal and measures his progress by the degree to which he gains moral awareness. He argues against the relativist and subjectivist: Because no one can know everything about right and wrong conduct, it does not follow that no knowledge is possible or that one person's opinion is as good as another's.

In the same way that we can differentiate between ethical relativism and objectivism, a distinction can be made between ethical objectivism and and a logical extension of that position called *universalism*. The theory of universalism maintains that actions that are intrinsically right are forever right. That is, an act that can be judged right in itself therefore is right for all people, at all times, and in all places. For example, if we value respect for another person's bodily integrity and this belief is a truly valid principle, then it holds true everywhere and for everyone. Consequently, the violent act of rape, which denies the factor of consent and violates a person's body, is wrong whenever it occurs.

The universalist is actually carrying objectivism one step further, asserting universality to intrinsically correct values. In linguistic terms it is the claim that "right" implies "ought": Whatever is right should always be done. It would be very odd, the universalist thinks, to claim that an act is valuable but to deny that everyone ought to do it. It would be equally peculiar to claim that an act is wrong in one place yet right in another (e.g., rape), or that something formerly wrong has become right. The moral nature of actions does not change even if our perception of them does. The difficult part lies in recognizing their essential nature and making value judgments that are correct in terms of that reality. But at least we have to assume that conduct correctly judged as right or wrong would be so absolutely and universally.

The lines of disagreement are thereby drawn, with the relativist and subjectivist on one side and the objectivist and universalist on the other. But which position is correct? Are there values that transcend time and place, are things right in themselves, or are all values arbitrary and dependent upon one's society or personal temperament? Can one make something trivial important by taking it seriously? Is an action right if people think it so or could people be mistaken in their moral judgments? Could an ideal be valuable whether or not anyone realizes it? Does conduct become right because of society's beliefs or could a society be wrong in what it believes, holding various acts to be commendable when in fact they are abominable?

Relativism in Greek Philosophy

In intellectual history the debate over this question goes back at least as far as Plato (c. 427–347 B.C.). We will discuss Plato's broader views later, but during that period of history there were a group of Greek thinkers who were known as Sophists—itinerant philosophers who taught the skills of practical success. They often were accused of being persuasive rather than logical in their reasoning and more concerned with their fees than with the integrity of teaching. (Sophistry, in fact, has become a name for fallacious arguments that have the appearance of being correct.) The important point for our purposes is that they shared a common belief in relativism and were the first philosophers to hold such a position.

In Plato's most famous dialogue, *The Republic*, a celebrated discussion takes place between Socrates and a Sophist named Thrasymachus over the issue of justice, and as the dialogue proceeds it comes to include the larger issue of ethical relativism. Socrates, who is either a spokesman for Plato's ideas or the person whose words Plato recorded, asks for a sound definition of justice. Thrasymachus replies that "justice is nothing else than the interest of the stronger." He then elaborates upon his position in political terms by saying

> "have you never heard that forms of government differ; there are tyrannies, and there are democracies, and there are aristocracies?"
> "Yes, I know." Socrates replies.
> "And the government is the ruling power in each state?"
> "Certainly."
> "And the different forms of government make laws democratical, aristocratical, tyrannical, with a view to their several interests; and these laws, which are made by them for their own interests, are the justice which they deliver to their subjects,

and him who transgresses them they punish as a breaker of the law, and unjust. And that is what I mean when I say that in all states there is the same principle of justice, which is the interest of the government; and as the government must be supposed to have power, the only reasonable conclusion is, that everywhere there is one principle of justice, which is the interest of the stronger."[3]

In this passage Thrasymachus claims that might makes right; whatever laws a government has the power to enforce thereby become just because of that power. Justice changes then according to the various forms of governments that are established and is wholly relative to the rulers' interests.

The Sophist Gorgias is another early representative of relativism and he expressed his views in three propositions for which he is renowned. The first proposition consists of the bald pronouncement that right and wrong have no objective validity. If an action were right then we would be morally bound to perform it whenever the occasion arose. But because ethical values are merely the product of tradition and custom, right and wrong have no claim upon us. There are only actions that further our purposes and those that obstruct our self-interest.

The second proposition is that even if there were universal standards of right and wrong we could never have knowledge of them. We can only accept the moral ideas that we have experienced in our own nation and are never able to transcend the limitations of that cultural experience. Different peoples hold different values because of the beliefs that prevail in their particular social environments and to escape into a realm of objective understanding is utterly impossible.

Gorgias addresses a final eventuality in his third proposition, that even if objective standards existed and they could be grasped by exceptional individuals such truths could never be communicated. For no one would be receptive to new insights that were at variance with the accepted customs and beliefs. The discoverers of such ideas would be shunned or persecuted as dangerous radicals, and their ideas would be condemned as heresy.[4]

These three propositions — that values do not exist, that if they did exist they would be unknowable, and that if they were knowable they would be incommunicable — clearly place Gorgias in the relativist camp. In an overall sense he is convinced that right and wrong are terms that merely reflect our personal advantage; to think otherwise, he believes, is hypocrisy.

Besides Thrasymachus and Gorgias, another Sophist named Protagoras appears to have been the father of the group as well as the most eminent and powerful spokesman for the relativist position. He is referred to as the Great Sophist and one of Plato's dialogues, named the *Protagoras*, offers a very sympathetic rendering of his views.

It was Protagoras who said, "Man is the measure of all things, of the existence of the things that are and the nonexistence of the things that are not." This *Homo Mensura* or Man–Measure theory was derived from Protagoras' views about perception. In the dialogue the *Theaetetus* Plato attributes to him the paradigm of the wind, which can be expressed as follows: When a wind blows it will be felt by a person with fever as chilly but to another person it will be perceived as refreshing. Now if the same wind can appear both chilly and refreshing, then the wind itself does not possess qualities but is what it appears to be to each person.

The same is true of the perception of tastes, textures, colors, aromas, and sounds. (This point sometimes is expressed by saying that to an ant silk is rough and a pin drop loud.)

Protagoras applies the same principle to moral values. Whether a child speaks Greek or Persian, he says, depends on the nation in which he is born, and by the same token, whether one believes in abandoning unwanted babies to die is a cultural accident. So long as a person holds certain beliefs they are true to him, for right and wrong are whatever we say they are.[5]

Relativism in Modern Philosophy

The relativist position did not die with the ancient thinkers. It has been argued by numerous philosophers throughout history and continues to be affirmed to the present day. Some of the most notable figures in the relativist camp were Thomas Hobbes (1588–1679), Benedict Spinoza (1632–1677), David Hume 1711–1776), and more contemporaneously the Pragmatists William James (1842–1910) and John Dewey (1859–1952), A. J. Ayer (1910–) the chief spokesman for Logical Positivism, and Jean-Paul Sartre (1905–1980) the dean of French Existentialism. Even the British philosopher Bertrand Russell at one time expressed a relativist position when he said, "there can be no such thing as 'sin' in any absolute sense; what one man calls 'sin' another may call 'virtue,' and though they may dislike each other on account of this difference, neither can convict the other of intellectual error."[6] It would be useful therefore to examine some of the arguments they offer, taking Hume as a representative of what is termed *modern* philosophy and A. J. Ayer as an example of contemporary philosophic thinking.

David Hume held a position of ethical relativism in the eighteenth century but from a very different standpoint than that of Thrasymachus. In the following celebrated passage from his book *An Enquiry Concerning Human Understanding* Hume first divides genuine knowledge into two categories:

> All the objects of human reason or inquiry may naturally be divided into two kinds, to wit, *Relations of Ideas*, and *Matters of Fact*. Of the first kind are the sciences of Geometry, Algebra, and Arithmetic; and in short, every affirmation which is either intuitively or demonstratively certain. *That the square of the hypothenuse is equal to the square of the two sides*, is a proposition which expresses a relation between these figures. *That three times five is equal to the half of thirty*, expresses a relation between these numbers. Propositions of this kind are discoverable by the mere operation of thought, without dependence on what is anywhere existent in the universe. Though there never were a circle or a triangle in nature, the truths demonstrated by Euclid would forever retain their certainty and evidence.
>
> Matters of fact, which are the second objects of human reason, are not ascertained in the same manner; nor is our evidence of their truth, however great, of a like nature with the foregoing. The contrary of every matter of fact is still possible; because it can never imply a contradiction, and is conceived by the mind with the same facility and distinctness, as if ever so conformable to reality. *That the sun will not rise tomorrow* is no less intelligible a proposition, and implies no more contradiction than the affirmation, *that it will rise. . . .* [7]

To paraphrase and update Hume's distinction, relations of ideas are judged according to the meaning of the terms involved. The sentence All circles are round is a true statement because part of the meaning of the term *circle* is that it is a round figure; the predicate of the sentence is contained in the subject. Because of the logic of the two concepts and their relation, we can assert that the proposition is true. The same can be said of All bachelors are unmarried males; All murals are on walls; and All mammals breathe air. These statements may be obvious and trivial but they also are necessarily true; the conceptual relationship makes them undeniable.

Matters of fact, on the other hand, are not established by examining the logic but by determining whether the proposition accurately describes the external world. For example, the truth of the statement All fish have dorsal fins cannot be determined by analyzing the concept of fish to see whether having dorsal fins is implied. Rather, we would have to check the facts. We might consult an ichthyologist, refer to a text on marine biology, or conduct a study ourselves of every species of fish. Whatever steps we took to find out, we would be comparing the statement to what is actually the case in the world.

Hume, incidentally, maintains that matters of fact are verified by showing a cause – effect connection between the statement and some fact that proves it. For instance, if we were to find a watch on a deserted island we would have to conclude that people had once been there, for the effect, that is the watch, could only have been caused by people having created it. The same type of proof applies to all factual assertions, Hume declares, therefore we should treat the study of cause – effect connections as crucial in testing the truth of matters of fact. Hume himself went on to develop one of the most radical concepts of causality ever devised.[8]

The application of Hume's distinction to ethics is that moral judgments are neither relations of ideas nor matters of fact. The truth of a principle such as Love thine enemy cannot be proven either by the meaning of the terms involved or by reference to external facts. Moral judgments therefore occupy a state of limbo; their truth lies beyond all verification. Hume writes:

> In every system of morality which I have hitherto met with, I have always remarked, that the author proceeds for some time in the ordinary way of reasoning, and establishes the being of a god, or makes observations concerning human affairs; when of a sudden I am surpriz'd to find, that instead of the usual copulations of propositions, *is* and *is not*, I meet with no proposition that is not connected with an *ought*, or an *ought not*. This change is imperceptible; but it is, however, of the last consequence. For as this ought or ought not, expresses some new relation or affirmation, 'tis necessary that it should be observed and explained . . . and [I] am persuaded that this small attention would subvert all the vulgar systems of morality, and let us see, that the distinction of vice and virtue is not founded merely on the relations of objects, nor is perceived by reason.[9]

Hume is implying here that ethical assertions (the *ought* and *ought not*) do not fall into either of the two categories of genuine knowledge. According to his view then, we can have no knowledge of any actual right or wrong.

In the history of philosophy, Hume's position has been echoed by numerous voices all of which reached the same skeptical conclusion regarding values. A theory known as *Positivism*, founded by the French philosopher Auguste Comte (1798 – 1857), was especially militant in maintaining that only scientific claims can be true. And Hume's position emerged again (but in "linguistic" form) in the twentieth century movement called *Logical Positivism*. A. J. Ayer was one of its leading spokesmen and in his influential book *Language, Truth and Logic* he presents a basic standard for determining when a sentence is meaningful and when it is meaningless. Ayer calls this the Verification Principle and describes it as follows:

> The criterion which we use to test the genuineness of apparent statements of fact is the criterion of verifiability. We say that a sentence is factually significant to any given person, if, and only if, he knows how to verify the proposition which it purports to express—that is, if he knows what observations would lead him, under certain conditions, to accept the proposition as being true, or reject it as being false. If, on the other hand, the putative proposition is of such a character that the assumption of its truth, or falsehood, is consistent with any assumption whatsoever concerning the nature of his future experience, then, as far as he is concerned, it is, if not a tautology, a mere pseudo-proposition. The sentence expressing it may be emotionally significant to him; but it is not literally significant.[10]

The implication of the Verification Principle is that various types of sentences previously regarded as perfectly meaningful were now to be regarded as meaningless. Sentences about religion, art, emotions, history—all were judged as nonsense because they could not be verified by any empirical (i.e., sense) observations. Most important for our purposes, value judgments were also declared meaningless on the same grounds: No empirical tests could confirm or deny them.

The Logical Positivists were arguing that a sentence such as The cat is on the mat is clearly meaningful, because we know how to go about verifying its truth. If we experience a certain shape and size, a mewing sound, a particular odor, and can feel soft fur then these sense particulars constitute proof that the proposition is true. But how can anyone test an alleged proposition such as Honesty is praiseworthy or To forgive is divine. Sentences of this kind are beyond all possible verification; therefore they are not false but, worse still, they are utterly senseless.

All ethical assertions fall into this category. They are meaningless and therefore incapable of being judged either true or false. It is as though we were saying, " 'Twas brillig, and the slithy toves/ Did gyre and gimble in the wabe," that is, expressing a parody of meaningful language. Ayer writes:

> If I say to someone, "You acted wrongly in stealing that money," I am not stating anything more than if I had simply said, "You stole that money." In adding that this action is wrong I am not making any further statement about it. I am simply evincing my moral disapproval of it. It is as if I had said "You stole that money," in a peculiar tone of horror. . . .
>
> It is clear that there is nothing said here which can be true or false. Another man may disagree with me about the wrongness of stealing, in the sense that he may not have the same feelings about stealing as I have, and he may quarrel with me on account of my moral sentiments. But he cannot, strictly speaking, contradict me. For in saying that a certain type of action is right or wrong, I am not making any factual statement, not even a statement about my own state of mind. I am merely expressing certain moral sentiments.[11]

Sociological and Anthropological Evidence

Numerous philosophers in the twentieth century have agreed with Ayer's conclusions and many more have supported relativism for other reasons, however, the main support for relativism has come not from philosophy but from anthropology and sociology. William Graham Sumner in *Folkways*, Vilfredo Pareto in *Mind and Society*, Karl Mannheim in *Sociology of Knowledge*, Ruth Benedict in *Patterns of Culture*, Talcott Parsons in *Evolution of Societies*, and Melville Herskovits in *Cultural Relativism* are just some of the figures who have supported the view that value judgments are always relative to the society. They do not just describe but prescribe a relativistic stance. As Ruth Benedict states, "There is no reason to suppose that any one culture has seized upon an eternal sanity and will stand in history as a solitary solution to the human problem," there are only "variant configurations of human culture."

The following selection from *Cultural Relativism* by a leading anthropologist, Melville Herskovits, can be taken as representative of this general view. Notice that Herskovits carefully differentiates his position from subjectivism but affirms a relativism in terms of one's culture.

Cultural Relativism and Cultural Values*

Cultural relativism, in all cases, must be sharply distinguished from concepts of the relativity of individual behavior, which would negate all social controls over conduct. . . . The very core of cultural relativism is the social discipline that comes of respect for differences—mutual respect. Emphasis on the worth of many ways of life, not one, is an affirmation of the values in each culture. Such emphasis seeks to understand and to harmonize goals, not to judge and destroy those that do not dovetail with our own.

All peoples form judgments about ways of life different from their own. When systematic study is undertaken, comparison gives rise to classification, and scholars have devised many schemes for classifying ways of life. Moral judgments have been drawn regarding the ethical principles that guide the behavior and mold the value systems of different peoples. Their economic and political structures and their religious beliefs have been ranked in order of complexity, efficiency, desirability. Their art, music, and literary forms have been weighed.

It has become increasingly evident, however, that evaluations of this kind stand or fall with the acceptance of the premises from which they derive. In addition, many of the criteria on which judgment is based are in conflict, so that conclusions drawn from one definition of what is desirable will not agree with those based on another formulation.

---

*Reprinted by permission from Melville Herskovits, *Cultural Relativism* (New York: Random House, 1972), 11–34, some footnotes have been deleted.

A simple example will illustrate this. There are not many ways in which the primary family can be constituted. One man may live with one woman, one woman may have a number of husbands, one man may have a number of wives. But if we evaluate these forms according to their function of perpetuating the group, it is clear that they perform their essential tasks. Otherwise, the societies wherein they exist would not survive.

Such an answer will, however, not satisfy all those who have undertaken to study cultural evaluation. What of the moral questions inherent in the practice of monogamy as against polygamy, the adjustment of children raised in households where, for example, the mothers must compete on behalf of their offspring for the favors of a common husband? If monogamy is held to be the desired form of marriage, the responses to these questions are predetermined. But when we consider these questions from the point of view of those who live in polygamous societies, alternative answers, based on different conceptions of what is desirable, may be given.

Let us consider, for example, the life of a plural family in the West African culture of Dahomey. . . . Here, within a compound, live a man and his wives. The man has his own house, as has each of the women and her children, after the basic African principle that two wives cannot successfully inhabit the same quarters. Each wife in turn spends a native week of four days with the common husband, cooking his food, washing his cloths, sleeping in his house, and then making way for the next. Her children, however, remain in their mother's hut. With pregnancy, she drops out of this routine, and ideally, in the interest of her child's health and her own, does not again visit her husband until the child has been born and weaned. This means a period of from three to four years, since infants are nursed two years and longer.

The compound, made up of these households, is a cooperative unit. The women who sell goods in the market, or make pottery, or have their gardens, contribute to its support. This aspect, though of great economic importance, is secondary to the prestige that attaches to the larger unit. This is why one often finds a wife not only urging her husband to acquire a second spouse but even aiding him by loans or gifts to make this possible.

Tensions do arise between the women who inhabit a large compound. Thirteen different ways of getting married have been recorded in this society, and in a large household those wives who are married in the same category tend to unite against all others. Competition for the regard of the husband is also a factor, when several wives try to influence the choice of an heir in favor of their own sons. Yet all the children of the compound play together, and the strength of the emotional ties between the children of the same mother more than compensates for whatever stresses may arise between brothers and sisters who share the same father but are of different mothers. Cooperation, moreover, is by no means a mere formality among the wives. Many common tasks are performed in friendly unison, and there is solidarity in the interest of women's prerogatives, or where the status of the common husband is threatened.

We may now return to the criteria to be applied in drawing judgments concerning polygamous as against monogamous families. The family structure of Dahomey is obviously a complex institution. If we but consider the possible lines of personal relations among the many individuals concerned, we see clearly how numerous are the ramifications of reciprocal right and obligation of the Dahomean family. The effectiveness of the Dahomean family is, however, patent. It has, for untold generations, performed its function of rearing the young; more than this, the very size of the group gives it economic resources and a resulting stability that might well be envied by those who live under different systems of family organization. Moral values are always difficult to establish, but at least in this society marriage is clearly distinguished from casual sex relations and from prostitution, in its supernatural sanctions and in the prestige it confers, to say nothing of the economic obligations toward spouse and prospective offspring explicitly accepted by one who enters into a marriage.

Numerous problems of adjustment do present themselves in an aggregate of this sort. It does not call for much speculation to understand the plaint of the head of one large compound when he said: "One must be something of a diplomat if one has many wives." Yet the sly digs in proverb and song, and the open quarreling, involve no greater stress than is found in any small rural community where people are also thrown closely together for long periods of time. Quarrels between co-wives are not greatly different from disputes over the back fence between neighbors. And Dahomeans who know European culture, when they argue for their system, stress the fact that it permits the individual wife to space her children in a way that is in accord with the best precepts of modern gynecology.

Thus polygamy, when looked at from the point of view of those who practice it, is seen to hold values that are not apparent from the outside. A similar case can be made for monogamy, however, when it is attacked by those who are enculturated to a different kind of family structure. And what is true of a particular phase of culture such as this, is also true of others. Evaluations are *relative* to the cultural background out of which they arise.

2

Cultural relativism is in essence an approach to the question of the nature and role of values in culture. It represents a scientific, inductive attack on an age-old philosophical problem, using fresh, cross-cultural data, hitherto not available to scholars, gained from the study of the underlying value-systems of societies having the most diverse customs. The principle of cultural relativism, briefly stated, is as follows: *Judgments are based on experience, and experience is interpreted by each individual in terms of his own enculturation.* Those who hold for the existence of fixed values will find materials in other societies that necessitate a re-investigation of their assumptions. Are there absolute moral standards, or are moral standards effective only as far as they agree with the orientations of a given people at a given period of their history? We even approach the problem of the ultimate nature of reality itself. Cassirer . . . holds that reality can only be experienced through the symbolism of language. Is reality, then, not defined and redefined by the ever-varied symbolisms of the innumerable languages of mankind? Answers to questions such as these represent one of the most profound contributions of anthropology to the analysis of man's place in the world. When we reflect that such intangibles as right and wrong, normal and

abnormal, beautiful and plain are absorbed as a person learns the ways of the
group into which he is born, we see that we are dealing here with a process
of first importance. Even the facts of the physical world are discerned
through the enculturative screen, so that the perception of time, distance,
weight, size, and other "realities" is mediated by the conventions of any
given group.

No culture, however, is a closed system of rigid molds to which the
behavior of all members of a society must conform. The psychological reality
of culture tells us that a culture, as such, can *do* nothing. It is but the
summation of the behavior and habitual modes of thought of the persons
who make up a particular society. Though by learning and habit these
individuals conform to the ways of the group into which they have been
born, they nonetheless vary in their reactions to the situations of living they
commonly meet. They vary, too, in the degree to which they desire change,
as whole cultures vary. This is but another way in which we see that culture
is flexible and holds many possibilities of choice within its framework, and
that to recognize the values held by a given people in no wise implies that
these values are a constant factor in the lives of succeeding generations of the
same group.

How the ideas of a people mediate their approach even to the physical
world can be made plain by a few examples. Indians living in the
southwestern part of the United States think in terms of *six* cardinal points
rather than four. In addition to north, south, east and west, they include the
directions "up" and "down." From the point of view that the universe is
three dimensional, these Indians are entirely realistic. Among ourselves, even
in airplane navigation, where three dimensions must be coped with as they
need not by those who keep to the surface of the earth, we separate direction
from height in instruments and in our thinking about position. We operate,
conceptually, on two distinct planes. One is horizontal — "We are traveling
ENE." One is vertical — "We are now cruising at 8000 feet."

Or take a problem in the patterning of sound. We accept the concept of
the wave length, tune pianos in accordance with a mechanically determined
scale, and are thus conditioned to what we call true pitch. Some persons, we
say, have absolute pitch; that is, a note struck or sung at random will
immediately be given its place in the scale — "That's B flat." A composition
learned in a given key, when transposed, will deeply trouble such a person,
though those who are musically trained but do not have true pitch will enjoy
such a transposed work, if the *relation* of each note to every other has not
been disturbed. Let us assume that it is proposed to study whether this ability
to identify a note is an inborn trait, found among varying but small
percentages of individuals in various societies. The difficulty of probing such
a question appears immediately once we discover that but few peoples have
fixed scales, and none other than ourselves has the concept of true pitch!
Those living in cultures without mechanically tuned and true instruments
are free to enjoy notes that are as much as a quarter-tone "off," as we would
say. As for the patterned progressions in which the typical scales and modal
orientations of any musical convention are set, the number of such systems,
each of which is consistent within its own limits, is infinite . . .

The very definition of what is normal or abnormal is relative to the
cultural frame of reference. As an example of this, we may take the

phenomenon of possession as found among African and New World Negroes. The supreme expression of their religious experience, possession, is a psychological state wherein a displacement of personality occurs when the god "comes to the head" of the worshipper. The individual thereupon is held to be the deity himself. This phenomenon has been described in pathological terms by many students whose approach is non-anthropological, because of its surface resemblance to cases in the records of medical practitioners, psychological clinicians, psychiatrists, and others. The hysteria-like trances, where persons, their eyes tightly closed, move about excitedly and presumably without purpose or design, or roll on the ground, muttering meaningless syllables, or go into a state where their bodies achieve complete rigidity, are not difficult to equate with the neurotic and even psychotic manifestations of abnormality found in Euroamerican society.

Yet when we look beneath behavior to meaning, and place such apparently random acts in their cultural frame of reference, such conclusions become untenable. For *relative to the setting in which these possession experiences occur, they are not to be regarded as abnormal at all*, much less psychopathological. They are *culturally* patterned, and often induced by learning and discipline. The dancing or other acts of the possessed persons are so stylized that one who knows this religion can identify the god possessing a devotee by the behavior of the individual possessed. Furthermore, the possession experience does not seem to be confined to emotionally unstable persons. Those who "get the god" run the gamut of personality types found in the group. Observation of persons who frequent the cults, yet who, in the idiom of worship "have nothing in the head" and thus never experience possession, seems to show that they are far less adjusted than those who do get possessed. Finally, the nature of the possession experience in these cultures is so disciplined that it may only come to a given devotee under particular circumstances. In West Africa and Brazil the gods come only to those who have been designated in advance by the priest of their group, who lays his hands on their heads. In Haiti, for an initiate not a member of the family group giving a rite to become possessed at a ceremony is considered extremely "bad form" socially and a sign of spiritual weakness, evidence that the god is not under the control of his worshipper.

The terminology of psychopathology, employed solely for descriptive purposes, may be of some utility. But the connotation it carries of psychic instability, emotional imbalance, and departure from normality recommends the use of other words that do not invite such a distortion of cultural reality. For in these Negro societies, the meaning this experience holds for the people falls entirely in the realm of understandable, predictable, *normal* behavior. This behavior is known and recognized by all members as an experience that may come to any one of them, and is to be welcomed not only for the psychological security it affords, but also for the status, economic gain, aesthetic expression, and emotional release it vouchsafes the devotee.

3

The primary mechanism that directs the evaluation of culture is *ethnocentrism*. Ethnocentrism is the point of view that one's own way of life is to be preferred to all others. Flowing logically from the process of early enculturation, it characterizes the way most individuals feel about their own culture, whether or not they verbalize their feeling. Outside the stream of Euroamerican culture, particularly among nonliterate peoples, this is taken for granted and is to be viewed as a factor making for individual adjustment and social integration. For the strengthening of the ego, identification with one's own group, whose ways are implicitly accepted as best, is all-important. It is when, as in Euroamerican culture, ethnocentrism is rationalized and made the basis of programs of action detrimental to the well-being of other peoples that it gives rise to serious problems.

The ethnocentrism of nonliterate peoples is best illustrated in their myths, folk tales, proverbs, and linguistic habits. It is manifest in many tribal names whose meaning in their respective languages signifies "human beings." The inference that those to whom the name does not apply are outside this category is, however, rarely, if ever, explicitly made. When the Suriname Bush Negro, shown a flashlight, admires it and then quotes the proverb: "White man's magic isn't black man's magic," he is merely reaffirming his faith in his own culture. He is pointing out that the stranger, for all his mechanical devices, would be lost in the Guiana jungle without the aid of his Bush Negro friends.

A myth of the origin of human races, told by the Cherokee Indians of the Great Smoky Mountains, gives another instance of this kind of ethnocentrism. The Creator fashioned man by first making and firing an oven and then, from dough he had prepared, shaping three figures in human form. He placed the figures in the oven and waited for them to get done. But his impatience to see the result of this, his crowning experiment in the work of creation, was so great that he removed the first figure too soon. It was sadly underdone—pale, an unlovely color, and from it descended the white people. His second figure had fared well. The timing was accurate, the form, richly browned, that was to be the ancestor of the Indians, pleased him in every way. He so admired it, indeed, that he neglected to take out of the oven the third form, until he smelled it burning. He threw open the door, only to find this last one charred and black. It was regrettable, but there was nothing to be done; and this was the first Negro.*

This is the more usual form that ethnocentrism takes among many peoples—a gentle insistence on the good qualities of one's own group, without any drive to extend this attitude into the field of action. With such a point of view, the objectives, sanctioned modes of behavior, and value systems of peoples with whom one's own group comes into contact can be considered in terms of their desirability, then accepted or rejected without any reference to absolute standards. That differences in the manner of achieving commonly sought objectives may be permitted to exist without a judgment being entered on them involves a reorientation in thought for those in the Euroamerican tradition, because in this tradition, a difference in belief or behavior too often implies something is worse, or less desirable, and must be changed.

*This unpublished myth was told F. M. Olbrechts of Brussels, Belgium, in the course of field work among the Cherokee. His having made it available is gratefully acknowledged. A similar tale has been recorded from the Albany Cree, at Moose Factory, according to information received from F. Voget.

The assumption that the cultures of nonliterate peoples are of inferior quality is the end product of a long series of developments in our intellectual history. It is not often recalled that the concept of progress, that strikes so deep into our thinking, is relatively recent. It is, in fact, a unique product of our culture. It is a part of the same historic stream that developed the scientific tradition and that developed the machine, thus giving Europe and America the final word in debates about cultural superiority. "He who makes the gun-powder wields the power," runs a Dahomean proverb. There is no rebuttal to an argument, backed by cannon, advanced to a people who can defend their position with no more than spears, or bows and arrows, or at best a flint-lock gun.

With the possible exception of technological aspects of life, however, the proposition that one way of thought or action is better than another is exceedingly difficult to establish on the grounds of any universally acceptable criteria. Let us take food as an instance. Cultures are equipped differently for the production of food, so that some peoples eat more than others. However, even on the subsistence level, there is no people who do not hold certain potential foodstuffs to be unfit for human consumption. Milk, which figures importantly in our diet, is rejected as food by the peoples of southeastern Asia. Beef, a valued element of the Euroamerican cuisine, is regarded with disgust by Hindus. Nor need compulsions be this strong. The thousands of cattle that range the East African highlands are primarily wealth to be preserved, and not a source of food. Only the cow that dies is eaten—a practice that, though abhorrent to us, has apparently done no harm to those who have been following it for generations.

Totemic and religious taboos set up further restrictions on available foodstuffs, while the refusal to consume many other edible and nourishing substances is simply based on the enculturative conditioning. So strong is this conditioning that prohibited food consumed unwittingly may induce such a physiological reaction as vomiting. All young animals provide succulent meat, but the religious abhorrence of the young pig by the Mohammedan is no stronger than the secular rejection of puppy steaks or colt chops by ourselves. Ant larvae, insect grubs, locusts—all of which have caloric values and vitamin content—when roasted or otherwise cooked, or even when raw, are regarded by many peoples as delicacies. We never eat them, however, though they are equally available to us. On the other hand, some of the same peoples who feed on these with gusto regard substances that come out of tin cans as unfit for human consumption. . . .

5

Before we terminate our discussion of cultural relativism, it is important that we consider questions that are raised when the cultural-relativistic position is advanced. "It may be true," it is argued, "that human beings live in accordance with the ways they have learned. These ways may be regarded by them as best. A people may be so devoted to these ways that they are ready to fight and die for them. In terms of survival value, their effectiveness may be admitted, since the group that lives in accordance with them continues to exist. But does this mean that all systems of moral values, all concepts of right and wrong, are founded on such shifting sands that there is no need for morality, for proper behavior, for ethical codes? Does not a relativistic philosophy, indeed, imply a negation of these?"

To hold that values do not exist because they are relative to time and place is to fall prey to a fallacy that results from a failure to take into account the positive contribution of the relativistic position. For cultural relativism is a philosophy that recognizes the values set up by every society to guide its own life and that understands their worth to those who live by them, though they may differ from one's own. Instead of underscoring differences from absolute norms that, however objectively arrived at, are nonetheless the product of a given time or place, the relativistic point of view brings into relief the validity of every set of norms for the people who have them, and the values these represent.

It is essential, in considering cultural relativism, that we differentiate absolutes from universals. *Absolutes* are fixed, and, as far as convention is concerned, are not admitted to have variation, to differ from culture to culture, from epoch to epoch. *Universals*, on the other hand, are those least common denominators to be extracted from the range of variation that all phenomena of the natural or cultural world manifest. If we apply the distinction between these two concepts in drawing an answer to the points raised in our question, these criticisms are found to lose their force. To say that there is no absolute criterion of values or morals, or even, psychologically, of time or space, does not mean that such criteria, in differing *forms*, do not comprise universals in human culture. Morality is a universal, and so is enjoyment of beauty, and some standard for truth. The many forms these concepts take are but products of the particular historical experience of the societies that manifest them. In each, criteria are subject to continuous questioning, continuous change. But the basic conceptions remain, to channel thought and direct conduct, to give purpose to living.

In considering cultural relativism, also, we must recognize that it has three quite different aspects, which in most discussions of it tend to be disregarded. One of these is methodological, one philosophical, and one practical. As it has been put:

> As method, relativism encompasses the principle of our science that, in studying a culture, one seeks to attain as great a degree of objectivity as possible; that one does not judge the modes of behavior one is describing, or seek to change them. Rather, one seeks to understand the sanctions of behavior in terms of the established relationships within the culture itself, and refrains from making interpretations that arise from a preconceived frame of reference. Relativism as philosophy concerns the nature of cultural values, and, beyond this, the implications of an epistemology that derives from a recognition of the force of enculturative conditioning in shaping thought and behavior. Its practical aspects involve are the application—the practice—of the philosophical principles derived from this method, to the wider, cross-cultural scene.

We may follow this reasoning somewhat further.

> In these terms, the three aspects of cultural relativism can be regarded as representing a logical sequence which, in a broad sense, the historical

development of the idea has also followed. That is, the methodological aspect, whereby the data from which the epistemological propositions flow are gathered, ordered and assessed, came first. For it is difficult to conceive of a systematic theory of cultural relativism — as against a generalized idea of live-and-let-live — without the pre-existence of the massive ethnographic documentation gathered by anthropologists concerning the similarities and differences between cultures the world over. Out of these data came the philosophical position, and with the philosophical position came speculation as to its implications for conduct.*

Cultural relativism, in all cases, must be sharply distinguished from concepts of the relativity of individual behavior, which would negate all social controls over conduct. Conformity to the code of the group is a requirement for any regularity in life. Yet to say that we have a right to expect conformity to the code of our day for ourselves does not imply that we need expect, much less impose, conformity to our code on persons who live by other codes. The very core of cultural relativism is the social discipline that comes of respect for differences — of mutual respect. Emphasis on the worth of many ways of life, not one, is an affirmation of the values in each culture. Such emphasis seeks to understand and to harmonize goals, not to judge and destroy those that do not dovetail with our own. Cultural history teaches that, important as it is to discern and study the parallelisms in human civilizations, it is no less important to discern and study the different ways man has devised to fulfill his needs.

That it has been necessary to consider questions such as have been raised reflects an enculturative experience wherein the prevalent system of morals is not only consciously inculcated, but its exclusive claim to excellence emphasized. There are not many cultures, for example, where a rigid dichotomy between good and evil, such as we have set up, is insisted upon. Rather it is recognized that good and evil are but the extremes of a continuously varied scale between these poles that produces only different degrees of greyness. We thus return to the principle enunciated earlier, that "judgments are based on experience, and experience is interpreted by each individual in terms of his enculturation." In a culture where absolute values are stressed, the relativism of a world that encompasses many ways of living will be difficult to comprehend. Rather, it will offer a field day for value judgments based on the degree to which a given body of customs resembles or differs from those of Euroamerican culture.†

Once comprehended, however, and employing the field methods of the scientific student of man, together with an awareness of the satisfactions the most varied bodies of custom yield, this position gives us a leverage to lift us

*M. J. Herskovits, 1951, p. 24.

†Instances of the rejection of relativism on philosophical grounds, by writers who attempt to reconcile the principle of absolute values with the diversity of known systems, are to be found in E. Vivas, 1950, pp. 27–42, and D. Bidney, 1953a, pp. 689–95, 1953b, pp. 423–29. Both of these discussions, also, afford examples of the confusion that results when a distinction is not drawn between the methodological, philosophical, and practical aspects of relativism. For a critical consideration of relativism that, by implication, recognizes these differences, see R. Redfield, 1953, pp. 144 ff.

out of the ethnocentric morass in which our thinking about ultimate values has for so long bogged down. With a means of probing deeply into all manner of differing cultural orientations, of reaching into the significance of the ways of living of different peoples, we can turn again to our own culture with fresh perspective, and an objectivity that can be achieved in no other manner.

Evaluation

Relativism appears to be a solid scientific theory with extensive philosophic support and a spirit congenial to the awareness of the twentieth century. It is certainly beneficial in promoting receptivity toward foreign codes of behavior and in reminding us of the diversity of moral viewpoints. We become much more flexible and much less self-righteous if we realize that our way of living is not the only way in which human life can be organized. And we are reluctant to force our values on others through missionaries or the military if we take all values as equally valid. A liberal, live-and-let-live attitude prevails in which we respect each individual's way of live — what the Germans call *leben und leben lassen.*

Nevertheless, although certain social gains follow from the relativist assumptions, the question of its truth must be addressed. An idea can be beneficial but not true, and ideas certainly aren't true because they are beneficial. Wishing does not make it so, any more than denying reality can make the truth disappear, which is the ostrich mentality. For good or ill, we must ask ourselves whether the relativist is correct in what he claims.

1. First of all with regard to the philosophic claims of David Hume and A. J. Ayer, both seem guilty of excluding the possibility of objective morality by peremptorily defining what is to count as a genuine or meaningful assertion. They both seem to say that the only claims worth considering (apart from logical relations of ideas) are those that can be tested by the senses, that is, empirically verifiable propositions. But that criterion is highly arbitrary and would eliminate an entire range of discourse. Statements such as The sunset is beautiful, The meal is delicious, and even I am in love with you would be considered worthless. This is hardly in keeping with our ordinary assumptions, and neither philosopher gives us any good reasons as to why the empirically verifiable alone is worth saying.

It has also been pointed out that neither Hume's classification of two types of genuine knowledge nor Ayer's Verification Principle is provable according to its author's own criterion. Neither one is based on empirical evidence (or logical relations) and, thus by the relativist's own standards, must be considered specious or meaningless.

2. Aside from the problems inherent in particular philosophic claims, relativism in its broadest sense can be charged with contradicting itself. For when the relativist argues that everything is relative and that this proposition is absolutely true, he becomes involved in affirming and denying his own claim. If everything is relative then nothing is absolutely true including that principle itself. Or differently put, in saying that everything is relative, the statement is not thought

to be relative but absolute; therefore not everything is relative. In the same way, it is logically inconsistent for the subjectivist to claim that his position is objectively true, if everything is a subjective matter.

If the relativist tries to make his position more consistent by saying that the statement everything is relative is also a relative statement, then no one need take it seriously. For the statement then becomes a trivial one, relative to the speaker's society or disposition.

The relativist then can be consistent but say very little or maintain that he is really right and contradict himself. Neither choice is a very happy one and neither one does much to make the relativist position rationally convincing.

The same logical problem, incidentally, confronts any skeptical position regarding knowledge. If the skeptic declares that there is no knowledge, then this statement is not knowledge either or he contradicts himself. And the situation is not improved by changing the claim to There is no truth.

3. Another problem arises if relativism is taken in the subjectivist sense of claiming that whatever an individual believes to be true is true to him. For this would produce the logically impossible situation in which two contradictory statements would both have to be judged as true if each was maintained by someone. We would have to say, for example, that a square has four sides and that a square does not have four sides if two people took opposing views about it. Both positions would have to be considered correct if it is assumed that each individual is right to himself, and this is patently absurd.

The lesson to be learned here is that thinking does not make it so. We can be mistaken in what we believe, and whether we have judged matters correctly or incorrectly is determined by the reality we are attempting to describe. This is apparent in the previous example when one realizes that two contradictory propositions cannot both be true; this Principle of Noncontradiction, as it is called, is one of the most basic laws of thought. No statement can be both true and false; at least one position would have to be mistaken. And the decision as to which position is incorrect would be made in terms of the actual state of affairs.

It should be added that even if everyone were in accord about an idea that would not establish it as so, because truth is not dependent on what people think is the case but on what the case happens to be. As one philosopher phrases it,

> A fundamental distinction must be drawn between the way the world is and what we say about it, even if we all happen to agree. We could all be wrong. Some of the most important commitments we make in our life could be based on error. What is true and what we think is true need not coincide. This simple statement seems self-evident, since it merely draws attention to human fallibility in general, and our own in particular.[12]

Socrates offers a similar criticism of the subjectivist view when he objects to the definition of justice offered by Thrasymachus. In the passage quoted earlier from *The Republic*, Thrasymachus had argued that justice is nothing other than the interests of the stronger. Socrates then proceeds to question this definition in the following way. He asks Thrasymachus,

> "Do you admit that it is just for subjects to obey their rulers?"
> "I do."

"But are the rulers of states absolutely infallible, or are they sometimes liable to error?"

"To be sure. . . . they are liable to err."

"Then in making their laws they may sometimes make them rightly, and sometimes not?"

"True."

"When they make them rightly, they make them agreeably to their interest; when they are mistaken, contrary to their interest; you admit that?"

"Yes."

"And the laws which they make must be obeyed by their subjects — and that is what you call justice?"

"Doubtless."

"Then justice, according to your argument, is not only obedience to the interest of the stronger but the reverse?"

"What is that you are saying? . . ."

"I am only repeating what you are saying, I believe. But let us consider: Have we not admitted that the rulers may be mistaken about their own interest in what they command, and also that to obey them is justice? Has not that been admitted?"

"Yes."

"Then you must also have acknowledged justice not to be the interest of the stronger, when the rulers unintentionally command things to be done which are to their own injury. For if, as you say, justice is the obedience which the subject renders to their commands, in that case, O wisest of men, is there any escape from the conclusion that the weaker are commanded to do, not what is for the interest, but what is for the injury of the stronger?"

In other words, doing what the stronger commands could mean doing what is good for them or doing what is bad for them, depending on whether they had understood where their best interests lie. Justice then could work out to be that which harms the stronger, which is just the opposite of what Thrasymachus intended.

For our purposes the important point is that no moral values are determined by what an individual asserts. Even if we hold the cynical view of values as mere self-interest (as Thrasymachus does with regard to justice), the individual would be correct or incorrect in his decision according to what his best interests actually were. And just as people can be mistaken about what is good for them, they can be mistaken about what is truly fair, equitable, or honest. In no case does believing something make it right; values are independent of the individual or the ruling political form. This is Plato's point and it applies equally well to the relativism of Protagoras and Gorgias.

4. Another criticism of ethical relativism has to do with the assumption that differing moral values among cultures show that no objective standards exist. Is that conclusion really justified?

To begin with, the diversity in values worldwide may be more apparent than actual. For example, it seems as though a society that condones a husband killing his wife's lover and a society that condemns such action are in fundamental disagreement. To the one the husband has behaved honorably, to the other he is a base criminal. However, these may be superficial differences masking common principles. Both societies will probably have laws prohibiting murder and have strong beliefs in the protection of human life. They will differ only in their definitions as to what constitutes murder, that is, taking life unjustifiably. In the same way, a tribe that practices hospitality toward neighboring tribes and one that acts with enmity toward its neighbors may appear to be exhibiting diverse values. However, both may share a common belief in the value of hospitality. To the first that would include adjacent tribes, whereas to the second it would only apply to other families within the tribe. The difference may be over what constitutes a neighbor and a stranger and who therefore is entitled to the gift of hospitality.

In other words the underlying values may be the same and the disagreement may not stem from moral differences at all. As some anthropologists have pointed out, there certainly seems to be widespread agreement over the worth of values such as group loyalty, courage, and parental affection for the young. Likewise, deceit, ingratitude, and stealing are broadly condemned. The evidence therefore points to a certain unanimity on fundamental moral principles, and what is taken as cultural diversity in values may only be differences in the application or meaning of those principles.

As a prime example it has been claimed that the Golden Rule is one of the oldest principles of a distinctly universal character. Witness the following comparative list, drawn mainly from chief religions of the world:

Confucianism

What you don't want done to yourself, don't do to others.

— SIXTH CENTURY B.C.

Buddhism

Hurt not others with that which pains thyself.

— FIFTH CENTURY B.C.

Jainism

In happiness and suffering, in joy and grief, we should regard all creatures as we regard our own self, and should therefore refrain from inflicting upon others such injury as would appear undesirable to us if inflicted upon ourselves.

— FIFTH CENTURY B.C.

Zoroastrianism

Do not do unto others all that which is not well for oneself.

— FIFTH CENTURY B.C.

Classical Philosophy

May I do to others as I would that they should do unto me.

Plato — FOURTH CENTURY B.C.

Hinduism

Do naught to others which if done to thee would cause thee pain.

Mahabharata — THIRD CENTURY B.C.

Judaism

> What is hateful to yourself, don't do to your fellow man.
>
> *Rabbi Hillel* — FIRST CENTURY B.C.

Christianity

> Whatsoever ye would that men should do to you, do ye even so to them.
>
> *Jesus of Nazareth* — FIRST CENTURY A.D.

Sikhism

> Treat others as thou wouldst be treated thyself.
>
> — SIXTEENTH CENTURY A.D.

However, even if moral disagreement does exist, disagreement that cannot be explained away in terms of a substratum of shared values, that still would not demonstrate the relativity of values. For the fact that societies disagree about values does not prove that each is right; it only shows that each society believes itself to be right. It still makes good sense to ask which has come closest to the truth and which is farthest away from the mark.

To take an analogy from science, the fact that disease used to be attributed to evil spirits or the influences of the four humors and that cures were thought of in terms of exorcism or bloodletting does not imply that disease has no real cause. The multiplicity of beliefs about these matters does not warrant the conclusion that everything is relative to the time and place and one person's opinion is as good as another's. Rather, the medical researcher assumes that diseases have actual causes and that cures can be effected by properly identifying those causes. He attributes the variety of past beliefs about disease to the greater clarity or dimness with which people have perceived the truth. At various times people may have been very ignorant and superstitious or remarkably perceptive (as with herbal remedies). But as a scientist he takes it for granted that there is a truth to be known and that assumption provides the motivation for his research.

In the same way the objectivist sees the multiplicity of moral beliefs not as evidence of relativism but as a manifestation of greater or lesser understanding of genuine values — values that he also tries to grasp in his systematic and rigorous way. Notice that he does not doubt the facts of cultural diversity but only the interpretation of those facts — that moral relativity follows from them.

5. But couldn't it be argued that the reverse might be true? Couldn't the diversity of moral views at different times and places indicate the relativity of morals and not any universal standard variously perceived? After all two interpretations are possible, so why choose the objectivist one?

This consideration introduces the concept of burden of proof which is usually taken as an argument against the relativist view. According to this concept, the burden of proof in a dispute is always on the side that takes the unusual position. For example, in an argument over what factors were responsible for World War II the person who says it was due to the astrological influence of the stars would have to prove that contention, otherwise it would be appropriate to assume that the economic conditions in Germany, the humiliation of the Treaty of Versailles, the charismatic leadership of Hitler, and so forth were responsible for the war. In other words, the person who adopts a theory that is out of the ordinary must prove his case, while the person who maintains a customary or common-sensical view is justified in holding that view until it is disproven.

In the dispute over the relativity or objectivity of values the burden of proof falls on the relativist, and the question is whether he has in fact established his position. For people ordinarily believe that certain values are truly important, that indiscriminate killing, for example, is terribly wrong and the preservation of life is a moral obligation. If assumptions of this kind are mistaken then that has to be proven, and it does not seem that the relativist has succeeded in demonstrating it. He has only shown the wide range of values among cultures and in different historical periods, and that does not prove all values are relative. Therefore, the objectivist position, which is in accord with common human experience, can be maintained with some confidence.

In summation then we can see that relativism is basically self-contradictory or inconsistent in numerous ways and that cultural diversity does not warrant the conclusion that values have no objective basis.

Oddly enough, relativism cannot even claim the social benefit of fostering tolerance, as several philosophers have shown.[13] For by advocating the value of tolerance the relativist is presupposing that this value has objective worth and denying his own position. He is extolling tolerance from the standpoint of a moral system that he believes everyone should accept. In other words, by claiming the virtue of tolerance for his position the relativist gives the game away, for tolerance at least is assumed to be objectively valuable.

Perhaps Socrates had the last laugh regarding relativism when he argued against Protagoras in the *Theaetetus* by saying "and the best of the joke is that he acknowledges the truth of their opinions who believe his own opinions to be false for he admits that the opinions of all men are true.[14] That is, if man is the measure of all things and whatever a person believes is true because he believes it, then the person who believes relativism is false would be correct in his belief. Relativism therefore collapses of its own weight.

Notes

1. Aristarchus of Samos was the first person to declare the sun a fixed point with the earth orbiting around it, but this view, originating in the third century B.C., was soon abandoned and a geocentric view was developed by the second century A.D. It is interesting to investigate why correct ideas were neglected or abandoned for centuries and then rediscovered. The atomic theory of Democritus in the fifth century B.C. is another case in point and Judaeo-Christians also would include the monotheism of the Egyptian pharaoh Ikhnaton (c. 1375–1358 B.C.).
2. The twentieth century British philosopher C. L. Stevenson argues that sentences that appear to affirm some ethical values are only asserting some subjective fact and, what's more, issuing a command or hortation. In other words, to say "X is right" actually means "I approve of X and I wish you would agree with me." See *Ethics and Language* (New Haven: Yale University Press, 1943), and A. Stroll, *The Emotive Theory of Ethics* (Berkeley: University of California Press, 1954). Bertrand Russell expresses the same sentiments in some of his writings, for example, in *Religion and Science* he writes: "When a man says 'This is good in itself,' . . . what the man really means is: 'I wish everybody to desire this,' or rather 'Would that everybody desired this.'"

3. In this passage from Book I *The Republic* and the ones that follow from Plato's works, the translation is by Benjamin Jowett, *The Dialogues of Plato* (New York: Scribner, Armstrong, 1874).

4. These three propositions of Gorgias are taken from a fragment of his writings that were preserved. See K. Freeman, *The Pre-Socratic Philosophers* (Cambridge: Harvard University Press, 1942), 359–61. Some scholarly debate has occurred over the actual philosophic position that Gorgias maintained.

5. *Protagoras* in Jowett, *Plato*. Benedict Spinoza echoed the sentiments of Protagoras when he stated, "Music is good to a person who is melancholy, bad to one who is mourning, while to a deaf man it is neither good nor bad." *Ethics*, Vol. 4 (London: G. Bell, 1884), Preface. The question of whether qualities reside in objects or in the perceiver became a major issue among the British empiricists, especially John Locke and Bishop Berkeley.

6. Bertrand Russell, *Religion and Science* (London: Butterworth, 1935), 230–31.

7. *An Enquiry Concerning Human Understanding* in *Philosophical Works of David Hume* (Boston: Little, Brown and Co., 1854).

8. Hume maintained that causation, in the usual sense, is an unwarranted assumption because we never actually see the cause of anything. Only the "constant conjunction" of two events is visible to us. For example, we see the hammer strike the nail and the nail sink into the wood but we do not see the hammer drive the nail into the wood. Since we have no empirical evidence that the first event forced the second to happen we cannot assume any causal relationship—here or elsewhere.

   Incidentally, Hume's example of the watch on the deserted island was developed by the theologian William Paley (1743–1805) to support one of St. Thomas Aquinas' arguments for the existence of God. This teleological proof, as it is termed, claimed that the design of the world implies a cosmic designer. Paley reinforced this argument by his celebrated watchmaker analogy. He pointed out that just as the intricacy of a watch implies a watchmaker, the complexity and precision of the world implies an earthmaker. Neither could have come about by chance. Hume, however, criticized this analogical argument in his *Dialogues Concerning Natural Religion* by drawing out the logical implications to the point of absurdity.

9. David Hume, *A Treatise of Human Nature* (Edinburgh: Black, Tait and Tait, 1726), 2:236. In this passage Hume is also credited with identifying a logical mistake called the naturalistic fallacy. According to this fallacy one cannot deduce values from facts; judgments as to what ought to be done cannot be derived from descriptions of what is done. See my *Deity and Morality* (London: George Allen and Unwin, 1968).

10. A. J. Ayer, *Language, Truth and Logic* (New York: Dover Publications, 1946), 35. Ayer succeeded in popularizing Logical Positivism but the originators of the movement were a group of men known as the Vienna Circle. They included Moritz Schlick, Rudolf Carnap, Otto Neurath, Friedrich Waismann, Herbert Feigl, and Kurt Godel.

11. Ayer, *Language*, 107.

12. Roger Trigg, *Reason and Commitment* (Cambridge: Cambridge University Press, 1973).

13. Cf. Geoffrey Harrison, "Relativism and Tolerance," in *Philosophy, Politics and Society*, eds. Peter Laslett and James Fishkin (New Haven: Yale University Press, 1979), 273–90.

14. *Theaetetus* in Jowett, *Plato*, 373. A similar way of putting the point is that relativism claims whatever is right for you is right, but that claim may not be right for you.

Bibliography

ASCH, SOLOMON. *Social Psychology*. New York: Prentice–Hall, 1952.

ATTFIELD, ROBIN. *"How Not To Be a Moral Relativist."* The Monist No. 62, 4 (1979): 510–21.

BAIER, KURT. *The Moral Point of View*. New York: Random House, 1965.

BARTON, JOHN. *"Reflections On Cultural Relativism."* Theology (March and May 1979).

BEATTIE, J. H. M. *Other Cultures*. New York: Free Press, 1964.

BENEDICT, RUTH. *Patterns of Culture*. Boston: Houghton Mifflin, 1934.

BIDNEY, D. *Theoretical Anthropology*. New York: Schocken Books, 1970.

BRANDT, R. *Ethical Theory*. Englewood Cliffs, N.J.: Prentice–Hall, 1959.

BURKE, T. E. *"The Limits of Relativism."* Philosophical Quarterly 29 (1979).

CASTAÑEDA, HECTOR-NERI. *The Structure of Morality*. Springfield, Ill.: Charles C Thomas, 1974.

COBURN, ROBERT. *"Relativism and the Basis of Morality."* Philosophical Review 85 (1976): 87–93.

COOPER, DAVID. *"Moral Relativism,"* Midwest Studies in Philosophy 3 (1978): 97–108.

DAVIDSON, DONALD. *"Reality Without Reference."* In Reference, Truth and Reality. Edited by Mark Platts. London: Routledge and Kegan Paul, 1980.

DEVITT, M. *Realism and Truth*. Princeton: Princeton University Press, 1984.

DONAGAN, ALAN. *The Theory of Morality*. Chicago: University of Chicago Press, 1977.

DUNCKER, KARL. "Ethical Relativity." *Mind* 48 (1939): 39–53.

EDEL, ABRAHAM. *Ethical Judgment*. Glencoe, Ill.: Free Press, 1955.

EDEL, MAY, AND ABRAHAM EDEL. *Anthropology and Ethics*. Cleveland: Press of Case Western Reserve University, 1968.

FOOT, PHILIPPA. "Moral Beliefs." *Proceedings of the Aristotelian Society* (1958–1959): 83–104.

FRANKENA, WILLIAM. *Perspectives on Morality*. South Bend, Ind.: Notre Dame University Press, 1976.

GERT, BERNARD. *The Moral Rules*. New York: Harper and Row, 1970.

GEWIRTH, ALAN. *Reason and Morality*. Chicago: University of Chicago Press, 1978.

GIFFORD, N. L. *When in Rome: An Introduction to Relativism and Knowledge*. Albany: State University of New York Press, 1983.

GINSBURG, MORRIS. *On the Diversity of Morals*. New York: Macmillan, 1956.

GOLDMAN, ALVIN, AND JAEGWON, KIM, EDS. *Values and Morals*. Dordrecht, Holland: D. Reidel, 1978.

HARE, R. M. *Freedom and Reason*. London: Oxford University Press, 1963.

HARMAN, GILBERT. "Moral Relativism Defended." *Philosophical Review* 84 (1975): 3–22.

HARRISON, GEOFFREY. "Relativism and Tolerance." *Ethics* 86 (1976): 122–35.

HOLLIS, M., AND S. LUKES, EDS. *Rationality and Relativism*. Cambridge: MIT Press, 1983.

HOWARD, ABE. "Do Anthropologists Become Relativists by Mistake?" *Inquiry* 11 (1968): 175–89.

JORDAN, JAMES E. "Protagoras and Relativism: Criticisms Good and Bad." *Southwestern Journal of Philosophy* 2 (1971): 7–29.

KAUFMAN, GORDAN. *Relativism, Knowledge, and Faith*. Chicago: University of Chicago Press, 1960.

KRAUSZ, MICHAEL. "Relativism and Rationality." *American Philosophical Quarterly* 10 (1973): 307–12.

LADD, JOHN. "The Issue of Relativism." *The Monist* 47 (1963): 585–609.

———. *Ethical Relativism*. Belmont, Calif.: Wadsworth, 1973.

LÉVY-BRUHL, L. *Primitive Mentality*. Translated by L. A. Clare, Chicago: University of Chicago Press, 1966.

LYONS, DAVID. "Ethical Relativism and the Problem of Incoherence." *Ethics* 86 (1976): 107–21.

MacIntyre, Alasdair. *After Virtue*. South Bend, Ind.: Notre Dame University Press, 1981.

Mackie, J. L. *Ethics: Inventing Right and Wrong*. Harmondsworth, England: Penguin, 1977.

Mannheim, Karl. *Ideology and Utopia*. New York: Harcourt Brace, 1949.

McClintock, Thomas. "The Argument for Ethical Relativism from the Diversity of Morals." *The Monist* 47 (1963): 528–44.

———. "How to Establish or Refute Ethical Relativism." *The Personalist* 54 (1973): 318–24.

Meiland, Jack. *Skepticism and Historical Knowledge*. New York: Random House, 1965.

———. "Concepts of Relative Truth." *The Monist* 60 (1977): 568–82.

Meyerson, Emile. *The Relativistic Deduction*. Dordrecht, Holland: Kluwer, 1984.

Moser, S. *Absolutism and Relativism in Ethics*. Springfield, Ill.: Charles C Thomas, 1968.

Murdoch, Iris. *The Sovereignty of the Good*. New York: Schocken Books, 1971.

Nielsen, Kai. "Varieties of Ethical Subjectivism." *Danish Yearbook of Philosophy* 7 (1970): 73–87.

———. "On the Diversity of Moral Beliefs." *Cultural Hermeneutics* 2 (1974): 281–303.

———. "Rationality and Relativism." *Philosophy of the Social Sciences* 4 (1974): 281–303.

Pareto, Vilfredo. *Mind and Society*. New York: Harcourt Brace, 1935.

Parsons, T. *The Social System*. London: Collier-Macmillan, 1951.

Redfield, Robert. *The Primitive World and Its Transformation*. Ithaca, N.Y.: Cornell University Press, 1953.

Roberts, George W. "Some Refutations of Private Subjectivism in Ethics." *Journal of Value Inquiry* 5 (1971): 292–309.

———. *The Nature of Morality*. New York: Oxford University Press, 1977.

Rotenstreich, Nathan. "On Ethical Relativism." *Journal of Value Inquiry* 11 (1977): 81–103.

Runciman, W. G. "Relativism: Cognitive and Moral." *Aristotelian Society Supplementary Volume* 48 (1974): 191–208.

Stace, W. T. *The Concept of Morals*. New York: Macmillan, 1962.

Strawson, P. F. *Skepticism and Naturalism*. New York: Columbia University Press, 1985.

Sumner, William G. *Folkways*. New York: Dover, 1906.

Taylor, Paul W. "Four Types of Ethical Relativism." *Philosophical Review* 63 (1954).

———. "Social Science and Ethical Relativism." *Journal of Philosophy* 55 (1958): 32–44.

Toulmin, S. *The Place of Reason in Ethics*. Cambridge: Harvard University Press, 1950.

Urmson, J. O. *The Emotive Theory of Ethics*. New York: Oxford University Press, 1968.

Vivas, Eliseo. *The Moral Life and the Ethical Life*. Chicago: University of Chicago Press, 1950.

Wellman, Carl. "The Ethical Implications of Cultural Relativity." *Journal of Philosophy* 60 (1963): 169–84.

Westermarck, Edward. *Ethical Relativity*. London: Routledge and Kegan Paul, 1932.

Williams, Bernard. *Morality: An Introduction to Ethics*. New York: Harper and Row, 1972.

———. "The Truth in Relativism." *Proceedings of the Aristotelian Society* (1974–75): 215–28.

Wilson, Bryan, ed. *Rationality*. New York: Harper and Row, 1970.

Wong, David B. *Moral Relativity*. Berkeley: University of California Press, 1984.

CHAPTER 2

Egoism

The analysis of relativism in the previous chapter has shown that values may well be objective, which then allows discussion to take place as to which values are really worth holding. However, another barrier must be cleared away before we can address that more ultimate question. This particular obstacle is erected by the egoist position in ethics, which maintains that it is either not possible or not desirable to pursue anyone's welfare but one's own. Since moral actions by their very nature are motivated by concern for others, this position would negate moral purpose in any form whatsoever. That is, if we cannot or should not act for the good of others but only for our own self-interest, then moral judgments become totally irrelevant and useless.

In discussing this position an important distinction must be made between psychological and ethical egoism. The *psychological egoist* maintains that human beings are so constituted that they cannot help but pursue their own advantage. To desire one's personal welfare is simply a psychological law of human nature. People may appear to be acting for the well being of others but at bottom they are only masking their selfish desires, pretending to the world or to themselves that they are generous and high minded. We may wish that it were otherwise, that man were closer to angels than to beasts, because our self-concept as a race or as individuals would be flattered by painting a nobler picture; nevertheless the facts do not bear that out. We always get something for ourselves out of what we do, otherwise we would not do it.

This egoistic view should not be confused with egotism, which is simply an exaggerated sense of self-importance or placing oneself first when deliberating about moral conduct. The position of psychological egoism claims that, whether we are self-important or humble, our motivation for action is always that of self-interest. Perhaps we should become our brother's keeper and love our neighbor as ourselves, but we simply are not made that way. We look out for number one and ask What's in it for me? whenever we act. And as George Bernard Shaw says, although we may blush for it we cannot help it because no other motivation is possible to us.

In contrast to psychological egoism, the *ethical egoist* maintains that everyone should pursue his own interests. Whether or not people do act solely for themselves nevertheless they ought to do so, since self-interest is the only justifiable mode of behavior. A life of altruism, in which an individual feels obliged to help others and place their welfare above his own, simply has no foundation—

although preachers and lofty moralists may try to persuade us otherwise. We have a primary obligation to act so that we benefit ourselves. If other people are benefited also then that's all well and good, but their welfare should never be the reason for our action. Only the well being of the individual should serve as motivation for conduct because that is the fundamental aim in living.

Egoism, then, can take two forms, and we will have to examine each one in turn.

Psychological: Everyone Is Out for Himself

As in so many cases, the ancient Greeks took the first steps in elucidating this theory. In Book II of Plato's *The Republic* one of Socrates' opponents presents the psychological egoist's viewpoint through a parable drawn from mythology. The man's name is Glaucon and the parable is known as the Ring of Gyges.

They say that to do injustice is, by nature, good; to suffer injustice, evil; but that the evil is greater than the good. And so when men have both done and suffered injustice and have had experience of both, not being able to avoid the one and obtain the other, they think that they had better agree among themselves to have neither; hence there arise laws and mutual covenants; and that which is ordained by law is termed by them lawful and just. This they affirm to be the origin and nature of justice; — it is a mean or compromise, between the best of all, which is to do injustice and not be punished, and the worst of all, which is to suffer injustice without the power of retaliation; and justice, being at a middle point between the two, is tolerated not as a good, but as the lesser evil, and honored by reason of the inability of men to do injustice. For no man who is worthy to be called a man would ever submit to such an agreement if he were able to resist; he would be mad if he did. Such is the received account, Socrates, of the nature and origin of justice.

Now that those who practise justice do so involuntarily and because they have not the power to be unjust will best appear if we imagine something of this kind: having given both to the just and the unjust power to do what they will, let us watch and see whither desire will lead them; then we shall discover in the very act the just and unjust man to be proceeding along the same road, following their interest, which all natures deem to be their good, and are only diverted into the path of justice by the force of law. The liberty which we are supposing may be most completely given to them in the form of such a power as is said to have been possessed by Gyges, the ancestor of Croesus the Lydian. According to the tradition, Gyges was a shepherd in the service of the king of Lydia; there was a great storm, and an earthquake made an opening in the earth at the place where he was feeding his flock. Amazed at the sight, he descended into the opening, where, among other marvels, he beheld a hollow brazen horse, having doors, at which he stooping and looking in saw a dead body of stature, as appeared to him, more than human, and having nothing on but a gold ring; this he took from the finger of the dead and reascended. Now the shepherds met together, according to custom, that they might send their monthly report about the flocks to the king; into their assembly he came having the ring on his finger, and as he was sitting among them he chanced to turn the collet of the ring inside his hand, when instantly he became invisible to the rest of the company and they began to speak of him as if he were no longer present. He was astonished at this, and again touching the ring he turned the collet outwards and reappeared; he made several trials of the ring, and always with the same result — when he turned the collet inwards he became invisible, when outwards he reappeared. Whereupon he contrived to be chosen one of the messengers who were sent to the court; where as soon as he arrived he seduced the queen, and with her help conspired against the king and slew him, and took the kingdom. Suppose now that there were two such magic rings, and the just put on one of them and the unjust the other; no man can be imagined to be of such an iron nature that he would stand fast in justice. No man would keep his hands off what was not his own when he could safely take what he liked out of the market, or go into houses and lie with any one at his pleasure, or kill or release from prison whom he would, and in all respects be like a God among men. Then the actions of the just would be as the actions of the unjust; they would both come at last to the same point. And this we may truly affirm to be a great proof that a man is just, not willingly or because he thinks that justice is any good to him individually, but of necessity, for wherever any one thinks that he can safely be unjust, there he is unjust. For all men believe in their hearts that injustice is far more profitable to the individual than justice, and he who argues as I have been supposing, will say that they are right. If you could imagine any one obtaining this power of becoming invisible, and never doing any wrong or touching what was another's, he would be thought by the lookers-on to be a most wretched idiot, although they would praise him to one another's faces, and keep up appearances with one another from a fear that they too might suffer injustice.[1]

In short, everyone would behave selfishly and with contempt for justice if they could. People restrain themselves only because they fear retaliation. We are selfish by our very nature and only involuntarily behave justly toward others. Anyone who had the Ring of Gyges would take what he wanted with no qualms of conscience.

Now a very likely objection to this thesis is that we sometimes find people who seem to be quite generous and would not behave in selfish ways even if they could get away with it. A parent, for example, will often give up money he could spend on himself in order to give his child a good college education, and he would not take the money back even if he could do so secretly. Surely such a parent is being genuinely unselfish here.

No he isn't, the egoist will reply, because the parent is proud of his child's accomplishments and derives satisfaction from the success of his offspring; it reflects favorably on himself. He is far more gratified by people knowing his child is attending college than he would be by spending the tuition fees on a car or a trip to the Bahamas.

But what about the case of someone who dedicates his leisure time to some charitable cause, helping to ship food to starving nations, volunteering as a fund-raiser for the Cancer Society, serving as a scout leader or a counsellor for alcoholics or runaways. Wouldn't that be evidence of concern for the welfare of others?

No, the psychological egoist would say, because people who do charity work are usually quite obvious about it, and the good reputation they acquire is the underlying motive for their generosity. Few people cast their bread upon the waters. They want acknowledgment on the concert program as financial contributors or insist on having their names on the scholarship fund they endowed or on the cornerstones of the library they had constructed. Even in those rare instances where individuals do perform acts of private generosity and never obtain the admiration of their neighbors, they still have the satisfaction of thinking well of themselves. Their self-image is enhanced by believing that they are humane and magnanimous individuals. They might also feel a sense of superiority over the people they have helped for, as the Swedish playwright Strindberg has pointed out, all assistance is humiliating and the giver inevitably feels proud that he is in a position to be charitable. To help those less fortunate than yourself means you are more fortunate than they are, and if the recipient is placed under some obligation, that adds still further to the personal satisfaction that the situation provides.

But what about more extreme examples of self-sacrifice, as in the case of a soldier who throws himself on a hand grenade to save his comrades, the fireman who risks his life to save a child, or the martyr who acts as Christ did and dies an excruciating death for the sake of mankind?

These also are examples of self-interest, the egoist claims, because such individuals are seeking fame. They would rather have a short, magnificent existence than a long, undistinguished one. To be anonymous in this world would constitute failure for them but glory would redeem their lives, and they could even hope for immortality in the life to come.

Using arguments such as these, the psychological egoist denies that the cases mentioned in any way discredit his view of universal self-interest. Overtly people sometimes appear kindhearted and willing to help their fellow man but upon analysis they only help others in order to benefit themselves. Just as the business organization cannot be trusted when it claims "we are here to serve you," no individual can be trusted to honestly state his underlying motives. We all rationalize our behavior and try to give the impression that we are good Samaritans when at heart everyone loves himself best and acts to enhance his own existence. To the egoist this is not cynicism but down-to-earth analysis.

In the history of philosophy this theory of human behavior has been repeated by many voices since Glaucon first articulated it in *The Republic*. Very often the assertions are made within the larger context of discussions on the basic nature of man. In his primal condition, in the "state of nature" prior to the development of human society, was man benevolent or malevolent? Does the young child exhibit a psychological propensity toward sharing or is he inclined to be grasping, in direct parallel to the infancy of the human race as a whole? The egoist takes the position that the character of man is fundamentally selfish; his drives and desires must be controlled by socialization and the power of government.

For example, one of the church fathers, St. Augustine (354–430), stressed man's basic impulse toward evil and traced it back to original sin. The Fall from grace in the Garden of Eden shows man's natural rebelliousness and self-love, so that the sacrifice of Christ was needed to bring about his salvation. Augustine also believed that in the secular realm a strong state is necessary to restrain these evil impulses—a corollary often made by those who distrust people's natural inclinations. If man were good then minimal controls would be needed and the government would be best that governed least.[2]

Niccolò Machiavelli (1469–1527), the famous politician and theorist of Renaissance Florence, expressed similar sentiments, especially in his work the *Discourses*. Here Machiavelli presents a list of aphorisms on the nature of man. For example, "All men are bad and ever ready to display their vicious nature, whenever they may find occasion for it" (I, 3); "Men act right only under compulsion" (I, 3); "Ambition [is a] passion so powerful in the hearts of men that it never leaves them" (I, 37); and "The fear to lose stirs the same passions in men as the desire to gain, as men do not believe themselves sure of what they possess, except by acquiring still more; and moreover, these new acquisitions are so many means of strength and power for abuses" (I, 5).[3] It should be added that Machiavelli thought of himself as no more than a realist, and his aim was to ensure the prosperity of the kingdom by knowing the motives of men.

Various other figures could be cited but the philosopher who is usually credited with the most complete advocacy of the egoistic position is the English philosopher Thomas Hobbes (1588 – 1679). Hobbes is celebrated chiefly for his writings on political philosophy, which he based on a psychological account of human nature. He wrote several books but the *Leviathan* is his principal work, and the following excerpt contains his description of man in a state of nature as well as his prescription for the form of government that will "cure" it.[4]

From *Leviathan**

CHAPTER 13

Of the Natural Condition of Mankind as Concerning Their Felicity, and Misery

Nature hath made men so equal, in the faculties of the body and mind; as that, though there be found one man sometimes manifestly stronger in body or of quicker mind than another, yet when all is reckoned together, the difference between man and man is not so considerable, as that one man can thereupon claim to himself any benefit, to which another may not pretend as well as he. For as to the strength of body, the weakest has strength enough to kill the strongest, either by secret machination, or by confederacy with others that are in the same danger with himself.

And as to the faculties of the mind — setting aside the arts grounded upon words, and especially that skill of proceeding upon general and infallible rules, called science; which very few have, and but in few things; as being not a native faculty, born with us; not attained, as prudence, while we look after somewhat else — I find yet a greater equality amongst men, than that of strength. For prudence is but experience, which equal time equally bestows on all men, in those things they equally apply themselves unto. That which may perhaps make such equality incredible, is but a vain conceit of one's own wisdom, which almost all men think they have in a greater degree than the vulgar; that is, than all men but themselves, and a few others, whom by fame, or for concurring with themselves, they approve. For such is the nature of men, that howsoever they may acknowledge many others to be more witty, or more eloquent, or more learned, yet they will hardly believe there be many so wise as themselves; for they see their own wit at hand, and other men's at a distance. But this proveth rather that men are in that point equal, than unequal. For there is not ordinarily a greater sign of the equal distribution of anything, than that every man is contented with his share.

*Reprinted from Thomas Hobbes, *Leviathan* (London: J. M. Dent, 1834).

From this equality of ability, ariseth equality of hope in the attaining of our ends. And therefore if any two men desire the same thing, which nevertheless they cannot both enjoy, they become enemies; and in the way to their end, which is principally their own conservation, and sometimes their delectation only, endeavor to destroy, or subdue one another. And from hence it comes to pass that where an invader hath no more to fear than another man's single power; if one plant, sow, build, or possess a convenient seat, others may probably be expected to come prepared with forces united, to dispossess and deprive him, not only of the fruit of his labor, but also of his life or liberty. And the invader again is in the like danger of another.

And from this diffidence of one another, there is no way for any man to secure himself so reasonable as anticipation; that is, by force or wiles to master the persons of all men he can, so long, till he see no other power great enough to endanger him: and this is no more than his own conservation requireth, and is generally allowed. Also because there be some, that taking pleasure in contemplating their own power in the acts of conquest, which they pursue farther than their security requires; if others, that otherwise would be glad to be at ease within modest bounds, should not by invasion increase their power, they would not be able long time, by standing only on their defence, to subsist. And by consequence, such augmentation of dominion over men being necessary to a man's conservation, it ought to be allowed him.

Again, men have no pleasure, but on the contrary a great deal of grief, in keeping company, where there is no power able to overawe them all. For every man looketh that his companion should value him at the same rate he sets upon himself; and upon all signs of contempt, or undervaluing, naturally endeavors, as far as he dares (which amongst them that have no common power to keep them in quiet, is far enough to make them destroy each other), to extort a greater value from his contemners by damage, and from others by the example.

So that in the nature of man, we find three principal causes of quarrel. First, competition; second, diffidence; thirdly, glory.

The first maketh men invade for gain; the second, for safety; and the third, for reputation. The first use violence to make themselves masters of other men's persons, wives, children, and cattle; the second, to defend them; the third, for trifles, as a word, a smile, a different opinion, and any other sign of undervalue, either direct in their persons, or by reflection in their kindred, their friends, their nation, their profession, or their name.

Hereby it is manifest that during the time men live without a common power to keep them all in awe, they are in that condition which is called war; and such a war as is of every man against every man. For *war* consisteth not in battle only, or the act of fighting, but in a tract of time wherein the will to contend by battle is sufficiently known, and therefore the notion of *time* is to be considered in the nature of war, as it is in the nature of weather. For as the nature of foul weather lieth not in a shower or two of rain, but in an inclination thereto of many days together; so the nature of war consisteth not in actual fighting, but in the known disposition thereto, during all the time there is no assurance to the contrary. All other time is *peace*.

Whatsoever therefore is consequent to a time of war, where every man is enemy to every man; the same is consequent to the time, wherein men live without other security than what their own strength and their own invention shall furnish them withal. In such condition there is no place for industry, because the fruit thereof is uncertain: and consequently no culture of the earth; no navigation, nor use of the commodities that may be imported by sea; no commodious building; no instruments of moving, and removing, such things as require much force; no knowledge of the face of the earth; no account of time; no arts; no letters; no society; and which is worst of all, continual fear, and danger of violent death; and the life of man, solitary, poor, nasty, brutish, and short.

It may seem strange to some man that has not well weighed these things, that nature should thus dissociate, and render men apt to invade and destroy one another; and he may therefore, not trusting to this inference, made from the passions, desire perhaps to have the same confirmed by experience. Let him therefore consider with himself, when taking a journey, he arms himself and seeks to go well accompanied; when going to sleep, he locks his doors; when even in his house he locks his chests; and this when he knows there be laws, and public officers, armed, to revenge all injuries shall be done him: what opinion he has of his fellow-subjects, when he rides armed; of his fellow citizens, when he locks his doors; and of his children, and servants, when he locks his chests. Does he not there as much accuse mankind by his actions, as I do by my words? But neither of us accuse man's nature in it. The desires, and other passions of man, are in themselves no sin. No more are the actions that proceed from those passions, till they know a law that forbids them: which till laws be made they cannot know; nor can any law be made, till they have agreed upon the person that shall make it.

It may preadventure be thought, there was never such a time nor condition of war as this; and I believe it was never generally so, over all the world: but there are many places where they live so now. For the savage people in many places of America, except the government of small families, the concord whereof dependeth on natural lust, have no government at all; and live at this day in that brutish manner, as I said before. Howsoever, it may be perceived what manner of life there would be, where there were no common power to fear; by the manner of life which men that have formerly lived under a peaceful government, use to degenerate into in a civil war.

But though there had never been any time wherein particular men were in a condition of war one against another; yet in all times, kings, and persons of sovereign authority, because of their independency, are in continual jealousies, and in the state and posture of gladiators; having their weapons pointing, and their eyes fixed on one another; that is, their forts, garrisons, and guns upon the frontiers of their kingdoms; and continual spies upon their neighbors; which is a posture of war. But because they uphold thereby the industry of their subjects, there does not follow from it that misery which accompanies the liberty of particular men.

To this war of every man against every man, this also is consequent: *that nothing can be unjust.* The notions of right and wrong, justice and injustice, have there no place. Where there is no common power, there is no law; where no law, no injustice. Force and fraud are in war the two cardinal virtues. Justice and injustice are none of the faculties neither of the body nor mind. If they were, they might be in a man that were alone in the world, as well as his senses and passions. They are qualities that relate to men in society, not in solitude. It is consequent also to the same condition, that there be no propriety, no dominion, no *mine* and *thine* distinct; but only that to be every man's, that he can get; and for so long as he can keep it. And thus much for the ill condition which man by mere nature is actually placed in; though with a possibility to come out of it, consisting partly in the passions, partly in his reason.

The passions that incline men to peace are fear of death, desire of such things as are necessary to commodious living, and a hope by their industry to obtain them. And reason suggesteth convenient articles of peace, upon which men may be drawn to agreement. These articles are they which otherwise are called the Laws of Nature; whereof I shall speak more particularly in the two following chapters.

CHAPTER 14

Of the First and Second Natural Laws, and of Contracts

The right of nature, which writers commonly call *jus naturale*, in the liberty each man hath to use his own power, as he will himself, for the preservation of his own nature; that is to say, of his own life; and consequently, of doing anything, which in his own judgment and reason, he shall conceive to be the aptest means thereunto.

By *liberty*, is understood, according to the proper signification of the word, the absence of external impediments: which impediments, may oft take away part of a man's power to do what he would; but cannot hinder him from using the power left him, according as his judgment, and reason shall dictate to him.

A *law of nature, lex naturalis*, is a precept of general rule, found out by reason, by which a man is forbidden to do that which is destructive of his life, or taketh away the means of preserving the same; and to omit that by which he thinketh it may be best preserved. For though they that speak of this subject, use to confound *jus* and *lex, right* and *law*; yet they ought to be distinguished: because *right* consisteth in liberty to do or to forbear, whereas *law* determineth and bindeth to one of them; so that law, and right differ as much as obligation and liberty; which in one and the same matter are inconsistent.

And because the condition of man, as hath been declared in the precedent chapter, is a condition of war of everyone against everyone; in which case everyone is governed by his own reason, and there is nothing he can make use of that may not be a help unto him in preserving his life against his enemies: it followeth, that in such a condition every man has a right to everything; even to one another's body. And therefore, as long as this natural right of every man to everything endureth, there can be no security to any man, how strong or wise soever he be, of living out the time which nature ordinarily alloweth men to live. And consequently it is a precept, or general rule of reason, *that every man ought to endeavor peace, as far as he has hope of obtaining it; and when he cannot obtain it, that he may seek and use all helps and advantages of war.* The first branch of which rule containeth the first and fundamental law of nature; which is, *to seek peace and follow it.* The second, the sum of the right of nature; which is, *by all means we can, to defend ourselves.*

From this fundamental law of nature, by which men are commanded to endeavor peace, is derived this second law; *that a man be willing, when others are so too, as far forth as for peace and defence of himself he shall think it necessary, to lay down this right to all things; and be contented with so much liberty against other men, as he would allow other men against himself.* For as long as every man holdeth this right, of doing anything he liketh, so long are all men in the condition of war. But if other men will not lay down their right, as well as he, then there is no reason for anyone to divest himself of his: for that were to expose himself to prey, which no man is bound to, rather than to dispose himself to peace. . . .

Whensoever a man transferreth his right, or renounceth it; it is either in consideration of some right reciprocally transferred to himself, or for some other good he hopeth for thereby. For it is a voluntary act; and of the voluntary acts of every man, the object is some *good to himself.* And therefore there be some rights which no man can be understood by any words, or other signs, to have abandoned or transferred. As first a man cannot lay down the right of resisting them that assault him by force, to take away his life; because he cannot be understood to aim thereby, at any good to himself. The same may be said of wounds, and chains, and imprisonment: both because there is no benefit consequent to such patience, as there is to the patience of suffering another to be wounded or imprisoned; as also because a man cannot tell, when he seeth men proceed against him by violence, whether they intend his death or not. And lastly the motive, an end for which this renouncing and transferring of right is introduced, is nothing else but the security of a man's person, in his life, and in the means of so preserving life as not to be weary of it. And therefore if a man by words, or other signs, seem to despoil himself of the end for which those signs were intended, he is not to be understood as if he meant it, or that it was his will, but that he was ignorant of how such words and actions were to be interpreted.

The mutual transferring of right, is that which men call *contract.*

CHAPTER 15

Of Other Laws of Nature

From that law of nature by which we are obliged to transfer to another such rights as, being retained, hinder the peace of mankind, there followeth a third; which is this, *that men perform their convenants made*: without which, convenants are in vain, and but empty words; and the right of all men to all things remaining, we are still in the condition of war.

And in this law of nature, consisteth the fountain and original of *justice.* For where no covenant hath preceded, there hath no right been transferred, and every man has right to everything; and consequently, no action can be unjust. But when a covenant is made, then to break it is *unjust*; and the definition of *injustice* is no other than *the not performance of covenant.* And whatsoever is not unjust, is *just.*

But because covenants of mutual trust, where there is a fear of not performance on either part, as hath been said in the former chapter, are invalid; though the original of justice be the making of covenants; yet injustice actually there can be none, till the cause of such fear be taken away; which while men are in the natural condition of war, cannot be done. Therefore before the names of just and unjust can have place, there must be some coercive power, to compel men equally to the performance of their covenants, by the terror of some punishment greater than the benefit they expect by the breach of their covenant; and to make good that propriety which by mutual contract men acquire, in recompense of the universal right they abandon: and such power there is none before the erection of a commonwealth. And this is also to be gathered out of the ordinary definition of justice in the Schools; for they say, that *justice is the constant will of giving to every man his own*. And therefore where there is no *own*, that is no propriety, there is no injustice; and where is no coercive power erected, that is, where there is no commonwealth, there is no propriety; all men having right to all things: therefore where there is no commonwealth, there nothing is unjust. So that the nature of justice consisteth in keeping of valid covenants; but the validity of covenants begins not but with the constitution of a civil power sufficient to compel men to keep them, and then it is also that propriety begins. . . .

. . .

CHAPTER 17

Of the Causes, Generation, and Definition of a Commonwealth

The final cause, end, or design of men who naturally love liberty and dominion over others, in the introduction of that restraint upon themselves in which we see them live in commonwealths, is the foresight of their own preservation, and of a more contented life thereby; that is to say, of getting themselves out from that miserable condition of war, which is necessarily consequent, as hath been shown in Chapter 13, to the natural passions of men, when there is no visible power to keep them in awe, and tie them by fear of punishment to the performance of their covenants and observation of those laws of nature set down in the fourteenth and fifteenth chapters.

For the laws of nature, as justice, equity, modesty, mercy, and, in sum, *doing to others as we would be done to*, of themselves, without the terror of some power to cause them to be observed, are contrary to our natural passions, that carry us to partiality, pride, revenge, and the like. And covenants, without the sword, are but words, and of no strength to secure a man at all. Therefore notwithstanding the laws of nature, which everyone hath then kept, when he has the will to keep them when he can do it safely; if there be no power erected, or not great enough for our security, every man will, and may, lawfully rely on his own strength and art, for caution against all men. . . .

The foundation of Hobbes' argument is that, in a natural state outside the bounds of civil society, man lives in continual conflict and danger of death. His condition is described as a *bellum omnium contra omnes* (a war of all against all). The reason for the constant turmoil is that each person acts in a self-seeking way, and the coverging lines of self-interest make life an endless and intolerable battleground. Hobbes wrote, "If any two men desire the same thing, which they nevertheless cannot both enjoy, they become enemies and . . . endeavor to destroy or subdue one another." The result is a life for man that is "solitary, poor, nasty, brutish, and short."

We recognize the fact that to satisfy our wants and to avoid pain and suffering, to ensure that we will be able to live securely both now and in the future, we need to obtain power. But no one can ever secure lasting power over anyone else; the abilities of people are too evenly matched. Life therefore becomes "a perpetual and restless desire of power after power, which ceases only in death." We long for peace and security, safety in our persons and property, and an end to the hate and fear that surround us. But we can never acquire sufficient power to attain that end or the more positive goal of fulfilling our desires. Everyone lives for himself alone and is engaged in a fruitless, lethal struggle with his neighbor.

Hobbes may not have meant that there was such a time in prehistory when everyone preyed upon everyone else; the "state of nature" may never have existed. However, his point was that such a state of chaos would exist if people acted solely in terms of their selfish desires, that is, their primary impulses.

Happily, Hobbes said, people escape from that state through the instrumentality of reason. They realize that they must agree to a "social contract" for the establishment of a common power "to keep them in awe, and to direct their actions to the Common Benefit." They therefore agree to set up the civil state, not out of a sense of community and brotherhood but for their mutual advantage. Reason tells them that only the power of a central government is sufficient to safeguard individual life.

Hobbes described in colorful detail the kinds of existence people enjoy outside and inside the state:

> Out of it, any man may rightly spoil or kill another; in it, none but one. Out of it, we are protected by our own forces; in it, by the power of all. Out of it, no man is sure of the fruit of his labors; in it, all men are. Lastly, out of it there is a dominion of passions, war, fear, poverty, slovenliness, solitude, barbarism, ignorance, cruelty; in it, the dominion of reason, peace, security, riches, decency, society, elegancy, sciences and benevolence.[5]

By saying that "none but one" may kill in an established state, Hobbes was alluding to his belief that a sovereign would be best as head of government, invested with the power of punishing citizens with death. That is, he believed that a single monarch would be most effective in maintaining authority and keeping people from warring against each other. A sovereign group of leaders might be sufficient but never a democratic form of government, and after weighing all the advantages and disadvantages he feels a monarch would probably be ideal.

Be that as it may, the main point for our purposes is that Hobbes saw human nature as essentially selfish to the point of violence. We cannot help wanting to advance our own interests even by trampling on other people, so that a communal agreement is needed as well as the power of the state to enforce it; otherwise our egoistic behavior could never be controlled.

Glaucon had argued that if we were invisible without the restraint of punishment, we would all be unjust, taking whatever we wanted. Hobbes reiterated this view and attributes this behavior to man's fundamentally greedy nature. We take advantage of situations and get as much as we can because we are beastlier than any beast. Man needs the control of law, which people accept not out of fellow feeling or a spirit of cooperation but because it is the best way for them to satisfy their personal wants.

Both Glaucon and Hobbes would agree that if man could do so he would always act selfishly thereby endorsing the basic thesis of psychological egoism: that human beings never act except in terms of their own interests.

Evaluation

1. The first point to notice about Hobbes' analysis is that it is grossly one sided, unfairly exaggerating the awfulness of human character. Even if man were in some peculiar state of nature, wearing the ring of Gyges, he would probably not behave as brutishly as Hobbes described. For man possesses tendencies other than the purely negative ones — tendencies toward understanding, mutual support, and comradeship, for example. We want to create not just destroy and to share as well as to take for ourselves. Our fraternal and gregarious inclinations are at least as strong as our predatory and acquisitive ones, and we feel as much sympathy for other people as we do hostility or aggression. Furthermore, people join together for the excellences of civilization not just to avoid the disadvantages of a solitary existence. We want to communicate with one another, to experience art, music, and literature, and generally enjoy the benefits of human society.

This is why Aristotle (384 – 322 B.C.) described man as the political animal and why philosophers such as Jean-Jacques Rousseau (1712 – 1778) and John Locke (1632 – 1704) could take such a positive view of human nature; they looked at the other side of the coin. To Rousseau, the "natural man" is a person of good instincts and wholesome, simple tastes. In direct contrast to Hobbes, he maintained that it is civilization that corrupts man's natural goodness, especially the acids of urban life, class distinctions, and governmental tyranny.[6] Locke also believed that the state of nature was relatively peaceful with people equal, free, and independent, behaving in a largely rational manner. "Men living together according to reason without a common superior on earth with authority to judge between them, is properly the state of nature." Rights, he thought, are not conferred by a sovereign who has saved people from themselves but exist as "natural rights" that government is entrusted to protect; if that trust is broken, and citizens are denied their life, health, liberty, or possessions, then revolution is justified.[7]

It could be added that the "noble savage" tradition, extolled by writers such as James Fenimore Cooper (1789 – 1851) and Robert Louis Stevenson (1850 – 1894), does not paint primitive man as ferocious and cruel but a creature of dignity and natural kindness. Certain anthropological and sociological evidence tend to support the view that benevolent traits are, in fact, present in early man and prehumans. And the picture that is emerging from recent studies in primatology shows that even chimpanzees help each other when they are injured, adopt orphan babies, and grieve when death occurs.

Perhaps the simplest denial of the Hobbesian view of man was made by the economic and political theorist Adam Smith (1723–1790). Smith's principal work is *The Wealth of Nations* but in *The Theory of Moral Sentiments* he described the basis of human sympathy as springing from a universal, psychological response of empathy.

How selfish soever man may be supposed, there are evidently some principles in his nature, which interest him in the fortune of others, and render their happiness necessary to him, though he derives nothing from it except the pleasure of seeing it. Of this kind is pity or compassion, the emotion which we feel for the misery of others, when we either see it, or are made to conceive it in a very lively manner. That we often derive sorrow from the sorrow of others, is a matter of fact too obvious to require any instances to prove it; for this sentiment, like all the other original passions of human nature, is by no means confined to the virtuous and humane, though they perhaps may feel it with the most exquisite sensibility. The greatest ruffian, the most hardened violator of the laws of society, is not altogether without it.

As we have no immediate experience of what other men feel, we can form no idea of the manner in which they are affected, but by conceiving what we ourselves should feel in the like situation. Though our brother is upon the rack, as long as we ourselves are at our ease, our senses will never inform us of what he suffers. They never did, and never can, carry us beyond our own person, and it is by the imagination only that we can form any conception of what are his sensations. Neither can that faculty help us to this other way, than by representing to us what would be our own, if we were in his case. It is the impressions of our own senses only, not those of his, which our imaginations copy. By the imagination we place ourselves in his situation, we conceive ourselves enduring all the same torments, we enter as it were into his body, and become in some measure the same person with him, and thence form some idea of his sensations, and even feel something which, though weaker in degree, is not altogether unlike them. His agonies, when they are thus brought home to ourselves, when we have thus adopted and made them our own, begin at last to affect us, and we then tremble and shudder at the thought of what he feels. For as to be in pain or distress of any kind excites the most excessive sorrow, so to conceive or to imagine that we are in it, excites some degree of the same emotion, in proportion to the vivacity or dullness of the conception.

That this is the source of our fellow-feeling for the misery of others, that it is by changing places in fancy with the sufferer, that we come either to conceive or to be affected by what he feels, may be demonstrated by many obvious observations, if it should not be thought sufficiently evident of itself. When we see a stroke aimed and just ready to fall upon the leg or arm of another person, we naturally shrink and draw back our own leg or our own arm; and when it does fall, we feel it in some measure, and are hurt by it as well as the sufferer. The mob, when they are gazing at a dancer on the slack rope, naturally writhe and twist and balance their own bodies, as they see him do, and as they feel that they themselves must do it in his situation. Persons of delicate fibres, and a weak constitution of body, complain, that in looking on the sores and ulcers which are exposed by beggars in the streets, they are apt to feel an itching or uneasy sensation in the correspondent part of their own bodies. The horror which they conceive at the misery of those wretches affects that particular part in themselves more than any other; because that horror arises from conceiving what they themselves would suffer, if they really were the wretches whom they are looking upon. . . .[8]

These claims by Adam Smith of a natural response of sympathy toward others or Rousseau or Locke's claim of positive cooperation not incessant competition, of a basic rationality and benevolence rather than continual malice, may be as distorted in their way as Hobbes is in his conception of universal selfishness. One can sin to the left as well as to the right. But at least they enable us to question Hobbes' base view of man by offering the opposite alternative. Perhaps the true answer lies halfway in between, that man is a mixed creature, neither good nor bad but "middling." There is trust as well as betrayal, friendship together with enmity, love alternating with hate. We are neither saintly nor devilish but simply human with complicated and diverse natures.

Or we might assume, as most contemporary psychologists do, that people are not born with any inherent moral nature but only with amoral drives and needs that are shaped by the social environment. The psychologists Jean Piaget and L. Kohlberg, for example, maintained that moral cognition occurs through a natural process of development. Instead of seeing people as sinful at birth then or "trailing clouds of glory" as Wordsworth says, we could maintain that man "grows" moral through the normal experience of socialization. Some recent studies have shown that personality traits can owe more to heredity than environment, but the verdict is not yet in on human nature.[9]

In the eighteenth century it was customary to ask about man's innate moral qualities but this approach ignored the variability and adaptibility of human beings. People can acquire characteristics through learning and build a moral nature. If there are original motives (in Hobbes' state of nature or Freud's concept of early childhood) they may be fundamentally different when we reach various stages of maturity.

Whichever position we adopt, at least we could not reasonably believe the Hobbesian evaluation of human behavior. The egoistic picture he paints seems too extreme to be accepted, especially in the light of the positive characteristics of man that are in evidence, either inherently or through social interaction. Society is held together by inner cohesion not just external force and part of that cohesion seems to stem from sympathy for one another.

2. Aside from Hobbes, the general position of psychological egoism can be criticized for the assumption that actions are only done for personal gratification. The psychological evidence simply does not support this analysis of human motivation nor does common sense and everyday experience.

This point can be made clear by taking the example of eating. Most times we eat because we are hungry not because we desire the satisfaction of eating. We do not consciously or even unconsciously seek the personal gratifications that eating provides in the way of pleasant taste sensations but simply want to consume the meat or vegetables on the plate. Sometimes we desire food for its taste and will choose a restaurant for its fine cooking, but more often the smell and texture and flavor is an accompaniment to eating and not the reason for it. In other words, our motive in eating is rarely that of satisfaction; in most cases we have a different reason, i.e., the drive of our appetite. Therefore the psychological egoist seems to be mistaken when he claims that people always act for the sake of satisfaction; eating appears to be a contrary case.

But this analysis is not limited to food; it appears to be correct with regard to many other objects. We play chess because we want to play chess; our aim is not the enjoyment that chess playing provides. We bathe to get clean and do not have in mind that satisfaction of getting clean. And when one adds to this understanding the fact that many actions are performed out of habit or in response to an obligation or promise, then the egoistic interpretation cannot hold up. Clearly, personal satisfaction is not the only purpose behind human action.

3. A related criticism has to do with the psychological egoist's argument that since all people act from personal desires therefore all people act for themselves. This conclusion simply does not follow from the premises. Even if people acted only in accordance with their own desires those desires could be for someone else's welfare. Perhaps we always do what we want but what we want could be another person's good.

In other words, just because all actions originate in personal desires that does not mean that the aim of all action is personal benefit. The psychological egoist is confusing the origin of an action with its objective or purpose and, because of that confusion, accusing everyone of selfishness. But selfishness consists in acting for oneself not merely from oneself, that is, from personal motives, and at least some of our purposes seem to be altruistic.

The following passage from the sermons of Bishop Joseph Butler (1692–1752) is often taken as the definitive statement on this point. Butler argued that the desire for "private good" is not necessarily in opposition to the "public good" but can actually include it. Self-love and benevolence do, in fact, coincide.

From this review and comparison of the nature of man as respecting self and as respecting society, it will plainly appear that there are as real and the same kind of indications in human nature that we were made for society and to do good to our fellow creatures, as that we were intended to take care of our own life and health and private good; and that the same objections lie against one of these assertions as against the other.

First, there is a natural principle of *benevolence* in man, which is in some degree to *society* what *self-love* is to the *individual*. And if there be in mankind any disposition to friendship; if there be any such thing as compassion, for compassion is momentary love; if there be any such thing as the paternal or filial affections; if there be any affection in human nature the object and end of which is the good of another — this is itself benevolence or the love of another. Be it ever so short, be it in ever so low a degree, or ever so unhappily confined, it proves the assertion and points out what we were designed for, as really as though it were in a higher degree and more extensive. I must however remind you that though benevolence and self-love are different, though the former tends most directly to public good, and the latter to private, yet they are so perfectly coincident that the greatest satisfactions to ourselves depend upon our having benevolence in a due degree, and that self-love is one chief security of our right behavior toward society. It may be added that their mutual coinciding, so that we can scarce promote one without the other, is equally a proof that we were made for both.

· · ·

Secondly, this will further appear, from observing that the *several passions and affections*, which are distinct both from benevolence and self-love, do in general contribute and lead us to *public* good as really as to *private*. It might be thought too minute and particular, and would carry us too great a length, to distinguish between and compare together the several passions or appetites distinct from benevolence, whose primary use and intention is the security and good of society; and the passions distinct from self-love, whose primary intention and design is the security and good of the individual. It is enough to the present argument that desire of esteem from others, contempt and esteem of them, love of society as distinct from affection to the good of it, indignation against successful vice—that these are public affections or passions, have an immediate respect to others, naturally lead us to regulate our behavior in such a manner as will be of service to our fellow creatures. If any or all of these may be considered likewise as private affections, as tending to private good, this does not hinder them from being public affections, too, or destroy the good influence of them upon society, and their tendency to public good. It may be added that as persons without any conviction from reason of the desirableness of life would yet of course preserve it merely from the appetite of hunger, so by acting merely from regard (suppose) to reputation, without any consideration of the good of others, men often contribute to public good. In both these instances they are plainly instruments in the hands of another, in the hands of Providence, to carry on ends, the preservation of the individual and good of society, which they themselves have not in their view or intention. The sum is, men have various appetites, passions, and particular affections, quite distinct both from self-love and from benevolence—all of these have a tendency to promote both public and private good, and may be considered as respecting others and ourselves equally and in common; but some of them seem most immediately to respect others, or tend to public good, others of them most immediately to respect self, or tend to private good; as the former are not benevolence, so the latter are not self-love; neither sort are instances of our love either to ourselves or others, but only instances of our Maker's care and love both of the individual and the species, and proofs that He intended we should be instruments of good to each other, as well as that we should be so to ourselves.

Thirdly, there is a principle of reflection in men by which they distinguish between, approve and disapprove, their own actions. We are plainly constituted such sort of creatures as to reflect upon our own nature. The mind can take a view of what passes within itself, its propensions, aversions, passions, affections, as respecting such objects and in such degrees, and of the several actions consequent thereupon. In this survey it approves of one, disapproves of another, and toward a third is affected in neither of these ways, but is quite indifferent. This principle in man by which he approves or disapproves his heart, temper, and actions, is conscience. . . . That this faculty tends to restrain men from doing mischief to each other, and leads them to do good, is too manifest to need being insisted upon. Thus a parent has the affection of love to his children; this leads him to take care of, to educate, to make due provision for them; the natural affection leads to this, but the reflection that it is his proper business, what belongs to him, that it is right and commendable so to do — this added to the affection becomes a much more settled principle and carries him on through more labor and difficulties for the sake of his children than he would undergo from that affection alone, if he thought it, and the course of action it led to, either indifferent or criminal. This indeed is impossible, to do that which is good and not to approve of it; for which reason they are frequently not considered as distinct, though they really are, for men often approve of the actions of others which they will not imitate, and likewise do that which they approve not. It cannot possibly be denied that there is this principle of reflection or conscience in human nature. Suppose a man to relieve an innocent person in great distress, suppose the same man afterwards, in the fury of anger, to do the greatest mischief to a person who had given no just cause of offense; to aggravate the injury, add the circumstances of former friendship and obligation from the injured person, let the man who is supposed to have done these two different actions coolly reflect upon them afterwards, without regard to their consequences to himself; to assert that any common man would be affected in the same way toward these different actions, that he would make no distinction between them, but approve or disapprove them equally, is too glaring a falsity to need being confuted. There is therefore this principle of reflection or conscience in mankind. . . .

If it be said that there are persons in the world who are in great measure without the natural affections toward their fellow creatures, there are likewise instances of persons without the common natural affections to themselves; but the nature of man is not to be judged of by either of these, but by what appears in the common world, in the bulk of mankind.[10]

Butler claimed that we cannot satisfy ourselves without expressing benevolence toward others for that is part of what pleases us. We may be acting out of personal desires but that does not mean only for our benefit; others are bound to profit also because their welfare is involved in what we desire.

4. Still another criticism has to do with the egoist's interpretation of allegedly unselfish actions. When the psychological egoist is confronted with the parent who sacrifices for his child, the person who contributes his time to charitable causes, or the martyr who gives up his life for humanity he will discount these cases on the grounds that the individual receives some benefit from his generosity. The personal gain is interpreted as the reason for the action.

However, even if we receive satisfaction from benefiting another person that does not imply that our aim was to achieve such satisfaction. The good we obtain for ourselves may very well be incidental and minor, a by-product or accidental result of an essentially unselfish action. For example, we might feel self-satisfied after helping in a civil rights struggle but it would be odd to assume that our objective was to feel that self-satisfaction. By the same token, if we were frustrated in our aims we would never assume that frustration was what we were seeking. In brief, the purpose of action should not be equated with its consequences.

5. Several more subtle criticisms of psychological egoism have been made, including the following: When the egoist claims that helping others is a means to personal gratification this argument can be turned back against him; he is Hoist with his own petar. For if a person derives satisfaction from attaining the goal of helping others this hardly shows selfishness but indicates unselfishness instead. It is the compassionate person who finds satisfaction in helping other people not the selfish one.

Also, the point could be made that the psychological egoist is inconsistent. For when the egoist says that although it is an unpleasant truth we always do what pleases us, he is presenting a truth that is not pleasing and thus denying his own statement. If he finds this fact painful but states it anyway then he does not always do what pleases him.

Still other objections could be mentioned, however a sufficient number of problems have been cited to at least cast doubt on psychological egoism as a viable description of human conduct. We must now turn to the sister doctrine of ethical egoism, which maintains that whether or not people do act only for themselves nevertheless they should, seeking their own advantage as the governing principle in all conduct.

Ethical: Why Should We Be Moral?

The egoist ethic maintains that an individual's sole obligation is to promote his own welfare. He is to act only in ways that further his personal advantage, obtaining the maximum amount of good for himself rather than concerning himself with other people's well being. Although moralists usually assume that we should be *altruistic* and act in ways that benefit others (especially the unfortunate), the ethical egoist recognizes no such responsibility. In his mind, pursuing our individual interests is paramount and life should be lived for oneself alone.

Sometimes he will argue that altruism is actually an impossible doctrine to carry out, for if everyone is self-sacrificing then no one is left to accept the sacrifice. It is utterly fruitless for everyone to give and no one to take. On the other hand, for each person to pursue his own good is perfectly feasible and will lead to the well being of all. For as each person looks after himself then everyone is necessarily enriched; the whole, after all, is the sum of its parts.

We should each look after ourselves then and not dedicate our lives to serving others. That kind of self-sacrifice is unjustified to the ethical egoist because our basic duty is to promote our own good. Sometimes our conduct will affect others in a favorable way, sometimes it will produce unfavorable consequences, but our purpose should always be to benefit ourselves. The ethical egoist will sometimes soften his doctrine by saying that the moral agent is to be the *primary* beneficiary of an action but he will never advocate a selfless dedication to others.

In contemporary terms, we might tell a person today not to be a chump, a patsy, a wimp, a loser. Look out for yourself, we say, because no one else will do it for you. Get smart. God helps those who help themselves. Do unto others before they do unto you. We only go round once so get what you can out of life.

The 1980s, in fact, have been characterized as the "me" era, in which people feel very little social conscience or responsibility toward others but want money, status, and material possessions for themselves. This is the modern attitude of ethical egoism in which corporations will fight antipollution regulations that decrease their profits; legislators with a belief in individualism will oppose subsidies for low-income housing, school lunch programs, and job retraining programs; and whites will reject affirmative action policies on the grounds that each person should make his own way on his own merits. Self-help not handouts is the contemporary motto. Many people feel a commitment to themselves and are willing to work hard to realize their aspirations but they feel no sense of solidarity with the world community; they are not their brother's keeper. They may share their earnings with their family but not with those starving to death in the third world; that is not their business.

A great deal of this unabashed selfishness and the lowering of moral standards is predicated on the belief that personal success is the most important factor in life, far more important than the way success is won (it's not how you play the game but whether you win or lose). In sports, business, politics, or elsewhere we are inclined to put our scruples in our pocket and pursue personal reward as our goal. Crime consists in getting caught not in stepping on others on your way to the top.

In the history of philosophy, one of the most blatant expressions of ethical egoism appears in the theories of Niccolò Machiavelli, the Italian Renaissance theorist whose ignoble view of man was mentioned previously. Like Hobbes, Machiavelli was chiefly a political theorist and his advice was couched in terms of the ideal for a ruler. But the ruler (or Prince as Machiavelli conceives him) should do what is necessary to maintain himself in power and the individual, at whatever level, should pursue his own advantage. It was Machiavelli who said "the ends justify the means," so that anything is permissible provided that it furthers one's purposes.

In the following excerpt from *The Prince and the Discourses* Machiavelli presented a handbook of rules for manipulating people out of hidden, self-serving motives.

The Prince*

It is necessary for a prince, who wishes to maintain himself, to learn how not to be good, and to use this knowledge and not use it, according to the necessities of the case. . . . Some things which seem virtues would, if

*Reprinted with permission from Niccolò Machiavelli; *The Prince*, in *The Prince and the Discourses*, trans. Luigi Ricci and C. E. Detmold (New York: Random House, 1940), Chapters 16–19.

followed, lead to one's ruin, and some others which appear vices result in one's great security and well being.

It Is Better to Be Feared than Loved

A prince must not mind incurring the charge of cruelty for the purpose of keeping his subjects united and faithful; for, with a very few examples, he will be more merciful than those who, from excess of tenderness, allow disorders to arise, from whence spring bloodshed and rapine; for these as a rule injure the whole community, while the executions carried out by the prince injure only individuals. And of all princes, it is impossible for a new prince to escape the reputation of cruelty, new states being always full of dangers. . . .

From this arises the question whether it is better to be loved more than feared, or feared more than loved. The reply is, that one ought to be both feared and loved, but as it is difficult for the two to go together, it is much safer to be feared than loved, if one of the two has to be wanting. For it may be said of men in general that they are ungrateful, voluble, dissemblers, anxious to avoid danger, and covetous of gain; as long as you benefit them, they are entirely yours; they offer you their blood, their goods, their life, and their children, as I have before said, when the necessity is remote; but when it approaches, they revolt. And the prince who has relied solely on their words, without making other preparations, is ruined; for the friendship which is gained by purchase and not through grandeur and nobility of spirit is bought but not secured, and at a pinch is not to be expended in your service. And men have less scruple in offending one who makes himself loved than one who makes himself feared; for love is held by a chain of obligation which, men being selfish, is broken whenever it serves their purpose; but fear is maintained by a dread of punishment which never fails.

Still, a prince should make himself feared in such a way that if he does not gain love, he at any rate avoids hatred; for fear and the absence of hatred may well go together, and will be always attained by one who abstains from interfering with the property of his citizens and subjects or with their women. . . . But above all he must abstain from taking the property of others, for men forget more easily the death of their father than the loss of their patrimony. . . .

I conclude, therefore, with regard to being feared and loved, that men love at their own free will, but fear at the will of the prince, and that a wise prince must rely on what is in his power and not on what is in the power of others, and he must only contrive to avoid incurring hatred, as has been explained.

The Disadvantages of Keeping Promises

You must know that there are two methods of fighting, the one by law, the other by force: the first method is that of men, the second of beasts; but as the first method is often insufficient, one must have recourse to the second. It is therefore necessary for a prince to know well how to use both the beast and the man. . . .

A prince being thus obliged to know well how to act as a beast must imitate the fox and the lion, for the lion cannot protect himself from traps, and the fox cannot defend himself from wolves. One must therefore be a fox to recognise traps, and a lion to frighten wolves. Those that wish to be only lions do not understand this. Therefore, a prudent ruler ought not to keep faith when by so doing it would be against his interest, and when the reasons which made him bind himself no longer exist. If men were all good, this precept would not be a good one; but as they are bad, and would not observe their faith with you, so you are not bound to keep faith with them. Nor have legitimate grounds ever failed a prince who wished to show colourable excuse for the non-fulfilment of his promise. Of this one could furnish an infinite number of modern examples, and show how many times peace has been broken, and how many promises rendered worthless, by the faithlessness of princes, and those that have been best able to imitate the fox have succeeded best. But it is necessary to be able to disguise this character well, and to be a great feigner and dissembler; and men are so simple and so ready to obey present necessities, that one who deceives will always find those who allow themselves to be deceived.

I will only mention one modern instance. Alexander VI did nothing else but deceive men, he thought of nothing else, and found the occasion for it; no man was ever more able to give assurances, or affirmed things with stronger oaths, and no man observed them less; however, he always succeeded in his deceptions, as he well knew this aspect of things.

It is not, therefore, necessary for a prince to have all the above-named qualities, but it is very necessary to seem to have them. I would even be bold to say that to possess them and always to observe them is dangerous, but to appear to possess them is useful. Thus it is well to seem merciful, faithful, humane, sincere, religious, and also to be so; but you must have the mind so disposed that when it is needful to be otherwise you may be able to change to the opposite qualities. And it must be understood that a prince, and especially a new prince, cannot observe all those things which are considered good in men, being often obliged, in order to maintain the state, to act against faith, against charity, against humanity, and against religion. And, therefore, he must have a mind disposed to adapt itself according to the wind, and as the variations of fortune dictate, and, as I said before, not deviate from what is good, if possible, but be able to do evil if constrained. . . .

In the actions of men, and especially of princes, from which there is no appeal, the end justifies the means. Let a prince therefore aim at conquering and maintaining the state, and the means will always be judged honourable and praised by every one, for the vulgar is always taken by appearances and the issue of the event; and the world consists only of the vulgar, and the few who are not vulgar are isolated when the many have a rallying point in the prince.

Niggardliness Is Superior to Liberality

It would be well to be considered liberal, nevertheless liberality such as the world understands it will injure you, because if used virtuously and in the proper way, it will not be known, and you will incur the disgrace of the contrary vice. But one who wishes to obtain the reputation of liberality among men, must not omit every kind of sumptuous display, and to such an extent that a prince of this character will consume by such means all his resources, and will be at last compelled, if he wishes to maintain his name for liberality, to impose heavy taxes on his people, become extortionate, and do everything possible to obtain money. This will make his subjects begin to hate him, and he will be little esteemed being poor, so that having by this liberality injured many and benefited but few, he will feel the first little disturbance and be endangered by every peril. If he recognises this and wishes to change his system, he incurs at once the charge of niggardliness.

A prince, therefore, . . . must not, if he be prudent, object to be called miserly. In course of time he will be thought more liberal, when it is seen that by his parsimony his revenue is sufficient, that he can defend himself against those who make war on him, and undertake enterprises without burdening his people, so that he is really liberal to all those from whom he does not take, who are infinite in number, and niggardly to all to whom he does not give, who are few. In our times we have seen nothing great done except by those who have been esteemed niggardly; the others have all been ruined. . . .

You may be very generous indeed with what is not the property of yourself or your subjects, as were Cyrus, Caesar, and Alexander; for spending the wealth of others will not diminish your reputation, but increase it, only spending your own resources will injure you. There is nothing which destroys itself so much as liberality, for by using it you lose the power of using it, and become either poor and despicable, or, to escape poverty, rapacious and hated. And of all things that a prince must guard against, the most important are being despicable or hated, and liberality will lead you to one or other of these conditions. It is, therefore, wiser to have the name of a miser, which produces disgrace without hatred, than to incur of necessity the name of being rapacious, which produces both disgrace and hatred.

Cunning and Deceit Are Superior to Force

I believe it to be most true that it seldom happens that men rise from low condition to high rank without employing either force or fraud, unless that rank should be attained either by gift or inheritance. Nor do I believe that force alone will ever be found to suffice, whilst it will often be the case that cunning alone serves the purpose; as is clearly seen by whoever reads the life of Philip of Macedon, or that of Agathocles the Sicilian, and many others, who from the lowest or most moderate condition have achieved thrones and great empires. Xenophon shows in his Life of Cyrus the necessity of deception to success: the first expedition of Cyrus against the king of Armenia is replete with fraud, and it was deceit alone, and not force, that enabled him to seize that kingdom. And Xenophon draws no other conclusion from it than that a prince who wishes to achieve great things must learn to deceive.

Notice that Machiavelli had no moral scruples regarding force, fraud, cruelty, intimidation, cunning, and deceit, and only advocated being "merciful, faithful, humane, sincere, [and] religious" when it is useful to seem or act that way. Whatever proves itself to be an effective instrument for success is justified precisely because it is expedient for gaining the advantage.

Machiavelli believed that all people act selfishly and offers realistic advice to rulers in the light of that perceived truth. He accepted the fact and does not condemn mankind, rather he advised rulers to be smart and act likewise because that is the way of the world: *così fan tutti.*

The German philosopher Friedrich Nietzsche (1844–1900) was another prominent representative of ethical egoism. Unlike Machiavelli, Nietzsche's writings were not primarily political but personal, advocating a certain mode of living as a reflection of his overall philosophic system. This system was developed in a passionate, sweeping way without much consistency and Nietzsche often resembled a gifted poet more than a rigorous thinker. Nevertheless, his insights have exerted a powerful influence on Western ideals as to how the individual ought to live.

Nietzsche's starting point lies in a concept as to the nature of reality as a whole. To his mind, ultimate reality consists of a perpetually striving will. This is not a will to live, as his predecessor Arthur Schopenhauer (1788–1860) had postulated and Darwinian evolutionism had suggested, but a will to power. This force permeates the universe and is responsible for every manifestation of striving and vitality, endurance, initiative, and vigor. The urge to preserve oneself, Nietzsche thought, is only incidental to nature's overall thrust of energy that aims at increased power. "A living thing seeks above all to *discharge* its strength," he wrote, "life itself is *Will to Power*; self-preservation is only one of the indirect and most frequent results thereof."

Since the will to power is the dominant force coursing through all living organisms including human beings, we should be free to employ any methods available for the expression and acquisition of that fundamental power. The individual should feel no qualms of conscience at using deceit, cruelty, lies, or violence since the drive for the enlargement of the self is the basic truth of our being. This is why Nietzsche wrote in a book entitled (tellingly) *Beyond Good and Evil*, "Exploitation does not belong to a depraved, or imperfect and primitive society: it belongs to the *nature* of the living being as a primary organic function; it is the consequence of the intrinsic Will to Power." Whatever is life enhancing or increases the fullness of our being is thereby justified because we are linking into the most elemental force of existence.

As a corollary to this doctrine advocating the uninhibited exercise of power, Nietzsche accepted the fact that a vigorous and perhaps brutal competition will result. But he welcomes this atmosphere because it would be a tonic to the development of the individual, stimulating excitement and creative energy; we breathe best in a thunderstorm. Not only will an exhilarating environment be produced but Nietzsche could foresee that humanity would become divided into the successful and the unsuccessful through the winnowing force of competition. As each person strove to expand his own power the lines of self-interest would converge and the outcome of that clash would be the creation of superior and inferior classes, the shepherds and the sheep. The two groups would not be separated by social or economic factors or by distinctions of birth but by the degree to which they possess the will to self-assertion.

The superior people or "masters" as Nietzsche called them would consist of those who have the courage to take charge of their lives and ignore the interests of other people for the sake of maximizing their own being. They would overcome the dictates of conscience, which only reflect conventional morality, and perform actions that spring from their personal code of plenitude and power. They would act for themselves and let others defend themselves with the force of their will, giving no quarter and asking none. Their harshness and aggression would be what they expect to encounter and their victory would justify their higher status because it demonstrates the superiority of their will.

The "slaves," on the other hand, would be those who lack the strength to develop themselves at someone else's expense and feel obliged to follow social rules. They are the people who honor values such as pity, consideration, and compassion because their will is flacid and weak. Values such as these are really nothing more than rationalizations masking a basic cowardice. The slaves are making a virtue of necessity, championing the self-denying tendencies they find most comfortable. To sacrifice for others gives them a sense of being needed and of belonging, salves their conscience, and makes them feel virtuous and admirable but it only hides their inability to be individuals and grasp life for themselves. Instead of taking risks they cringe in fear of being hurt and settle for the safety of kindness to others, meekness, deference, and humility. They are the ones who glorify service over self and feel morally self-satisfied when in fact they have abdicated authority over their lives and denied the primal will to power.

Since two levels of humanity exist, Nietzsche felt that two different ethics must be acknowledged. It would be a mistake to have a general morality that ignores this distinction and proclaims an absolute set of principles for everyone. "Moral systems must be compelled first of all to bow before the *gradations of rank*; their presumption must be driven home to their conscience — until they thoroughly understand at last that it is *immoral* to say that 'what is right for one is proper for another.'"

Nietzsche was here rejecting the golden rule that Whatsoever ye would that men should do to you, do ye even so to them or, negatively stated, What is hateful to yourself, don't do to your fellow man. In his approach, different rules apply for master morality and for slave morality. The masters should be hard and domineering; the slaves, deferential and ingratiating. The masters are daring, innovative, powerful, and intelligent; the slaves lack originality, resist all change, and follow their leaders obsequiously. Above all, the masters have the right to pursue their self-interest through the free exercise of their power whereas the slaves have surrendered that right through their cowardice and frailty; they are subjugated to the ambition of the masters.

In taking as his ideal the individualism of master morality, Nietzsche vehemently rejected both democracy and Christianity. He interpreted them as being allied with slave virtues because they regard every person as equally valuable and not separable into superior and inferior categories. Democracy assumes that all men are created equal and every citizen is qualified to serve on juries and vote for the leaders of government, and Christianity holds as an article of faith that all souls are equally precious in the sight of god. Therefore in his *Twilight of the Gods* Nietzsche wrote, "Modern democracy is the historic form of the decay of the state" and "The equality of souls before God, this lie, this screen for the [rancour] of all the base-minded, this anarchist bomb of a concept, which has become the last revolution, the modern idea and principle of the whole social order — this is Christian dynamite.''

In addition, Christianity tells its followers to be compassionate, obliging, patient, charitable — all the negative and pusillanimous virtues that Nietzsche identified as the slave sickness. The religious leaders reassure the faithful that the meek shall inherit the earth instead of inspiring them to master the earth through forceful action. Above all, Christianity preaches belief in a nonexistent god and denies people the satisfactions of earthly life, extolling them to put their trust in a mythical heaven. In order to save one's soul one must lose the world including the physical joys of the body.

In place of the slave morality promulgated by democracy and Christianity, Nietzsche defended the ideal of a personal will to power as a nobler, more vital aim in living. The individual counts not the masses and oddly enough it is the superior individual, serving himself, who will bring humanity to progressively higher levels of civilization. Nietzsche's ethic of the dominant will is ultimately for the betterment of civilization.

In the following selection from *The Gay Science* Nietzsche presented some of his ideas in a typically lyrical and aphoristic form.

The Gay Science*

[283]

Preparatory men. I welcome all signs that a more manly, a warlike, age is about to begin, an age which, above all, will give honor to valor once again. For this age shall prepare the way for one yet higher, and it shall gather the strength which this higher age will need one day — this age which is to carry heroism into the pursuit of knowledge and *wage wars* for the sake of thoughts and their consequences. To this end we now need many preparatory valorous men who cannot leap into being out of nothing — any more than out of the sand and slime of our present civilization and metropolitanism: men who are bent on seeking for that aspect in all things which must be *overcome*; men characterized by cheerfulness, patience, unpretentiousness, and contempt for all great vanities, as well as by magnanimity in victory and forbearance regarding the small vanities of the vanquished; men possessed of keen and free judgment concerning all victors and the share of chance in every victory and every fame; men who have their own festivals, their own weekdays, their own periods of mourning, who are accustomed to command with assurance and are no less ready to obey when necessary, in both cases equally proud and serving their own cause; men who are in greater danger, more fruitful, and happier! For, believe me, the secret of the greatest fruitfulness and the greatest enjoyment of existence is: to *live dangerously*! Build your cities under Vesuvius! Send your ships into uncharted seas! Live at war with your peers and yourselves. Be robbers and conquerors, as long as you cannot be rulers and owners, you lovers of knowledge. Soon the age will

*Reprinted with permission from Friedrich Nietzsche, *The Gay Science*, in *The Portable Nietzsche* (New York: Viking Press, 1954), 97–99.

be past when you could be satisfied to live like shy deer, hidden in the woods! At long last the pursuit of knowledge will reach out for its due: it will want to *rule* and *own*, and you with it!

[290]

One thing is needful. "Giving style" to one's character—a great and rare art! It is exercised by those who see all the strengths and weaknesses of their own natures and then comprehend them in an artistic plan until everything appears as art and reason and even weakness delights the eye. Here a large mass of second nature has been added; there a piece of original nature has been removed: both by long practice and daily labor. Here the ugly which could not be removed is hidden; there it has been reinterpreted and made sublime. . . . It will be the strong and domineering natures who enjoy their finest gaiety in such compulsion, in such constraint and perfection under a law of their own; the passion of their tremendous will relents when confronted with stylized, conquered, and serving nature; even when they have to build palaces and lay out gardens, they demur at giving nature a free hand. Conversely, it is the weak characters without power over themselves who *hate* the constraint of style. . . . They become slaves as soon as they serve; they hate to serve. Such spirits—and they may be of the first rank—are always out to interpret themselves and their environment as *free* nature—wild, arbitrary, fantastic, disorderly, astonishing; and they do well because only in this way do they please themselves. For one thing is needful: that a human being attain his satisfaction with himself—whether it be by this or by that poetry and art; only then is a human being at all tolerable to behold. Whoever is dissatisfied with himself is always ready to revenge himself therefore; we others will be his victims, if only by always having to stand his ugly sight. For the sight of the ugly makes men bad and gloomy.

• • •

[4]

What preserves the species. The strongest and most evil spirits have so far advanced humanity the most: they have always rekindled the drowsing passions—all ordered society puts the passions to sleep; they have always reawakened the sense of comparison, of contradiction, of joy in the new, the daring, and the untried; they force men to meet opinion with opinion, model with model. For the most part by arms, by the overthrow of boundary stones, and by offense to the pieties, but also by new religions and moralities. The same "malice" is to be found in every teacher and preacher of the new. . . . The new is always *the evil*, as that which wants to conquer, to overthrow the old boundary stones and the old pieties; and only the old is the good. The good men of every age are those who dig the old ideas deep down and bear fruit with them, the husbandmen of the spirit. But all land is finally exhausted, and the plow of evil must always return.

There is a fundamentally erroneous doctrine in contemporary morality, celebrated particularly in England: according to this, the judgments "good" and "evil" are condensations of the experiences concerning "expedient" and "inexpedient"; what is called good preserves the species, while what is called evil is harmful to the species. In truth, however, the evil urges are expedient and indispensable and preserve the species to as high a degree as the good ones—only their function is different.

[7]

Something for the industrious. . . . So far, everything that has given color to existence still lacks a history: or, where could one find a history of love, of avarice, of envy, of conscience, of piety, or of cruelty?

Both Nietzsche and Machiavelli therefore are proponents of the ethical egoist doctrine. Machiavelli stressed its application to political manipulation while Nietzsche championed an individualism that pivots round the concept of power. In all fairness, Nietzsche's version of ethical egoism has a large admixture of dedication to the growth of culture and civilization. Nevertheless the masters are not mainly a means for humanity's advancement but rather humanity will benefit from the will to power of the masters; it is the individual that Nietzsche wants to enliven to a vibrant life of color, depth, and excellence.

Ethical egoism has received substantial support from both thinkers as well as profiting from the philosophies of modern figures such as J. Kalin, E. Regis, and Ayn Rand (1905 – 1982). For example, in elaborating her theory of Objectivism Rand wrote,

> The basic *social* principle of the Objectivist ethics is that just as life is an end in itself, so every living being is an end in himself, not the means to the end or the welfare of others—and, therefore, that man must live for his own sake, neither sacrificing himself to others nor sacrificing others to himself. To live for his own sake means that *the achievement of his own happiness is man's highest moral purpose.*[11]

This approach is rather typical of contemporary egoistic positions and in Rand's case enabled her to become a champion of the current individualistic capitalism.

Ayn Rand's philosophy has achieved a certain popularity, mainly through her novels *The Fountainhead* and *Atlas Shrugged*. In the latter work her alter ego, John Galt, makes a speech in which he advocates many of the tenets of the Objectivist position. Witness the following extract, which marries egoism with capitalism.

John Galt's Speech*

"Just as I support my life, neither by robbery nor alms, but by my own effort, so I do not seek to derive my happiness from the injury or the favor of others, but earn it by my own achievement. Just as I do not consider the pleasure of others as the goal of my life, so I do not consider my pleasure as the goal of the lives of others. Just as there are no contradictions in my

---

*Ayn Rand, *Atlas Shrugged* (New York: Random House, 1957). Copyright 1985 by the Estate of Ayn Rand. Reprinted with permission from the Estate of Ayn Rand.

values and no conflicts among my desires—so there are no victims and no conflicts of interest among rational men, men who do not desire the unearned and do not view one another with a cannibal's lust, men who neither make sacrifices nor accept them.

"The symbol of all relationships among such men, the moral symbol of respect for human beings, is *the trader*. We, who live by values, not by loot, are traders, both in matter and in spirit. A trader is a man who earns what he gets and does not give or take the undeserved. A trader does not ask to be paid for his failures, nor does he ask to be loved for his flaws. A trader does not squander his body as fodder or his soul as alms. Just as he does not give his work except in trade for material values, so he does not give the values of his spirit—his love, his friendship, his esteem—except in payment and in trade for human virtues, in payment for his own selfish pleasure, which he receives from men he can respect. The mystic parasites who have, throughout the ages, reviled the traders and held them in contempt, while honoring the beggars and the looters, have known the secret motive of their sneers: a trader is the entity they dread—a man of justice.

"Do you ask what moral obligation I owe to my fellow men? None— except the obligation I owe to myself, to material objects and to all of existence: rationality. I deal with men as my nature and theirs demands: by means of reason. I seek or desire nothing from them except such relations as they care to enter of their own voluntary choice. It is only with their mind that I can deal and only for my own self-interest, when they see that my interest coincides with theirs.

• • •

"Accept the fact that the achievement of your happiness is the only *moral* purpose of your life, and that *happiness*—not pain or mindless self-indulgence—is the proof of your moral integrity, since it is the proof and the result of your loyalty to the achievement of your values. Happiness was the responsibility you dreaded, it required the kind of rational discipline you did not value yourself enough to assume—and the anxious staleness of your days is the monument to your evasion of the knowledge that there is no moral substitute for happiness, that there is no more despicable coward than the man who deserted the battle for his joy, fearing to assert his right to existence, lacking the courage and the loyalty to life of a bird or a flower reaching for the sun. Discard the protective rags of that vice which you called a virtue: humility—learn to value yourself, which means: to fight for your happiness—and when you learn that *pride* is the sum of all virtues, you will learn to live like a man.

• • •

"But to win it requires your total dedication and a total break with the world of your past, with the doctrine that man is a sacrificial animal who exists for the pleasure of others. Fight for the value of your person. Fight for the virtue of your pride. Fight for the essence of that which is man: for his sovereign rational mind. Fight with the radiant certainty and the absolute rectitude of knowing that yours is the Morality of Life and that yours is the battle for any achievement, any value, any grandeur, any goodness, any joy that has ever existed on this earth.

"You will win when you are ready to pronounce the oath I have taken at the start of my battle — and for those who wish to know the day of my return, I shall now repeat it to the hearing of the world:

"I swear — by my life and my love of it — that I will never live for the sake of another man, nor ask another man to live for mine."

Evaluation

Ethical egoism then has considerable support from diverse sources. In addition, it seems down to earth and practical, a realistic ethic that accepts the selfishness of human desires and builds a normative system around that raw truth. Instead of feeling apologetic about self-seeking behavior, the ethical egoist declares this to be the ideal for every human life. Nevertheless, certain criticisms do apply to the egoist ethic, among which are the following.

1. Some philosophers have pointed out that strictly speaking ethical egoism is not an ethical position at all but rather the absence of ethics. Not only does it endorse selfishness, which has generally been considered the opposite of moral behavior, it even fails to acknowledge any moral obligations independent of our own welfare. Perhaps it is not so much ethical as a nonethical because it rejects moral responsibility in any of the usual senses. Or from another perspective, to talk about responsibility to oneself is really an abuse of language since being responsible implies "to others." In the same way, an ethic of selfishness is actually a conflict in terms.

But isn't this merely a semantic quibble over labels? Regardless of whether the egoism described is called ethical or nonethical isn't the important point whether the position itself is worth holding? No, because the egoist should not be allowed the advantage of presenting his theory as a type of ethic when in fact it is the antithesis of all ethical approaches to living. And once it is seen as a blatant proposal to look out for oneself alone, then it can be judged more clearly.

The doctrine then is one of total selfishness, which presumably requires a very convincing argument in order to be accepted. But the "ethical" egoist offers no such argument. Machiavelli gave us a handbook of practical advice for rulers who want to maintain their power without showing why the ruler is justified in using any expediency required to keep him in power. He simply assumes that because everyone from prince to peasant tends to behave selfishly, therefore everyone should behave in a selfish way, which is hardly convincing logic. The only justification Nietzsche (sometimes) offered is that humanity as a whole would be enriched by each individual exercising his power to the utmost. That reasoning does not support egoism at all but favors an altruistic ethic instead. It implies that if humanity would be better served by generosity than by exploitation, then generosity would be called for.

In point of fact, we *would* all be better off if we considered each other's needs and not just our own, so if the good of humanity is our goal then egoism does not seem to be the means of achieving it. But in any case, the egoist theory needs to offer a good reason for itself as the end of life, and none of the egoists, including Nietzsche and Machiavelli, has provided that. Egoism therefore fails in demonstrating that it is superior to a genuine ethical theory that shows concern for the good of others.

2. Another basic difficulty with egoism has to do with the matter of offering advice. An important aspect of morality concerns the type of advice that one person should give to another about problems confronted in daily living. Whether it is a pastor advising a parishoner, a clinical psychologist offering therapeutic counseling, or simply one friend concerned about the well being of another, the question arises as to what sort of advice should be offered.

Now the egoist would only say what is to his own advantage, which is hardly satisfactory in this context. For example, if an alcoholic came for professional help and the counselor were an egoist with shares in a liquor distillery, he would advise the person to drink more. A doctor who wanted to increase his income would prescribe the wrong medication so that his patients remained sick and in need of continued treatment. And an egoistic coach would give his team all the wrong advice and place a large bet on the opposing side. Sometimes, of course, "enlightened" or "rational" self-interest would modify these recommendations if the egoist found he would be better off in the long run by giving good advice, but if this were not the case then nothing would prevent him from harming others for his own benefit.

We recognize this possibility in people when we say "Don't ask the barber whether you need a haircut," but society could not really function if those we depend upon for sound advice told us only what furthered their own advantage. Egoism therefore is deficient in not being able to fulfill this important aspect of human interaction; it cannot serve as the basis for any advice giving.

3. Another argument against egoism is that it contains an internal inconsistency. The problem is not one of self-contradiction because that would mean affirming and denying a statement at the same time (for example, be selfish and do not be selfish) but rather that it cannot be maintained in a consistent way. This objection usually takes the following form.

Ethical theories, if they are to be genuine at all, are recommendations as to how people ought to behave. They are not private value systems, referring only to standards that the individual (or prince or master) feels he should adopt but prescriptions that apply to everyone. When we say, for instance, "don't be prejudiced" or "deceit is an awful practice," we intend these as universal judgments; we mean that no one should be prejudiced or deceitful in his dealings with others.

Now if we try to promulgate the theory of egoism it immediately produces an inconsistency. For how can we urge others to act only for themselves when that could mean acting against us? If we really believed in doing what is best for ourselves, then we should recommend that others behave altruistically; in that way we could receive the benefit of their unselfish conduct. But to recommend altruism would violate our moral theory as to how people ought to act, which is egoistically.

In other words, we are caught in a neat dilemma. To preach the doctrine of egoism could well be contrary to our personal welfare, and self-interest after all is the heart of the egoist position. On the other hand, to advocate a policy of altruism, which would be in our best interests, is inconsistent with the theory of egoism.

Of course, if other people acted for their own good it might coincide with our own welfare. For example, for people in a foreign nation to try to avoid war could certainly be to their advantage as well as to our own; when nations are peaceful we are all better off — especially in a nuclear age. To advocate egoism in that situation would not conflict with our individual good at all but be consistent with it. However, such cases are the exception not the rule. For when other people assiduously look after their own interests in all probability this would not work to our maximum advantage. A far safer course would be to recommend that others serve us in an altruistic way; then we are most likely to benefit personally. But then we are also back in the logical predicament of recommending altruism when we believe in egoism.

The theory of egoism is thus seen to be absurd. The egoist, for the most part, cannot advocate self-interest without thwarting his own aims, and to promote the goal of self-interest would mean not advocating the doctrine of egoism.[12]

4. At this point the egoist might fall back to the position known as "enlightened egoism." This is the view that by serving others one is also benefiting oneself, therefore no conflict exists between altruism and egoism. Although the motive may be selfish, nevertheless other people's good is promoted and in the final analysis that is what counts. One is pursuing other people's interests out of self-interest but the bottom line is that everyone is better off. It is a doctrine cleverly presented by Bernard Mandeville (c. 1670–1733) in *The Fable of the Bees: or Private Vices, Public Benefits.*

Some moralists have tried to make a case for this position, arguing that the best way to help yourself is to help others, that your good deeds will always come back to you and be repaid a hundredfold. If you scratch someone else's back they will scratch yours; society is a system of reciprocity. Regardless of whether your concern for others is based on such expectations, you are contributing to the general good of humanity, and if we all did likewise then everyone would benefit and be content. We would each be getting more than we gave, and instead of resenting our generosity as self-sacrifice, we would recognize that our best interests were served that way.

Although both capitalism and Christianity have been argued on these grounds,[13] the truth is that one does not always help oneself by helping others. Perhaps virtue is its own reward but the individual is not necessarily rewarded by the external world. And wrongdoing could bring enormous personal advantages — far more than the chance effects of niceness. Some people will repay generosity in kind and with interest but many will not; to the scoundrel the charitable person is a fool.

Enlightened egoism also commits the inconsistency outlined previously of advocating altruism while being committed to egoism, but the main difficulty lies in ignoring the facts. Those who give do not necessarily receive, and they certainly do not always receive more than they give. Kindness may be rewarded in the next life but in this world people will exploit it as readily as they will be kind in return. Even in a Christian heaven the enlightened egoist cannot expect to receive his reward because he is acting out of selfishness not love and that would be unacceptable to god.

Overall it seems to make more sense to say that we should pursue the good of others because such action is valuable in itself and not because of what we can get out of it. In the same way, we should not hurt other people for the very good reason that other people would be hurt and that is something we ought to care about. Regardless of the personal gain that follows from kindness or cruelty, we should choose the one and avoid the other out of a common sympathy for our fellow man. Anything else seems calculating and callous.

Before we leave the topic of egoism a final point needs to be made. We should not conclude on the the basis of our discussion that love for oneself is something shameful that should be eliminated from our character in favor of love for others. The selfishness at the core of the egoist theory is what has been criticized, the attitude of ignoring the needs of others or getting ahead by stepping on other people. Eating a gourmet meal could be perfectly innocent but refusing to share the food with starving people around you would be selfish. The egoist carries self-interest this far, maintaining that he alone counts, that no one should ever help anyone but himself. It is precisely at this point that his doctrine becomes reprehensible.

Self-love however must be distinguished from selfishness as something normal and worthwhile, and this distinction has been made most effectively by the psychologist Erich Fromm. In the following excerpt from one of his well known writings, Fromm described the nature of love and its manifestation in the love of oneself; in his view, egoistic selfishness is quite a different matter.

Selfishness and Self-Love*

Love, like character-conditioned hatred, is rooted in a basic attitude which is constantly present; a readiness to love, a *basic sympathy* as one might call it. It is started, but not caused, by a particular *object*. The ability and readiness to love is a character trait just as is the readiness to hate. . . . It is difficult to say what the conditions favoring the development of this *basic sympathy* are. It seems that there are two main conditions, a positive and a negative one. The positive one is simply to have experienced love from others as a child. While conventionally, parents are supposed to *love* their children as a matter of course, this is rather the exception than the rule. The positive condition is, therefore, frequently absent. The negative condition is the absence of all those factors, discussed above, which make for the existence of a chronic hatred. The observer of childhood experiences may well doubt that the absence of these conditions is frequent.

From the premise that actual love is rooted in a *basic sympathy* there follows an important conclusion with regard to the *objects* of love. The conclusion is, in principle, the same as was stated with regard to the objects of chronic hatred: the objects of love do not have the quality of exclusiveness. To be sure, it is not accidental that a certain person becomes the *object* of manifest love. The factors conditioning such a specific choice are too numerous and

---

*Reprinted with permission from Erich Fromm, ''Selfishness and Self-Love,'' *Psychiatry*, 2(1939):521.

too complex to be discussed here. The important point, however, is that love for a particular *object* is only the actualization and concentration of lingering love with regard to one person; it is not, as the idea of *romantic love* would have it, that there is only *the* one person in the world whom one could love, that it is the great chance of one's life to find that person, and that love for him or her results in a withdrawal from all others. The kind of love which can only be experienced with regard to one person demonstrates by this very fact that it is not love, but a symbiotic attachment. The basic affirmation contained in love is directed toward the beloved person as an incarnation of essentially human qualities. Love for one person implies love for man as such. The kind of "division of labor" as William James calls it; namely, to love one's family, but to be without feeling for the "stranger," is a sign of a basic inability to love. Love for man as such is not, as it is frequently supposed to be, an abstraction coming "after" the love for a specific person, or an enlargement of the experience with a specific *object*; it is its premise, although, generally, it is acquired in the contact with concrete individuals.

From this, it follows that my own self, in principle, is as much an object of my love as another person. The affirmation of my own life, happiness, growth, freedom is rooted in the presence of the basic readiness of and ability for such an affirmation. If an individual has this readiness, he has it also toward himself; if he can only *love* others, he cannot love at all. In one word, love is as indivisible as hatred with regard to its *objects*.

• • •

One last question remains to be discussed. Granted that love for oneself and for others in principle runs parallel, how do we explain the kind of *selfishness* which obviously is in contradiction to any genuine concern for others. The *selfish* person is only interested in himself, wants everything for himself, is unable to give with any pleasure but is only anxious to take; the world outside himself is conceived only from the standpoint of what he can get out of it; he lacks interest in the needs of others, or respect for their dignity and integrity. He sees only himself, judges everyone and everything from the standpoint of its usefulness to him, is basically unable to love. This selfishness can be manifest or disguised by all sorts of unselfish gestures; dynamically it is exactly the same. It seems obvious that with this type of personality there is a contradiction between the enormous concern for oneself and the lack of concern for others. Do we not have the proof here that there exists an alternative between concern for others and concern for oneself? This would certainly be the case if selfishness and self-love were identical. But this assumption is the very fallacy which has led to so many mistaken conclusions with regard to our problem. Selfishness and self-love far from being identical, actually are opposites.

Selfishness is one kind of greediness. . . . Like all greediness, it contains an insatiability, as a consequence of which there is never any real satisfaction. Greed is a bottomless pit which exhausts the person in an endless effort to satisfy the need without ever reaching satisfaction. This leads to the crucial point: close observation shows that while the selfish person is always anxiously concerned with himself, he is never satisfied, is always restless, always driven by the fear of not getting enough, of missing something, of being deprived of something. He is filled with burning envy of anyone who might have more. If we observe still closer, especially the unconscious dynamics, we find that this type of person is basically not fond of himself but deeply dislikes himself. The puzzle in this seeming contradiction is easy to solve. The selfishness is rooted in this very lack of fondness for oneself. The person who is not fond of himself, who does not approve of himself, is in a constant anxiety concerning his own self. He has not the inner security which can exist only on the basis of genuine fondness and affirmation. He must be concerned about himself, greedy to get everything for himself, since basically his own self lacks security and satisfaction.

This is an important difference to bear in mind. There is absolutely nothing wrong in wanting a great deal from life; on the contrary, desiring a full, rich existence out of love for oneself is healthy and positive. Selfishness however shows an unhealthy insecurity and self-dislike. To love oneself is not opposed to generosity but is a condition for it and selfishness is an opposite mental state. The selfish person does not love himself and because of this lack of fondness or self-regard is forever greedy to acquire more, even at other people's expense.

Egoism then can be extensively criticized, as this chapter has shown, but that does not mean that we should reject our personal wants and needs as selfish. Personal enjoyment is not necessarily selfish enjoyment. We should feel comfortable in our self-love and that will carry over to a human sympathy for others who are, after all, very like ourselves.

Notes

1. Plato, *The Republic*, in *The Dialogues of Plato* trans. Benjamin Jowett (New York: Scribner, Armstrong, 1874), Book II.
2. It is worth underscoring that those who are suspicious of human nature and fear man's basic tendencies will usually opt for a strong central government as Augustine and Machiavelli did. Democracy assumes man is sufficiently rational and moral to govern himself. This same division separates the Church of Rome and Protestantism; the former stresses a strict hierarchy, the latter private conscience.
3. Niccolò Machiavelli, "Aphorisms on the Nature of Man," in *The Prince and the Discourses*, trans. Luigi Ricci and C. E. Detmold (New York: Random House, 1940).
4. In recent years a Hobbesian position (that man is territorial and aggressive) has been taken in Robert Ardrey's *The Territorial Imperative*, Konrad Lorenz's *On Aggression*, Desmond Morris' *The Naked Ape*, and Lionel Tiger and Robin Fox's *The Imperial Animal*.
5. Thomas Hobbes, *De Cive* (New York: Appleton Century Crofts, 1949), 114.
6. See Rousseau's early essays and his novels, especially *The New Heloise* and *Émile*.
7. See John Locke, *Two Treatises of Government* (Cambridge: Cambridge University Press, 1967), Second Treatise.
8. Adam Smith, *The Theory of Moral Sentiments* (London: A. Miller, A. Kincaid, and J. Bell, 1759), Part I, Chapter 1.

9. See Jean Piaget, *The Moral Judgment of the Child* (New York: Free Press, 1965), and Lawrence Kohlberg *The Philosophy of Moral Development* (San Francisco: Harper and Row, 1981). See also the studies on the role of genes in human behavior done at the Minnesota Center for Twin and Adoption Research.

10. Joseph Butler, *Fifteen Sermons* (London: Macmillan and Co., 1913), 27–35.

11. Ayn Rand, "The Objectivist Ethics," in *The Virtue of Selfishness* (New York: New American Library, 1964), p.

12. For an excellent analysis of this inconsistency, see Brian Medlin, "Ultimate Principles and Ethical Egoism," *Australasian Journal of Philosophy* 35 (1957): 111–18.

13. Most advocates of capitalism believe this very strongly, including entrepreneurs such as Henry Ford. In Christianity the most extreme version perhaps was expressed by Abraham Tucker. In *The Light of Nature Pursued*, Tucker argued that all the happiness men have enjoyed is deposited in "the bank of the universe." Whenever a person increases the happiness of others he also increases the total stock of happiness, and since god has arranged to divide this stock equally, he is increasing his own share. To Tucker, we are all shareholder in the great happiness bank, presided over by god as chairman of the board.

Bibliography

BAIER, KURT. *The Moral Point of View*. Ithaca, N.Y.: Cornell University Press, 1958, Chapter 8.

BAUMER, W. H. "Indefensible Impersonal Egoism." *Philosophical Studies* 18 (1967): 72–75.

BAUMRIN, BERNARD, ED. *Hobbes' Leviathan: Interpretation and Criticism*. Belmont, Calif.: Wadsworth Publishing Co., 1969.

BENDITT, THEODORE. "Egoism's Inconsistencies." *Personalist* 57 (1976): 43–50.

BRANDEN, NATHANIEL. "Rational Egoism." *Personalist* 51 (1970): 196–211, 305–13.

BRADLEY, F. H. *"Why Should I Be Moral." Essay 2 in Ethical Studies*. Oxford: Oxford University Press, 1927.

BRANDT, RICHARD. *Ethical Theory*. Englewood Cliffs, N.J.: Prentice-Hall, 1959, Chapter 14.

BROAD, C. D. "Egoism as a Theory of Human Motives." In *Ethics and the History of Philosophy*. London: Routledge and Kegan Paul, 1952.

BROWN, NORMAN J. "Psychological Egoism Revisited." *Philosophy* 54 (1979): 293–309.

BRUNTON, J. A. "Egoism and Morality." *Philosophical Quarterly* 6 (1956): 289–303.

CAMPBELL, RICHMOND. "A Short Refutation of Ethical Egoism." *Canadian Journal of Philosophy* 2 (1972): 249–54.

CARLSON, GEORGE R. "Ethical Egoism Reconsidered." *American Philosophical Quarterly* (1973): 25–33.

DUNCAN-JONES, AUSTIN. *Butler's Moral Philosophy*. Harmondsworth, England: Penguin Books, 1952.

DWYER, WILLIAM. "Criticisms of Egoism." *Personalist* 56 (1975): 214–27.

EDEL, ABRAHAM. "Two Traditions in the Refutation of Egoism." *Journal of Philosophy* 34 (1937): 617–28.

EMMONS, DONALD. "Refuting the Egoist." *Personalist* 50 (1969): 301–19.

GAUTIER, DAVID, ED. *Morality and Rational Self-Interest*. Englewood Cliffs, N.J.: Prentice-Hall, 1970.

GLASGOW, W. D. "The Contradiction in Ethical Egoism," *Philosophical Studies* 19 (1968): 81–85.

HOSPERS, JOHN. "Baier and Medlin on Ethical Egoism." *Philosophical Studies* 12 (1961): 10–16.

KALIN, JESSE. "On Ethical Egoism." *American Philosophical Quarterly, Monograph Series No. 1: Studies in Moral Philosophy* (1968): 26–41.

MACHAN, TIBOR. "Recent Work in Ethical Egoism." *American Philosophical Quarterly* 16 (1979): 1–15.

MACINTYRE, ALISDAIR. *A Short History of Ethics.* New York: Macmillan, 1966.

McCLINTOCK, T. "The Egotists Psychological Argument." *American Philosophical Quarterly* 8 (1971): 79–85.

MIDGLEY, MARY. *Wickedness, A Philosophical Essay.* London: Routledge and Kegan Paul, 1984.

MILO, RONALD D., ED. *Egoism and Altruism.* Belmont, Calif.: Wadsworth Publishing Co., 1973.

NAGEL, THOMAS. *The Possibility of Altruism.* Oxford: Clarendon Press, 1970.

NOZICK, ROBERT. "On The Randian Argument." *Personalist* 52 (1971): 282–304.

OLSON, ROBERT G. *The Morality of Self-Interest.* New York: Harcourt Brace Jovanovich, 1965.

QUINN, WARREN. "Egoism and an Ethical System." *Journal of Philosophy* 71 (1974): 456–72.

RACHELS, JAMES. "Two Arguments Against Ethical Egoism," *Philosophia* 4 (1974): 297–314.

REGIS, EDWARD, JR. "What Is Ethical Egoism?" *Ethics* 91 (1980): 50–62.

SANDERS, STEVEN. "Egoism's Conception of Self." *Personalist* 58 (1977): 59–67.

SCHUTTE, OFELIA. *Beyond Nihilism: Nietzsche Without Masks.* Chicago: University of Chicago Press, 1984.

SIDGWICK, HENRY. *The Methods of Ethics.* New York: Macmillan, 1874, Book 2.

SLOTE, MICHAEL. "An Empirical Basis for Psychological Egoism." *The Journal of Philosophy* 61 (1964): 530–37.

CHAPTER 3

Determinism

In the same way the relativism and egoism are an undermining influence on ethics, the theory of determinism also poses a significant threat. For the determinist maintains that all of our choices and actions are the necessary result of prior factors and for that reason wholly beyond our control. These factors or antecedent conditions make all of our decisions unavoidable; it would be impossible that they could be otherwise. Therefore we cannot assume responsibility for any of our behavior—including our moral behavior. We can neither be praised nor blamed because strictly speaking the action did not emanate from us.

To elaborate this position, the determinist claims that every allegedly "free" choice can be traced back to a combination of factors that forced the particular act to occur. We may not always be aware of these forces but they exist nonetheless and can be identified once we analyze our behavior more acutely. For example, a married couple may feel that they made an independent decision to have a child when in fact they were merely giving in to pressure by their parents for a grandchild, conforming to social expectations, expressing their sexual urges, gratifying their psychological need for parenting, and perhaps fulfilling a biological drive to perpetuate the species. Whatever factors lie behind the decision, the couple themselves were not responsible for the choice at all.

One could say that they were not actually doing what they wanted to do or, more subtly, that what they wanted was completely determined by outside forces. This is the meaning of the statement by the German philosopher Arthur Schopenhauer (1788–1860) that impressed and convinced Einstein: "A man can surely do what he wills to do, but he cannot determine what he wills." The question is *why* people want this or that, and the answer must always be because they cannot help it. We may have any number of desires but it is not in our power to choose whether to have those desires or to choose among the desires we have.

The determinist is actually denying that people possess *free will*, and it is worth noting that this is a very different doctrine than the denial of *freedom*. The term *freedom* usually refers to the opportunity to exercise one's choice rather than the power to choose voluntarily. For this reason freedom is often used in a political sense to indicate the rights that a government confers or protects. For example, we speak about freedom of religion or freedom of speech, meaning that we should be able to worship as we please or to express our opinions without fear of force being used against us by a repressive government. Here we make distinctions between freedom from and freedom to and refer to a free marketplace, a free country, or freedom as opposed to imprisonment.

The determinist however rejects the belief that human beings possess the *free will* to make their own choices and to act upon them. He claims that people are in some way "programmed" to think and behave as they do and, in that sense, never act of their own volition.

Libertarianism is the theory that stands in direct contrast to determinism, for it holds that man's choices are essentially free. The libertarian believes that human beings are basically in control of their lives and that their decisions proceed from themselves as autonomous entities. He does not assert that all ideas and actions are free since people can be unconsciously manipulated and controlled, but he does assert that human beings possess free will and have the potential to think and act freely. Choices are made through a "creative act of will" and are initiated by the individual. The determinist, on the other hand, denies free will and maintains that all decisions are a direct consequence of prior factors and are therefore beyond our control.

It is the determinist position that has damaging implications for ethics in various, related ways. First, if a person's will is forced rather than free, then his judgment as to what is morally right or good is not a genuine judgment at all. It is a necessary conclusion that the person was compelled to reach not a moral evaluation arrived at through rational reflection and the deliberate assessment of relevant factors.

Second, no one can be commended or criticized for his ethical ideas or actions because he is not responsible for them. Praise and blame, reward and punishment become utterly pointless if the individual was unable to do otherwise. "I could not help it" is a complete excuse. Aristotle (384 – 322 B.C.) pointed this out in his *Nicomachean Ethics* when he said that people are not responsible for behavior done through ignorance or compulsion, and the determinist maintains that all of our emotions, beliefs, and physical behavior fall into the category of the compelled and unavoidable. More recent writers such as G. E. Moore and P. H. Nowell-Smith have reiterated the point stating that no one is responsible for an action unless "they could have done differently if they had chosen to do differently."

Third, not only does determinism imply that people cannot be blamed or commended for their behavior but no behavior could possibly be *recommended*. If people have been determined to be good or bad, to hold the values they hold and to act in certain necessary ways, then any advice or prescription as to how they should conduct themselves is useless. As the philosopher Immanuel Kant (1724 – 1804) declared, "Ought implies can." One can only tell a person that he ought to do something if he can do it. To ask a bedridden man to save a drowning child, for example, would be foolish because that is something impossible for him to do. In the same way, if people have no choice, as the determinist maintains, then it is meaningless to ever suggest that they should behave differently. Since a great deal of ethics consists of suggestions and recommendations about the kinds of values that are worth holding and the kind of life worth living, the determinist position would make ethics largely futile.

We have already encountered this problem in our discussion of psychological egoism. There we found that if people must always act in terms of self-interest, that because of man's selfish nature they have no other option, then advising them to be altruistic is meaningless. For it is surely a waste of time to tell people that they should or should not act selfishly when it is impossible for them to act differently. The same problem is inherent in determinism. There is no point in making any moral recommendations if everyone must think and act as they do, if their behavior is unavoidable and unchangeable.

This is the nature of the determinist threat to ethics. Strictly speaking, determinism is a metaphysical position—a theory as to the nature of reality or that which is ultimately real. But as we have seen, its consequences for the field of ethics are enormous.

Fatalism: Destiny Governs Our Lives

A special version of determinism that has features substantially different from the main position just described is that of fatalism. This theory, which is sometimes called predestination (although that implies the design of a personal god), maintains that nothing ever occurs either by chance or by choice but only in accordance with destiny's decrees. It is not that our behavior is determined by environmental or hereditary factors but that, in a cosmic sense, everything we do is dictated by forces that render it inescapable.

For example, the person who accepts the theory of fatalism believes it is inevitable that each of us be born just as it is necessary that we all will die—and at a predetermined time, place, and manner. Our success or failure in life is also fated as well as whether we will marry, be healthy or sickly throughout our lives, have one child or several or none, travel or stay at home, be injured or spared in a catastrophe, and so forth. A psychic or astrologer or clairvoyant can foresee what must happen in our future. It may be "written in the stars" (as in the "star-crossed" lovers Romeo and Juliet), inscribed in the Book of Fate, or dictated by a divine providence but, whatever forces are thought responsible for what happens, our lives are fixed and unalterable. Each individual existence was meant to be exactly as it is, a thread in the tapestry of destiny. We may think that events occur by accident, unexpectedly, by some fluke of luck, but everything happens for a reason in accordance with the grand design of the universe. As the Persian poet Omar Khayyám wrote in the *Rubáiyát*,

> With earth's first clay they did the last man knead,
> And there of the last harvest sowed the seed.
> And the first morning of creation wrote
> What the last dawn of reckoning shall read.

Numerous cultures have believed in predestination as can be seen even in linguistic phrases: the Spanish, for example, say *que será, será* (what will be, will be), meaning that the future is as unalterable as the past. The French have the expression *c'était écrit* (this was written), and the Germans speak about *seinem Schicksal entgegengehen* (going to one's fate). The Arabs have the term *kismet*, which stands for destiny, and say *inchallah* meaning that whatever occurs is Allah's will.

However, the most celebrated affirmation of universal fate is probably that of ancient Greece. The Greeks called it *moira* and it was thought to rule not just the lives of men but the activities of the gods; even the power of Zeus was circumscribed by *moira*. The plays of Sophocles and Euripides clearly display this underlying belief, for mortals are shown to be the playthings of fate — an inscrutable, inexorable fate handed down from Mount Olympus by the gods or sometimes despite the gods. The choruses in the dramas ruminate about the mysteries of destiny, and seers sometimes foretell the events, but no explanations are offered as to why things happen as they do and there is no escaping what has been foreordained. The three goddesses called The Fates are inscrutable in determining the course of human life but their will, or the agency of an impersonal *moira*, is absolutely inviolable.

In Sophocles' play *Oedipus Rex*, for example, Oedipus could not escape the prophecy that he would one day kill his father and marry his mother. Although he left what he thought was his home in order to thwart this destiny, we see that he was only playing into destiny's hands, realizing his fate in trying to escape it. His doom was sealed from the outset and fate used him as an unwitting tool throughout. The seer Tiresias knows this and also knows that there is nothing he could say or not say to avoid the inevitable.

To emphasize that a drama of destiny is being enacted the chorus chants of Oedipus at several points "O dread fate for men to see. . . . Who is the unearthly foe that, with a bound of more than mortal range, hath made thine ill-starred life his prey?" and "the son of Zeus is springing on him, all armed with fiery lightnings, and with him come the dread, unerring Fates."[1]

In all his plays Sophocles articulated the Greek sense that the course of our lives depends on a "riddle of destiny," some "dark dealings of the immortals" far beyond us and, as Homer said repeatedly in the *Iliad*, "the lot they spin for man is full of sorrow." This Greek vision in turn is representative of the general belief in cosmic destiny prevalent in the ancient world.

Predestination in Christianity

Fatalistic beliefs of various forms also appear in several of the major religious systems that claim that a god or spiritual force ordains the history of men and nations. There are elements of this kind in Buddhism, Hinduism, Judaism, and Islam. In most Indian religions, for example, there is the notion of *karma*, a force generated by a person's actions that perpetuates transmigration and determines a person's destiny in his next existence. However, the most interesting manifestation in terms of our Western tradition occurs in the development of Christianity. Here questions of predestination arose in connection with three primary attributes that were considered essential to a personal and perfect god: absolute goodness, omnipotence, and omniscience.

With regard to divine goodness, it would be incongruous if not contradictory to imagine that god would perpetrate or allow evil in the world. By his very nature he is wholly loving, so evil is not a possible choice to him; rather, the creation of an ideal world would be necessary and unavoidable. It is not that god couldn't create evil if he tried but that, given his wholly loving character, he could never try.

The philosopher Benedict de Spinoza (1632–1677) maintained this position, arguing that god could not have made creation different than it is, given his

essence as god. But the philosopher who developed this position most extensively was G. W. Leibniz (1646–1716) who maintained that, on the assumption
that god is absolutely good, the world that exists is "the best of all possible
worlds."

Since life on earth did not seem ideal to many people Leibniz offered an
explanation of human suffering in the following terms. He argued that natural
evils such as floods and earthquakes, disease and death are necessary for the
punishment of man's wickedness. The world we have has been arranged by god
with complete justice so that sinful humanity is punished exactly as it deserves. If
there were more natural evil then the punishment would be excessive; if there
were less then the punishment would be out of proportion to the amount of sin.
Instead we have the precise degree that fairness requires, neither too much nor
too little, and the world is the best it can be. With our limited intelligence we may
not think the scheme is operating justly but, sub specie aeternitatis, each and
every aspect is fair and necessary. We must have faith that the whole is good
because, in the last analysis, god is precluded from doing otherwise.[2]

The poet Alexander Pope (1688–1744) expressed Leibniz' position in his
"Essay on Man," the last stanza of which is as follows:

> All Nature is but Art, unknown to thee;
> All Chance, Direction which thou canst not see;
> All Discord, Harmony not understood;
> All partial Evil, universal Good:
> And, spite of Pride, in erring Reason's spite,
> One truth is clear, whatever is, is RIGHT.

For our purposes, the point is not that we should trust in god despite appearances, or that Pope and Leibniz were able to "vindicate the ways of God to
man," but that a morally perfect being is compelled to produce only good. That
necessity, and the corresponding inability to produce evil, constitutes a logical
form of predeterminism.

As for god's omniscience entailing a denial of free will in man, this has been a
persistent point of debate within Christianity. For it has been argued that if god
is all knowing, as he is believed to be, then that omniscience would include
knowledge of the future. God would know everything that is going to happen
including the choices and actions of each human being. But if god knows what
we are going to do that means we cannot do otherwise and are compelled rather
than free in our behavior. In other words, if we could act in ways that are
different than what god foresees, then he does not really know what we will do,
but if he actually knows then, in some sense, our action is unavoidable and not
free. God himself may not be compelling our choices but his foreknowledge
means that our choices are already fixed.

Since a conclusion of that sort would mean the end of all preaching for people
to act righteously and would make god's judgment of man entirely unjust, some
Christian theologians have argued against it vehemently. Their argument
usually takes this form: God can predict what a person *will* do but that is not what
the person *must* do; god simply knows in advance the free choice the person will
make. An individual could do differently if he chose to but god knows that he
will not make any other choice. Thus divine foreknowledge does not imply
foreordination.

To illustrate this point an analogy can be made with the common experience of predicting a friend's conduct. If you know a person well you know his characteristic choices, that is, the decisions he consistently makes. But that does not imply that your friend must choose as he does; it only means that you know he will not choose differently. The fact that you can accurately predict his behavior does not mean that his behavior is forced or in any respect diminish his responsibility. In the same way, if god in his omniscience knows how we will act nevertheless the decision is still our own. Human beings therefore are responsible for their choices even though god knows ahead of time every choice they will make.

This sounds persuasive but is it logically correct? If god knows what decision we will reach then, even if he is not compelling us, something must be or he could not know in advance what we will decide. If our choice could not be otherwise (as evidenced by the fact that he foresees it), then we are not free to choose between alternatives but forced to only one, that is, we are not actually choosing. To revert to our analogy, if you truly know that your friend would never choose differently then he is acting under compulsion and could not choose differently; in fact, he has no choice.

Chaucer in the *Canterbury Tales* (the "Nun's Priest's Tale") put the dilemma this way, "in the schools there's a great altercation in this regard and much high disputation. . . . Whether the fact of God's great foreknowing makes it right needful that I do a thing (by needful, I mean, of necessity); or else, if a free choice be granted me, to do that same thing, or to do it not, though God foreknew before the thing was wrought."

A great deal more could be said but at this point we must leave the relation between predestination and religion with some questions unresolved. At least we can say that if god's foreknowledge does imply foreordination then human beings are not accountable for their behavior.[3]

The third aspect of predestination in Christianity has to do with the concept of omnipotence. Many theologians in the history of the church have denied free will in man because they found it incompatible with the absolute power of god. This includes St. Augustine who had argued earlier that foreknowledge and free will can logically occur together, but here Augustine holds rather typically that man's power is nothing compared to the supreme, divine power. Unless the grace of god is present, he declares, people have no choice but to sin; they are the instruments of the devil.

The first human beings were free and could have resisted temptation, Augustine believed, but when Adam and Eve tested the forbidden fruit they lost free will for all mankind. (In the seventeenth century the Jansenist sect held a similar position—that Adam's fall felled us all, losing freedom for man through original sin.) At this stage in the history of humanity, Augustine says, we can only be raised to goodness and achieve salvation by the power of god.[4]

Within the Protestant tradition the same type of position was taken by Martin Luther (1483–1546) and John Calvin (1509–1564), although their differences opened up two distinct pathways in Reformation theology. Both men emphasized the power, sovereignty, and righteousness of God and, to a lesser extent, his mercy and love. They argued that to assume any free will on man's part, any capability to win salvation through meritorious works, would be to compromise the power of god to grant salvation through grace. God must be viewed as having supreme power and man as devoid of the ability to become good by his own efforts; the state of man's soul as well as his actions are ultimately dependent on his maker. Heaven cannot be gained through man's own efforts but only by the spirit of god "in the souls of the elect and of them alone."

Luther compared the human will to that of a beast of burden that can be ridden by god or Satan. If he is ridden by god he goes where god directs him; if ridden by Satan he travels in the opposite direction. But in neither case does the beast choose its rider or have the power to go where it wills; his path is predetermined.[5]

Although these are the classic formulations of predestination in Christian thought, most contemporary theologians tend not to accept them. Belief in predestination would mean that people are not accountable for their behavior and should not receive heavenly rewards or the punishment of eternal damnation, and such a view runs counter to some very basic tenets of Christian teaching. The modern view is to call man free and to hold him responsible for his goodness or badness, his salvation or damnation. God is viewed as possessing final authority but that does not mean human beings have no control over their character, their conduct, or their ascension to paradise.

The issue has never been clearly settled. Debate still takes place over the extent of god's providence and man's ability to choose his own way. Is every hair of our head numbered and is there an ultimate purpose behind all that we do, a meaning known only to god who sees the scheme entire, or is the future unformed and open ended, the consequence of our free choice? Must love triumph over evil in the end, the good things throw the last stone, or as the American philosopher William James (1842–1910) asked rhetorically, Does what we do make a difference in the final outcome? Are god and the devil locked in combat over men's souls with the end undecided or is it inevitable that god will be victorious?

Speculations of this kind induced John Milton to write in *Paradise Lost* (Book I, 1, 555), describing the expulsion of Satan,

> Others apart sat on a hill retir'd,
> In thought more elevate, the reason'd high
> Of providence, foreknowledge, will and fate,
> Fix'd fate, free will, foreknowledge absolute,
> And found no end, in wand'ring mazes lost.

Although fatalism is often tied to a religious faith it does not have to be. There are inner, cosmic dimensions to it and a sense of the spiritual nature of the universe but our fortune need not lie in the lap of any gods. In fact, no intelligence has to be presupposed as the dictator of events, a master puppeteer pulling the strings. All events are said to happen by necessity, because of the ineluctable workings of fate, but fate is not another name for god and god does not always operate with the instrument of fate. Rather, the process seems to be more mechanical than premeditated, with principles that unfold according to strict laws, and humanity is held within the grip of that purposive machine.

Nevertheless, fatalism is always "telic" in nature, meaning that it assumes an end or aim toward which all events are tending. Whether we realize it or not, we all serve some overarching purpose and are part of a set direction that is inherent in the scheme of things. Cicero (106–43 B.C.) was representative of this telic attitude when he said that a sick man has no need of a physician since he is either going to die or not, and in the former case a physician will be futile, in the latter case superfluous.

Most fatalistic schemes are thoroughgoing and apply to all events, but it should be mentioned that there is a modified version that restricts our free will but does not deny it altogether. According to this doctrine, fate determines the outcome of events but the details involved in the fulfillment of fate's decrees are left to chance or the individual. For example, we may be destined to die at age forty five but how we die may remain open. It could be by drowning in a flood, from lung cancer due to smoking, or as a result of a congenital heart disorder. (And if "our number is not up" then it does not matter whether we smoke three packs of cigarettes a day or are on the front line in a war; we will live a charmed life.) In other words, a modified fatalism claims that the final results are predetermined but the particular means have not been fixed.

Evaluation

Since fatalism is not a consistently developed philosophic theory its claims are difficult to assess in a formal way. Few laymen or philosophers accept this view today; it seems to have been abandoned more than refuted and to have died of neglect. Perhaps the paucity of evidence makes it difficult to accept (or reject) or perhaps the simple experience of living makes it ludicrous to think that whatever we do was meant to be; we feel freer than that.

The only contemporary theory of any significance to endorse the fatalistic view is Marxism, and even the Marxists hesitate to adopt a strict version. The Marxist does claim that the eventual overthrow of the capitalist state is inevitable because of certain socio-economic forces moving in a rigid "dialectic" pattern through history, but there is nothing of a cosmic character connected with them. Furthermore, Marxists urge the workers to unite against their capitalist oppressors, that they have nothing to loose but their chains, and this implies that the worker is free to help or hinder the revolution.

By and large, predestination survives as a folk relic, appearing in literature about the occult or in astrological claims about the influence of the stars. And although we may enjoy believing in such notions, they have little scientific support. People will also turn to fatalism occasionally when they are under acute stress, for instance, if they are flying in a plane that develops engine trouble. In times like these there is some consolation in the thought that if one's time is up there is nothing to be done and if one is not meant to die then it will not matter how severe the disaster might be. But the reassurance that fatalism brings is not proof of its truth, rather it is a testimony to human weakness.

We are also inclined to turn to fatalism when we want to escape responsibility for our lives, but the following passage from *King Lear* might serve as an appropriate summation of that attitude as well as a resounding rejection of fatalism altogether:

> This is the excellent foppery of the world, that when we are sick in fortune — often the surfeit of our own behavior — we make guilty of our disasters the sun, the moon, and the stars, as if we were villains by necessity, fools by heavenly compulsion, knaves, thieves and treachers by spherical predominance, drunkards, liars,

and adulterers by an enforced obedience of planetary influence, and all that we are evil in by a divine thrusting on. An admirable evasion of whoremaster man, to lay his goatish disposition to the charge of a star!

Scientific Causation: Nature Times Nurture

In contrast to the theory of predestination, the position of scientific determinism holds that all desires, choices, and behavior have antecedent *causes* and are not a matter of voluntary decision. In other words, the scientific determinist does not claim that a cosmic destiny rules our lives but rather that all occurrences including human actions are the effect of casual agents and for that reason wholly determined. No event is uncaused, springing into being out of nothing, but everything comes about as the result of prior factors, and the internal and external events of human life are no exception to that cause–effect system.

For example, a social scientist might claim that people who commit crimes cannot help it; they are simply the victims of their background. A particular criminal might have been born with congenital defects, raised in a ghetto and rejected by his mother, forced to attend an inadequate school that never prepared him for a decent job, and had friends who were all involved in drugs, street violence, and prostitution. The inevitable effect of this background was that he too turned to crime. Given his genetic inheritance and the conditions of his upbringing, he could hardly have done anything else; the fact that he is a criminal is not his fault.

As for why other people raised in the same conditions did not become criminals, the scientific determinist maintains that the circumstances of life are always different. No two backgrounds are ever the same because there are countless variables in the human environment. But even though we may not know what impelled one person to become a murderer and take life and another to become a doctor and preserve life, we do know that different causal factors were present. Our ignorance of the specific causes involved does not prove that there were none but only that we do not know what they are.

In this connection the determinist will point out that the whole of science proceeds on the assumption that events must have a cause, otherwise there could be no theories or hypotheses or predictions or even simple experimentation. It would be extremely odd, for example, for a chemist to say "There was no cause behind that explosion; it just happened by itself." Rather the chemist would assume that some chemical agents in combination produced a large-scale, rapid, and spectacular expansion. He would then try to determine exactly which agents were responsible so that he might be able to prevent its future occurrence. To eliminate the effect he would try to isolate the causes, presupposing throughout that a cause–effect connection must exist. In the same way, an economist, psychologist, or historian who investigates human conduct would never reach the conclusion that certain events had no cause. He would find it more difficult to identify the causes because human behavior is so complex, but he would never even begin his research unless he thought that some factors existed that could account for the occurrence.

The determinist also argues that in our everyday lives we act as though people do respond to causal agents. Laws are enacted and penalties imposed for violation of those laws because we believe this will cause people to behave accordingly. Companies spend millions of dollars on advertising because they know they can effect a substantial increase in sales that way. Priests and ministers will deliver homilies on the rewards of heaven or the punishments of hell, using a carrot or a stick to get people to behave righteously. Furthermore, we send our children to school because we expect education to have an effect on them, just as we try to guide their choice of friends, type of entertainment, eating habits, expression, and so forth on the assumption that it makes a difference. In a broad sense, whenever we depend upon people, we believe they will respond in certain predictable ways; in fact to know a person means understanding the springs of his behavior, the causal pattern underlying his actions.

Thus the determinist claims that all human behavior is the result of antecedent factors not individual choice. We only flatter ourselves when we claim to be in control and "free as nature first made man." In fact, we are an integral part of the physical world and no less subject to cause–effect laws than the falling of a ripe apple. The image of the autonomous individual, freely deciding his life, is a flattering myth; in the light of scientific analysis it must be regarded as outmoded.

As for the specific form of these antecedent conditions, the scientific determinist maintains that it consists of nature and nurture, our biological inheritance as well as the various social, psychological, political, economic, and cultural forces that play upon us. Many lists have been drawn up but the typical causal factors that are cited would include the physical environment, cultural effects, psychological factors, and genetic determinants.

The Physical Environment

In the first place, the effect of *climate and geography* has been extensively described as a significant factor in human behavior — although considerable controversy exists over its precise effect. People who inhabit cool regions of the world tend to be brisk, industrious, and efficient, with strong goal orientation and the need for meaningful work. They are characteristically serious and organized and have highly developed social, economic, and political systems. However, in warm climates people are inclined to be very relaxed, to value enjoyment over accomplishment, to live sensuously rather than intellectually, and generally to adopt a lighter, slower, easier style of living. One thinks of northern Europe as opposed to the South Pacific, North America in contrast to Central America or equatorial Africa. Even the differences in temperature within a nation can produce very different personalities as, for example, in the case of severe New England and the sunny South, the "Prussian" north of Germany and the easier air of Bavaria (fostering Gemütlichkeit), northern France with Paris at the hub and the balmy Mediterranean provinces.

The amount of rainfall can also be a determining factor, for people who live in a rainy climate tend to develop a more gloomy disposition, to be ingrown, and to prefer indoor activities. A sunny climate on the other hand gives people a brighter outlook and inclines them toward more active pursuits. If there is too much sun, heat, and humidity, of course, people will be reduced to a state of torpor and inactivity, while cool, dry weather is invigorating.

In the same way, the geographical area in which a person lives will determine the type of person he becomes. People in mountainous regions are generally independent and self-reliant, strong, introspective, and reserved, while those raised on lush plains tend to be more communicative, extroverted, and mutually dependent. In the landlocked, central portion of the country the people will develop conservative, parochial attitudes, while those living along the borders or seacoast will be more open minded and liberal in their thinking, having been exposed to foreign influences.

Besides these obvious factors, a whole range of other climatic and geographical features will shape a people, including the size, shape, outline, and location of a nation, the winds, elevation, soil, vegetation, surface configuration, and type of precipitation.

In presenting this type of analysis the determinist is not declaring that every person exposed to particular conditions will exhibit a set personality. (Not all Brazilians will have sunny dispositions and not all Englishmen will be withdrawn, retreating from the rain.) But he is saying that by and large people raised in different climatic and geographical conditions will act differently from one another. The physical environment does not explain everything but it does contribute to our understanding of the determinants of personality and behavior.

Toward the beginning of the twentieth century a number of theorists put forward hypotheses concerning the influence of geography on world history and the formation of cultures. Among the most important figures were Sir Halford Mackinder, William Morris Davis, Alfred Hettner, and Arnold Toynbee.[6] All of them posited an environment cause producing social effects.

Mackinder, for example, presented the concept of "the geographical pivot of history" by which he meant that the "pivot region of the world's politics [is] that vast area of Euro-Asia which is inaccessible to ships, but in antiquity lay open to the horse-riding nomads, and is today about to be covered with a network of railroads." This "heartland" has always determined the way of life of the surrounding civilizations, and if it were now coupled with access to the sea, Mackinder argued, it would become not only the political determinant of the "World-Island" of Europe and Asia but the nodal focus on the entire world. In a formula that held sway for about forty years he stated,

> Who rules East Europe commands the Heartland:
> Who rules the Heartland commands the World-Island:
> Who rules the World-Island commands the World.

Perhaps the most interesting member of this group however was Arnold Toynbee (1889–1975), who developed this aspect of determinism extensively in his book *A Study of History*. Toynbee wanted to discover a pattern for the growth and decay of civilizations throughout history, and to do this he undertook an empirical and comparative analysis of twenty-one developed civilizations and five "arrested" ones. He concluded that the challenge of the environmental conditions is responsible, at least with regard to the initial stage of growth. The conditions cannot be so severe that development is stifled nor so easy that creativity is inhibited but they must be sufficiently difficult to stimulate progress. Soft conditions will produce soft people but challenge will result in the creation of a great culture. What are sometimes thought of as stumbling blocks are actually the stepping stones of civilization.

In fairness to Toynbee it should be pointed out that he included the human as well as the physical in his concept of environment. He said, for instance, that disintegration occurs when a people are forcibly unified into a universal state and when fringe groups gradually encroach on the periphery of the civilization. Nevertheless, he placed great stress on the climatic and geographical causes, and his idea of challenge is centered on these physical factors.

In the excerpt that follows Toynbee first illustrates the thesis that wherever nature has reasserted itself over a civilization we can see evidence of the tremendous effort that was needed intially in its development. He later goes on to give direct examples of hard conditions that generated particular civilizations.

A Study of History

At various times and places, recalcitrant Nature, once broken in by human heroism, has broken loose again because later generations have ceased for some reason to keep up the constant exertions required of them in order to maintain the mastery which had been won for them and transmitted to them by the pioneers. In such cases of reversion, the primeval state of Nature, as it was before Man ever took it in hand, can be seen to-day — not merely in the mirror of some similar piece of Nature which has happened to remain in its virgin state — but by direct observation on the very spot which has temporarily been the scene of a signal human achievement. Such spectacles, in which the primeval state of Nature and the subsequent works of Man and the eventual reversion of Nature to her primeval state are all displayed together on one spot like geological strata, are certainly more striking, as visual demonstrations, than the spectacle — striking though this is — of the contrast between the present state of Egypt and the present state of the Bahr-al-Jabal, in which the two objects that have to be brought into simultaneous focus lie a thousand miles apart. Where Nature has actually reasserted her ascendancy over some spot that has once been the birth-place of a civilization or the scene of some other signal human achievement, it is impossible to behold Nature flaunting her ultimate triumph over these works of Man and still to doubt that here, at any rate, the conditions in which those human works were performed were not unusually easy but unusually difficult. We will therefore try to clinch our argument by passing a few instances of such reversions under review.

*Dr. Ellsworth Huntington suggests that the Nature whom the fathers of the Mayan Civilization once put to flight was a different (and less formidable) antagonist from the Nature who has since got the better of these men's descendants in the selfsame region. . . .

In Central America

One remarkable instance is the present state of the birth-place of the Mayan Civilization. Far different from the dykes and fields of Egypt and Shinar, which are still being kept in order by Man and still duly serving his purpose in yielding him a livelihood, the works of the Mayas are no longer 'going concerns' to-day. Their sole surviving monuments are the ruins of the immense and magnificently decorated public buildings which now stand, far away from any present human habitations, in the depths of the tropical forest. The forest, like some sylvan boa-constrictor, has literally swallowed them up, and now it is dismembering them at its leisure: prising their fine-hewn, close-laid stones apart with its writhing roots and tendrils. The contrast between the present aspect of the country and the aspect which it must have worn when the Mayan Civilization was in being is so great that it is almost beyond imagination.** There must have been a time when these immense public buildings stood in the heart of large and populous cities, and when those cities lay in the midst of vast stretches of cultivated land which furnished them with their food-supplies. The masterpieces of Mayan architecture which are now being strangled by the forest must have been built as works of super-erogation with the surplus of an energy which, for leagues around, had already transformed the forest into fruitful fields. They were trophies of Man's victory over Nature; and, at the moment when they were raised, the retreating fringe of the vanquished and routed sylvan enemy was perhaps barely visible on the horizon, even from the highest platforms of the palaces or from the summits of the temple-pyramids. To the human beings who looked out over the World from those vantage-points then, the victory of Man over Nature must have seemed utterly secure; and the transitoriness of human achievements and the vanity of human wishes are poignantly exposed by the ultimate return of the forest, engulfing first the fields and then the houses, and finally the palaces and the temples themselves. Yet that is not the most significant or even the most obvious lesson to be learnt from the present state of Copan or Tikal or Palenque. The ruins speak still more eloquently of the intensity of the struggle with the physical environment which the creators of the Mayan Civilization must have waged victoriously in their day. In her very revenge, which reveals her in all her gruesome power, Tropical Nature testifies unwillingly to the courage and the vigour of the men who once, if only for a season, succeeded in putting her to flight and keeping her at bay.* . . .

On Easter Island

In a different environment again, we may draw a corresponding conclusion concerning the origins of the Polynesian Civilization from the present state of

**See Routledge, S.: *The Mystery of Easter Island* (London 1919, Sifton Praed); and Brown, J. Macmillan: *The Riddle of the Pacific* (London 1924, Fisher Unwin).

*Reprinted with permission from Arnold J. Toynbee, *A Study of History* (London: Oxford University Press, 1935), Vol. 2: 3–4, 12–14, 22–23, 31.

Easter Island.** At the time of its discovery by modern Western explorers, Easter Island was inhabited by two races: a race of flesh-and-blood and a race of stone; an apparently primitive human population of Polynesian physique, and a highly accomplished population of statues. The living inhabitants in that generation possessed neither the art of carving statues such as these nor the science of navigating the thousand miles of open sea that separate Easter Island from the nearest sister-island of the Polynesian Archipelago. Before its discovery by the seamen of the West, Easter Island had been isolated from the rest of the World for an unknown length of time. Yet its dual population of flesh and stone testifies, just as clearly as the ruins of Palmyra or Copan, to a vanished past which must have been utterly different from the visible present.

Those human beings must have been begotten, and those figures must have been carved, by Polynesian navigators who once found their way across the Pacific to Easter Island in flimsy open canoes, without chart, compass or chronometer and with no other motorpower than the wind behind their sails and the muscular force that plied their paddles. And this voyage can hardly have been an isolated adventure which brought one boat-load of Polynesian pioneers to Easter Island by a stroke of luck that was not repeated; for on that supposition it would really be impossible to account both for the presence of the population of statues and for the inability of the latter-day population of human beings to carve them. The art of sculpture must have been brought to Easter Island by the pioneers, and lost on Easter Island by their descendants, together with the art of navigation. The relapse of these distant colonists from the cultural level of the Polynesian Society elsewhere must have been due to the breaking of their contact with the rest of Polynesia. On the other hand, the population of statues is so numerous that it must have taken many generations to produce; and during these generations the art of sculpture, which has been lost in this latter-day age of isolation, must have been kept alive on Easter Island by continual transmarine intercourse. Taken together, these considerations point to a previous state of affairs in which the navigation across those thousand miles of open sea was carried on regularly over a long period of time. Eventually, for some reason which still remains a mystery to us, the sea, once traversed victoriously by Man, closed in round Easter Island, as the desert closed in round Palmyra and the forest round Copan. Yet, here again, Nature's reassertion of her power bears testimony to the prowess of Man in once overcoming her and thus indicates that there were certain features of unusual difficulty in the physical environment in which the Polynesian Civilization came to birth.

The truth thus proclaimed in unison by Past and Present on Easter Island is, of course, in flat contradiction to the popular Western view that the South Sea Islands are an earthly paradise and their inhabitants children of Nature in the legendary state of Adam and Eve before the Fall. Perhaps this view arises from a mistaken assumption that one portion of the Polynesian environment constitutes the whole of it. The physical environment of the

---

**The imaginative feat of conveying this contrast in words has been accomplished by Mr. Rudyard Kipling in his description of 'the Cold Lairs': a fictitious Hindu city which the Indian Jungle has swallowed up. (Read the story called 'Kaa's Hunting' in *The Jungle Book*.)

Polynesian Society consists, in reality, of water as well as land: water which presents a formidable challenge to any human beings who propose to cross it without possessing any better means of navigation than those, described above, which were actually the only means at the Polynesian navigators' command. It was by responding boldly and successfully to this challenge of the estranging sea — by achieving, with their rudimentary means of navigation, the *tour de force* of establishing a regular maritime traffic across the open waters between island and island — that the Polynesian pioneers won their footing on the specks of dry land which are scattered through the vast watery wilderness of the Pacific Ocean almost as rarely as the stars are scattered through the depths of Space.

. . .

The Temptations of Odysseus

This fable of the Persians' Choice, like the true story of Hannibal's Army at Capua, signifies that when human beings who have been living under pressure are set at ease, their energies are not released but are rather relaxed by this pleasurable change in their conditions of life. The same conception appears in a work of classical literature that is older and more famous than the histories of Herodotus and Livy. It is the theme of those four books of the *Odyssey* . . . in which the hero tells Alcinous the story of his wanderings from the day when he sailed with his companions from Troy to the day when he was washed up, the sole survivor, on the shores of Calypso's island.

In that long series of adventures it is not when he is encountering his difficulties and dangers — running the gauntlet of the Laestrygons or confronting the Cyclops or making the passage between Scylla and Charybdis — that Odysseus comes nearest to failure in his struggle to make his way home to Ithaca. Rather, these ordeals speed him on his course towards the goal of his endeavours by calling his faculties of audacity and nimbleness of wit and endurance and ingenuity into action . . . He comes nearest to failure when the resolution to persevere on the difficult and dangerous course towards the journey's end has to compete with the attractions of an assured and immediate ease.

Thus, when the three companions whom he sent out on a reconnaissance into the land of the lotus-eaters fell in with the inhabitants,

> the lotus-eaters did not bethink them to do our companions to death, but gave them of the lotus to taste. And which soever of them did eat that honey-sweet fruit, he no longer had the will to bring back tidings nor in any wise to return; but their will was to remain there with the lotus-eaters, feeding on lotus, and to think no more of the homeward voyage. So I took them to the ships weeping, under duress, and in the hollow ships I dragged them under the benches and bound them there. And then I bade the rest of my companions come aboard the swift ships with all speed, lest any man should lose thought of the voyage home by eating of the lotus.

. . .

A Plan of Operations

> We have now perhaps established decisively the truth that ease is inimical to civilization. The results of our investigation up to this point appear to warrant the proposition that, the greater the ease of the environment, the weaker the stimulus towards civilization which that environment administers to Man . . . [and] that the stimulus towards civilization grows stronger in proportion as the environment grows more difficult.

Cultural Effects

In addition to the forces of our physical environment that can give rise to grand philosophies of history such as that of Toynbee, another factor that shapes us is the *society and culture* to which we belong. Each person is a part of a social group with particular beliefs and customs, institutions and traditions, and this societal context exerts a powerful effect on the person's ideas, values, and behavior.

For example, someone raised in a rural village in India, speaking Urdu and following Hinduism, will become an entirely different person than an Italian from Rome, who is descended from the nobility and a firm believer in the Roman Catholic faith. Similarly, an Eskimo in northern Alaska is very different from a Polynesian, an Ethiopian from a Chinaman, and the difference lies mainly in their having been formed by different cultures. Even when the climate and geography are essentially the same, people will turn out differently depending upon their societal background.

More specifically, the individual will not freely decide how to dress but will conform to the culture's styles. He will wear a burnoose in Morocco, a sarape in Mexico, a kimono in Japan, and pants and shirt in the United States. Some variation will occur in the range of dress within a culture but in global terms it will be relatively little. Certainly with regard to past styles of dress, a person will not wear a loin cloth, a toga, or a powdered wig. With regard to sports, the Spaniard will like bullfighting, the Englishman cricket, and the American football. With regard to concepts of beauty, the Indian woman will wear heavy jewelry and perhaps a nose ornament, the African may have ritual scarification on her face, and the American woman will paint her lips red and her eyelids blue. The same social pressures will determine a person's latitude of political opinion, religious convictions, moral code, work and recreation, sexual attitudes, sense of humor, habits, expression, and so forth.

Another major cultural effect comes about through the use of language. Each culture possesses a language with a built-in framework for understanding and evaluating the world, and this framework orders the mind of the language user. Certain ideas are almost unthinkable in Chinese which would be temptations of thought in English, and whenever a person learns a new language his field of thought is altered and expanded. A theory has been proposed in fact, called the Sapir-Whorf hypothesis, which maintains that language determines thought instead of thought determining language. A society does not see the world in a particular way then invent a language to express that perspective, but has a certain perspective because of the language used.[7] And Ludwig Wittgenstein (1889–1951), one of the founders of the movement of linguistic analysis, claimed that language traps us into making conceptual mistakes; he believed that the task of philosophy is to show the fly the way out of the fly-bottle.[8] In both cases, the effect of language is emphasized and our culture decides the language we speak. Each person in the culture repeatedly "traces round the picture frame" because language and thought are so intimately connected.

A great deal more could be said about the influence of language but the overall point is that, in addition to factors in the physical environment, one's culture and society also determine one's ideas and conduct. The determinist is doing nothing more than stating the obvious, that the effect of society upon the individual cannot be denied.

The force of culture so impressed the sociologist Émile Durkheim that he said, "The individual does not exist." In a milder vein the anthropologist Ruth Benedict stated:

> No man ever looks at the world with pristine eyes. He sees it edited by a definite set of customs and institutions and ways of thinking. . . . The life history of the individual is first and foremost an accomodation to the patterns and standards traditionally handed down in his community. From the moment of his birth the customs into which he is born shape his experience and behaviour. By the time he can talk, he is the little creature of his culture, and by the time he is grown and able to take part in its activities, its habits are his habits, its beliefs his beliefs, its impossibilities his impossibilities. Every child that is born into his group will share them with him, and no child born into one on the opposite side of the globe can ever achieve the thousandth part.

Benedict went on to say that even with regard to characteristics which we would usually regard as self-chosen, the cultural model holds true.

Recent important experiments dealing with personality traits have shown that social determinants are crucial even in the traits of honesty and leadership. Honesty in one experimental situation gave almost no indication whether the child would cheat in another. There turned out to be not honest–dishonest persons, but honest–dishonest situations. In the same way in the study of leaders there proved to be no uniform traits that could be set down as standard even in our own society. The rôle developed the leader, and his qualities were those that the situation emphasized. In these 'situational' results it has become more and more evident that social conduct even in a selected society is 'not simply the expression of a fixed mechanism that predetermines to a specific mode of conduct, but rather a set of tendencies aroused in variable ways by the specific problem that confronts us.'

When these situations that even in one society are dynamic in human behaviour are magnified into contrasts between cultures opposed to one another in goals and motivations to such a degree as Zuñi and the Kwakiutl, for instance, the conclusion is inescapable. If we are interested in human behaviour, we need first of all to understand the institutions that are provided in any society. For human behaviour will take the forms those institutions suggest, even in extremes of which the observer, deep-dyed in the culture of which he is a part, can have no intimation.[9]

Psychological Factors

In recent intellectual history the field of psychology has offered a great deal of support for determinism.[10] In particular, the theories of *behaviorism* and *Freudian psychology* have been fertile breeding grounds for deterministic thinking. It is important therefore to understand broadly what each position claims.

Behaviorism is associated with Ivan Pavlov (1849–1936), J. B. Watson (1878–1958), and more recently B. F. Skinner (1904–   ). The central thesis of the behaviorist is that human conduct can be understood, not through introspective evidence or the analysis of cognition or consciousness, but through the scientific study of responses to stimuli. Psychology, it is claimed, is the examination of human behavior not speculation about a "ghost in the machine" that people call "mind."

Starting with Pavlov who conditioned dogs to salivate at the sound of a bell that signaled food, the behaviorists have amassed an impressive array of data showing how both human and animal behavior is a conditioned response to given stimuli. The strongest stimulus always wins. When people are frequently rewarded for their conduct that strong (positive) reinforcement will confirm and fix the behavior. In aversive (negative) conditioning the experience of punishment acts as a discouragement and can cause the behavior to be extinguished.

According to the behaviorist, whatever we do is the effect of reinforcement, a stimulus–response process that is mechanical and exhaustive. The conditioning can be more or less random as it is in contemporary society or quite deliberate as, for example, Skinner advocated in *Walden II*, but no one can escape the conditioning process. Free choice, outside of all conditioning, is an illusion that we maintain for the sake of our pride and in order to differentiate ourselves from animals and objects. But it is an illusion nonetheless, for people are stimulus–response organisms and through conditioned responses build up predictable patterns of behavior. In the same way that rats and mice can be conditioned to negotiate a maze in an experimental laboratory, people are conditioned to perform successfully in the labyrinth of society.

The following selection from *Beyond Freedom and Dignity* by B. F. Skinner provides a succinct expression of the behaviorist position. Skinner is the reigning dean of behaviorism and the title of his book is instructive in itself.

Beyond Freedom and Dignity*

Almost all living things act to free themselves from harmful contacts. A kind of freedom is achieved by the relatively simple forms of behavior called reflexes. A person sneezes and frees his respiratory passages from irritating substances. He vomits and frees his stomach from indigestible or poisonous food. He pulls back his hand and frees it from a sharp or hot object. More

*Reprinted with permission from B. F. Skinner, *Beyond Freedom and Dignity* (New York: Alfred Knopf, 1971), 26–29, 199–201, 211–12.

elaborate forms of behavior have similar effects. When confined, people struggle ("in rage") and break free. When in danger they flee from or attack its source. Behavior of this kind presumably evolved because of its survival value; it is as much a part of what we call the human genetic endowment as breathing, sweating, or digesting food. And through conditioning similar behavior may be acquired with respect to novel objects which could have played no role in evolution. These are no doubt minor instances of the struggle to be free, but they are significant. We do not attribute them to any love of freedom; they are simply forms of behavior which have proved useful in reducing various threats to the individual and hence to the species in the course of evolution.

A much more important role is played by behavior which weakens harmful stimuli in another way. It is not acquired in the form of conditioned reflexes, but as the product of a different process called operant conditioning. When a bit of behavior is followed by a certain kind of consequence, it is more likely to occur again, and a consequence having this effect is called a reinforcer. Food, for example, is a reinforcer to a hungry organism; anything the organism does that is followed by the receipt of food is more likely to be done again whenever the organism is hungry. Some stimuli are called negative reinforcers; any response which reduces the intensity of such a stimulus — or ends it — is more likely to be emitted when the stimulus recurs. Thus, if a person escapes from a hot sun when he moves under cover, he is more likely to move under cover when the sun is again hot. The reduction in temperature reinforces the behavior it is "contingent upon" — that is, the behavior it follows. Operant conditioning also occurs when a person simply avoids a hot sun — when, roughly speaking, he escapes from the *threat* of a hot sun.

Negative reinforcers are called aversive in the sense that they are the things organisms "turn away from." The term suggests a spatial separation — moving or running away from something — but the essential relation is temporal. In a standard apparatus used to study the process in the laboratory, an arbitrary response simply weakens an aversive stimulus or brings it to an end. A great deal of physical technology is the result of this kind of struggle for freedom. Over the centuries, in erratic ways, men have constructed a world in which they are relatively free of many kinds of threatening or harmful stimuli — extremes of temperature, sources of infection, hard labor, danger, and even those minor aversive stimuli called discomfort.

Escape and avoidance play a much more important role in the struggle for freedom when the aversive conditions are generated by other people. Other people can be aversive without, so to speak, trying: they can be rude, dangerous, contagious, or annoying, and one escapes from them or avoids them accordingly. They may also be "intentionally" aversive — that is, they may treat other people aversively because of what follows. Thus, a slave driver induces a slave to work by whipping him when he stops; by resuming work the slave escapes from the whipping (and incidentally reinforces the slave driver's behavior in using the whip). A parent nags a child until the child performs a task; by performing the task the child escapes nagging (and reinforces the parent's behavior). The blackmailer threatens exposure unless the victim pays; by paying, the victim escapes from the threat (and reinforces the practice). A teacher threatens corporal punishment or failure until his students pay attention; by paying attention the students escape from the threat of punishment (and reinforce the teacher for threatening it). In one form or another intentional aversive control is the pattern of most social coordination—in ethics, religion, government, economics, education, psychotherapy, and family life.

A person escapes from or avoids aversive treatment by behaving in ways which reinforce those who treated him aversively until he did so, but he may escape in other ways. For example, he may simply move out of range. A person may escape from slavery, emigrate or defect from a government, desert from an army, become an apostate from a religion, play truant, leave home, or drop out of a culture as a hobo, hermit, or hippie. Such behavior is as much a product of the aversive conditions as the behavior the conditions were designed to evoke. The latter can be guaranteed only by sharpening the contingencies or by using stronger aversive stimuli.

• • •

The picture which emerges from a scientific analysis is not of a body with a person inside, but of a body which is a person in the sense that it displays a complex repertoire of behavior. The picture is, of course, unfamiliar. The man thus portrayed is a stranger, and from the traditional point of view he may not seem to be a man at all. . . . What is being abolished is autonomous man—the inner man, the homunculus, the possessing demon, the man defended by the literatures of freedom and dignity. His abolition has long been overdue. Autonomous man is a device used to explain what we cannot explain in any other way. He has been constructed from our ignorance, and as our understanding increases, the very stuff of which he is composed vanishes. Science does not dehumanize man, it de-homunculizes him, and it must do so if it is to prevent the abolition of the human species. To man *qua* man we readily say good riddance. Only by dispossessing him can we turn to the real causes of human behavior. Only then can we turn from the inferred to the observed, from the miraculous to the natural, from the inaccessible to the manipulable. . . .

Science has probably never demanded a more sweeping change in a traditional way of thinking about a subject, nor has there ever been a more important subject. In the traditional picture a person perceives the world around him, selects features to be perceived, discriminates among them, judges them good or bad, changes them to make them better (or, if he is careless, worse), and may be held responsible for his action and justly rewarded or punished for its consequences. In the scientific picture a person is a member of a species shaped by evolutionary contingencies of survival, displaying behavioral processes which bring him under the control of the environment in which he lives, and largely under the control of a social environment which he and millions of others like him have constructed and maintained during the evolution of a culture. The direction of the controlling relation is reversed: a person does not act upon the world, the world acts upon him.

It is difficult to accept such a change simply of intellectual grounds and nearly impossible to accept its implications. The reaction of the traditionalist is usually described in terms of feelings. One of these, to which the Freudians have appealed in explaining the resistance to psychoanalysis, is wounded vanity. Freud himself expounded, as Ernest Jones has said, "the three heavy blows which narcissism or self-love of mankind had suffered at the hands of science. The first was cosmological and was dealt by Copernicus; the second was biological and was dealt by Darwin; the third was psychological and was dealt by Freud." (The blow was suffered by the belief that something at the center of man knows all that goes on within him and that an instrument called will power exercises command and control over the rest of one's personality.) But what are the signs or symptoms of wounded vanity, and how shall we explain them? What people *do* about such a scientific picture of man is call it wrong, demeaning, and dangerous, argue against it, and attack those who propose or defend it. They do so not out of wounded vanity but because the scientific formulation has destroyed accustomed reinforcers. If a person can no longer take credit or be admired for what he does, then he seems to suffer a loss of dignity or worth, and behavior previously reinforced by credit or admiration will undergo extinction. Extinction often leads to aggressive attack.

On this model of behavior, then, we have gone beyond the "antique" notion of human autonomy and accepted the hard truth of science that causal determinants in the form of conditioned responses control all thought and action.

Freudian psychology shares with behaviorism a belief in determinism but the reasons offered are very different. According to Sigmund Freud (1856–1939) there is a mind behind behavior and it consists of three energy systems: the id, ego, and super ego. The id is the "dark, inaccessible part of the personality," a "cauldron full of seething excitations"; it is the primary source of our psychic energy and seeks gratification continually and indiscriminately. The excitations are basically sexual in the nature and operate from infancy on, at which time the psychic organism is "polymorphously perverse." Although its operations remain deeply hidden within the recesses of the mind, evidence of it can be seen in forgetting, slips of the tongue, jokes, and so forth, which always have an underlying reason. Above all, the power of the id can be seen in dreams, which are the unconscious representation of repressed desires.

The ego is the reasonable element of the mind, modifying the id's desire for pleasure or the discharge of excitation with a practical appraisal of the surrounding circumstances. It interacts with the external world and finds the least punishing way of expressing the demands of the id. Without ever extinguishing the id's desires, it effectively channels them so that the psyche obtains maximum satisfaction within the context of external reality.

The super ego is the embodiment of social sanctions and prohibitions, a regulating force that constrains the elemental desires so that they conform to the group's standards. Parents are proxies of society, disciplining the child in accordance with the prevailing rules of conduct, fostering the culture's ideals and instilling a conscience within him. That conscience will punish the child with guilt if he violates the social norms and the ideals he has assimilated will make him feel proud of himself when he meets social expectations.

The ego has the difficult task of mediating between the demands of the id and the super ego, guiding the psyche to the maximum satisfaction of desires within the constraints of outside reality and societal regulation. If the ego is successful then a proper equilibrium or homeostasis will be achieved that is called normalcy. But if it is unsuccessful the person will be unbalanced the neurosis or psychosis will occur; this Freud described as "the return of the repressed."

In all cases, the person is ruled by these three energy systems even though he assumes that his conscious mind is in control. It is the unconscious that determines what we do, and all our vaunted logic is mere rationalization for the forces that drive us along. The human condition is most aptly portrayed in the metaphor of the crippled man sitting on the shoulders of the blind giant.

Such are the basic tenets of the Freudian view of mind. Its specific implications to ethics are to deny free will altogether, and these implications have been drawn most forcefully by the contemporary philosopher John Hospers. The following passage, taken from an article by Hospers which has had some influence on discussions of responsibility, explains this point quite clearly.

We have always been conscious of the fact that we are not masters of our fate in every respect — that there are many things which we cannot do, that nature is more powerful than we are, that we cannot disobey laws without danger of reprisals, etc. We have become "officially" conscious, too, though in our private lives we must long have been aware of it, that we are not free with respect to the emotions that we feel — whom we love or hate, what types we admire, and the like. More lately still we have been reminded that there are unconscious motivations for our basic attractions and repulsions, our compulsive actions or inabilities to act. But what is not welcome news is that our very acts of volition, and the entire train of deliberations leading up to them, are but façades for the expression of unconscious wishes, or rather, unconscious compromises and defenses.

. . .

We talk about free will, and we say, for example, the person is free to do so-and-so if he can do so *if* he wants to — and we forget that his wanting to is itself caught up in the stream of determinism, that unconscious forces drive him into the wanting or not wanting to do the thing in question. The analogy of the puppet whose motions are manipulated from behind by invisible wires, or better still, by springs inside, is a telling one at almost every point.

And the glaring fact is that it all started so early, before we knew what was happening. The personality structure is inelastic after the age of five, and comparatively so in most cases after the age of three. Whether one acquires a neurosis or not is determined by that age — and just as involuntarily as if it had been a curse of God . . . only the psychiatrist knows what puppets people really are; and it is no wonder that the protestations of philosophers that "the act which is the result of a volition, a deliberation, a conscious decision, is free" leave these persons, to speak mildly, somewhat cold.

. . . Now, what of the notion of responsibility? What happens to it in our analysis?

Let us begin with an example, not a fictitious one. A woman and her two-year-old baby are riding on a train to Montreal in midwinter. The child is ill. The woman wants badly to get to her destination. She is, unknown to herself, the victim of a neurotic conflict whose nature is irrelevant here except for the fact that it forces her to behave aggressively toward the child, partly to spite her husband whom she despises and who loves the child, but chiefly to ward off super-ego charges of masochistic attachment. Consciously she loves the child, and when she says this she says it sincerely, but she must behave aggressively toward it nevertheless, just as many children love their mothers but are nasty to them most of the time in neurotic pseudo-aggression. The child becomes more ill as the train approaches Montreal; the heating system of the train is not working, and the conductor pleads with the woman to get off the train at the next town and get the child to a hospital at once. The woman refuses. Soon after, the child's condition worsens, and the mother does all she can to keep it alive, without, however, leaving the train, for she declares that it is absolutely necessary that she reach her destination. But before she gets there the child is dead. After that, of course, the mother grieves, blames herself, weeps hysterically, and joins the church to gain surcease from the guilt that constantly overwhelms her when she thinks of how her aggressive behavior has killed her child.

Was she responsible for her deed? In ordinary life, after making a mistake, we say, "Chalk it up to experience." Here we should say, "Chalk it up to the neurosis." *She* could not help it if her neurosis forced her to act this way — she didn't even know what was going on behind the scenes, her conscious self merely acted out its assigned part. This is far more true than is generally realized: criminal actions in general are not actions for which their agents are responsible; the agents are passive, not active — they are victims of a neurotic conflict. Their very hyperactivity is unconsciously determined.

· · ·

Heretofore it was pretty generally thought that, while we could not rightly blame a person for the color of his eyes or the morality of his parents, or even for what he did at the age of three, or to a large extent what impulses he had and whom he fell in love with, one *could* do so for other of his adult activities, particularly the acts he performed voluntarily and with premeditation. Later this attitude was shaken. Many voluntary acts came to be recognized, at least in some circles, as compelled by the unconscious. Some philosophers recognized this too — Ayer talks about the kleptomaniac being unfree, and about a person being unfree when another person exerts a habitual ascendancy over his personality. But this is as far as he goes. The usual examples, such as the kleptomaniac and the schizophrenic, apparently satisfy most philosophers, and with these exceptions removed, the rest of mankind is permitted to wander in the vast and alluring fields of freedom and responsibility. So far the inroads upon freedom left the vast majority of humanity untouched; they began to hit home when psychiatrists began to realize, though philosophers did not, that the domination of the conscious by the unconscious extended, not merely to a few exceptional individuals, but to all human beings, that the "big three behind the scenes" are not respecters of persons, and dominate us all, even including that *sanctum sanctorum* of freedom, our conscious will. To be sure, the domination by the unconscious in the case of "normal" individuals is somewhat more benevolent than the tyranny and despotism exercised in neurotic cases, and therefore the former have evoked less comment; but the principle remains in all cases the same: the unconscious is the master of every fate and the caption of every soul.[11]

Genetic Determinants

In addition to the effects of geography and climate the social environment, and psychological factors, our *genetic inheritance* is also identified as contributing to the forces that determine us.

In a broad sense, we are strongly determined by the chemical, anatomical, and physiological characteristics that are our biological endowment. These traits would include especially our skeletal structure, nervous system, glandular activity, brain capacity, sense organs, chemical metabolism, sex, and secondary sexual characteristics. It would also include our hereditary body type, classified by W. H. Sheldon as ectomorphic (a slender, angular, fragile, light build); endomorphic (a round, soft body with a tendency toward fat); or mezomorphic (a muscular, large-boned physique).[12]

On this reading, a person with a low intelligence quotient could never become an astrophysicist, neurosurgeon, a corporation executive, or an engineer but would have to work at some menial job suited to his mental capability. Someone with a small, ectomorphic body, slow reflexes, and an underactive thyroid would not become a basketball player, a jet pilot, or a short order cook. In this sense, biology is destiny. Not only would these individuals be excluded from the respective fields by the requirements but they would never choose to enter these fields, given their physical traits. In other words, they would not only lack the freedom of entry to certain careers but also the freedom to decide in favor of them. A person with a poor sense of taste and smell would never think of becoming a wine expert; it simply would not be a viable option.

In recent years a new field of biological science has been developed with similar implications for the free will–determinism argument. This is the field of *sociobiology* which tries to unite biological and cultural explanations for human behavior. E. O. Wilson, R. Dawkins, W. D. Hamilton, Irven De Vore, D. P. Barash, and others of this breed have succeeded in creating a startling new theory.[13] It has been criticized as racist and sexist, antireligious and antihumanist, but despite the surrounding controversy its claims have commanded the attention of the academic community.

Using data drawn largely from genetics, anthropology, and field biology, the sociobiologists have constructed a unique explanation for the social behavior of man. Their overall thesis is that species are controlled by their genes, which regulate behavior so as to ensure the perpetuation of the gene type. Individual members of species are manipulated to produce more genes and function as the housing that the genes require. The raison d'etre of all organisms is the continued existence of the genetic strain—and that includes the human organism as well.

Instead of explaining the characteristics of species in terms of the classic survival-of-the-fittest process described by Darwin, the sociobiologist modifies evolutionary theory and uses the action of the gene as the main principle of selection. What R. Dawkins called "the selfish gene" accounts for the attributes and behavior that has been selected-for in all species.[14]

The uniqueness of sociobiological theory can be seen in the case of altruism. In traditional evolutionary accounts the kind of characteristics carried forward are those that increase fitness. If an individual's fitness is enhanced then survival is more likely and offspring are produced that possess the gene that determined the behavior. However, altruism appears to contradict this explanation because it has been perpetuated in species yet it works against the survival of the altruistic member. Why then does it still exist?

For example, animals will frequently share food with members of their group. Biological studies of ants and honeybees, for instance, show that newly fed workers will surrender a portion of their food to their nestmates, even without being begged and even though this places their food level below that of the colony average. This altruistic conduct benefits the group but does not increase the individual's fitness for survival. If the standard theory of evolution were correct, the individuals possessing that gene would have been eliminated long ago, and food sharing would not exist in ants, honeybees, or any other species. The same appears to be true for the human animal. Self-sacrificing people will not compete as successfully as selfish ones (nice guys finish last), yet people persist in being generous even to their own detriment. Why then should altruism still be a strain in the human species?

The answer given by the sociobiologist is that gene types are perpetuated by the sacrifice of individuals. The mechanism for achieving this is called *inclusive fitness* and it operates in the following way.

The kind of genes possessed by an individual are shared by his relatives in direct proportion to the closeness of the relation. The individual is therefore driven to perform altruistic acts even though they are dangerous to himself because protection is thereby provided to his relatives who are carrying his genotype. In this way the genes are saved even though the individual may be lost. Altruism therefore, is attributable to the action of the genes just as the genes are responsible for every mode of behavior of man and the other biological species.

According to the sociobiologist, what we formerly ascribed to the free, unfettered choice of individuals is rooted deep in the structure of the genes. Altruism is not a decision made after a recognition of our moral obligations but, like every other value, is something compelled for the continued survival of the gene types. In his recent book *On Human Nature* E. O. Wilson wrote, "The genes hold culture on a leash. The leash is very long, but inevitably values will be constrained in accordance with their effect on the human gene pool."

In his definitive work, *Sociobiology: The New Synthesis*, Wilson offered a similar explanation for such cultural manifestations as religion, tribalism, warfare, genocide, cooperation, competition, entrepeneurship, conformity, and ethics in general. The following excerpt shows some of the principles and evidence that are used by Wilson, who can be taken as representative of the sociobiological perspective.

The Morality of the Gene*

Camus said that the only serious philosophical question is suicide. That is wrong even in the strict sense intended. The biologist, who is concerned with questions of physiology and evolutionary history, realizes that self-knowledge is constrained and shaped by the emotional control centers in the hypothalamus and limbic system of the brain. These centers flood our consciousness with all the emotions—hate, love, guilt, fear, and others—that are consulted by ethical philosophers who wish to intuit the standards of good and evil. What, we are then compelled to ask, made the hypothalamus and limbic system? They evolved by natural selection. That simple biological statement must be pursued to explain ethics and ethical philosophers, if not epistemology and epistemologists, at all depths. Self-existence, or the suicide that terminates it, is not the central question of philosophy. The hypothalamic–limbic complex automatically denies such logical reduction by countering it with feelings of guilt and altruism. In this one way the philosopher's own emotional control centers are wiser than his solipsist consciousness, "knowing" that in evolutionary time the individual organism counts for almost nothing. In a Darwinist sense the organism does not live for itself. Its primary function is not even to reproduce other organisms; it reproduces genes, and it serves as their temporary carrier. Each organism generated by sexual reproduction is a unique, accidental subset of all the genes constituting the species. Natural selection is the process whereby certain genes gain representation in the following generations superior to that of other genes located at the same chromosome positions. When new sex cells are manufactured in each generation, the winning genes are pulled apart and reassembled to manufacture new organisms that, on the average, contain a higher proportion of the same genes. But the individual organism is only their vehicle, part of an elaborate device to preserve and spread them with the least possible biochemical perturbation. Samuel Butler's famous aphorism, that the chicken is only an egg's way of making another egg, has been modernized: the organism is only DNA's way of making more DNA. More to the point, the hypothalamus and limbic system are engineered to perpetuate DNA.

In the process of natural selection, then, any device that can insert a higher proportion of certain genes into subsequent generations will come to characterize the species. One class of such devices promotes prolonged individual survival. Another promotes superior mating performance and care of the resulting offspring. As more complex social behavior by the organism is added to the genes' techniques for replicating themselves, altruism becomes increasingly prevalent and eventually appears in exaggerated forms. This brings us to the central theoretical problem of sociobiology: how can altruism, which by definition reduces personal fitness, possibly evolve by natural selection? The answer is kinship: if the genes

*Reprinted with permission from Edward O. Wilson, *Sociobiology: The New Synthesis* (Cambridge: Harvard University Press, 1975), 125, 129. References cited within the text have been deleted.

causing the altruism are shared by two organisms because of common descent, and if the altruistic act by one organism increases the joint contribution of these genes to the next generation, the propensity to altruism will spread through the gene pool. This occurs even though the altruist makes less of a solitary contribution to the gene pool as the price of its altruistic act.

To his own question, "Does the Absurd dictate death?" Camus replied that the struggle toward the heights is itself enough to fill a man's heart. This arid judgment is probably correct, but it makes little sense except when closely examined in the light of evolutionary theory. The hypothalamic–limbic complex of a highly social species, such as man, "knows," or more precisely it has been programmed to perform as if it knows, that its underlying genes will be proliferated maximally only if it orchestrates behavioral responses that bring into play an efficient mixture of personal survival, reproduction, and altruism. Consequently, the centers of the complex tax the conscious mind with ambivalences whenever the organisms encounter stressful situations. Love joins hate; aggression, fear; expansiveness, withdrawal; and so on; in blends designed not to promote the happiness and survival of the individual, but to favor the maximum transmission of the controlling genes.

· · ·

I have raised a problem in ethical philosophy in order to characterize the essence of sociobiology. Sociobiology is defined as the systematic study of the biological basis of all social behavior. For the present it focuses on animal societies, their population structure, castes, and communication, together with all of the physiology underlying the social adaptations. But the discipline is also concerned with the social behavior of early man and the adaptive features of organization in the more primitive contemporary human societies. Sociology *sensu stricto*, the study of human societies at all levels of complexity, still stands apart from sociobiology because of its largely structuralist and nongenetic approach. It attempts to explain human behavior primarily by empirical description of the outermost phenotypes and by unaided intuition, without reference to evolutionary explanations in the true genetic sense. It is most successful, in the way descriptive taxonomy and ecology have been most successful, when it provides a detailed description of particular phenomena and demonstrates first-order correlations with features of the environment. Taxonomy and ecology, however, have been reshaped entirely during the past forty years by integration into neo-Darwinist evolutionary theory — the "Modern Synthesis," as it is often called — in which each phenomenon is weighed for its adaptive significance and then related to the basic principles of population genetics. It may not be too much to say that sociology and the other social sciences, as well as the humanities, are the last branches of biology waiting to be included in the Modern Synthesis. One of the functions of sociobiology, then, is to reformulate the foundations of the social sciences in a way that draws these subjects into the Modern Synthesis. Whether the social sciences can be truly biologicized in this fashion remains to be seen.

· · ·

Altruistic Behavior

Armed with existing theory, let us now reevaluate the reported cases of altruism among animals. In the review to follow each class of behavior will insofar as possible be examined in the light of two or more competing hypotheses that counterpoise altruism and selfishness.

Thwarting Predators

The social insects contain many striking examples of altruistic behavior evolved by family-level selection. The altruistic responses are directed not only at offspring and parents but also at sibs and even nieces, nephews, and cousins. . . . The soldier caste of most species of termites and ants is mostly limited in function to colony defense. Soldiers are often slow to respond to stimuli that arouse the rest of the colony, but when they do react, they normally place themselves in the position of maximum danger. When nest walls of higher termites such as *Nasutitermes* are broken open, for example, the white, defenseless nymphs and workers rush inward toward the concealed depths of the nests, while the soldiers press outward and mill aggressively on the outside of the nest. W. L. Nutting (personal communication) witnessed soldiers of *Amitermes emersoni* in Arizona emerge well in advance of the nuptial flights, wander widely around the nest vicinity, and effectively engage in combat all foraging ants that might have endangered the emerging winged reproductives. I have observed that injured workers of the fire ant *Solenopsis invicta* leave the nest more readily and are more aggressive on the average than their uninjured sisters. Dying workers of the harvesting ant *Pogonomyrmex badius* tend to leave the nest altogether. Both effects may be no more than nonadaptive epiphenomena, but it is also likely that the responses are altruistic. To be specific, injured workers are useless for more functions other than defense, while dying workers pose a sanitary problem. Honeybee workers possess barbed stings that tend to remain embedded in their victims when the insects pull away, causing part of their viscera to be torn out and the bees to be fatally injured. . . . The suicide seems to be a device specifically adapted to repel human beings and other vertebrates, since the workers can sting intruding bees from other hives without suffering the effect. . . . A similar defensive maneuver occurs in the ant *P. badius* and in many polybiine wasps, including *Synoeca surinama* and at least some species of *Polybia* and *Stelopolybia*. . . . The fearsome reputation of social bees and wasps is due to their general readiness to throw their lives away upon slight provocation.

Although vertebrates are seldom suicidal in the manner of the social insects, many place themselves in harm's way to defend relatives. The dominant males of chacma baboon troops (*Papio ursinus*) position themselves in exposed locations in order to scan the environment while the other troop members forage. If predators or rival troops approach, the dominant males warn the others by barking and may move toward the intruders in a threatening manner, perhaps accompanied by other males. As the troop retreats, the dominant males cover the rear. . . . Essentially the same behavior has been observed in the yellow baboon (*P. cynocephalus*) by the Altmanns. . . . When troops of hamadryas baboons, rhesus macaques, or vervets meet and fight, the adult males lead the combat. . . . The adults of many ungulates living in family groups, such as musk oxen, moose, zebras, and kudus, interpose themselves between predators and the young. When males are in charge of harems, they usually assume the role; otherwise the females are the defenders. This behavior can be rather easily explained by kin selection. Dominant males are likely to be the fathers or at least close relatives of the weaker individuals they defend. . . .

Parental sacrifice in the face of predators attains its clearest expression in the distraction displays of birds. . . . A distraction display is any distinctive behavior used to attract the attention of an enemy and to draw it away from an object that the animal is trying to protect. In the great majority of instances the display directs a predator away from the eggs or young. Bird species belonging to many different families have evolved their own particular bag of tricks. The commonest is injury feigning, which varies according to the species from simple interruptions of normal movements to the exact imitation of injury or illness. The female nighthawk (*Chordeiles minor*) deserts her nest when approached, flies conspicuously at low levels, and finally settles on the ground in front of the intruder (and away from her nest) with wings drooping or outstretched. . . . Wood ducks (*Aix sponsa*) and black-throated divers (*Gavia arctica*) spread one wing as if broken and paddle around in circles as if they were crippled. The prairie warbler (*Dendroica discolor*) plummets from the nest to the ground and grovels frantically in front of the observer. These performances can be quite affecting. New Zealand pied stilts (*Himantopus picatus*) are among the great actors of the animal world. Guthrie-Smith . . . has described their response to intrusion in the vicinity of the nest as follows:

> Dancing, prancing, galumphing over one spot of ground, the stricken bird seems simultaneously to jerk both legs and wings, as strange toy beasts can be agitated by elastic wires, the extreme length of the bird's legs producing extraordinary effects. It gradually becomes less and less able to maintain an upright attitude. Lassitude, fatigue, weariness, faintings—lackadaisical and fine ladyish—supervene. The end comes slowly, surely, a miserable flurry and scraping, the dying Stilt, however, even in *articulo mortis*, contriving to avoid inconvenient stones and to select a pleasant sandy spot upon which decently to expire. When on some shingle bank well removed from eggs and nests half a dozen Stilts—for they often die in companies—go through their performances, agonizing and fainting, the sight is quaint indeed.

Other behavior patterns besides injury feigning are utilized as distraction displays. Oystercatchers (*Haematopus ostralegus*) and dunlins (*Calidris alpina*) perform display flights of the kind usually limited to courtship. Many kinds of shore birds alternate injury feigning with squatting on the ground as though they were brooding eggs. Short-eared owls (*Asio flammeus*) and Australian splendid blue wrens (*Malurus splendens*) even pretend to *be* young birds, quivering their wings as though begging for food. Anecdotes in the literature indicate that predators are indeed attracted by the various kinds of distraction displays, and there can be little doubt that the adults engaging in the displays endanger their own lives while reducing the risk for their young.

· · ·

Cooperative Breeding

The reduction of personal reproduction in order to favor the reproduction of others is widespread among organisms and offers some of the strongest indirect evidence of kin selection. The social insects, as usual, are clear-cut in this respect. The very definition of higher sociality ("eusociality") in termites, ants, bees, and wasps entails the existence of sterile castes whose basic functions are to increase the oviposition rate of the queen, ordinarily their mother, and to rear the queen's offspring, ordinarily their brothers and sisters. The case of "helpers" among birds is also strongly suggestive. . . . Among the many cases of helpers assisting other birds to rear their young, including moorhens, Australian blue wrens, thornbills, anis, and others, the assistance is typically rendered by young adults to their parents. Consequently, just as in the social insects, the cooperators are rearing their own brothers and sisters. . . .

In some respects "aunt" and "uncle" behavior in monkeys and apes superficially resembles the cooperative brood care of social insects and birds. Childless adults take over the infants of others for short periods during which they carry the young about, groom them, and play with them. The baby-sitting may seem to be altruistic, but there are other explanations. Adult males of the Barbary macaque use infants in ritual presentations to conciliate other adult males. The "aunts" of rhesus and Japanese macaques also use baby-sitting to form alliances with mothers of superior rank. Furthermore, the possibility cannot be excluded that aunting behavior provides training in the manipulation of infants that improves the performance of young females when they bear their first young. . . .

Outright adoption of infants and juveniles has also been recorded in a few mammal species. Jane van Lawick-Goodall . . . recorded three cases of adult chimpanzees adopting young orphaned siblings at the Gombe Stream Reserve. As she noted, it is strange (but significant for the theory of kin selection) that the infants were adopted by siblings rather than by an experienced female with a child of her own, who could supply the orphan with milk as well as with more adequate social protection. During studies of African wild dogs in the Ngorongoro Crater conducted by Estes and Goddard . . ., a mother died when her nine pups were only five weeks old. The adult males of the pack continued to care for them, returning to the den each day with food until the pups were able to join the pack on hunting trips. The small size of wild dog packs makes it probable that the males were fathers, uncles, cousins, or other similarly close relatives. Males of the hamadryas baboon normally adopt juvenile females. . . . This unusual adaptation is clearly selfish in nature, since in hamadryas society adoption is useful for the accumulation of a harem. . . .

The Field of Righteousness

In conclusion, although the theory of group selection is still rudimentary, it has already provided insights into some of the least understood and most disturbing qualities of social behavior. Above all, it predicts ambivalence as a way of life in social creatures. Like Arjuna faltering on the Field of Righteousness, the individual is forced to make imperfect choices based on irreconcilable loyalties—between the "rights" and "duties" of self and those of family, tribe, and other units of selection, each of which evolves its own code of honor. No wonder the human spirit is in constant turmoil. Arjuna agonized, "Restless is the mind, O Krishna, turbulent, forceful, and stubborn; I think it no more easily to be controlled than is the wind." And Krishna replied, "For one who is uncontrolled, I agree the Rule is hard to attain; but by the obedient spirits who will strive for it, it may be won by following the proper way." In the opening chapter of this book, I suggested that a science of sociobiology, if coupled with neurophysiology, might transform the insights of ancient religions into a precise account of the evolutionary origin of ethics and hence explain the reasons why we make certain moral choices instead of others are particular times. Whether such understanding will then produce the Rule remains to be seen. For the moment, perhaps it is enough to establish that a single strong thread does indeed run from the conduct of termite colonies and turkey brotherhoods to the social behavior of man.

Before evaluating the determinist position with its support from people such as Toynbee, Skinner, Freud, and Wilson some distinctions should be made that have become standard bench marks of exposition. One classification often used is to identify as "hard" determinism the customary version of the doctrine and to distinguished that from "soft" determinism, which allows people responsibility for their actions. This distinction was originally made by the American philosopher William James (1842–1910),[15] although he mentioned it only to refute it.

Hard determinism maintains that all thoughts, motives, attitudes, desires, actions, and so forth are caused by factors beyond the person's control and that praise or blame is therefore unreasonable; no one is responsible for what he is compelled to do. As the colorful trial lawyer Clarence Darrow put it, "the laws that control human behavior are as fixed and certain as those that control the physical world" and "if we were all-wise and all-understanding we could not condemn"; everyone is "morally blameless."[16] This is the theory we have been considering as the basic position of scientific determinism. *Soft* determinism however holds that although all human behavior is the inevitable consequence of antecedent causes nevertheless human beings are responsible for their conduct. The reasons offered for this position are that the person himself can be the causal agent behind an action. It is not that actions are uncaused but that the causes can be internal, residing in the individual. The person is not outside the cause–effect chain but is himself a cause for events, and if his decision caused an event to occur then he is responsible for it.

The advocate of this soft version is not so much refuting determinism as reinterpreting it so that moral responsibility remains. Determinism is judged to be true but in such a way that people are the authors of their behavior and can be held accountable for what they do. Some would even say that if the causes reside within the person then he is *free* and at the same time a part of the determined, cause–effect world.

The philosophers David Hume (1711–1776), John Locke (1632–1704), and John Stuart Mill (1806–1873) are said to have advocated a determinism of this type that "resolved" the free will–determinism controversy, and it is popular with a number of contemporary philosophers as well.[17] Nevertheless, soft determinism has come in for its share of criticisms. The main problem is that if human beings are part of the causal chain then even those causes that lie within human beings are the necessary effect of prior causes. These causal agents within people could not have been otherwise, and if so then people are unable to choose freely and are not responsible for what they do. For example, even though the cause of an action might be a person's greed, that greed would be caused by antecedent conditions that made him greedy. The greedy action therefore was ultimately beyond the person's control (he could not help being greedy), and to hold him responsible for the act would be unfair. For this reason the alleged solution to the problem may not work; determinism and responsibility are not necessarily compatible — even when the determinism is soft.

Another discrimination often made is to contrast determinism (hard or soft) with indeterminism and to claim that the latter is a more accurate view of the human condition. *Indeterminism* maintains that necessity does not apply to persons but only to those objects and events that are wholly material in nature. Physical and chemical causes are responsible for the growth of plants or an avalanche of rocks, but human behavior cannot be reduced to such mechanistic explanations. Human actions, the indeterminist claims, are unique in that they occur for no reason. People act spontaneously, in surprising and original ways, having no necessary relation to their backgrounds or circumstances.

Sometimes the indeterminist will go further and deny that causation exists for anything, maintaining that randomness or chance is characteristic of the universe at large. Such a view will not just deny common sense but in some instances have scientific support. For example, the physicist Werner Heisenberg declared that indeterminacy operates at the subatomic level and some theorists have extended that Principle of Indeterminacy as a general law of physics. At an earlier point, the historian J. B. Bury in his *Later Roman Empire* also spoke of the elements of coincidence and surprise in history. This made the search for historical principles (such as Toynbee's hypothesis) completely futile; according to Bury, there are no general causes of events.[18]

However, indeterminism is very difficult to prove and in any case would not show that people are free or responsible. For if human actions (let alone electrons or the fall of Rome) are due to pure chance, then it would be unreasonable to attribute them to any definable person. If these acts are wholly accidental intrusions into the order of the world, then the individual is no more responsible for them than if they were ineluctably caused. A genuinely free action seems to be purposeful activity that is neither random nor determined.

For these reasons neither soft determinism nor indeterminism allows people free will or responsibility. Only a libertarian view provides this – the view that we are not determined at all.

Evaluation

1. To begin with, serious criticisms have been leveled against each of the sources of determinism. Toynbee, for example, has been faulted by geographers and historians for using the Greeks and Romans as universal models; employing myths and metaphors as being comparable to factual data; presum-

ing that Western Christianity is the highest expression of religion; and defining *civilization* and *culture* in ambiguous ways. Furthermore, his thesis that challenging environments foster civilization is extremely questionable as a law of world history. Obstacles do not always bring about cultural advances or improve people, unless one wants to beg the question by claiming that all contrary cases couldn't have been as easy as they seem. Toynbee may have fallen victim to the fallacy that pleasure leads to decadence and suffering is character-building, that the bitter medicine is the one that does you good. This is rather like the religious doctrine of the punishment of the body to improve the soul. The playwrite George Bernard Shaw believed this to be a particularly British mistake and writes in *Man and Superman*, "An Englishman always thinks he is being moral when, in fact, he is only uncomfortable."

Extensive critiques have also been made of Freudian psychology, which has been called more admirable in its detail than in its generalizations. For one thing, Freud has been upbraided for basing his theory on "contaminated" evidence; his patients were highly repressed, Viennese women, living during the late nineteeth and early twentieth centuries. This is hardly a representative sampling on which to base general truths for all humanity. What's more, he shows extreme bias against women by viewing them as a deficient sex, lacking male genitals. He also dismisses the phenomenon of religion in a high-handed way by treating it as an infantile neurosis, and overemphasizes the significance of sexuality in human life and the creation of culture. For our purposes his most flagrant mistake consists in claiming that actions always occur for unconscious motives. We are indebted to Freud for pointing out that many of the reasons we give for our behavior are, in fact, rationalizations for the satisfaction of desires, but it is extreme to maintain that conduct always arises from the unconscious impulses of the id. It should be added that no real evidence exists for an id, ego, or super ego, either as dynamic principles that explain the psyche or as some actual mysterious entity. The latter is called the error or reification, treating a theoretical object as if it were concrete, and Freud often commits this mistake.

Sociobiology has also come in for its share of criticism. It has been charged, for example, with championing the status quo — legitimizing the competition, racism, hierarchical organization, male-domination, and entrepeneurial practices of contemporary society. As one critical study stated,

> If men dominate women, it is because they must. If employers exploit their workers, it is because evolution has built into us the genes for entrepreneurial activity. If we kill each other in war, it is the force of our genes for territoriality, xenophobia, tribalism, and aggression. . . . We are bound by our biology . . . "lumbering robots" containing genes that "control us, body and mind."[19]

Most of the other criticisms of sociobiology fasten on its questionable scientific basis. As the Harvard geologist Stephen Jay Gould wrote in a review of Wilson's book, "Human sociobiology is not merely bedeviled by unfortunate implications, it is unsupported." For instance, to claim that there are specific genes for traits such as aggression, homosexuality, and altruism has not been proven, much less a mysterious "Dahlberg gene" responsible for success and status.

Unfortunately, it is beyond the scope of our study to trace the criticisms further or to describe the attacks that have also been made on behaviorism and cultural determinism. However, these examples will serve to illustrate that serious problems do exist in the theories that the determinist uses as the foundation for his position. And certainly the determinist cannot use all the theories combined because they often conflict; Freud claims, for example, that we are compelled to seek selfish pleasure while sociobiologists claim we are programmed to be altruistic.

2. Aside from specific defects in the supporting theories, determinism also suffers from a number of intrinsic problems. One logical difficulty is that the determinist cannot claim that after a deliberate and rational assessment of the evidence he has concluded that determinism is true. For if all ideas as well as actions are determined then the determinist was not free to reach this conclusion but was determined to accept it. To claim that upon careful reflection determinism has been judged to be correct is to argue that one has freely chosen a doctrine that denies the possibility of free choice, and this is plainly self-contradictory.

In fact, the more the determinist argues for his position the more apparent it becomes that he believes his opponent is free to change his mind. In order to be consistent, he would have to assume that he was determined to believe in determinism just as others are determined to believe in free will. He would assume that rational discussion is useless and remain silent. But he isn't silent at all, and the more arguments he uses the more he indicates his assumption of the opposite position.

A sophisticated determinist might respond that his arguments could *cause* his opponent to change his mind and that, on these grounds, arguing for determinism is consistent. But the rational consideration of arguments and the act of making a judgment based upon them is an example of free will not determinism. It could also be pointed out that one isn't even forced to agree to anything by the logic of an argument since the individual decides whether or not to abide by the rules of logic.

Another point often made against determinism is that it claims to be a scientific theory accounting for human conduct and if so it should be testable in a scientific way. In science, evidence is marshaled to support the theory being proposed and the type of evidence that would refute the theory is also known. But in the case of determinism, although we are given evidence for it, no conceivable evidence could count against it.

More precisely, the determinist presents examples of behavior caused by antecedent factors as proof of his thesis. The person in Brazil is lackadaisical because of the climate and perhaps his glandular secretions, the attorney chose his profession because of parental conditioning, the criminal is the helpless victim of social deprivation, underprivileged and disadvantaged. But what about the case of an energetic Brazilian, an attorney whose parents wanted him to be a musician, a slum dweller who grew up to become a minister? Here the determinist will say that we may not know the casual determinants but they must be there; we simply have not found them yet. But if the former cases count for the theory that everyone is determined, then the latter cases should count against the theory, otherwise it is not scientific or even rational.

In short, the determinist insulates himself against all possible disproof, keeping his theory out of harm's way. No conceivable evidence could contradict it, and when that situation exists a theory becomes valueless. It cannot be said to make any truth – claim about human behavior at all but occupies the status of a definition, a rule, or a tautology. It is as though the determinist were saying "All behavior is determined because behavior means that which is determined; therefore there cannot be a case of undetermined behavior."

A related problem is that the determinist argues backward in presenting his proof, claiming after the fact that a person's actions were due to certain prior conditions and therefore unavoidable. He is far less successful in arguing forward, predicting what a person will do given certain conditions. One of the chief tests of a scientific theory is its predictive power — its ability to anticipate that, given factors A, B, C, then x and y are certain to occur.

Again, the determinist will defend himself by saying that the complete list of determinants is not known in the case of man but as we acquire more knowledge prediction will become more accurate. But this is a matter of faith not a matter of fact. The inability to make accurate predictions of human behavior may not be due to unknown factors but the capability of human beings to act in free, undetermined ways. In other words, it may not be the investigator's ignorance that makes behavior unpredictable but man's capacity for novel choice.

3. In contrast to the claims of determinism the *libertarian* position is that human beings are the sources of their actions and are not compelled to act as they do. Man is capable of creating his own character and serving as the originator of his actions. Antecedent factors certainly exist and undeniably affect people but they cannot be said to compel people. Intentions and purposes lie behind human behavior and that places man outside the mechanistic, cause–effect system. We are not just acted upon but are beings who act in the world and not from provocations or stimuli but in order to accomplish chosen ends. Intending, deciding, acting, and so forth arise from an autonomous self, and the person is therefore responsible for the choices he makes.

To elaborate on some of these points, the libertarian argues that human beings are unique in being able to reflect upon the various factors influencing them and to select those they want to be dominant. At that point of consciousness, when one is aware of the surrounding and antecedent conditions, one is no longer controlled by those conditions but able to make a free choice. The person who comes to realize how his politics or religion has been formed by the nation in which he was raised is then free to affirm or reject those political or religious beliefs; to that extent, the social forces are disarmed of power over him. The person who understands the impact of climate on behavior will be in a position to resist or yield to that pressure and can even move to another place with a climate more conducive to his chosen way of living. The person who recognizes the constrictions of his super ego or the conditioned responses that have character-ized his behavior is then able to "change his mind" so that he is genuinely acting instead of psychologically reacting. As W. E. Hocking (1873 – 1966) put it, "there is nothing in the field of natural causation entering into me upon which I may not thus reflect. And to discover a cause in the act of affecting me is to be upon my guard against its action . . . [thus] the description of a man as a set of reactions becomes untrue when he becomes aware that he is being so described."[20]

From a somewhat different vantage point, the libertarian is asserting that, once we know the forces operating upon us, there can be reasons for our actions not just causes. Having reasons implies some process of reflection whereby a person deliberately weighs the various alternatives, then freely decides among them. To speak of causes, on the other hand, presupposes a strict, mechanical system of cause and effect with no room for self-initiated acts of human beings — acts that do not result from some prior causes. According to libertarianism, people's actions are not necessarily the effects of antecedent causes even though physical matter may operate that way; people can have explanations for what they do. Birds are compelled by instinct to build a nest but human beings have a purpose in mind when they decide to build a home.

What's more, the libertarian points out that a causal sequence has not been shown to occur in the case of human actions. Rather, he charges the determinist with committing a common fallacy called *post hoc, ergo propter hoc* (after this, therefore caused by this). It is the logical mistake of assuming that when one event follows another, the earlier event must have caused the later one. A savage, for example, might assume that dancing causes rain because it eventually rained following a rain dance. The determinist is accused of making this mistake when he assumes that because certain conditions preceded an act therefore these conditions caused the act. To establish a genuine causal connection as distinct from a temporal sequence the determinist would have to show that the first event made the second event happen, and this he has not done. He has not proven that given certain conditions it would be impossible for a person to act differently and thus has not demonstrated a necessary cause – effect relationship.

In a general sense, the libertarian points to the logical defects in the determinist argument as described here and elsewhere in our evaluation and stresses the introspective, common-sense support for assuming free will and personal responsibility. We commonly feel that external forces may limit our choices but the final decision between alternatives is always our own doing; we can kick the stone or not kick it, just as we please. We also experience a sense of obligation to one another as, for example, the moral requirement to preserve life not destroy it, and these obligations would be senseless if we had no capacity to choose our own conduct. In addition we would have to abandon numerous concepts that seem authentic and worth retaining, for example, purpose, creativity, deliberation, selfhood, ideals, rationality, initiative, responsibility, and so forth. Before we do that we should have better grounds than the determinist has provided.

For these reasons determinism does not seem to be the most persuasive theory to hold. Therefore, we can proceed with our discussion of the various life purposes reasonably confident that they offer a real choice for our consideration. As for the question of which ideal is best, that remains to be decided, but at least we seem justified in thinking that a decision can be made.

Notes

1. References to fatalism are scattered throughout *Oedipus Rex* as well as in *Oedipus at Colonus* and *Philoctetes*. See also *Helen* and *Medea* by Euripides. In the latter play the concluding statement by the chorus is "Many a fate doth Zeus dispense, high on his Olympian throne; oft do the gods bring things to pass beyond man's

expectation; that, which we thought would be, is not fulfilled, while for the unlooked-for god finds out a way; and such hath been the issue of this matter."

2. See G. W. Leibniz, *Discourse on Metaphysics*, trans. by G. Montgomery (Chicago: Open Court, 1924), and *Theodicy*, trans. by E. M. Huggard (London: Routledge and Kegan Paul, 1952).

3. The following books contain excellent discussions of the issue: C. F. d'Arcy, *God and Freedom in Human Experience* (London: E. Arnold, 1915), and D. Von Hildebrand, *Christian Ethics* (New York: McKay, 1935).

4. See St. Augustine "On Free Will," in *Free Will*, S. Morgenbesser and James Walsh, eds. (Englewood Cliffs, N.J.: Prentice-Hall, 1962). Cf. Augustine's *The City of God*, Book XI, Chapter 21, and *Treatise on the Predestination of the Saints*.

5. See Martin Luther, *Discourse on Free Will*, trans. E. F. Winter (New York: Scribner's, 1961), and John Calvin, *Institutes of the Christian Religion*, trans. C. Beveridge (Grand Rapids: Eerdmans, 1953), end of Book 3. Highlights of the celebrated exchange on this topic between Erasmus and Luther can be found in E. F. Winter, ed., *Erasmus–Luther—Discourse on Free Will* (New York: Ungar, 1961). St. Thomas Aquinas seems to have been of two minds for he wrote in *Summa Theologica*, "Man has free choice; or otherwise counsels, exhortations, commands, prohibitions, rewards, and punishments would be in vain," (I, 83, 1). But then he contradicted himself by saying "It is fitting that God should predestine men. For all things are subject to his providence" (I, 23, 1).

6. Paul Vidal de la Blanche was also a member of his group but he argued that the geographical environment presented a variety of possibilities rather than an unalterable, determined path. His followers were consequently known as environmental possibilists.

7. See E. Sapir, *Culture, Language, and Personality* (Berkeley: University of California Press, 1970).

8. For an exposition of this concept see A. Flew, *Logic and Language* (Oxford: Basil Blackwell, 1961), vol. 2, especially Gilbert Ryle, F. Waismann, J. Austin, J. O. Urmson.

9. R. Benedict, *Patterns of Culture* (London: Routledge and Sons, 1935), 2–3, 236. See also A. Montagu, *The Biosocial Nature of Man* (New York: Grove Press, 1956) 74–75.

10. Notable exceptions are the humanistic or existential psychologists such as Rollo May, Erich Fromm, Abraham Maslow, Ludwig Binswanger, Carl Rogers, and R. D. Laing.

11. John Hospers, "Meaning and Free Will," *Philosophy and Phenomenological Research* 10 (1950): 307, 328, 329.

12. W. H. Sheldon, *The Varieties of Human Physique* (New York: Harper and Brothers, 1940).

13. See W. D. Hamilton, "The Genetical Theory of Social Behavior," *Journal of Theoretical Biology* 7 (1964): 1–52; E. O. Wilson, *On Human Nature* (Cambridge: Harvard University Press, 1978); P. D. Barash, *Sociobiology and Behavior* (Amsterdam: Elsevier, 1977); R. Dawkins, *The Extended Phenotype* (San Francisco: Freeman, 1981); I. DeVore, *Sociobiology and the Social Sciences* (Chicago: Aldine Atherton, 1979).

14. R. Dawkins, *The Selfish Gene* (Oxford: Oxford University Press, 1976).

15. William James, "The Dilemma of Determinism," in *The Will To Believe* (New York: Longmans Green, 1921), 145.

16. Clarence Darrow, *Crime, Its Cause and Treatment* (Montclair, N.J.: Patterson Smith, 1972), xxi, xxii. See also Chapters 3–6.

17. See John Locke, *Essay Concerning Human Understanding*, Chapter 21; David Hume, *Treatise of Human Nature*, Book 2, Part 3, and *Inquiry Concerning Human*

Understanding, Section 8; John Stuart Mill, *System of Logic*, Book 6, Chapter 2. Cf. Thomas Hobbes, "Of Liberty and Necessity," and W. T. Jones, *Morality and Freedom in the Philosophy of Kant* (London: Oxford University Press, 1940). For more modern treatments, see W. D. Ross, *Foundations of Ethics* (Oxford: Clarendon Press, 1939); A. J. Ayer, *Philosophical Essays* (London: Macmillan, 1954); and R. B. Brandt, *Ethical Theory* (Englewood Cliffs, N.J.: Prentice-Hall, 1954), Chapter 20.

18. Werner Heisenberg (1901–1976), a physicist at the University of Leipzig, received a Nobel Price in 1932 for his work in quantum physics. John Bagnell Bury (1861–1927), an Irish historian, taught ancient history at Cambridge. For a similar denial of historical predictability, see the American philosopher Karl Popper who argued that prediction is theoretically impossible because of new knowledge that introduces novelty.

19. R. C. Lewontin, Steven Rose, and Leon Kamin, *Not in Our Genes* (New York: Pantheon Books, 1983), 237, 287.

20. W. E. Hocking, *The Self: Its Body and Freedom* (New Haven: Yale University Press, 1928).

Bibliography

ADLER, M. J. *The Idea of Freedom*. Garden City, N.Y.: Doubleday, 1961.

ANSCOMBE, G. E. M. *Intention*. Oxford: Blackwell, 1957.

AYER, A. J. *"Freedom and Necessity."* In *Philosophical Essays*, 271–84. New York: Macmillan, 1954.

AYERS, N. *The Refutation of Determinism: An Essay in Philosophical Logic*. London: Methuen, 1968.

BENNETT, W. *Religion and Free Will*. Oxford: Clarendon Press, 1913.

BERGSON, HENRI. *Time and Free Will*. New York: Macmillan, 1921.

BERLIN, I. *Historical Inevitability*. London: Oxford University Press, 1954.

BEROFSKY, B., ED. *Free Will and Determinism*. New York: Harper & Row, 1966.

DANTO, A. "Basic Actions." *American Philosophical Quarterly* 2 (1965): 141–48.

DAVIDSON, D. "How Is Weakness of the Will Possible?" In *Moral Concepts*, Joel Feinberg, ed., 93–113. Oxford: Oxford University Press, 1970.

DENNETT, DANIEL C. *Elbow Room, The Varieties of Free Will Worth Wanting*. Cambridge: MIT Press, 1984.

DWORKIN, G., ED. *Determinism, Free Will and Moral Responsibility*. Englewood Cliffs, N.J.: Prentice-Hall, 1970.

EDDINGTON, A. *Nature of the Physical World*. New York: Macmillan, 1928, Chapter 14.

ELLIS, E. *Rational Decision and Causality*. Cambridge: Bradford/MIT Press, 1981.

FISCHER, J. *"Responsibility and Control."* Journal of Philosophy (January 1982): 24–40.

FLEW, A. "Divine Omniscience and Human Freedom." In *New Essays in Philosophical Theology*, A. Flew and A. MacIntyre, eds., 141–169. London: SCM Press, 1955.

FOOT, PHILIPPA. "Free Will as Involving Determinism." *Philosophical Review* 66 (1957): 439–50.

FRANKFURT, H. "Freedom of the Will and the Concept of a Person." *Journal of Philosophy* 65 (1971): 5–20.

GIBBS, J. P. *Crime, Punishment, and Deterrence*. New York/Oxford/Amsterdam: Elsevier, 1975.

GOMBERG, P. "Free Will as Ultimate Responsibility," *American Philosophical Quarterly* 15 (1978): 208.

GREENSPAN, P. "Behavior Control and Freedom of Action." *Philosophical Review* 87 (1978): 25–40.

HAMPSHIRE, S. *Thought and Action*. London: Chatto and Windus, 1959.

HART, H. L. A. *Punishment and Responsibility*. Oxford: Oxford University Press, 1968.

HOBART, R. E. "Free Will as Involving Determinism and as Inconceivable Without It." *Mind* 43 (1934): 1–27.

HOBBES, T. "The Question Concerning Liberty, Necessity, and Chance." In *The English Works of Thomas Hobbes*, vol. 5, edited by Sir W. Molesworth. London: John Bohn, 1841.

HOFSTADTER, D. R. *Gödel, Escher, Bach: An Eternal Golden Braid*. New York: Basic Books, 1979.

HONDERICH, T., ED. *Essays on Freedom of Action*. London: Routledge and Kegan Paul, 1973.

HOLMSTROM, N. "Firming up Soft Determinism." *The Personalist* 58 (1977): 39–51.

HOOK, S., ED. *Determinism and Freedom in the Age of Modern Science*. New York: Collier, 1961.

JAMES, W. "The Dilemma of Determinism." In *The Will to Believe*, 145–83. New York: Longmans, Green, 1921.

JONES, ERNEST. "Free Will and Determinism." In *Essays in Applied Psychoanalysis*, vol 2. London: Hogarth Press, 1951.

LEWONTIN, R. C., STEVEN ROSE, AND LEON J. KAMIN. *Not in Our Genes*. New York: Pantheon Books, 1984.

LUCAS, J. R. *The Freedom of the Will*. Oxford: Clarendon, 1970.

MACINTYRE, A. "Determinism." *Mind* 66 (1957): 28–41.

MELDEN, A. I. *Free Action*. London: Routledge and Kegan Paul, 1961.

MONOD, J. *Chance and Necessity*. New York: Alfred Knopf, 1972.

MORGENBESSER, S., AND J. WALSH, EDS. *Free Will*. Englewood Cliffs, N.J.: Prentice-Hall, 1962.

MORRIS, HERBERT, ED. *Freedom and Responsibility*. Stanford, Calif.: Stanford University Press, 1961.

MUNN, A. M. *Free Will and Determinism*. London: Macgibbon and Kee, 1960.

NOWELL-SMITH, P. H. "Free Will and Moral Responsibility." *Mind* (1948).

NOZICK, R. *Philosphical Explanations*. Cambridge: Harvard University Press, 1981.

PEARS, D. F., ED. *Freedom and the Will*. London: Macmillan, 1963.

PLANTINGA, A. *God, Freedom and Evil*. New York: Harper & Row, 1974.

POPPER, K., AND J. ECCLES. *The Self and Its Brain*. New York: Springer, 1977.

RAAB, F. V. "Free Will and the Ambiguity of 'Could'." *Philosophical Review* 64:60–77.

RANKIN, K. W. *Choice and Chance*. Oxford: Blackwell, 1961.

RORTY, A., ED. *The Identities of Persons*. Berkeley: University of California Press, 1976.

RUSE, M. *Sociobiology: Sense or Nonsense*. London: D. Reidel, 1979.

SLOTE, M. "Selective Necessity and Free Will." *Journal of Philosophy* 74 (1982): 5–24.

STRAWSON, P. F. *Individuals*. London: Methuen, 1959.

THOMSON, JUDITH J. "Remarks on Causation and Liability." *Philosophy and Public Affairs* 13 (1983): 101–13.

THORP, J. *Free Will: A Defense Against Neurophysiological Determinism*. London and Boston: Routlege and Kegan Paul, 1980.

TRUSTED, J. *Free Will and Responsibility*. Oxford: Oxford University Press, 1984.

VAN INWAGEN, P. "The Incompatibility of Free Will and Determinism." *Philosophical Studies* 27 (1975): 185–199.

——. *An Essay of Free Will*. Oxford: Clarendon, 1983.

WATSON, G., ED. *Free Will*. Oxford: Oxford University Press, 1982.

WILLIAMS, B. *Moral Luck*. Cambridge: Cambridge University Press, 1981.

WOLF, S. "The Importance of Free Will." *Mind* 190 (1981): 386–78.

WOOLDRIDGE, D. *Mechanical Man: The Physical Basis of Intelligent Life*. New York: McGraw-Hill, 1968.

PART II

Ideals in Living

CHAPTER 4

Hedonism

One of our most basic assumptions is that pleasure or happiness is the goal in life, and this belief constitutes the core of hedonist philosophy. The hedonist maintains that nothing else is ultimately worth striving for, that happiness or pleasure are natural goals, which any person of common sense recognizes as supremely valuable. He assumes that a truism of this type hardly requires justification, that everyone acknowledges a life of happiness to be good and a life of pain and misery to be unequivocally bad. "I just want to be happy," says the person in the street, and that seems the ordinary, sane, and appropriate response to the question of what to live for. Even the masochist does not contradict this truth but simply finds pain as his mode of increasing the amount of pleasure.

Reasons for Choosing Hedonism

When the hedonist does attempt to justify his goal of happiness he is likely to point out that, not only is this attitude universally accepted, but from the time of early childhood "good" and "pleasurable" are inseparably linked in our minds. The birthday cake is "good" the child exclaims, meaning pleasurable to taste, and declares that he had a "good time" at the party when he had a lot of fun. In the same way, adults will ask one another whether they had a "good" vacation, that is, an enjoyable one, or whether they are in a good mood, that is, a happy frame of mind. In all of these cases, the good and the pleasurable are taken to be synonymous and, conversely, things such as a bad cake or a bad vacation are assumed to mean not very enjoyable.

Of course, the hedonist does not claim that good is always used to mean enjoyable. He would admit that a good operation is not necessarily a pleasurable one and the subject matter of a good modern painting could be very disturbing. A good set of beliefs, a good exercise program, or a good mathematical formula do not have to involve the notion of enjoyment. But, he maintains, whenever we use the term *good* to mean a positive life experience, an element of pleasure is implied.

The hedonist further claims that even if people feel they want something out of life besides pleasure or happiness a careful analysis will show that their goal contains a strong component of pleasure. An artistic life, for instance, in which the individual develops his creative abilities, is usually an enjoyable one overall. Furthermore, these supposedly different aims can be seen in reality as mere means for the attainment of pleasure and not alternatives to pleasure as the goal in living. For example, those people who believe that they want to serve god rather than pursue pleasure are actually obtaining pleasure through service to god. Similarly, a life of dedication to humanity will bring joy to the individuals who act on those principles, and the happiness they experience will be the real reason for their commitment.

Not only does the hedonist maintain that pleasure and the good are habitually linked and that pleasure accompanies and ultimately accounts for other types of goals, but he also argues that pleasure and pain are simple feelings, incapable of being reduced to more basic psychological parts. Moreover, these simple elements evoke the same reactions in people. The individual who experiences pleasure regards it as something good; the person who undergoes feelings of pain judges that experience as bad. It would be very unusual, the hedonist points out, to come across anyone with the opposite kind of reactions, and if we did encounter people who wanted to be miserable and avoided happiness at all costs we would probably regard them as emotionally disturbed.

Aristotle (c. 435–356 B.C.) gave the hedonists additional evidence in his *Nicomachean Ethics* (Book I) in connection with the ideal of *eudaimonia*. Although Aristotle favored an ethic of self-realization (as we shall see in Chapter 6) and *eudaimonia* is more properly rendered as "vital well being," nevertheless some philosophers have translated the concept as happiness. This enabled hedonists to use his arguments as further support for their theory.

First, Aristotle argued, happiness is a self-sufficient state. If people are genuinely happy they feel completely satisfied and do not want anything further. If something else is desired then they are not truly happy. "A self-sufficient thing," Aristotle wrote, "we take to be one which on its own footing tends to make life desirable and lacking in nothing. And we regard happiness as such a thing." In other words, if all striving and desire ceases with the attainment of happiness, so that we do not feel unfulfilled or incomplete in any respect, then happiness is self-sufficient and for that reason the final aim in life.

The other argument concerns the relation between means and ends. We all know, for example, that in order to climb a mountain we would have to scale some cliffs and that eating and drinking is a necessary means of sustaining life. But from another viewpoint, doing such things as scaling cliffs is the end that a person may have in mind in climbing a mountain and the French are sometimes accused of living to eat rather than eating to live. Is a chicken really a way in which an egg builds another egg, as sociobiologists claim? In all of these cases, we are not sure which is the means and which is the end.

Aristotle spent some time trying to refine this distinction, after which he asserted that happiness is the ultimate end, that for which everything else is done. Happiness (or vital well being) is never a means toward the attainment of anything further but rather all activities aim at that final goal of happiness. Since the attainment of a happy life is always an end, Aristotle declared happiness to be *the* end — that all-encompassing good toward which all of our energies are and should be directed.

The hedonist uses still other arguments besides those of Aristotle concerning happiness as self-sufficient and the final end of all activities and the arguments mentioned previously: the identification between good and enjoyable, the fact that all goals involve pleasure, are actually done for pleasure, and that pleasure is a simple feeling normally judged to be good. However, these are the main arguments that are used, and it should be reemphasized that most hedonists do not feel that an elaborate network of proofs is necessary in any case. Like most people, they take it as self-evident that a good life is a happy one.

Psychological and Ethical Hedonism

Embedded in the hedonist account are a number of different points that need to be separated, and in the history of hedonism these distinctions have in fact been made. In the first place, the hedonist is sometimes describing how people *do* or *must* behave. When this is done, an analysis is being offered of man's natural motivation and conduct, and such a position is known as *psychological hedonism.* The psychological hedonist maintains that human nature is so constituted that people cannot help but pursue pleasure and avoid pain; it is simply the nature of the beast, a universal law without any exceptions. No one ever knowingly brings about his own discomfort but rather all choices are made in the hope of obtaining satisfaction. The psychological hedonist takes this as the most fundamental cause of action, such that pleasure seeking is considered an unavoidable fact of human behavior.

Again, common sense seems to support this hedonistic position. No one in his right mind wants to be miserable and all people act in ways they hope will make them happy. Even Freudian psychology is in agreement, for Freud wrote: "We may ask whether in the operation of our mental apparatus a main purpose can be detected, and we may reply as a first approximation that that purpose is directed to obtaining pleasure. It seems as though our total mental activity is directed toward achieving pleasure and avoiding unpleasure." This master mechanism, which automatically regulates our behavior, Freud called the "pleasure principle."[1] Although it may be modified by other parts of the mind it cannot be eliminated and always remains the mainspring of our conduct.

Sometimes, however, the hedonist is not describing but prescribing how people *ought* to behave in order to get the most out of life, and this position is called *ethical hedonism.* The ethical hedonist maintains that, whether or not people do pursue pleasure, they certainly should do so because that is the greatest good attainable. Pleasure or happiness is here recommended as the primary purpose in living — the ideal that people should strive to achieve.

A certain number of the hedonist philosophers try to link psychological and ethical hedonism, arguing that the psychological law that determines our behavior also shows us what is valuable. If, as Freud said, our minds directs us to seek pleasure, then pleasure is what we ought to seek. They do not ignore the distinction between "is" and "ought" but claim that the one furnishes the grounds for the other; the ethical principle is rooted in the psychological fact.

For example, the French hedonist Claude Adrien Helvétius (1715–1771), whose doctrine of sensualism or sensationalism caused his books to be publicly burned, maintained that an overall design inclines us toward pleasure seeking. This inclination is all to the good because the pursuit of pleasure and the avoidance of pain is a principle on which "the order and happiness of the moral world depends." In his major book *De l'Espirit* he presented this concept by writing as if god had said to man at the beginning of creation: "I endow you with sensation, the blind instrument of my will, in order that you may accomplish my designs despite your inability to know what they are. I am putting you under the guardianship of pleasure and pain. Both of them will watch over your thoughts and your actions; they will excite your passions, your friendships, your tenderness and aversion; they will kindle your desires and your hopes."[2]

The same type of connection between our need for pleasure and the worth of pleasure was made by the English philosophers Jeremy Bentham (1748–1832) and John Stuart Mill (1806–1873); their hedonistic theories will be examined in the following chapter.

Individualistic and Universalistic Hedonism

Another distinction that has been made historically is between the individualistic and the universalistic versions of hedonism. Both are ethical doctrines, advocating pleasure or happiness as the goal in living, but the *individualistic hedonist* believes that these goals should be sought for the person alone. That is, the individualistic hedonist maintains that we should try to obtain pleasure for ourselves and not be concerned with providing pleasure to others. If in the course of securing our own happiness we happen to bring happiness to other people that would be all right, or if part of our happiness came from making others happy then that would be justified. But the purpose of our actions should always be to promote our personal enjoyment in living. In those cases where other people are involved, they should be treated as only incidental to the primary goal of individual happiness.

For example, a defense attorney should work for his client's acquittal if that would increase the attorney's reputation, allow him to charge higher fees in the future, and ultimately add to the sum total of his happiness, but it would be wrong, according to the individualistic hedonist, for the attorney to be primarily concerned with his client's happiness and to defend him for that reason. We should never expect this, any more than we should expect the client to want to be acquitted so that the attorney could benefit from the victory. Attorneys, like everyone else, should be acting for their own sakes not for the sake of anyone else, for life is nothing more than the happiness one gets out of it.

As justification for this attitude the individualistic hedonist points out that we never really know what will make other people happy so there is little point in trying to please them. It is difficult enough to determine what we ourselves might like, let alone figure out what someone else would enjoy. If, for instance, a man were to invite a woman for a roast beef dinner she may be offended because she is a vegetarian; if he orders wine she may be outraged because she is a teetotaler; and if he pays the check he may discover that she is a rabid feminist who considers his conduct patronizing and chauvinistic. No one can tell then what another person will enjoy, so it is far better to concentrate on our own pleasures and not waste time attempting to satisfy other people's wants. (There is also no point in judging others by ourselves because, as Noel Coward remarked, "Do not do unto others as you would have them do unto you; they may not have the same tastes.")

In passing it should be noted that this argument is not very convincing. We may not be able to determine exactly what people want or be correct in all cases, but we can know people well enough to make a reasonable prediction as to what they would find enjoyable. And human nature is sufficiently similar so that we can use ourselves as representative. Most people would not enjoy feeling sick or threatened, for example, but would enjoy personal relationships and a high standard of living. All legislation is based on the assumption that legislators can know what most people would like and can pass laws accordingly, promoting health, prosperity, security, and general social well being. It would be very odd for a congressman to throw up his hands and say "How should I know whether anyone will find this law beneficial?"

The *universalistic hedonist* has no such qualms and maintains not only that we can know what pleases other people but, more significantly, that we should always try to bring pleasure or happiness to others by our actions. According to the universalistic hedonist, the purpose of our lives ought to be the maximization of happiness for society as a whole. Instead of a selfish existence in which we are only concerned with our own enjoyment we should dedicate ourselves to the happiness of everyone. This does not exclude ourselves but neither does it mean that our own happiness is most important. Rather, we should think of ourselves as just one among those affected by an action and neither more nor less deserving than anyone else. Every person's happiness should be promoted equally, and our conduct must be viewed in terms of its value to all of the people affected by it.

If a choice should arise between our own happiness and that of a number of other people we should always be prepared to be self-sacrificing. For instance, if an entrepeneur had an opportunity to corner the market on some commodity, it certainly would bring him pleasure because he could then make a fortune, but it would diminish the happiness of all those forced to buy the commodity at an inflated and exorbitant price. The universalistic hedonist would therefore recommend that the entrepeneur restrain himself from enriching himself at other people's expense. The happiness of all should be our basic concern in all areas of life, including the conduct of business.

Of course, some universalistic hedonists argue that self-sacrifice is never really needed in pursuing the goal of general happiness because the good of the individual is always identical with the good of the group. By creating happiness for the society at large one is also ensuring one's personal happiness as a member of that society, therefore no conflict arises between selfishness and generosity. Helping others means helping oneself and harming others will inevitably rebound against the person who causes the harm.

However, as was shown in the Evaluation of Ethical Egoism in Chapter 2 this argument seems a bit strained. We do not necessarily increase our own happiness by bringing happiness to others; in fact we may decrease it. Aside from the gain that comes from virtue being its own reward, we do not always reap personal benefits from selfless conduct. Because of the size and complexity of society, the good we do by way of increasing the happiness of others may not come back to us at all but flow outward or bypass us altogether. And we could be a member of the minority whose happiness is not increased when the majority is made happier. The entrepeneur who decides not to corner the market and become wealthy is not necessarily a happier person because of his choice; in all likelihood his example will not make society an appreciably happier place in which he can live. His decision may be right according to the principles of universalistic hedonism but his happiness is not likely to be augmented; obtaining a fortune, on the other hand, could help quite a bit. Although it may be true that money cannot buy happiness, nevertheless "he that wants money is without a good friend," as Shakespeare says. With a lot of good friends happiness becomes easier—even if it isn't guaranteed.

Whether we always benefit from generosity or whether generosity sometimes involves self-sacrifice, the universalistic hedonist advocates that our motive in action should always be the happiness of the group as a whole. The individualistic hedonist may please others too but as previously mentioned that would only be a chance consequence or a means of increasing his own pleasure. The universalistic hedonist however takes the happiness of others as his primary goal, and although he may obtain pleasure from doing so that is not his purpose. The way in which one can tell the difference between the two is that the individualistic hedonist would not bring pleasure to others unless he derived pleasure himself, whereas the universalistic hedonist would continue to bring pleasure to others even though it did not bring pleasure to himself.

The Cyrenaics: Maximizing Sensuous Pleasure

The view that pleasure should be enjoyed for its own sake is not only common but very ancient. As a school of thought it first appeared in Greek philosophy in the fourth and third centuries B.C., specifically in the teachings of Aristippus of Cyrene (c. 435–350 B.C.) in what is now Libya. The name *Cyrenaics* was applied to the disciples of Aristippus, the most notable of whom were his daughter Arete, Aristippus the younger (a grandson called mother-taught), Bio, Aethiops of Ptolemais, and Antipater of Cyrene; in later years, various versions of the doctrine were formulated by Theodorus, Hegesias, and Anniceris.

In developing his ideas Aristippus was apparently influenced by the Socratic teaching that happiness is one of the ends of moral action, but he took this to mean that pleasure is the basic aim in life. Not only did he interpret one end as the only end, but he largely rejected the goal of happiness and emphasized pleasure instead. Hedonism endorses both but Aristippus affirmed pleasure primarily and thought happiness much less important—even something to be avoided at times.

When a distinction is made between the two, *happiness* is taken to mean an overall state of well being and contentment in life. It is long lasting and accompanies distinctively human activities such as creative expression, personal relationships, intelligent work, free and conscious choices, and so forth. *Pleasure,* by contrast, means physical satisfaction at the fulfillment of some desire. It is not a persistent, enduring state but a momentary condition that occurs at a particular time and is strongly related to the gratification of sensuous desire. One can name happy years in one's life but one talks about moments of pleasure, and one can refer to the inner happiness that comes from achieving a goal but drinking good wine is a pleasure of the senses. As far as Aristippus was concerned, pleasure is far more important. A physical life in which we indulge our emotions, act on our impulses, and gratify our bodily desires seemed to him the best kind of existence imaginable. Happiness might be acceptable as the sum of pleasures but not as a superior alternative to pleasure as the ideal.

The grounds on which the Cyrenaic claim is based are largely epistemic in nature, that is, they relate to a certain theory of knowledge. The Cyrenaics did say that all living things are instinctively drawn by pleasure ("from our youth up we are attracted to it"), thus supporting ethical hedonism with psychological hedonism, but they defended their position largely in terms of the type of knowledge possible to us. Our understanding, they argued, is restricted to private sensations, so that we cannot claim that an object contains certain qualities but only be aware of what we ourselves experience. For example, we can reliably state that we feel cold or are experiencing the taste of sweetness, but we cannot maintain that the snow is cold or the honey sweet. Our senses are not dependable enough to detect characteristics in things but can only report what we know subjectively. Personal sensations then are our only trustworthy guide, and we must act solely in terms of those feelings.[3]

Specifically, we should be responsive to the sensations the Cyrenaics described as "rough" and "smooth." The rough sensations are painful and repellent and should be avoided; the smooth are pleasant and attractive and should be sought as the best experience obtainable. The end of life, Aristippus said, is "the smooth motion resulting in sensation." Since pleasurable feelings are knowable and desirable, they constitute the ideals in living.

When the Cyrenaics come to define the type of pleasures that are best, they conclude that the pleasures of the moment are better than any anticipated ones. As Horace later phrased it, *"Carpe diem, quam minimum credula postero"* (enjoy the present day, trusting as little as possible to what tomorrow may bring). Sensuous satisfaction here and now was what mattered not the pleasures of a previous time or those that might come some day. The past is only a memory and should provoke neither satisfaction nor regret, the future is a dream without the power to incite any effort; only the knife-edge instant of the present is real and can stimulate our feelings.

In addition to arguing for immediate, brief, bodily pleasure, the Cyrenaics also stressed that stronger sensations are more desirable. The greater the intensity of one's pleasure the better the experience. This is one reason why physical pleasure is better than mental happiness: the feelings are more concentrated and acute. And one pleasure is preferable to another only in the degree of vividness and force. The source of the pleasure or even its rightness does not matter. So long as the physical excitement is vivid and strong, that is all that counts.

The Cyrenaics did say however that the mind should be employed to some extent in rationally choosing those experiences that will provide maximum pleasure. Our practical intelligence should be trained to manipulate circumstances and cleverly adapt ourselves to them for our own hedonistic ends. Present gratification is extremely important but we must take into consideration the consequences of our actions and not be self-defeating in our choices. Domination over one's pleasures should be the rule rather than avoidance or enslavement to them, and this requires rational control. "The master of a ship or horse," Aristippus said, "is not one who does not use them, but he who guides them wherever he wishes." Or as he stated with regard to his mistress, "I have Laïs, not she me; and it is not abstinence from pleasure that is best, but mastery over them without ever being worsted."[4]

The Cyrenaics therefore did operate in the light of reason to some extent, nevertheless it never bulked very large in their teaching. Pleasure was basically viewed as a fortunate addiction, not completely under our control, and the pleasures that we are sure of now are always superior to uncertain ones in the future. Similarly, they believed that we shouldn't really endure present pain for the sake of future pleasure. On one occasion when Aristippus' servant was carrying a heavy load of money, he said, "Pour away the greater part, and carry no more than you can manage." The discomfort was real and immediate and the benefits could be an illusion, so the feelings of the moment should be the deciding factor. Aristippus was characterized, in fact, as a person who "derived pleasure from what was present, and did not toil to procure the enjoyment of something not present," and this seems to be the main thrust of the Cyrenaic teaching. They would agree with the Persian poet Omar Khyaam in the *Rubiayatt* when he wrote,

> Ah, make the most of what we yet may spend,
> Before we too into the Dust descend;
> Dust Into Dust and under Dust to lie,
> Sans Wine, sans Song, sans Singer, and — sans End.

For the Cyrenaic, immediate, momentary, intense, physical pleasure was what mattered most and not a tranquil life of passive enjoyment and subtle, pleasant experiences.

In the selection that follows, the philosophy of the Cyrenaics is described in the best source we have on their views, *The Lives of Eminent Philosophers* by Diogenes Laertius. In addition to presenting the ideals of Aristippus, the subsequent modifications of Hegesias, Anniceris, and Theodorus are also discussed. Hegesias developed a rather pessimistic view of the world, claiming that "the body is infected with (so) much suffering" that "happiness cannot be realized." The best we can do is avoid pain rather than cultivate pleasure, pursue our own interests, and adopt the proper attitude to external circumstances. Anniceris had a sunnier outlook, holding that the enjoyment of individual pleasures was both possible and wonderful, especially the pleasures of friendship and patriotism. He even introduced an altruistic element by saying that, "a friend should be cherished not merely for his utility." Finally, Theodorus returned to a self-centered doctrine, rejecting friendship (and belief in anything divine) and advocating "theft, adultery, and sacrilege" if need be in order to indulge our passions. Joy and grief to him are the supreme good and evil that the self-sufficient person can control for his own advantage.

Aristippus and the Cyrenaic School*

Aristippus was by birth a citizen of Cyrene and, as Aeschines informs us, was drawn to Athens by the fame of Socrates. Having come forward as a lecturer or sophist, as Phanias of Eresus, the Peripatetic, informs us, he was the first of the followers of Socrates to charge fees and to send money to his master. And on one occasion the sum of twenty minae which he had sent was returned to him, Socrates declaring that the supernatural sign would not let him take it; the very offer, in fact, annoyed him. Xenophon was no friend to Aristippus; and for this reason he has made Socrates direct against Aristippus

*Reprinted with permission from diogenes Laertius, *The Lives of Eminent Philosophers,* trans. R. D. Hicks (Cambridge: Harvard University Press, 1950), vol. 2:65–68, 73–77, 86–99.

the discourse in which he denounces pleasure. Not but what Theodorus in his work *On the Sects* abuses him, and so does Plato in the dialogue *On the Soul,* as has been shown elsewhere.

He was capable of adapting himself to place, time and person, and of playing his part appropriately under whatever circumstances. Hence he found more favour than anybody else with Dionysius, because he could always turn the situation to good account. He derived pleasure from what was present, and did not toil to procure the enjoyment of something not present. Hence Diogenes called him the king's poodle** Timon, too, sneered at him for luxury in these words:

"Such was the delicate nature of Aristippus, who groped after error by touch."†

He is said to have ordered a partridge to be bought at a cost of fifty drachmae, and, when someone censured him, he inquired, "Would not you have given an obol for it?" and, being answered in the affirmative, rejoined. "Fifty drachmae are no more to me." And when Dionysius gave him his choice of three courtesans, he carried off all three, saying, "Paris paid dearly for giving the preference to one out of three." And when he had brought them as far as the porch, he let them go. To such lengths did he go both in choosing and in disdaining. Hence the remark of Strato, or by some accounts of Plato, "You alone are endowed with the gift to flaunt in robes or go in rags." He bore with Dionysius when he spat on him, and to one who took him to task he replied, "If the fishermen let themselves be drenched with sea-water in order to catch a gudgeon, ought I not to endure to be wetted with negus in order to take a blenny?"‡

Diogenes, washing the dirt from his vegetables, saw him passing and jeered at him in these terms, "If you had learnt to make these your diet, you would not have paid court to kings," to which his rejoinder was, "And if you knew how to associate with men, you would not be washing vegetables." Being asked what he had gained from philosophy, he replied, "The ability to feel at ease in any society." Being reproached for his extravagance, he said, "If it were wrong to be extravagant, it would not be in vogue at the festivals of the gods."

To one who accused him of living with a courtesan, he put the question, "Why, is there any difference between taking a house in which many people have lived before and taking one in which nobody has ever lived?" The answer being "No," he continued, "Or again, between sailing in a ship in which ten thousand persons have sailed before and in one in which nobody has ever sailed?" "There is no difference." "Then it makes no difference," said he, "whether the woman you live with has lived with many or with nobody." To the accusation that, although he was a pupil of Socrates, he took fees, his rejoinder was, "Most certainly I do, for Socrates, too, when

---

**Or "royal cynic." It is impossible to preserve the double entendre here, for *κιων*, dog, also means "cynic"; in fact the very name of that sect proclaims that they gloried in their dog-like attributes, especially in snarling and biting. [Translator's note.]

†This alludes to his doctrine of sensation, sometimes called "internal touch." [Translator's note.]

‡[A gudgeon is a small European fish related to carps; a blenny is an elongated, scaleless fish found along the rocky shores of Greece.]

certain people sent him corn and wine, used to take a little and return all the rest; and he had the foremost men in Athens for his stewards, whereas mine is my slave Eutychides." He enjoyed the favours of Laïs, as Sotion states in the second book of his Successions of Philosophers. To those who censured him his defence was, "I have Laïs, not she me; and it is not abstinence from pleasures that is best, but mastery over them without ever being worsted." To one who reproached him with extravagance in eating, he replied, "Wouldn't you have bought this if you could have got it for three obols?" The answer being in the affirmative, "Very well, then," said Aristippus, "I am no longer a lover of pleasure, it is you who are a lover of money." One day Simus, the steward of Dionysius, a Phrygian by birth and a rascally fellow, was showing him costly houses with tesselated pavements, when Aristippus coughed up phlegm and spat in his face. And on his resenting this he replied, "I could not find any place more suitable."

When Charondas (or, as others say, Phaedo) inquired, "Who is this who reeks with unguents?" he replied, "It is I, unlucky wight, and the still more unlucky Persian king. But, as none of the other animals are at any disadvantage on that account, consider whether it be not the same with man. Confound the effeminates who spoil for us the use of good perfume." Being asked how Socrates died, he answered, "As I would wish to die myself." Polyxenus the sophist once paid him a visit and, after having seen ladies present and expensive entertainment, reproached him with it later. After an interval Aristippus asked him, "Can you join us today?" On the other accepting the invitation, Aristippus inquired, "Why, then, did you find fault? For you appear to blame the cost and not the entertainment." When his servant was carrying money and found the load too heavy — the story is told by his Lectures — Aristippus cried, "Pour away the greater part, and carry no more than you can manage."

· · ·

Having written his life, let me now proceed to pass in review the philosophers of the Cyrenaic school which sprang from him, although some call themselves followers of Anniceris, others again of Theodorus. . . .

Those then who adhered to the teaching of Aristippus and were known as Cyrenaics held the following opinions. They laid down that there are two states, pleasure and pain, the former a smooth, the latter a rough motion, and that pleasure does not differ from pleasure nor is one pleasure more pleasant than another. The one state is agreeable and the other repellent to all living things. However, the bodily pleasure which is the end is, according to Panactius is his work *On the Sects,* not the settled pleasure following the removal of pains, or the sort of freedom from discomfort which Epicurus accepts and maintains to be the end. They also hold that there is a difference between "end" and "happiness." Our end is particular pleasure, whereas happiness is the sum total of all particular pleasures, in which are included both past and future pleasures.

Particular pleasure is desirable for its own sake, whereas happiness is desirable not for its own sake but for the sake of particular pleasures. That pleasure if the end is proved by the fact that from our youth up we are instinctively attracted to it, and, when we obtain it, seek for nothing more, and shun nothing so much as its opposite, pain. Pleasure is good even if it proceed from the most unseemly conduct, as Hippobotus says in his work *On the Sects.* For even if the action be irregular, still, at any rate, the resultant pleasure is desirable for its own sake and is good. The removal of pain, however, which is put forward in Epicurus, seems to them not to be pleasure at all, any more than the absence of pleasure is pain. For both pleasure and pain they hold to consist in motion, whereas absence of pleasure like absence of pain is not motion, since painlessness is the condition of one who is, as it were, asleep. They assert that some people may fail to choose pleasure because their minds are perverted; not all mental pleasures and pains, however, are derived from bodily counterparts. For instance, we take disinterested delight in the prosperity of our country which is as real as our delight in our own prosperity. Nor again do they admit that pleasure is derived from the memory or expectation of good, which was a doctrine of Epicurus. For they assert that the movement affecting the mind is exhausted in course of time. Again they hold that the pleasure is not derived from sight or from hearing alone. At all events, we listen with pleasure to imitation of mourning, while the reality causes pain. They gave the names of absence of pleasure and absence of pain to the intermediate conditions. However, they insist that bodily pleasures are far better than mental pleasures, and bodily pains far worse than mental pains, and that this is the reason why offenders are punished with the former. For they assumed pain to be more repellent, pleasure more congenial. For these reasons they paid more attention to the body than to the mind. Hence, although pleasure is in itself desirable, yet they hold that the things which are productive of certain pleasures are often of a painful nature, the very opposite of pleasure; so that to accumulate the pleasures which are productive of happiness appears to them a most irksome business.

They do not accept the doctrine that every wise man lives pleasantly and every fool painfully, but regard it as true for the most part only. It is sufficient even if we enjoy but each single pleasure as it comes. They say that prudence is a good, though desirable not in itself but on account of its consequences; that we make friends from interested motives, just as we cherish any part of the body so long as we have it; that some of the virtues are found even in the foolish; that bodily training contributes to the acquisition of virtue; that the sage will not give way to envy or love or superstition, since these weaknesses are due to mere empty opinion; he will, however, feel pain and fear, these being natural affections; and that wealth too is productive of pleasure, though not desirable for its own sake.

They affirm that mental affections can be known, but not the objects from which they come; and they abandoned the study of nature because of its apparent uncertainty, but fastened on logical inquiries because of their utility. But Meleager in his second book *On Philosophical Opinions,* and Clitomachus in his first book *On the Sects,* affirm that they maintain Dialectic as well as Physics to be useless, since, when one has learnt the theory of good and evil, it is possible to speak with propriety, to be free from superstition, and to escape the fear of death. They also held that nothing is just or honourable or base by nature, but only by convention and custom.

Nevertheless the good man will be deterred from wrong-doing by the penalties imposed and the prejudices that it would arouse. Further that the wise man really exists. They allow progress to be attainable in philosophy as well as in other matters. They maintain that the pain of one man exceeds that of another, and that the senses are not always true and trustworthy.

The school of Hegesias, as it is called, adopted the same ends, namely pleasure and pain. In their view there is no such thing as gratitude or friendship or beneficence, because it is not for themselves that we choose to do these things but simply from motives of interest, apart from which such conduct is nowhere found. They denied the possibility of happiness, for the body is infected with much suffering, while the soul shares in the sufferings of the body and is a prey to disturbance, and fortune often disappoints. From all this it follows that happiness cannot be realized. Moreover, life and death are each desirable in turn. But that there is anything naturally pleasant or unpleasant they deny; when some men are pleased and others pained by the same objects, this is owing to the lack or rarity of surfeit of such objects. Poverty and riches have no relevance to pleasure; for neither the rich not the poor as such have any special share in pleasure. Slavery and freedom, nobility and low birth, honour and dishonour, are alike indifferent in a calculation of pleasure. To the fool life is advantageous, while to the wise it is a matter of indifference. The wise man will be guided in all he does by his own interests, for there is none other whom he regards as equally deserving. . . .

. . . The wise man will not have so much advantage over others in the choice of goods as in the avoidance of evils, making it his end to live without pain of body or mind. This then, they say, is the advantage accruing to those who make no distinction between any of the objects which produce pleasure. . . .

The school of Anniceris in other respects agreed with them, but admitted that friendship and gratitude and respect for parents do exist in real life, and that a good man will sometimes act out of patriotic motives. Hence, if the wise man receive annoyance, he will be none the less happy even if few pleasures accrue to him. The happiness of a friend is not in itself desirable, for it is not felt by his neighbour. Instruction is not sufficient in itself to inspire us with confidence and to make us rise superior to the opinion of the multitude. Habits must be formed because of the bad disposition which has grown up in us from the first. A friend should be cherished not merely for his utility — for, if that fails, we should then no longer associate with him — but for the good feeling for the sake of which we shall even endure hardships. Nay, though we make pleasure the end and are annoyed when deprived of it, we shall nevertheless cheerfully endure this because of our love to our friend.

The Theodoreans derived their name from Theodorus, who has already been mentioned, and adopted his doctrines. Theodorus was a man who utterly rejected the current belief in the gods. And I have come across a book of his entitled *Of the Gods* which is not contemptible. From that book, they say, Epicurus borrowed most of what he wrote on the subject.

Theodorus was also a pupil of Anniceris and of Dionysius the dialectician, as Antisthenes mentions in his *Successions of Philosophers*. He considered joy and grief to be supreme good and evil, the one brought about by wisdom, the other by folly. Wisdom and justice he called goods, and their opposites evils, pleasure and pain being intermediate to good and evil. Friendship he rejected because it did not exist between the unwise nor between the wise; with the former, when the want is removed, the friendship disappears, whereas the wise are self-sufficient and have no need of friends. It was reasonable, as he thought, for the good man not to risk his life in the defence of his country, for he would never throw wisdom away to benefit the unwise.

He said the world was his country. Theft, adultery, and sacrilege would be allowable upon occasion, since none of these acts is by nature base, if once you have removed the prejudice against them, which is kept up in order to hold the foolish multitude together. The wise man would indulge his passion openly without the least regard to circumstances.

The Epicureans: Enjoying Peace of Mind

The Epicureans developed a rival theory to that of the Cyrenaics and founded an actual school of philosophy in Athens in 307–306 B.C. Although both were hedonistic and shared a number of basic assumptions, their differences provoked considerable antagonism and eventually the Epicurean viewpoint prevailed as the dominant ideal of the time. In addition to Epicurus himself, the chief proponents of the school were Hermarchus, Polystratus, and Metrodorus, although the best known disciple was the Latin poet, T. Lucretius Carus (91–51 B.C.). In his poem *De Rerum Natura*, Lucretius expressed the essential Epicurean teaching in affective form.

From some of the fragments of his writings and correspondence (including charred remnants recovered from the eruption of Vesuvius in 79 A.D.), Epicurus appears to have been a charismatic leader and a warm, generous friend. He was venerated in his lifetime, and after his death a cultlike devotion to the Epicurean doctrine developed among his followers. Monthly feasts were held to honor his memory and his disciples adhered to his beliefs in a strict orthodoxy. During his life he used his own Garden as the center of the community, and this became the model for Epicurean groups throughout Greece. Women, slaves, even courtesans were welcome, for fellowship was prized far more than social distinctions. Some sense of the man can be glimpsed in a letter written on his deathbed to a friend: "On this last, yet blessed, day of my life, I write to you. Pains and tortures of the body I have to the full, but there is set over against these the joy of my heart at the memory of our happy conversations in the past. Do you, if you would be worthy of your devotion to me and philosophy, take care of the children of Metrodorus."

In addition to his teachings on ethics, Epicurus was celebrated in antiquity for his metaphysical theory, that is, his view that reality consists of tiny atoms that are the building blocks of all matter. The philosopher Democritus is usually credited with originating this atomic theory but the earliest account of it appears in a letter from Epicurus to Herodotus. And Epicurus certainly added an original note when he asserted that the atoms do not always fall in a steady, parallel rain but sometimes swerve voluntarily or by chance, thus colliding and combining. In any case, this brilliant conjecture that atoms are the basic reality was later verified by modern physics after being ignored for over 2,000 years.

As for his ethical views, Epicurus agreed with the Cyrenaics that immediate experience is the test for all ideas. Specifically, our knowledge of good and evil depends upon pleasure and pain and our judgments are only meaningful in terms of these feelings. "We affirm that pleasure is the beginning and end of living happily," Epicurus wrote, "for we have recognized this as the first good connate with us; and it is with reference to it that we begin every choice and avoidance." This places Epicurus clearly within the hedonist tradition, and by stressing our common responsiveness to pleasure his ethical theory is grounded in psychological facts.

Where he differed from the Cyrenaics was with regard to the kind of pleasure that is most desirable. The Epicureans in fact affirmed happiness *instead* of pleasure even though they used a term commonly translated as pleasure. For they rejected voluptuous, high living, the physical life of sense gratification. As Epicurus wrote in his *Letter to Menoeceus,* "When therefore we maintain that pleasure is an end, we do not mean the pleasures of profligates and those that consist in sensuality." Rather, it was intellectual enjoyment that the Epicureans sought, "not continuous drinkings, nor the satisfaction of lusts, . . . but sober reasonings." Much more important than physical pleasures were the satisfactions of the mind, just as the avoidance of mental distress mattered more than bodily pain. The most we could expect from the body was perfect health whereas the mind could give us freedom from anxiety.[5]

In an interesting aside Epicurus said that the worst the body can produce is death, which is not a real evil. Death is actually neither good nor bad; it is "nothing to us, since so long as we exist death is not with us, but when death comes then we no longer exist." The mind, however, can plague us with memories of past evils and the fear of future pain.

Mental happiness then is most significant and the Epicureans endorsed the refined life of the cultured person. The notion of an Epicurean as someone who wallows in sensuous delights is a modern misconception based on slanders of later Greek writers. Much more typical is the following fragment from a letter by Epicurus. "Send me some cheese of Cythnos that I may be able to fare sumptuously when I like." Simple, modest meals that can be relished spiritually more than physically, freedom from all cares and distress, the gratification of kindness, justice, and companionship, tranquil and enduring satisfactions of every description — these are the inward joys that make life worthwhile. Far from being debauched and depraved, the Epicureans were virtuous people who led lives of temperance and moderation that bordered on the ascetic. They actually reduced their needs to a minimum rather than risk the disappointment that could come with a multitude of desires.

Not only were the fulfillments of the mind thought to be superior to the pleasures of the body, but the intellect was also viewed as a discriminating instrument which should reject and avoid those pleasures that are likely to produce subsequent misery and persuade us to endure certain pains for the sake of an overall happiness. For example, drinking heavily might be enjoyable for a time, but it could lead to an unhealthy state — what we recognize today as alcoholism and cirrhosis of the liver. Conversely, having a tooth pulled might involve considerable discomfort but it could prevent greater agony later on.

The mind is needed to make these differentiations and not simply allow our natural inclinations to determine our behavior. "At times we pass over many pleasures when any difficulty is likely to ensue from them," Epicurus wrote, "and we think many pains better than pleasures when a greater pleasure follows them."

Enjoyment is always better than suffering of course, but we have to be wise in making our selections, and not in the sense that one experience is morally better than another. We simply need to look ahead toward the long-term good, the lasting happiness we want in our lives as a whole, and that calls for prudence and self-control in our choices. "Every pleasure is therefore a good on account of its own nature, but it does not follow that every pleasure is worthy of being chosen; just as every pain is an evil, and yet every pain must not be avoided."

This emphasis on the role of the intellect in choosing experiences led quite naturally to a central tenet of the Epicurean ethic, namely that *ataraxia,* or peace of mind, is of supreme value in living. The Epicureans believed that happiness is essentially a comfortable state of mental tranquility in which we are not disturbed by any harshness or outside strife. The goal was not so much to seek pleasure as to avoid pain, and if we were not uncomfortable we could consider ourselves well off. The absence of physical discomfort and mental disturbance constitutes serenity (ataraxia), which is the best state one can attain. Positive enjoyment comes very seldom, the Epicureans thought, and during the long intervals we should strive for equilibrium and peace, the balanced, rationally controlled life that yields "freedom from disquietude of the soul."

The Garden of Epicurus is often considered a fitting symbol of this negative philosophy because its walls did not keep enjoyment in so much as keep troubles out. It was an oasis, a haven, what one philosopher calls homecoming rather than shipwreck. Happiness meant being sheltered in a delightful and safe retreat, where one could withdraw from the vicissitudes of life, enjoy the company of gifted and noble friends, and find profound peace.

Friendship in particular was considered an important ingredient in this contentment, for as a practical matter it is much pleasanter to live among people you like and trust. This is why Epicurus wrote,

> He who desires to live tranquilly without having anything to fear from other men, ought to make himself friends; those whom he cannot make friends of, he should, at least, avoid rendering enemies. . . . The happiest men are they who have arrived at the point of having nothing to fear from those who surround them. Such men live with one another most agreeably, having the firmest grounds of confidence in one another, enjoying the advantages of friendship in all their fullness.

The Epicureans did not value friendship as such but only insofar as it had utility, which is fundamentally an egoistic reason. When Epicurus said, "Of all things which wisdom provides for the happiness of the whole life, by far the most important is the acquisition of friendship," he meant that a secure and serene life for oneself requires a society of friends.[6]

However, even if the Epicureans were doing the right thing for the wrong reasons, the stress they placed on friendship made them agreeable companions. They affirmed other virtues as well, which were based on selfishness but in practice worked out for the social good. Justice, honor, kindness, and fair conduct of every kind were prized because no person could live a happy life unless he acted in accordance with such virtues. "Injustice is not intrinsically bad," Epicurus declared candidly, "it has this character only because there is joined with it a fear of not escaping those who are appointed to punish actions marked with that character. . . . The just man is freest of all men from disquietude; but the unjust man is a perpetual prey to it." Or as he stated in another passage, "It is not possible to live pleasantly without living prudently, and honorably, and justly; nor to live prudently, and honorably, and justly, without living pleasantly." The wise man therefore is a moral man, because he knows that in order to have a tranquil life he must treat others well.

The aim of a calm, secure life also led the Epicureans to oppose ordinary religion as an evil because it oppressed people, making them anxious about the anger and jealousy of the gods. But the immortal gods themselves should not be rejected, merely redefined in a way conducive to peace of mind. We should believe that the gods do not control nature or intervene in human life but live in utter tranquility far above the world (rather like the Indian image of the Buddha on the lotus flower, rising above the Sea of Sorrow). They are removed from any concern for humanity, having attained the ultimate beatitude possible to conscious beings. The ideal of human life is to realize that same state of bliss and become godlike ourselves, aloof, balanced, rational, and wholly serene. As in a number of philosophic systems, a link to the cosmos validates a set of ideals.

In the selection that follows, the principal themes of the Epicurean ethic are struck: the primacy of mental happiness, the need for rational choice among actions so that overall enjoyment is achieved, ataraxia as the specific kind of happiness that should be sought, the role of friendship and other virtues in attaining the goal of ataraxia, and the most satisfying interpretation to hold of the gods. These are the fundamental ideas just discussed and the main ways in which the Epicureans differed from the Cyrenaics.

Two documents of Epicurus are included here, both of which were preserved by Diogenes Laertius: the *Letter to Menoeceus* and the *Principal Doctrines*. They are the main extant sources for our knowledge of the Epicurean ethic.

Letter to Menoeceus*

"Epicurus to Menoeceus, greeting.

"Let no one be slow to seek wisdom when he is young nor weary in the search thereof when he is grown old. For no age is too early or too late for the health of the soul. And to say that the season for studying philosophy has not yet come, or that it is past and gone, is like saying that the season for happiness is not yet or it is now no more. Therefore, both old and young ought to seek wisdom, the former in order that, as age comes over him, he may be young in good things because of the grace of what has been, and the latter in order that, while he is young, he may at the same time be old, because he has no fear of the things which are to come. So we must exercise ourselves in the things which bring happiness, since, if that be present, we

*Reprinted with permission from Diogenes Laertius, *The Lives of Eminent Philosophers*, trans. R. D. Hicks (Cambridge: Harvard University Press, 1950), vol. 2: 121–39.

have everything, and, if that be absent, all our actions are directed toward attaining it.

"Those things which without ceasing I have declared unto thee, those do, and exercise thyself therein, holding them to be the elements of right life. First believe that God is a living being immortal and blessed, according to the notion of a god indicated by the common sense of mankind; and so believing, thou shalt not affirm of him aught that is foreign to his immortality or that agrees not with blessedness, but shalt believe about him whatever may uphold both his blessedness and his immortality. For verily there are gods, and the knowledge of them is manifest; but they are not such as the multitude believe, seeing that men do not steadfastly maintain the notions they form respecting them. Not the man who denies the gods worshipped by the multitude, but he who affirms of the gods what the multitude believes about them is truly impious. For the utterances of the multitude about the gods are not true preconceptions but false assumptions; hence it is that the greatest evils happen to the wicked and the greatest blessings happen to the good from the hand of the gods, seeing that they are always favourable to their own good qualities and take pleasure in men like unto themselves, but reject as alien whatever is not of their kind.

"Accustom theyself to believe that death is nothing to us, for good and evil imply sentience, and death is the privation of all sentience; therefore a right understanding that death is nothing to us makes the mortality of life enjoyable, not by adding to life an illimitable time, but by taking away the yearning after immortality. For life has no terrors for him who has thoroughly apprehended that there are no terrors for him in ceasing to live. Foolish, therefore, is the man who says that he fears death, not because it will pain when it comes, but because it pains in the prospect. Whatsoever causes no annoyance when it is present, causes only a groundless pain in the expectation. Death, therefore, the most awful of evils, is nothing to us, seeing that, when we are, death is not come, and, when death is come, we are not. It is nothing, then, either to the living or to the dead, for with the living it is not and the dead exist no longer. But in the world, at one time men shun death as the greatest of all evils, and at another time choose it as a respite from the evils in life. The wise man does not deprecate life nor does he fear the cessation of life. The thought of life is no offence to him, nor is the cessation of life regarded as an evil. And even as men choose of food not merely and simply the larger portion, but the more pleasant, so the wise seek to enjoy the time which is most pleasant and not merely that which is longest. And he who admonishes the young to live well and the old to make a good end speaks foolishly, not merely because of the desirableness of life, but because the same exercise at once teaches to live well and to die well. Much worse is he who says that it were good not to be born, but when once one is born to pass with all speed through the gates of Hades. For if he truly believes this, why does he not depart from life? It were easy for him to do so, if once he were firmly convinced. If he speaks only in mockery, his words are foolishness, for those who hear believe him not.

"We must remember that the future is neither wholly ours nor wholly not ours, so that neither must we count upon it as quite certain to come nor despair of it as quite certain not to come.

"We must also reflect that of desires some are natural, others are groundless; and that of the natural some are necessary as well as natural, and some natural only. And of the necessary desires some are necessary if we are to be happy, some if the body is to be rid of uneasiness, some if we are even to live. He who has a clear and certain understanding of these things will direct every preference and aversion toward securing health of body and tranquility of mind, seeing that his is the sum and end of a blessed life. For the end of all our actions is to be free from pain and fear, and, when once we have attained all this, the tempest of the soul is laid; seeing that the living creature has no need to go in search of something that is lacking, nor to look for anything else by which the good of the soul and of the body will be fulfilled. When we are pained because of the absence of pleasure, then, and then only, do we feel the need of pleasure. Wherefore we call pleasure the alpha and the omega of a blessed life. Pleasure is our first and kindred good. It is the starting-point of every choice and of every aversion, and to it we come back, inasmuch as we make feeling the rule by which to judge of every good thing. And since pleasure is our first and native good, for that reason we do not choose every pleasure whatsoever, but ofttimes pass over many pleasures when a greater annoyance ensues from them. And ofttimes we consider pains superior to pleasures when submission to the pains for a long time brings us as a consequence a greater pleasure. While therefore all pleasure because it is naturally akin to us is good, not all pleasure is choiceworthy, just as all pain is an evil and yet not all pain is against another, and by looking at the conveniences and inconveniences, that all these matters must be judged. Sometimes we treat the good as an evil, and the evil, on the contrary, as a good. Again, we regard independence of outward things as a great good, not so as in all cases to use little, but so as to be contented with little if we have not much, being honestly persuaded that they have the sweetest enjoyment of luxury who stand least in need of it, and that whatever is natural is easily procured and only the vain and worthless hard to win. Plain fare gives as much pleasure as a costly diet, when once the pain of want has been removed, while bread and water conger the highest possible pleasure when they are brought to hungry lips. To habituate one's self, therefore, to simple and inexpensive diet supplies all that is needful for health, and enables a man to meet the necessary requirements of life without shrinking, and it places us in a better condition when we approach at intervals a costly fare and renders us fearless of fortune.

"When we say, then, that pleasure is the end and aim, we do not mean the pleasures of the prodigal or the pleasures of sensuality, as we are understood to do by some through ignorance, prejudice, or willful misrepresentation. By pleasure we mean the absence of pain in the body and of trouble in the soul. It is not an unbroken succession of drinking-bouts and of revelry, not sexual love, not the enjoyment of the fish and other delicacies of a luxurious table, which produce a pleasant life; it is sober reasoning, searching out the ground of every choice and avoidance, and banishing those beliefs through which the greatest good is prudence. Wherefore prudence is a more precious thing even than philosophy; from it spring all other virtues, for it teaches that we cannot lead a life of pleasure which is not also a life of prudence, honour, and justice; nor lead a life of prudence, honour, and justice, which is not also a life of pleasure. For the virtues have grown into one with a pleasant life, and a pleasant life is inseperable from them.

"Who, then, is superior in thy judgment to such a men? He holds a holy belief concerning the gods, and is altogether free from the fear of death. He has diligently considered the end fixed by nature, and understands how easily the limit of good things can be reached and attained, and how either the duration or the intesity of evils is but slight. Destiny, which some introduce as sovereign over all things, he laughs to scorn, affirming rather that some things happen of necessity, others by chance, others through our own agency. For he sees that chance or fortune is inconstant; whereas our own actions are free, and it is to them that praise and blame naturally attach. It were better, indeed, to accept the legends of the gods than to bow beneath the yoke of destiny which the natural philosophers have imposed. The one holds out some faint hope that we may escape if we honour the gods, while the necessity of the naturalists is deaf to all entreaties. Nor does he hold chance to be a god, as the world in general does, for in the acts of a god there is no disorder; nor to be a cause, though an uncertain one, for he believes that no good or evil is dispensed by chance to men so as to make life blessed, though it supplies the starting-point of great good and great evil. He believes that the misfortune of the wise is better than the prosperity of the fool. It is better, in short, that what is well judged in action should not owe its successful issue to the aid of chance.

"Exercise thyself in these and kindred precepts day and night, both by thyself and with him who is like unto thee; then never, either in waking or in dream, wilt thou be disturbed, but wilt live as a god among men. For man loses all semblance of mortality by living in the midst of immortal blessing."

Elsewhere he rejects the whole of divination, as in the short epitome, and says, "No means of predicting the future really exists, and if it did, we must regard what happens according to it as nothing to us."

Such are his views on life and conduct; and he has discoursed upon them at greater length elsewhere.

He differs from the Cyrenaics with regard to pleasure. They do not include under the term the pleasure which is a state of rest, but only that which consists in motion. Epicurus admits both; also pleasure of mind as well as of body, as he states in his work *On Choice and Avoidance* and in that *On the Ethical End,* and in the first book on his work *On Human Life* and in the epistle to his philosopher friend in Mytilene. So also Diogenes in the seventeenth book of his *Epilecta,* and Metrodorus in his *Timocrates,* whose actual words are: "Thus pleasure being conceived both as that species which consists in motion and that which is a state of rest." The words of Epicurus in his work *On Choice* are: "Peace of mind and freedom from pain are pleasures which imply a state of rest; joy and delight are seen to consist in motion and activity."

He further disagrees with the Cyrenaics in that they hold that pains of the body are worse than mental pains; at all events evil-doers are made to suffer bodily punishment; whereas Epicurus holds the pains of the mind to be worse; at any rate the flesh endures the storms of the present alone, the mind those of the past and future as well as the present. In this way also he holds mental pleasure to be greater than those of the body. And as proof that pleasure is the end he adduces the fact that living things, so soon as they are born, are well content with pleasure and are at enmity with pain, by the prompting of nature and apart from reason. Left to our own feelings, then, we shun pain; as when even Heracles, devoured by the poisoned robe, cries aloud,

> *And bites and yells, and to rock resounds,*
> *Headlands of Loeris and Euboean cliffs.*

And we choose the virtues too on account of pleasure and not for their own sake, as we take medicine for the sake of health. So too in the twentieth book of *Epilecta* says Diogenes, who also calls education (ἀγωγή) recreation (διαγωγή). Epicurus describes virtue as the sine qua non of pleasure, i. e., the one thing without which pleasure cannot be, everything else, food, for instance, being separable, i. e., not indispensable to pleasure.

Principal Doctrines*

Come, then, let me set the seal, so to say, on my entire work as well as on this philosopher's life by citing his Sovran Maximus,** therewith bringing the whole work to a close and making the end of it to coincide with the beginning of happiness.

1. A blessed and eternal being has no trouble himself and brings no trouble upon any other being; hence he is exempt from movements of anger and partiality, for every such movement implies weakness. [Elsewhere he says that the gods are discernible by reason alone, some being numerically distinct, while others result uniformly from the continuous influx of similar images direct to the same spot and in human form.]

2. Death is nothing to us; for the body, when it has been resolved into its elements, has no feeling, and that which has no feeling is nothing to us.

3. The magnitude of pleasure reaches its limit in the removal of all pain. When pleasure is present, so long as it is uninterrupted, there is no pain either of body or of mind or of both together.

4. Continuous pain does not last long in the flesh; on the contrary, pain, if extreme, is present a very short time, and even that degree of pain which barely outweighs pleasure in the flesh does not last for many days together. Illness of long duration even permit of an excess of pleasure over pain in the flesh.

*Reprinted with permission from Diogenes Laertius, *The Lives of Eminent Philosophers* (Cambridge: Harvard University Press, 1950), vol. 2: 139–54.

**This collection of forty of the most important articles of faith in the Epicurean creed was famous in antiquity. It consists of extracts from the voluminous writings of Epicurus, and may have been put together by a faithful disciple. On the other hand, Epicurus laid great stress (35, 36) on epitomes of his doctrine being committed to memory; so that his passion for personal direction and supervision of the studies of his pupils may have induced him to furnish them with such an indispensable catechism. [Translator's note]

5. It is impossible to live a pleasant life without living wisely and well and justly, and it is impossible to live wisely and well and justly without living pleasantly. Whenever any one of these is lacking, when, for instance, the man is not able to live wisely, though he lives well and justly, it is impossible for him to live a pleasant life.

6. In order to obtain security from other men any means whatsoever of procuring this was a natural good.

7. Some men have sought to become famous and renowned, thinking that thus they would make selves secure against their fellow-men. If, then, the life of such persons really was secure, they attained natural good; if, however, it was insecure, they have not attained the end which by nature's own prompting they originally sought.

8. No pleasure is in itself evil, but the things which produce certain pleasures entail annoyances many times greater than the pleasures themselves.

9. If all pleasure had been capable of accumulation, — if this had gone on not only by recurrence in time, but all over the frame or, at any rate, over the principal parts of man's nature, there would never have been any difference between one pleasure and another, as in fact there is.

10. If the objects which are productive of pleasures to profligate persons really freed them from fears of the mind, — the fears, I mean, inspired by celestial and atmospheric phenomena, the fear of death, the fear of pain; if, further, they taught them to limit their desires, we should never have any fault to find with pleasures to overflowing on all sides and would be exempt from all pain, whether of body or mind, that is, from all evil.

11. If we had never been molested by alarms at celestial and atmospheric phenomena, nor by the misgiving that death somehow affects us, nor by neglect of the proper limits of pains and desires, we should have had no need to study natural science.

12. It would be impossible to banish fear on matters of the highest importance, if a man did not know the nature of the whole universe, but lived in dread of what the legends tells us. Hence without the study of nature there was no enjoyment of unmixed pleasures.

13. There would be no advantage in providing security against our fellow-men, so long as we were alarmed by occurrences over our heads or beneath the earth or in general by whatever happens in the boundless universe.

14. When tolerable security against our fellow-men is attained, then on a basis of power sufficient to afford support and of material prosperity arises in most genuine form the security of a quiet private life withdrawn from the multitude.

15. Nature's wealth at once has its bounds and is easy to procure; but the wealth of vain fancies recedes to an infinite distance.

16. Fortune but seldom interferes with the wise man: his greatest and highest interests have been, are, and will be, directed by reason throughout the course of his life.

17. The just man enjoys the greatest peace of mind, while the unjust is full of the utmost disquietude.

18. Pleasure in the flesh admits no increase when once the pain of want has been removed; after that it only admits of variation. The limit of pleasure in the mind, however, is reached when we reflect on the things themselves and their congeners which cause the mind the greatest alarms.

19. Unlimited time and limited time afford an equal amount of pleasure, if we measure the limits of that pleasure by reason.

20. The flesh receives as unlimited the limits of pleasure; and to provide it requires unlimited time. But the mind, grasping in thought what the end and limit of flesh is, and banishing the terrors of futurity, procures a complete and perfect life, and has no longer any need of unlimited time. Nevertheless it does not shun pleasure, and even in the hour of death, when ushered out of existence by circumstances, the mind does not lack enjoyment of the best life.

21. He who understands the limits of life knows how easy it is to procure enough to remove the pain of want and make the whole of life complete and perfect. Hence he has no longer any need of things which are not to be won save by labour and conflict.

22. We must take into account as the end all that really exists and all clear evidence of sense to which we refer our opinions; for otherwise everything will be full of uncertainty and confusion.

23. If you fight against all of your sensations, you will have no standard to which to refer, and thus no means of judging even those judgements which you pronounce false.

24. If you reject absolutely any single sensation without stopping to discriminate with respect to that which awaits confirmation between matter of opinion and that which is already present, whether in sensation or in feelings or in any presentative perception of the mind, you will throw into confusion even the rest of your sensations by your groundless belief and so you will be rejecting the standard of truth altogether. If in your ideas based upon opinions you hastily affirm as true all that awaits confirmation as well as that which does not, you will not escape error, as you will be maintaining complete ambiguity whenever it is a case of judging between right and wrong opinion.

25. If you do not on every separate occasion refer each of your actions to the end prescribed by nature, but instead of this in the act of choice or avoidance swerve aside to some other end, your acts will not be considered with your theories.

26. All such desires as lead to no pain when they remain ungratified are unnecessary, and the longing is easily got rid of, when the thing desired is difficult to procure or when the desires seem likely to produce harm.

27. Of all the means which are procured by wisdom to ensure happiness throughout the whole of life, by far the most important is the acquisition of friends.

28. The same conviction which inspires confidence that nothing we have to fear is eternal or even of long duration, also enables us to see that even in our limited conditions of life nothing enhances our security so much as friendship.

29. Of our desires some are natural and necessary; others are natural, but not necessary; others, again, are neither natural nor necessary, but are due to illusory opinion. [Epicurus regards as natural and necessary desires which bring relief from pain, as e.g. drink when we are thirsty; while by natural and not necessary he means desires for crowns and the erection of statues in one's honour.]

30. Those natural desires which entail no pain when not gratified, though their objects are vehemently pursued, are also due to illusory opinion; and when they are not got rid of, it is not because of their own nature, but because of the man's illusory opinion.

31. Natural justice is a symbol or expression of expediency, to prevent one man from harming or being harmed by another.

32. Those animals which are incapable of making covenants with one another, to the end that they may neither inflict nor suffer harm, are without either justice or injustice. And those tribes which either could not or would not form mutual covenants to the same end are in like case.

33. There never was an absolute justice, but only an agreement made in reciprocal intercourse in whatever localities now and again from time to time, providing against the infliction or suffering of harm.

34. Injustice is not in itself an evil, but only in its consequence, viz, the terror which is excited by apprehension that those appointed to punish such offences will discover the injustice.

35. It is impossible for the man who secretly violates any article of the social compact to feel confident that he will remain undiscovered, even if he has already escaped ten thousand times; for right on to the end of his life he is never sure he will be detected.

36. Taken generally, justice is the same for all, to wit, something found expedient in mutual intercourse; but in its application to particular cases of locality or conditions of whatever kind, it varies under different circumstances.

37. Among the things accounted just by conventional law, whatever in the needs of mutual intercourse is attested to be expedient, is thereby stamped as just, whether or not it be the same for all; and in case any law is made and does not prove suitable to the expediences of mutual intercourse, then this is no longer just. And should the expediency which is expressed by the law vary and only for a time correspond with the prior conception, nevertheless for the time being it was just, so long as we do not trouble ourselves about empty words, but look simply at the facts.

38. Where without any change in circumstances the conventional laws, when judged by their consequences, were seen not to correspond with the notion of justice, such laws were not really just; but wherever the laws have

ceased to be expedient in consequence of change in circumstances, in that case the laws were for the time being just when they were expedient for the mutual intercourse of the citizens, and subsequently ceased to be just when they ceased to be expedient.

39. He who best knew how to meet fear of external foes made into one family all the creatures he could; and those he could not, he at any rate did not treat as aliens; and where he found even this impossible, he avoided all intercourse, and, so far as was expedient, kept them at a distance.

40. Those who were best able to provide themselves with the means of security against their neighbours, being thus in possession of the surest guarantee, passed the most agreeable life in each other's society; and their enjoyment of the fullest intimacy was such that, if one of them died before his time, the survivors did not lament his death as if it called for commiseration.

Evaluation

The Cyrenaic and Epicurean alternatives in hedonism point up each other's strengths and weaknesses and form a useful intellectual counterpoint. On the one hand, the Epicurean approach seems much more sensible and adult, insisting on the more profound satisfactions of the mind and the superficiality of physical pleasure. Mental happiness is richer and more enduring, and the intellect can choose experiences that benefit the person in the long run rather than for the moment. Furthermore, the Epicurean maintains quite correctly that tranquil enjoyment tends to carry over to similarly pleasurable states whereas intense pleasures may well be followed by intense pains. For example, a promiscuous life could result in venereal disease, the drifter who stays in a job only as long as the excitement lasts may find himself destitute and homeless, but the cultivation of friendship will provide a steady source of joy, and plain rather than rich food will maintain health much longer. We should not be shortsighted, seduced by brief, trite, hollow, animal pleasures that betray our humanity and work against our overall welfare. The serene, inner happiness accessible to man alone and persisting throughout our lifetime is a nobler and wiser aim.

On the other hand, however, the Cyrenaic argues that Epicurean premeditation tends to destroy the excitement in living. We may be better off in a calculating way but we do not experience much vitality or sheer fun. Spontaneity is lost and what is achieved in avoiding negative consequences does not compensate for it. Furthermore, the Cyrenaic claims, tangible pleasure is immediate, powerful, and intense, a saturation of tonic emotions, whereas intellectual enjoyment is tame, sedate, and dull. Such enjoyment may be mature but it is also very boring — a truth that kills. Why settle for the absence of discomfort as the highest state attainable? We should say yes to life not no and seek positive experiences that enhance our existence, action, thrills, a variety of stimulations. Instead of protecting ourselves from mistakes, we ought to take risks and live for today because that is the only way that excitement can be had; when nothing is ventured, nothing is gained. From the point of view of the Cyrenaic, the Epicurean thinks he is leading a good life when all he is doing is avoiding a bad one. He is taking his enjoyments too seriously and not satisfying his whims, indulging his follies. At least with a Cyrenaic attitude we can live before we die and not spend our time in the twilight realm of peace and safety.

Such is the reply of the Cyrenaic and in a sense it is the answer vigorous youth gives to wise old age. The time curve of our lives tends to run from Cyrenaic early on to Epicurean in our later years, so that adolescents typically want a fast paced, loud, and active life, while their grandparents prefer peace and quiet; in that sense the debate is between a younger and an older mentality. But aside from what we are inclined to want at various stages in life, the philosophic question is Which theory is preferrable?

Presumably we cannot evade a decision by trying to combine the two in a compromise solution. There cannot be a brief, intense pleasure that is at the same time extended and tranquil, and to alternate between Cyrenaic and Epicurean experiences would produce an inconsistent, even contradictory life. (It just wouldn't work, for example, to be Cyrenaic on Monday, Wednesday, and Friday and Epicurean on Tuesday, Thursday, and Saturday, with Sunday divided half and half!) When conflicts arise between the two sets of values, a choice has to be made, and that calls for an overall judgment by the individual as to which has greater worth.

Of course, it could be that neither position should be chosen, that hedonism in whatever version is not a suitable goal for human existence. There are, in fact, numerous criticisms of the hedonistic system.

1. To begin with, the psychological hedonist may be mistaken in thinking that happiness or pleasure is our only possible motivation. Seemingly, people do want other things out of life such as power, self-development, recognition, social justice, and so forth, and these are not necessarily means toward securing happiness. It seems much more likely that they are actual ends that people want to realize, and although happiness may accompany their attainment they are not sought as a means of deriving happiness. The person who is concerned with social justice, for example, may enjoy the fruits of his victory when the ideals he has fought for finally come about, but it is very doubtful that such enjoyment was his aim in seeking those ideals. As was pointed out with regard to psychological egoism, pleasure can be a by-product of the pursuit of other goals, an accidental consequence of their attainment, or a feeling that goes along with the struggle, but it is not necessarily the only reason why things are done. It has been suggested that perhaps people never seek pleasure but only *value* because they cannot enjoy anything without first valuing it, and if they cannot respect what they are doing they cannot enjoy it. In any case, happiness or pleasure do not seem to be the only goals that human beings can or do pursue.

The psychological hedonist will sometimes reply to this objection that people are not always conscious of having pleasure as their purpose. Nonetheless, they want pleasure in whatever they do and would never perform an act unless they thought it would produce pleasure in the end. The fact that they do not articulate their motives and prefer to present themselves as having loftier aims does not prove that pleasure isn't their hidden or unconscious goal.

But as we have seen, the burden of proof is always on the person who denies an apparent truth to prove his case. That is, it seems that someone such as Albert Schweitzer working with poor Africans in the tropics or Mother Theresa helping malnourished or dying children in India are truly dedicated people. If they are really pleasure-seekers underneath that must be established, otherwise we are justified in thinking that what seems to be the case is the case — that they are actually committed to serving humanity. The psychological hedonist has not proven his claim with regard to individuals such as Schweitzer and Mother Theresa or the countless others who appear to be genuinely altruistic people. He is only saying "for all we know the dedicated person may be seeking personal gratification" but the logical reply is "yes, but as far as we know his motive is to help mankind not gratify himself." Therefore, our ordinary assumptions can stand that some people at least pursue other goals in life besides pleasure.

2. A second point that should be made has to do with the type of ethical hedonism that is based on psychological hedonism. To say that people ought to do what they have to do is a largely meaningless statement. If we haven't a choice but must of necessity pursue pleasure and avoid pain then it is pointless to recommend this as a goal in life. Unless we could do otherwise all urging and persuasion becomes irrelevant. At best the hedonist could commend the actions we are forced to perform but, because there is no alternative, he cannot recommend these actions above all others.

Another problem arises if the hedonist claims, not that everyone is compelled to seek pleasure, but that everyone actually does, and pleasure therefore is a worthwhile goal. Upon analysis, this argument also seems faulty. Just because people do pursue pleasure that does not imply that they should. Even if it were a natural and widespread tendency it might not be a good thing at all. For example, the desire to take advantage of others, to be aggressive and exploitative for one's own self-interest may be a general human tendency, nevertheless we would not consider this behavior to be worthwhile. The point is that how people actually behave (even universally) never tells us how they ought to behave; it cannot be taken as a sound reason for valuing their conduct.

People can desire all sorts of things that are bad for them or harmful to others, so that having a desire does not necessarily mean the object is desirable, that is, worthy of being desired. For example, I might want a high meat diet but the cholestrol would not be beneficial for my health or I might want to rob a bank but that would involve taking money that belongs to other people and could mean a long jail sentence for me. Having a desire, then, does not automatically mean that the desire is for something good. In the same way, the fact that people desire happiness does not in itself guarantee that happiness is worth pursuing. If everyone wanted to be cruel, we would never think of arguing that cruelty must therefore be a good thing.

Overall, then, genuine defects can be seen in the position of psychological hedonism and in the attempt to base ethical hedonism upon it.

3. Still another criticism of the hedonistic ethic concerns its relationship to morality. Both the Cyrenaics and the Epicureans are individualistic hedonists, unconcerned with other people's welfare. They advocate actions solely in terms of the enjoyment that the person might derive from them. If personal happiness or pleasure is produced then the action is justified ipso facto; if not, then the action should be avoided. Neither the Cyrenaic nor the Epicurean is concerned about injuring others in the process or with any possibility of self-sacrifice for someone else's good. All that matters is the well being of the agent, the person performing the action, not the rightness or wrongness that is involved. If torturing another person provides pleasure there is nothing in the hedonistic approach to prohibit it. The fact that a pleasure might be harmful, sordid,

unhealthy, or ugly is of no consequence. Even killing would be acceptable if pleasure could be derived that way — provided, of course, that no punishment interfered with the killer's enjoyment.

A philosophy of this kind that could ignore moral considerations and humane feeling is seriously deficient as an ideal for living. As an individualistic doctrine it would not only fail to serve others but would willingly destroy others for the sake of personal happiness. This absence of restraint makes it a grossly selfish and immoral theory.

4. A final criticism has to do with an ironic psychological fact called the "hedonistic paradox." The paradox, quite simply, is that if one tries to be happy chances are that one will not be. Happiness or pleasure tends to elude direct pursuit and only comes about indirectly, as the side effect of some other goal. If we forget about seeking happiness and become involved in composing music, raising children, helping the church, starting a business, competing in sports, and so forth then we may find that we are happy. But if our aim in life is happiness that is almost a sure formula for making ourselves miserable.

Numerous analogies can be used to illustrate the point. For example, we cannot hold onto sand by squeezing it hard in our hand; the stronger our grip the more it will sift through our fingers. If we want to keep the sand we must stop trying to grasp it. In the same way, we cannot make ourselves fall asleep; sleep will only come once we forget about sleeping. Happiness appears to function in a similar way. People who look for a good time rarely find one. They get in their own way by the very deliberate, conscious effort they are making.

John Stuart Mill, who was himself a hedonist, expressed the point this way:

> Those only are happy . . . who have their minds fixed on some object other than their own happiness; on the happiness of others, on the improvement of mankind, even on some art or pursuit, followed not as a means, but as itself an ideal end. Aiming thus at something else, they find happiness by the way. The enjoyments of life . . . are sufficient to make it a pleasant thing, when they are taken *en passant*, without being made a principal object. Once make them so, and they are immediately felt to be insufficient. They will not bear a scrutinizing examination. Ask yourself whether you are happy, and you cease to be so. The only chance is to treat, not happiness, but some end external to it, as the purpose of life.[7]

For this reason happiness is sometimes pictured as a blue bird that turns black when you try to catch it.

Thus the paradox arises of trying to be happy or of recommending to others that they should seek happiness; it is almost sure to be self-defeating. And a theory that is impossible to follow without interfering with the goal of the theory itself is rather useless.

In the next chapter we will see whether Utilitarianism, a nineteenth century form of hedonism, can meet these objections successfully.

Notes

1. S. Freud, *The Complete Introductory Lectures on Psychoanalysis,* trans. J. Strachey (New York: W. W. Norton, 1966), 356.
2. Claude Adrien Helvétius, *De l'Espirit: Or Essays on the Mind and Its Several Faculties* (New York: B. Franklin, 1970 [from 1758 edition]), Essay II, Chapter 9.

3. This epistemological position may have been derived from Plato's *Theaetetus* and was discussed most fully in philosophic history by the British empiricists. See especially John Locke, *An Essay Concerning Human Understanding*, Book 2, Chapters 1–8, Book 4, Chapters 4 and 11; and George Berkeley, *A Treatise Concerning the Principles of Human Knowledge*, "Of Principles of Human Knowledge."

4. The philosopher who is usually attributed with presenting the most thorough exposition of reason controlling the passions is Benedict de Spinoza (1632–1677). See his *Ethics*, "Of Human Bondage." For a literary counterpart read the novel by Somerset Maugham of the same name.

5. An interesting and useful distinction is made by Epicurus between "kenetic" pleasures such as eating rich and exotic food and "catastemic" pleasures such as not being hungry or thirsty. The former depend on some activity and last only the duration of that activity while the latter come from a state of being and can be extended indefinitely. The Epicureans obviously endorsed catastemic pleasures with the pinnacle being ataraxia, the enduring pleasures of the mind.

6. It is worth noting that the two major points in the Epicurean philosophy were made previously by the Cyrenaics. Hegesias pointed out the superior virtue of avoiding pain rather than seeking pleasure and Anniceris championed the joys of friendship.

7. *Autobiography of John Stuart Mill* (New York: Columbia University Press, 1924), 100.

Bibliography

ATKINSON, R. F. *Conduct: An Introduction to Moral Philosophy*. London: Macmillan, 1969.

BAIER, KURT. *The Moral Point of View*. Ithaca: Cornell University Press, 1958, 266–77.

BAILEY, C. *The Greek Atomists and Epicurus*. Oxford: Clarendon Press, 1928, Part 2, Chapter 10.

BEDFORD, ERROL. "Pleasure and Belief." *Proceedings of the Aristotelian Society* Supp. 33 (1959): 281–304.

BLAKE, R. M. "Why Not Hedonism? A Protest." *International Journal of Ethics*, 37 (1926–27): 1–18.

BOURKE, V. J. *History of Ethics*, Vol. 1. New York: Doubleday, 1970.

BURNET, JOHN. *Early Greek Philosophy*. London: A. and C. Black, 1930.

CARRITT, E. F. *Ethical and Political Thinking*. Oxford: Clarendon Press, 1947, Chapters 4 and 8.

CORNFORD, F. M. *Before and After Socrates*. New York: Macmillan, 1932.

DE WITT, N. W. *Epicurus and His Philosophy*. Minneapolis: University of Minnesota Press, 1954.

DIGBY, JOHN. *Epicurus's Morals*. London: 1712.

EDWARDS, REM B. *Pleasures and Pains: A Theory of Qualitative Hedonism*. Ithaca: Cornell University Press, 1979.

FESTUGIERE, A. J. *Epicurus and His Gods*. Cambridge: Harvard University Press, 1956.

EPICURUS. *The Extant Remains*, trans. C. Bailey. Oxford: Clarendon Press, 1926.

FRANKEL, CHARLES. *The Case for Modern Man*. New York: Harper and Brothers, 1956.

FRANKENA, W. K., AND J. T. GRANROSE, EDS. *Introductory Readings in Ethics*. Englewood Cliffs, N.J.: Prentice-Hall, 1974.

FULLER, B. A. G. *History of Greek Philosophy: Thales to Democritus*. New York: Henry Holt, 1923.

GALLIE, W. B. "Pleasure." *Proceedings of the Aristotelian Society* 28 (1954): 147–64.

GALLOP, DAVID. "True and False Pleasures." *Philosophical Quarterly* 10 (1960): 331–42.

GOSLING. J. C. B., AND C. C. W. TAYLOR. *The Greeks on Pleasure.* Oxford: Clarendon
    Press, 1982.
HIBLER, RICHARD W. *Happiness Through Tranquility: The School of Epicurus.*
    Washington, D.C.: University Press of America, 1984.
HICKS, R. D. *Stoic and Epicurean.* New York: Russell and Russell, 1962, Chapter 5.
HOLT, E. B. *The Freudian Wish and Its Place in Ethics.* New York: Henry Holt, 1915.
ISENBERG, A., KENNICK W., AND TERENCE PENELHUM. "Pleasure and Falsity." *American
    Philosophical Quarterly* 1 (1964): 81–100.
LONG, A. A. *Hellenistic Philosophy: Stoics, Epicureans, Sceptics.* London: Duckworth,
    1974, Chapter 2.
MACINTYRE, ALASDAIR. *A Short History of Ethics.* New York: Macmillan, 1966.
MANSER, A. R. "Pleasure." *Proceedings of the Aristotelian Society* 61 (1960–61): 223–38.
MAYO, THOMAS F. *Epicurus in England 1650–1725.* Dallas: University of Texas Press,
    1934.
McNAUGHTON, R. M. "A Metrical Concept of Happiness." *Philosophy and
    Phenomenological Research* 14 (1953): 172–83.
MOORE, G. E. *Principia Ethica.* Cambridge: Cambridge University Press, 1903,
    Chapter 3.
NICHOLS, JAMES H. *Epicurean Political Philosophy.* Ithaca: Cornell University Press, 1977.
NOWELL-SMITH, P. H. *Ethics.* Harmondsworth, England: Penguin Books, 1954,
    Chapter 10.
OATES, WHITNEY J., ED. *The Stoic and Epicurean Philosophers.* New York: Random
    House, 1940.
PANICHAS, G. A. *Epicurus.* New York: Twayne, 1967.
PATER, WALTER. *Marius the Epicurean.* New York: Macmillan, 1928.
PENELHUM, TERENCE. "The Logic of Pleasure." *Philosophy and Phenomenological
    Research* 17 (1957): 488–503.
PERRY, B. B. *General Theory of Value.* New York: Longmans Green, 1926, Chapter 21.
PERRY, DAVID L. *The Concept of Pleasure.* The Hague, Holland: Mouton, 1967.
PRATT, J. B. *Reason in the Art of Living.* New York: Macmillan, 1949, Chapters 10–12
    and 13.
RIST, J. M. *Epicurus.* London: Cambridge University Press, 1972, Chapter 6.
ROBIN, L. *Greek Thought.* London: Kegan Paul, 1928.
RUSSELL, BERTRAND. *The Conquest of Happiness.* London: Allen and Unwin, 1930.
SIDGWICK, H. *The Methods of Ethics.* New York: Macmillan, 1901.
STACE, W. T. *A Critical History of Greek Philosophy.* New York: Macmillan, 1920.
TAYLOR, A. E. *Epicurus.* London: Constable, 1911.
THALBERG, IRVING. "False Pleasures." *Journal of Philosophy* 59 (1962): 65–74.
VAUGHAN, FREDERICK. *The Tradition of Political Hedonism.* New York: Fordham
    University Press, 1982.
WALLACE, W. *Epicureanism.* New York: Pott, Young, 1880.
WATSON, JOHN. *Hedonistic Theories from Aristippus to Spencer.* Glasgow: 1898.
WILLIAMS, B. A. O. "Pleasure and Belief." *Proceedings of the Aristotelian Society* Supp.
    33 (1959): 57–72.
YUTANG, LIN. *The Importance of Living.* New York: Day, 1937.
ZELLER, E. *Outlines of the History of Greek Philosophy.* New York: Henry Holt, 1931.

CHAPTER 5

Utilitarianism

The hedonistic ethic did not undergo any significant changes during the Middle Ages or the Renaissance and appears to have lapsed into a dormant state. This is mainly due to the bad name it acquired from Christianity. Not only was hedonism viewed as a self-centered rather than a god-centered approach to living (stemming from pagan roots), but it was seen as basically a sensuous philosophy, encouraging the enjoyment of bodily pleasure. To the early Christian, the temptations of the flesh were Satan's instruments for corrupting man's soul. The body was the seat of sin while the spirit was as an aspect of the Holy Ghost resident in man. If a purification of the soul was to take place and man made fit to live in eternity with god, the flesh had to be mortified and mastered; it could not be indulged in its desires. Hedonism, as a philosophy associated with the voluptuous, simply had no place in this pure cosmic vision.

Some development of the theory took place in the seventeenth century philosophies of Thomas Hobbes (1588–1679), John Locke (1632–1704), and Pierre Gassendi (1592–1655), and again in the eighteenth century writings of Francis Hutcheson (1694–1746) and David Hume (1711–1776), although Hume merely described the basis of moral judgments. However, significant changes did not take place until the nineteenth century when two outstanding English philosophers, Jeremy Bentham (1748–1832) and his intellectual offspring John Stuart Mill (1806–1873), virtually transformed hedonism into a highly moral doctrine, radically different from that of the ancient Greeks.

Specifically, Bentham and Mill rewrote the hedonistic ethic along practical, humanitarian lines, developing a social hedonism that Mill christened *utilitarianism*. Bentham's "principle of utility," which forms the core of the utilitarian system, is described as "that principle which approves or disapproves of every action whatsoever, according to the tendency which it appears to have to augment or diminish the happiness of the party whose interest is in question." Or as it was more simply rendered, we ought to seek "the greatest amount of happiness for the greatest number of persons." Instead of desiring happiness for ourselves alone we should foster it for humanity in general, and this happiness should be as full and as extensive as possible. Success in living is to be gauged by the degree to which we have made other people happy not just ourselves.

The term *utilitarian* that Mill used has, in fact, a much wider meaning in philosophy. It signifies the broad ethical view that acts should be judged in terms of whether they produce good or bad results. That is, if an action leads to a worthwhile end then it is judged to be morally right; if, on the other hand, unfavorable consequences result then it is considered wrong. Mill actually affirmed a hedonistic version of utilitarianism, which states that actions should be evaluated according to whether they promote or hinder the specific end of happiness. However, his theory became so influential that it is now practically synonymous with utilitarianism in general, and when *utilitarian* is used today it usually designates someone who endorses the "greatest happiness" principle.

In any case, Bentham and Mill obviously held a much more altruistic and humane doctrine than that of the Cyrenaics and Epicureans. The latter were concerned with whether enjoyment should be physical, mental, immediate, extended, and so forth, but it was always enjoyment for the individual that was at issue. The utilitarians, by contrast, wanted happiness for the community not just for themselves. The agent performing the act is only one person and does not matter any more or any less than anyone else. Therefore, it is not a question of sacrificing oneself for one's fellow man (as in Christian martyrdom) or putting oneself first (as in Greek hedonism) but of treating oneself as equally deserving of happiness. Everyone's happiness is important, including one's own, or as the utilitarians put it, each is to count for one and none for more than one.

Mill described the utilitarian position in the following terms: "the happiness which forms the utilitarian standard of what is right in conduct is not the agent's own happiness but that of all concerned. As between his own happiness and that of others, utilitarianism requires him to be as strictly impartial as a disinterested and benevolent spectator." He then went on to identify this altruism with the highest Christian principles. "In the golden rule of Jesus of Nazareth, we read the complete spirit of the ethics of utility. 'To do as you would be done by,' and 'to love your neighbor as yourself,' constitute the ideal perfection of utilitarian morality."[1]

According to the distinction made previously, we can clearly see that the utilitarians are universalistic rather than individualistic hedonists. They transmuted a self-centered philosophy that extolled enjoyment for the individual into an other-directed ethic aimed at social improvement. Although the utilitarians continued to regard themselves as hedonists (from *hedone,* "pleasure"), they conflated happiness and pleasure, treating them interchangeably, and attempted to apply the principles of universalistic hedonism to effect political change. Their aim was to reduce the amount of misery for mankind and increase the sum of human happiness.

Bentham, for instance, worked continuously for the adoption of prison reform and the abolition of the notorious Botany Bay system of penology then in effect. He was especially interested in revising the system of classifying crimes; to his mind, the gravity of the offense should not be the criterion used but the unhappiness and misery that the crime caused to the victims. In addition, he organized a political party called the democratic or philosophical radicals, which elected to Parliament several strong spokesmen for social programs based entirely on utilitarian principles. Mill also was politically involved, serving as a member of the House of Commons during three sessions and supporting passage of the Reform Bill of 1865, which transferred power from the landed gentry to the urban bourgeoisie. He even tried to add an amendment to the bill dealing with women's voting rights, and although he was not successful his efforts resulted in the formation of the National Society for Women's Suffrage. In his estimation, as reported in his *Autobiography*, this was "by far the most important, perhaps the only really important, public service I performed."[2]

In both theory and practice then the utilitarians were committed to the standard of universal happiness not some abstract concept far removed from human welfare. They were men with a strong social conscience, dedicated to increasing human happiness through direct legislative action and the more indirect influence of their ideas. The ancient Greeks could write manuals for personal enjoyment in living but the utilitarians wanted to enlarge the circle of happiness to include the whole of humanity. Mill was typical when he wrote that "his object in life [was] to be a reformer of the world." In this respect he resembled his contemporary Karl Marx, whose primary aim was not so much to understand the world as to change it. In short, he was no armchair philosopher but a concerned activist.

The utilitarians also tried to be down-to-earth in laying the groundwork for their principles, basing their ethics on the psychological facts of human behavior. In a famous passage in his *Introduction to the Principles of Morals and Legislation* (a selection from which appears in this chapter) Jeremy Bentham wrote, "Nature has placed mankind under the guidance of two sovereign masters, *pain* and *pleasure*. It is for them alone to point out what we ought to do, as well as to determine what we shall do." In saying this, Bentham was claiming that the value of pleasure as a good can be seen in the fact that people are dominated by the desire for pleasure. Since people *do* seek pleasure then pleasure *ought* to be sought; the psychological description furnishes the grounds for the ethical value.

The corresponding passage in John Stuart Mill's *Utilitarianism*, which also will be quoted more fully, is as follows:

> The only proof capable of being given that an object is visible is that people actually see it. The only proof that a sound is audible is that people hear it; and so of the other sources of our experience. In like manner, I apprehend, the sole evidence it is possible to produce that anything is desirable is that people do actually desire it. . . . No reason can be given why the general happiness is desirable except that each person, so far as he believes it to be attainable, desires his own happiness.

Here again the proof of the worth of happiness is said to lie in the fact that everyone desires it.

We can see that the utilitarians were not only universalistic rather than individualistic hedonists but endorsed both psychological and ethical hedonism, the former assumed to prove the latter. But this juxtaposition presented a problem for them. If pleasure and pain are our sovereign masters and everyone seeks his own happiness, how then is it possible for people to want happiness for others? How can the utilitarian combine both psychological and universal hedonism.

To solve this problem Bentham described four "sanctions" or "sources of pain and pleasure," three of which would induce the individual to seek the happiness of the community:

1. The "physical" sanction refers to the effects of natural causes such as pleas-

ant weather or tasty food or on the other hand calamities such as floods and famines that affect us because of our susceptibility to pain.

2. The "political" sanction stems from governmental authority that can reward or punish us in accordance with the power of the state.
3. "Moral" or "popular" sanctions arise from the interaction with people in our social environment — our neighbors who may be a hindrance or a help according to their response to our moral character.
4. The final sanction is the "religious" one by which god can bless or punish us, or even cause anxiety through the dread of punishment to come.

In order to get people to serve the ends of the community and not just themselves political, moral, and religious sanctions are used. Each one exerts a powerful influence on individual behavior. For example, the government ensures that those who harm others are suitably punished so that the pain or fear of pain exceeds the pleasure obtained from the selfish act. Likewise, the popular sentiments of society control the person by approval and disapproval, inclusion and ostracism; everyone is judged by his fellow man according to whether his motives embrace the public good or are only rooted in personal gain. Finally, the institution of religion exercises a restraining force on the individual, plaguing the sinner's conscience in this life and threatening him with eternal torment in the next.

In describing these sanctions as the way in which people can be made to consider the interests of others, Bentham is not actually demonstrating how altruistic motives can be built into people. His account only shows how a social conscience can be formed through enlightened self-interest. His universalistic hedonism is founded on psychological hedonism in the sense that he believes a personal concern with obtaining pleasure and avoiding pain will make utilitarianism work.

John Stuart Mill used a rather unusual line of reasoning in this connection, arguing that "Happiness is a good; each person's happiness is a good to that person, and the general happiness, therefore, a good to the aggregate of persons." But as the Scottish essayist Thomas Carlyle pointed out, this is equivalent to saying that if each pig wants all the swill in the trough for itself, then a litter of pigs will desire each member to have its share of the swill. Unsound reasoning of this kind is surprising in Mill, whose book *A System of Logic* was a standard work in the field for many years.

Perhaps a closer rendering of Mill's views on the relation between personal wants and the general welfare can be found in the following passage: "The utilitarian morality does recognize in human beings the power of sacrificing their own greatest good for the good of others. It only refuses to admit that the sacrifice is itself a good. A sacrifice which does not increase or tend to increase the sum total of happiness, it considers as wasted." Mill's position seems to be that although all people want personal happiness they can choose otherwise. Self-sacrifice is possible, but it should only be for the happiness of mankind not in the service of some abstract virtue. In other words, his psychological hedonism is not absolute but a description of the general desires that motivate human beings. The individual is capable of resigning his portion of happiness and on occasion should do so to increase the amount of happiness in the world at large.

Fortunately, self-sacrifice is rarely needed because "the social feelings of mankind; the desire to be in unity with our fellow-creatures [is] a powerful principle of human nature." Promoting the common good therefore tends to make us happy because we are naturally social beings.

Although the utilitarians wanted to make their theory as logically consistent as possible, their main concern was to translate theory into practice, and for this they needed a concrete program. For Bentham such a program entailed the construction of a scientific method for determining which actions would actually increase human happiness. He was very impressed with the emerging science of his day and wanted to incorporate its precision into his philosophy; in this way he could increase the likelihood that more pleasure would be obtained for more people.[3] Mill also wanted to offer a practical system of utilitarian ethics and all of his writings are designed for that purpose. As we shall see, however, he was less concerned with being scientific than with doing justice to human values and feelings.

Jeremy Bentham: The Greatest Happiness for the Greatest Number

The scheme Bentham devised for assessing the pleasure quotient of actions he termed the "hedonic calculus" or "calculus of pleasures." By using this mathematical model he believed he could scientifically measure the amount of pleasure or pain that any action would yield. Those actions that provided more pleasure obviously were preferable to those that brought less. Regardless of the agent's motive, the worth of an action was to be judged in terms of its pleasurable consequences and this the hedonic calculus would determine.

More specifically, Bentham thought he could reduce pleasure to certain elements that might be called *hedons,* units of pleasure or pain capable of being added and subtracted. Furthermore, he wanted to isolate each of the factors involved in pleasure and to rate actions according to the number of hedons provided by all the factors combined. Being aware of the history of hedonism, Bentham knew that the Cyrenaics had identified some important considerations such as intensity and immediacy and that the Epicureans had also included good points in their definition of happiness, that tranquility, duration, and the like were also worthwhile. To Bentham, it was not a matter of pitting the two against each other as mutually exclusive alternatives but of taking each school of thought into account; an action was to be given numerical values relative to the degree of pleasure or pain that both Cyrenaic and Epicurean features provided.

Bentham found that, upon analysis, seven factors emerged that appeared significant, and he called them his seven "marks." The first of these marks was *intensity,* which was, of course, stressed more strongly by the Cyrenaics. All else being equal, we would want our pleasures to be as strong as possible. *Duration,* the second factor, refers to the length of the pleasure, whether extended or brief. A pleasure that lasts longer is normally better than one of short duration, and this consideration counted heavily with the Epicureans. By its very nature, duration stands in opposition to intensity but both seem to be important factors, and some activities involve acuteness of sensation while others tend toward prolongation.

Certainty or *uncertainty* is another mark, the meaning of which is self-evident. An experience that we are certain to enjoy would be given a much higher rating than one that we are unsure about. In this case Bentham is recognizing the Cyrenaic concern with enjoyment we can depend upon rather than the kind that is dubious or merely possible. The certainty or uncertainty of a pleasure could be a function of its nearness, and this leads to Bentham's fourth mark, *propinquity* or *remoteness*. This mark means that a pleasurable experience that can be enjoyed immediately is superior to that which one hopes to obtain at some future time. The greater the proximity the better, because when we defer pleasures, hoping to enjoy them at some future point, we run the risk of never actually experiencing them at all. Nearer pleasures stand a much better chance of being enjoyed, as the Cyrenaics pointed out.

A fifth factor, *fecundity* (or fruitfulness), refers to the tendency of a pleasure to be "followed by sensations of the *same* kind: That is, pleasures, if it be pleasures: pains, if it be a pain." If a pleasant or disagreeable experience leads to similar experiences rather than those of an opposite kind, then it can be rated high in fecundity. Here Bentham was acknowledging the merit of the Epicurean point that we must be concerned with future effects. Some pleasures should be avoided because they lead to subsequent misery (for example, hard drugs), whereas some pains should be endured because of future benefits (for example, the struggle to obtain a college education); seminal pleasures that contain the seeds for additional pleasures are, of course, best of all.

By including fecundity Bentham also was counterbalancing the factor of intensity. For as intensity increases, fecundity tends to decrease; the two vary in inverse ratio. That is, the greater the intensity of the pleasure the more likely it is to be followed by feelings of pain and the lower it is in fecundity. To take a modern example, the faster a person drives, looking for the thrill of speed, the greater the chance of being injured in a crash. In metaphorical terms, the taller the mountain the deeper the valley, the higher the wave the lower the trough. Fecundity as well as duration then counterbalance Bentham's endorsement of intensity.[4]

Still another factor included in Bentham's list is *purity*, which is defined as the chance a pleasure or pain has "of *not* being followed by sensations of the *opposite* kinds: that is, pains, if it be a pleasure: pleasures, if it be a pain." This too pays deference to the Epicurean concern with the effects of action and the overall pleasure content of our lives. (See the Epicurean critique of Cyrenaic hedonism described in Chapter 4.)

The final mark is *extent*, meaning the number of persons to whom the pleasure or pain extends. A pleasurable action that affects more people is preferable to one affecting fewer people, whereas painful actions are undesirable and their extent should be minimized. As a utilitarian, of course, Bentham was committed to the principle of happiness for the greatest number of people.

Bentham assumed that these seven marks exhaustively accounted for the main factors involved in the attainment of pleasure. He also believed that he had culled the best of the hedonistic thought of the past since he had incorporated into his system the Cyrenaic factors of intensity, certainty, and propinquity and the Epicurean values of duration, fecundity, and purity. In addition he had added his own utilitarian factor of extent in order to ensure that the happiness of all would be a consideration.

Having determined the relevant factors Bentham then employed them in his hedonic calculus in the following way. A person would draw up a list of all the pleasures that could be derived from a given action. The value of each pleasure would then be determined by applying each of the seven marks and the number of hedons would thereby be determined. The same process would be carried out with regard to the pains. Finally, the total number of negatives would be subtracted from the total of positives to see whether the act was pleasurable overall. If a total of positive hedons resulted then the act could be considered justified, but if the net result showed pain to predominate then the act should not be performed.

Two points about this hedonic calculus should be made in passing. First, the individual is the one who decides the number of hedons to award for each factor, but the factors involved in the action are an objective matter. Thus, there is a blend of subjectivity and objectivity in the system, and two people might well assign very different numbers. Second, in using this scheme people should give an honest appraisal of the number of hedons entailed for each mark and not "rig" the figures. In other words, one should not be biased in favor of an act and assign numbers so as to prove that it is highly enjoyable. This could be self-defeating and would negate the purpose of the calculus, which is to establish scientifically which actions will, in fact, yield the most pleasure.

If this scheme were used in the right way, Bentham believed, the aims of utilitarianism would be effectively fostered. We could then predict with mathematical accuracy which actions would prove more pleasurable. The greatest happiness for the greatest number, which was the highest ethical ideal, could be realized through the instrument of the calculus.

In the selection that follows from *An Introduction to the Principles of Morals and Legislation* we will let Bentham speak for himself, describing the nature, foundation, inducements, and measurement of his utilitarian philosophy. Other writings of Bentham include *Defence of Usury* (1787), *A Table of the Springs of Action* (1815), and *Constitutional Code for the Use of All Nations* (1830).

Introduction to Morals and Legislation*

CHAPTER I

Of the Principle of Utility

I. Nature has placed mankind under the governance of two sovereign masters, *pain* and *pleasure*. It is for them alone to point out what we ought to do, as well as to determine what we shall do. On the one hand the standard of right and wrong, on the other the chain of causes and effects, are fastened to their throne. They govern us in all we do, in all we say, in all we think: every effort we can make to throw off our subjection, will serve but to demonstrate and confirm it. In words a man may pretend to abjure their

*Reprinted from Jeremy Bentham, *An Introduction to the Principles of Morals and Legislation* (Oxford: Oxford University Press, 1823).

empire: but in reality he will remain subject to it all the while. The *principle of utility* recognizes this subjection, and assumes it for the foundation of that system, the object of which is to rear the fabric of felicity by the hands of reason and of law. Systems which attempt to question it, deal in sounds instead of sense, in caprice instead of reason, in darkness instead of light.

But enough of metaphor and declamation: it is not by such means that moral science is to be improved.

II. The principle of utility is the foundation of the present work: it will be proper therefore at the outset to give an explicit and determinate account of what is meant by it. By the principle of utility is meant that principle which approves or disapproves of every action whatsoever, according to the tendency which it appears to have to augment or diminish the happiness of the party whose interest is in question: or, what is the same thing in other words, to promote or to oppose that happiness. I say of every action whatsoever; and therefore not only of every action of a private individual, but of every measure of government.

III. By utility is meant that property in any object, whereby it tends to produce benefit, advantage, pleasure, good, or happiness, (all this in the present case comes to the same thing) or (what comes again to the same thing) to prevent the happening of mischief, pain, evil, or unhappiness to the party whose interest is considered: if that party be the community in general, then the happiness of the community: if a particular individual, then the happiness of that individual.

IV. The interest of the community is one of the most general expressions that can occur in the phraseology of morals: no wonder that the meaning of it is often lost. When it has a meaning, it is this. The community is a fictitious *body*, composed of the individual persons who are considered as constituting as it were its *members*. The interest of the community then is, what? — the sum of the interests of the several members who compose it.

V. It is in vain to talk of the interest of the community, without understanding what is the interest of the individual. A thing is said to promote the interest, or to be *for* the interest, of an individual, when it tends to add to the sum total of his pleasures: or, what comes to the same thing, to diminish the sum total of his pains.

VI. An action then may be said to be conformable to the principle of utility, or, for shortness sake, to utility, (meaning with respect to the community at large) when the tendency it has to augment the happiness of the community is greater than any it has to diminish it.

VII. A measure of government (which is but a particular kind of action, performed by a particular person or persons) may be said to be conformable to or dictated by the principle of utility, when in like manner the tendency which it has to augment the happiness of the community is greater than any which it has to diminish it.

VIII. When an action, or in particular a measure of government, is supposed by a man to be conformable to the principle of utility, it may be convenient, for the purposes of discourse, to imagine a kind of law or dictate, called a law or dictate of utility: and to speak of the action in question, as being conformable to such law or dictate.

IX. A man may be said to be a partisan of the principle of utility, when the approbation or disapprobation he annexes to any action, or to any measure, is determined by and proportioned to the tendency which he conceives it to have to augment or to diminish the happiness of the community: or in other words, to its conformity or unconformity to the laws or dictates of utility.

X. Of an action that is conformable to the principle of utility one may always say either that it is one that ought to be done, or at least that it is not one that ought not to be done. One may say also, that it is right it should be done; at least that it is not wrong it should be done: that it is a right action; at least that it is not a wrong action. When thus interpreted, the words *ought*, and *right* and *wrong*, and others of that stamp, have a meaning: when otherwise, they have none.

XI. Has the rectitude of this principle been ever formally contested? It should seem that it had, by those who have not known what they have been meaning. Is it susceptible of any direct proof? it should seem not: for that which is used to prove every thing else, cannot itself be proved: a chain of proofs must have their commencement somewhere. To give such proof is as impossible as it is needless.

XII. Not that there is or ever has been that human creature breathing, however stupid or perverse, who has not on many, perhaps on most occasions of his life, deferred to it. By the natural constitution of the human frame, on most occasions of their lives men in general embrace this principle, without thinking of it: if not for the ordering of their own actions, yet for the trying of their own actions, as well as those of other men. There have been, at the same time, not many, perhaps, even of the most intelligent, who have been disposed to embrace it purely and without reserve. There are even few who have not taken some occasion or other to quarrel with it, either on account of their not understanding always how to apply it, or on account of some prejudice or other which they were afraid to examine into, or could not bear to part with. For such is the stuff that man is made of: in principle and in practice, in a right track and in a wrong one, the rarest of all human qualities is consistency.

XIII. When a man attempts to combat the principle of utility, it is with reasons drawn, without his being aware of it, from that very principle itself. His arguments, if they prove any thing, prove not that the principle is *wrong*, but that, according to the applications he supposes to be made of it, it is *misapplied*. Is it possible for a man to move the earth? Yes; but he must first find out another earth to stand upon.

XIV. To disprove the propriety of it by arguments is impossible; but, from the causes that have been mentioned, or from some confused or partial view of it, a man may happen to be disposed not to relish it. Where this is the case, if he thinks the settling of his opinions on such a subject worth the trouble, let him take the following steps, and at length, perhaps, he may come to reconcile himself to it.

1. Let him settle with himself, whether he would wish to discard this principle altogether; if so, let him consider what it is that all his reasonings (in matters of politics especially) can amount to?

2. If he would, let him settle with himself, whether he would judge and act without any principle, or whether there is any other he would judge and act by?

3. If there be, let him examine and satisfy himself whether the principle he thinks he has found is really any separate intelligible principle; or whether it be not a mere principle in words, a kind of phrase, which at bottom expresses neither more nor less than the mere averment of his own unfounded sentiments; that is, what in another person he might be apt to call caprice?

4. If he is inclined to think that his own approbation or disapprobation, annexed to the idea of an act, without any regard to its consequences, is a sufficient foundation for him to judge and act upon, let him ask himself whether his sentiment is to be a standard of right and wrong, with respect to every other man, or whether every man's sentiment has the same privilege of being a standard to itself?

5. In the first case, let him ask himself whether his principle is not despotical, and hostile to all the rest of the human race?

6. In the second case, whether it is not anarchical, and whether at this rate there are not as many different standards of right and wrong as there are men? and whether even to the same man, the same thing, which is right to-day, may not (without the least change in its nature) be wrong tomorrow? and whether the same thing is not right and wrong in the same place at the same time? and in either case, whether all argument is not at an end? and whether, when two men have said, 'I like this,' and 'I don't like it,' they can (upon such a principle) have any thing more to say?

7. If he should have said to himself, No: for that the sentiment which he proposes as a standard must be grounded on reflection, let him say on what particulars the reflection is to turn? if on particulars having relation to the utility of the act, then let him say whether this is not deserting his own principle, and borrowing assistance from that very one in opposition to which he sets it up: or if not on those particulars, on what other particulars?

8. If he should be for compounding the matter, and adopting his own principle in part, and the principle of utility in part, let him say how far he will adopt it?

9. When he has settled with himself where he will stop, then let him ask himself how he justifies to himself the adopting it so far? and why he will not adopt it any farther?

10. Admitting any other principle than the principle of utility to be a right principle, a principle that it is right for a man to pursue; admitting (what is not true) that the word *right* can have a meaning without reference to utility,

let him say whether there is any such thing as a *motive* that a man can have to pursue the dictates of it: if there is, let him say what that motive is, and how it is to be distinguished from those which enforce the dictates of utility: if not, then lastly let him say what it is this other principle can be good for?

. . .

CHAPTER III

Of the Four Sanctions or Sources of Pain and Pleasure

I. It has been shown that the happiness of the individuals, of whom a community is composed, that is their pleasures and their security, is the end and the sole end which the legislator ought to have in view: the sole standard, in conformity to which each individual ought, as far as depends upon the legislator, to be *made* to fashion his behaviour. But whether it be this or any thing else that is to be *done,* there is nothing by which a man can ultimately be *made* to do it, but either pain or pleasure. Having taken a general view of these two grand objects (viz. pleasure, and what comes to the same thing, immunity from pain) in the character of *final* causes; it will be necessary to take a view of pleasure and pain itself, in the character of *efficient* causes or means.

II. There are four distinguishable sources from which pleasure and pain are in use to flow: considered separately, they may be termed the *physical,* the *political,* the *moral,* and the *religious:* and inasmuch as the pleasures and pains belonging to each of them are capable of giving a binding force to any law or rule of conduct, they may all of them be termed sanctions.*

III. If it be in the present life, and from the ordinary course of nature, not purposely modified by the interposition of the will of any human being, nor by any extraordinary interposition of any superior invisible being, that the pleasure or the pain takes place or is expected, it may be said to issue from or to belong to the *physical sanction.*

---

*Sanctio, in Latin, was used to signify the *act of binding,* and, by a common grammatical transition, *any thing which serves to bind a man:* to wit, to the observance of such or such a mode of conduct. According to a Latin grammarian, the import of the word is derived by rather a far-fetched process (such as those commonly are, and in a great measure indeed must be, by which intellectual ideas are derived from sensible ones) from the word *sanguis,* blood: because, among the Romans, with a view to inculcate into the people a persuasion that such or such a mode of conduct would be rendered obligatory upon a man by the force of what I call the religious sanction (that is, that he would be made to suffer by the extraordinary interposition of some superior being, if he failed to observe the mode of conduct in question) certain ceremonies were contrived by the priests: in the course of which ceremonies the blood of victims was made use of.

A Sanction then is a source of obligatory powers or *motives:* that is, of *pains* and *pleasures:* which, according as they are connected with such or such modes of conduct, operate, and are indeed the only things which can operate, as *motives.*

IV. If at the hands of a *particular* person or set of persons in the community, who under names correspondent to that of *judge,* are chosen for the particular purpose of dispensing it, according to the will of the sovereign or supreme ruling power in the state, it may be said to issue from the *political sanction.*

V. If at the hands of such *chance* persons in the community, as the party in question may happen in the course of his life to have concerns with, according to each man's spontaneous disposition, and not according to any settled or concerted rule, it may be said to issue from the *moral* or *popular sanction.***

VI. If from the immediate hand of a superior invisible being, either in the present life, or in a future, it may be said to issue from the *religious sanction.*

VII. Pleasures or pains which may be expected to issue from the *physical, political,* or *moral* sanctions, must all of them be expected to be experienced, if ever, in the *present* life: those which may be expected to issue from the *religious* sanction, may be expected to be experienced either in the *present* life or in a *future.*

VIII. Those which can be experienced in the present life, can of course be no others than such as human nature in the course of the present life is susceptible of: and from each of these sources may flow all the pleasures or pains of which, in the course of the present life, human nature is susceptible. With regard to these then (with which alone we have in this place any concern) those of them which belong to any one of those sanctions, differ not ultimately in kind from those which belong to any one of the other three: the only difference there is among them lies in the circumstances that accompany their production. A suffering which befalls a man in the natural and spontaneous course of things, shall be styled, for instance, a *calamity:* in which case, if it be supposed to befall him through any imprudence of his, it may be styled a punishment issuing from the physical sanction. Now this same suffering, if inflicted by the law, will be what is commonly called a *punishment;* if incurred for want of any friendly assistance, which the misconduct, or supposed misconduct, of the sufferer has occasioned to be withholden, a punishment issuing from the *moral* sanction; if through the immediate interposition of a particular providence, a punishment issuing from the religious sanction.

IX. A man's goods, or his person, are consumed by fire. If this happened to him by what is called an accident, it was a calamity; if by reason of his own imprudence (for instance, from his neglecting to put his candle out) it may be styled a punishment of the physical sanction: if it happened to him by the sentence of the political magistrate, a punishment belonging to the political sanction; that is, what is commonly called a punishment: if for want of any

***Better termed *popular,* as more directly indicative of its constituent cause; as likewise of its relation to the more common phrase *public opinion,* in French *opinion publique,* the name there given to that tutelary power, of which of late so much is said, and by which so much is done. The latter appellation is however unhappy and inexpressive; since if *opinion* is material, it is only in virtue of the influence it exercises over action, through the medium of the affections and the will.

assistance which his *neighbour* withheld from him out of some dislike to his *moral* character, a punishment of the *moral* sanction: if by an immediate act of *God's* displeasure, manifested on account of some *sin* commited by him, or through any distraction of mind, occasioned by the dread of such displeasure, a punishment of the *religious* sanction.

X. As to such of the pleasures and pains belonging to the religious sanction, as regard a future life, of what kind these may be we cannot know. These lie not open to our observation. During the present life they are matter only of expectation: and, whether that expectation be derived from natural or revealed religion, the particular kind of pleasure or pain, if it be different from all those which lie open to our observation, is what we can have no idea of. The best ideas we can obtain of such pains and pleasures are altogether unliquidated in point of quality. In what other respects our ideas of them *may* be liquidated will be considered in another place.

XI. Of these four sanctions the physical is altogether, we may observe, the ground-work of the political and the moral: so is it also of the religious, in as far as the latter bears relation to the present life. It is included in each of those other three. This may operate in any case, (that is, any of the pains or pleasures belonging to it may operate) independently of *them:* none of *them* can operate but by means of this. In a word, the powers of nature may operate of themselves; but neither the magistrate, nor men at large, *can* operate, nor is God in the case in question *supposed* to operate, but through the powers of nature.

XII. For these four objects, which in their nature have so much in common, it seemed of use to find a common name. It seemed of use, in the first place, for the convenience of giving a name to certain pleasures and pains, for which a name equally characteristic could hardly otherwise have been found: in the second place, for the sake of holding up the efficacy of certain moral forces, the influence of which is apt not to be sufficiently attended to. Does the political sanction exert an influence over the conduct of mankind? The moral, the religious sanctions do so too. In every inch of his career are the operations of the political magistrate liable to be aided or impeded by these two foreign powers: who, one or other of them, or both, are sure to be either his rivals or his allies. Does it happen to him to leave them out in his calculations? he will be sure almost to find himself mistaken in the result. Of all this we shall find abundant proofs in the sequel of this work. It behooves him, therefore, to have them continually before his eyes; and that under such a name as exhibits the relation they bear to his own purposes and designs.

CHAPTER IV

Value of a Lot of Pleasure or Pain, How to Be Measured

I. Pleasures then, and the avoidance of pains, are the *ends* which the legislator has in view: it behooves him therefore to understand their *value.*

Pleasures and pains are the *instruments* he has to work with: it behooves him therefore to understand their force, which is again, in other words, their value.

II. To a person considered *by himself*, the value of a pleasure or pain considered *by itself*, will be greater or less, according to the four following circumstances:*

1. Its *intensity.*
2. Its *duration.*
3. Its *certainty* or *uncertainty.*
4. Its *propinquity* or *remoteness.*

III. These are the circumstances which are to be considered in estimating a pleasure or a pain considered each of them by itself. But when the value of any pleasure or pain is considered for the purpose of estimating the tendency of any *act* by which it is produced, there are two other circumstances to be taken into the account; these are,

5. Its *fecundity*, or the chance it has of being followed by sensations of the *same* kind: that is, pleasures, if it be a pleasure: pains, if it be a pain.

6. Its *purity*, or the chance it has of *not* being followed by sensations of the *opposite* kind: that is, pains, if it be a pleasure: pleasures, if it be a pain.

These two last, however, are in strictness scarcely to be deemed properties of the pleasure or the pain itself; they are not, therefore, in strictness to be taken into the account of the value of that pleasure or that pain. They are in strictness to be deemed properties only of the act, or other event, by which such pleasure or pain has been produced; and accordingly are only to be taken into the account of the tendency of such act or such event.

IV. To a *number* of persons, with reference to each of whom the value of a pleasure or a pain is considered, it will be greater or less, according to seven circumstances: to wit, the six preceding ones; viz.

1. Its *intensity.*
2. Its *duration.*
3. Its *certainty* or *uncertainty.*
4. Its *propinquity* or *remoteness.*
5. Its *fecundity.*
6. Its *purity*

---

*These circumstances have since been denominated *elements* or *dimensions* of *value* in a pleasure or a pain.

Not long after the publication of the first edition, the following memoriter verses were framed, in the view of lodging more effectually, in the memory, these points, on which the whole fabric of morals and legislation may be seen to rest.

> *Intense, long, certain, speedy, fruitful, pure—*
> Such marks in *pleasures* and in *pains* endure.
> If it be *public*, wide let them *extend.*
> Such *pains* avoid, whichever be thy view:
> If pains *must* come, let them *extend* to few.

And one other; to wit:

7. Its *extent;* that is, the number of persons to whom it *extends;* or (in other words) who are affected by it.

V. To take an exact account then of the general tendency of any act, by which the interests of a community are affected, proceed as follows. Begin with any one person of those whose interests seem most immediately to be affected by it: and take an account.

1. Of the value of each distinguishable *pleasure* which appears to be produced by it in the *first* instance.

2. Of the value of each *pain* which appears to be produced by it in the *first* instance.

3. Of the value of each pleasure which appears to be produced by it *after* the first. This constitutes the *fecundity* of the first *pleasure* and the *impurity* of the first *pain.*

4. Of the value of each *pain* which appears to be produced by it after the first. This constitutes the *fecundity* of the first *pain,* and the *impurity* of the first *pleasure.*

5. Sum up all the values of all the *pleasures* on the one side, and those of all the *pains* on the other. The balance, if it be on the side of pleasure, will give the *good* tendency of the act upon the whole, with respect to the interests of that *individual* person; if on the side of the pain, the *bad* tendency of it upon the whole.

6. Take an account of the *number* of persons whose interests appear to be concerned; and repeat the above process with respect to each. *Sum up* the numbers expressive of the degrees of *good* tendency which the act has, with respect to each individual, in regard to whom the tendency of it is *good* upon the whole: . . . do this again with respect to each individual, in regard to whom the tendency of it is *bad* upon the whole. Take the *balance;* which, if on the side of *pleasure,* will give the general *good tendency* of the act, with respect to the total number or community of individuals concerned; if on the side of pain, the general *evil tendency,* with respect to the same community.

VI. It is not to be expected that this process should be strictly pursued previously to every moral judgment, or to every legislative or judicial operation. It may, however, be always kept in view: and as near as the process actually pursued on these occasions approaches to it, so near will such process approach to the character of an exact one.

VII. The same process is alike applicable to pleasure and pain, in whatever shape they appear: and by whatever denomination they are distinguished: to pleasure, whether it be called *good* (which is properly the cause or instrument of pleasure) or *profit* (which is distant pleasure, or the cause or instrument of distant pleasure,) or *convenience,* or *advantage, benefit, emolument, happiness,* and so forth: to pain, whether it be called *evil,* (which corresponds to *good)* or *mischief,* or *inconvenience,* or *disadvantage,* or *loss,* or *unhappiness,* and so forth.

VIII. Nor is this a novel and unwarranted, any more than it is a useless theory. In all this there is nothing but what the practice of mankind, wheresoever they have a clear view of their own interest, is perfectly conformable to. An article of property, an estate in land, for instance, is valuable, on what account? On account of the pleasures of all kinds which it enables a man to produce, and what comes to the same thing the pains of all kinds which it enables him to avert. But the value of such an article of property is universally understood to rise or fall according to the length or shortness of the time which a man has in it: the certainty or uncertainty of its coming into possession: and the nearness or remoteness of the time at which, if at all, it is to come into possession. As to the *intensity* of the pleasures which a man may derive from it, this is never thought of, because it depends upon the use which each particular person may come to make of it; which cannot be estimated till the particular pleasures he may come to derive from it, or the particular pains he may come to exclude by means of it, are brought to view. For the same reason, neither does he think of the *fecundity* or *purity* of those pleasures.

. . .

CHAPTER X

Of Motives

2. *No motives either constantly good or constantly bad*

IX. In all this chain of motives, the principal or original link seems to be the last internal motive in prospect: it is to this that all the other motives in prospect owe their materiality: and the immediately acting motive its existence. This motive in prospect, we see is always some pleasure, or some pain; some pleasure, which the act in question is expected to be a means of continuing or producing: some pain which it is expected to be a means of discontinuing or preventing. A motive is substantially nothing more than pleasure or pain, operating in a certain manner.

X. Now, pleasure is in *itself* a good: nay, even setting aside immunity from pain, the only good: pain is in itself an evil; and, indeed, without exception, the only evil; or else the words good and evil have no meaning. And this is alike true of every sort of pain, and of every sort of pleasure. It follows, therefore, immediately and incontestably, that *there is no such thing as any sort of motive that is in itself a bad one.*

XI. It is common, however, to speak of actions as proceeding from *good* or *bad* motives: in which case the motives meant are such as are internal. The expression is far from being an accurate one; and as it is apt to occur in the consideration of almost every kind of offence, it will be requisite to settle the precise meaning of it, and observe how far it quadrates with the truth of things.

XII. With respect to goodness and badness, as it is with everything else that is not itself either pain or pleasure, so is it with motives. If they are good or bad, it is only on account of their effects: good, on account of their tendency to produce pleasure, or avert pain: bad, on account of their tendency to produce pain, or avert pleasure. Now the case is, that from one and the same motive, and from every kind of motive, may proceed actions that are good, others that are bad, and others that are indifferent.

John Stuart Mill: Qualitatively Higher Happiness

Mill staunchly defended Bentham's utilitarian scheme partly out of loyalty to his father, James Mill, who was one of its most earnest supporters and partly out of sincere conviction.[5] However, it is one of the wry happenings in philosophic history that in defending Bentham against his critics Mill changed utilitarianism into a substantially different doctrine.

The strongest criticism against Bentham was that his only concern was to maximize the sheer quantity of pleasure and that he did not allow for the higher pleasures accesible to man. For this reason it was denounced as "pig philosophy," a theory that made no distinction between the pleasures of a pig and those of a person. To Bentham, all pleasures are equal and the only question worth asking is whether one activity will yield more pleasure than another. He even went so far as to claim in a celebrated passage that "Prejudice apart, the game of push-pin is of equal value with the arts and sciences of music and poetry." This assertion was widely interpreted as the endorsement of a vulgar ethic. Bentham was baldly stating that, pushpin, a trivial child's game resembling jackstraws or pick-up-sticks, was as valuable as any intellectual or aesthetic experience so long as it offered an equal amount of enjoyment to the person.

Since Bentham had died by the time the storm broke, Mill assumed the responsibility of answering his critics, charging them with a misrepresentation of the utilitarian position. In his *Utilitarianism*, which is excerpted later, Mill argued that "the accusation supposes human beings to be capable of no pleasures except those of which swine are capable." But "a beast's pleasures do not satisfy a human being's conceptions of happiness"; we are beings with "faculties more elevated than the animal appetites" and are able to enjoy more civilized types of pleasure. "The pleasures of the intellect, of the feelings and imagination, and of the moral sentiments [have] a much higher value as pleasure than do those of mere sensation," Mill wrote. Furthermore, he claimed, "it is quite compatible with the principle of utility to recognize the fact, that some kinds of pleasure are more desirable and more valuable than others."

In other words, Mill maintained that the kind or level or quality of enjoyment is important to utilitarianism. "It would be absurd," he wrote, "that, while in estimating all other things quality is considered as well as quantity, the estimation of pleasures should be supposed to depend on quantity alone." Human beings should lead more elevated lives, preferring the types of experiences that are unique to man. In his famous phrase, "It is better to be a human being dissatisfied than a pig satisfied; better to be Socrates dissatisfied than a fool satisfied."

It is doubtful whether Mill was correct in thinking that such a view was consistent with Bentham's "moral arithmetic" but at least it was a refinement that utilitarianism sorely needed to make it more respectable. The next question of course was how could one determine which of two pleasures is qualitatively higher; the criterion of "feelings," "imagination," and certain "sentiments" was simply too vague. It was difficult enough to discover which experience contained more pleasure, but deciding on superior and inferior pleasures would seem hopeless. It also smacked of elitism and snobbery to even make such distinctions.

In response to this question, Mill wrote, "there is but one possible answer. Of two pleasures, if there be one to which all or almost all who have experience of both give a decided preference, irrespective of any feeling of moral obligation to prefer it, that is the more desirable pleasure." That is, to identify the finer pleasure ask the person who has experienced both pleasures, for he is in a position to tell which of the two is better. Mill further maintained that these "knowledgeable" people would never select a lower over a higher pleasure even if a greater amount of happiness lay that way. "Few human creatures would consent to be changed into any of the lower animals for a promise of the fullest allowance of a beast's pleasures."

Mill seemed to be saying that although we might sometimes envy the joyous energy of animals we would not want to trade places with a dog or horse, even if we knew that they enjoyed their lives more. Once we have experienced both sides, the physicality of animals and the intellectuality of man, we realize that a cultured life that involves our higher faculties is far better. The same holds true when we are confronted with any two possibilities: competent judges will choose the finer pleasure in almost all instances.

In effect, Mill's utilitarianism advocates the *highest* happiness for the greatest number. Just as Bentham substantially improved hedonism by making it a universalistic theory, Mill elevated utilitarianism by introducing considerations of quality. The finer kind of life was best to Mill, even if that meant being a Socrates dissatisfied. He also believed so strongly in a Christian ideal of love for humanity that he favored the renunciation of our personal happiness when the happiness of our fellow man was at stake.

These are all admirable modifications but is it still the same position as that devised by Bentham? Could Mill claim that he had remained faithful to the original theory or had his utilitarianism died the death of a thousand qualifications? If we change the head of an axe and then change the handle it is not the same axe. Perhaps Mill had so altered hedonism that it should be called a different theory altogether. If so, he has sacrificed consistency to honesty, recognizing the worth of other values beside pleasure. Mill was a sensitive and humane man and, ironically enough, his breadth of understanding may have worked against the systematic development of his ethics.

In the selection from *Utilitarianism*, that follows Mill's basic position is presented. In reading it, bear in mind the sincerity, good sense, and perceptiveness that Mill showed as well as the various tensions that this created in his thought.

In addition to his main ethical work, *Utilitarianism*, Mill's important books include *The Principles of Political Economy* (1848), *On Liberty* (1859), *Examination of Sir William Hamilton's Philosophy* (1865), and his *Logic* (1843) and *Autobiography* (1873), which were mentioned previously.

Utilitarianism*

CHAPTER II

What Utilitarianism Is

· · ·

The creed which accepts as the foundation of morals 'utility' or the 'greatest happiness principle' holds that actions are right in proportion as they tend to promote happiness; wrong as they tend to produce the reverse of happiness. By happiness is intended pleasure and the absence of pain; by unhappiness, pain and the privation of pleasure. To give a clear view of the moral standard set up by the theory, much more requires to be said; in particular, what things it includes in the ideas of pain and pleasure, and to what extent this is left an open question. But these supplementary explanations do not affect the theory of life on which this theory of morality is grounded—namely, that pleasure and freedom from pain are the only things desirable as ends; and that all desirable things (which are as numerous in the utilitarian as in any other scheme) are desirable either for pleasure inherent in themselves or as means to the promotion of pleasure and the prevention of pain.

Now such a theory of life excites in many minds, and among them in some of the most estimable in feeling and purpose, inveterate dislike. To suppose that life has (as they express it) no higher end than pleasure—no better and nobler object of desire and pursuit—they designate as utterly mean and groveling, as a doctrine worthy only of swine, to whom the followers of Epicurus were, at a very early period, contemptuously likened; and modern holders of the doctrine are occasionally made the subject of equally polite comparisons by its German, French, and English assailants.

When thus attacked, the Epicureans have always answered that it is not they, but their accusers, who represent human nature in a degrading light, since the accusation supposes human beings to be capable of no pleasures except those of which swine are capable. If this supposition were true, the charge could not be gainsaid, but would then be no longer an imputation; for if the sources of pleasure were precisely the same to human beings and to swine, the rule of life which is good enough for the one would be good enough for the other. The comparison of the Epicurean life to that of beasts is felt as degrading, precisely because a beast's pleasures do not satisfy a human being's conceptions of happiness. Human beings have faculties more elevated than the animal appetites and, when once made conscious of them, do not regard anything as happiness which does not include their gratification. I do not, indeed, consider the Epicureans to have been by any means faultless in drawing out their scheme of consequences from the utilitarian principle. To do this in any sufficient manner, many Stoic, as well as Christian, elements require to be included. But there is no known Epicurean theory of life which does not assign to the pleasures of the

*Reprinted from John Stuart Mill, *Utilitarianism* (London, 1897).

intellect, of the feelings and imagination, and of the moral sentiments a much higher value as pleasures than to those of mere sensation. It must be admitted, however, that utilitarian writers in general have placed the superiority of mental over bodily pleasures chiefly in the greater permanency, safety, uncostliness, etc., of the former — that is, in their circumstantial advantages rather than in their intrinsic nature. And on all these points utilitarians have fully proved their case; but they might have taken the other and, as it may be called, higher ground with entire consistency. It is quite compatible with the principle of utility to recognize the fact that some kinds of pleasure are more desirable and more valuable than others. It would be absurd that, while in estimating all other things quality is considered as well as quantity, the estimation of pleasure should be supposed to depend on quantity alone.

If I am asked what I mean by difference of quality in pleasures, or what makes one pleasure more valuable than another, merely as a pleasure, except its being greater in amount, there is but one possible answer. Of two pleasures, if there be one to which all or almost all who have experience of both give a decided preference, irrespective of any feeling of moral obligation to prefer it, that is the more desirable pleasure. If one of the two is, by those who are competently acquainted with both, placed so far above the other that they prefer it, even though knowing it to be attended with a greater amount of discontent, and would not resign it for any quantity of the other pleasure which their nature is capable of, we are justified in ascribing to the preferred enjoyment a superiority in quality so far outweighing quantity as to render it, in comparison, of small account.

Now it is an unquestionable fact that those who are equally acquainted with and equally capable of appreciating and enjoying both do give a most marked preference to the manner of existence which employs their higher faculties. Few human creatures would consent to be changed into any of the lower animals for a promise of the fullest allowance of a beast's pleasures; no intelligent human being would consent to be a fool, no instructed person would be an ignoramus, no person of feeling and conscience would be selfish and base, even though they should be persuaded that the fool, the dunce, or the rascal is better satisfied with his lot than they are with theirs. They would not resign what they possess more than he for the most complete satisfaction of all the desires which they have in common with him. If they ever fancy they would, it is only in cases of unhappiness so extreme that to escape from it they would exchange their lot for almost any other, however undesirable in their own eyes. A being of higher faculties requires more to make him happy, is capable probably of more acute suffering, and certainly accessible to it at more points, than one of an inferior type; but in spite of these liabilities, he can never really wish to sink into what he feels to be a lower grade of existence. We may give what explanation we please of this unwillingness; we may attribute it to pride, a name which is given indiscriminately to some of the most and to some of the least estimable feelings of which mankind are capable; we may refer it to the love of liberty and personal independence, an appeal to which was with the Stoics one of the most effective means for the inculcation of it; to the love of power or to the love of excitement, both of which do really enter into and contribute to it;

but its most appropriate appellation is a sense of dignity, which all human beings possess in one form or other, and in some, though by no means in exact, proportion to their higher faculties, and which is so essential a part of the happiness of those in whom it is strong that nothing which conflicts with it could be otherwise than momentarily an object of desire to them. Whoever supposes that this preference takes place at a sacrifice of happiness—that the superior being, in anything like equal circumstances, is not happier than the inferior—confounds the two very different ideas of happiness and content. It is indisputable that the being whose capacities of enjoyment are low has the greatest chance of having them fully satisfied; and a highly endowed being will always feel that any happiness which he can look for, as the world is constituted, is imperfect. But he can learn to bear its imperfections, if they are at all bearable; and they will not make him envy the being who is indeed unconscious of the imperfections, but only because he feels not at all the good which those imperfections qualify. It is better to be a human being dissatisfied than a pig satisfied; better to be Socrates dissatisfied than a fool satisfied. And if the fool, or the pig, are of a different opinion, it is because they only know their own side of the question. The other party to the comparison knows both sides.

It may be objected that many who are capable of the higher pleasures occasionally, under the influence of temptation, postpone them to the lower. But this is quite compatible with a full appreciation of the intrinsic superiority of the higher. Men often, from infirmity of character, make their election for the nearer good, though they know it to be the less valuable; and this no less when the choice is between two bodily pleasures than when it is between bodily and mental. They pursue sensual indulgences to the injury of health, though perfectly aware that health is the greater good. It may be further objected that many who begin with youthful enthusiasm for everything noble, as they advance in years, sink into indolence and selfishness. But I do not believe that those who undergo this very common change voluntarily choose the lower description of pleasures in preference to the higher. I believe that, before they devote themselves exclusively to the one, they have already become incapable of the other. Capacity for the nobler feelings is in most natures a very tender plant, easily killed, not only by hostile influences, but by mere want of sustenance; and in the majority of young persons it speedily dies away if the occupations to which their position in life has devoted them, and the society into which it has thrown them, are not favorable to keeping that higher capacity in exercise. Men lose their high aspirations as they lose their intellectual tastes, because they have not time or opportunity for indulging them; and they addict themselves to inferior pleasures, not because they deliberately prefer them, but because they are either the only ones to which they have access or the only ones which they are any longer capable of enjoying. It may be questioned whether anyone who has remained equally susceptible to both classes of pleasures ever knowingly and calmly preferred the lower, though many, in all ages, have broken down in an ineffectual attempt to combine both.

From this verdict of the only competent judges, I apprehend there can be no appeal. On a question which is the best worth having of two pleasures, or which of two modes of existence is the most grateful to the feelings, apart from its moral attributes and from its consequences, the judgment of those who are qualified for knowledge of both, or, if they differ, that of the majority among them, must be admitted as final. And there needs be the less hesitation to accept this judgment respecting the quality of pleasures, since there is no other tribunal to be referred to even on the question of quantity. What means are there of determining which is the acutest of two pains, or the intensest of two pleasurable sensations, except the general suffrage of those who are familiar with both? Neither pains nor pleasures are homogeneous, and pain is always heterogeneous with pleasure. What is there to decide whether a particular pleasure is worth purchasing at the cost of a particular pain, except the feelings and judgment of the experienced? When, therefore, those feelings and judgment declare the pleasures derived from the higher faculties to be preferable *in kind,* apart from the question of intensity, to those of which the animal nature, disjoined from the higher faculties, is susceptible, they are entitled on this subject to the same regard.

I have dwelt on this point as being a necessary part of a perfectly just conception of utility or happiness considered as the directive rule of human conduct. But it is by no means an indispensable condition to the acceptance of the utilitarian standard; for that standard is not the agent's own greatest happiness, but the greatest amount of happiness altogether; and if it may possibly be doubted whether a noble character is always the happier for its nobleness, there can be no doubt that it makes other people happier, and that the world in general is immensely a gainer by it. Utilitarianism, therefore, could only attain its end by the general cultivation of nobleness of character, even if each individual were only benefited by the nobleness of others, and his own, so far as happiness is concerned, were a sheer deduction from the benefit. But the bare enunciation of such an absurdity as this last renders refutation superfluous.

According to the greatest happiness principle, as above explained, the ultimate end, with reference to and for the sake of which all other things are desirable — whether we are considering our own good or that of other people — is an existence exempt as far as possible from pain, and as rich as possible in enjoyments, both in point of quantity and quality; the test of quality and the rule for measuring it against quantity being the preference felt by those who, in their opportunities of experience, to which must be added their habits of self-consciousness and self-observation, are best furnished with the means of comparison. This, being according to the utilitarian opinion the end of human action, is necessarily also the standard of morality, which may accordingly be defined 'the rules and precepts for human conduct,' by the observance of which an existence such as has been described might be, to the greatest extent possible, secured to all mankind; and not to them only, but, so far as the nature of things admits, to the whole sentient creation.

· · ·

I must again repeat what the assailants of utilitarianism seldom have the justice to acknowledge, that the happiness which forms the utilitarian standard of what is right in conduct is not the agent's own happiness but that of all concerned. As between his own happiness and that of others, utilitarianism requires him to be as strictly impartial as a disinterested and benevolent spectator. In the golden rule of Jesus of Nazareth, we read the complete spirit of the ethics of utility. 'To do as you would be done by,' and 'to love your neighbor as yourself,' constitute the ideal perfection of utilitarian morality. As the means of making the nearest approach to this ideal, utility would enjoin, first, that laws and social arrangements should place the happiness or (as speaking practically, it may be called) the interest of every individual as nearly as possible in harmony with the interest of the whole; and, secondly, that education and opinion, which have so vast a power over human character, should so use that power as to establish in the mind of every individual an indissoluble association between his own happiness and the good of the whole, especially between his own happiness and the practice of such modes of conduct, negative and positive, as regard for the universal happiness prescribes; so that not only he may be unable to conceive the possibility of happiness to himself, consistently with conduct opposed to the general good, but also that a direct impulse to promote the general good may be in every individual one of the habitual motives of action, and the sentiments connected therewith may fill a large and prominent place in every human being's sentient existence. If the impugners of the utilitarian morality represented it to their own minds in this its true character, I know not what recommendation possessed by any other morality they could possibly affirm to be wanting to it; what more beautiful or more exalted developments of human nature any other ethical system can be supposed to foster, or what springs of action, not accessible to the utilitarian, such systems rely on for giving effect to their mandates.

The objectors to utilitarianism cannot always be charged with representing it in a discreditable light. On the contrary, those among them who entertain anything like a just idea for its disinterested character sometimes find fault with its standard as being too high for humanity. They say it is exacting too much to require that people shall always act from the inducement of promoting the general interests of society. But this is to mistake the very meaning of a standard of morals and confound the rule of action with the motive of it. It is the business of ethics to tell us what are our duties, or by what test we may know them; but no system of ethics requires that the sole motive of all we do shall be a feeling of duty; on the contrary, ninety-nine hundredths of all our actions are done from other motives, and rightly so done if the rule of duty does not condemn them. It is the more unjust to utilitarianism that this particular misapprehension should be made a ground of objection to it, inasmuch as utilitarian moralists have gone beyond almost all others in affirming that the motive has nothing to do with the morality of the action, though much with the worth of the agent. He who saves a fellow creature from drowning does what is morally right, whether his motive be duty or the hope of being paid for his trouble; he who betrays the friend that trusts him is guilty of a crime, even if his object be to serve another friend to whom he is under greater obligations. But to speak only of actions done from the motive of duty, and in direct obedience to principle: it is a misapprehension of the utilitarian mode of thought to conceive it as implying that people should fix their minds upon so wide a generality as the world, or society at large. The great majority of good actions are intended not for the benefit of the world, but for that of individuals, of which the good of the world is made up; and the thoughts of the most virtuous man need not on these occasions travel beyond the particular persons concerned, except so far as is necessary to assure himself that in benefiting them he is not violating the rights, that is, the legitimate and authorized expectations, of anyone else. The multiplication of happiness is, according to the utilitarian ethics, the object of virtue: the occasions on which any person (except one in a thousand) has it in his power to do this on an extended scale—in other words, to be a public benefactor—are but exceptional; and on these occasions alone is he called onto consider public utility; in every other case, private utility, the interest or happiness of some few persons, is all he has to attend to. Those alone the influence of whose actions extends to society in general need concern themselves habitually about so large an object. In the case of abstinences indeed—of things which people forbear to do from moral considerations, though the consequences in the particular case might be beneficial—it would be unworthy of an intelligent agent not to be consciously aware that the action is of a class which, if practiced generally, would be generally injurious, and that this is the ground of the obligation to abstain from it. The amount of regard for the public interest implied in this recognition is no greater than is demanded by every system of morals, for they all enjoin to abstain from whatever is manifestly pernicious to society.

The same considerations dispose of another reproach against the doctrine of utility, founded on a still grosser misconception of the purpose of a standard of morality and of the very meaning of the words 'right' and 'wrong.' It is often affirmed that utilitarianism renders men cold and unsympathizing; that it chills their moral feelings toward individuals; that it makes them regard only the dry and hard consideration of the consequences of actions, not taking into their moral estimate the qualities from which those actions emanate. If the assertion means that they do not allow their judgment respecting the rightness or wrongness of an action to be influenced by their opinion of the qualities of the person who does it, this is a complaint not against utilitarianism, but against any standard of morality at all; for certainly no known ethical standard decides an action to be good or bad because it is done by a good or a bad man, still less because done by an amiable, a brave, or a benevolent man, or the contrary. These considerations are relevant, not to the estimation of actions, but of persons; and there is nothing in the utilitarian theory inconsistent with the fact that there are other things which interest us in persons besides the rightness and wrongness of their actions. The Stoics, indeed, with the paradoxical misuse of language which was part of their system, and by which they strove to raise themselves above all concern about anything but virtue, were fond of saying that he who has that has everything; that he, and only he, is rich, is beautiful, is a king. But no claim of this description is made for the virtuous man by the utilitarian doctrine. Utilitarians are quite aware that there are other desirable possessions and qualities besides virtue, and are perfectly willing to allow to all of them their full worth. They are also aware that a right action does not necessarily indicate a virtuous character, and that actions which are blamable often proceed from qualities entitled to praise. When this is apparent in any particular case, it modifies their estimation, not certainly of the act, but of the agent. I grant that they are, notwithstanding, of opinion that in the long run the best proof of a good character is good actions; and resolutely refuse to consider any mental disposition as good of which the predominant tendency is to produce bad conduct. This makes them unpopular with many people, but it is an unpopularity which they must share with everyone who regards the distinction between right and wrong in a serious light; and the reproach is not one which a conscientious utilitarian need be anxious to repel.

• • •

CHAPTER III

Of the Ultimate Sanction of the Principle of Utility

The question is often asked, and properly so, in regard to any supposed moral standard — What is its sanction? what are the motives to obey? or, more specifically, what is the source of its obligation? whence does it derive its binding force? It is a necessary part of moral philosophy to provide the answer to this question, which, though frequently assuming the shape of an objection to the utilitarian morality, as if it had some special applicability to that above others, really arises in regard to all standards. It arises, in fact, whenever a person is called on to *adopt* a standard, or refer morality to any basis on which he has not been accustomed to rest it. For the customary morality, that which education and opinion have consecrated, is the only one which presents itself to the mind with the feeling of being *in itself* obligatory; and when a person is asked to believe that this morality *derives* its obligation from some general principle round which custom has not thrown the same halo, the assertion is to him a paradox; the supposed corollaries seem to have a more binding force than the original theorem; the superstructure seems to stand better without than with what is represented as its foundation. He says to himself, I feel that I am bound not to rob or murder, betray or deceive; but why am I bound to promote the general happiness? If my own happiness lies in something else, why may I not give that the preference?

If the view adopted by the utilitarian philosophy of the nature of the moral sense be correct, this difficulty will always present itself until the influences which form moral character have taken the same hold of the principle which they have taken of some of the consequences — until, by the improvement of education, the feeling of unity with our fellow creatures shall be (what it cannot be denied that Christ intended it to be) as deeply rooted in our character, and to our own consciousness as completely a part of our nature, as the horror of crime is in an ordinarily well-brought-up young person. In the meantime, however, the difficulty has no peculiar application to the doctrine of utility, but is inherent in every attempt to analyze morality and reduce it to principles; which, unless the principle is already in men's minds invested with as much sacredness as any of its applications, always seems to divest them of a part of their sanctity.

The principle of utility either has, or there is no reason why it might not have, all the sanctions which belong to any other system of morals. Those sanctions are either external or internal. Of the external sanctions it is not necessary to speak at any length. They are the hope of favor and the fear of displeasure from our fellow creatures or from the Ruler of the universe, along with whatever we may have of sympathy or affection for them, or of love and awe of Him, inclining us to do His will independently of selfish consequences. There is evidently no reason why all these motives for observance should not attach themselves to the utilitarian morality as completely and as powerfully as to any other. Indeed, those of them which refer to our fellow creatures are sure to do so, in proportion to the amount of general intelligence; for whether there be any other ground of moral obligation than the general happiness or not, men do desire happiness; and however imperfect may be their own practice, they desire and commend all conduct in others toward themselves by which they think their happiness is promoted. With regard to the religious motive, if men believe, as most profess to do, in the goodness of God, those who think that conduciveness to the general happiness is the essence or even only the criterion of good must necessarily believe that it is also that which God approves. The whole force therefore of external reward and punishment, whether physical or moral, and whether proceeding from God or from our fellow men, together with all that the capacities of human nature admit of disinterested devotion to either, become available to enforce the utilitarian morality, in proportion as that morality is recognized; and the more powerfully, the more the appliances of education and general cultivation are bent to the purpose.

So far as to external sanctions. The internal sanction of duty, whatever our standard of duty may be, is one and the same—a feeling in our own mind; a pain, more or less intense, attendant on violation of duty, which in properly cultivated moral natures rises, in the more serious cases, into shrinking from it as an impossibility. This feeling, when disinterested and connecting itself with the pure idea of duty, and not with some particular form of it, or with any of the merely accessory circumstances, is the essence of conscience; though in that complex phenomenon as it actually exists, the simple fact is in general all encrusted over with collateral associations derived from sympathy, from love, and still more from fear; from all the forms of religious feeling; from the recollections of childhood and of all our past life; from self-esteem, desire of the esteem of others, and occasionally even self-abasement. This extreme complication is, I apprehend, the origin of the sort of mystical character which, by a tendency of the human mind of which there are many other examples, is apt to be attributed to the idea of moral obligation, and which leads people to believe that the idea cannot possibly attach itself to any other objects than those which, by a supposed mysterious law, are found in our present experience to excite it. Its binding force, however, consists in the existence of a mass of feeling which must be broken through in order to do what violates our standard of right, and which, if we do nevertheless violate that standard, will probably have to be encountered afterwards in the form of remorse. Whatever theory we have of the nature or origin of conscience, this is what essentially constitutes it.

The ultimate sanction, therefore, of all morality (external motives apart) being a subjective feeling in our own minds, I see nothing embarrassing to those whose standard is utility in the question, What is the sanction of that particular standard? We may answer, the same as of all other moral standards—the conscientious feelings of mankind. Undoubtedly this sanction has no binding efficacy on those who do not possess the feelings it appeals to; but neither will these persons be more obedient to any other moral principle than to the utilitarian one. On them morality of any kind has no hold but through the external sanctions. Meanwhile the feelings exist, a fact in human nature, the reality of which, and the great power with which they are capable of acting on those in whom they have been duly cultivated, are proved by experience. No reason has ever been shown why they may not be cultivated to as great intensity in connection with the utilitarian as with any other rule of morals.

There is, I am aware, a disposition to believe that a person who sees in moral obligation a transcendental fact, an objective reality belonging to the province of 'things in themselves,' is likely to be more obedient to it than one who believes it to be entirely subjective, having its seat in human consciousness only. But whatever a person's opinion may be on this point of ontology, the force he is really urged by is his own subjective feeling, and is exactly measured by its strength. No one's belief that duty is an objective reality is stronger than the belief that God is so; yet the belief in God, apart from the expectation of actual reward and punishment, only operates on conduct through, and in proportion to, the subjective religious feeling. The sanction, so far as it is disinterested, is always in the mind itself; and the notion, therefore, of the transcendental moralists must be that this sanction will not exist in the mind unless it is believed to have its root out of the mind; and that if a person is able to say to himself, 'That which is restraining me and which is called my conscience is only a feeling in my own mind,' he may possibly draw the conclusion that when the feeling ceases the obligation ceases, and that if he find the feeling inconvenient, he may disregard it and endeavor to get rid of it. But is this danger confined to the utilitarian morality? Does the belief that moral obligation has its seat outside the mind make the feeling of it too strong to be got rid of? The fact is so far otherwise that all moralists admit and lament the ease with which, in the generality of minds, conscience can be silenced or stifled. The question, 'Need I obey my conscience?' is quite as often put to themselves by persons who never heard of the principle of utility as by its adherents. Those whose conscientious feelings are so weak as to allow of their asking this question, if they answer it affirmatively, will not do so because they believe in the transcendental theory, but because of the external sanctions.

It is not necessary, for the present purpose, to decide whether the feeling of duty is innate or implanted. Assuming it to be innate, it is an open question to what objects it naturally attaches itself; for the philosophic supporters of that theory are now agreed that the intuitive perception is of principles of morality and not of the details. If there be anything innate in the matter, I see no reason why the feeling which is innate should not be that of regard to the pleasures and pains of others. If there is any principle of morals which is intuitively obligatory, I should say it must be that. If so, the intuitive ethics would coincide with the utilitarian, and there would be no further quarrel between them. Even as it is, the intuitive moralists, though they believe that there are other intuitive moral obligations, do already believe this to be one; for they unanimously hold that a large *portion* of morality turns upon the consideration due to the interests of our fellow creatures. Therefore, if the belief in the transcendental origins of moral obligation gives any additional efficacy to the internal sanction, it appears to me that the utilitarian principle has already the benefit of it.

On the other hand, if, as is my own belief, the moral feelings are not innate but acquired, they are not for that reason the less natural. It is natural to man to speak, to reason, to build cities, to cultivate the ground, though these are acquired faculties. The moral feelings are not indeed a part of our nature in the sense of being in any perceptible degree present in all of us; but this, unhappily, is a fact admitted by those who believe the most strenuously in their transcendental origin. Like the other acquired capacities above referred to, the moral faculty, if not a part of our nature, is a natural outgrowth from it; capable, like them, in a certain small degree, of springing up spontaneously; and susceptible of being brought by cultivation to a high degree of development. Unhappily it is also susceptible, by a sufficient use of the external sanctions and of the force of early impressions, of being cultivated in almost any direction, so that there is hardly anything so absurd or so mischievous that it may not, by means of these influences, be made to act on the human mind with all the authority of conscience. To doubt that the same potency might be given by the same means to the principle of utility, even if it had no foundation in human nature, would be flying in the face of all experience.

But moral associations which are wholly of artificial creation, when the intellectual culture goes on, yield by degrees to the dissolving force of analysis; and if the feeling of duty, when associated with utility, would appear equally arbitrary; if there were no leading department of our nature, no powerful class of sentiments, with which that association would harmonize, which would make us feel it congenial and incline us not only to foster it in others (for which we have abundant interested motives), but also to cherish it in ourselves—if there were not, in short, a natural basis of sentiment for utilitarian morality, it might well happen that this association also, even after it had been implanted by education, might be analyzed away.

But there is this basis of powerful natural sentiment; and this it is which, when once the general happiness is recognized as the ethical standard, will constitute the strength of the utilitarian morality. This firm foundation is that of the social feelings of mankind—the desire to be in unity with our fellow creatures, which is already a powerful principle in human nature, and happily one of those which tend to become stronger, even without express inculcation, from the influences of advancing civilization.

· · ·

CHAPTER IV

Of What Sort of Proof the Principle of Utility Is Susceptible

It has already been remarked that questions of ultimate ends do not admit of proof, in the ordinary acceptation of the term. To be incapable of proof by reasoning is common to all first principles, to the first premises of our knowledge, as well as to those of our conduct. But the former, being matters of fact, may be the subject of a direct appeal to the faculties which judge of fact—namely, our senses and our internal consciousness. Can an appeal be made to the same faculties on questions of practical ends? Or by what other faculty is cognizance taken of them?

Questions about ends are, in other words, questions what things are desirable. The utilitarian doctrine is that happiness is desirable, and the only thing desirable, as an end; all other things being only desirable as means to that end. What ought to be required of this doctrine, what conditions is it requisite that the doctrine should fulfill—to make good its claim to be believed?

The only proof capable of being given that an object is visible is that people actually see it. The only proof that a sound is audible is that people hear it; and so of the other sources of our experience. In like manner, I apprehend, the sole evidence it is possible to produce that anything is desirable is that people do actually desire it. If the end which the utilitarian doctrine proposes to itself were not, in theory and in practice, acknowledged to be an end, nothing could ever convince any person that it was so. No reason can be given why the general happiness is desirable, except that each person, so far as he believes it to be attainable, desires his own happiness. This, however, being a fact, we have not only all the proof which the case admits of, but all which it is possible to require, that happiness is a good, that each person's happiness is a good to that person, and the general happiness, therefore, a good to the aggregate of all persons. Happiness has made out its title as *one* of the ends of conduct and, consequently, one of the criteria of morality.

But it has not, by this alone, proved itself to be the sole criterion. To do that, it would seem, by the same rule, necessary to show, not only that people desire happiness, but that they never desire anything else. Now it is palpable that they do desire things which, in common language, are decidedly distinguished from happiness. They desire, for example, virtue and the absence of vice no less really than pleasure and the absence of pain. The desire of virtue is not as universal, but it is as authentic a fact as the desire of happiness. And hence the opponents of the utilitarian standard deem that they have a right to infer that there are other ends of human action besides happiness, and that happiness is not the standard of approbation and disapprobation.

But does the utilitarian doctrine deny that people desire virtue, or maintain that virtue is not a thing to be desired? The very reverse. It maintains not only that virtue is to be desired, but that it is to be desired disinterestedly, for itself. Whatever may be the opinion of utilitarian moralists as to the original conditions by which virtue is made virtue, however they may believe (as they do) that actions and dispositions are only virtuous because they promote another end than virtue, yet this being granted, and it having been decided, from considerations of this description, what *is* virtuous, they not only place virtue at the very head of the things which are good as means to the ultimate end, but they also recognize as a psychological fact the possibility of its being, to the individual, a good in itself, without looking to any end beyond it; and hold that the mind is not in a right state, not in a state comfortable to utility, not in the state most conducive to the general happiness, unless it does love virtue in this manner—as a thing desirable in itself, even although, in the individual instance, it should not produce those other desirable consequences which it tends to produce, and on account of which it is held to be virtue. This opinion is not, in the smallest degree, a departure from the happiness principle. The ingredients of happiness are very various, and each of them is desirable in itself, and not merely when considered as swelling an aggregate. The principle of utility does not mean that any given pleasure, as music for instance, or any given exemption from pain, as for example health, is to be looked upon as means to a collective something termed happiness, and to be desired on that account. They are desired and desirable in and for themselves; besides being means, they are a part of the end. Virtue, according to the utilitarian doctrine, is not naturally and originally part of the end, but it is capable of becoming so; and in those who live it disinterestedly it has become so, and is desired and cherished, not as a means to happiness, but as a part of their happiness.

To illustrate this further, we may remember that virtue is not the only thing originally a means, and which if it were not a means to anything else would be and remain indifferent, but which by association with what it is a means to comes to be desired for itself, and that too with the utmost intensity. What, for example, shall we say of the love of money? There is nothing originally more desirable about money than about any heap of glittering pebbles. Its worth is solely that of the things which it will buy; the desires for other things than itself, which it is a means of gratifying. Yet the love of money is not only one of the strongest moving forces of human life, but money is, in many cases, desired in and for itself; the desire to possess it is often stronger than the desire to use it, and goes on increasing when all the desires which point to ends beyond it, to be compassed by it, are falling off. It may, then, be said truly that money is desired not for the sake of an end, but as part of the end. From being a means to happiness, it has come to be itself a principle ingredient of the individual's conception of happiness. The same may be said of the majority of the great objects of human life: power, for example, or fame, except that to each of these there is a certain amount of immediate pleasure annexed, which has at least the semblance of being naturally inherent in them—a thing which cannot be said of money. Still, however, the strongest natural attraction, both of power and of fame, is the immense aid they give to the attainment of our other wishes; and it is the strong association thus generated between them and all our objects of desire which gives to the direct desire of them the intensity it often assumes, so as in some characters to surpass in strength all other desires. In these cases the means have become a part of the end, and a more important part of it than any of the things which they are means to. What was once desired as an instrument for the attainment of happiness has come to be desired for its own sake. In being desired for its own sake it is, however, desired as *part* of happiness. The person is made, or thinks he would be made, happy by its mere possession; and is made unhappy by failure to obtain it. The desire of it is not a different thing from the desire of happiness any more than the love of music or the desire of health. They are included in happiness. They are some of the elements of which the desire of happiness is made up. Happiness is not an abstract idea but a concrete whole; and these are some of its parts. And the utilitarian standard sanctions and approves their being so. Life would be a poor thing, very ill provided with sources of happiness, if there were not this provision of nature by which things originally indifferent, but conductive to, or otherwise associated with, the satisfaction of our primitive desires, become in themselves sources of pleasure more valuable than the primitive pleasures, both in permanency, in the space of human existence that they are capable of covering, and even in intensity.

Virtue, according to the utilitarian conception, is a good of this description. There was no original desire of it, or motive to it, save its conduciveness to pleasure, and especially to protection from pain. But through the association thus formed it may be felt a good in itself, and desired as such with as great intensity as any other good; and with this difference between it and the love of money, of power, or of fame—that all of these may, and often do, render the individual noxious to the other members of the society to which he belongs, whereas there is nothing which makes him so much a blessing to them as the cultivation of the disinterested love of virtue. And consequently, the utilitarian standard, while it tolerates and approves those other acquired desires, up to the point beyond which they would be more injurious to the general happiness than promotive of it, enjoins and requires the cultivation of the love of virtue up to the greatest strength possible, as being above all things important to the general happiness.

It results from the preceding considerations that there is in reality nothing desired except happiness. Whatever is desired otherwise than as a means to some end beyond itself, and ultimately to happiness, is desired as itself a part of happiness, and is not desired for itself until it has become so. Those who desire virtue for its own sake desire it either because the consciousness of it is a pleasure, or because the consciousness of being without it is a pain, or for both reasons united; as in truth the pleasure and pain seldom exist separately, but almost always together—the same person feeling pleasure in the degree of virtue attained, and pain in not having attained more. If one of these gave him no pleasure, and the other no pain, he would not love or desire virtue, or would desire it only for the other benefits which it might produce to himself or to persons whom he cared for.

We have now, then, an answer to the question, of what sort of proof the principle of utility is susceptible. If the opinion which I have now stated is psychologically true—if human nature is so constituted as to desire nothing which is not either a part of happiness or a means of happiness—we can have no other proof, and we require no other, that these are the only things desirable. If so, happiness is the sole end of human action, and the promotion of it the test by which to judge of all human conduct; from whence it necessarily follows that it must be the criterion of morality, since a part is included in the whole.

Act and Rule Utilitarianism

Before we go on to evaluate Bentham and Mill's utilitarian ethic an important distinction must be made that emerged subsequent to the nineteenth century. In contemporary discussion, two different versions of utilitarianism are distinguished: act and rule. According to *act utilitarianism,* which was espoused by Bentham, every act should be evaluated in terms of the greatest happiness principle. If the consequences of a single action are pleasurable to people then that action is justified. *Rule utilitarianism,* on the other hand, as advocated by Mill, claimed that the greatest happiness principle should be used to establish general rules of behavior. The test of an action does not lie in its individual consequences but in the application of a moral rule or what Mill calls a "secondary principle." We should adopt those rules that will enhance human happiness and regard as wrong all rules that tend to produce the opposite.[6]

The following example will illustrate the difference. Suppose you are an airline pilot who has just discovered a serious mechanical problem with the aircraft and must announce to the passengers why it is necessary to return to the airport. You know that, in general, lying is not a good policy because human society functions far better when there is honesty among people. But in this instance, to tell the truth would result in terror and panic, whereas a "white lie" (for instance, that bad weather conditions ahead are responsible) would reassure everyone that all is well. What do you do?

If you were an act utilitarian you would lie — and with an easy conscience. For you believe the suffering that the lie prevents is sufficient justification for the act, and what's more, you would feel a moral responsibility to lie as convincingly as possible. However, if you were a rule utilitarian you would probably tell the truth because you are guided by general precepts; truth-telling is more conducive to human happiness and you would apply that principle as your rule of conduct even in extreme circumstances.

Of course, the rule utilitarian is bound to encounter cases where two rules will conflict. For example, the doctor who has pledged in the Hippocratic Oath to preserve life and alleviate pain and finds that he cannot do both. He may have a terminally ill patient in an excruciating condition that no medical treatment can relieve. In this situation he must either put the patient out of his misery with a lethal injection or preserve the patient's life along with his pain.

In order to cover such cases, the rule utilitarian will usually develop a hierarchy of rules whereby the more important values take precedence over the less important ones. In the last example, for instance, the doctor might feel that the alleviation of pain is an overriding principle, that the quality of life matters much more than its sheer length. If two rules appear of equal value, so that the same action was required by one rule and prohibited by another, then Mill, for one, would abandon all reliance on rules (secondary principles) and use the pleasure or displeasure of the act as the ultimate test (first principles).

Despite some of its awkwardness, most utilitarians today have adopted the rule approach. For one thing they have found that many actions have a moral similarity and tend to fall under common principles, so that the act utilitarian soon finds himself using a system of general rules in any case. For another thing, the rule method gives utilitarianism the status it needs as an ethical ideal. High moral precepts can be shown to be consistent with the goal of happiness, in fact, to have their basis in the greatest happiness standard. Cheating, stealing, and killing, for example, are wrong because they have harmful consequences, producing widespread unhappiness. On the other hand, respect for life and property are right because they benefit the bulk of mankind, augmenting people's happiness. Instead of relying upon some intuitive grasp of the rightness or wrongness of actions, the utilitarian can offer concrete reasons for ethical judgments. This makes utilitarianism not only a practical doctrine but shows that it has sufficient moral dignity to serve as the goal of life.

Evaluation

1. To begin with, each of the utilitarians can be faulted separately for difficulties that are endemic to their particular schemes. Bentham's neglect of the qualitative aspect of pleasure has already been shown in Mill's modification of the doctrine; by adding the factor of quality, Mill effectively criticized Bentham's purely quantitative approach. In addition, Bentham's hedonic calculus was not an actual scientific system but a form of pseudo-science. The amount of pleasure that an action might yield is simply not measurable in exact numbers, and although we can judge that economic prosperity, for example, would create more happiness than dire poverty, we cannot specify precisely how much more happiness it will provide. Would it deliver six hedons worth or thirty-eight, seventeen or fifty-seven? In short, pleasure cannot be measured by numbers in a calculus because feelings do not lend themselves to scientific exactitude. As Aristotle said, we can only expect the amount of precision that the subject matter allows. Bentham violated that rule and asked more of pleasure than it can provide.

But even if the hedonic calculus could be made to work it still would not offer all the information that Bentham wanted. For the calculus might tell us whether the greatest happiness would result from a given action but not whether it would be for the greatest number of people, and as a utilitarian Bentham is presumably interested in both. The reason for this defect is that the factor of "extent" is only one of seven marks and would not necessarily be decisive in the final summation. In other words, extent counts only one seventh among all the factors that must be considered, so that the result of a calculation could well be the endorsement of an action that yields pleasure to fewer people (although that pleasure would be considerable). In this way the universalistic aspect of utilitarianism is minimized in the hedonic calculus when Bentham is committed to having it maximized. (It should be added that Mill also betrayed universalistic hedonism by his concern with quality; happiness was limited to the appreciative few.)

In addition, Bentham's calculus of pleasures is extremely time consuming and cumbersome to operate; it eliminates impulsiveness and makes all choices very deliberate in a way reminiscent of Epicurean premeditation. Bentham did not expect people to use the system for every decision but simply kept in mind, nevertheless that is enough to take the spontaneity and adventure out of living. No one wants to go through life marking down numbers of hedons in a little black book before taking a step or even doing mental arithmetic.

2. Mill in turn committed some serious mistakes in his ethical system, mainly in connection with the introduction of qualitative considerations. In the first place, he used as his standard for higher pleasures the choices of qualified people, that is, those who have experienced both pleasures being considered, and he believed that such people will almost always choose the better of the two. But this does not seem to be borne out by the evidence. Assuming that art galleries offer a superior mode of enjoyment than football games, most people

will prefer the football game; having experienced both, they still choose the "lower" over the "higher" pleasure. The same holds true for television soap operas that have a larger audience than serious drama, fast food places that are more crowded than gourmet restaurants, cheap novels that sell much better than good literature, horror movies that gross far more money than artistic films, and so on. A good argument could be made for saying that public taste is, by and large, bad taste, and cultured pleasures are usually enjoyed by the minority. It is an open question as to how far we want to carry this reasoning, but at least Mill's basic assumption can be disputed. People who have known two pleasures do not necessarily choose the qualitatively higher one. What society values and what society does are often not the same.

In criticizing Mill's criterion for higher pleasures, the whole question of better and worse pleasures is raised. Are certain pleasures really better than others in quality and, if so, by what standard? It seems patronizing and undemocratic to maintain such a distinction but unless we do we are forced to agree with Bentham that only the amount of pleasure matters; poetry is as good as pushpin.[7]

A second way in which Mill's qualitative concerns are problematic has to do with his statement that it is better to be an outstanding person dissatisfied than a fool or a pig satisfied. We might want to agree with this idea (and it certainly reflects credit on Mill) but at the same time it is not the position we would expect a hedonist to take. Mill is saying that unhappiness can be better than happiness (so long as the higher human faculties are involved), which directly contradicts the hedonist theory. It seems to be a genuine conviction of Mill's that the richness of living, provided by our intellectual, spiritual, and aesthetic sensibilities, should be sought by all humanity, but in maintaining this position he has abandoned his hedonistic ethic. His ultimate philosophy seems to be that the fundamental standard for behavior is the finer existence accessible to man — whether or not it makes us happy.

Thus in trying to dignify hedonism and utilitarianism Mill has actually placed himself outside their camp, maintaining all the while that he is not only hedonism's defender but a loyal follower of Bentham as well. In these circumstances, one does not know whether to admire the nobility of his feelings or to deplore the self-deception in his beliefs. In any case, because Mill did not believe that the "basest" pleasures are on a par with the more refined pleasures, he was forced to use another criterion of selection besides pleasure.

3. An additional problem faced by both Bentham and Mill stems from their reliance on psychological hedonism as the foundation of their ethical hedonism. As we saw in the preceding chapter, this derivation does not work in terms of sound logic. Specifically, Bentham made the mistake of arguing that since we are determined by nature to seek pleasure, this indicates that pleasure is what we ought to seek. But as we have seen, if people must pursue pleasure then it is pointless to recommend that they should pursue it as their goal. And just because we are compelled to seek pleasure that does not prove pleasure is valuable. Mill committed a similar mistake when he argued that because people desire pleasure this shows pleasure is desirable. But from the fact that people seek pleasure we cannot conclude that they should.

Mill's reasoning in particular deserves closer examination. He claimed that a visible object is one that is seen, something audible is that which is heard, and whatever is desirable is proven by the fact that it is desired. Each person desires his own happiness, therefore happiness is desirable.

The argument appears very persuasive but it rests on a subtle equivocation. What is seen is visible and what is heard is audible but what is desired may not be desirable, that is, *worthy* of being desired. The term *desirable* functions differently than *visible* or *audible* because it is an evaluative term not just a descriptive one. As a contemporary linguistic analyst would say, it occupies a different logical category. The objects that people desire may not be worth desiring at all, for example, cigarettes or junk food, and an object may be desirable even though no one desires it; if the time came when no one appreciated classical music, Mozart and Beethoven would still be valuable, "like an old gold coin that retains its value even though it is no longer current."

Mill's main error lay in thinking that whatever people want is worthwhile by virtue of the fact that they want it. This subjectivist position has obvious difficulties. What we do desire is not necessarily what we ought to desire, otherwise we would never need to be persuaded to choose better goals. For instance, a life of drug abuse is not desirable even if the addict desires to be in a continual stupor.[8]

4. Aside from flaws in Bentham and Mill's systems of thought, utilitarianism in general can be criticized for several reasons. One of the recurrent and important questions about utilitarianism concerns its moral dimension. One would think that a universalistic hedonism would be on high moral ground because of its altruistic nature but seeking the greatest happiness for the greatest number can mean ignoring the rights of minorities. For example, the majority might derive happiness from enslaving the minority but that hardly shows slavery to be a moral institution. Blacks were imported from Africa as slaves partly with justification of this kind, which shows the inherent moral weakness in the utilitarian system.

Even if the denial of a minority's rights would produce widespread happiness nevertheless those rights must be respected. One mark of a nation's level of civilization is its treatment of minorities, that is, its commitment to humane principles regardless of the social benefits that might accrue from annulling them.[9]

It should be added that the distinction between act and rule utilitarianism does not provide the moral element that is needed. For not even rule utilitarianism would prevent the abuse of minority rights if that brought more happiness to more people. Even the principle of slavery would be acceptable to a rule utilitarian, regardless of its assault on human dignity and freedom; the general happiness of society is what counts and that alone is the measure of morality. On utilitarian grounds then one could approve of everything from Salem witch hunts to the murder of Jews in Nazi Germany.[10]

5. A final criticism of utilitarianism follows from the points just made but includes wider considerations. In the field of ethics a threefold division is made in the way that actions may be judged. *Intentionalism* is the view that the intent or motive of the agent is the most important element in evaluating the worth of actions. If a person "means well," if his "heart is in the right place," then we should praise the behavior. In contrast, *formalism* or *deontologism* is the position

that the nature of the act is most important, its inherent rightness or wrongness. Our moral obligation to perform an action springs from its essential character, and actions should be judged in terms of their embodiment of principles that are intrinsically correct. *Teleologism,* in contradistinction to both of these theories, claims that the value of actions depends upon their consequences. If an action tends to produce good results rather than bad then it is considered worthwhile.

The charge leveled against utilitarianism is that it fails to consider either the agent's intention or formal elements in judging action and focuses exclusively on the teleological aspect. That is, the utilitarian is solely concerned with the happiness that results and neglects both the purpose of the act and its rightness.

With regard to intention Bentham stated at the end of the selection included here (Chapter 10, No. 10) *"there is no such thing as any sort of motive that is in itself a bad one,"* provided that pleasure is produced. This sentiment was echoed by Mill when he said, "the motive has nothing to do with the morality of the action, though much with the worth of the agent"; if happiness is multiplied then the action is worthwhile (Chapter 2). This attitude seems rather extreme because it implies that if a good result were achieved by someone with bad intentions then the act should be praised. For example, we should have to say that a corrupt congressman who accepts a bribe for a military contract has done a fine thing if the weapons help the national defense.[11]

More significant still is utilitarianism's adoption of a teleological ethic and its rejection of formalism. According to the formalist charge, the utilitarian fails to recognize that actions should be valued according to their inherent nature and not their consequences for human happiness. We should do what is right in itself, the formalist claims, for if we choose actions in terms of their ability to produce good results then we have no principles at all; we do whatever expediency requires. We are then prepared to lie if the truth would hurt, to steal for our family's welfare, to kill for the benefit of the group, in short, to perform any evil act if the outcome seems beneficial. The ends justify the means.

The formalist on the contrary maintains that a principle should be followed because it is right without reference to the practical implications it might have. In general, good consequences follow from right actions and bad consequences from wrong actions, but an action does not derive its moral quality from those consequences. Acts are correct in themselves or according to the principle under which they fall and are independent of time, place, circumstances, and results.

A more subtle way of expressing the formalist critique is to say that utilitarianism does not successfully explain why we feel that moral rules should not be broken. When people assert that justice, promise-keeping, or respect for life are important principles to maintain, they do not mean that happiness will be lessened if we violate these principles. They mean that we have a moral obligation to honor such values regardless of any pleasure that may be produced by adhering to them.

The attitude that people take toward the punishment of criminals can be used to illustrate the difference between a formalistic and a teleological approach. A formalist will judge the severity of a person's crime and on that basis reach a decision as to what would constitute an appropriate form of punishment. A teleologist, on the other hand, will adjust the punishment to the person's need for reform, using the nature of the offence as an index of that need. In deciding on the penalty for murder, for example, a formalist might conclude that a death sentence is the only just punishment, not out of a desire for vengeance but because the death penalty is thought proportional in severity to the taking of life. A teleologist, however, would probably set a prison term of sufficient length to reform and rehabilitate the murderer and to deter potential murderers in society. For the formalist, punishment must always be fair; for the teleologist, it need only be effective.

In essence, the formalist charges that the utilitarian is solely concerned with the good consequences of actions and not with their rightness. He feels that this creates a functional, pragmatic approach to ethics in which principles have no meaning except as classes of actions that have the effect of increasing pleasure or reducing pain. To the formalist, however, what is right cannot be reduced to what is good.

The debate between formalism and teleologism is ongoing and we will return to it when we examine the Kantian ethic of duty. At this point it is sufficient to notice that if the formalist is correct, then utilitarianism can be faulted for being so teleologically oriented. At the very least we can say that the intrinsic worth of an action (and the intention behind it) should be given more weight in an ethical system.

Despite the internal difficulties that utilitarianism suffers under, it still stands as one of the great systems of thought and continues to exercise a strong influence in the field of ethics. It has been attacked persistently in philosophic history yet regularly survives attack, emerging each time in a purer and more energetic form. Such tenacity is probably a reflection of its real strengths and of the psychological appeal that happiness holds as an ideal for human existence. In the final analysis, there are worse goals in life than trying to maximize happiness for all of mankind.

Notes

1. This passage appears in the selection included in this chapter and shows how Mill believes utilitarianism to be in keeping with Christian ethics. At a subsequent point in the same section he writes, "If it be a true belief that God desires, above all things, the happiness of his creatures, and that this was his purpose in their creation, utility is not only not a godless doctrine, but more profoundly religious than any other." Oddly enough, Immanuel Kant, whose philosophy is largely opposed to utilitarianism, believes that his theory embodies the Christian ethic.

2. See Mill's *Autobiography* for an account of his political involvment. Note also his tribute to the influence of his wife, especially on his *Principles of Political Economy* and his essay *On Liberty*.

3. To Bentham, ethics in the past had been too inexact and the time was ripe for introducing scientific rigorousness. In attempting to make philosophy scientific he is in company with numerous philosophers including Descartes, Leibniz, Spencer, Comte, Bradley, Ayer, and Russell.

4. Intensity does not vary in exact inverse ratio to fecundity and duration but only in a general way. With regard to duration, for example, an experience of five minutes will not necessarily be lower in intensity than one of two minutes, but an experience that lasts an hour will probably be less intense. The same inexactitude applies to the factor of fecundity.

5. Again, Mill's *Autobiography* should be consulted for a description of his extraordinary early education and the way in which his father groomed him to be a disciple of Bentham.

6. For excellent discussions of the act–rule debate, see J. J. C. Smart and Bernard Williams, *Utilitarianism: For and Against* (New York: Cambridge University Press, 1973), especially Smart's "Act-Utilitarianism"; Richard Brandt, *Theory of the Good and the Right* (Oxford: Oxford University Press, 1979), 286–305, especially Brandt's defense of rule utilitarianism; and John Rawls, "Two Concepts of Rules," *The Philosophical Review* 64 (1955): 3–32. One of the major contributions of Henry Sidgwick's *Methods of Ethics* is to show how intuitionism and universalistic hedonism are compatible, that the axioms of utilitarianism are self-evident.

7. Another question involved is whether a great quantity of pleasure is more desirable than a modest amount of sophisticated enjoyment; e.g., a sumptuous meal versus a mediocre chamber concert.

8. Another mistake Mill made was to assume that objects are only visible if they are seen, audible if they are heard. Something can be capable of being heard or seen even though no one has, in fact, heard or seen it, for example, an astronomical object. The dark side of the moon was visible before anyone had seen it.

9. In a contemporary work, *Theory of Justice*, John Rawls adds a "fairness principle" to utilitarianism, which stipulates that some actions are wrong to do regardless of the amount of happiness that may result from them. This seems to be an extremely useful corrective. It would certainly protect minority rights, and we are all members of a minority in some respects, whether as stamp collectors, mountain climbers, or opera goers.

10. This is a point of debate among utilitarians. Some would argue that people cannot be happy if they live in fear that one day they will part of a minority group. Therefore respect for minority rights would have to be a utilitarian principle.

11. Edward Westermarck has commented on Mill's statement that the distinction between acts and agents is a false one. "It cannot be admitted" he writes, "that 'he who saves a fellow creature from drowning does what is morally right, whether his motive be duty, or the hope of being paid for his trouble.' He ought, of course, to save the other person from drowning, but at the same time he ought to save him for a better motive than a wish for money . . . moral judgments are really passed upon men as acting or willing, not upon acts or volitions in the abstract." Edward Westermarck, *The Origin and Development of the Moral Ideas* (London: Macmillan, 1912), vol. 1: 209.

Bibliography

ANSCHUTZ, RICHARD. *The Philosophy of John Stuart Mill.* Oxford: Clarendon Press, 1953.

AYER, A. J. "The Principle of Utility." In *Philosophical Essays.* New York: St. Martin's Press, 1955.

BAUMGARDT, D. *Bentham and the Ethics of Today.* Princeton, N. J.: Princeton University Press, 1952.

BAYLES, MICHAEL D., ED. *Contemporary Utilitarianism.* New York: Anchor Doubleday, 1968.

BRANDT, RICHARD. *Ethical Theory.* Englewood Cliffs, N. J.: Prentice-Hall, 1960.

BRITTON, KARL. *Mill.* Baltimore: Penguin Books, 1953.

BROCK, DAN. "Recent Work in Utilitarianism." *American Philosophical Quarterly* 18 (1973): 241–76.

BRODY, BARUCH, ED. *Moral Rules and Particular Circumstances.* Englewood Cliffs, N. J.: Prentice-Hall, 1970.

ELLERY, JOHN. *John Stuart Mill.* Boston: Twayne, 1964.

EWING, ALFRED. "Utilitarianism." *Ethics* 58 (1948): 100–11.

GOROVITZ, SAMUEL, ED. *John Stuart Mill: Utilitarianism with Critical Essays.* Indianapolis: Bobbs-Merrill, 1971.

HARE, R. M. *Moral Thinking: Its Levels, Method and Point.* New York: Oxford University Press, 1981.

HARRISON, J. "Utilitarianism, Universalization and Our Duty to Be Just." *Proceedings of the Aristotelian Society* 53 (1952–53): 105–34.

HASLETT, D. W. *Moral Rightness.* The Hague, Holland: Martinus Nijhoff, 1974.

HEARN, THOMAS, ED. *Studies in Utilitarianism.* New York: Appleton-Century-Crofts, 1971.

HENSON, RICHARD. "Utilitarianism and the Wrongness of Killing." *Philosophical Review* 80 (1971): 320–37.

HODGSON, I. H. *Consequences of Utilitarianism.* London: Oxford University Press, 1967.

JONES, H. "Mill's Argument for the Principle of Utility." *Philosophy and Phenomenological Research* 38 (1977–78): 338–54.

LYONS, DAVID. *Forms and Limits of Utilitarianism.* London: Oxford University Press, 1965.

MacCUNN, JOHN. *Six Radical Thinkers.* London: E. Arnold, 1910.

MACK, MARY. *Jeremy Bentham, An Odyssey of Ideas.* New York: Columbia University Press, 1963.

MOORE, G. E. *Ethics,* Chapters 1 and 2. London: Oxford University Press, 1912.

NARVESON, JAN. *Morality and Utility.* Baltimore: Johns Hopkins University Press, 1967.

PLAMENATZ, J. *The English Utilitarians,* Chapter 4. Oxford: Basil Blackwell, 1966.

RASHDALL, H. *The Theory of Good and Evil,* vol. 1, Chapter 2. Oxford: Clarendon Press, 1907.

ROBSON, JOHN. *Improvement of Mankind: The Social and Political Thought of John Stuart Mill.* Toronto: University of Toronto Press, 1968.

ROSEN, BERNARD. *Strategies of Ethics.* Boston: Houghton Mifflin, 1978.

SCHNEEWIND, J. B., ED. *Mill's Ethical Writings.* New York: Collier Books, 1965.

SIDGWICK, HENRY. *The Methods of Ethics,* Book 4. 7th ed. London: Macmillan, 1874.

SINGER, M. G. *Generalization in Ethics.* New York: Alfred Knopf, 1961.

SMART, J. J. C. *Outlines of a Utilitarian System of Ethics.* London: Cambridge University Press, 1961.

————, and BERNARD WILLIAMS. *Utilitarianism: For and Against.* Cambridge: Cambridge University Press, 1973.

SMITH, JAMES M., and ERNEST SOSA, EDS. *Mill's Utilitarianism: Text and Criticism.* Belmont, Calif.: Wadsworth, 1969.

SOBEL, J. H. "Utilitarianism, Simple and General." *Inquiry* 13 (1970): 394–449.

SORLEY, W. R. *A History of English Philosophy.* New York: Putnam, 1920.

STEINTRAGER, J. *Bentham.* London: Allen and Unwin, 1977.

STEPHEN, L. *The English Utilitarians,* vol. 1, Chapters 5 and 6. London: Duckworth, 1900.

WATSON, JOHN. *Hedonistic Theories from Aristippus to Spencer.* Glasgow: 1898.

WEDER, SVEN. *Duty and Utility.* Lund, Sweden: 1952.

CHAPTER 6

Self-Realization

One of the overall defects of hedonism is that it seems trite and cheap as a reason for living. Even in its highest form, as utilitarianism, it cannot escape the stigma of being superficial and commonplace. On the other hand, a morality that ignores human happiness and decides actions solely in terms of principle seems overly austere.

Since one should sin neither to the right nor to the left a compromise is needed, and this is achieved through the theory of self-realization. Here a finer type of existence is endorsed but along with personal fulfillment.

According to the self-realizationist the purpose of living is the full realization of our potentialities. Each person possesses talents, interests, and capabilities that can be developed and made substantial. We must recognize those abilities, dredging them to the light of consciousness through the process of introspection, and by deliberate, carefully chosen actions make those potentialities into actualities. The more of ourselves we can become, the better our lives will be.

Although this doctrine is usually called self-realization it is also referred to as self-actualization, which is almost a synonym; energism, which means engaging all of man's energies; perfectionism, which implies striving to become one's ideal self; and eudaimonism, which literally means "possession of a good genius" or more freely the vital well being enjoyed by a fully functioning human being. Each of these labels suggests that the capacities of the individual should be realized so that a complete, integrated, and unified self is brought into being. Above all, the aim is to understand one's essential nature and to become in actuality the kind of person one discovers oneself to be.

For example, a person might have artistic talent but never try to paint in a serious way, or be good at playing tennis but seldom go out on the courts because other activities seem more immediate or necessary, or be basically quite social, enjoying the company of other people but be too shy to join groups and form friendships. The self-realizationist would say that such a person should recognize that these creative, athletic, and social interests and abilities are important to express, and that such major parts of oneself should always be given priority over the lesser ones. We must all discover our dominant potentialities and cluster our activities around their development, keeping as a central pivot what is most fundamental to ourselves. It would be wrong, from the standpoint of self-realization, to act in ways that express the peripheral parts of our nature and to allow our essential being to remain latent and unactualized.

In this process of development it is not our *present* self that should be realized but our *ideal* self, not the self as it exists at any given moment but the self we could imagine becoming if we were at our best. This ideal, of course, can never become an actuality for we will never be perfect, but it provides us with a goal and an overall orientation for our conduct. Obviously we never achieve completeness, never reach that state of full maturity for there is always more that we could do and be. As the French philosopher Jean-Paul Sartre (1905–1980) pointed out, you cannot expect an animal to be anything more than it is; a frog or squirrel reaches the limits of its possibilities at the time it is born and cannot develop beyond its predetermined nature. But a human being is always less than he can conceive himself to be, forever deficient in his own eyes, so that a gap exists throughout our lifetime between what we are and what we wish we were.[1]

The person who wants to be a millionaire may someday be able to say "At last I have achieved my aim, I have a million dollars," but the self-realizationist knows that his dream will never come true. For he has set his sights on the horizon and the horizon line moves as he does. He throws the ball ahead of himself each time then races after it again. Nevertheless, in trying to reach goals that are progressively more distant his self is challenged and enriched. By trying to realize himself as completely as possible he feels very much alive because he is continually growing.

Another distinction that can be made besides that of the present and ideal self has to do with whether one's *individuality* should be realized or one's *humanness*. That is, we can decide to develop our individual qualities and become more of the unique person we are or we can choose as our goal becoming manifestly more human.

Most self-realizationists maintain that we should focus on our individuality, which means that we should try to understand the particular qualities intrinsic to our identity. We have to ask the question What is it without which I would not be me? Once we have isolated those factors necessary to being ourselves, then we know who we are and what we must do to confirm and express that special self.

That is not to say we should turn inward and develop our private being in isolation from others. We may find that gregariousness is an inseparable part of ourselves or that compassion, belonging, or generosity is essential to our nature. In these cases we should become involved with those around us, participate extensively in community activities that will promote personal interaction. Whatever the development of our particular nature requires should be done whether it means involvement with others or a solitary life of contemplation and creation.

A minority of self-realizationists, however, are in favor of our becoming more completely human, which means understanding the qualities that constitute humanness and striving to emulate them. This is not the same as fulfilling ourselves because some of our characteristics could differ from the general character of humanity. If a discrepancy does arise then, according to this version, the human should be given priority.

The question of what differentiates human beings from other forms of life is a difficult one, as we shall see. It has been proposed that man is the rational animal, the language user, the tool maker (*homo faber*), the aesthetic, political, or religious creature, and so forth. However, no matter what humanness might be we must take it as our model, avoiding the life of animals even though we might have a personal predilection for it. Aristotle is the philosopher most closely identified with this kind of self-realization theory, and he writes that even if we show ourselves "utterly slavish in [our] preference for the life of brute beasts" it is the existence of the human being that must form the standard for our conduct.

Aristotle's self-realization theory will be examined in the latter part of this chapter. It is the most thorough system ever devised of this type, but most followers of the self-realization ethic disagree and believe that our individual natures rather than our human nature should be cultivated and made to bloom.

Those self-realizationists who are in this mainstream have another decision to make, which is whether individuals should develop their dominant *interests* or their major *abilities*. In an ideal world the two would coincide, and even in our imperfect one people will often like the things they do well and vice versa. But sometimes a person will prefer an activity (or even an occupation) for which he has very little talent. For example, someone who was a first-rate insurance salesman and a second-rate guitarist might still prefer playing the guitar; making music could be more gratifying to him even though he does not do it very well. On the other hand, a person might choose to work in the expanding field of computers even though it is not his primary interest. If he has a particular aptitude for it he may feel that it is a smart career choice. Perhaps the study of history is his main love but he could decide to develop his most promising skills instead. Not only would this make more practical sense but it could be viewed as the actualization of potentialities that are central to himself.

The self-realizationists do not provide a very clear signal as to which choice is preferrable, and the issue is decided differently by different theorists. Perhaps the purer form of self-realization favors the development of one's abilities; doing whatever one likes could be a brand of hedonism.

Being Diversified or Focused

One major issue over which self-realizationists will often divide is whether people should focus on developing their principal interests and abilities (and subordinating the rest) or whether they should realize the full spectrum of their potentialities instead. The latter approach suggests that we should be *diversified*, exploring every facet of ourselves and enjoying the complete range of possibilities available to us. It advocates openness and experimentation, a willingness to try everything for the sake of becoming a well-rounded individual. Rather than being limited to some narrow specialization we should be generalists with a breadth of understanding and a variety of skills and talents to our credit. Only the person with a broad range of experiences and achievements can be called complete. The overall design of our lives must resemble the striations in a block of marble, variegated with a network of colorings and markings that nevertheless form a polished whole.

This interpretation of self-realization was perhaps best exemplified during the Renaissance, the period of history between the fourteenth and seventeenth centuries in which painting, music, and architecture flourished, modern science had its beginnings, and classical humanism was revived. According to the Renaissance ideal, the individual was supposed to be active and forceful, to pursue earthly success more than heavenly bliss, but along with the acquisition of wealth and status he was also expected to seek self-fulfillment through diversity and creative acts. At the time there was a sense of life as a fine art and careful attention was paid to the amenities and cultural aspects of daily living. Beauty was thought to be an important ingredient in a gratifying existence and knowledge, especially of classical literature, was the hallmark of the truly civilized person. To the Renaissance mind, autonomy consisted in reaching a state of completeness, and a successful existence meant not the amassing of power (although one should not be ineffectual) but the attainment of excellence.[2]

The epitome of the Renaissance man is probably Leonardo da Vinci (1452–1519), who was an artist, architect, writer, engineer, scientist, and mathematician. His accomplishments range from studies in meteorology, hydraulics, and anatomy to the construction of canals and cathedrals to the creation of fine sculptures and paintings. His talent was enormously diverse and almost everything he produced was superb.

Perhaps an even better example of breadth and excellence can be found in the ideal on which Renaissance values were largely based — that of ancient Greece during the fifth century B.C., the Age of Pericles. As the Athenian culture in particular has come down to us, it appears to have been characterized by an unusually varied and harmonious perspective on the world. The Athenian was very concerned to develop the diverse parts of himself in a consistent way and achieved remarkable scope and balance. In Matthew Arnold's phrase, the Athenian seemed to "see life steadily and as a whole." This concern with personal development and with proportion in thought and action is one of the main achievements of Athenian society.

To take one illustration, the way in which the Athenians viewed the Sophists is particularly instructive. As was mentioned in Chapter 1, the Sophists were generally regarded with contempt, not just because they taught people how to argue persuasively rather than logically but because they were one sided, being solely concerned with methods for practical success. In other words, they were wholly "commercial" in their attitudes, valuing only what paid. They neglected abstract subjects that showed man's relation to the world or those that "merely" developed the individual's capacity to appreciate the richness of life. The Athenians believed that both are necessary: training in practical skills for effectiveness in our work and theoretical understanding to allow a broader perspective on our lives. As Thucydides (born c. 471 B.C.) stated, the Athenian had "the power of adapting himself to the most varied form of action with the utmost versatility and grace" because he was at home in a multiplicity of circumstances.[3]

To be diversified and balanced, to have a fruitful mix of the social aspect of life with the personal and private, aesthetic creation and political involvement, the economic and the spiritual, a sound mind within a healthy body (*mens sana in corpore sano*) — all this was essential for a fully realized and unified human being.

Attractive as this ideal might be, however, most self-realizationists maintain that *focusing* and *concentration* is superior to diversity, even if those diverse interests are combined in a harmonious way. For very few people can achieve excellence in a number of different fields, and the attempt to participate in a broad array of activities usually produces shallowness; the Leonardo da Vinci's of this world are few and far between. More often single-minded dedication is needed to create something outstanding. Today especially, when an enormous amount of knowledge exists in every field, specialization is essential; one must find a "major" as the primary focus of one's energies, with other subjects taking second place. The person who tries to know everything and do everything winds up having a shallow and trivial understanding. He becomes a jack of all trades and a master of none.

Furthermore, the individual who divides his time among the social, the personal, the aesthetic, the political, the economic, the spiritual, the mental, and the physical is simply spreading himself too thin; he will usually fail to achieve satisfaction in any of these areas. Not only will his efforts produce only passable work but he will not experience the gratification that comes from following his special bent. Developing his strongest interests, that is, devoting most of his time to doing what he likes best, is a more promising approach to a good life.

The self-realizationist who favors concentration also points out that unless we give priority to our dominant tendencies we would have no principle for selecting between competing interests. In other words, we cannot do everything at the same time or even in one lifetime so choices have to be made. In his *Psychology* William James puts the point this way:

"I am often confronted by the necessity of standing by one of my empirical selves and relinquishing the rest. Not that I would not, if I could, be both handsome and fat and well dressed, and a great athlete, and make a million a year, be a wit, a *bon-vivant,* and a lady-killer, as well as a philosopher; a philanthropist, statesman, warrior, and African explorer, as well as a 'tone-poet' and saint. But the thing is simply impossible. The millionaire's work would run counter to the saint's; the *bon-vivant* and the philanthropist would trip each other up; the philosopher and the lady-killer could not well keep house in the same tenement of clay. Such different characters may conceivably at the outset of life be alike possible to a man. But to make any one of them actual, the rest must more or less be suppressed.

However, if we know our major abilities and tendencies and put them foremost, then we are able to make choices, for the various activities are ranked and we can decide which ones deserve more attention. Unless we do this, at worst, we would be paralyzed in our choices since all aspects of our being would have an equal claim to be realized. At best, we might then follow the inclinations of the moment but we would not necessarily do what would maximize our development. An impossible situation would exist, in which one activity is equal to another and no standard can be used to decide between them.

As a final point it is also argued that being a generalist means that we never achieve any personal identity. For if we are a little bit of everything then we are totally amorphous and devoid of definition, a crazy quilt pattern without a coherent design. In the same way, if we assume a receptive and flexible stance, open to a variety of possibilities and uncommitted to any overall direction, then it is hard to imagine what type of person we would be. We must decide what we are and what we are not, what is consistent with ourselves and what should be excluded from our lives; otherwise we have no character and can hardly be regarded as individuals. In short, we have to close the door on certain options and not experience every possibility; only in that way can a definite self be created.

The American philosopher George Santayana (1863–1952) explains this point in the following way. In speaking of Goethe's *Faust* and of the ideal of maximum experience expressed there Santayana says,

> It is characteristic of the absolute romantic spirit that when it has finished with
> something it must invent a new interest. It beats the bush for fresh game; it is always
> on the verge of being utterly bored. . . . [However] man is constituted by his
> limitations, by his station contrasted with all other stations, and his purposes cho-
> sen from amongst all other purposes. . . . His understanding may render him
> universal; his life never can. To be at all you must be something in particular.[4]

Santayana seems to be saying that identity is formed in part through negative
decisions, by refusing various alternatives as foreign to our makeup. We must
reject some things and stand for others. He is reminding us of the simple truth
that if we try to be everything in general we will be nothing in particular.

For all of these reasons most of the proponents of self-realization favor the
more selective approach of concentrating on what is most intimate and important to our selves. They advocate the full development of the individual but
always under the guidance of his dominant interests or abilities. We should
always engage in those actions that will realize more of our essential selves rather
than selecting activities that will foster what is minor or inconsequential. They
fully agree that we must develop ourselves as widely as possible but with the
qualification that the actualization of our more basic parts is more important
than the range of our development.

Whether diversification or concentration is chosen, the self-realizationists are
in agreement that the desires we fulfill must be harmonious with one another.
For example, we should not develop our interest in savoring rich French food
cooked with creamy sauces and eaten with full bodied wines and at the same time
start a program of heavy training for athletic competition. The one would
obstruct and conflict with the other. However, if we liked history, debate, and
law these could be made congruent quite easily; we could enter the field of
politics and make use of all three. That is not to say that our interests must have
strong similarities, but rather that their realization should produce a mutually
consistent and harmonious self; we do not want a mass of activities that hinder or
block one another. The aim is to develop ourselves in a completely harmonious
way.

An analogy that is relevant in this connection is with a work of architecture. If
we were to design a cathedral with a medieval vaulted ceiling, a glass and steel
exterior, and a New England colonial steeple, it would not be a wonderful
mosaic of styles but a mass of incongruities. Art, like people, must make sense
and as the aesthetician G.-L. Buffon has said an artist's style is the person himself
("*Le style est l'homme même*"). A good work of art always expresses an identity and
is unified and integrated in its purpose. In the same way people should combine
those aspects of themselves that can create a singular and consonant whole.

As we can see the decision to adopt self-realization involves a number of
distinctions and subsequent choices. We must differentiate between our present
and our ideal self, whether we should develop our individuality or our humanness, our dominant interests or major abilities, and finally whether to be a
diversified person or to concentrate and achieve expertise.

Self-Realization and Hedonism

Sometimes it is mistakenly assumed that the ultimate purpose of self-realization
is to bring about the goal of hedonism, viz., the happiness of the individual, that
self-realization is desirable because it is a means to the end of happiness. In fact,

self-realization is not considered an instrument for producing happiness but an ultimate end in itself; like a mountain peak, it leads nowhere. Instead of pursuing a life of happiness, the self-realizationist wants to make his potentialities into actualities. If in the process of realizing his capacities he also finds happiness that would be a marvelous additional benefit, but it is not his purpose.

Very often the two will, in fact, coincide, and we can find happiness in the realization of our selves but that is not always the case. Sometimes self-fulfillment will run counter to the attainment of happiness because actions may be required that are not pleasurable at all. For example, a woman might be tempted by a marriage proposal from a man whom she knows will make her happy but in the end decide not to accept for fear that her personal development would be stifled. He may be wealthy and promise to provide her with a very comfortable existence but she could feel that, like the bird in the gilded cage, a life of luxury might entail the end of her self-respect. The pleasures that wealth provides could militate against her becoming a worthwhile person, seducing her to a life of ease rather than one of accomplishment. She might know her weaknesses and realize that in those circumstances she would not be able to resist indulging herself but that she would be far better off struggling to improve herself instead. It is not that she is afraid she will be unhappy in the life offered to her but that she is afraid she will be happy and, because of that happiness, become stunted in her growth as a person.

In other words, self-realization and happiness could diverge, leading in opposite directions, and a person could elect to take the path of greatest development rather than the line of least resistance. We can see, therefore, that self-realization is a separate life purpose, which people could prefer to that of hedonism. We should not ask then why someone wants to develop himself, implying that it must be for the sake of some further end. Self-realization is itself a final goal of conduct and stands on a par with happiness, an alternative theory as to what constitutes a good life.

In an extreme form, the self-realizationist does not want to *be* anything at all, whether happy, dutiful, natural, or whatever; he wants to exist in a continual state of *becoming,* to feel gratified by growing into a fuller, richer, more profound person throughout his life. This means that self-realization can differ not just from hedonism but from most ethical theories by stressing process as more important. The point lies in the going not the goal, the journey not the arrival. The adventure of unfolding oneself is what seems to offer excitement and fulfillment. To some self-realizationists the self is the universe in miniature, the macrocosm in the microcosm, so that in progressively understanding oneself one is actually revealing the heart of life like Tennyson's "Flower in the crannied wall" that contains everything of god and man, or William Blake's "World in a Grain of sand,/And a Heaven in a Wild Flower,/ . . . Infinity in the palm of your hand,/And Eternity in an hour." This attitude is reminiscent of much of Eastern thought where the inner and the outer are thought to be identical, that by exploring our interior spirit through a series of illuminations we also come to comprehend the divine universe surrounding us.

For most self-realizationists of the present day, however, the matter is much less mystical. They conceive of the self and the world in a natural way without any assumption that there are cosmic implications to self-development. They simply want the maximum fulfillment of the human self as it moves through its earthly life. The goal is not happiness but neither is it a disclosure that the individual soul and the World Soul are one.

Individual: Actualizing Our Potentialities

In the contemporary age this straightforward approach to self-realization has gained a great deal of support from certain prominent psychologists. People such as Abraham Maslow (1908–1970), Carl Rogers (1902–1987), and Erich Fromm (1900–1980) have advocated this philosophy much more than any philosophers have done. They were, in fact, its major spokesmen, writing numerous books on self-realization as a liberating, healthy-minded, emotionally enriching approach to life. In the 1960s and early 1970s the "be yourself" doctrine was particularly prevalent and it continues to be a popular philosophy today. We can take their writings then as representative of the form that self-realization has assumed in recent years. Sometimes these psychologists are called existential, sometimes humanistic, but their position is more essentially self-realizationist in character.

Carl Rogers, for example, has a book entitled *On Becoming a Person* with a chapter called "To Be That Self Which One Truly Is"; Erich Fromm's orientaion can be seen in his *Man for Himself, To Have or to Be* and *The Anatomy of Human Destructiveness;* and Abraham Maslow has written *Toward a Psychology of Being* and *Motivation and Personality,* the latter presenting a blueprint for the stages of development leading to self-actualization.

The following selections from Maslow's writings may be taken as representative of this psychological approach. In presenting what he described as a newly emerging concept of mental health Maslow wrote:

First of all and most important of all is the strong belief that man has an essential nature of his own, some skeleton of psychological structure that may be treated and discussed analogously with his physical structure, that he has some needs, capacities, and tendencies that are in part genetically based, some of which are characteristic of the whole human species, cutting across all cultural lines, and some of which are unique to the individual. These basic needs are on their face good or neutral rather than evil. Second, there is involved the conception that full health and normal and desirable development consist in actualizing this nature, in fulfilling these potentialities, and in developing into maturity along the lines that this hidden, covert, dimly seen essential nature dictates, growing from within rather than being shaped from without. Third, it is now seen clearly that most psychopathology results from the denial or the frustration or the twisting of man's essential nature. By this concept what is good? Anything that conduces to this desirable development in the direction of actualization of the inner nature of man. What is bad or abnormal? Anything that frustrates or blocks or denies the essential nature of man. What is psychopathological? Anything that disturbs or frustrates or twists the course of self-actualization. What is psychotherapy, or for that matter any therapy or growth of any kind? Any means of any kind that helps to restore the person to the path of self-actualization and of development along the lines that his inner nature dictates.

. . .

Now coming back to the question with which we started, the nature of normality, we have come close to identifying it with the highest excellence of which we are capable. But this ideal is not an unattainable goal set out far ahead of us; rather it is actually within us, existent but hidden, as potentiality rather than as actuality.

One last point. The key concepts in the newer dynamic psychology are spontaneity, release, naturalness, self-choice, self-acceptance, impulse-awareness, gratification of basic needs. They *used* to be control, inhibition, discipline, training, shaping, on the principle that the depths of human nature were dangerous, evil, predatory, and ravenous.[5]

Maslow is well known for his theory of a "hierarchy of needs," which culminates in the need for self-actualization. He described the physiological need for food as a primary need and declared that "it is quite true that man lives by bread alone — when there is no bread." He next described the need for safety, which includes the desire for security, stability, dependency, protection, freedom from fear, from anxiety and chaos, and so forth. If the physiological and safety needs are satisfied the need for love and belonging begins to appear, a hunger for affection and contact with one's fellow man. A further characteristic of the human organism is the need for self-esteem. We desire strength, achievement, mastery, and confidence as well as prestige, status, and appreciation. Ideally, this self-esteem is not based on determination and a resulting competence won through will power but arises naturally from a person's inner nature.

Finally, if the need for food, safety, love, and self-esteem have all been met an ultimate need emerges, which is "the need for self-actualization." Maslow stated,

a new discontent and restlessness will soon develop, unless the individual is doing what *he*, individually, is fitted for. A musician must make music, an artist must paint, a poet must write, if he is to be ultimately at peace with himself. What a man *can* be, he *must* be. He must be true to his own nature. This need we may call self-actualization. . . . It refers to man's desire for self-fulfillment, namely, to the tendency for him to become actualized in what he is potentially. This tendency might be phrased as the desire to become more and more what one idiosyncratically is, to become everything that one is capable of becoming.[6]

This psychological theory of self-realization was developed in a parallel way by Rogers and Fromm and it appeared in their work as both a theory of personality and a psychotherapeutic technique for promoting balance and wholeness. Carl Rogers, for instance, in describing "A Therapist's View of the Good Life: The Fully Functioning Person," said:

The good life, from the point of view of my experience, is the process of movement in a direction which the human organism selects when it is inwardly free to move in any direction, and the general qualities of this selected direction appear to have a certain universality.

• • •

In the first place, the process seems to involve an increasing openness to experience. This phrase has come to have more and more meaning for me. It is the polar opposite of defensiveness. Defensiveness I have described in the past as being the organism's response to experiences which are perceived or anticipated as threatening, as incongruent with the individual's existing picture of himself, or of himself in relationship to the world. These threatening experiences are temporarily rendered harmless by being distorted in awareness, or being denied to awareness. I quite literally cannot see, with accuracy, those experiences, feelings, reactions in myself which are significantly at variance with the picture of myself which I already possess. A large part of the process of therapy is the continuing discovery by the client that he is experiencing feelings and attitudes which heretofore he has not been able to be aware of, which he has not been able to "own" as being a part of himself.

If a person could be fully open to his experience, however, every stimulus — whether originating within the organism or in the environment — would be freely relayed through the nervous system without being distorted by any defensive mechanism. There would be no need of the mechanism of "subception" whereby the organism is forewarned of any experience threatening to the self. On the contrary, whether the stimulus was the impact of a configuration of form, color, or sound in the environment on the sensory nerves, or a memory trace from the past, or a visceral sensation of fear or pleasure or disgust, the person would be "living" it, would have it completely available to awareness.

Thus, one aspect of this process which I am naming "the good life" appears to be a movement away from the pole of defensiveness toward the pole of openness to experience. The individual is becoming more able to listen to himself, to experience what is going on within himself. He is more open to his feelings of fear and discouragement and pain. He is also more open to his feelings of courage, and tenderness, and awe. He is free to live his feelings subjectively, as they exist in him, and also free to be aware of these feelings. He is more able fully to live the experiences of his organism rather than shutting them out of awareness.

• • •

One last implication I should like to mention is that this process of living in the good life involves a wider range, a greater richness, than the constricted living in which most of us find ourselves. To be a part of this process means that one is involved in the frequently frightening and frequently satisfying experience of a more sensitive living, with greater range, greater variety, greater richness. It seems to me that clients who have moved significantly in therapy live more intimately with their feelings of pain, but also more vividly with their feelings of ectasy; that anger is more clearly felt, but so also is love; that fear is an experience they know more deeply, but so is courage. And the reason they can thus live fully in a wider range is that they have this underlying confidence in themselves as trustworthy instruments for encountering life.

I believe it will have become evident why, for me, adjectives such as happy, contented, blissful, enjoyable, do not seem quite appropriate to any general description of this process I have called the good life, even though the person in this process would experience each one of these feelings at appropriate times. But the adjectives which seem more generally fitting are adjectives such as enriching, exciting, rewarding, challenging, meaningful. This process of the good life is not, I am convinced, a life for the faint-hearted. It involves the stretching and growing of becoming more and more of one's potentialities. It involves the courage to be. It means launching oneself fully into the stream of life. Yet the deeply exciting thing about human beings is that when the individual is inwardly free, he chooses as the good life this process of becoming.[7]

Aside from distinguished figures in psychology, self-realization has also had representatives among the philosophers. The philosophic figures include people such as J. H. Muirhead, Bernard Bosanquet, H. J. Paton, T. H. Green, W. E. Hocking, W. K. Wright and J. M. E. McTaggart, most of whom wrote toward the beginning of the twentieth century. In their separate ways, they all took an *idealistic* view of the development of self.[8]

The term idealism is generally used to mean high ethical aims but in philosophic terms it stands for the theory that reality is fundamentally spiritual not material in nature. Reality is said to consist of ideas or mind, perhaps individual minds on which the world is dependent or the absolute mind of god. The self is part of this essential idealistic reality, and it cannot attain fulfillment unless it merges with the general spirituality of the universe.

J. H. Muirhead (1855–1940), for example, maintained that the self is not an "isolated atom" that can stand alone and attain its realization apart from others and society. "Individuality must be sought for not in separation from the whole," Muirhead wrote, "but in a whole-hearted acceptance of a definite station within it. It is from his unity with the whole that the individual draws his substance." He went on to say that "it is impossible to will an individual good . . . all good is social"; that the good, which is "the fulfillment or realization of the self as a whole" can only come about through participation and absorption in the social unit "which corresponds to [our] deepest needs to be an individual."[9] Using the same organic view T. H. Green linked the realization of the self to a conception of deity. God is that totality and completeness of being that the human spirit aspires toward, Green argued. He is the perfectly realized entity, therefore to approach one's ideal self is to approach the divine.

In this same idealistic tradition were certain better known philosophers such as G. W. F. Hegel (1770–1831), Josiah Royce (1855–1916), and F. H. Bradley (1846–1924), who presented more complete philosophic systems of thought.

Hegel was by far the most prominent of the group but his writings are at times extremely obscure; it is difficult to tell, for example, what he means by spirit.

Sometimes he appears to be referring to the human spirit and the stages necessary for its refinement, although at other times spirit seems synonymous with god. F. H. Bradley, on the other hand, has a very lucid style and can be taken as a more accessible representative of the idealistic approach to self-realization.

Like many British philosophers of the period, Bradley was a convert to the Hegelian metaphysics. He accepted the idealist's thesis that reality is spiritual in nature and emphasized that it formed an essential unity. The *absolute,* or the totality of everything, is the only actual reality; everything else, including all of the parts, he calls mere appearance. The title of his principal book, *Appearance and Reality,* is expressive of this dichotomy and shows how the elements within the comprehensive whole are not at variance with one another but form a consistent and connected network of relations.

Bradley then drew the implications to ethics, that we cannot live a good life by taking an individualistic stance. Human life is only worthwhile when it fulfills its obligations as a part of the larger whole. Once the person recognizes his place within the "scheme of things entire" and strives to realize himself in the light of that embracing reality, then and only then will he make his existence meaningful. More specifically, the self must be realized through its membership in society and the state, which is "an organic unity of spiritual beings," and then pass upwards to a confluence with the highest spirituality of religion.

The selection that follows from Bradley's *Ethical Studies* is often considered the best short statement of the idealistic ethic and even expresses the basic Hegelian position.

My Station and Its Duties*

• • •

The 'individual' man, the man into whose essence his community with others does not enter, who does not include relation to others in his very being, is, we say, a fiction, and in the light of facts we have to examine him. Let us take him in the shape of an English child as soon as he is born; for I suppose we ought not to go further back. Let us take him as soon as he is separated from his mother, and occupies a space clear and exclusive of all other human beings. At this time, education and custom will, I imagine, be allowed to have not as yet operated on him or lessened his "individuality." But is he now a mere 'individual,' in the sense of not implying in his being identity with others? We can not say that, if we hold to the teaching of modern physiology. Physiology would tell us, in one language or another, that even now the child's mind is no passive 'tabula rasa'; he has an inner, a yet undeveloped nature, which must largely determine his future individuality. What is this inner nature? Is it particular to himself? Certainly not all of it, will have to be the answer. The child is not fallen from heaven. He is born of certain parents who come of certain families, and he has in him the qualities of his parents, and, as breeders would say, of the strains from both sides. Much of it we can see, and more we believe to be latent, and, given certain (possible

*Reprinted from F. H. Bradley, *Ethical Studies* (Oxford: Clarendon Press, 1927, first published 1876).

or impossible) conditions, ready to come to light. On the descent of mental qualities, modern investigation and popular experience, as expressed in uneducated vulgar opinion, altogether, I believe, support one another, and we need not linger here. But if the intellectual and active qualities do descend from ancestors, is it not, I would ask, quite clear that a man may have in him the same that his father and mother had, the same that his brothers and sisters have? And if any one objects to the word 'same', I would put this to him. If, concerning two dogs allied in blood, I were to ask a man, 'Is that of the same strain or stock as this?' and were answered, 'No, not the same, but similar', should I not think one of these things, that the man either meant to deceive me, or was a 'thinker', or a fool?

But the child is not merely the member of a family; he is born into other spheres, and (passing over the subordinate wholes, which nevertheless do in many cases qualify him) he is born a member of the English nation. It is, I believe, a matter of fact that at birth the child of one race is not the same as the child of another; that in the children of the one race there is a certain identity, a developed or undeveloped national type, which may be hard to recognize, or which at present may even be unrecognizable, but which nevertheless in some form will appear. If that be the fact, then again we must say that one English child is in some points, though perhaps it does not as yet show itself, the same as another. His being is so far common to him with others; he is not a mere 'individual'.

We see the child has been born at a certain time of parents of a certain race, and that means also of a certain degree of culture. It is the opinion of those best qualified to speak on the subject, that civilization is to some not inconsiderable extent hereditary; that aptitudes are developed, and are latent in the child at birth; and that it is a very different thing, even apart from education, to be born of civilized and of uncivilized ancestors. These 'civilized tendencies', if we may use the phrase, are part of the essence of the child: he would only partly (if at all) be himself without them; he owes them to his ancestors, and his ancestors owe them to society. The ancestors were made what they were by the society they lived in. If in answer it be replied, 'Yes, but individual ancestors were prior to their society', then that, to say the least of it, is a hazardous and unproved assertion, since man, so far as history can trace him back, is social; and if Mr. Darwin's conjecture as to the development of man from a social animal be received, we must say that man has never been anything but social, and society never was made by individual men. Nor, if the (baseless) assertion of the priority of individual men were allowed, would that destroy our case; for certainly our more immediate ancestors were social; and, whether society was manufactured previously by individuals or not, yet in their case it certainly was not so. They at all events have been so qualified by the common possessions of social mankind that, as members in the organism, they have become relative to the whole. If we suppose then that the results of the social life of the race are present in a latent and potential form in the child, can we deny that they are common property? Can we assert that they are not an element of sameness in all? Can we say that the individual is this individual, because he is exclusive, when, if we deduct from him what he includes, he loses characteristics which make him himself, and when again he does include what the others include, and therefore does (how can we escape the consequences?) include in some sense the others also, just as they include him? By himself, then, what are we to call him? I confess I do not know, unless we name him a theoretical attempt to isolate what can not be isolated; and that, I suppose, has, out of our heads, no existence. But what he is really, and not in mere theory, can be described only as the specification or particularization of that which is common, which is the same amid diversity, and without which the 'individual' would be so other than he is that we could not call him the same.

Thus the child is at birth; and he is born not into a desert, but into a living world, a whole which has a true individuality of its own, and into a system and order which it is difficult to look at as anything else than an organism, and which, even in England, we are now beginning to call by that name. And I fear that the 'individuality' (the particularness) which the child brought into the light with him, now stands but a poor chance, and that there is no help for him until he is old enough to become a 'philosopher'. We have seen that already he has in him inherited habits, or what will of themselves appear as such; but, in addition to this, he is not for one moment left alone, but continually tampered with; and the habituation which is applied from the outside is the more insidious that it answers to this inborn disposition. Who can resist it? Nay, who but a 'thinker' could wish to have resisted it? And yet the tender care that receives and guides him is impressing on him habits, habits, alas, not particular to himself, and the 'icy chains' of universal custom are hardening themselves round his cradled life. As the poet tells us, he has not yet thought of himself; his earliest notions come mixed to him of things and persons, not distinct from one another, nor divided from the feeling of his own existence. The need that he can not understand moves him to foolish, but not futile, cries for what only another can give him; and the breast of his mother, and the soft warmth and touches and tones of his nurse, are made one with the feeling of his own pleasure and pain; nor is he yet a moralist to beware of such illusion, and to see in them mere means to an end without them in his separate self. For he does not even think of his separate self; he grows with his world, his mind fills and orders itself; and when he can separate himself from that world, and know himself apart from it, then by that time his self, the object of his self-consciousness, is penetrated, infected, characterized by the existence of others. Its content implies in every fibre relations of community. He learns, or already perhaps has learnt, to speak, and here he appropriates the common heritage of his race, the tongue that he makes his own is his country's language, it is (or it should be) the same that others speak, and it carries into his mind the ideas and sentiments of the race (over this I need not stay), and stamps them in indelibly. He grows up in an atmosphere of example and general custom, his life widens out from one little world to other and higher worlds, and he apprehends through successive stations the whole in which he lives, and in which he has lived. Is he now to try and develop his 'individuality', his self which is not the same as other selves? Where is it? What is it? Where can he find it? The soul within him is saturated, is filled, is qualified by, it has assimilated, has got its substance, has built itself up from, it *is* one and the same life with the universal life, and if he turns against this he turns against himself; if he thrusts it from him, he tears his own vitals; if he attacks it, he sets his weapon against his own heart. He has found his life in the life of the whole, he lives that in himself, 'he is a pulse-beat of the whole system, and himself the whole system'.

'The child, in his character of the form of the possibility of a moral individual, is something subjective or negative; his growing to manhood is the ceasing to be of this form, and his education is the discipline or the compulsion thereof. The positive side and the essence is that he is suckled at the breast of the universal Ethos, lives in its absolute intuition, as in that of a foreign being first, then comprehends it more and more, and so passes over into the universal mind.' The writer proceeds to draw the weighty conclusion that virtue 'is not a troubling oneself about a peculiar and isolated morality of one's own, that the striving for a positive morality of one's own is futile, and in its very nature impossible of attainment; that in respect of morality the saying of the wisest men of antiquity is the only one which is true, that to be moral is to live in accordance with the moral tradition of one's country; and in respect of education, the one true answer is that which a Pythagorean gave to him who asked what was the best education for his son, If you make him the citizen of a people with good institutions'.*

But this is to anticipate. So far, I think, without aid from metaphysics, we have seen that the 'individual' apart from the community is an abstraction. It is not anything real, and hence not anything that we can realize, however much we may wish to do so. We have seen that I am myself by sharing with others, by including in my essence relations to them, the relations of the social state. If I wish to realize my true being, I must therefore realize something beyond my being as a mere this or that; for my true being has in it a life which is not the life of any mere particular, and so must be called a universal life.

What is it then that I am to realize? We have said it in 'my station and its duties'. To know what a man is (as we have seen) you must not take him in isolation. He is one of a people, he was born in a family, he lives in a certain society, in a certain state. What he has to do depends on what his place is, what his function is, and that all comes from his station in the organism. Are there then such organisms in which he lives, and if so, what is their nature? Here we come to questions which must be answered in full by any complete system of Ethics, but which we can not enter on. We must content ourselves by pointing out that there are such facts as the family, then in a middle position a man's own profession and society, and, over all, the larger community of the state. Leaving out of sight the question of a society wider than the state, we must say that a man's life with its moral duties is in the main filled up by his station in that system of wholes which the state is, and that this, partly by its laws and institutions, and still more by its spirit, gives him the life which he does live and ought to live. That objective institutions exist is of course an obvious fact; and it is a fact which every day is becoming plainer that these institutions are organic, and further, that they are moral. The assertion that communities have been manufactured by the addition of exclusive units is, as we have seen, a mere fable; and if, within the state, we take that which seems wholly to depend on individual caprice, e.g.

*Hegel.

marriage,* yet even here we find that a man does give up his self so far as it excludes others; he does bring himself under a unity which is superior to the particular person and the impulses that belong to his single existence, and which makes him fully as much as he makes it. In short, man is a social being; he is real only because he is social, and can realize himself only because it is as social that he realizes himself. The mere individual is a delusion of theory; and the attempt to realize it in practice is the starvation and mutilation of human nature, with total sterility or the production of monstrosities.

• • •

The non-theoretical person, if he be not immoral, is at peace with reality; and the man who in any degree has made this point of view has own, becomes more and more reconciled to the world and to life, and the theories of 'advanced thinkers' come to him more and more as the thinnest and most miserable abstractions. He sees evils which can not discourage him, since they point to the strength of the life which can endure such parasites and flourish in spite of them. If the popularizing of superficial views inclines him to bitterness, he comforts himself when he sees that they live in the head, and but little, if at all, in the heart and life; that still at the push the doctrinaire and the quacksalver go to the wall, and that even that too is as it ought to be. He sees the true account of the state (which holds it to be neither mere force nor convention, but the moral organism, the real identity of might and right) unknown or 'refuted', laughed at and despised, but he sees the state every day in its practice refute every other doctrine, and do with the moral approval of all what the explicit theory of scarcely one will morally justify. He sees instincts are better and stronger than so-called 'principles.' He sees in the hour of need what are called 'rights' laughed at, 'freedom', the liberty to do what one pleases, trampled on, the claims of the individual trodden under foot, and theories burst like cobwebs. And he sees, as of old, the heart of a nation rise high and beat in the breast of each one of her citizens, till her safety and her honour are dearer to each than life, till to those who live her shame and sorrow, if such is allotted, outweigh their loss, and death seems a little thing to those who go for her to their common and nameless grave. And he knows that what is stronger than death is hate or love, hate here for love's sake, and that love does not fear death, because already it is the death into life of what our philosophers tell us is the only life and reality.

Yes, the state is not put together, but it lives; it is not a heap nor a machine; it is no mere extravagance when a poet talks of a nation's soul. It is the objective mind which is subjective and self-conscious in its citizens: it feels and knows itself in the heart of each. It speaks the word of command and gives the field of accomplishment, and in the activity of obedience it has and bestows individual life and satisfaction and happiness.

First in the community is the individual realized. He is here the embodiment of beauty, goodness, and truth: of truth, because he corresponds

---

*Marriage is a contract to pass out of the sphere of contract; and this is possible only because the contracting parties are already beyond and above the sphere of mere contract.

to his universal conception; of beauty, because he realizes it in a single form to the senses or imagination; of goodness, because his will expresses and is the will of the universal.

'The realm of morality is nothing but the absolute spiritual unity of the essence of individuals, which exists in the independent reality of them. . . . The moral substance, looked at abstractedly from the mere side of its universality, is the law, and, as this, is only thought; but none the less is it, from another point of view, immediate real self-consciousness or custom: and conversely the individual exists as this single unit, in as much as it is conscious in its individuality of the universal consciousness as its own being, in as much as its action and existence are the universal Ethos. . . . They (the individuals) are aware in themselves that they possess this individual independent being because of the sacrifice of their individuality, because the universal substance is their soul and essence: and, on the other side, this universal is their individual action, the work that they as individuals have produced.

'The merely individual action and business of the separate person is concerned with the needs he is subject to as a natural being, as an individuality which exists. That even these his commonest functions do not come to nothing, but possess reality, is effected solely by the universal maintaining medium, by the power of the whole people. But it is not simply the form of persistence which the universal substance confers on his action; it gives also the content — what he does *is* the universal skill and custom of all. This content, just so far as it completely individualizes itself, is in its reality interlaced with the action of all. The work of the individual for his needs is a satisfaction of the needs of others as much as of his own; and he attains the satisfaction of his own only through the work of the others. The individual in his individual work thus accomplishes a universal work — he does so here *unconsciously*; but he also further accomplishes it as his *conscious* object: the whole as the whole is his work for which he sacrifices himself, and from which by that very sacrifice he gets again his self restored. Here there is nothing taken which is not given, nothing wherein the independent individual, by and in the resolution of his atomic existence, by and in the negation of his self, fails to give himself the positive significance of a being which exists by and for itself. This unity — on the one side of the being for another, or the making oneself into an outward thing, and on the other side of the being for oneself — this universal substance speaks its universal language in the usages and laws of his people: and yet this unchanging essence is itself nought else than the expression of the single individuality, which seems at first sight its mere opposite; the laws pronounce nothing but what every one *is* and does. The individual recognizes the substance not only as his universal outward existence, but he recognizes also himself in it, particularized in his own individuality and in that of each of his fellow citizens. And so in the universal mind each one has nothing but self-certainty, the assurance of finding in existing reality nothing but himself. In all I contemplate independent beings, that are such, and are for themselves, only in the very same way that I am for myself; in them I see existing free unity of self with others, and existing by virtue of me and by virtue of the others alike. Them as myself, myself as them.

'In a free people, therefore, reason is realized in truth; it is present living mind, and in this not only does the individual find his destination, i.e. his universal and singular essence, promulgated and ready to his hand as an outward existence, but he himself is this essence, and has also reached and fulfilled his destination. Hence the wisest men of antiquity have given judgment that wisdom and virtue consist in living agreeably to the Ethos of one's people.*

Once let us take the point of view which regards the community as the real moral organism, which in its members knows and wills itself, and sees the individual to be real just so far as the universal self is in his self, as he in it, and we get the solution of most, if not all, of our previous difficulties. There is here no need to ask and by some scientific process find out what is moral, for morality exists all round us, and faces us, if need be, with a categorical imperative, while it surrounds us on the other side with an atmosphere of love.

The belief in this real moral organism is the one solution of ethical problems. It breaks down the antithesis of despotism and individualism; it denies them, while it preserves the truth of both. The truth of individualism is saved, because, unless we have intense life and self-consciousness in the members of the state, the whole state is ossified. The truth of despotism is saved, because, unless the member realizes the whole by and in himself, he fails to reach his own individuality. Considered in the main, the best communities are those which have the best men for their members, and the best men are the members of the best communities. Circle as this is, it is not a vicious circle. The two problems of the best man and best state are two sides, two distinguishable aspects of the one problem, how to realize in human nature the perfect unity of homogeneity and specification; and when we see that each of these without the other is unreal, then we see that (speaking in general) the welfare of the state and the welfare of its individuals are questions which it is mistaken and ruinous to separate. Personal morality and political and social institutions can not exist apart, and (in general) the better the one the better the other. The community is moral, because it realizes personal morality; personal morality is moral, because and in so far as it realizes the moral whole.

It is here we find a *partial* answer to the complaint of our day on the dwindling of human nature. The higher the organism (we are told), the more are its functions specified, and hence narrowed. The man becomes a machine, or the piece of a machine; and, though the world grows, 'the individual withers'. On this we may first remark that, if what is meant is that, the more centralized the system, the more narrow and monotonous is the life of the member, that is a very questionable assertion. If it be meant that the individual's life can be narrowed to 'file-packing', or the like, without detriment to the intensity of the life of the whole, that is even more questionable. If again it be meant that in many cases we have a one-sided specification, which, despite the immediate stimulus of particular function, implies ultimate loss of life to the body, that, I think, probably is so, but it is doubtful if we are compelled to think it always must be so. But the root of the whole complaint is a false view of things. The moral organism is not a

*Hegel.

mere animal organism. In the latter (it is no novel remark) the member is not aware of itself as such, while in the former it knows itself, and therefore knows the whole in itself. The narrow external function of the man is not the whole man. He has a life which we can not see with our eyes; and there is no duty so mean that it is not the realization of this, and knowable as such. What counts is not the visible outer work so much as the spirit in which it is done. The breadth of my life is not measured by the multitude of my pursuits, nor the space I take up amongst other men; but by the fullness of the whole life which I know as mine. It is true that less now depends on each of us, as this or that man; it is not true that our individuality is therefore lessened, that therefore we have less in us.

Let us now consider our point of view in relation to certain antagonistic ideas; and first against the common error that there is something 'right in itself' for me to do, in the sense that either there must be some absolute rule of morality the same for all persons without distinction of times and places, or else that all morality is 'relative', and hence no morality. Let us begin by remarking that there is no such fixed code or rule of right. It is abundantly clear that the morality of one time is not that of another time, that the men considered good in one age might in another age not be thought good, and what would be right for us here might be mean and base in another country, and what would be wrong for us here might there be our bounden duty. This is clear fact, which is denied only in the interest of a foregone conclusion. The motive to deny it is the belief that it is fatal to morality. If what is right here is wrong there, then all morality (such is the notion) becomes chance and convention, and so ceases. But 'my station and its duties' holds that *unless* morals varied, there could be no morality; that a morality which was *not* relative would be futile, and I should have to ask for something 'more relative than this'.

Let us explain. We hold that man is φνσει πολιτικός [by nature political], that apart from the community he is θεὸς η θήριον [a god or a beast], no man at all. We hold again that the true nature of man, the oneness of homogeneity and specification, is being wrought out in history; in short, we believe in evolution. The process of evolution is the humanizing of the bestial foundation of man's nature by carrying out in it the true idea of man; in other words, by realizing man as an infinite whole. This realization is possible only by the individual's living as member in a higher life, and this higher life is slowly developed in a series of stages. Starting from and on the basis of animal nature, humanity has worked itself out by gradual advances of specification and systematization; and any other progress would, in the world we know, have been impossible. The notion that full-fledged moral ideas fell down from heaven is contrary to all the facts with which we are acquainted. If they had done so, it would have been for their own sake; for by us they certainly could not have been perceived, much less applied. At any given period to know more than he did, man must have been more than he was; for a human being is nothing if he is not the son of his time; and he must realize himself as that, or he will not do it at all.

Morality is 'relative', but is none the less real. At every stage there is the solid fact of a world so far moralized. There is an objective morality in the accomplished will of the past and present, a higher self worked out by the infinite pain, the sweat and blood of generations, and now given to me by free grace and in love and faith as a sacred trust. It comes to me as the truth of my own nature, and the power and the law, which is stronger and higher than any caprice or opinion of my own.

'Evolution', in this sense of the word, gives us over neither to chance nor alien necessity, for it is that self-realization which is the progressive conquest of both. But, on another understanding of the term, we can not help asking, Is this still the case, and is 'my station' a tenable point of view?

Wholly tenable, in the form in which we have stated it, it is not. For if, in saying Morality has developed, all we mean is that something has happened different from earlier events, that human society has changed, and that the alterations, so far as we know them, are more or less of a certain sort; if 'progress' signifies that an advance has been set going and is kept up by chance in an unknown direction; that the higher is, in short, what *is* and what before was not, and that what will be, of whatever sort it is, will still be a step in progress; if, in short, the movement of history towards a goal is mere illusion, and the stages of that movement are nothing but the successes of what from time to time somehow happens to be best suited to the chance of circumstances—then it is clear in the first place that, teleology being banished, such words as evolution and progress have lost their own meaning, and that to speak of humanity realizing itself in history, and of myself finding in that movement the truth of myself worked out, would be simply to delude oneself with hollow phrases.

Thus far, we must say that on such a view of 'development' the doctrine of 'my station' is grievously curtailed. But is it destroyed? Not wholly; though sorely mutilated, it still keeps its ground. We have rejected teleology, but have not yet embraced individualism. We still believe that the universal self is more than a collection or an idea, that it is reality, and that apart from it the 'individuals' are the fictions of a theory. We have still the fact of the one self particularized in its many members; and the right and duty of gaining self-realization through the real universal is still as certain as is the impossibility of gaining it otherwise. And so 'my station' is after all a position, not indeed satisfactory, but not yet untenable.

But if the larger doctrine be the truth, if evolution is more than a tortured phrase, and progress to a goal no mere idea but an actual fact, then history is the working out of the true human nature through various incomplete stages towards completion, and 'my station' is the one satisfactory view of morals. Here (as we have seen) all morality is and must be 'relative', because the essence of realization is evolution through stages, and hence existence in some one stage which is not final; here, on the other hand, all mortality is 'absolute', because in every stage the essence of man *is* realized, however imperfectly: and yet again the distinction of right in itself against relative morality is not banished, because, from the point of view of a higher stage, we can see that lower stages failed to realize the truth completely enough, and also, mixed and one with their realization, did present features contrary to the true nature of man as we now see it. Yet herein the morality of every stage is justified for that stage; and the demand for a code of right in itself, apart from any stage, is seen to be the asking for an impossibility.

The next point we come to is the question, How do I get to know in particular what is right and wrong? And here again we find a strangely erroneous preconception. It is thought that moral philosophy has to accomplish this task for us; and the conclusion lies near at hand, that any system which will not do this is worthless. Well, we first remark, and with some confidence, that there cannot be a moral philosophy which will tell us what in particular we are to do, and also that it is not the business of philosophy to do so. All philosophy has to do is 'to understand what is', and moral philosophy has to understand morals which exist, not to make them or give directions for making them. Such a notion is simply ludicrous. Philosophy in general has not to anticipate the discoveries of the particular sciences nor the evolution of history; the philosophy of religion has not to make a new religion or teach an old one, but simply to understand the religious consciousness; and aesthetic has not to produce works of fine art, but to theorize the beautiful which it finds; political philosophy has not to play tricks with the state, but to understand it; and ethics has not to make the world moral, but to reduce to theory the morality current in the world. If we want it to do anything more, so much the worse for us; for it can not possibly construct new morality, and, even if it could to any extent codify what exists (a point on which I do not enter), yet it surely is clear that in cases of collision of duties it would not help you to know what to do. Who would go to a learned theologian, as such, in a practical religious difficulty; to a system of aesthetic for suggestions on the handling of an artistic theme; to a physiologist, as such, for a diagnosis and prescription; to a political philosopher in practical politics; or to a psychologist in an intrigue of any kind? All these persons no doubt might be the best to go to, but that would not be because they were the best theorists, but because they were more. In short, the view which thinks moral philosophy is to supply us with particular moral prescriptions confuses science with art, and confuses, besides, reflective with intuitive judgment. That which tells us what in particular is right and wrong is not reflection but intuition.

We know what is right in a particular case by what we may call an immediate judgment, or an intuitive subsumption. These phrases are perhaps not very luminous, and the matter of the 'intuitive understanding' in general is doubtless difficult, and the special character of moral judgments not easy to define; and I do not say that I am in a position to explain these subjects at all, nor, I think, could any one do so, except at considerable length. But the point that I do wish to establish here is, I think, not at all obscure. The reader has first to recognize that moral judgments are not discursive; next, that nevertheless they do start from and rest on a certain basis; and then if he puts the two together, he will see that they involve what he may call the 'intuitive understanding', or by any other name, so long as he keeps in sight the two elements and holds them together.

On the head that moral judgments are not discursive, no one, I think, will wish me to stay long. If the reader attends to the facts he will not want anything else; and if he does not, I confess I can not prove my point. In practical morality no doubt we *may* reflect on our principles, but I think it is not too much to say that we *never* do so, except where we have come upon a difficulty of particular application. If any one thinks that a man's *ordinary* judgment, 'this is right or wrong,' comes from the having a rule *before* the mind and bringing the particular case under it, he may be right; and I can not try to show that he is wrong. I can only leave it to the reader to judge for himself. We say we 'see' and we 'feel' in these cases, not we 'conclude'. We prize the advice of persons who can give us no reasons for what they say. There is a general belief that the having a reason for all your actions is pedantic and absurd. There is a general belief that to try to have reasons for all that you do is sometimes very dangerous. Not only the woman but the man who 'deliberates' may be 'lost'. First thoughts are often the best, and if once you begin to argue with the devil you are in a perilous state. And I think I may add (though I do it in fear) that women in general are remarkable for the fineness of their moral perceptions* and the quickness of their judgments, and yet are or (let me save myself by saying) 'may be' not remarkable for corresponding discursive ability.

Taking for granted then that our ordinary way of judging in morals is not by reflection and explicit reasoning, we have now to point to the other side of the fact, viz. that these judgments are not mere isolated impressions, but stand in an intimate and vital relation to a certain system, which is their basis. Here again we must ask the reader to pause, if in doubt, and consider the facts for himself. Different men, who have lived in different times and countries, judge or would judge a fresh case in morals differently. Why is this? There is probably no 'why' before the mind of either when he judges; but *we* perhaps can say, 'I know why A said so and B so', because we find some general rule or principle different in each, and in each the basis of the judgment. Different people in the same society may judge points differently, and we sometimes know why. It is because A is struck by one aspect of the case, B by another, and one principle is (not *before*, but) *in* A's mind when he judges, and another in B's. Each has subsumed, but under a different head; the one perhaps justice, the other gratitude. Every man has the morality he has made his own in his mind, and he 'sees' or 'feels' or 'judges' accordingly, though he does not reason explicitly from data to a conclusion.

I think this will be clear to the reader; and so we must say that on their perceptive or intellectual side (and that, the reader must not forget, is the one side that we are considering) our moral judgments are intuitive subsumptions.

To the question, How am I to know what is right? the answer must be, By the αἴσθησις [perception] of the φρόνιμος [man of practical wisdom]; and the φρόνιμος is the man who has identified his will with the moral spirit of the community, and judges accordingly. If an immoral course be suggested to him, he 'feels' or 'sees' at once that the act is not in harmony with a good will, and he does not do this by saying, 'this is a breach of rule A, *therefore*, &c'; but the first thing he is aware of is that he 'does not like it'; and what he has done, without being aware of it, is (at least in most cases) to seize the quality of the act, that quality being a general quality. Actions of a particular kind he does not like, and he has instinctively referred the particular act to that kind. What is right is perceived in the same way; courses suggest themselves, and one is approved of, because intuitively judged to be of a certain kind, which kind represents a principle of the good will.

*Not, perhaps, on *all* matters. Nor, again, will it do to say that *everywhere* women are pre-eminently intuitive, and men discursive. But in *practical* matters there seems not much doubt that it is so.

If a man is to know what is right, he should have imbibed by precept, and still more by example, the spirit of his community, its general and special beliefs as to right and wrong, and, with this whole embodied in his mind, should particularize it in any new case, not by a reflective deduction, but by an intuitive subsumption, which does not know that it is a subsumption; by a carrying out of the self into a new case, wherein what is before the mind is the case and not the self to be carried out, and where it is indeed the whole that feels and sees, but all that is seen is seen in the form of *this* case, *this* point, *this* instance. Precept is good, but example is better; for by a series of particulars (as such forgotten) we get the general spirit, we identify ourselves on the sides both of will and judgment with the basis, which basis (be it remembered) has not got to be explicit.*

There are a number of questions which invite consideration** here, but we can not stop. We wished to point out briefly the character of our common moral judgments. This (on the intellectual side) is the way in which they are ordinarily made; and, in the main, there is not much practical difficulty. What is moral *in any particular given case* is seldom doubtful. Society pronounces beforehand; or, after some one course has been taken, it can say whether it was right or not; though society can not generalize much, and, if asked to reflect, is helpless and becomes incoherent. But I do not say there are no cases where the morally-minded man has to doubt; most certainly such do arise, though not so many as some people think, far fewer than some would be glad to think. A very large number arise from reflection, which wants to act from an explicit principle, and so begins to abstract and divide, and, thus becoming one-sided, makes the relative absolute. Apart from this, however, collisions must take place; and here there is no guide whatever but the intuitive judgment of oneself or others.†

This intuition must not be confounded with what is sometimes miscalled 'conscience'. It is not mere individual opinion or caprice. It presupposes the morality of the community as its basis, and is subject to the approval thereof. Here, if anywhere, the idea of universal and impersonal morality is realized. For the final arbiters are the φρόνιμοι [men of practical wisdom], persons with a will to do right, and not full of reflections and theories. If they fail you, you must judge for yourself, but practically they seldom do fail you. Their private peculiarities neutralize each other, and the result is an intuition which does not belong merely to this or that man or collection of men. 'Conscience' is the antipodes of this. It wants you to have no law but yourself, and to be better than the world. But this intuition tells you that, if

---

*It is worth while in this connexion to refer to the custom some persons have (and find useful) of calling before the mind, when in doubt, a known person of high character and quick judgment, and thinking what they would have done. This no doubt both delivers the mind from private considerations and also is to act in the spirit of the other person (so far as we know it), i.e. from the general basis of his acts (certainly *not* the mere memory of his particular acts, or such memory plus inference).

**One of these would be as to how progress in morality is made.

†I may remark on this (after Erdmann, and I suppose Plato) that collisions of duties are avoided mostly by each man keeping to his own immediate duties, and not trying to see from the point of view of other stations than his own.

you could be as good as your world, you would be better than most likely you are, and that to wish to be better than the world is to be already on the threshold of immorality.

This perhaps 'is a hard saying', but it is least hard to those who know life best; it is intolerable to those mainly who, from inexperience or preconceived theories, can not see the world as it is. Explained it may be by saying that enthusiasm for good dies away — the ideal fades —

> Dem Herrlichsten, was auch der Geist empfangen,
> Drängt immer fremd und fremder Stoff sich an; ‡

but better perhaps if we say that those who have seen most of the world (not one side of it) — old people of no one-sided profession nor of immoral life — know most also how much good there is in it. They are tolerant of new theories and youthful opinions that everything would be better upside down, because they know that this also is as it should be, and that the world gets good even from these. They are intolerant only of those who are old enough, and should be wise enough, to know better than that they know better than the world; for in such people they can not help seeing the self-conceit which is pardonable only in youth.

Let us be clear. What is that wish to be better, and to make the world better, which is on the threshold of immorality? What is the 'world' in this sense? It is the morality already existing ready to hand in laws, institutions, social usages, moral opinions and feelings. This is the element in which the young are brought up. It has given moral content to themselves, and it is the only source of such content. It is not wrong, it is a duty, to take the best that there is, and to live up to the best. It is not wrong, it is a duty, standing on the basis of the existing, and in harmony with its general spirit, to try and make not only oneself but also the world better, or rather, and in preference, one's own world better. But it is another thing, starting from oneself, from ideals in one's head, to set oneself and them against the moral world. The moral world with its social institutions, &c., is a fact; it is real; our 'ideals' are not real. 'But we will make them real.' We should consider what we are, and what the world is. We should learn to see the great moral fact in the world, and to reflect on the likelihood of our private 'ideal' being anything more than an abstraction, which, because an abstraction, is all the better fitted for our heads, and all the worse fitted for actual existence.

We should consider whether the encouraging oneself in having opinions of one's own, in the sense of thinking differently from the world on moral subjects, be not, in any person other than a heaven-born prophet, sheer self-conceit. And though the disease may spend itself in the harmless and even entertaining silliness by which we are advised to assert our social 'individuality', yet still the having theories of one's own in the face of the world is not far from having practice in the same direction; and if the latter is (as it often must be) immorality, the former has certainly but stopped at the threshold.

But the moral organism is strong against both. The person anxious to throw off the yoke of custom and develop his 'individuality' in startling

‡[Substance, more and more alien, worms its infectious way into that which is the most sublime, which the spirit would likewise fold into its embrace.]

directions, passes as a rule into the common Philistine, and learns that Philistinism is after all a good thing. And the licentious young man, anxious for pleasure at any price, who, without troubling himself about 'principles', does put into practice the principles of the former person, finds after all that the self within him can be satisfied only with that from whence it came. And some fine morning the dream is gone, the enchanged bower is a hideous phantasm, and the despised and common reality has become the ideal.

We have thus seen the community to be the real moral idea, to be stronger than the theories and the practice of its members against it, and to give us self-realization. And this is indeed limitation; it bids us say farewell to visions of superhuman morality, to ideal societies, and to practical 'ideals' generally. But perhaps the unlimited is not the perfect, not the true ideal. And, leaving 'ideals' out of sight, it is quite clear that if anybody wants to realize himself as a perfect man without trying to be a perfect member of his country and all his smaller communities, he makes what all sane persons would admit to be a great mistake. There is no more fatal enemy than theories which are not also facts; and when people inveigh against the vulgar antithesis of the two, they themselves should accept their own doctrine, and give up the harbouring of theories of what should be and is not. Until they do that, the vulgar are in the right; for a theory of that which (only) is to be, is a theory of that which in fact is not, and that I suppose is only a theory.

There is nothing better than my station and its duties, nor anything higher or more truly beautiful. It holds and will hold its own against the worship of the 'individual', whatever form that may take. It is strong against frantic theories and vehement passions, and in the end it triumphs over the fact, and can smile at the literature, even of sentimentalism, however fulsome in its impulsive setting out, or sour in its disappointed end. It laughs at its frenzied apotheosis of the yet unsatisfied passion it calls love; and at that embitterment too which has lost its illusions, and yet can not let them go — with its kindness for the genius too clever in general to do anything in particular, and its adoration of star-gazing virgins with souls above their spheres, whose wish to be something in the world takes the form of wanting to do something with it, and who in the end do badly what they might have done in the beginning well; and, worse than all, its cynical contempt for what deserves only pity, sacrifice of a life for work to the best of one's lights, a sacrifice despised not simply because it has failed, but because it is stupid, and uninteresting, and altogether unsentimental.[10]

Evaluation

1. To take F. H. Bradley's writings first, we know from modern psychological research that he is clearly wrong when he states at the beginning of his essay "at birth the child of one race is not the same as a child of another; that in the children of the one race there is a certain identity, a developed or undeveloped national type . . . one English child is in some points, though perhaps it does not as yet show itself, the same as another. His being is so far common to him with others; he is not a mere 'individual'." He goes on to say "civilization is to some not inconsiderable extent hereditary . . . it is a very different thing, even apart from education, to be born of civilized and of uncivilized ancestors. These

'civilized tendencies', if we may use the phrase, are part of the essence of the child: he would only partly (if at all) be himself without them; he owes them to his ancestors, and his ancestors owe them to society.''

These late nineteenth century beliefs have now been largely discredited. The English are a nation not a race and British civilization is not biologically inherited; the cultural environment is responsible for its formation.[11]

Apart from mistakes of fact, Bradley's selection also slights the ability of the individual to reach independent and correct moral judgments even if they are at variance with those of the society. Bradley wrote that "the spirit of the community" tells us what is right, pronounces it beforehand. Having opinions of one's own, he said, is sheer conceit. "We have thus seen the community to be the real moral idea, to be stronger than the theories and the practice of its members against it, and to give us self-realization."

This type of doctrine seriously undermines personal judgment and private conscience, treating the individual as a cell in the organism of the state, and that seems not only a mistake but a very dangerous card to play. Politically it can be used to glorify a totalitarian government and to deny any status to individual rights. It easily justifies the concept that the citizen exists for the state rather than the state for its citizens. We have seen a terrifying example of this in Nazi Germany, where dissent was not allowed and the worth of the individual was measured in his contribution to the nation-state.

As a corollary to this, another charge frequently leveled against idealistic ethics is that it overestimates the degree to which the individual is a part of society and therefore overestimates the amount of social involvement necessary for self-realization. It may be true as Bradley claimed that apart from the political and community life man is hardly man at all, but that does not mean that society is superior to the individual or that self-realization only comes about when the individual dedicates himself to the general welfare. Some social relations and commitments are certainly necessary but the idealistic ethic seems to equate self-realization with self-sacrifice. This smacks of George Orwell's *1984* where war is peace and slavery is freedom. It is also reminiscent of the mystic's paradox that if you surrender yourself you gain yourself (which is taken from the Biblical idea "Whosoever will save his life shall loose it, and whosoever will loose his life shall find it"). But as the Cambridge philosopher Henry Sidgwick remarked, it is hard to tell the difference between a paradox that conveys some higher truth and a plain self-contradiction. At the very least, we can say that idealists like Bradley seem inconsistent when they argue that our individual development is only achieved by sacrificing our individuality in the service of the state and ultimately to the embrace of the "universal."

2. Apart from the highly questionable notion of self used in idealistic philosophy, the general ethic of self-realization has a very "woolly" concept of selfhood as well. We have seen how Bradley seemed to blur the line between the person and society, and such confusion about the nature of the self characterizes most forms of self-realization. This is obviously an important matter, for if we cannot find a clear definition of the self, then we do not know what it is that should be realized.

The question of selfhood is a metaphysical one with roots that run deep in the history of philosophy and the self-realizationist has not settled the issue at all. To understand what is at stake we have to divide the concept into two parts: the self in "space" and the self in "time."

The question of the self in space has to do with the dimensions encompassed: What is included as part of the self and what would be excluded as extraneous to it? Is the self that inner entity, spiritual or mental, that feels emotions, thinks, imagines, remembers, reflects, and is aware of itself performing these operations? Is our real self anchored somewhere just behind our eyes, looking through them at the external world (and visible to others when they gaze through these "windows of the soul")? It sometimes seems so, because the inability to reason as a result of brain damage or the loss of memory in amnesia changes the person in a radical way. And the person who is in a coma, lacking all consciousness, is hardly himself. So perhaps the self resides within the body, our sanctum sanctorum or private, inner being known only to ourselves.[12]

But shouldn't our physical body be included in the definition of the self? Isn't it more than a dwelling or shell within which we live? Our body certainly seems to be something that we are and not just something we have. We do, in fact, identify with our bodies and especially our faces and treat our physical appearance as a true representation of ourselves. When we look in a mirror we call the image we see "me", and if we play football, make love, break an arm, win a beauty contest, and so forth we believe that these things are happening to us. Furthermore, when we contemplate our deaths we do not feel that we are just "chained to a dying animal"; in some real sense, we are the mortal animal that will die.

Is the self, then, that which lies within as religion often claims in affirming that man will one day "shuffle off this mortal coil," or is the body an inseparable part of the self, perhaps the whole of the person as behavioral psychology maintains? We are left as perplexed as Oscar Wilde when he wrote,

> Soul and body, body and soul — how mysterious they were! There was animalism in the soul, and the body had its moments of spirituality. The senses could refine, and the intellect could degrade. Who could say where the fleshy impulse ceased, or the physical impulse began? How shallow are the arbitrary definitions of ordinary psychologists! And yet how difficult to decide between the claims of the various schools! Was the soul a shadow seated in the house of sin? Or was the body really in the soul, as Giordano Bruno thought? The separation of spirit from matter was a mystery, and the union of spirit and matter were a mystery also.[13]

If we believe that the self embraces both mind and body, then we might wonder whether it might include still more. Perhaps we are a part of everyone we have met and they of us, especially those we have come to love whose successes are our successes and whose suffering fills us with pain. Perhaps the self should be seen to include a home that is precious to us, the books we have read, the tools we used throughout a lifetime, the places to which we have traveled, the land we have worked with our own hands, or a musical instrument that gave us a means of expression. In a genuine sense, all these things could be said to make up our selves. We could even perceive the entire world to lie within us as in the Hindu principle "that art thou" (*tat tvam asi*), meaning that the inner and the outer are one, or believe as some Christians do that God is immanent in our hearts and we are part and parcel of God.

It was this sense of unity that made the English poet John Donne write "No man is an island, entire of itself; every man is a piece of the continent, a part of the main; if a clod be washed away by the sea, Europe is the less, as well as if a promontory were; as well as if a manor of thy friends or of thine own; any man's death diminishes me, because I am involved in mankind; and therefore never send to know for whom the bell tolls; it tolls for thee." The socialist Eugene Debs had a similar idea in mind when he said "While there is a lower class I am in it; while there is a criminal element I am of it; while there is a soul in prison, I am not free."[14]

Would we want to enlarge the self to this extent, and, if not, where would be the appropriate cutoff point. This is one of the principal problems regarding the self that has vexed philosophers for generations; it remains unresolved and may be unresolvable. An individual is "the sum total of all that he can call his" according to the American philosopher William James, but the question remains as to what one should call one's own.

Just as we are puzzled about the dimensions of the self in "space," we also find it hard to identify the continuous element in the self that persists through time. Here the question becomes What is it in anyone that remains constant, that entitles us to say he is the same person from birth to death? That is, in order to recognize someone as the same individual now that existed before there must be something about him that has not changed, some common denominator by virtue of which we are justified in saying he is the same person. The problem lies in finding that golden thread, that continuity in the midst of change without which he would not be himself.

It seems as though everything about a person changes. His thoughts and attitudes, aspirations and values alter radically between childhood and old age, so they cannot be the persistent element in the self. Certainly what a person regards as important changes significantly between six, sixteen, and sixty. Likewise we cannot say that an individual's disposition constitutes his self because if his disposition changes, say from optimism to pessimism as a result of a brutal prison experience, we would still call him the same person only with a different disposition. Cynics may be former idealists but they are not different selves.

A similar situation exists if we identify the self with our physical being, for our body changes continuously as it develops, matures, and decays. Our skin first expands then wrinkles, our hair becomes dense then thins and changes color, our muscles grow strong then atrophy, and our senses increase in acuteness then gradually degenerate as we age. The composition of our organs changes as well, and we cannot even claim that our cells are the same since they are completely replaced within seven years, including even basic elements such as the RNA in nerve cells.

Nothing about a person then seems to remain constant which makes us wonder whether we are the same selves at all, persisting through time with a continuous identity. A simple analogy might make the point clearer. If we owned a sailboat and put in a new deck when we found the original one was rotten, then replaced the sails to increase the wind area, then gave it an entirely different hull for a shallower draft and greater speed, then built a comfortable cabin, installed a modern mast, new rigging, and so forth, we would reach a point where it would no longer be the same boat. Similarly, if we had an axe and changed the head, then the handle, it would be a different axe. If every part of an object is different then the object itself is not the same — whether that object is a boat, an axe, or a human being.

Formidable problems therefore exist concerning the nature of the self, both spatially and temporally. And the fact that selfhood is so problematic creates a major stumbling block for all forms of self-realization.

3. Perhaps the most damning indictment of the ethic, however, is that it is intrinsically selfish and immoral, justifying actions that could be harmful to others so long as they are beneficial to the individual himself. For example, suppose that a person's principal interests and abilities center round deceiving people, and he decides to become a confidence man so that his potentialities can be realized to the full. He could work as a propagandist but that might not entail as much deception or give him the excitement he craves. Only the life of a swindler lets him realize himself completely — as well as offering high pay for very little work. He is finally able to be, in Fromm's phrase, "that self which [he] truly is." Or the person with an aptitude and propensity for killing might find life with the Mafia to his liking, providing him with maximum opportunities for realizing his talent. If it were wartime he could join the army, but in time of peace working as a Mafia hit man might be an ideal occupation; there he could become self-actualized in terms of his dominant abilities. In Maslow's words he would be "doing what *he,* individually, is fitted for."

The self-realizationist will try to answer this charge by saying that the individual cannot be himself at other people's expense but only through identifying with society and serving others. But this is hardly true; it does seem possible for personal fulfillment to come about in ways that are antisocial. The individual is not precluded from realizing himself by the fact that he is harming others, in fact there are many ponts where the realization of one self means the suppression of another.[15]

We have seen how idealists sometimes try to eliminate the problem of selfishness in this way by claiming that the self is a social self, and that the individual cannot develop except through pursuing humanity's welfare. However, this is not in keeping with the facts. And the martyr who sacrifices himself for some cause may be benefiting mankind but he is certainly not developing himself. If he is dead and the self is extinct then all self-realization comes to an end.

We can see, then, that people do not just develop themselves when they do what is right but can develop themselves by doing what is wrong, and that means the doctrine of self-realization does not always lead to moral behavior. A related problem is that someone such as a drunkard or a miser could justify his existence by saying that he is merely developing his major aptitudes and interests. But if self-realization can be used to justify a bad life then the good cannot be equated with self-realization.

Our conclusion must be that people will not necessarily do what is right or lead a life that is good by following the self-realization ethic.

Human: Realizing Our Essential Humanness

Another kind of self-realization theory does not fasten on the unique self as the entity to be actualized but upon the humanness all people share in common. According to this doctrine we should try to become fully realized by understanding and developing those qualities that make us essentially human. Here the goal is to develop ourselves to the greatest extent possible, not in terms of any animal tendencies (even if they are central to our self) and not behaving as angels or robots either but in accordance with the character of a human being.

The Greek philosopher Aristotle (384–322 B.C.) was the most prominent representative of this type of self-realization doctrine. Together with Plato, Aristotle is considered one of the greatest philosophers in the ancient world, and just as Plato founded the Academy in Athens, which was the first school of philosophy in existence, Aristotle established his Lyceum, which gradually became its rival. (In these names can be seen the origin of the English word *academic* and the French *lycée*, which is a school modeled along Aristotelian lines). Aristotle was, in fact, a student of Plato before going on to develop a separate system of thought, which among its many effects profoundly influenced the theology of St. Thomas Aquinas and much of the Catholic church. Although Aristotle greatly admired his teacher he refused to follow his ideas slavishly; as he remarked, "Plato is dear to me, but dearer still is truth."

The members of the Lyceum adopted the unusual practice of walking around during their discussions and for this reason they became known as *peripatetics* (those who walk up and down); subsequently, the whole of Aristotle's teachings came to be called Peripatetic Philosophy. All of the extant writings of Aristotle were first presented in this way, as "pacing" lectures in the Lyceum, and they were later recorded by his disciples from the notes that had been taken. One of these manuscripts that managed to be preserved in complete form is the *Nicomachean Ethics,* which is named for the student who edited and compiled them, Aristotle's son Nicomachus. It is considered the most thorough system of ethics ever written and contains a complete exposition of Aristotle's ideal of self-realization.

Aristotle was a very practical, down-to-earth philosopher who used what he considered plain facts and common sense in formulating the good for man. For him the everyday ethical questions were most compelling—questions of how one ought to live and why people fail to do what they ought to do. And the ideas people normally hold or the common opinions of society provide the basis on which the judgment of value can be built; "it is by the practical experience of life and conduct," he said, "that the truth is really tested." Furthermore, he believed that correct behavior is always rooted in our natural tendencies, for "every ideal has a natural basis, and everything natural has an ideal development." It was not a matter of antagonism between the man's nature and a worthwhile life but rather a basic compatibility, for the fulfillment of our inner nature is itself an ideal existence.

This viewpoint led Aristotle to ask What is the final end which is truly intrinsic to man's nature, the goal sought by human beings universally? The bridlemaker aims at fashioning good bridle equipment, the soldier tries to acquire skill in arms, the medical practitioner seeks health, and so forth. But all of these activities are means to some higher end. Bridlemaking, for example, is a means to the art of horsemanship and horsemanship is a means to victory in war. The basic question is What is the ultimate end for which all else is done, the good "at which everything aims"?

Aristotle's answer was *eudaimonia,* a concept that is often translated as happiness but more literally means having a good inner principle of selection. A more accurate rendering of this Greek term might be "vital well being" or the awareness of the enlivened person at the fulfillment of his humanness.

However, although people might agree that the good is some form of well being, opinions differ as to how that can be brought about and the exact form that it might take. There is a consensus, Aristotle thought, that man needs to participate in a social community, as best exemplified in the "polis" or city-state of ancient Greece. "No one would choose to live without friends," Aristotle wrote, and "no one would choose to have every conceivable good thing on condition that he remain solitary, for man is a political creature, designed by nature to live with others." Furthermore, Aristotle's *Ethics* is one half of a single work the other half of which is the *Politics*, which shows how intimate he believed the connection to be between the individual and the society. "In the natural order of things," he wrote, "the State is prior to the household and the individual, as the whole is prior to the part."[16] Nevertheless, there is no common agreement as to the type of life that will produce eudaimonia for the citizens living within the city-state.

Many people think that well being consists of obtaining pleasure, and Aristotle admitted that pleasure certainly is a strong desire in everyone. But the pleasurable life is vulgar and animalistic, "a life fit only for cattle." That is not to say that pleasure is unimportant, in fact "pleasure and life are inseparably united," but people make a mistake when they assume it is the end or aim of human existence. To Aristotle, pleasure accompanies the healthy exercise of our natural function but it is not sufficiently deep or dignified to be our object in living. As mentioned previously, when people are hungry they want to satisfy their appetite not to obtain the pleasure of eating. In the same way, when our basic tendencies are fulfilled then pleasure will follow as a sign and consequence of that fulfillment "like the bloom of health in the young and vigorous."

A smaller proportion of people believe that well being is achieved through honor and success, and such people are certainly necessary to the state. For every society needs politicians who are motivated by fame or a place in history, soldiers looking for glory (as Shakespeare said, "Seeking the bubble reputation/Even in the cannon's mouth"), and merchants whose dominating aim is to be successful in business. But Aristotle also rejected this possibility on the grounds that it hinges too much on other people and not enough on one's own efforts. That is, being honored for one's accomplishments depends upon recognition by others, which can be more a matter of luck than merit.

A third type of life is that of money seeking, but Aristotle did not regard this as ideal either even though it is quite common. For one thing, money is not a goal or end of activity, "for it is good only as being useful, as a means to something else." It is what philosophers call an instrumental good rather than an intrinsic good. A person who has acquired money still must decide how to spend it in order to live well, and some people have a Midas touch for making money but lead vacuous lives because they spend it so badly. In addition, money seeking is extremely time consuming, which means that a major portion of a person's life can be taken up with an activity that, after all, is only a means. A contemporary example might be the executive who puts in ten hours a day and brings home work on weekends, neglecting his family and allowing himself very little leisure time, all for the sake of a high income. Too often he will die a few years after retirement, just when he is beginning to enjoy the fruits of his long labor.

In terms of this analysis Aristotle rejected lives of pleasure, honor, and money seeking. Instead of these possibilities, Aristotle chose the reflective life or *theoretikos* as the ultimate end appropriate to man. This is a rational existence where one engages in pure philosophic contemplation and enjoys the exercise of reason for its own sake. Aristotle wrote, "Now the activity of philosophic reflection or wisdom is admittedly the most pleasant of excellent activities; at all events it is held that philosophy or the pursuit of wisdom provides pleasures of marvelous purity and permanence . . . it is the activity of reason that constitutes complete human eudaimonia."

Aristotle reached this conclusion by asking the question What is the function of man? He assumed from his studies in biology that every organism as well as every body part had a function, so it seemed sensible to ask this question of the human species. For example, the function of gills is to obtain oxygen from water and the function of wings is to enable the bird to fly, just as axes function to chop wood and houses function to provide shelter. Aristotle's assumption here is termed *teleology* from the Greek word *telos*, which means end or goal, and it stands for the metaphysical idea that everything has a function or purpose that is its reason for being (cf. pp. 170–72). All phenomena are said to have tendencies, aims, or implicit purposes, and human beings are no exception.

To Aristotle's mind, the notion of function meant something unique to each species, not a feature shared with other forms of life. This means that in the case of man his function was not connected with nourishment and growth because that was the vegetative existence of plants. Likewise it could not be the fact of having feelings or emotions or the ability to perceive the external world using the senses, for that was the mode of existence common to animals. Therefore man's essential function could only be the life of reason, the unique ability that separates human beings from all other organisms and places them at the top of the earth's hierarchy.

Reason then is man's function since it is particularly characteristic of the human species and its proper employment can lead to the summum bonum or highest good, which is vital well being. Having reached this conclusion, however, Aristotle then said that this rational nature possessed by human beings can be expressed in two directions. It can be used for reflective contemplation as described earlier or it can be employed to control our animal impulses and appetites, the irrational beast within the human form. The first leads to intellectual virtue and is the highest mode of functioning possible to man, but the second produces moral virtue and that too must be cultivated if we are to be practically successful as human beings. Aristotle, in fact, devoted a considerable portion of the *Nicomachean Ethics* to discussing practical reason, and it forms the most interesting part of his theory.

To exercise our function of reason in this practical sense we must first of all strive for *arete* or excellence in its employment. If the function of a harpist is to play the harp, Aristotle said, then that of a good harpist is to play the harp well. In the same way, if man's function is to be rational he must apply his rationality in an excellent manner, controlling his emotions with calm good sense.

Second and more specifically, the excellent use of our rational faculties consists in following the path of moderation or the "golden mean" in selecting states and activities in our lives. We must use our rationality to strike the proper balance between the extremes that the passions tend to promote, choosing the "middle way" in each and every action. Our rationality should guide us to the mean, carefully adjudicating between conflicting feelings and finding the area of sensible behavior between excesses and deficiencies.

Moderation is best, Aristotle believed, for just as it can be said of a good work "that nothing could be taken from it or added to it, implying that excellence is destroyed by excess or deficiency, but secured by observing the mean," so in action we must aim at the mean under the governance of reason.

> For instance, it is possible to feel fear, confidence, desire, anger, pity, and generally to be affected pleasantly and painfully, either too much or too little, in either case wrongly; but to be thus affected at the right times, and on the right occasions, and toward the right persons, and with the right object, and in the right fashion, is the mean course and the best course . . . excess is wrong and deficiency also is blamed, but the mean amount is priased and is right.[17]

However, since this advice is rather general and Aristotle wanted to provide a virtual handbook of morality, he then specified the particular states and actions that would be covered by his doctrine. With regard to feelings of fear and confidence, the mean would be courage, the excess a foolhardiness, and the deficiency cowardice. With respect to pleasures and pains the mean would be temperance, the excess profligacy (dissipation), and the deficiency, Aristotle said, has not been given a name because it is hardly every found (sic!). In money matters involving large sums, moderation is magnificence and the excess and deficiency are vulgarity and meanness, respectively. With regard to honor and disgrace, the mean is pride, the excess vanity, and the deficiency humility.

Aristotle supplied us with an extensive list including wit as a mean between buffoonery and boorishness, friendliness as the moderate path between obsequiousness and quarrelsomeness, and so forth. In all cases steering a middle course (the Middle Path as the Buddhists call it) constitutes rational and virtuous behavior. Aristotle did not say that we should aim for a precise midpoint between extremes but rather a middle range along the continuum from deficiency to excess. Being courageous, for example, includes a broad span depending upon our tendencies.

By exercising our rationality in this way (and by making a habit of virtuous choices) we will develop our humanness to the greatest extent and reach that state of eudaimonia in which our capacities approach full realization.

In the following selection from the *Nicomachean Ethics* Aristotle presented the scheme that has been discussed. Notice that the translator used the term *happiness* as the highest good but as we have seen Aristotle is more accurately described as advocating a self-realization ethic in which vital well being is the goal of the developed human being.

In addition to the *Ethics*, Aristotle is celebrated for his *Metaphysics, Politics,* and *Poetics*—the last an extremely influential book in aesthetic theory.

Aristotle's *Ethics**

BOOK I

1 | Every art and every inquiry, and similarly every action and pursuit, is
thought to aim at some good; and for this reason the good has rightly been

*Reprinted from *The Works of Aristotle*, vol. 9, *Ethica Nicomachae*, trans. W. D. Ross (London: Oxford University Press, 1963, first edition 1915).

declared to be that at which all things aim. But a certain difference is found
among ends; some are activities, others are products apart from the activities
that produce them. Where there are ends apart from the actions, it is the   5
nature of the products to be better than the activities. Now, as there are
many actions, arts, and sciences, their ends also are many; the end of the
medical art is health, that of shipbuilding a vessel, that of strategy victory,
that of economics wealth. But where such arts fall under a single
capacity—as bridle-making and the other arts concerned with the   10
equipment of horses fall under the art of riding, and this and every military
action under strategy, in the same way other arts fall under yet others—in
all of these the ends of the master arts are to be preferred to all the
subordinate ends; for it is for the sake of the former that the latter are   15
pursued. It makes no difference whether the activities themselves are the
ends of the actions, or something else apart from the activities, as in the case
of the sciences just mentioned.

2   If, then, there is some end of the things we do, which we desire for its own
sake (everything else being desired for the sake of this), and if we do not
choose everything for the sake of something else (for at that rate the process   20
would go on to infinity, so that our desire would be empty and vain), clearly
this must be the good and the chief good. Will not the knowledge of it, then,
have a great influence on life? Shall we not, like archers have a great
influence on life? Shall we not, like archers who have a mark to aim at, be
more likely to hit upon what is right? If so, we must try, in outline at least, to   25
determine what it is, and of which of the sciences or capacities it is the
object. It would seem to belong to the most authoritative art and that which
is most truly the master art. And politics appears to be of this nature; for it is
this that ordains which of the sciences should be studied in a state, and which
each class of citizens should learn and up to what point they should learn
them; and we see even the most highly esteemed of capacities to fall under
5   this, e.g. strategy, economics, rhetoric; now, since politics uses the rest of the
sciences, and since, again, it legislates as to what we are to do and what we
are to abstain from, the end of this science must include those of the others,
so that this end must be the good for man. For even if the end is the same
for a single man and for a state, that of the state seems at all events
something greater and more complete whether to attain or to preserve;
though it is worth while to attain the end merely for one man, it is finer and
10   more godlike to attain it for a nation or for city-states. These, then, are the
ends at which our inquiry aims, since it is political science, in one sense of
that term.
       Our discussion will be adequate if it has as much clearness as the   3
subject-matter admits of, for precision is not to be sought for alike in all
discussions, any more than in all the products of the crafts. Now fine and just
15   actions, which political science investigates, admit of much variety and
fluctuation of opinion, so that they may be thought to exist only by
convention, and not by nature. And goods also give rise to a similar
fluctuation because they bring harm to many people; for before now men
have been undone by reason of their wealth, and others by reason of their
courage. We must be content, then, in speaking of such subjects and with
20   such premises to indicate the truth roughly and in outline, and in speaking
about things which are only for the most part true and with premises of the

same kind to reach conclusions that are no better. In the same spirit, therefore, should each type of statement be *received;* for it is the mark of an educated man to look for precision in each class of things just so far as the nature of the subject admits; it is evidently equally foolish to accept probable reasoning from a mathematician and to demand from a rhetorician scientific proofs. . . .

Let us resume our inquiry and state, in view of the fact that all knowledge and every pursuit aims at some good, what it is that we say political science aims at and what is the highest of all goods achievable by action. Verbally there is very general agreement; for both the general run of men and people of superior refinement say that it is happiness, and identify living well and doing well with being happy; but with regard to what happiness is they differ, and the many do not give the same account as the wise. For the former think it is some plain and obvious thing, like pleasure, wealth, or honour; they differ, however, from one another—and often even the same man identifies it with different things, with health when he is ill, with wealth when he is poor; but, conscious of their ignorance, they admire those who proclaim some great ideal that is above their comprehension. Now some thought that apart from these many goods there is another which is self-subsistent and causes the goodness of all these as well. To examine all the opinions that have been held were perhaps somewhat fruitless; enough to examine those that are most prevalent or that seem to be arguable. . . .

Let us, however, resume our discussion from the point at which we digressed. To judge from the lives that men lead, most men, and men of the most vulgar type, seem (not without some ground) to identify the good, or happiness, with pleasure; which is the reason why they love the life of enjoyment. For there are, we may say, three prominent types of life—that just mentioned, the political, and thirdly the contemplative life. Now the mass of mankind are evidently quite slavish in their tastes, preferring a life suitable to beasts, but they get some ground for their view from the fact that many of those in high places share the tastes of Sardanapallus. A consideration of the prominent types of life shows that people of superior refinement and of active disposition identify happiness with honour; for this is, roughly speaking, the end of the political life. But it seems too superficial to be what we are looking for, since it is thought to depend on those who bestow honour rather than on him who receives it, but the good we divine to be something proper to a man and not easily taken from him. Further, men seem to pursue honour in order that they may be assured of their goodness; at least it is by men of practical wisdom that they seek to be honoured, and among those who know them, and on the ground of their virtue; clearly, then, according to them, at any rate, virtue is better. And perhaps one might even suppose this to be, rather than honour, the end of the political life. But even this appears somewhat incomplete; for possession of virtue seems actually compatible with being asleep, or with lifelong inactivity, and, further, with the greatest sufferings and misfortunes; but a man who was living so no one would call happy, unless he were maintaining a thesis at all costs. But enough of this; for the subject has been sufficiently treated even in the current discussions. Third comes the contemplative life, which we shall consider later.

The life of money-making is one undertaken under compulsion, and

wealth is evidently not the good we are seeking; for it is merely useful and
for the sake of something else. And so one might rather take the aforenamed
objects to be ends; for they are loved for themselves. But it is evident that
10   not even these are ends; yet many arguments have been thrown away in
support of them. Let us leave this subject, then. . . .

7   Let us again return to the good we are seeking, and ask what it can be. It   15
seems different in different actions and arts; it is different in medicine, in
strategy, and in the other arts likewise. What then is the good of each? Surely
that for whose sake everything else is done. In medicine this is health, in
strategy victory, in architecture a house, in any other sphere something else,   20
and in every action and pursuit the end; for it is for the sake of this that all
men do whatever else they do. Therefore, if there is an end for all that we
do, this will be the good achievable by action, and if there are more than
one, these will be the goods achievable by action.

So the argument has by a different course reached the same point; but we
must try to state this even more clearly. Since there are evidently more than
one end, and we choose some of these (e.g. wealth, flutes, and in general   25
instruments) for the sake of something else, clearly not all ends are final
ends; but the chief good is evidently something final. Therefore, if there is
only one final end, this will be what we are seeking, and if there are more
than one, the most final of these will be what we are seeking. Now we call that   30
which is in itself worthy of pursuit more final than that which is worthy of
pursuit for the sake of something else, and that which is never desirable for
the sake of something else more final than the things that are desirable both
in themselves and for the sake of that other thing, and therefore we call final
without qualification that which is always desirable in itself and never for the
sake of something else.

Now such a thing happiness, above all else, is held to be; for this we choose
always for itself and never for the sake of something else, but honour,
pleasure, reason, and every virtue we choose indeed for themselves (for if
nothing resulted from them we should still choose each of them), but we
5   choose them also for the sake of happiness, judging that by means of them
we shall be happy. Happiness, on the other hand, no one chooses for the sake
of these, nor, in general, for anything other than itself.

From the point of view of self-sufficiency the same result seems to follow;
for the final good is thought to be self-sufficient. Now by self-sufficient we
do not mean that which is sufficient for a man by himself, for one who lives a
10   solitary life, but also for parents, children, wife, and in general for his friends
and fellow citizens, since man is born for citizenship. But some limit must be
set to this; for if we extend our requirement to ancestors and descendants
and friends' friends we are in for an infinite series. Let us examine this
question, however, on another occasion; the self-sufficient we now define as
15   that which when isolated makes life desirable and lacking in nothing; and
such we think happiness to be; and further we think it most desirable of all
things, without being counted as one good thing among others — if it were so
counted it would clearly be made more desirable by the addition of even the
20   least of goods; for that which is added becomes an excess of goods, and of
goods the greater is always more desirable. Happiness, then, is something
final and self-sufficient, and is the end of action.

25 Presumably, however, to say that happiness is the chief good seems a platitude, and a clearer account of what it is is still desired. This might perhaps be given, if we could first ascertain the function of man. For just as for a flute-player, a sculptor, or any artist, and, in general, for all things that have a function or activity, the good and the 'well' is thought to reside in the function, so would it seem to be for man, if he has a function. Have the carpenter, then, and the tanner certain functions or activities, and has man

30 none? Is he born without a function? Or as eye, hand, foot, and in general each of the parts evidently has a function, may one lay it down that man similarly has a function apart from all these? What then can this be? Life seems to be common even to plants, but we are seeking what is peculiar to man. Let us exclude, therefore, the life of nutrition and growth. Next there would be a life of perception, but *it* also seems to be common even to the horse, the ox, and every animal. There remains, then, an active life of the element that has a rational principle; of this, one part has such a principle in the sense of being obedient to one, the other in the sense of possessing one and exercising thought. And, as 'life of the rational element' also has two 5 meanings, we must state that life in the sense of activity is what we mean; for this seems to be the more proper sense of the term. Now if the function of man is an activity of soul which follows or implies a rational principle, and if we say 'a so-and-so' and 'a good so-and-so' have a function which is the same in kind, e.g. a lyre-player and a good lyre-player, and so without qualification in all cases, eminence in respect of goodness being added to the name of the 10 function (for the function of a lyre-player is to play the lyre, and that of a good lyre-player is to do so well): if this is the case, [and we state the function of man to be a certain kind of life, and this to be an activity or actions of the soul implying a rational principle, and the function of a good man to be the good and noble performance of these, and if any action is well performed 15 when it is performed in accordance with the appropriate excellence: if this is the case,] human good turns out to be activity of soul in accordance with virtue, and if there are more than one virtue, in accordance with the best and most complete.

But we must add 'in a complete life'. For one swallow does not make a summer, nor does one day; and so too one day, or a short time, does not make a man blessed and happy.[18]

• • •

BOOK II

2 Since, then, the present inquiry does not aim at theoretical knowledge like the others (for we are inquiring not in order to know what virtue is, but in order to become good, since otherwise our inquiry would have been of no use), we must examine the nature of actions, namely how we ought to do

30 them; for these determine also the nature of the states of character that are produced, as we have said. Now, that we must act according to the right rule is a common principle and must be assumed—it will be discussed later, i.e. both what the right rule is, and how it is related to the other virtues. But this must be agreed upon beforehand, that the whole account of matters of

conduct must be given in outline and not precisely, as we said at the very
beginning that the accounts we demand must be in accordance with the
subject-matter; matters concerned with conduct and questions of what is good
for us have no fixity, any more than matters of health. The general account   5
being of this nature, the account of particular cases is yet more lacking in
exactness; for they do not fall under any art or precept but the agents
themselves must in each case consider what is appropriate to the occasion, as
happens also in the art of medicine or of navigation.

But though our present account is of this nature we must give what help   10
we can. First, then, let us consider this, that it is the nature of such things to
be destroyed by defect and excess, as we see in the case of strength and of
health (for to gain light on things imperceptible we must use the evidence of
sensible things); both excessive and defective exercise destroys the strength,   15
and similarly drink or food which is above or below a certain amount
destroys the health, while that which is proportionate both produces and
increases and preserves it. So too is it, then, in the case of temperance and
courage and the other virtues. For the man who flies from and fears
everything and does not stand his ground against anything becomes a   20
coward, and the man who fears nothing at all but goes to meet every danger
becomes rash; and similarly the man who indulges in every pleasure and
abstains from none becomes self-indulgent, while the man who shuns every
pleasure, as boors do, becomes in a way insensible; temperance and courage,
then, are destroyed by excess and defect, and preserved by the mean.   25

But not only are the sources and causes of their origination and growth
the same as those of their destruction, but also the sphere of their
actualization will be the same; for this is also true of the things which are
more evident to sense, e.g. of strength; it is produced by taking much food
and undergoing much exertion, and it is the strong man that will be most
able to do these things. So too is it with the virtues; by abstaining from
pleasures we become temperate, and it is when we have become so that we
are most able to abstain from them; and similarly too in the case of courage;   35
for by being habituated to despise things that are terrible and to stand our
ground against them we become brave, and it is when we have become so
that we shall be most able to stand our ground against them.

We must take as a sign of states of character the pleasure or pain that   3
ensues on acts; for the man who abstains from bodily pleasures and delights   5
in this very fact is temperate, while the man who is annoyed at it is
self-indulgent, and he who stands his ground against things that are terrible
and delights in this or at least is not pained is brave, while the man who is
pained is a coward. For moral excellence is concerned with pleasures and
pains; it is on account of the pleasure that we do bad things, and on account   10
of the pain that we abstain from noble ones. Hence we ought to have been
brought up in a particular way from our very youth, as Plato says, so as both
to delight in and to be pained by the things that we ought; for this is the
right education.

· · ·

6 | We must, however, not only describe virtue as a state of character, but also

say what sort of state it is. We may remark, then, that every virtue or excellence both brings into good condition the thing of which it is the excellence and makes the work of that thing be done well; e.g. the excellence of the eye makes both the eye and its work good; for it is by the excellence of the eye that we see well. Similarly the excellence of the horse makes a horse both good in itself and good at running and at carrying its rider and at awaiting the attack of the enemy. Therefore, if this is true in every case, the virtue of man also will be the state of character which makes a man good and which makes him do his own work well.

How this is to happen we have stated already, but it will be made plain also by the following consideration of the specific nature of virtue. In everything that is continuous and divisible it is possible to take more, less, or an equal amount, and that either in terms of the thing itself or relatively to us; and the equal is an intermediate between excess and defect. By the intermediate in the object I mean that which is equidistant from each of the extremes, which is one and the same for all men; by the intermediate relatively to us that which is neither too much not too little—and this is not one, nor the same for all. For instance, if ten is many and two is few, six is the intermediate, taken in terms of the object; for it exceeds and is exceeded by an equal amount; this is intermediate according to arithmetical proportion. But the intermediate relatively to us is not to be taken so; if ten pounds are too much for a particular person to eat and two too little, it does not follow that the trainer will order six pounds; for this also is perhaps too much for the person who is to take it, or too little—too little for Milo,* too much for the beginner in athletic exercises. The same is true of running and wrestling. Thus a master of any art avoids excess and defect, but seeks the intermediate and chooses this—the intermediate not in the object but relatively to us.

If it is thus, then, that every art does its work well—by looking to the intermediate and judging its works by this standard (so that we often say of good works of art that it is not possible either to take away or to add anything, implying that excess and defect destroy the goodness of works of art, while the mean preserves it; and good artists, as we say, look to this in their work), and if, further, virtue is more exact and better than any art, as nature also is, then virtue must have the quality of aiming at the intermediate. I mean moral virtue; for it is this that is concerned with passions and actions, and in these there is excess, defect, and the intermediate. For instance, both fear and confidence and appetite and anger and pity and in general pleasure and pain may be felt both too much and too little, and in both cases not well; but to feel them at the right times, with reference to the right objects, towards the right people, with the right motive, and in the right way, is what is both intermediate and best, and this is characteristic of virtue. Similarly with regard to actions also there is excess, defect, and the intermediate. Now virtue is concerned with passions and actions, in which excess is a form of failure, and so is defect, while the intermediate is praised and is a form of success; and being praised and being successful are both characteristics of virtue. Therefore virtue is a kind of mean, since, as we have seen, it aims at what is intermediate.

*A famous wrestler. [Translator's note.]

Again, it is possible to fail in many ways (for evil belongs to the class of the unlimited, as the Pythagoreans conjectured, and good to that of the limited), while to succeed is possible only in one way (for which reason also one is easy 30 and the other difficult—to miss the mark easy, to hit it difficult); for these reasons also, then, excess and defect are characteristic of vice, and the mean of virtue;

For men are good in but one way, but bad in many.   35

Virtue, then, is a state of character concerned with choice, lying in a mean, i.e. the mean relative to us, this being determined by a rational principle, and by that principle by which the man of practical wisdom would determine it. Now it is a mean between two vices, that which depends on excess and that which depends on defect; and again it is a mean because the vices respectively fall short of or exceed what is right in both passions and actions, while virtue both finds and chooses that which is intermediate. Hence in   5 respect of its substance and the definition which states its essence virtue is a mean, with regard to what is best and right an extreme.

But not every action nor every passion admits of a mean; for some have names that already imply badness, e.g. spite, shamelessness, envy, and in the 10 case of actions adultery, theft, murder; for all of these and suchlike things imply by their names that they are themselves bad, and not the excesses or deficiences of them. It is not possible, then, ever to be right with regard to them; one must always be wrong. Nor does goodness or badness with regard 15 to such things depend on committing adultery with the right woman, at the right time, and in the right way, but simply to do any of them is to go wrong. It would be equally absurd, then, to expect that in unjust, cowardly, and 20 voluptuous action there should be a mean, an excess, and a deficiency; for at that rate there would be a mean of excess and of deficiency, an excess of excess, and a deficiency of deficiency. But as there is no excess of excess and a deficiency of temperance and courage because what is intermediate is in a sense an extreme, so too of the actions we have mentioned there is no mean 25 nor any excess and deficiency, but however they are done they are wrong; for in general there is neither a mean of excess and deficiency, nor excess and deficiency of a mean.

We must, however, not only make this general statement, but also apply it 7 to the individual facts. For among statements about conduct those which are 30 general apply more widely, but those which are particular are more genuine, since conduct has to do with individual cases, and our statements must harmonize with the facts in these cases. We may take these cases from our table. With regard to feelings of fear and confidence courage is the mean; of the people who exceed, he who exceeds in fearlessness has no name (many of the states have no name), while the man who exceeds in confidence is rash, and he who exceeds in fear and falls short in confidence is a coward. With regard to pleasures and pains—not all of them, and not so much with 5 regard to the pains—the means is temperance, the excess self-indulgence. Persons deficient with regard to the pleasures are not often found; hence such persons also have received no name. But let us call them 'insensible'.

With regard to giving and taking of money the mean is liberality, the

excess and the defect prodigality and meanness. In these actions people   10
exceed and fall short in contrary ways; the prodigal exceeds in spending and
falls short in taking, while the mean man exceeds in taking and falls short in
spending. (At present we are giving a mere outline or summary, and are
satisfied with this; later these states will be more exactly determined.) With   15
regard to money there are also other dispositions—a mean, magnificence
(for the magnificent man differs from the liberal man; the former deals with
large sums, the latter with small ones), an excess, tastelessness and vulgarity,
and a deficiency, niggardliness; these differ from the states opposed to   20
liberality, and the mode of their difference will be stated later.

 With regard to honour and dishonour the mean is proper pride, the excess
is known as a sort of 'empty vanity'. and the deficiency is undue humility;
and as we said liberality was related to magnificence, differing from it by
dealing with small sums, so there is a state similarly related to proper pride,   25
being concerned with small honours while that is concerned with great. For it
is possible to desire honour as one ought, and more than one ought, and less,
and the man who exceeds in his desires is called ambitious, the man who falls
short unambitious, while the intermediate person has no name. The
dispositions also are nameless, except that that of the ambitious man is called   30
ambition. Hence the people who are at the extremes lay claim to the middle
place; and we ourselves sometimes call the intermediate person ambitious
and sometimes unambitious, and sometimes praise the ambitious man and
sometimes the unambitious. The reason of our doing this will be stated in
what follows; but now let us speak of the remaining states according to the
method which has been indicated.

 With regard to anger also there is an excess, a deficiency, and a mean.
Although they can scarcely be said to have names, yet since we call the   5
intermediate person good-tempered let us call the mean good temper; of the
persons at the extremes let the one who exceeds be called irascible, and his
vice irascibility, and the man who falls short an inirascible sort of person, and
the deficiency inirascibility.

10 There are also three other means, which have a certain likeness to one
another, but differ from one another: for they are all concerned with
intercourse in words and actions, but differ in that one is concerned with
truth in this sphere, the other two with pleasantness; and of this one kind is
exhibited in giving amusement, the other in all the circumstances of life. We
must therefore speak of these too, that we may the better see that in all
15 things the mean is praiseworthy, and the extremes neither praiseworthy nor
right, but worthy of blame. Now most of these states also have no names, but
we must try, as in the other cases, to invent names ourselves so that we may
20 be clear and easy to follow. With regard to truth, then, the intermediate is a
truthful sort of person and the mean may be called truthfulness, while the
pretence which exaggerates is boastfulness and the person characterized by it
a boaster, and that which understates is mock modesty and the person
characterized by it mock-modest. With regard to pleasantness in the giving
of amusement the intermediate person is ready-witted and the disposition
25 ready wit, the excess is buffoonery and the person characterized by it a
buffoon, while the man who falls short is a sort of boor and his state is
boorishness. With regard to the remaining kind of pleasantness, that which is

exhibited in life in general, the man who is pleasant in the right way is friendly and the mean is friendliness, while the man who exceeds is an obsequious person if he has no end in view, a flatterer if he is aiming at his own advantage, and the man who falls short and is unpleasant in all circumstances is a quarrelsome and surly sort of person.

30   There are also means in the passions and concerned with the passions; since shame is not a virtue, and yet praise is extended to the modest man. For even in these matters one man is said to be intermediate, and another to exceed, as for instance the bashful man who is ashamed of everything; while he who falls short or is not ashamed of anything at all is shameless, and the intermediate person is modest. Righteous indignation is a mean between   35 envy and spite, and these states are concerned with the pain and pleasure that are felt at the fortunes of our neighbors; the man who is characterized by righteous indignation is pained at undeserved good fortune, the envious man, going beyond him, is pained at all good fortune, and the spiteful man   5 falls so far short of being pained that he even rejoices. But these states there will be an opportunity of describing elsewhere; with regard to justice, since it has not one simple meaning, we shall, after describing the other states, distinguish its two kinds and say how each of them is a mean; and similarly we shall treat also of the rational virtues. . . .   10

20   That moral virtue is a mean, then, and in what sense it is so, and that it is a 9 mean between two vices, the one involving excess, the other deficiency, and that it is such because its character is to aim at what is intermediate in passions and in actions, has been sufficiently stated. Hence also it is no easy task to be good. For in everything it is no easy task to find the middle, e.g. to   25 find the middle of a circle is not for every one but for him who knows; so, too, any one can get angry—that is easy—or give or spend money; but to do this to the right person, to the right extent, at the right time, with the right motive, and in the right way, *that* is not for every one, nor is it easy; wherefore goodness is both rare and laudable and noble.

    Hence he who aims at the intermediate must first depart from what is the   30 more contrary to it, as Calypso advises—

> *Hold the ship out beyond that surf and spray.*

For of the extremes one is more erroneous, one less so; therefore, since to hit the mean is hard in the extreme, we must as a second best, as people say, take the least of the evils; and this will be done best in the way we describe.   35

    But we must consider the things towards which we ourselves also are easily carried away; for some of us tend to one thing, some to another; and this will be recognizable from the pleasure and the pain we feel. We must drag ourselves away to the contrary extreme; for we shall get into the   5 intermediate state by drawing well away from error, as people do in straightening sticks that are bent.

    Now in everything the pleasant or pleasure is most to be guarded against; for we do not judge it impartially. We ought, then, to feel towards pleasure as the elders of the people felt towards Helen, and in all circumstances repeat their saying; for if we dismiss pleasure thus we are less likely to go astray. It is by doing this, then, (to sum the matter up) that we shall best be able to hit the mean.

But this is no doubt difficult, and especially in individual cases; for it is not easy to determine both how and with whom and on what provocation and 15 how long one should be angry; for we too sometimes praise those who fall short and call them good-tempered, but sometimes we praise those who get angry and call them manly. The man, however, who deviates little from goodness is not blamed, whether he do so in the direction of the more or of 20 the less, but only the man who deviates more widely; for *he* does not fail to be noticed. But up to what point and to what extent a man must deviate before he becomes blameworthy it is not easy to determine by reasoning, any more than anything else that is perceived by the senses; such things depend on particular facts, and the decision rests with perception. So much, then, is plain, that the intermediate state is in all things to be praised, but that we 25 must incline sometimes towards the excess, sometimes towards the deficiency; for so shall we most easily hit the mean and what is right.

Evaluation

From our earlier description of self-realization we can see that Aristotle's theory is certainly not the standard type. However, it does belong within the self-realization category because Aristotle advocated the development of man's essential nature and by that means the achievement of personal well being. He was not concerned with the individual developing himself in ways that distinguish him from other human beings but with each person realizing himself *as* a human being.

More specifically, Aristotle claimed that if we use our unique reasoning ability to find the mean between extremes then we will be employing our rationality in an excellent manner and fulfilling ourselves as human beings. The equilibrium of the person controlling the appetitive side of his nature, the overall harmony in feelings and actions of the poised individual living according to reason — this is absolutely essential. If we go to extremes then our balance is destroyed and our development will become distorted. But to live in such a way that we achieve just the right amount, at the proper time and place, guided by the dominant rationality of human nature, that will provide success in living.

1. However, the first question we might ask is whether moderation is always best. The idea certainly has great appeal and conventional wisdom tells us that we should not be extremists or radicals but temperate and reasonable in our behavior. We should not spend our money like water or be miserly and hoard it, not clown all the time or be overly serious, not accept every dare (and think we are being brave) or hang back timidly at every danger. It makes sense to say that people should be intelligent about spending their money, witty in their humor, and neither fearless nor too fearful. We ought to keep everything in proper perspective and maintain a sense of proportion; even in romance we should love wisely not too well.

This approach to life certainly appears to be nothing more than common sense but on closer examination the ideal of moderation seems rather bland and boring. It is a value dear to the middle class, the middle aged, and middlebrow, anyone who is opposed to risk and afraid of his own emotions. As we saw in

Epicurean hedonism, a restrained life may be commendable as something mature and sensible but it is also very pedestrian and dull like tepid tea. Adolescent vices can be better than grown-up virtues, and Aristotle's middle-of-the-road approach is uninspiring as an ideal in living.

The outstanding figures in human history certainly did not follow the path of moderation but chose extreme dedication to their fields whether science, music, religion, politics, or even Aristotelian philosophy. Major painters such as van Gogh and Gauguin, for example, went to extremes in their passion for art, and Galileo and Newton were devoted to science in a single-minded, exceptional way.

In championing the mean, then, as the virtuous Aristotle became a spokesman for a commonplace, banal ethic. We surely feel that we should not be moderate in the pursuit of excellence any more than in matters of truth, goodness, rationality, justice, or virtue itself.

Aristotle tried to protect himself by saying that certain states or actions (such as truth and justice) are good in themselves and can be taken to extremes; moderation in them would be a vice. But this implies that moderation is not always best, which is inconsistent with Aristotle's general position. And how do we know in advance the things that are good in themselves and should not be done in moderation when virtuous behavior has been defined as that which is moderate? It seems as though Aristotle had already decided what is right and then took these preestablished virtues and fitted them into an ingenious arrangement of means and extremes. The conclusion came first and the reasons came second in the form of the Aristotelian system. But the system itself seems unable to tell us how to conduct ourselves, for sometimes virtue lies in moderation and sometimes moderation would be a vice.

2. Another issue that has been raised in connection with Aristotelianism has to do with the assumption of a teleological universe. Aristotle held that every object in creation had a function: gills allow the fish to draw oxygen from water, wings enable the bird to fly, and so forth. But although this may hold true for gills and wings, we are not sure that everything in the natural world has a function. In fact there may not be a function to anything in Aristotle's sense of a governing purpose. Perhaps the universe is not purposive but "tychistic," with chance characterizing all reality. That is, there may not be a reason for all that exists, an inherent end toward which all objects tend; things might exist for no reason.

What is the intrinsic function of a rock, for example? It can be put to various uses such as building a wall or throwing at a snarling dog or laying in a stream as a stepping-stone but does it have an inner function? The same question can be asked of any natural object from artichokes to elephants. Human artifacts such as axes have a purpose because they were designed for one but does that hold true of things found in nature? Obviously the same human mind that invents axes can find a use for rocks or artichokes or elephants but do these objects have some inherent function, an aim that is their reason for being? Or, differently put, when we utilize these objects are we finding a useful function they can serve or are we discovering the function they were meant to serve?

The answer to this question may depend upon one's religious views. If we assume there is a god, that assumption could carry the corollary that nothing is created senselessly but each object has its appointed place and purpose in the overall scheme of things. (As Tennyson writes in his *In Memoriam* "That nothing walks with aimless feet . . . When God hath made the pile complete" "That not a worm is cloven in vain . . . Or but subserves another's gain.") Nonbelievers, on the other hand, will usually assume that the universe and all its parts are chance occurrences, thrown out by natural forces; if the roll of the dice were different then a different world would have resulted. They would claim that nothing in the universe has any intrinsic purpose that should be realized — including the human species.

This is a profound question and one that has no decisive answer, but at least we can say that in the twentieth century A.D. we do not have the same confidence in a teleological universe that Aristotle had in the fourth century B.C. (And we are not sure that uniqueness is the index of any designated function man might have, especially when our uniqueness might consist in being more predatory than any other creature.) To illustrate some of the contemporary resistance to this notion let us take the issue of the role of women.

Conservative members of society will often argue that a woman's function is to be a mother (and a wife). Since women are uniquely capable of bearing children that is seen as a woman's purpose and the way in which she can achieve her greatest fulfillment. On this view, a woman without a child is hardly a woman because she has not realized her basic function. But the feminist will reply that woman was not intended to be anything at all. Rather, women have a wide range of capabilities and should be free to develop themselves along the lines they choose. If a woman decides to follow the traditional role and have children that is her option not her obligation, and the woman who chooses a career does not necessarily lead an unfulfilled life. On this reading, there are no inherent purposes for the female sex and perhaps none for the male sex or humanity either.

3. This leads to a third criticism of Aristotle, which concerns his failure to provide a sound definition of humanness. He claims that human beings are unique in possessing reason and that man's essence and function therefore consist in being rational, but we are not so certain of this any more.[19] Although human beings may be the most rational creatures that does not make them unique in kind but only places them at the upper end of an intelligence spectrum that runs throughout the animal kingdom. Chimpanzees, for example, have shown some remarkable skills in problem solving. They will select a pointed stick, strip off the bark, and insert it into a termites nest; when the termites clamp onto the intruding object the chimpanzee will withdraw the stick and eat the termites. They will also insert leaves into cavities too small for their hands to absorb the rainwater that has collected there; they then suck the water from the leaf. This behavior not only displays intelligence but also shows a tool using and tool making capability that anthropologists used to take as the hallmark of man. In laboratory conditions chimpanzees have also proven themselves capable of learning language and have progressed to the level of a four-year-old child. Because they lack the necessary vocal apparatus they cannot produce speech but they can be taught sign language, even to the point of symbolizing abstract concepts. This certainly indicates a high level of intellectual ability.[20]

Aristotle's account of humanness then has not held up through time, and such an account is needed by any self-realization ethic based on the development of one's humanness. For unless we know what a human being is we cannot develop into a superb example of the species.

In all fairness, Aristotle can hardly be blamed for failing to settle the issue. The question of man's nature has perplexed thinkers for generations (see Chapter 2) and we are still debating the question, especially in the context of abortion and euthanasia. (It makes a significant difference whether we think that a human being is involved or merely living tissue.) In the long history of the debate man has been called the political or inquisitive animal (following Aristotle who said, "All men by nature desire to know"), the aesthetic animal, the religious animal, the social animal, the noble animal, and the aggressive animal. We are also told that to err is human or learning from one's mistakes, to be conscious is human and to be self-conscious, to use speech, to create art objects, to be bored, to laugh, to curse, to play, to have imagination. Human beings have been referred to as apes or angels, heaven's masterpiece or nature's sole mistake, the creature that makes progress or is a bundle of self-contradictions, the only creature that is ashamed of himself — or needs to be, the only creature that eats when he isn't hungry, drinks when he isn't thirsty, and makes love all year round!

No firm definition has emerged from this welter of suggestions, and the person who wants to be a fine human being is left without clear direction. It is a problem that parallels that of the more common self-realization theory in which the concept of the self remains far too vague.

In the light of this analysis we can see that Aristotle's theory has a number of disadvantages and defects. Whether these weaknesses render his position unadoptable is a moot point; it can only be decided by the individual once he knows basically what is involved. In a larger sense, it certainly seems admirable for an ethic to recommend that we lead balanced and reasonable lives as ideal human beings.

Notes

1. See Jean-Paul Sartre, *Existentialism and Human Emotions,* trans. B. Frechtman (New York: Philosophical Library, 1957), 12–23.
2. Books on the Renaissance abound but one that stresses the "excellence in diversity" of the period is Walter Pater's *The Renaissance* (London: Macmillan, 1917). Pater is a noted stylist and his famous conclusion to the book is "to burn always with this hard, gemlike flame, to maintain this ecstasy, is success in life."
3. See *Thucydides,* trans. B. Jowett (Boston: D. Lothrop, 1883), ii, 40.
4. George Santayana, *Three Philosophical Poets* (Cambridge: Harvard University Press, 1910), Chapter 4, passim. In the play *Peer Gynt* by Heinrich Ibsen, the same idea is expressed through the figure of the Button Molder who melts down all souls who, instead of being true to their essential selves, had sought diverse experience instead.
5. Abraham Maslow, *Motivation and Personality* (New York: Harper & Row, 1970), 269–70, 279.
6. Maslow, ibid., 46. K. Goldstein is credited with inventing the concept of self-actualization. See his *Human Nature from the Point of View of Psychopathology* (Cambridge: Harvard University Press, 1940), and *The Organism* (New York: American Book Co., 1939).

7. Carl Rogers, *On Becoming A Person* (Boston: Houghton Mifflin, 1961), 187–88, 195–96. Reprinted with permission.

8. For representative works see J. H. Muirhead, *Rule and End in Morals* (London: Oxford University Press, 1932); B. Bosanquet, *Some Suggestions in Ethics* (London: Macmillan, 1919); and H. J. Paton, *The Good Will* (New York: Macmillan, 1927).

9. J. H. Muirhead, *Elements of Ethics* (London: John Murray, and New York: Charles Scribner's Sons, 1932), 178, 180, 232.

10. It should be mentioned that Bradley departed from the Hegelian position described here in his next essay, "Ideal Morality."

11. Bradley tried to hedge his bets by saying that these hereditary characteristics may "not as yet" show themselves in the child, but a move of this kind would allow him to say that all characteristics are due to heredity and simply appeared late.

12. For the classic exposition of this view see René Descartes, *Meditations On First Philosophy*, especially Meditation II. John Stuart Mill said in this connection that we cannot be just a series of feelings since we are conscious of having those feelings. "I feel" is not the same as "I know that I feel."

13. Oscar Wilde, *The Picture of Dorian Gray* (New York: William H. Wise, 1931), 108–109.

14. See John Donne's *Devotions* (London: William Pichenng, 1870), Meditation XVII; and Eugene Debs, *On Labor and Freedom* (London: Macmillan, 1932). In the light of this progression we can see how an idealistic view of self can be derived.

15. Whenever a doctrine claims that one should help others as a means of helping oneself, the implication is that if we do not derive any benefit then we should not help others. And treating others as a means to self-realization is not the most praiseworthy morality.

16. In this he followed Plato, whose *The Republic* is a discussion of justice in the state that parallels justice in the individual. The state is considered the individual "writ large."

17. Aristotle, *Nicomachean Ethics*, Book 2: 6.

18. Aristotle added here (1099b) that happiness also "needs the external goods as well; for it is impossible, or not easy, to do noble acts without the proper equipment. In many actions we use friends and riches and political power as instruments; and there are some things the lack of which takes the lustre from happiness, as good birth, goodly children, beauty; for the man who is very ugly in appearance or ill-born or solitary and childless is not very likely to be happy . . . still less likely if he had thoroughly bad children or friends or had lost good children or friends by death."

19. Aristotle has been criticized for excessively emphasizing reason and for having contempt for the emotional side of man, which is a rather cold attitude to take. His idea of *theoria* as the highest rational function has been especially criticized as an elitist idea, fit only for those with sufficient leisure time to engage in rational contemplation.

20. For excellent accounts of research in primatology see D. Premack, *Intelligence in Ape and Man* (New York: Erlbaum Assoc., 1976), R. E. Passingham, *The Human Primate* (San Francisco: W. H. Freeman, 1982); and A. J. Premack, *Why Chimps Can Read* (New York: Harper and Row, 1976).

Bibliography

ADLER, FELIX. *An Ethical Philosophy of Life.* New York: Appleton and Co., 1918.

BLANSHARD, BRAND. *Reason and Goodness.* New York: Macmillan, 1961.

BOSANQUET, B. *Some Suggestions in Ethics.* London: Macmillan, 1919.

CALKINS, MARY. *The Good Man and the Good.* New York: Macmillan, 1918.

CAMPBELL, CHARLES. "Moral Intuition and the Principle of Self Realization." *Proceedings of the British Academy* 34 (1948): 23–56.

CROCE, BENEDETTO. *The Philosophy of the Practical*, trans. D. Ainslee. London: Macmillan, 1913.

ELIOT, T. S. *Knowledge and Experience in the Philosophy of F. H. Bradley.* London: Faber and Faber, 1963.

EVERETT, W. G. *Moral Values.* New York: Henry Holt, 1918.

FROMM, ERICH. *Man for Himself.* New York: Holt, Rinehart and Winston, 1947.

GINSBERG, MORRIS. "The Function of Reason in Morals." *Proceedings of the Aristotelian Society* 39 (1938–39).

GOLDSTEIN, K. *Human Nature from the Point of View of Psychopathology.* Cambridge: Harvard University Press, 1940.

GREEN, T. H. *Lectures on the Principles of Political Obligation.* London: Longmans, Green, 1941.

———. *Prolegomena to Ethics.* London: Oxford University Press, 1883.

HARDIE, W. F. R. *Aristotle's Ethical Theory.* Oxford: University Press, 1968.

———. "Aristotle on the Best Life for a Man." *Philosophy* 54 (1979): 35–50.

HARTSHORNE, CHARLES. *The Logic of Perfection and Other Essays in Neoclassical Metaphysics.* La Salle, Ill.: Open Court, 1962.

HUBY, PAMELA. *Greek Ethics.* London: Macmillan, 1967.

JAEGER, W. *Aristotle.* London: Barnes and Noble, 1922.

LAIRD, JOHN. "Rationalism in Ethics." *Journal of Philosophical Studies* 4 (1929).

MANSER, A., AND G. STOCK. *The Philosophy of F. H. Bradley.* Oxford: Oxford University Press, 1984.

MARSHALL, THOMAS. *Aristotle's Theory of Conduct.* London: T. F. Unwin, 1906.

MASLOW, A. H. *Motivation and Personality.* New York: Harper and Row, 1970.

———. *Toward a Psychology of Being.* New York: Van Nostrand Reinhold, 1968.

MORAVSCIK, J., ED. *Aristotle.* New York: Doubleday, 1966.

MUIRHEAD, J. H. *Elements of Ethics.* London: John Murray, 1932.

OATES, W. J. *Aristotle and the Problem of Value.* Princeton, N.J.: Princeton University Press, 1963.

PASSMORE, JOHN. *The Perfectibility of Man.* New York: Scribners, 1970.

PATON, H. J. "Can Reason Be Practical?" *Proceedings of the British Academy* 1945.

———. *The Good Will.* London: Allen and Unwin, 1927.

RANDALL, J. H. *Aristotle.* New York: Columbia University Press, 1960.

ROGERS, CARL. *On Becoming a Person.* Boston: Houghton Mifflin, 1961.

ROYCE, J. *The World and the Individual.* New York: Macmillan, 1900.

SIDGWICK, HENRY. *Lectures on the Ethics of T. H. Green, Mr. Herbert Spencer, and J. Martineau.* London: Macmillan, 1902.

———. *Outlines of the History of Ethics.* London: Macmillan, 1931.

VEATCH, H. B. *Rational Man: A Modern Interpretation of Aristotelian Ethics.* Bloomington: University of Indiana Press, 1962.

VON WRIGHT, G. H. *The Varieties of Goodness.* London: Humanities Press, 1963.

WALLACE, JAMES D. "Excellences and Merit." *Philosophical Review* 83 (1974): 182–99.

WALSH, J. J., AND H. L. SHAPIRO. *Aristotle's Ethics: Issues and Interpretations.* Belmont, Calif.: Wadsworth, 1967.

WILLIAMS, B. A. O. "Aristotle on the Good." *Philosophical Quarterly* 12 (1962): 289–96.

WRIGHT, W. K. *General Introduction to Ethics.* New York: Macmillan, 1929.

CHAPTER 7

Naturalism

After the introspective and ingrown ethic of self-realization it seems a breath of fresh air to turn to naturalism, a philosophy that takes the natural world as its ideal. According to this theory, nature in its various manifestations is the model for human conduct. To "be natural," "let nature take its course," "live naturally," "do whatever feels natural," "return to nature" — these are the common phrases that declare the natural life is best.

But *naturalism* is a term that has a multitude of meanings. The naturalistic movement in art includes any work that faithfully copies the external world, that is representational, mimetic, and realistic. Most of the paintings of Andrew Wyeth and Edward Hopper fall into this category as well as the illustrations of Normal Rockwell, the "slice-of-life" literary works of Hart Crane, Theodore Dreiser, John Steinbeck, and Erskine Caldwell, and even the musical compositions of Aaron Copland and Leonard Bernstein. Naturalism in theology means studying nature to understand god, apart from any special revelation, and naturalism in philosophy means, broadly speaking, any theory of reality that claims objects and events are physical phenomena without supernatural significance.[1] A natural scale in music has neither sharps nor flats (e.g., C major); a natural law is a physical principle such as that governing gravity or electromagnetism; and a natural reaction in a person is spontaneous without artificiality or affectation. There is also a natural born citizen, one's natural child, a natural affinity or aversion, and natural and unnatural love.

The first task then in exploring the territory of ethical naturalism is to find out where the land lies. One way of doing this is to divide naturalism into two parts: (1) the position that our lives should follow the course of nature (as it appears outside us and flows within us); and (2) that we should live in accordance with nature's principle of development, especially the evolutionary process. Both of these positions will be examined in turn.

Living Naturally: Letting Nature Be Our Guide

Perhaps the most straightforward meaning of naturalism is that we ought to return to an earlier time when people lived in closer harmony with the natural environment. It is vital, the theory states, that we get back to the basics of life, the necessities of food, clothing, and shelter, and satisfy them in plain, elemental

223

ways. Instead of the elaborate and sophisticated structure that civilized man has erected we should live more simply, even primitively so that we are at one with nature which is our home.

This theory trades upon the very strong sense today that we have overshot the mark, gone too far in our scientific and technological progress so that our roots have been severed, and we now wander aimlessly and disconnected in our man-made world. Nature has become alien to us and we even pride ourselves on not behaving like animals, but at the same time we cannot feel comfortable in surroundings that are totally artificial; the world of synthetics is even more foreign and threatening to us. If we live in an apartment high up in a glass and steel "box" in some urban center we feel the need to have flowers in vases or grow plants indoors, keep pets such as dogs, cats, fish, or canaries, and travel to the country or the beach on weekends (or at least sit under a tree in the park). According to this theory, such behavior shows a deep-seated longing for a primal environment and points up the need to restore to human life a sense of rapport with our origins in nature; in short, the ineradicable desire to live more naturally and less artificially. We are feeling homesick, it is said, because we have strayed too far from mother earth, and the only cure is to return to our beginnings.

This ethical theory, in which nature is taken as the model for an ideal existence, has had recent expression in the populist movement of the late 1960s and early 1970s. At that time many young people in the United States and Europe took a stand against the prevailing values and formed what Theodore Rozak called a "counter culture."[2] One of its features was a return to a natural way of living, and the effects of this outlook can be seen in our contemporary preference for natural fabrics and materials, for exercise and outdoor sports, healthy foods, a pure environment, ecological balance, and so forth.

The participants in this movement can be described as advocating

> "the authenticity of the country over the falseness of urban life, the rhythm of the days and seasons as their measure of time, the tenderness of making love in place of the violence of making war, and the simplicity and space and silence of the land to make them gentle, balanced, sensitive, and tranquil. They want to eat organic foods without pesticides or preservatives, to drink pure water and breathe unpolluted air, and to maintain good health through balanced nutrition and physical activity, with minimum reliance on machines. They also want to express themselves through folk crafts and popular music rather than being spectators of high art, and to wear comfortable, working clothes instead of dressing up in the latest expensive fashions; following Thoreau they say that security does not consist in what you have but in what you can do without. There is an emphasis on joy instead of status, feeling rather than intellect, emotional communion in place of verbal communication, and direct experience rather than ideas contained in books. They also believe in magic and, perhaps, the insights obtained through hallucinogenic drugs rather than the methods of science and discursive reasoning. Culture, learning, sophistication, achievement, and urbanity are all suspect as artificial overlays on natural man, whereas plainness, simplicity, openness, and rusticity are prized as elemental and good.[3]

Obviously this type of naturalism is not a formal academic philosophy but a grass roots movement in reaction to certain negative features of modern life — industrial pollution, chemical additives in food, overcrowded, noisy, unsafe cities, for example. However, it does have foundations in the history of philosophy, especially in the writings of Jean-Jacques Rousseau (1712–1778) and Henry David Thoreau (1817–1862). Both of these men can be taken as major figures within naturalism, and each in his own way has helped shape our modern "be natural" mentality.

Jean-Jacques Rousseau

Rousseau was a philosopher, essayist, musician, and novelist who led an unusually volatile and stormy life, moving from place to place in Europe, quarreling with enemies and friends, changing his religious and intellectual convictions repeatedly. However, he did maintain as a rather consistent principle that nature is essentially good and consequently that human beings possess a natural goodness from the moment of birth. Everything, in fact, that comes from the hands of nature is positive and human beings are no exception. He does not state that man in his original savage state has an ideal life, for there are natural inequalities and primitive man lives by appetites, impulses, and instincts not justice, morality, and reason. But man is endowed with free will and perfectibility so that if the proper social communities are established his natural virtue will flower. If, on the other hand, political societies develop in opposition to man's nature (as Rousseau believed was the case), then people will become divided into rich and poor, powerful and weak, and ultimately masters and slaves. This is worse than the state of nature for at least primitive man was basically happy there, living in accordance with his primary needs (for food and sex) and establishing an equilibrium with his environment.

Early man led an isolated existence in the forests, Rousseau believed, in a condition of self-sufficiency, comfortable with disease and death, and never inflicting unnecessary harm on his fellow man; his drive toward self-preservation was always modified by a natural pity. Despotism, that tragic trait, only came into being with the development of a society that did not "follow the natural progress of the human heart." In short, man is eternally good but society is wicked and its influence has led to the perversion of men; "vice and error, alien to man's constitution, [were] introduced into it from outside."

Rousseau's naturalism focuses on man's innate goodness, which must be cultivated; it does not stress the emulation of the external characteristics of nature as many naturalisic theories do. Left in a state of nature we would remain kind to each other but in society we are forced to be hypocritical, to keep up appearances, make pretenses, and generally betray and exploit one another. Such things as poverty, slums, unemployment, the rigid division of labor that allows some men to consume rich food and others to work themselves to death — all of these artificially created conditions make it almost impossible for us to realize "nature within us." It is not completely impossible because "conscience persists in following the order of nature in spite of all the laws of man." Nevertheless, the complete scale of misery and immorality of modern civilization can be traced back to man's departure from his natural state. Man is noble as a savage but deplorable in civilization.

In his *Social Contract* Rousseau tried to lay out the conditions for a community that would support the unfolding of man's inner nature, and in his book *Emile* he described a system of education that would develop what he saw as the natural virtues of human beings. For our purposes, *Emile* is the more relevant work (although the interested reader should also consult *Discourse on the Origin of Inequality Among Men* and *Julie or the New Heloise*). Here Rousseau explicated an educational philosophy that is permissive, simple, utilitarian, and close to nature. By following the "dictates of the heart" rather than the teachings of "intellectual culture" he believed that basic truths can be understood. The student has the cause and effect model of nature before him and an innate ability to grasp realities — realities that for Rousseau include god, freedom, and immortality.

More specifically, Rousseau described the optimal education of a boy, Emile, who is separated from the ordinary social influences that contaminate a child's purity and raised by a tutor under strictly controlled conditions. This process is described as *negative education,* where Emile is protected by a "sanitary cordon" from any impediments to his natural growth. The tutor, who is obviously a surrogate for Rousseau, bases the boy's early education on the senses alone, forcing him to concentrate on his immediate existence and to learn through a process of trial and error. Books are avoided and understanding is brought about through example and direct experience. Only the book of nature should be read — that and Daniel Defoe's *Robinson Crusoe* for its lessons in primitive self-reliance. (Emile learns, for example, that a farmer or a blacksmith or a carpenter is more useful on a desert island than a shopkeeper, an engraver, or a watchmaker.) But as a general principle "Reading is the scourge of childhood," Rousseau wrote, because it inculcates and perpetuates all of society's evils. As Shakespeare said in *As You Like It,* one should find tongues in trees, books in the running brooks, sermons in stones, and good in everything.

A *positive education* begins when Emile becomes aware of relationships with other people, but even here reason plays a very small part. It is the "sensibilities" that are engaged, especially the innate feelings of pity or compassion that give rise to the virtues of generosity, clemency, humanity, benevolence, and friendship. Gradually Emile is then led to a fuller life in the community as his emotional capacity, intelligence, and imagination develop. Each stage is carefully timed so that the boy's natural tendencies are fulfilled in an orderly manner rather than being disciplined, thwarted, and perverted as in the customary process of education.

It is important to note that Rousseau did not want Emile to remain in a natural, instinctive state. Part of his autonomous tendencies were to interact with others and to live in a harmonious relationship with his fellow man. Nature intends that human beings should have a moral and communal life, and only through participation at this higher level can Emile fulfill his inner nature.

The following selection from *Emile* will illustrate some of Rousseau's contentions. Not only does it show Rousseau's faith in nature but it presents one of the most original and provocative philosophies of education ever devised.

The Education of Children*

Everything is good as it comes from the hands of the Maker of the world but degenerates once it gets into the hands of man. Man makes one land yield the products of another, disregards differences of climates, elements and

*Reprinted with permission from Jean-Jacques Rousseau, *Émile*, trans. W. Boyd (New York: Columbia University Press, 1976), 11–15, 17, 33–34, 36–40.

seasons, mutilates his dogs and horses, perverts and disfigures everything. Not content to leave anything as nature has made it, he must needs shape man himself to his notions, as he does the trees in his garden.

But under present conditions, human beings would be even worse than they are without this fashioning. A man left entirely to himself from birth would be the most misshapen of creatures. Prejudices, authority, necessity, example, the social institutions in which we are immersed, would crush out nature in him without putting anything in its place. He would fare like a shrub that has grown up by chance in the middle of a road, and got trampled under foot by the passers-by.

Plants are fashioned by cultivation, men by education. We are born feeble and need strength; possessing nothing, we need assistance; beginning without intelligence, we need judgment. All that we lack at birth and need when grown up is given us by education. This education comes to us from nature, from men, or from things. The internal development of our faculties and organs is the education of nature. The use we learn to make of this development is the education of men. What comes to us from our experience of the things that affect us is the education of things. Each of us therefore is fashioned by three kinds of teachers. When their lessons are at variance the pupil is badly educated, and is never at peace with himself. When they coincide and lead to a common goal he goes straight to his mark and lives single-minded. Now, of these three educations the one due to nature is independent of us, and the one from things only depends on us to a limited extent. The education that comes from men is the only one within our control, and even that is doubtful. Who can hope to have the entire direction of the words and deeds of all the people around a child?

It is only by good luck that the goal can be reached. What is this goal? It is nature's own goal. Since the three educations must work together for a perfect result, the one that cannot be modified determines the course of the other two. But perhaps 'nature' is too vague a word. We must try to fix its meaning. Nature, it has been said, is only habit. Is that really so? Are there not habits which are formed under pressure, leaving the original nature unchanged? One example is the habit of plants which have been forced away from the upright direction. When set free, the plant retains the bent forced upon it; but the sap has not changed its first direction and any new growth the plant makes returns to the vertical. It is the same with human inclinations. So long as there is no change in conditions the inclinations due to habits, however unnatural, remain unchanged, but immediately the restraint is removed the habit vanishes and nature reasserts itself.

We are born capable of sensation and from birth are affected in diverse ways by the objects around us. As soon as we become conscious of our sensations we are inclined to seek or to avoid the objects which produce them: at first, because they are agreeable or disagreeable to us, later because we discover that they suit or do not suit us, and ultimately because of the judgments we pass on them by reference to the idea of happiness or perfection we get from reason. These inclinations extend and strengthen with the growth of sensibility and intelligence, but under the pressure of habit they are changed to some extent with our opinions. The inclinations before this change are what I call our nature. In my view everything ought to be in conformity with these original inclinations.

There would be no difficulty if our three educations were merely different. But what is to be done when they are at cross purposes? Consistency is plainly impossible when we seek to educate a man for others, instead of for himself. If we have to combat either nature or society, we must choose between making a man or making a citizen. We cannot make both. There is an inevitable conflict of aims, from which come two opposing forms of education: the one communal and public, the other individual and domestic.

To get a good idea of communal education, read Plato's *Republic*. It is not a political treatise, as those who merely judge books by their titles think. It is the finest treatise on education ever written. Communal education in this sense, however, does not and can not now exist. There are no longer any real fatherlands and therefore no real citizens. The words 'fatherland' and 'citizen' should be expunged from modern languages.

I do not regard the instruction given in those ridiculous establishments called colleges as 'public,' any more than the ordinary kind of education. This education makes for two opposite goals and reaches neither. The men it turns out are double-minded, seemingly concerned for others, but really only concerned for themselves. From this contradiction comes the conflict we never cease to experience in ourselves. We are drawn in different directions by nature and by man, and take a midway path that leads us nowhere. In this state of confusion we go through life and end up with our contradictions unsolved, never having been any good to ourselves or to other people.

There remains then domestic education, the education of nature. But how will a man who has been educated entirely for himself get on with other people? If there were any way of combining in a single person the twofold aim, and removing the contradictions of life, a great obstacle to happiness would be removed. But before passing judgment on this kind of man it would be necessary to follow his development and see him fully formed. It would be necessary, in a word, to make the acquaintance of the natural man. This is the subject of our quest in this book.

What can be done to produce this very exceptional person? In point of fact all we have to do is to prevent anything being done.

• • •

The Natural Educators

It is not enough merely to keep children alive. They should be fitted to take care of themselves when they grow up. They should learn to bear the blows of fortune; to meet either wealth or poverty, to live if need be in the frosts of Iceland or on the sweltering rock of Malta. The important thing is not to ward off death, but to make sure they really live. Life is not just breathing: it is action, the functioning of organs, senses, faculties, every part of us that gives the consciousness of existence. The man who gets most out of life is not the one who has lived longest, but the one who has felt life most deeply.

Man's wisdom is but servile prejudice: his customs but subjection and restraint. From the beginning to the end of life civilised man is a slave.

• • •

Observe nature and follow the path she marks out. She keeps on disciplining the children all the time. She hardens their temperaments by ordeals of every kind. She shows them the meaning of pain and suffering in their early years. Their teeth as they come through give them fever. Sharp colics cause convulsions. Racking coughs choke them. Worms torment them. Ferments in the blood cause dangerous eruptions. Early childhood is beset with sickness and danger. Half the children born die before eight. It is only after the child has succeeded in passing these tests and has won through to strength that life becomes more secure.

This is nature's way. Why set yourself against it? Do you not see that in attempting to improve on her work you are destroying it and defeating the provision she has made? So long as you do not go beyond the measure of the child's strength there is less risk in employing it than in husbanding it. Train the children, then, for the hardships they will one day have to endure. Harden them to the rigours of the seasons, the climate, the elements. Inure them to hunger, thirst and fatigue. Dip them in the waters of Styx.

The babe comes into the world with a cry, and his first days are spent in tears. Sometimes he is dandled and caressed to soothe him. At other times he is threatened and beaten to keep him quiet. Either we do what pleases him, or we make him do what pleases us. He gives orders, or he gets them: there is no middle way for us. His first ideas are either of mastery or of servitude. Before he can speak he commands: before he can act he obeys. Sometimes he is punished for faults before he knows anything about them and even before he is able to commit them. That is how we put into the young heart the passions we afterwards impute to nature. Having taken pains to make the child bad we complain about his badness.

If you want the child to keep his original character watch over him from the moment he enters the world. Get hold of him as soon as he is born and never leave him till he is a man. Short of that, you will not succeed.

· · ·

Happiness in Childhood

Another advance at this time which makes crying less necessary is increase in strength. The more children can do for themselves the less help they need from other people. Added strength brings with it the sense needed for its direction. With the coming of self-consciousness at this second stage individual life really begins. Memory extends the sense of identity over all the moments of the child's existence. He becomes one and the same person, capable of happiness or sorrow. From this point on it is essential to regard him as a moral being.

· · ·

Your first duty is to be humane. Love childhood. Look with friendly eyes on its games, its pleasures, its amiable dispositions. Which of you does not sometimes look back regretfully on the age when laughter was ever on the lips and the heart free of care? Why steal from the little innocents the enjoyment of a time that passes all too quickly?

Excessive severity and excessive indulgence are equally to be avoided. If you let children suffer you endanger health and life. If you are over-careful in shielding them from trouble of every kind you are laying up much unhappiness for the future: you are withdrawing them from the common lot of man, to which they must one day become subject in spite of you.

· · ·

The surest way to make your child unhappy is to accustom him to get everything he wants. With desire constantly increasing through easy satisfaction, lack of power will sooner or later force you to a refusal in spite of yourself, and the unwonted refusal will cause him deeper annoyance than the mere lack of what he desires. First he will want the stick in your hand, then the bird that flies past, then the star that shines above him. Everything he sees he will want: and unless you were God you could never hope to satisfy him. How could such a child possibly be happy? Happy! He is a despot, at once the meanest of slaves and the most wretched of creatures. Let us get back to the primitive way. Nature made children to be loved and helped, not to be obeyed and feared. Is there in the world a being more feeble and unhappy, more at the mercy of his environment, more in need of pity and protection than a child? Surely then there is nothing more offensive or more unseemly than the sight of a dictatorial headstrong child, issuing orders to those around him and assuming the stone of a master to people without whom he would perish.

On the other hand, it should be obvious that with the many restrictions imposed on children by their own weakness it is barbarous for us to add subjection to our caprices to the natural subjection, and take from them such limited liberty as they possess. Social servitude will come with the age of reason. Why anticipate it by a domestic servitude? Let one moment of life be free from this yoke which nature has not imposed, and leave the child to the enjoyment of his natural liberty.

· · ·

Nature wants children to be children before they are men. If we deliberately depart from this order we shall get premature fruits which are neither ripe nor well flavoured and which soon decay. We shall have youthful sages and grown up children. Childhood has ways of seeing, thinking and feeling peculiar to itself: nothing can be more foolish that to seek to substitute our ways for them. I should as soon expect a child of ten to be five feet in height as to be possessed of judgment.

· · ·

It is strange that all the time people have been bringing up children nobody has thought of any instruments for their direction but emulation, jealousy, envy, vanity, greed or base fear; most dangerous passions all of them, sure to corrupt the soul. Foolish teachers think they are working wonders when they are simply making the children wicked in the attempt to teach them about goodness. Then they announce gravely: such is man. Yes, such is the man you have made. All the instruments have been tried but one, and that as it happens is the only one that can succeed: well regulated liberty.

Avoid verbal lessons with your pupil. The only kind of lesson he should get is that of experience. Never inflict any punishment, for he does not know what it is to be at fault. Being devoid of all morality in his actions he can do nothing morally wrong, nothing that deserves either punishment or reprimand.

Let us lay it down as an incontestable principle that the first impulses of nature are always right. There is no original perversity in the human heart. Of every vice we can say how it entered and whence it came. The only passion natural to man is self-love, or self-esteem in a broad sense. This self-esteem has no necessary reference to other people. In so far as it relates to ourselves it is good and useful. It only becomes good or bad in the social application we make of it. Until reason, which is the guide of self-esteem, makes its appearance, the child should not do anything because he is seen or heard by other people, but only do what nature demands of him. Then he will do nothing but what is right.

Henry David Thoreau

Rousseau is important as an exponent of the natural goodness in man, the belief that we should behave naturally and follow the voice of nature inside us. However, most naturalistic ethics concentrate more on nature as an external model for our behavior in the way that the "back to nature" movement interpreted it.

Here the emphasis is on living physically close to nature in a country setting and working at jobs that put us in contact with the earth. We should be farmers, ranchers, and fishermen; carpenters, leather workers, and craftsmen of all kinds; we should live in houses built with our own hands out of natural materials of wood or stone, hide or soil or ice; and we should chop our own firewood, draw our own water from the well, use candles or oil lamps for light, preserve our meat in a smokehouse and our vegetables in a root cellar. Our clothing should be simple and practical not fashionable, we should decorate ourselves with simple jewellery such as turquoise beads but not gold necklaces, and our art should consist of naive painting, storytelling, and folk music not impressionist exhibits or classical concerts.

The closer we can approximate the mode of living of early man the more fulfilling our lives will be, for the natural world is the source of man's deepest pleasure. It is our joy, our comfort, our teacher, our best medicine "wise in every part."

Some of these sentiments were expressed in a higher way by outstanding British poets of the nineteenth century such as Wordsworth, Keats, Shelley, and Byron. William Wordsworth, for example, in "The Tables Turned" declared that we learn much more from nature than from books. If only we open ourselves to receive nature's lessons we will understand the most profound truths:

> Books! t'is a dull and endless strife:
> Come, hear the woodland linnet,
> How sweet his music! on my life.
> There's more of wisdom in it . . .

One impulse from a vernal wood
May teach you more of man,
Of moral evil and of good,
Than all the sages can . . .

Enough of Science and of Art;
Close up those barren leaves;
Come forth, and bring with you a heart
That watches and receives.

John Keats also celebrated nature, for example, in his famous "Poem to Endymion" where he described the restorative powers of nature's forms, the way in which their beauty has the power to cure our despondency:

A thing of beauty is a joy forever:
Its loveliness increases; it will never
Pass into nothingness; but still will keep
A bower quiet for us, and a sleep
Full of sweet dreams, and health, and quiet breathing.
Therefore, on every morrow, are we wreathing
A flowery band to bind us to the earth,
Spite of despondence, of the inhuman dearth
Of noble natures . . .
Some shape of beauty moves away the pall
From our dark spirits. Such the sun, the moon,
Trees old, and young, sprouting a shady boon
For simple sheep; and such are daffodils
With the green world they live in; and clear rills
That for themselves a cooling covert make
'Gainst the hot season . . .
Whether there be shine, or gloom o'ercast,
They always must be with us, or we die.

Wordsworth again in "Tintern Abbey" broadly extolled nature as

The anchor of my purest thoughts, the nurse,
The guide, the guardian of my heart, and soul
Of all my moral being.

Elsewhere in the same poem he wrote

For nature then
(The coarser pleasures of my boyish days,
And their glad animal movements all gone by)
To me was all in all. — I cannot paint
What then I was. The sounding cataract
Haunted me like a passion: the tall rock,
The mountain, and the deep and gloomy wood,
Their colours and their forms, were then to me
An appetite: a feeling and a love,
That had no need of a remoter charm,
By thought supplied, nor any interest
Unborrowed from the eye.

Idealizing nature then can run the gamut from the praise of a rustic life to a lyrical celebration of nature's depth and richness. The common factor throughout is that man should follow nature, copying its features and patterns in order to live well. Rousseau had said that we should not be divided from our own natural being but here the stress is placed on not being divided from our natural home. The so-called progress of modern life has only lured man away from the basic source of his gratification, so we must return to a condition in which we can have immediate contact with the natural world. The ways of nature must once again be given centrality and become our guide to a fulfilling existence.

The figure who perhaps best exemplifies this approach to successful living as well as epitomizing its eclectic character is the nineteenth century American philosopher Henry David Thoreau. His book *Walden, or, Life in the Woods* is a classic document of nature philosophy, not so much because it lays down the governing principles but because it provides a superb testament to the natural way of life.

Thoreau is usually labeled a *transcendentalist* in the classification of American philosophers and this is true as far as it goes. Transcendentalism is a metaphysical view that links naturalism and theism, seeing god within nature. It maintains that a divine spirit permeates the natural world, giving it direction and purpose. God is not behind nature but within it; his mind is its active power, his body its physical form. Transcendentalism also maintains a strong belief in the inherent morality of nature, which caused many of its adherents to protest against slavery and war as contrary to nature's intentions. "At the center of nature lies the moral law, radiating to the circumference," and injustice is an affront to nature itself.

In addition to Thoreau, the American transcendentalists are said to include Ralph Waldo Emerson (1803–1882), William Ellery Channing (1780–1842), Margaret Fuller (1810–1850), Theodore Parker (1810–1860), and A. B. Alcott (1799–1888). Emerson was the leading figure of this New England movement, and his books *Nature* (1836) and *Essays* (1841 and 1844) exerted a strong influence on American thought of the period. The transcendentalists formed a loosely organized club, published a magazine, *The Dial*, and even attempted a utopian experiment in the colony of Brook Farm; it was designed as a model of "plain living and high thinking."

Thoreau shared a great many of the assumptions of the transcendentalists. Nature had spiritual significance for him too, and he believed that insofar as man is a part of nature he carries a divine spark. He agreed with Emerson's mysticism that "every natural fact is a symbol of some spiritual fact," that "the whole of nature is a metaphor of the human mind" and "within man is the soul of the whole." Like the others he actively protested against slavery and defied the Fugitive Slave Law, believing that the desecration of the human spirit was an offence against nature in man. His celebrated essay "Civil Disobedience" draws out the implications of this moral position and influenced Gandhi in his doctrine of passive resistance.

However, the transcendentalists were concerned with improving society in the light of the reality revealed by nature, whereas Thoreau gave centrality to living within nature; he was not concerned with forming an ideal community. It was of primary importance to him that the individual lead a real existence, and that could only happen in natural surroundings where communion with nature could take place. He wanted a natural mode of life rather than being in any American or European society, however well organized it might be, for nature was the setting within which authenticity could be achieved.

In short, he was in individualist who wanted people to work out the ideal terms of their personal existence by returning to the "basics," and that meant living in harmony with nature. He extolled the right of man to withdraw from civilization and the conventions of society in order to become genuine once more. Freedom and self-reliance were needed, independent thought rather than conformity to the prevailing ways of living. In his famous phrases, "If a man does not keep pace with his companions, perhaps it is because he hears a different drummer. Let him step to the music he hears, however measured or far away."

To Thoreau, most people are slaves to commerce, "that incessant business" of making money. Earning money is certainly necessary but only a minimum amount of time should be spent on it. (He wrote that "to have done anything by which you earned money merely is to have been truly idle, or worse," and suggests elsewhere that he did not believe in the dignity of labor per se.) But people spend an inordinate amount of their time working in order to support a wasteful, superfluous, artificial existence in towns. They have been diverted from the satisfaction of their primary needs into rounds of frivolity and superficial pleasures, needless luxuries and debilitating comforts. Modern society causes people to squander their lives, laboring incessantly for goods that are unnecessary: fashionable clothing, large houses, an excessive amount of food. For this reason "The mass of men lead lives of quiet desperation," Thoreau wrote. "What is called resignation is confirmed desperation." Driven to maintain a "civilized" standard of living, people dissipate their strength, grow weak and dependent, and above all lose sight of what is essential in life — the basic terms of existence that are made plain by living in a natural state.[4]

We need to return, therefore, to more elemental conditions, to simplify our lives, clarify our senses, become one with nature once again. Human beings should regard themselves as "an inhabitant, or a part and parcel of Nature, rather than a member of society." The freedom of the wilderness is what is needed to make us more spontaneous and alive, more independent and original.

Thoreau best expressed these ideas in the following passages drawn from his book *Walden*, a work widely regarded as a masterpiece of American literature. It was written to make people reconsider their assumptions about the proper way to live, to rouse them from their "dogmatic slumbers." For as Thoreau says: "When we consider what, to use the words of the catechism, is the chief end of man, and what are the true necessaries and means of life, it appears as if men had deliberately chosen the common mode of living because they preferred it to any other. Yet they honestly think there is no choice left. But alert and healthy natures remember that the sun rose clear. It is never too late to give up our prejudices."

From Walden Pond*

When I wrote the following pages, or rather the bulk of them, I lived alone, in the woods, a mile from any neighbor, in a house which I had built myself,

*Reprinted from Henry David Thoreau, *Walden, or, Life in the Woods* (New York: Random House, 1937; originally published, 1854), 3, 5–11, 76–89, 277.

on the shore of Walden Pond, in Concord, Massachusetts, and earned my living by the labor of my hands only. I lived there two years and two months. At present I am a sojourner in civilized life again.

• • •

When first I took up my abode in the woods, that is, began to spend my nights as well as days there, which, by accident, was on Independence Day, or the Fourth of July, 1845, my house was not finished for winter, but was merely a defence against the rain, without plastering or chimney, the walls being of rough, weather-stained boards, with wide chinks, which made it cool at night. The upright white hewn studs and freshly planed door and window casings gave it a clean and airy look, especially in the morning, when its timbers were saturated with dew, so that I fancied that by noon some sweet gum would exude from them. To my imagination it retained throughout the day more or less of this auroral character, reminding me of a certain house on a mountain which I had visited a year before. This was an airy and unplastered cabin, fit to entertain a travelling god, and where a goddess might trail her garments. The winds which passed over my dwelling were such as sweep over the ridges of mountains, bearing the broken strains, or celestial parts only, of terrestrial music. The morning wind forever blows, the poem of creation is uninterrupted; but few are the ears that hear it. Olympus is but the outside of the earth everywhere.

The only house I had been the owner of before, if I except a boat, was a tent, which I used occasionally when making excursions in the summer, and this is still rolled up in my garret; but the boat, after passing from hand to hand, has gone down the stream of time. With this more substantial shelter about me, I had made some progress toward settling in the world. This frame, so slightly clad, was a sort of crystallization around me, and reacted on the builder. It was suggestive somewhat as a picture in outlines. I did not need to go outdoors to take the air, for the atmosphere within had lost none of its freshness. It was not so much within-doors as behind a door where I sat, even in the rainiest weather. The Harivansa says, "An abode without birds is like a meat without seasoning." Such was not my abode, for I found myself suddenly neighbor to the birds; not by having imprisoned one, but having caged myself near them. I was not only nearer to some of those which commonly frequent the garden and the orchard, but to those wilder and more thrilling songsters of the forest which never, or rarely, serenade a villager,— the wood thrush, the veery, the scarlet tanager, the field sparrow, the whip-poor-will, and many others.

I was seated by the shore of a small pond, about a mile and a half south of the village of Concord and somewhat higher than it, in the midst of an extensive wood between that town and Lincoln, and about two miles south of that our only field known to fame, Concord Battle Ground; but I was so low in the woods that the opposite shore, half a mile off, like the rest, covered with wood, was my most distant horizon. For the first week, whenever I looked out on the pond it impressed me like a tarn high up on the side of a mountain, its bottom far above the surface of other lakes, and, as the sun arose, I saw it throwing off its nightly clothing of mist, and here and there, by degrees, its soft ripples or its smooth reflecting surface was revealed, while the mists, like ghosts, were stealthily withdrawing in every direction into the woods, as at the breaking up of some nocturnal conventicle. The very dew seemed to hang upon the trees later into the day than usual, as on the sides of mountains.

. . .

Every morning was a cheerful invitation to make my life of equal simplicity, and I may say innocence, with Nature herself. I have been as sincere a worshipper of Aurora as the Greeks. I got up early and bathed in the pond; that was a religious exercise, and one of the best things which I did. They say that characters were engraven on the bathing tub of King Tching-thang to this effect: "Renew thyself completely each day; do it again, and again, and forever again." I can understand that. Morning brings back the heroic ages. I was as much affected by the faint hum of a mosquito making its invisible and unimaginable tour through my apartment at earliest dawn, when I was sitting with door and windows open, as I could be by any trumpet that ever sang of fame. It was Homer's requiem; itself an Iliad and Odyssey in the air, singing its own wrath and wanderings. There was something cosmical about it; a standing advertisement, till forbidden, of the everlasting vigor and fertility of the world. The morning, which is the most memorable season of the day, is the awakening hour. Then there is least somnolence in us; and for an hour, at least, some part of us awakes which slumbers all the rest of the day and night.

. . .

We must learn to reawaken and keep ourselves awake, not by mechanical aids, but by an infinite expectation of the dawn, which does not forsake us in our soundest sleep. I know of no more encouraging fact than the unquestionable ability of man to elevate his life by a conscious endeavor. It is something to be able to paint a particular picture, or to carve a statue, and so to make a few objects beautiful; but it is far more glorious to carve and paint the very atmosphere and medium through which we look, which morally we can do. To affect the quality of the day, that is the highest of arts. Every man is tasked to make his life, even in its details, worthy of the contemplation of his most elevated and critical hour. If we refused, or rather used up, such paltry information as we get, the oracles would distinctly inform us how this might be done.

I went to the woods because I wished to live deliberately, to front only the essential facts of life, and see if I could not learn what it had to teach, and not, when I came to die, discover that I had not lived. I did not wish to practise resignation, unless it was quite necessary. I wanted to live deep and suck out all the marrow of life, to live so sturdily and Spartan-like as to put to rout all that was not life, to cut a broad swath and shave close, to drive life into a corner, and reduce it to its lowest terms, and, if it proved to be mean, why then to get the whole and genuine meanness of it, and publish its meanness to the world; or if it were sublime, to know it by experience, and be able to give a true account of it in my next excursion. For most men, it appears to me, are in a strange uncertainty about it, whether it is of the devil or of God, and have *somewhat hastily* concluded that it is the chief end of man here to "glorify God and enjoy him forever."

Still we live meanly, like ants; though the fable tells us that we were long ago changed into men; like pygmies we fight with cranes; it is error upon error, and clout upon clout and our best virtue has for its occasion a superfluous and evitable wretchedness. Our life is frittered away by detail. An honest man has hardly need to count more than his ten fingers, or in extreme cases he may add his ten toes, and lump the rest. Simplicity, simplicity, simplicity! I say, let your affairs be as two or three, and not a hundred or a thousand; instead of a million count half a dozen, and keep your accounts on your thumb-nail. In the midst of this chopping sea of civilized life, such are the clouds and storms and quicksands and thousand-and-one items to be allowed for, that a man has to live, if he would not founder and go to the bottom and not make his port at all, by dead reckoning, and he must be a great calculator indeed who succeeds. Simplify, simplify. Instead of three meals a day, if it be necessary eat but one; instead of a hundred dishes, five; and reduce other things in proportion. Our life is like a German Confederacy, made up of petty states, with its boundary forever fluctuating, so that even a German cannot tell you how it is bounded at any moment. The nation itself, with all its so-called internal improvements, which, by the way, are all external and superficial, is just such an unwieldy and overgrown establishment, cluttered with furniture and tripped up by its own traps, ruined by luxury and heedless expense, by want of calculation and a worthy aim, as the million households in the land; and the only cure for it, as for them, is in a rigid economy, a stern and more than Spartan simplicity of life and elevation of purpose. It lives too fast. Men think that it is essential that the *Nation* have commerce, and export ice, and talk through a telegraph, and ride thirty miles an hour, without a doubt, whether *they* do or not; but whether we should live like baboons or like men, is a little uncertain. If we do not get out sleepers, and forge rails, and devote days and nights to the work, but go to tinkering upon our *lives* to improve *them,* who will build railroads? And if railroads are not built, how shall we get to Heaven in season? But if we stay at home and mind our business, who will want railroads? We do not ride on the railroad; it rides upon us. Did you ever think what those sleepers are that underlie the railroad? Each one is a man, an Irishman, or a Yankee man. The rails are laid on them, and they are covered with sand, and the cars run smoothly over them. They are sound sleepers, I assure you. And every few years a new lot is laid down and run over; so that, if some have the pleasure of riding on a rail, others have the misfortune to be ridden upon. And when they run over a man that is walking in his sleep, a supernumerary sleeper in the wrong position, and wake him up, they suddenly stop the cars, and make a hue and cry about it, as if this were an exception. I am glad to know that it takes a gang of men for every five miles to keep the sleepers down and level in their beds as it is, for this is a sign that they may sometime get up again.

Why should we live with such hurry and waste of life? We are determined to be starved before we are hungry. Men say that a stitch in time saves nine, and so they take a thousand stitches to-day to save nine to-morrow. As for *work,* we haven't any of any consequence. We have the Saint Vitus' dance, and cannot possibly keep our heads still.

• • •

For my part, I could easily do without the post-office. I think that there are very few important communications made through it. To speak critically, I never received more than one or two letters in my life — I wrote this some years ago — that were worth the postage. The penny-post is, commonly, an institution through which you seriously offer a man that penny for his thoughts which is so often safely offered in jest. And I am sure that I never read any memorable news in a newspaper. If we read of one man robbed, or murdered, or killed by accident, or one house burned, or one vessel wrecked, or one steamboat blown up, or one cow run over on the Western Railroad, or one mad dog killed, or one lot of grasshoppers in the winter, — we never need read of another. One is enough. If you are acquainted with the principle, what do you care for a myriad instances and applications? To a philosopher all *news,* as it is called, is gossip, and they who edit and read it are old women over their tea.

• • •

What news! how much more important to know what that is which was never old! "Kieou-he-yu (great dignitary of the state of Wei) sent a man to Khoung-tseu to know his news. Khoung-tseu caused the messenger to be seated near him, and questioned him in these terms: What is your master doing? The messenger answered with respect: My master desires to diminish the number of his faults, but he cannot come to the end of them. The messenger being gone, the philosopher remarked: What a worthy messenger! What a worthy messenger!" The preacher, instead of vexing the ears of drowsy farmers on their day of rest at the end of the week, — for Sunday is the fit conclusion of an ill-spent week, and not the fresh and brave beginning of a new one, — with this one other draggle-tail of a sermon, should shout with thundering voice, "Pause! Avast! Why so seeming fast, but deadly slow?"

Shams and delusions are esteemed for soundest truths, while reality is fabulous. If men would steadily observe realities only, and not allow themselves to be deluded, life, to compare it with such things as we know, would be like a fairy tale and the Arabian Nights' Entertainments. If we respected only what is inevitable and has a right to be, music and poetry would resound along the streets. When we are unhurried and wise, we perceive that only great and worthy things have any permanent and absolute existence, that petty fears and petty pleasures are but the shadow of the reality. This is always exhilarating and sublime. By closing the eyes and slumbering, and consenting to be deceived by shows, men establish and confirm their daily life of routine and habit everywhere, which still is built on purely illusory foundations. Children, who play life, discern its true law and relations more clearly than men, who fail to live it worthily, but who think that they are wiser by experience, that is, by failure. I have read in a Hindoo book, that "there was a king's son, who, being expelled in infancy from his native city, was brought up by a forester, and, growing up to maturity in that state, imagined himself to belong to the barbarous race with which he lived. One of his father's ministers having discovered him, revealed to him what he was, and the misconception of his character was removed, and he knew himself to be a prince. So soul," continues the Hindoo philosopher, "from the circumstances in which it is placed, mistakes its own character, until the truth is revealed to it by some holy teacher, and then it knows itself to be *Brahme*." I perceive that we inhabitants of New England live this mean life that we do because blunt vision does not penetrate the surface of things. We think that that *is* which *appears* to be. If a man should walk through this town and see only the reality, where, think you, would the "Mill-dam" go to? If he should give us an account of the realities he beheld there, we should not recognize the place in his description. Look at a meeting-house, or a court-house, or a jail, or a shop, or a dwelling-house, and say what that thing really is before a true gaze, and they would all go to pieces in your account of them. Men esteem truth remote, in the outskirts of the system, behind the farthest star, before Adam and after the last man. In eternity there is indeed something true and sublime. But all these times and places and occasions are now and here. God himself culminates in the present moment, and will never be more divine in the lapse of all the ages. And we are enabled to apprehend at all what is sublime and noble only by the perpetual instilling and drenching of the reality that surrounds us. The universe constantly and obediently answers to our conceptions; whether we travel fast or slow, the track is laid for us. Let us spend our lives in conceiving then. The poet or the artist never yet had so fair and noble a design but some of his posterity at least could accomplish it.

Let us spend one day as deliberately as Nature, and not be thrown off the track by every nutshell and mosquito's wing that falls on the rails. Let us rise early and fast, or break fast, gently and without perturbation; let company come and let company go, let the bells ring and the children cry,—determined to make a day of it. Why should we knock under and go with the stream? Let us not be upset and overwhelmed in that terrible rapid and whirlpool called a dinner, situated in the meridian shallows. Weather this danger and you are safe, for the rest of the way is down hill. With unrelaxed nerves, with morning vigor, sail by it, looking another way, tied to the mast like Ulysses. If the engine whistles, let it whistle till it is hoarse for its pains. If the bell rings, why should we run? We will consider what kind of music they are like. Let us settle ourselves, and work and wedge our feet downward through the mud and slush of opinion, and prejudice, and tradition, and delusion, and appearance, that alluvion which covers the globe, through Paris and London, through New York and Boston and Concord, through Church and State, through poetry and philosophy and religion, till we come to a hard bottom and rocks in place, which we can call *reality*, and say, This is, and no mistake; and then begin, having a *point d'appui*, below freshet and frost and fire, a place where you might found a wall or a state, or set a lamp-post safely, or perhaps a gauge, not a Nilometer, but a Realometer, that future ages might know how deep a freshet of shams and appearances had gathered from time to time. If you stand right fronting and face to face to a fact, you will see the sun glimmer on both its surfaces, as if it were a cimeter, and feel its sweet edge dividing you through the heart and marrow, and so you will happily conclude your mortal career. Be it life or death, we crave only reality. If we are really dying, let us hear the rattle in our throats and feel cold in the extremities; if we are alive, let us go about our business.

Time is but the stream I go a-fishing in. I drink at it; but while I drink I see the sandy bottom and detect how shallow it is. Its thin current slides away, but eternity remains. I would drink deeper; fish in the sky, whose bottom is pebbly with stars. I cannot count one. I know not the first letter of the alphabet. I have always been regretting that I was not as wise as the day I was born. The intellect is a cleaver; it discerns and rifts it way into the secret of things. I do not wish to be any more busy with my hands than is necessary. My head is hands and feet. I feel all my best faculties concentrated in it. My instinct tells me that my head is an organ for burrowing, as some creatures use their snout and fore paws, and with it I would mine and burrow my way through these hills. I think that the richest vein is somewhere hereabouts; so by the divining-rod and thin rising vapors I judge; and here I will begin to mine.

. . .

The first sparrow of spring! The year beginning with younger hope than ever! The faint silvery warblings heard over the partially bare and moist fields from the bluebird, the song sparrow, and the red-wing, as if the last flakes of winter tinkled as they fell! What at such a time are histories, chronologies, traditions, and all written revelations? The brooks sing carols and glees to the spring. The marsh hawk, sailing low over the meadow, is already seeking the first slimy life that awakes. The sinking sound of melting snow is heard in all dells, and the ice dissolves apace in the ponds. The grass flames up on the hillsides like a spring fire, — "et primitus oritur herba imbribus primoribus evocata," — as if the earth sent forth an inward heat to greet the returning sun; not yellow but green is the color of its flame; — the symbol of perpetual youth, the grass-blade, like a long green ribbon, streams from the sod into the summer, checked indeed by the frost, but anon pushing on again, lifting its spear of last year's hay with the fresh life below. It grows as steadily as the rill oozes out of the ground. It is almost identical with that, for in the growing days of June, when the rills are dry, the grass-blades are their channels, and from year to year the herds drink at this perennial green stream, and the mower draws from it be-times their winter supply. So our human life but dies down to its root, and still puts forth its green blade to eternity.

Evaluation

1. To begin with Rousseau, the main criticism leveled against his brand of naturalism is that he overstated the goodness of man in an aboriginal state. The "noble savage" idea (celebrated in the *Leatherstocking Tales* of James Fenimore Cooper) may be more romantic than realistic; some savages are extremely savage just as some brutes can be senselessly brutal. As we found in Chapter 2, it

seems as unbalanced for Machiavelli and Hobbes to claim that all men are bad and act rightly only under compulsion as for Rousseau to maintain that natural man is a creature of good instincts and corrupted by society. In point of fact, man's nature appears to be a mixture of good and bad or else develops through socialization and has no innate moral character at all. At least we cannot be confident that man in a state of nature is pure and righteous, or that following our natural feelings will lead to something good; the vein may not be pure gold.

It should also be mentioned that Rousseau's general philosophy, trading upon his view of man, has had a very checkered reception. He has been criticized especially for his sentimentality, his exaggerations, his paradoxes and self-contradictions that detract enormously from the force of his ideas. Even Rousseau's belief in man's natural goodness is questionable because he also writes "self-will and evil soon make their appearance in the child. This self-will, this germ of evil, must be broken and destroyed by discipline." And this position in turn led Rousseau to a political theory, expressed in *The Social Contract,* that approaches totalitarianism. For he advocated the imposition of order on human life, the "general will," which can be different from majority rule and can require a dictator to enforce. By some odd quirks of logic, Rousseau's begins by trusting in man's nature and ends up advocating an authoritarian government, so that Bertrand Russel could say "Hitler is an outcome of Rousseau.[5]

2. Thoreau's more general naturalism, which advocates living close to nature and far from civilization, has also come in for its share of criticism. Is a primitive life really best, a life in which we have only the necessities for survival? Should we live like hermits in the woods and dissociate ourselves from human society, turning our backs on the developments that have taken place in civilization over the past 4,000 years?

In the American temper there is an urge to do precisely that, to throw off the traces of civilization and strike out into the wilderness, to be mountain men, drifters, cowboys, trappers, self-sufficient loners who make their own way and feel threatened at the prospect of settling down with a family and a secure, established position. We want to test ourselves against the elements and rely upon our own abilities to survive, to be individualists, nonconformists, mavericks, ready to fight against any encroachment on our personal freedom. Some of that spirit was responsible for people leaving the cultured society of Europe for the virgin land that America represented, and it lay behind the push westward to the new frontier when the colonies became too developed and settled. A strong undercurrent still persists in the American psyche that favors the rough over the refined, the simple over the elaborate, the direct over the subtle, action over reflection, the emotions over the intellect, the individual over the social organization. The dream is to live alone, far from the demands of cities, in a rough hewn cabin set in some remote, idyllic valley, and to survive through nothing but our own ingenuity and effort. It is the American Shangri-la, our Green Mansions, Innisfree — or Walden Pond.[6]

But in our sober and rational moments we wonder whether such ideals are worth embracing. To "Go forth, under the open sky, and list/To Nature's teachings," as William Cullen Bryant puts it, is intriguing as an escapist's dream but could be harsh in actuality. Living in the country might be bucolic and serene but it is more likely to mean arduous labor for the satisfaction of our simplest needs. An enormous amount of time and effort would have to be spent in sheer survival. If we did not have running water, electric lights, indoor plumbing, or central heating, and if we did without refrigerators, stoves, washing machines, or motors of any kind our lives would entail a great deal of brute drudgery. At least some technological devices free us from fatiguing, repetitive, routine work, and enable us to rise above the purely biological level of subsistence; they give us the leisure time to live the higher, more complex life of a human being. Rejecting modern advances and leading a primitive life, on the other hand, would hardly result in independence for the person but reduction to a near animal level. It could well be a squalid and exhausting affair, not to mention monotonous, deadening, and lonely.

Furthermore, we would not have access to the benefits of civilization that enhance human existence. We could not go to concerts, art galleries, theaters, or museums. There would be no possibility of seeing fine architecture or films or dance. We could not buy a variety of different foods or enjoy dining in good restaurants, and we could not obtain any of the extraordinary range of products and services routinely available to the urban resident.

In addition, modern dental and medical care would not be available to us, highly trained doctors and well-equipped hospitals, and the advantages of excellent schools, social services, and transportation and communication facilities would be inaccessible to us. We could commune with nature but we could not hold intelligent conversations the way that civilized people do on a daily basis.

Finally, freedom may not consist in what we can do without, as Thoreau claims, for reducing our belongings to a bare minimum can impoverish our lives and reduce the extent of our freedom. Having a spacious, well-decorated house, with material belongings that include paintings, musical instruments, and books can allow us to express ourselves more fully than any sparsely furnished shack, even if the latter is more natural. A material life of "conspicuous consumption" is certainly deplorable but there is a sense in which "money is freedom to those who have it and slavery to those who do not."

3. Another defect present in nature philosophy, whether of Thoreau or others, is that no clear definition is given as to what "being natural" consists of. We are not given any firm criterion as to how elemental or primitive we should be in order to lead a truly natural life. Should we only gather fruits and nuts and berries rather than raising cattle and crops? If we eat meat must it be raw? Is it enough to work the land using a hand plow with an iron tip rather than a tractor or should we use a stick in order to farm the natural way? Should we do without metal for our tools, without fire or the wheel? Can we build houses and can they have windows or should we live in caves? When we travel can we simply forego trains, planes, and cars, using horses instead or must we walk? Is it natural to use boats and build bridges or must we swim across rivers? Should we go without shoes and clothing even in winter or can we use animal skins? Should we abandon all courtesy and manners, bathe very seldom, pay little attention to sanitary conditions, and never undergo surgery or use any medication other than herbs? Must we abandon the use of silverwear and plates, or even tables, chairs, and beds in order to live like early man?

In short, we do not know how far back in history we ought to go in order to reach the natural state. Should we strive to resemble an eighteenth century peasant, an ancient Egyptian, Neanderthal Man, an ape, an amphibian or fish, the tropic life of a plant, or perhaps an inanimate stone?

The question of what is natural has never been decided by the naturalists. At one extreme it is sometimes claimed that whatever man discovers in his physical environment is natural but whatever he alters thereby becomes unnatural. For example, rocks are a natural building material but steel is not because it is a processed alloy of iron and carbon. But using this criterion we would have to ban the use of glass, chromium, plastic, aluminum, and brass; we could not have the most effective antibiotics, vitamins, or anaesthetics, drink pasteurized milk or eat meat that has been processed to prevent trichinosis or anthrax. We might not even be permitted to transform the stone into a house or make clothing from cotton or wool (much less polyester) since that would involve altering the found object and therefore rendering it unnatural. Our music could only be bird songs but not symphonies, our art could be panoramas but not landscape paintings, and poetry and literature would be unknown.

Because of these implications an opposite definition has been suggested that whatever man is able to do becomes natural by virtue of the fact that it is a natural product of the human mind. But this definition hardly fares any better than the other. On these grounds every development in science and culture would be natural, nuclear reactors as much as solar energy. No distinction could then be made between living naturally and living unnaturally; whatever people did would be natural ipso facto. And this means that there could be no signposts showing us the path to a worthwhile life.

4. A final difficulty with the naturalistic philosophy has to do with its championing of nature as the model for human conduct. We are told to let nature take its course and to emulate it in our everyday affairs, that it constitutes an ideal that should inspire us. But is nature really admirable in all of its operations? Aren't there a number of respects in which nature appears cruel and brings suffering rather than comfort to people?

In the philosophy of religion the issue of human suffering from natural causes is called "the problem of evil" and it is a difficult dilemma for the person who believes in an omnipotent, omniscient, and wholly benevolent god. (Why, then, would the almighty, loving father allow his children to experience so much pain?) We need not explore that thorny question, but the facts that create the problem are that nature presents various types of conditions hostile to man:

1. Catastrophes such as earthquakes, volcanic eruptions, avalanches, tidal waves, floods, forest fires, and hurricanes;
2. illnesses including cancer, heart disease, cholera, yellow fever, tuberculosis, leprosy, and so forth;
3. inhospital regions on the earth, for example, deserts, jungles, and Arctic wastes;
4. and savage creatures such as tigers, crocodiles, bears, cobras, scorpions, and so forth.

The point that we should notice is that if all of these things are a part of the natural world then we cannot call nature unequivocally good. In fact, we might conclude, as John Stuart Mill did, that nature is largely destructive and should not be imitated. In his essay "Nature" he wrote:

In sober truth, nearly all the things which men are hanged or imprisoned for doing to one another, are nature's every day performances. Killing, the most criminal act recognized by human laws, Nature does once to every human being that lives; and in a large portion of cases, after protracted tortures. . . . Nature impales men, breaks them as if on the wheel, casts them to be devoured by wild beasts, burns them to death, crushes them with stones like the first Christian martyr, starves them with hunger, freezes them with cold, poisons them by the quick or slow venom of her exhalations, and has hundreds of other hideous deaths in reserve. . . . All this Nature does with the most supercilious disregard both of mercy and justice, emptying her shafts upon the best and noblest indifferently with the meanest and worst. . . . Next to taking life (equal to it according to a high authority) is taking the means by which we live; and Nature does this too on the largest scale and with the most callous indifference. A single hurricane destroys the hopes of a season; a flight of locusts, or an inundation, desolates a district; a trifling chemical change in an edible root, starves a million of people. . . . Everything in short, which the worst men commit either against life or property is perpetrated on a larger scale by natural agents.[7]

Mill may be exaggerating the point, nevertheless nature does have its destructive side, which means that we should not necessarily copy nature's ways. We have to introduce a qualification, that the good aspects of nature should be copied, which suggests another criterion of selection must be used in constructing a worthwhile life. The fact that an activity is consonant with nature is not sufficient. The ultraviolet light from the sun and radon from the earth are both sources of cancer, and if something as basic as the sun and earth can't be trusted then perhaps nature shouldn't be our guide.

We have seen in Rousseau and Thoreau and the criticisms of them some rather extreme views with regard to the natural life. Rousseau believed that we should trust our own nature while Hobbes distrusted human nature altogether; for Thoreau nature was a blessing, while to Mill it was a curse. The city dweller points to the values of culture, technological conveniences, and the overall benefits of civilization; the country dweller cites the beauty and tranquility, the space and silence and simplicity of life in a natural setting.

Surely the truth lies somewhere in between. It might be fair to conclude that not everything natural is good just as the artificial is not automatically bad. We have to be discriminating and choose what is worthwhile from each category. It would be as silly to refuse medical treatment because it is unnatural as to welcome a flood because it is natural. Perhaps nature is our best teacher but the good student does not admire his teacher blindly; he only accepts what his judgment tells him is sound.

Evolutionism: Survival of the Fittest

A second type of naturalism does not recommend that people follow the natural way of living but that they conform to the principle of development inherent in nature. This has been interpreted in any number of ways by Taoists, Stoics, Pantheists, and Hopi Indians. It also appears in the specialized theories of Henri Bergson (1859–1941) in *Creative Evolution* and John Dewey (1859–1952) in *Experience and Nature* and *Human Nature and Conduct*. However, the most prominent philosophic form is that of evolutionism. According to evolutionary ethics the best life consists in furthering the course of evolution and not impeding its momentum and progress.

In order to understand this position we must first examine evolutionary theory. Evolution first of all is a scientific hypothesis that explains the emergence of all biological organisms as a process of continuous development from lower, simpler forms to higher, more complex ones, culminating in the human species. Furthermore, it offers a mechanism to account for this development called the theory of natural selection.

It was probably originated by the Greek philosopher Heraclitus (c. 575–641 B.C), who claimed that all life evolved through a continuous state of flux (and change was the ruler of all), then elaborated by Aristotle (384–322 B.C.), who speculated that man developed from a succession of simpler organisms. Lucretius (c. 96–55 B.C.), the Roman philosophical poet, expounded the theory in his *De Rerum Natura* (*On the Nature of Things*), and it was then carried forward through Erasmus (c. 1466–1536), G.-L. Buffon (1707–1788) and J. W. Goethe (1749–1832), Chevalier de Lamarck (1744–1829), and Alfred Wallace (1823–1913) to Charles Darwin (1809–1882). Herbert Spencer (1820–1903) and T. H. Huxley (1825–1895) then expanded on its social implications.

The name *Darwin* of course has become synonymous with evolution for he was primarily responsible for developing and establishing it as the basic theory of biological development in the modern world. In his landmark publications, *The Origin of Species* (1859) and *The Descent of Man* (1871), Darwin argued that all species had evolved from lower to higher forms in a natural and dynamic process of change. This included the human species for "Man is descended from some less highly organized form." He did not just say that changes occurred in the varieties within each species (in nature and in domestic breeding) but that new species had emerged progressively throughout biological history.

Furthermore, Darwin proposed an explanatory principle for the development—a principle that came to him while reading the British economist Thomas Malthus. "Being well prepared to appreciate the struggle for existence which everywhere goes on from long continued observation of the habits of animals and plants," Darwin wrote "it at once struck me that under these circumstances favorable variations would tend to be preserved, and unfavorable ones to be destroyed. The result of this would be the formation of a new species."[8]

In other words, natural selection was postulated as responsible for the development of species from some simple origin. Because far more organisms are created by nature than the environment can sustain, competition results within and between species—competition over territory, mates, food, dominance, and so forth. In the struggle for survival those organisms favored by chance variations are able to survive and produce offspring; those organisms that are not as well equipped perish along the way. Only the fittest survive—that is, the strongest, cleverest, fastest, best camouflaged, most adaptable, and so on—and to the victors belong the spoils: their strain is carried forward as the principal form that the species assumes. If a strain becomes sufficiently differentiated as the result of cumulative changes over thousands of years, then it becomes a new species altogether, taking its place in the multiplicity of life forms. By the same token, if a species cannot meet the challenge of the environment, as in the case of dinosaurs, then it becomes extinct and only fossil records remain to show that it once existed.

To our contemporary mentality this theory does not appear revolutionary but in the nineteenth century it created a scandal. Up to that time the major scientific and religious doctrines had assumed that each species had been independently created; they were thought to be immutable, fixed and final, not evolving or passing out of existence. After some hesitation the scientific community accepted Darwin's dynamic theory but theologians adamantly opposed it. In 1925 fundamentalist religious leaders fought against the teaching of evolution in the schools, which culminated in the sensational Scopes trial, pitting William Jennings Bryan against Clarence Darrow, and the debate between creationism and evolutionism has resurfaced in the present day.

The reason for the strong reaction has to do with the Biblical account of creation described in Genesis that said, "God made the beast of the earth after its kind, and the cattle after their kind, and every thing that creepeth upon the ground after its kind." (At the time of the flood all the species were rescued by Noah who kept them in the ark until the waters subsided.) Therefore, every species that exists on earth was formed in an instantaneous act of special creation which occurred on "October 23, 4004 B.C. at 9:00 in the morning."[9] This was the belief that Darwin challenged by claiming that organisms had evolved from the first specks of protoplasmic jelly in the scum of tides (the primal soup) into more and more sophisticated species and that this evolutionary process had taken millions of years. Since every part of scripture came from god and was infallible, Darwin was seen as denying that the bible was divinely inspired; some theologians even said he was accusing god of lying.

Deeper still, Darwinism contradicted one of the intellectual mainstays of belief in god, the "teleological argument"—first formulated by St. Thomas Aquinas (1225?–1274) in *Summa Theologica* as the last of his "five ways" and later popularized by the English theologian William Paley (1743–1805) in his *Natural Theology*. The teleological argument proceeds from the premise that the world has an organized character to the conclusion that a conscious mind is responsible for that organization. In other words, the regularity, harmony, symmetry, and structure of the world suggests a conscious purpose and a being who devised the scheme; such organization could not have come about by chance. If we can perceive the outlines of a grand plan then there must be a divine planner; since nature is orderly there must be an orderer, and if the earth is a work of art there must exist a cosmic artist. In brief, since the natural world exhibits evidence of design we must assume the reality of a designer, namely god. For only god possesses the wisdom and power needed to create the earth in its fullness and splendor.

To take Paley's version as the more directly relevant, Paley used an analogy to support the teleological argument. He began by saying that if we found a stone while crossing a heath we would not pay much attention to it, but if we found a watch we would infer that someone had made the watch for the purpose of measuring time. The parts could not have come together accidentally in the exact combination and relation that were needed. Paley wrote that if the gears were properly positioned so as to interlock, the teeth, pointer, and balance were of the right shape to regulate the motion, the wheels were made of brass to keep them from rusting, the spring was of flexible steel, and there was glass over the face where a transparent material was required, we would be forced to conclude "that the watch must have had a maker . . . who formed it for the purpose which we find it actually to answer." In the same way, when we come upon the intricate mechanism of the world we must also infer that it had a creator who designed it for some reason. "There cannot be design without a designer" Paley asserted, "contrivance without a contriver; order without choice; arrangement without anything capable of arranging." We must assume "the presence of intelligence and mind" or the world makes no sense.[10]

Paley went on to say that we do not have to see the watch being made to know that it had been constructed because that is obvious from its complexity. Even if the watch is defective we would still assume that it was designed and even if we do not understand the purpose of some of its parts we would nevertheless believe that the parts had a purpose. By analogy, then, we need not be present at creation or see the goodness or purpose of everything in order to acknowledge a god behind the natural world.

Darwin however offered an alternative explanation for the orderliness that exists. He argued that through the process of natural selection various life forms emerged with the characteristics that were necessary for survival. These organisms were well equipped for survival because if they had not been they would not have survived. In the long history of evolution, Darwin reasoned, harmful features died out (sometimes together with the species that possessed them), while favorable qualities, which gave organisms an advantage in the struggle for survival, were perpetuated. Therefore it is not surprising that creatures that exist are as well ordered as a watch; if they were not they would never have survived. To be amazed, for example, that giraffes are perfectly fitted to reach the leaves at the tops of trees is like being surprised that all Olympic winners are good athletes; obviously, if they were not good athletes they would never have become Olympic winners. Or to find it uncanny that turtles have the protection they need in their hard shell is like being astonished that there are so many navigable rivers next to large cities; if the rivers had not been navigable the cities would never have become large. In other words, natural law can account for the orderliness without having to assume a supernatural purpose. The survival of the fittest doctrine can explain the structure of the natural world so that the hypothesis of a guiding hand becomes superfluous.

Some religious thinkers tried to meet this attack by accepting evolutionary theory and claiming that, rather than supplanting god, it simply revealed his method of creation. They began with evolution and argued it was a part of his plan, that the six days of creation in the life of god are equal to millions of years in the life of man. This approach caused considerable debate over whether god was needed in order to explain the world or whether the naturalistic principles of evolution were sufficient. A certain number of theologians argued that some reality had to lie behind evolution, a force responsible for the origin of life and its unfolding, a law-giver who enacted the natural law Darwin described. As the poet W. H. Carruth wrote in *Each in His Own Tongue*, "Some call it Evolution, and others call it God."

More secular thinkers however, using Occam's Razor, argued that explanations should not be compounded beyond what is required—that the simplest, most elegant theory is best—and concluded that god was an unnecessary hypothesis. In any case, Darwinism made it clear that we cannot necessarily infer the existence of god from the presence of order in the world. Evolution offered an alternative explanation that was concrete, simple, and natural.[11]

It is no wonder, then, that the theory of evolution created a furor. It offered a new concept of species that involved dynamic development not fixed categories, introduced a principle called *natural selection* to account for the process, and challenged traditional religious concepts as contained in the bible and in the teleological argument for the existence of god. For Darwinists, variation and selection were responsible for all life forms including man and both were accidental not planned.

Evolutionary Ethics

The idea of the human being as simply a higher form of animal among thousands of other life forms in the natural world was radical enough but the evolutionary theory was taken a step further when its ethical implications were drawn. A doctrine called *Social Darwinism* was developed, trading largely on the notions of competition and the principle that Herbert Spencer labeled *survival of the fittest*. Since there is a close similarity between man and the lower creatures and intense competition occurs among animals in nature, the same must be said of human life. Man too struggles for the means of existence, individually and as a group, and the most vigorous and best adapted are able to survive. Furthermore these individuals *should* be the ones who survive since that is nature's device for ensuring that the species is strengthened and improved. If only the fittest remain then the human race will progress and human history will show an increasingly upward tendency.

Therefore, the misfits and weaklings, the lazy and stupid, all the biologically defective specimens should be allowed to perish so that their genetic line will die out. Only the competent and accomplished should exist to enrich the human race with their genes. We know who these individuals are because they constitute the successful members of the species, and all that is needed is to allow them their success. The capable people must be permitted to rise to the top without any hindrance from society, and the failures should be allowed to fall without any misguided humanitarian programs supporting them artificially. The principle of survival of the fittest should operate freely and then mankind will improve and advance.

The industrial entrepreneurs or "robber barons" of the late nineteenth century used Social Darwinism to justify their positions, arguing that by being successful they demonstrated they were the fittest and therefore deserved the rewards they received from their wealth. The poor, on the other hand, were regarded as the unfit and their low status was justified on evolutionary grounds; if people did not "have what it takes" then they became impoverished and were prone to illness and death. It was the law of the jungle.

Evolutionary theory was also used to confirm the laissez-faire doctrine of economics, which called for the free operation of the marketplace without any government regulation. And the same justification was used to condemn minimum wage laws, social security programs, retirement benefits, and workmen's compensation laws (much less the welfare, medicare, and graduated income tax we have today); even unions were considered immoral because the weak were banding together against the strong. All of these actions were thought to be contrary to nature because they interfered with the progress of evolution, help-ing the feebler members of the species and weakening the human race.

To many people at the time evolutionism was no more than common sense and a scientific vindication of the middle-class notion that "the universe was designed to reward hard work, thrift, intelligence, and self-help and to punish laziness, waste, stupidity, and reliance on charity." Even Herbert Spencer, an evolutionist who was extremely compassionate in many respects, wrote

> the law by conformity to which the species is preserved, is that among adults the individuals best adapted to the conditions of their existence shall prosper most, and individuals least adapted to the conditions of their existence shall prosper least. . . . Pervading all Nature we may see at work a stern discipline which is often a little cruel that it may be very kind. . . . The ultimate result of shielding men from folly is to fill the world with fools.[12]

Some Social Darwinists even went so far as to recommend a eugenics program whereby the fit would be encouraged to have children and the unfit would not; compulsory sterilization would be practiced on the "idiots, the feeble-minded, and the insane." A still more extreme and sinister idea was that some groups were innately higher and had a right, in fact an obligation, to subjugate others. This took the form of identifying certain races or nation-states as superior and culminated in Hitler's belief that the fair-haired "Aryans" were the master race, destined by their biological ascendancy to rule the world; others such as Jews, Slavs, and Gypsies could be exterminated. If Germany had won World War II that would have proven its rightness, for the verdict of history was thought to be decisive.

But even short of Nazism, various leaders proclaimed their group as the elite, with finer physical and mental traits than other human beings. Whites in Europe sometimes argued this way in justifying the colonization of Africa and Asia, and imperialists such as Cecil Rhodes held that a world populated exclusively by Anglo-Saxons would be an ideal place. In America various Darwinian biologists wrote of the inherent inferiority of the negro, which gave fuel to racist doctrines and justified the institution of slavery. The idea of naturally better and naturally worse groups also influenced the Immigration Act of 1924, which set high quotas for northern Europeans and very low quotas for southern Europeans, eastern Europeans, and nonwhites. The finest specimens were thought to be the tall, blonde, thin-nosed, long-headed Nordic types, who were "a race of soldiers, sailors, adventurers and explorers, but above all, of rulers, organizers and aristocrats."[13]

Most Social Darwinists of course did not take their doctrine this far. They simply wanted to further the direction of evolution rather than reverse its flow, and this meant allowing the better qualified individuals to achieve the success that their abilities deserved. If there was free competition the fittest alone would survive, which was what nature intended.

Herbert Spencer

The philosopher who is usually credited with developing the ethical implications of evolutionism most fully is the nineteenth century English thinker Herbert Spencer. In his *Principles of Ethics* he removed many of the abrasive elements of

Social Darwinism and developed a theory that combined qualitative factors, a hedonistic element of pleasure, and above all the importance of cooperation rather than competition.

Specifically, Spencer tried to ground ethics in the objective facts of the natural world instead of in the airy realms of intuition or emotion. He found the basis he sought in scientific evolution and maintained that the standard of morality is evolutionary progress. "The conduct to which we apply the name good is the relatively more evolved conduct;" Spencer wrote, "bad is the name we apply to conduct which is relatively less evolved" and "other things equal, conduct is right or wrong according as its special acts . . . do or do not further the general end of self-preservation."

However, Spencer did not interpret evolutionary progess to mean just self-preservation; the continued existence of an individual or a group for a certain length of time is not the only criterion for success. Fullness or *breadth* of life also counts, perhaps even more than longevity or duration. That is, richness of living is crucially important, "the sum of vital activities," or the "aggregates of thought, feeling, and action."

To illustrate his notion of breadth of life Spencer used some biological examples. An oyster may live longer than a cuttlefish, he observed, because the oyster simply streams nutrients within its protective shell. Nevertheless, the cuttlefish has a richer life, with broader, more numerous and diverse experiences. In the same way, an earthworm may outlive an insect, but the insect "during its existence as larva and imago, may experience a greater quantity of the changes which constitute life." Man of course enjoys the fullest type of life (even if a redwood tree does live for hundreds of years), and the life of modern man is more complex and therefore better than that of the savage. Right conduct then, must promote not only increased length but richness of life: "the performance of every function is, in a sense, a moral obligation."

Spencer went on to say that, happily enough, an increase in fullness of life also produces an increase in longevity; the two always work hand in hand. "Each further evolution of conduct widens the aggregate of actions while conducing to elongation of it." What's more, he interpreted this richness of development to include the cooperative not competitive development of human beings. That is, evolution in its tendency toward fullness promotes concern for the welfare of others in the harmonious development of the species. It is not the survival of the individual member or even his breadth of life that nature favors but that of all individuals composing the human race. Predating the sociobiologists Spencer claimed that nature prescribes altruistic behavior for the general good, because "self-sacrifice is no less primordial than self-preservation" and works for the advancement of the entire species. The line of evolution leads not to a selfish individualism but to cooperation and community, which are essential to the survival and satisfaction of human beings, individually and collectively.

In shifting the focus from the person to the group, Spencer introduced a strong moral element as part of the evolutionary ethic instead of the "dog eat dog" approach of Social Darwinism. In all fairness however, Darwin himself favored mutual consideration and justice among men as the only way that healthy, vigorous individuals could be reared; it was some of Darwin's followers who interpreted evolution as savage competition among members of the species.

In any case, Spencer argued that when a community cooperates everyone benefits from the well being of the whole, so that as each individual works "to further the complete living of others" he indirectly benefits himself as well as furthering the progress of mankind. Conversely, immoral actions harm both the species and its members. For example, murder is wrong because it militates against the good of society and creates an insecure environment for the individual. At the same time, refraining from murdering does not involve any great self-sacrifice and makes the group more stable.

As a final point, Spencer maintains that right actions also tend to be accompanied by pleasure. We should not act to obtain pleasure but those activities that promote survival happen to correlate with pleasure. For example, the act of eating is enjoyable and at the same time provides our bodies with the nourishment necessary to existence. Sex is a pleasure and functions for the continuation of the species. Rest provides refreshment from fatigue, shelter offers the comfort of warmth and protection, and both are needed to maintain the life of the organism. Spencer also pointed out that the pleasures that accompany being married, rearing children, and accumulating property, all promote the survival of the species; they leave "a large balance of advantage, private and public, after making allowance for all the drawbacks." This is a fortunate concatenation for otherwise the human race would have become extinct long ago. Spencer wrote, "those races of beings only can have survived in which, on the average, agreeable or desired feelings went along with activities conducive to the maintenance of life, while disagreeable and habitually avoided feelings went along with activities directly or indirectly destructive of life."

Length and breadth of life, cooperation among members of a species, pleasurable feelings—all these fall together when we act in accordance with natural evolution. Moral behavior therefore consists in following the direction in which evolution points. As Spencer expressed it, we should further evolutionary development as it moves from the confused to the orderly, and from the lower and simpler to the higher and more complex structures. In fact, evolution is the process in which "matter passes from an indefinite, incoherent homogeneity to a definite, coherent heterogeneity," and that is what must be promoted.

The following excerpt is from *The Principles of Ethics* which, together with *The Data of Ethics*, presents Spencer's basic moral philosophy. (His other works include *System of Synthetic Philosophy* and *First Principles*.) Note the way in which Spencer used natural facts to demonstrate that evolution shows us the objective standard of correct behavior.[14]

Ethics and Survival*
The Evolution of Conduct

IV

Already the question — What constitutes advance in the evolution of conduct, as we trace it up from the lowest types of living creatures to the highest? has been answered by implication. A few examples will now bring the answer into conspicuous relief.

*Reprinted from Herbert Spencer, *The Principles of Ethics* (New York: D. Appleton, 1986), vol. 1:10–28, 30–32.

We saw that conduct is distinguished from the totality of actions by excluding purposeless actions; but during evolution this distinction arises by degrees. In the very lowest creatures most of the movements from moment to moment made, have not more recognizable aims than have the struggles of an epileptic. An infusorium swims randomly about, determined in its course not by a perceived object to be pursued or escaped, but, apparently, by varying stimuli in its medium; and its acts, unadjusted in any appreciable way to ends, lead it now into contact with some nutritive substance which it absorbs, and now into the neighbourhood of some creature by which it is swallowed and digested. Lacking those developed senses and motor powers which higher animals possess, ninety-nine in the hundred of these minute animals, severally living but for a few hours, disappear either by innutrition or by destruction. The conduct is constituted of actions so little adjusted to ends, that life continues only as long as the accidents of the environment are favourable. But when, among squatic creatures, we observe one which, though still low in type, is much higher that the infusorium — say a rotifer — we see how, along with larger size, more developed structures, and greater power of combining functions, there goes an advance in conduct. We see how by its whirling cilia it sucks in as food these small animals moving around; how by its prehensile tail it fixes itself to some object; how by withdrawing its outer organs and contracting its body, it preserves itself from this or that injury from time to time threatened; and how thus, by better adjusting its own actions, it becomes less dependent on the actions going on around, and so preserves itself for a longer period.

· · ·

Among vertebrate animals we similarly trace up, along with advance in structures and functions, this advance in conduct. A fish roaming about at hazard in search of something to eat, able to detect it by smell or sight only within short distances, and now and again rushing away in alarm on the approach of a bigger fish, makes adjustments of acts to ends that are relatively few and simple in their kinds; and shows us, as a consequence, how small is the average duration of life. So few survive to maturity that, to make up for destruction of unhatched young and small fry and half-grown individuals, a million ova have to be spawned by a cod-fish that two may reach the spawning age. Conversely, by a highly-evolved mammal, such as an elephant, those general actions performed in common with the fish are far better adjusted to their ends. By sight as well, probably, as by odour, it detects food at relatively great distances; and when, at intervals, there arises a need for escape, relatively-great speed is attained. But the chief difference arises from the addition of new sets of adjustments. We have combined actions which facilitate nutrition — the breaking off of succulent and fruit-bearing branches, the selecting of edible growths throughout a comparatively wide reach; and, in case of danger, safety can be achieved not by flight only, but, if necessary, by defence or attack: bringing into combined use tusks, trunk, and ponderous feet. Further, we see various subsidiary acts adjusted to subsidiary ends — now the going into a river for coolness, and using the trunk as a means of projecting water over the body; now the employment of a bough for sweeping away flies from the back; now the making of signal sounds to alarm the herd, and adapting the actions to such sounds when made by others. Evidently, the effect of this more highly-evolved conduct is to secure the balance of the organic actions throughout far longer periods.

And now, on studying the doings of the highest of mammals, mankind, we not only find that the adjustments of acts to ends are both more numerous and better than among lower mammals; but we find the same thing on comparing the doings of higher races of men with those of lower races. If we take any one of the major ends achieved, we see greater completeness of achievement by civilized than by savage; and we also see an achievement of relatively numerous minor ends subserving major ends. Is it in nutrition? The food is obtained more regularly in response to appetite; it is far higher in quality; it is free from dirt; it is greater in variety; it is better prepared. Is it in warmth? The characters of the fabrics and forms of the articles used for clothing, and the adaptations of them to requirements from day to day and hour to hour, are much superior. Is it in dwellings? Between the shelter of boughs and grass which the lowest savage builds, and the mansion of the civilized man, the contrast in aspect is not more extreme than is the contrast in number and efficiency of the adjustments of acts to ends betrayed in their respective constructions. And when with the ordinary activities of the savage we compare the ordinary civilized activities—as the business of the trader, which involves multiplied and complex transactions extending over long periods, or as professional avocations, prepared for by elaborate studies and daily carried on in endlessly-varied forms, or as political discussions and agitations, directed now to the carrying of this measure and now to the defeating of that,—we see sets of adjustments of acts to ends, not only immensely exceeding those seen among lower races of men in variety and intricacy, but sets to which lower races of men present nothing analogous. And along with this greater elaboration of life produced by the pursuit of more numerous ends, there goes that increased duration of life which constitutes the supreme end.

• • •

V

Turn we now to a further aspect of the phenomena, separate from, but necessarily associated with, the last. Thus far we have considered only those adjustments of acts to ends which have for their final purpose complete individual life. Now we have to consider those adjustments which have for their final purpose the life of the species.

Self-preservation in each generation has all along depended on the preservation of offspring by preceding generations. And in proportion as evolution of the conduct subserving individual life is high, implying high organization, there must previously have been a highly-evolved conduct subserving nurture of the young. Throughout the ascending grades of the animal kingdom, this second kind of conduct presents stages of advance like those which we have observed in the first. Low down, where structures and functions are little developed, and the power of adjusting acts to ends but slight, there is no conduct, properly so named, furthering salvation of the species. Race-maintaining conduct, like self-maintaining conduct, arises gradually out of that which cannot be called conduct: adjusted actions are preceded by unadjusted ones. Protozoa spontaneously divide and sub-divide, in consequence of physical changes over which they have no control; or, at other times, after a period of quiescence, break up into minute portions which severally grow into new individuals. In neither case can conduct be alleged. Higher up, the process is that of ripening, at intervals, germ-cells and sperm-cells, which, on occasion, are sent forth into the surrounding water and left to their fate: perhaps one in ten thousand surviving to maturity. Here, again, we see only development and dispersion going on apart from parental care. Types above these, as fish which choose fit places in which to deposit their ova, or as the higher crustaceans which carry masses of ova about until they are hatched, exhibit adjustments of acts to ends which we may properly call conduct; though it is of the simplest kind. Where, as among certain fish, the male keeps guard over the eggs, driving away intruders, there is an additional adjustment of acts to ends; and the applicability of the name conduct is more decided. Passing at once to creatures far superior, such as birds which, building nests and sitting on their eggs, feed their broods for considerable periods, and give them aid after they can fly; or such as mammals which, suckling their young for a time, continue afterwards to bring them food or protect them while they feed, until they reach ages at which they can provide for themselves; we are shown how this conduct which furthers race-maintenance evolves hand-in-hand with the conduct which furthers self-maintenance. That better organization which makes possible the last, makes possible the first also. Mankind exhibit a great progress of like nature. Compared with brutes, the savage, higher in his self-maintaining conduct, is higher too in his race-maintaining conduct. A larger number of the wants of offspring are provided for; and parental care, enduring longer, extends to the disciplining of offspring in arts and habits which fit them for their conditions of existence. Conduct of this order, equally with conduct of the first order, we see becoming evolved in a still greater degree as we ascend from savage to civilized. The adjustments of acts to ends in the rearing of children become far more elaborate, alike in number of ends met, variety of means used, and efficiency of their adaptations; and the aid and oversight are continued throughout a much greater part of early life.

In tracing up the evolution of conduct, so that we may frame a true conception of conduct in general, we have thus to recognize these two kinds as mutually dependent. Speaking generally, neither can evolve without evolution of the other; and the highest evolutions of the two must be reached simultaneously.

VI

To conclude, however, that on reaching a perfect adjustment of acts to ends subserving individual life and the rearing of offspring, the evolution of conduct becomes complete, is to conclude erroneously. Or rather, I should say, it is an error to suppose that either of these kinds of conduct can assume its highest form, without its highest form being assumed by a third kind of conduct yet to be named.

The multitudinous creatures of all kinds which fill the Earth, cannot live wholly apart from one another, but are more or less in presence of one another—are interfered with by one another. In large measure the adjustments of acts to ends which we have been considering, are components of that "struggle for existence" carried on both between members of the same species and between members of different species; and, very generally, a successful adjustment made by one creature involves an unsuccessful adjustment made by another creature, either of the same kind or of a different kind. That the carnivore may live herbivores must die; and that its young may be reared the young of weaker creatures must be orphaned. Maintenance of the hawk and its brood involves the deaths of many small birds; and that small birds may multiply, their progeny must be fed with innumerable sacrificed worms and larvae. Competition among members of the same species has allied, though less conspicuous, results. The stronger often carries off by force the prey which the weaker has caught. Monopolizing certain hunting grounds, the more ferocious drive others of their kind into less favourable places. With plant-eating animals, too, the like holds: the better food is secured by the more vigorous individuals, while the less vigorous and worse fed, succumb either directly from innutrition or indirectly from resulting inability to escape enemies. That is to say, among creatures whose lives are carried on antagonistically, each of the two kinds of conduct delineated above, must remain imperfectly evolved. Even in such few kinds of them as have little to fear from enemies or competitors, as lions or tigers, there is still inevitable failure in the adjustments of acts to ends towards the close of life. Death by starvation from inability to catch prey, shows a falling short of conduct from its ideal.

This imperfectly-evolved conduct introduces us by antithesis to conduct that is perfectly evolved. Contemplating these adjustments of acts to ends which miss completeness because they cannot be made by one creature without other creatures being prevented from making them, raises the thought of adjustments such that each creature may make them without preventing them from being made by other creatures. That the highest form of conduct must be so distinguished, is an inevitable implication; for while the form of conduct is such that adjustments of acts to ends by some necessitate non-adjustments by others, there remains room for modifications which bring conduct into a form avoiding this, and so making the totality of life greater.

From the abstract let us pass to the concrete. Recognizing men as the beings whose conduct is most evolved, let us ask under what conditions their conduct, in all three aspects of its evolution, reaches its limit. Clearly while the lives led are entirely predatory, as those of savages, the adjustments of acts to ends fall short of this highest form of conduct in every way. Individual life, ill carried on from hour to hour, is prematurely cut short; the fostering of offspring often fails, and is incomplete when it does not fail; and in so far as the ends of self-maintenance and race-maintenance are met, they are met by destruction of other beings, of different kind or of like kind. In social groups formed by compounding and re-compounding primitive hordes, conduct remains imperfectly evolved in proportion as there continue antagonisms between the groups and antagonisms between members of the same group—two traits necessarily associated; since the nature which prompts international aggression prompts aggression of individuals on one another. Hence the limit of evolution can be reached by conduct only in permanently peaceful societies. That perfect adjustment of acts to ends in maintaining individual life and rearing new individuals, which is effected by each without hindering others from effecting like perfect adjustments, is, in its very definition, shown to constitute a kind of conduct that can be approached only as war decreases and dies out.

A gap in this outline must now be filled up. There remains a further advance not yet even hinted. For beyond so behaving that each achieves his ends without preventing others from achieving their ends, the members of a society may give mutual help in the achievement of ends. And if, either indirectly by industrial co-operation, or directly by volunteered aid, fellow citizens can make easier for one another the adjustments of acts to ends, then their conduct assumes a still higher phase of evolution; since whatever facilitates the making of adjustments by each, increases the totality of the adjustments made, and serves to render the lives of all more complete.

. . .

Guided by the truth that as the conduct with which Ethics deals is part of conduct at large, conduct at large must be generally understood before this part can be specially understood; and guided by the further truth that to understand conduct at large we must understand the evolution of conduct; we have been led to see that Ethics has for its subject-matter, that form which universal conduct assumes during the last stages of its evolution. We have also concluded that these last stages in the evolution of conduct are those displayed by the highest type of being, when he is forced, by increase of numbers, to live more and more in presence of his fellows. And there has followed the corollary that conduct gains ethical sanction in proportion as the activities, becoming less and less militant and more and more industrial, are such as do not necessitate mutual injury or hindrance, but consist with, and are furthered by, co-operation and mutual aid.

These implications of the Evolution-Hypothesis, we shall now see harmonize with the leading moral ideas men have otherwise reached.

Good and Bad Conduct

VIII

By comparing its meanings in different connexions and observing what they have in common, we learn the essential meaning of a word; and the essential meaning of a word that is variously applied, may best be learnt by comparing with one another those applications of it which diverge most widely. Let us thus ascertain what good and bad mean.

In which cases do we distinguish as good, a knife, a gun, a house? And what trait leads us to speak of a bad umbrella or a bad pair of boots? The characters here predicated by the words good and bad, are not intrinsic characters; for apart from human wants, such things have neither merits nor demerits. We call these articles good or bad according as they are well or ill adapted to achieve prescribed ends. The good knife is one which will cut; the good gun is one which carries far and true; the good house is one which duly yields the shelter, comfort, and accommodation sought for. Conversely, the badness alleged of the umbrella or the pair of boots, refers to their failures in fulfilling the ends of keeping off the rain and comfortably protecting the feet, with due regard to appearances. So is it when we pass from inanimate objects to inanimate actions. We call a day bad in which storms prevent us from satisfying certain of our desires. A good season is the expression used when the weather has favoured the production of valuable crops. If from lifeless things and actions we pass to living ones, we similarly find that these words in their current applications refer to efficient subservience. The goodness or badness of a pointer or a hunter, of a sheep or an ox, ignoring all other attributes of these creatures, refer in the one case to the fitness of their actions for effecting the ends men use them for, and in the other case to the qualities of their flesh as adapting it to support human life. And those doings of men which, morally considered, are indifferent, we class as good or bad according to their success or failure. A good jump is a jump which remoter ends ignored, well achieves the immediate purpose of a jump; and a stroke at billiards is called good when the movements are skillfully adjusted to the requirements. Oppositely, the badness of a walk that is shuffling and an utterance that is indistinct, is alleged because of the relative non-adaptations of the acts to the ends.

Thus recognizing the meanings of good and bad as otherwise used, we shall understand better their meanings as used in characterizing conduct under its ethical aspects. Here, too, observation shows that we apply them according as the adjustments of acts to ends are, or are not, efficient. This truth is somewhat disguised. The entanglement of social relations is such, that men's actions often simultaneously affect the welfares of self, of offspring, and of fellow-citizens. Hence results confusion in judging of actions as good or bad; since actions well fitted to achieve ends of one order, may prevent ends of the other orders from being achieved. Nevertheless, when we disentangle the three orders of ends, and consider each separately, it becomes clear that the conduct which achieves each kind of end is regarded as relatively good; and is regarded as relatively bad if it fails to achieve it.

Take first the primary set of adjustments — those subserving individual life. Apart from approval or disapproval of his ulterior aims, a man who fights is said to make a good defence, if his defence is well adapted for self-preservation; and, the judgments on other aspects of his conduct remaining the same, he brings down on himself an unfavourable verdict, in so far as his immediate acts are concerned, if these are futile. The goodness ascribed to a man of business, as such, is measured by the activity and ability with which he buys and sells to advantage; any may coexist with a hard treatment of dependents which is reprobated. Though in repeatedly lending money to a friend who sinks one loan after another, a man is doing that which, considered in itself is held praiseworthy; yet, if he does it to the extent of bringing on his own ruin, he is held blameworthy for a self-sacrifice carried too far. And thus is it with the opinions we express from hour to hour on those acts of people around which bear on their health and personal welfare. "You should not have done that;" is the reproof given to one who crosses the street amid a dangerous rush of vehicles. "You ought to have changed your clothes;" is said to another who has taken cold after getting wet. "You were right to take a receipt;" "you were wrong to invest without advice;" are common criticisms. All such approving and disapproving utterances make the tacit assertion that, other things equal, conduct is right or wrong according as its special acts, well or ill adjusted to special ends, do or do not further the general end of self-preservation.

These ethical judgments we pass on self-regarding acts are ordinarily little emphasized; partly because the promptings of the self-regarding desires, generally strong enough, do not need moral enforcement, and partly because the promptings of the other-regarding desires, less strong, and often over-ridden, do need moral enforcement. Hence results a contrast. On turning to that second class of adjustments of acts to ends which subserve the rearing of offspring, we no longer find any obscurity in the application of the words good and bad to them, according as they are efficient or inefficient. The expressions good nursing and bad nursing, whether they refer to the supply of food, the quality and amount of clothing, or the due ministration to infantine wants from hour to hour, tacitly recognize as special ends which ought to be fulfilled, the furthering of the vital functions, with a view to the general end of continued life and growth. A mother is called good who, ministering to all the physical needs of her children, also adjusts her behavior in ways conducive to their mental health; and a bad father is one who either does not provide the necessaries of life for his family, or otherwise acts in a manner injurious to their bodies or minds. Similarly of the education given to them, or provided for them. Goodness or badness is affirmed of it (often with little consistency, however) according as its methods are so adapted to physical and psychical requirements, as to further the children's lives for the time being, while preparing them for carrying on complete and prolonged adult life.

Most emphatic, however, are the applications of the words good and bad to conduct throughout that third division of it comprising the deeds by which men affect one another. In maintaining their own lives and fostering their offspring, men's adjustments of other men, that insistance on the needful limitations has to be perpetual; and the mischiefs caused by men's interferences with one another's life-subserving actions are so great, that the interdicts have to be peremptory. Hence the fact that the words good and bad have come to be specially associated with acts which further the complete living of others and acts which obstruct their complete living. Goodness, standing by itself, suggests, above all other things, the conduct of one who aids the sick in re-acquiring normal vitality, assists the unfortunate to recover the means of maintaining themselves, defends those who are threatened with harm in person, property, or reputation, and aids whatever promises to improve the living of all his fellows. Contrariwise, badness brings to mind, as its leading correlative, the conduct of one who, in carrying on his own life, damages the lives of others by injuring their bodies, destroying their possessions, defrauding them, calumniating them.

Always, then, acts are called good or bad, according as they are well or ill adjusted to ends; and whatever inconsistency there is in our uses of the words, arises from inconsistency of the ends. Here, however, the study of conduct in general, and of the evolution of conduct, have prepared us to harmonize these interpretations. The foregoing exposition shows that the conduct to which we apply the name good, is the relatively more evolved conduct; and that bad is the name we apply to conduct which is relatively less evolved. We saw that evolution, tending ever towards self-preservation, reaches its limit when individual life is the greatest, both in length and breadth; and now we see that, leaving other ends aside, we regard as good the conduct furthering self-preservation, and as bad the conduct tending to self-destruction. It was shown that along with increasing power of maintaining individual life, which evolution brings, there goes increasing power of perpetuating the species by fostering progeny, and that in this direction evolution reaches its limit when the needful number of young, preserved to maturity, are then fit for a life that is complete in fulness and duration; and here it turns out that parental conduct is called good or bad as it approaches or falls short of this ideal result. Lastly, we inferred that establishment of an associated state, both makes possible and requires a form of conduct such that life may be completed in each and in his offspring, not only without preventing completion of it in others, but with furtherance of it in others; and we have found above, that this is the form of conduct most emphatically termed good. Moreover, just as we there saw that evolution becomes the highest possible when the conduct simultaneously achieves the greatest totality of life in self, in offspring, and in fellow men; so here we see that the conduct called good rises to the conduct conceived as best, when it fulfills all three classes of ends at the same time.

• • •

There is one postulate in which pessimists and optimists agree. Both their arguments assume it to be self-evident that life is good or bad, according as it does, or does not, bring a surplus of agreeable feeling. The pessimist says he condemns life because it results in more pain than pleasure. The optimist defends life in the belief that it brings more pleasure than pain. Each makes the kind of sentiency which accompanies life the test. They agree that the justification for life as a state of being, turns on this issue — whether the average consciousness rises above indifference-point into pleasurable feeling or falls below it into painful feeling. The implication common to their antagonist views is, that conduct should conduce to preservation of the individual, of the family, and of the society, only supposing that life brings more happiness than misery.

• • •

And here we are brought round to those primary meanings of the words good and bad, which we passed over when considering their secondary meanings. For on remembering that we call good and bad the things which immediately produce agreeable and disagreeable sensations, and also the sensations themselves—a good wine, a good appetite, a bad smell, a bad headache—we see that by referring directly to pleasures and pains, these meanings harmonize with those which indirectly refer to pleasures and pains. If we call good the enjoyable state itself, as a good laugh—if we call good the proximate cause of an enjoyable state, as good music—if we call good any agent which conduces immediately or remotely to an enjoyable state, as a good shop, a good teacher—if we call good considered intrinsically, each act so adjusted to its end as to further self-preservation and that surplus of enjoyment which makes self-preservation desirable—if we call good every kind of conduct which aids the lives of others, and do this under the belief that life brings more happiness than misery; then it becomes undeniable that, taking into account immediate and remote effects on all persons, the good is universally the pleasurable.

XI

Sundry influences—moral, theological, and political—conspire to make people disguise from themselves this truth. As in narrower cases so in this widest case, they become so pre-occupied with the means by which an end is achieved, as eventually to mistake it for the end. Just as money, which is a means of satisfying wants, comes to be regarded by a miser as the sole thing to be worked for, leaving the wants unsatisfied; so the conduct men have found preferable because most conducive to happiness, has come to be thought of as intrinsically preferable: not only to be made a proximate end (which it should be), but to be made an ultimate end, to the exclusion of the true ultimate end. And yet cross-examination quickly compels everyone to confess the true ultimate end. Just as the miser, asked to justify himself, is obliged to allege the power of money to purchase desirable things, as his reason for prizing it; so the moralist who thinks this conduct intrinsically good and that intrinsically bad, if pushed home, has no choice but to fall back on their pleasure-giving and pain-giving effects. To prove this it needs but to observe how impossible it would be to think of them as we do, if their effects were reversed.

Suppose that gashes and bruises caused agreeable sensations, and brought in their train increased power of doing work and receiving enjoyment; should we regard assault in the same manner as at present? Or suppose that self-mutilation, say by cutting off a hand, was both intrinsically pleasant and furthered performance of the processes by which personal welfare and the welfare of dependents is achieved; should we hold as now, that deliberate injury to one's own body is to be reprobated? Or again, suppose that picking a man's pocket excited in him joyful emotions, by brightening his prospects; would theft be counted among crimes, as in existing law-books and moral codes? In these extreme cases, no one can deny that what we call the badness of actions is ascribed to them solely for the reason that they entail pain, immediate or remote, and would not be so ascribed did they entail pleasure.

If we examine our conceptions on their obverse side, this general fact forces itself on our attention with equal distinctness. Imagine that ministering to a sick person always increased the pains of illness. Imagine that an orphan's relatives who took charge of it, thereby necessarily brought miseries upon it. Imagine that liquidating another man's pecuniary claims on you redounded to his disadvantage. Imagine that crediting a man with noble behavior hindered his social welfare and consequent gratification. What should we say to these acts which now fall into the class we call praiseworthy? Should we not contrariwise class them as blameworthy?

Using, then, as our tests, these most pronounced forms of good and bad conduct, we find it unquestionable that our ideas of their goodness and badness really originate from our consciousness of the certainty or probability that they will produce pleasures or pains somewhere.

Evaluation

1. To begin with Social Darwinism, those entrepreneurs who argue that individuals who are successful demonstrate thereby that they are the fittest and deserve their superior socio-economic status are ignoring the actual factors that produce success. Although some ability is certainly needed, social circumstances are much more significant in determining who will succeed and who will fail — even in the United States, the land of opportunity and upward mobility. If a person is born with a silver spoon in his mouth, has good family connections and is introduced to influential people, if he has considerable financial resources at his disposal from an inheritance, if he has been educated at prep schools and socially prestigious colleges, if he is a white, Anglo-Saxon, Protestant male, and if luck and timing are in his favor (being at the right place at the right time), his chances of success are enormously increased. A black woman from a poor home in an inner city slum without any of these advantages would be unlikely to advance, regardless of her natural intelligence or general fitness. Although we like to think that the rags to riches stories of Horatio Alger typify the American experience that is much more the exception than the rule.

In other words no necessary correlation exists between success and natural ability. Those at the top of the social and economic scale do not necessarily deserve their privileges by virtue of having superior qualities and the poor are not necessarily poor because of any biological deficiencies; many are victims and casualties of social forces. And because the financially successful people are not always the best specimens of Homo sapien their genes cannot be said to enrich the human race more than the genes of the poor. In short, those who survive and thrive are not automatically the fittest biologically; they may only be the most fortunate. Success in fact is more a mark of a person's opportunities than an indicator of his abilities, just as good luck can be more important than hard work.

2. Not only can we question whether the successful people are the fittest biologically but, even if that were true, we wonder whether a society founded on such an equation would be ethically sound. That is, would a just society allow success to be based on natural abilities? Should survival of the fittest be the governing principle for the distribution of wealth?

The concept of the "fittest" has been subject to various criticisms including the fact that it is circular, for an organism is called fit because it survives, and it survives because it is fit. But a more substantive criticism has to do with the assumption that the fittest means the best. When one considers this proposition it hardly rings true that the victors in the struggle for survival are the finest members of the species — especially when it comes to the human species. Someone who is ruthless and deceitful, unscrupulous and manipulative may have the qualities for success in a competitive society but that is not the picture we would paint of an admirable person. The fact that such an individual may succeed is not proof that he deserves his success; the worst people can win and nice guys may finish last. In other words, applying the criterion of survival of the fittest would in no way guarantee life and prosperity to decent people but only to the strongest, who use every means possible, fair and foul. The Mafia godfather may be the "fittest" as evidenced by his wealth and power but he is hardly an ideal human being.

Now we certainly would not want the human race to consist of fine people unable to survive, for that would lead to the extinction of the species, but neither would we want humanity composed of individuals with survival capabilities but terrible characters. In the latter case, the human race would continue in existence but would hardly be worth preserving. Rather than having either of these extremes we should aim at producing worthwhile individuals with sufficient ability to survive (and the human race along with them). That is, we should value moral qualities above survival skills while not neglecting the need to succeed in the struggle for existence. Social Darwinism effectively ignores the moral aspect of man and focuses entirely on survival of the fittest, which as we have seen does not mean survival of the finest

3. As for Herbert Spencer's evolutionary ethic, it certainly presents a more humane standard of behavior. Cooperation and mutual helpfulness are advocated as part of the increasing complexity of evolution rather than ruthless, individual competition. However, does nature in the main exhibit these tender virtues that Spencer ascribes to her? Creatures such as ants and bees may live in cooperative communities but others such as tigers and cobras are more solitary and savage, and it is an open question as to which is more representative. Other philosophers refer to nature as "the tyrannically inconsiderate and relentless enforcement of the claims of power" (Friedrich Nietzsche) or "ruthless self-assertion," a "thrusting aside, or treading down" of all competitors, a "gladiatorial" existence (T. H. Huxley).

Even if nature preserves the species through such devices as cooperation she does not do very much to preserve the members. "Individuality seems to be Nature's whole aim — and she cares nothing for individuals," Goethe wrote, which is a sentiment echoed by Wordsworth; "So careful of the type she seems,/So careless of the single life." These considerations certainly call into question the benevolent strains that Spencer describes; the "law of tooth and claw" may be closer to the mark.

Nature in general may not give us a moral model at all even though certain parts may be worth emulating (for example, the care given by animals to their offspring). She may even be morally neutral as scientists such as Stephen Jay Gould maintain. Therefore, instead of trying to use nature as our ideal perhaps we should try to improve upon her example with the compassion that is part of human civilization. We should try to build a garden in the jungle instead of importing the jungle into our garden.

4. Spencer also may have been mistaken about the inevitable line of ascendancy in nature from "incoherent homogeneity" to "coherent heterogeneity." He was optimistic about continual improvement in the way that Darwin was when he concluded *The Origin of Species* by stating, "we may look with some confidence to a secure future of great length. And as natural selection works solely by and for the good of each being, all corporeal and mental endowments will tend to progress toward perfection."

Since the nineteenth century, however, nuclear weapons have given us the power to reverse the advancement on our planet and revert to more elementary forms of life. We have also polluted the earth to the point where we may have done irreparable damage to the ecological balance necessary to maintain ourselves and other highly developed species in being. What's more, we have become increasingly aware of a counterevolutionary force in nature, called *entropy,* which works toward disorder, degrading matter and energy toward an ultimate state of inert uniformity.

In the light of these developments we cannot share Spencer's confidence that nature proceeds onward and upward, that evolution rather than devolution characterizes the universe. And if everything is degenerating then nature certainly is not the example we should follow, for it would lead us to nihilism and destructiveness.

The same point, incidentally, applies to Spencer's concept of breadth. Not only is this notion difficult to measure, but nature may not be tending toward greater breadth at all. For instance, we are not sure that modern man has a fuller life than say Renaissance man or that children today are better educated and more cultured than their parents or grandparents.

It is interesting to speculate as to whether Spencer would still endorse breadth of life as desirable even if it were not indicated by evolution. In making this refinement he parallels John Stuart Mill who tried to introduce qualitative distinctions into hedonism. Would Spencer also judge this factor so valuable that he would contradict his theory in order to support it?

5. Finally, Spencer may be challenged in maintaining that pleasurable activities are also conducive to evolutionary survival, for we know that pleasure often accompanies activities that do not promote survival. For example, driving a car at high speed can be pleasurable but it is also dangerous; the same is true of mountain climbing or sky diving, smoking cigarettes, or taking hard drugs. And some pleasurable activites although beneficial in some respects are dangerous in others. A simple example is that of food. Since eating is extremely enjoyable the temptation is to eat excessively and to eat good tasting food even if it is harmful to the body. As a result, obesity has become a major health problem in America today, and a link has been established between poor dietary habits and certain forms of cancer and heart disease. In these cases, pleasure does not work for our survival but against it.

Despite the numerous defects in evolutionary ethics it has the strong merit of being grounded in physical facts. To know what is right we simply look at the direction of evolution. Instead of consulting the dictates of our conscience or vague principles of correct behavior we use the objective reality of nature as our guide. And to link our actions to the movements of the natural world, the ethical to the actual, brings a sense of integration and wholeness, a feeling of oneness with the universe at large. What nature does we do, in parallel steps, mirror images, and our lives become a reflection of the whole. Rather than being alienated from the world of nature we feel at home once more, because the same principles of development are being used in animal and human life.

Oddly enough, this major psychological strength that all nature theories share can also be construed as a logical weakness. As David Hume (1711–1776) and other philosophers have pointed out, we cannot judge that an action is good simply because it conforms to some description of the world. To do so is called *the naturalistic fallacy*. That is, whatever *is* the case does not furnish the grounds for judging what *ought* to be the case; values cannot be derived from facts. This means that even if survival of the fittest is the law of nature, that does not justify establishing it as the moral law that mankind should follow. On ethical grounds, we might want to separate ourselves from nature in this respect and introduce principles of pity and compassion, for example, that may not be characteristic of the natural order. Instead of allowing the weak and defenseless to fall by the wayside we might feel morally obliged to offer them help—whether or not nature does the same.

Notes

1. A type of naturalism is also associated with John Dewey and George Santayana, and in technical terms naturalism is the ethical view that moral judgments are about natural rather than supernatural qualities.
2. Theodore Roszak, *The Making of a Counter Culture* (New York: Doubleday, 1969).
3. See Burton F. Porter, *The Good Life* (New York: Macmillan, 1980), Chapter 8.
4. In one amusing passage Thoreau shows how even farmers can misunderstand what is essential. "One farmer says to me, 'You cannot live on vegetable food solely, for it furnishes nothing to make bones with;' and so he religiously devotes a part of his day to supplying his system with the raw materials of bones; walking all the while he talks behind his oxen, which, with vegetable-made bones, jerk him and his lumbering plow along in spite of every obstacle."
5. Bertrand Russell, *A History of Western Philosophy* (New York: Simon and Schuster, 1945), 685. The question of whether Rousseau is democratic or totalitarian is a subject of endless debate in political philosophy. Often the issue devolves to whether he shares the antidemocratic views of G. W. F. Hegel in the latter's *The Philosophy of Right*. See J. L. Talmon, *The Rise of Totalitarian Democracy* (Boston: Beacon Press, 1952); John Chapman, *Rousseau—Totalitarian or Liberal* (New York: Columbia University Press, 1956); and James Miller, *Rousseau: Dreamer of Democracy* (New Haven: Yale University Press, 1984).
6. See *Lost Horizon* by James Hilton, *Green Mansions* by W. Hudson, and "The Lake Isle of Innisfree" by W. B. Yeats. The last mentioned contains the lines:

> I will arise and go now, and go to Innisfree,
> And a small cabin build there, of clay and wattles made:
> Nine bean rows will I have there, a hive for the honey-bee,
> And live all alone in the bee-loud glade.

7. John Stuart Mill, *Nature, The Utility of Religion, and Theism* (London: Longmans Green, 1874), 28–29.
8. William Dampier, *A History of Science* (Cambridge: University Press, 1929), 295. It should be mentioned that Alfred Russel Wallace discovered the principle of natural selection simultaneously with Darwin, and the first paper on evolution was written by them jointly.
9. A. White, *The History of the Warfare Between Science and Religion* (New York: D. Appleton, 1896), vol. 2: 9.
10. William Paley, *Natural Theology* (London: J. Faulder, 1809), 3 and 11; also Chapters 8–10, 19–22. In addition compare the statement by Cleanthes in David Hume, *Dialogues Concerning Natural Religion* (New York: Social Sciences Publishers, 1948), 143 ff. and 146.
11. Evolutionary theory also had the advantages of explaining evils such as physical catastrophes as natural phenomena and explaining dead ends in creation such as dinosaurs and other extinct species; it appeared more plausible to say that dinosaurs could not cope with radical changes in the environment than to argue that god broke off the line of reptiles and began to develop mammals.
12. Herbert Spencer, *The Principles of Ethics* (New York: D. Appleton, 1896), section 257.
13. Madison Grant, *The Passing of the Great Race* (New York: Charles Scribner's Sons, 1921), 229. It is interesting to note that the Western ideal of beauty is the fair, blue-eyed, Scandinavian type, and even Christ is frequently pictured this way, more often a blonde Apollo than a dark Semitic figure.
14. Also compare J. S. Huxley, *Evolutionary Ethics* (London: Oxford University Press, 1943).

Bibliography

ALLAND, ALEXANDER, JR. *Human Nature: Darwin's View.* New York: Columbia University Press, 1985.

ALLEE, W. C. *Cooperation Among Animals: With Human Applications.* London: H. Schumann, 1951.

ATKINSON, BROOKS. *Henry Thoreau: A Cosmic Yankee.* Darby, Pa.: Arden Library, 1978.

BORST, RAYMOND. *Henry David Thoreau: A Descriptive Bibliography.* Pittsburgh: University of Pittsburgh Press, 1981.

BRIDGMAN, RICHARD. *Dark Thoreau.* Lincoln: University of Nebraska Press, 1982.

CASTELL, A. *Selections From the Essays of T. H. Huxley.* New York: F. S. Crofts, 1948.

CAVELL, STANLEY. *The Senses of Walden.* Berkeley, Calif.: North Point Press, 1981.

CHAPMAN, JOHN W. *Rousseau—Totalitarian or Liberal.* New York: Columbia University Press, 1956.

CHARPENTIER, JOHN. *Rousseau: The Child of Nature.* Philadelphia: R. West, 1931.

CLODD, EDWARD. *Pioneers of Evolution from Thales to Huxley.* Freeport, N.Y.: Books for Libraries, 1972.

COMPAYRE, G. *Jean-Jacques Rousseau and Education from Nature.* New York: B. Franklin, 1907.

DARWIN, CHARLES. *Autobiography.* London: Watts, 1937.

———. *The Origin of Species.* New York: Collier, 1902 (original edition 1859).

DAVIDSON, I. *Rousseau and Education According to Nature.* Houston: Scholarly Publications, 1970.

DESHUMBERT, M. *An Ethical System Based on the Laws of Nature* trans. by L. Giles. Chicago: Open Court, 1917.

FARBER, MARVIN. *Naturalism and Subjectivism.* Springfield, Ill.: C. C. Thomas, 1959.

FLEW, ANTHONY. *Evolutionary Ethics*. London: Macmillan, 1967.

GODDARD, HAROLD CLARKE. *Studies In New England Transcendentalism*. New York: Humanities Press, 1969.

HALDANE, J. B. S. *Science and Ethics*. London: Watts, 1928.

HUXLEY, JULIAN. *The Living Thoughts of Darwin*. New York: Longmans, Green, 1939.

————. *Evolutionary Ethics*. London: Oxford University Press, 1943.

HUXLEY, T. H. *Evolution and Ethics*. New York: D. Appleton, 1929.

KEITH, ARTHUR. *Evolution and Ethics*. New York: Putnam, 1947.

KRIKORIAN, Y. *Naturalism and the Human Spirit*. New York: Columbia University Press, 1944.

KROPOTKIN, P. *Mutual Aid, A Factor of Evolution*. London: William Heineman, 1915.

————. *Ethics, Origin and Development*. New York: Dial Press, 1926.

LAMPRECHT, STERLING. *The Metaphysics of Naturalism*. New York: Appleton-Century-Crofts, 1967.

McINTOSH, JAMES. *Thoreau as Romantic Naturalist*. Ithaca, N.Y.: Cornell University Press, 1974.

MAXWELL, MARY. *Human Evolution: A Philosophical Anthropology*. New York: Columbia University Press, 1984.

MILLER, JIM. *Rousseau: Dreamer of Democracy*. New Haven: Yale University Press, 1984.

OSPOVAT, D. *The Development of Darwin's Theory: Natural History, Natural Theology, and Natural Selection*. Cambridge: Cambridge University Press, 1981.

PRATT, JAMES B. *Naturalism*. New Haven: Yale University Press, 1939.

RANDALL, JOHN HERMAN. *Nature and Historical Experience: Essays in Naturalism and in the Theory of History*. New York: Columbia University Press, 1958.

RICE, RICHARD A. *Rousseau and the Poetry of Nature in Eighteenth Century France*. Folcroft, Pa.: 1925.

ROACH, MARILYNNE. *Down to Earth at Walden*. Boston: Houghton-Mifflin, 1980.

ROUSSEAU, JEAN-JACQUES. *The Social Contract*. New York: Dutton, 1950.

————. *Emile*. New York: Dutton, 1970.

————. *Reveries of a Solitary Walker*, trans. C. Butterworth. New York: New York University Press, 1979.

ROYCE, JOSIAH. *Herbert Spencer, An Estimate and Review*. New York: Fox, Duffield, 1904.

SALT, HENRY S. *Life of Henry David Thoreau*. New York: Hasnell, 1969, reprint of 1890 edition.

SCHWEITZER, ALBERT. *Civilization and Ethics*, trans. J. Naish. London: A. and C. Black, 1923.

SIMPSON, GEORGE. *The Meaning of Evolution: Its Significance for Man*. New Haven: Yale University Press, 1950.

SMUTS, JAN. *Holism and Evolution*. New York: Macmillan, 1926.

SPENCER, HERBERT. *The Data of Ethics*. New York: Appleton, 1889.

————. *The Evolution of Society*. Chicago: University of Chicago Press, 1967.

THOREAU, HENRY DAVID. *The Maine Woods*. Boston: Houghton, Mifflin, 1892.

————. *Cape Cod*. New York: Houghton, Mifflin, 1914.

WADDINGTON, C. H. *Science and Ethics*. London: Allen and Unwin, 1942.

WOLF, WILLIAM J. *Thoreau: Mystic, Prophet, Ecologist*. New York: Pilgrim, 1974.

ZWINGER ANN, AND EDWIN W. TEALE. *A Conscious Stillness: Two Naturalists on Thoreau's River*. Amherst: University of Massachusetts Press, 1984.

CHAPTER 8

Rationalism

One persistent weakness that we detected in the naturalistic ethic is its failure to differentiate between aspects of nature that are beneficial and those that are harmful; not everything that is natural is good, so the good cannot be defined as whatever is natural. The same weakness afflicts the ethical ideal of self-realization. Some dimensions of our self are worth developing (for our own well being and that of others) and some are not, which means that the good is not necessarily the completely realized self. In both cases discrimination is needed using our reasoning abilities, which suggests that rationality itself might be central to a worthwhile life. Perhaps we should subject ourselves to the governance of reason, allowing our rational faculties to choose the path that leads to an ideal existence. Or more important, perhaps being rational is itself the ideal in living, not a means to a good life but the end or essence of it.

Rationalism is the term used for this approach to ethics — although it stands for much more in philosophy generally. With respect to questions of knowledge it embraces the view that the reasoning mind, using deductive logic and canons of consistency, should be trusted far more than the evidence of the senses in yielding truth about the world. The intellect here is considered a separate source of knowledge, inherently more reliable than sense experience, that is, empiricism. Sometimes in this connection rationality is also contrasted with imaginative, authoritarian, intuitive, or mystical ways of knowing and again judged to be the most trustworthy channel to understanding. It can also be considered the opposite of skepticism or emotivism insofar as it claims that reason can distinguish reality from illusion and discover what is actually the case.

In the field of ethics however rationalism means the view that the highest good in life is to be a rational human being. It is not that we should use reason as a method for distinguishing good from bad (although that too is important) but that we should conduct ourselves rationally. If our thoughts and actions are in keeping with reason, if we allow the intellect to assume a preeminent role in our decisions, then our lives will be successful.

We have already seen how Aristotle defined man as the rational animal, viewing reason as unique to human beings and central to their nature; it functions excellently, he claimed, in reflective contemplation and when it chooses the Golden Mean. The goal for Aristotle is eudaimonia or the vital well being of the fully functioning organism, but reason is crucial in its attainment and could even be regarded as part of the goal itself. Insofar as Aristotle stressed the importance of man's reason he was part of the rationalist tradition (while being a self-realizationist essentially). The philosophers René Descartes (1596–1650), G. W. Leibniz (1646–1716), Benedict de Spinoza (1632–1677), and Immanuel Kant (1724–1804) are also part of this school. However, the ethical positions most closely identified with rationalism are Stoicism and Platonism. In both theories reason occupies the principal place, for they each maintain that the good life is the rational life.

Both Stoicism and Platonism began in ancient Athens in the fourth century B.C., which is hardly a coincidence. At that time the Greeks were emerging from barbarism to become one of the first civilizations in human history and reason was widely held to be the characteristic that set the civilized man apart. Rather than the emotions or the will governing the person the Greeks cherished the rule of mind. Rationality was a cultural virtue and the value placed upon it led to the development of numerous systems of thought in which reason was awarded the dominant place.

Stoicism: Equanimity Even in the Face of Catastrophe

One of these systems of thought, Stoicism, was officially begun by the philosopher Zeno (336–264 B.C.) when he founded his school in Athens around 300 B.C. Zeno's followers used to gather at the *Stoa Poikile* (Painted Porch) and hence became known as Stoics or "men of the porch."

But the roots of Stoicism go back to an earlier philosophic movement, called Cynicism, which is associated with Antisthenes (c. 444–336 B.C.), who was its founder, and his famous disciple Diogenes (c. 412–323 B.C.), who gave the philosophy its name. For Diogenes was nicknamed "the Dog" which in Greek is *cynic*, presumably because of his biting wit, unkempt appearance, and refusal to participate in most human conventions.[1] This was rather typical of all the Cynics who were known for their attacks on society and their championing of self-sufficiency and the freedom of the individual. To their mind, all the accretions of civilization should be abandoned including worldly possessions, money, home, and property, as well as decency, education, community, and respect for authority. Only in that way could the individual be free. The fewer needs and desires the person had, the more he reduced his vulnerability and took charge of his own destiny.

Of course, a great deal of rational control was needed to minimize one's desires and renounce luxury altogether, but through continual discipline an ascetic, untroubled life could be attained. "I would rather go mad than feel pleasure," Antisthenes is reputed to have stated, which is a far cry from his contemporaries the Cyrenaics. On another occasion he is alleged to have said that the rational individual will rid himself "not only of artificial wants which complicate and enervate life, but of all ties whatsoever that bind him to the rest of the world," not troubling himself about "the material goods of life nor the attitude of his fellow men toward him. He will rather master himself, controlling his desires so that nothing outside can disturb him."[2]

A celebrated story about Diogenes and Alexander the Great illustrates some of the Cynic philosophy. Diogenes was sunning himself in a large tub (in which, reputedly, he lived) when Alexander rode up on his horse. "I am Alexander the great king," he declared. "And I," replied the other calmly, "am Diogenes the dog." "Are you then not afraid of me?" Alexander asked. "Why, what are you, something good or something evil?" "Something good, of course," "Well," responded Diogenes, "who would be so foolish as to fear anything good?" Alexander was so impressed by his composure and good sense that he said, "Ask anything you wish of me, and I will grant it." "Then be so good," Diogenes replied, "as to stand out of my sunlight." To this day the word *cynic* refers not only to someone distrustful of generous motives but to a caustic person with an independent mind and a wry contempt for the trappings of wealth and power.

A great many of the Cynics' ideas were incorporated into Stoicism as it was developed by Zeno and subsequent philosophers of Greece and Rome. The ideas of ascetic discipline, self-control, and the rational suppression of desires were especially significant in Stoic thought. But unlike the Cynic philosophy, which remained a minor, opposition doctrine, Stoicism became one of the dominant philosophies in the Graeco-Roman world. Initially its chief competitor was the Epicurean ethic, which in many ways functioned as its opposite and foil, and in Rome it rivaled Christianity for a time and influenced the formulation of Christian theology. The influence of Stoicism can be seen particularly in the Epistles of St. Paul, who prior to his conversion had been raised in the Stoic philosophy. It remained a major intellectual force in the early Christian era, and did not decline until the third century A.D.

During the forty years that Zeno directed the Stoic school he systematically defined the orthodox doctrine, but the philosophy was further refined by his successor Cleanthes and then by Chrysippus (c. 280–207 B.C.) who offered ingenious proofs in its defense. Even more important to the development of Stoicism was its importation into Rome where it flourished through the influence of Cicero (106–43 B.C.) and Cato (95–46 B.C.) and most importantly Seneca (c. 54 B.C.–39 A.D.), Epictetus (c. 55–135 A.D.), and Marcus Aurelius (121–180 A.D.). Of these figures, Epictetus, the Greek slave, is considered the most significant followed by Marcus Aurelius, the Roman emperor.

The Nature of the Universe

The Stoics were united in the belief that the universe displays a lawful order and not a haphazard arrangement of elements, that a World Reason pervades the cosmos and radiates within each human being. The finite reason that each person possesses is part of the natural law of reason — the inner manifestation or psychological counterpart of the metaphysical reality. The World Reason contains justice and wisdom in its operations and therefore commands our obedience. We have an obligation to follow its direction, uniting our human reason with cosmic rationality and achieving a harmony of the whole.

The Stoics further maintained that this enduring rational principle is the same as god. The deities in the Greek pantheon should not be worshiped as such, they declared, because Zeus, Apollo, Poseidon, and the rest are mere personifications of an underlying order and purpose that is the divine. It is not that god has created the structure of the universe and enacted the rational laws governing it (although the Stoics sometimes give that impression) but rather that he is coextensive with that lawfulness. World Reason is identical with divine wisdom, universal law is inherently spiritual and sacred, so that in conforming to reason

one is showing reverence for the will of god. Witness the following expression of
the unity of reason and religion in the *Hymn to Zeus* written by Cleanthes:

> O King, most High, nothing is done without Thee,
> Neither in heaven or on earth, nor in the sea,
> Except what the wicked do in their foolishness.
> Thou makest order out of disorder,
> And what is worthless becomes precious in thy sight;
> For Thou hast fitted together good and evil into one,
> And hast established one law that exists forever.
> But the wicked fly from Thy law, unhappy ones,
> And though they desire to possess what is good,
> Yet they see not, neither do they hear, the universal law of God.
> They go astray, each after his own devices, —
> Some vainly striving after reputation,
> Others turning aside after gain excessively,
> Others after riotous living and wantonness.
> Nay, but O Zeus, giver of all things,
> Deliver men from this foolishness,
> Scatter it from their souls and grant them to obtain wisdom,
> For by wisdom Thou dost rightly govern all things.
> Nor is there, for mortal men or for the gods, greater thing than this—
> Rightly to adore the universal law.

This document resembles some of the finest Hebrew and Christian scriptures
and is especially remarkable in that it was written at a time of polytheistic
worship in Greece and Rome.

The rational order of the universe, then, is divine in nature and deference to
reason is synonymous with the worship of god. A spark of the "original fire of
wisdom" is in every person, and it can illuminate everyones life in intelligent
thought and behavior.

The Stoic goes on to say that since the universe is rational and divine it must
also be good. God is known to be a benevolent force, the Stoic asserts, and
whatever is rational is certainly good. Therefore to call any aspect of life evil is a
mistake. The pain that we experience from poverty, sickness, and death is only
apparent harm; in the total scheme of things it is necessary and justified. If we
were sensible and pious we would regard evil as something unreal, a mistaken
judgment made by a limited mind that fails to see the intelligible whole. Just as a
musical composition can be richer because of its dissonance, so the universe
attains its ideal form through the suffering and injustice on earth. From a cosmic
perspective there are no defects in the universe, only the rational perfection of
god. In a parallel to Christianity, our suffering is redeemed in the fullness of
time. The true Stoic therefore says, "Do your worst, pain, do your worst: you
will never compel me to acknowledge that you are an evil." If we take the right
attitude, nothing will ever disturb us.

In addition to its intrinsic goodness the universe also posesses the characteristic of mechanical inevitability in the unfolding of its design. Cosmic rationality
makes no mistakes and does not swerve from its course, which means that every
event must happen as it does. A divine providence orders all things, or more
precisely, since no personal being stands behind destiny, all occurrences are
controlled by fate.

In classical mythology the Fates were three goddesses who decided the course of human life: Clotho spins the thread of life, Lachesis decides on its length, and Atropos cuts it off at the end. The fatalism accepted by the Stoics had a different origin. On the one hand, they argued that every event has a cause and all of reality is bound together by a cause–effect chain. The network of causes and effects in the past is certainly unchangeable now and what occurs in the present is dictated by that frozen past. In the same way, the future is the inevitable result of past and present causes, so whatever events take place in the future have already been determined to occur by this causal train. Everything, in fact, must happen as it does, for there is no escaping the iron law of causation.

On the other hand, the Stoics believed in fate on the grounds that all past events are unalterable (as the English poet John Dryden said, "Not heaven itself upon the past has power") and many future events also are inevitable. For example, the statement Man invented the wheel is true and cannot be made false, and the same can be said of the statement All men will die. But if all past events and some future ones are unchangeable, then maybe all events have this character. That is, perhaps all statements are already true or false, and as events occur we realize which judgment is correct. Rather than statements becoming true in the future their truth exists at present, which implies that everything is already so — that is, fated.

However unsound these arguments might be, the Stoics found them persuasive and believed in an eternal order that dictates every event in the universe, a rational system both mechanical and divine that controls not only the behavior of objects but the affairs of men. Whatever human beings do has already been destined to occur, a thread in the tapestry of creation, and the notion that we have control over our actions is a vain illusion.

The Stoic Ethic

In the light of this reality how ought human beings to live? According to the Stoic metaphysics, it does not seem as if we have any choice, but the Stoic stops short of declaring that every aspect of life is determined. On the contrary, he maintains that only external circumstances are fated to be as they are: our attitude toward the inevitable is entirely in our hands. We do not have any *freedom* (of action) but we do possess the *free will* to respond positively or negatively to fated events. In other words, we cannot change what will happen to us but we do have control over our reaction to those happenings. Here we have power over ourselves and are the masters of our fate, the captains of our soul.

Everything depends, then, on distinguishing between what is within our own power and what is not; that is, differentiating between our mental attitude and outside events. Our well being depends entirely on rationally controlling our reactions to those things we cannot change. For example, nothing can be done about a drought or a plague, but we can cultivate the right response toward them, achieving peace of mind even in the face of disaster.

The same holds true for poverty, which only affects us if we allow it to do so; having the proper attitude makes the crucial difference and that depends entirely on ourselves. "No man finds poverty a trouble to him but he that thinks it so," Seneca wrote, "and he that thinks it so, makes it so. He that is not content in poverty, would be so neither in plenty; for the fault is not in the thing but in the mind. If anyone be sickly, remove him from a kennel to a palace; he is at the same pass, for he carries his disease along with him."

Even death should be regarded this way. It certainly cannot be avoided but we can avoid poisoning our lives with the fear of death. Epictetus wrote that "Men are disturbed not by things, but by the view which they take of things," including death, which "is nothing terrible else it would have appeared so to Socrates. But the terror consists in our notion of death." If we can conduct ourselves with self-control, calmness, and rationality, and not yield to the weaknesses of desire and emotion, then even death will leave us undisturbed. We will view it with tranquil detachment as part of the order of life, an event that is part of universal perfection. By not letting it defeat us we become superior to our fate, transcending it through the power of our rational mind. "Ask not that events should happen as you will," Epictetus advised us, "but let your will be that events should happen as they do, and you shall have peace."[3]

To the Stoic we are always free in our response to events, and if we are wise we will respond in a positive and intelligent way. We could rail against our fate, which is the natural reaction when tragedies occur, but that would be foolish as well as sacrilegious. Since we cannot do anything about the disease or disaster that afflicts us we should be sensible and accept it with a certain poise and equilibrium. "There's no sense complaining, it won't do any good," we tell each other; "no use crying over spilt milk," "worrying won't help," which is sound Stoic advice when faced with a situation we can neither escape nor avoid. Even if we could oppose fate we should not do so because everything happens for the best in the long run.

The only rational and ethical response therefore is to maintain our equanimity and actually praise whatever occurs. We should not simply tolerate our lot in life with a calm resignation but positively endorse whatever fate decrees. If we are able to rationally control our feelings in all situations and know that we are in complete command of ourselves, not the slave of appetites and desires, then we will have attained that state of serenity that the stoic calls *apatheia*. It is an inner dignity and peace that comes from the realization that no misfortunes can harm us, not even death, so long as we emulate the disinterested divine reason that orders the universe. And once we have achieved apatheia then we have gained mastery over life. Such is the polished sphere of Stoic thought.

In the selection that follows from the *Encheiridion* or *Manual* of Epictetus we can see the strands of Stoic thought clearly displayed. Epictetus never actually wrote anything himself and all of his extant works are taken from the notes of Flavius Arrian, one of his pupils. But the *Encheiridion* together with the *Discourses* summarize Epictetus' basic teachings and constitute the principal source of the Stoic ethic.

Encheiridion (Manual)*

Of all existing things some are in our power, and others are not in our power. In our power are thought, impulse, will to get and will to avoid, and, in a word, everything which is our own doing. Things not in our power

*Reprinted from Epictetus, *The Discourses and Manual,* trans. by P. E. Matheson (Oxford: Oxford University Press, 1916), vol. 2: 213–20, 224–29, 235.

include the body, property, reputation, office, and, in a word, everything which is not our own doing. Things in our power are by nature free, unhindered, untrammelled; things not in our power are weak, servile, subject to hindrance, dependent on others. Remember then that if you imagine that what is naturally slavish is free, and what is naturally another's is your own, you will be hampered, you will mourn, you will be put to confusion, you will blame gods and men; but if you think that only your own belongs to you, and that what is another's is indeed another's, no one will ever put compulsion or hindrance on you, you will blame none, you will accuse none, you will do nothing against your will, no one will harm you, you will have no enemy, for no harm can touch you.

Aiming then at these high matters, you must remember that to attain them requires more than ordinary effort; you will have to give up some things entirely, and put off others for the moment. And if you would have these also—office and wealth—it may be that you will fail to get them, just because your desire is set on the former, and you will certainly fail to attain those things which alone bring freedom and happiness.

Make it your study then to confront every harsh impression with the words, 'You are but an impression, and not at all what you seem to be'. Then test it by those rules that you possess; and first by this—the chief test of all—'Is it concerned with what is in our power or with what is not in our power?' And if it is concerned with what is not in our power, be ready with the answer that it is nothing to you.

Remember that the will to get promises attainment of what you will, and the will to avoid promises escape from what you avoid; and he who fails to get what he wills is unfortunate, and he who does not escape what he wills to avoid is miserable. If then you try to avoid only what is unnatural in the region within your control, you will escape from all that you avoid; but if you try to avoid disease or death or poverty you will be miserable.

Therefore let your will to avoid have no concern with what is not in man's power; direct it only to things in man's power that are contrary to nature. But for the moment you must utterly remove the will to get;[2] for if you will to get something not in man's power you are bound to be unfortunate; while none of the things in man's power that you could honourably will to get is yet within your reach. Impulse to act and not to act, these are your concern; yet exercise them gently and without strain, and provisionally.

When anything, from the meanest thing upwards, is attractive or serviceable or an object of affection, remember always to say to yourself, 'What is its nature?' If you are fond of a jug, say you are fond of a jug; then you will not be disturbed if it be broken. If you kiss your child or your wife, say to yourself that you are kissing a human being, for then if death strikes it you will not be disturbed.

When you are about to take something in hand, remind yourself what manner of thing it is. If you are going to bathe put before your mind what happens in the bath—water pouring over some, others being jostled, some reviling, others stealing; and you will set to work more securely if you say to yourself at once: 'I want to bathe, and I want to keep my will in harmony with nature,' and so in each thing you do; for in this way, if anything turns up to hinder you in your bathing, you will be ready to say, 'I did not want only to bathe, but to keep my will in harmony with nature, and I shall not so keep it, if I lose my temper at what happens'.

What disturbs men's minds is not events but their judgements on events. For instance, death is nothing dreadful, or else Socrates would have thought it so. No, the only dreadful thing about it is men's judgement that it is dreadful. And so when we are hindered, or disturbed, or distressed, let us never lay the blame on others, but on ourselves, that is on our own judgements. To accuse others for one's own misfortunes is a sign of want of education; to accuse oneself shows that one's education has begun; to accuse neither oneself nor others shows that one's education is complete.

Be not elated at an excellence which is not your own. If the horse in his pride were to say, 'I am handsome', we could bear with it. But when you say with pride, 'I have a handsome horse', know that the good horse is the ground of your pride. You ask then what you can call your own. The answer is — the way you deal with your impressions. Therefore when you deal with your impressions in accord with nature, then you may be proud indeed, for your pride will be in a good which is your own.

When you are on a voyage, and your ship is at anchorage, and you disembark to get fresh water, you may pick up a small shellfish or a truffle by the way, but you must keep your attention fixed on the ship, and keep looking towards it constantly, to see if the Helmsman calls you; and if he does, you have to leave everything, or be bundled on board with your legs tied like a sheep. So it is in life. If you have a dear wife or child given you, they are like the shellfish or the truffle, they are very well in their way. Only, if the Helmsman call, run back to your ship, leave all else, and do not look behind you. And if you are old, never go far from the ship, so that when you are called you may not fail to appear.

Ask not that events should happen as you will, but let your will be that events should happen as they do, and you shall have peace.

Sickness is a hindrance to the body, but not to the will, unless the will consent. Lameness is a hindrance to the leg, but not to the will. Say this to yourself at each event that happens, for you shall find that though it hinders something else it will not hinder you.

When anything happens to you, always remember to turn to yourself and ask what faculty you have to deal with it. If you see a beautiful boy or a beautiful woman, you will find continence the faculty to exercise there; if trouble is laid on you, you will find endurance; if ribaldry, you will find patience. And if you train yourself in this habit your impressions will not carry you away.

Never say of anything, 'I lost it', but say, 'I gave it back'. Has your child died? It was given back. Has your wife died? She was given back. Has your estate been taken from you? Was not this also given back? But you say, 'He who took it from me is wicked'. What does it matter to you through whom the Giver asked it back? As long as He gives it you, take care of it, but not as your own; treat it as passers-by treat an inn.

If you wish to make progress, abandon reasonings of this sort; 'If I neglect my affairs I shall have nothing to live on'; 'If I do not punish my son, he will be wicked.' For it is better to die of hunger, so that you be free from pain and free from fear, than to live in plenty and be troubled in mind. It is better for your son to be wicked than for you to be miserable. Wherefore begin with little things. Is your drop of oil spilt? Is your sup of wine stolen? Say to yourself, 'This is the price paid for freedom from passion, this is the price of a quiet mind.' Nothing can be had without a price. When you call your slave-boy, reflect that he may not be able to hear you, and if he hears you, he may not be able to do anything you want. But he is not so well off that it rests with him to give you peace of mind.

If you wish to make progress, you must be content in external matters to seem a fool and a simpleton; do not wish men to think you know anything, and if any should think you to be somebody, distrust yourself. For know that it is not easy to keep your will in accord with nature and at the same time keep outward things; if you attend to one you must needs neglect the other.

It is silly to want your children and your wife and your friends to live for ever, for that means that you want what is not in your control to be in your control, and what is not your own to be yours. In the same way if you want your servant to make no mistakes, you are a fool, for you want vice not to be vice but something different. But if you want not to be disappointed in your will to get, you can attain to that.

Exercise yourself then in what lies in your power. Each man's master is the man who has authority over what he wishes or does not wish, to secure the one or to take away the other. Let him then who wishes to be free not wish for anything or avoid anything that depends on others; or else he is bound to be a slave.

Remember that you must behave in life as you would at a banquet. A dish is handed round and comes to you; put out your hand and take it politely. It passes you; do not stop it. It has not reached you; do not be impatient to get it, but wait till your turn comes. Bear yourself thus towards children, wife, office, wealth, and one day you will be worthy to banquet with the gods. But if when they are set before you, you do not take them but despise them, then you shall not only share the gods' banquet, but shall share their rule. For by so doing Diogenes and Heraclitus and men like them were called divine and deserved the name.

When you see a man shedding tears in sorrow for a child abroad or dead, or for loss of property, beware that you are not carried away by the impression that it is outward ills that make him miserable. Keep this thought by you; 'What distresses him is not the event, for that does not distress another, but his judgement on the event.' Therefore do not hesitate to sympathize with him so far as words go, and if it so chance, even to groan with him; but take heed that you do not also groan in your inner being. . . .

Remember that you are an actor in a play, and the Playwright chooses the manner of it: if he wants it short, it is short; if long, it is long. If he wants you to act a poor man you must act the part with all your powers; and so if your part be a cripple or a magistrate or a plain man. For your business is to act the character that is given you and act it well; the choice of the cast is Another's.

When a raven croaks with evil omen, let not the impression carry you away, but straightway distinguish in your own mind and say, 'These portents mean nothing to me; but only to my bit of a body or my bit of property or name, or my children or my wife. But for me all omens are favourable if I will, for, whatever the issue may be, it is in my power to get benefit therefrom.'

You can be invincible, if you never enter on a contest where victory is not in your power. Beware then that when you see a man raised to honour or great power or high repute you do not let your impression carry you away. For if the reality of good lies in what is in our power, there is no room for envy or jealousy. And you will not wish to be praetor, or perfect or consul, but to be free; and there is but one way to freedom—to despise what is not in our power.

Remember that foul words or blows in themselves are no outrage, but your judgement that they are so. So when any one makes you angry, know that it is your own thought that has angered you. Wherefore make it your first endeavour not to let your impressions carry you away. For if once you gain time and delay, you will find it easier to control yourself.

Keep before your eyes from day to day death and exile and all things that seem terrible, but death most of all, and then you will never set your thoughts on what is low and will never desire anything beyond measure.

. . .

In everything you do consider what comes first and what follows, and so approach it. Otherwise you will come to it with a good heart at first because you have not reflected on any of the consequences, and afterwards, when difficulties have appeared, you will desist to your shame. Do you wish to win at Olympia? So do I, by the gods, for it is a fine thing. But consider the first steps to it, and the consequences, and so lay your hand to the work. You must submit to discipline, eat to order, touch no sweets, train under compulsion, at a fixed hour, in heat and cold, drink no cold water, nor wine, except by order; you must hand yourself over completely to your trainer as you would to a physician, and then when the contest comes you must risk getting hacked, and sometimes dislocate your hand, twist your ankle, swallow plenty of sand, sometimes get a flogging, and with all this suffer defeat. When you have considered all this well, then enter on the athlete's course, if you still wish it. If you act without thought you will be behaving like children, who one day play at wrestlers, another day at gladiators, now sound the trumpet, and next strut the stage. Like them you will be now an athlete, now a gladiator, then orator, then philosopher, but nothing with all your soul. Like an ape, you imitate every sight you see, and one thing after another takes your fancy. When you undertake a thing you do it casually and half-heartedly, instead of considering it and looking at it all round. In the same way some people, when they see a philosopher and hear a man speaking like Euphrates (and indeed who can speak as he can?), wish to be philosophers themselves.

Man, consider first what it is you are undertaking; then look at your own powers and see if you can bear it. Do you want to compete in the pentathlon or in wrestling? Look to your arms, your thighs, see what your loins are like. For different men are born for different tasks. Do you suppose that if you do this you can live as you do now—eat and drink as you do now, indulge desire and discontent just as before? Nay, you must sit up late, work hard, abandon your own people, be looked down on by a mere slave, be ridiculed by those who meet you, get the worst of it in everything—in honour, in office, in justice, in every possible thing. This is what you have to consider: whether you are willing to pay this price for peace of mind, freedom, tranquillity. If not, do not come near; do not be, like the children, first a philosopher, then a tax-collector, then an orator, then one of Caesar's procurators. These callings do not agree. You must be one man, good or bad; you must develop either your Governing Principle, or your outward endowments; you must study either your inner man, or outward things—in a word, you must choose between the position of a philosopher and that of a mere outsider.

Appropriate acts are in general measured by the relations they are concerned with. 'He is your father.' This means you are called on to take care of him, give way to him in all things, bear with him if he reviles or strikes you.

'But he is a bad father.'

Well, have you any natural claim to a good father? No, only to a father.

'My brother wrongs me.'

Be careful then to maintain the relation you hold to him, and do not consider what he does, but what you must do if your purpose is to keep in accord with nature. For no one shall harm you, without your consent; you will only be harmed, when you think you are harmed. You will only discover what is proper to expect from neighbour, citizen, or praetor, if you get into the habit of looking at the relations implied by each.

For piety towards the gods know that the most important thing is this: to have right opinions about them—that they exist, and that they govern the universe well and justly—and to have set yourself to obey them, and to give way to all that happens, following events with a free will, in the belief that they are fulfilled by the highest mind. For thus you will never blame the gods, nor accuse them of neglecting you. But this you cannot achieve, unless you apply your conception of good and evil to those things only which are in our power, and not to those which are out of our power. For if you apply your notion of good or evil to the latter, then, as soon as you fail to get what you will to get or fail to avoid what you will to avoid, you will be bound to blame and hate those you hold responsible. For every living creature has a natural tendency to avoid and shun what seems harmful and all that causes it, and to pursue and admire what is helpful and all that causes it. It is not possible then for one who thinks he is harmed to take pleasure in what he thinks is the author of the harm, any more than to take pleasure in the harm itself. That is why a father is reviled by his son, when he does not give his son a share of what the son regards as good things; thus Polynices and Eteocles were set at enmity with one another by thinking that a king's throne was a good thing. That is why the farmer, and the sailor, and the merchant, and those who lose wife or children revile the gods. For men's religion is bound up with their interest. Therefore he who makes it his concern rightly to direct his will to get and his will to avoid, is thereby making piety his concern. But it is proper on each occasion to make libation and sacrifice and to offer first-fruits according to the custom of our fathers, with purity and not in slovenly or careless fashion, without meanness and without extravagance.

When you make use of prophecy remember that while you know not what the issue will be, but are come to learn it from the prophet, you do know before you come what manner of thing it is, if you are really a philosopher. For if the event is not in our control, it cannot be either good or evil. Therefore do not bring with you to the prophet the will to get or the will to avoid, and do not approach him with trembling, but with your mind made up, that the whole issue is indifferent and does not affect you and that, whatever it be, it will be in your power to make good use of it, and no one shall hinder this. With confidence then approach the gods as counsellors, and further, when the counsel is given you, remember whose counsel it is, and whom you will be disregarding if you disobey. And consult the oracle, as Socrates thought men should, only when the whole question turns upon the issue of events, and neither reason nor any art of man provides opportunities for discovering what lies before you. Therefore, when it is your duty to risk your life with friend or country, do not ask the oracle whether you should risk your life. For if the prophet warns you that the sacrifice is unfavourable, though it is plain that this means death or exile or injury to some part of your body, yet reason requires that even at this cost you must stand by your friend and share your country's danger. Wherefore pay heed to the greater prophet, Pythian Apollo, who cast out of his temple the man who did not help his friend when he was being killed.

Lay down for yourself from the first a definite stamp and style of conduct, which you will maintain when you are alone and also in the society of men. Be silent for the most part, or, if you speak, say only what is necessary and in a few words. Talk, but rarely, if occasion calls you, but do not talk of ordinary things — of gladiators, or horse-races, or athletes, or of meats or drinks — these are topics that arise everywhere — but above all do not talk about men in blame or compliment or comparison. If you can, turn the conversation of your company by your talk to some fitting subject; but if you should chance to be isolated among strangers, be silent. Do not laugh much, nor at many things, nor without restraint.

Refuse to take oaths, altogether if that be possible, but if not, as far as circumstances allow.

Refuse the entertainments of strangers and the vulgar. But if occasion arise to accept them, then strain every nerve to avoid lapsing into the state of the vulgar. For know that, if your comrade have a stain on him, he that associates with him must needs share the stain, even though he be clean in himself.

For your body take just so much as your bare need requires, such as food, drink, clothing, house, servants, but cut down all that tends to luxury and outward show.

• • •

The ignorant man's position and character is this: he never looks to himself for benefit or harm, but to the world outside him. The philosopher's position and character is that he always looks to himself for benefit and harm.

The signs of one who is making progress are: he blames none, praises none, complains of none, accuses none, never speaks of himself as if he were somebody, or as if he knew anything. And if any one compliments him he laughs in himself at his compliment; and if one blames him, he makes no defence. He goes about like a convalescent, careful not to disturb his constitution on its road to recovery, until it has got firm hold. He has got rid of the will to get, and his will to avoid is directed no longer to what is beyond our power but only to what is in our power.

Evaluation

The Stoic philosophy is extremely tempting on a number of counts, especially in the amount of personal freedom that it offers. For, ironically enough, even though Stoicism denies that we have any control over external events it ends up giving us considerable power over our lives by claiming that our attitude is free—and attitude is everything. Whether we have peace of mind depends entirely upon ourselves, regardless of what happens. Some people are miserable even though they are strong and healthy; others are content even when they are sick with some awful disease. Some people complain about aging, others say you are as old as you feel, that it's all a matter of how you look at it. The latter of course is the Stoic approach where one feels at ease in any circumstances because of an inner serenity.

1. One question that arises however is whether too high a price is being paid for control and inner peace. That is, perhaps we are giving up too much of our emotional life, withdrawing from the world into an impervious shell in order to avoid the possibility of suffering. Rather than repressing our feelings in this way, it might be better to risk the pain and disappointment and involve ourselves in the external world. Instead of trying to avoid unhappiness (which seems to be the Stoic's aim) we might be better off trying to gain fulfillment. We do get what

we strive for some of the time, perhaps most of the time, and those satisfactions can make up for a multitude of disappointments.

For example, when a man and a woman become emotionally involved they know that they risk being terribly hurt if the relationship does not work out, but they take that chance because of the satisfaction they find in being together. And if the relationship should end they will withdraw for a time, licking their wounds, but then be willing to take another chance with someone else. This seems a healthy pattern, and the person who is so afraid of being injured that he will never reach out again leads a tragic and stunted existence from that time on, safe but extremely sad. Such a person will renounce love because it makes him too vulnerable and in Buddhist fashion try to reduce or eliminate all desires since they render him liable to pain. But a protective, defensive life of this kind hardly seems worthwhile. As the children's tale teaches us, the turtle only moves forward by sticking its neck out.

In the same way, if we are worried about someone who is late in arriving the Stoic would advise us to suppress our feelings because they do no good. It is wasted emotion, he would say, serving no useful purpose; to get upset helps neither ourselves nor the person we care about. But if we are anxious, it is not because we think it will do any good but out of affection for the person. Our concern is not meant to *cause* any result but is the *effect* of our feelings for him. And as an expression of those feelings it seems a perfectly appropriate response —certainly more appropriate than indifference.

Most psychologists, in fact, will say that the emotions are at least as important as the intellect and cannot be repressed without bringing harm to the organism as a whole. To allow ourselves to feel only those emotions that are useful, to govern our responses to the point where everything is premeditated and nothing is spontaneous is hardly a desirable way to live.

> Such an attitude is characteristic of the authoritarian person who is highly controlled, rational, and deliberate. The authoritarian (as contrasted with the democratic) personality has such a rigid structure of responses that any genuine reactions are deeply buried beneath an extensive defense system. To be affected by genuine emotions means to risk a crack in the foundation of the personality, threatening it with collapse, therefore, a strict, strong, implacable, enameled surface is presented to the world. But such strength is basically weakness for it is grounded in anxiety about exposing oneself; the person is most afraid of being unguarded, that is, of being himself and vulnerable. The real person lies cowering behind an elaborate network of fortifications.
>
> And, oddly enough, this self-protective attitude which is assumed to provide freedom from injury becomes the opposite of authentic freedom, for the person locks himself away from others and himself, becoming separate and self-alienated. The fortress is actually a prison with little nourishment being delivered from outside the walls; the person feeds off of himself like a snake swallowing its own tail. He cannot be injured very readily but he also cannot communicate with others or be touched by them. In gaining the invulnerability of a citadel the authoritarian personality loses his reality as a person. Petrified by fear, he becomes part of the fortress itself, unassailable and less than human.[4]

It seems more promising, therefore, to cultivate the full range of our emotions and not impoverish ourselves by limiting our feelings to the sensible ones.

"Wasted emotion" is the price we pay for a rich human life, so in a larger sense the emotion is not wasted at all.

2. Another criticism of Stoicism has become so standard that it has acquired a name: the lazy argument. The argument claims that laziness would be the only proper response to the Stoic view, for if destiny governs everything then there is no point in trying to accomplish anything. If the event is fated it will happen regardless of what one does, and if it is not fated then no effort on the person's part will make it happen. The only sensible approach then is to stretch out in bed and do nothing.

As corollary, no one would ever be responsible for his actions, and praise as well as blame would be irrelevant. We should not honor people for service to humanity any more than we should imprison them for criminal actions — unless, of course, it was argued that the punishment is as inevitable as the crime. But then the punishment would not be justified only necessary in the scheme of things, and there would be no moral reason for it.

3. As we can see, the entire system becomes extremely paradoxical once a radical separation is made between will and action, when what one tries to do is thought to have no relation to what one actually does. And this theory can certainly be questioned, for it runs counter to our ordinary, commonsense assumptions. If we decide to kick a stone then our foot swings in an arc, comes in contact with the stone, and the stone flies through the air; we assume that a cause – effect sequence took place, that the stone moved because of our decision to kick it. The Stoic however would claim that the two events (one mental, one physical) just happened to coincide or were independent and synchronized.

Now common sense may not be correct in all cases but the Stoic claim strains our credibility to the breaking point. It seems much more plausible that a causal connection exists between the internal decision and the external happening, not just in relation to kicking stones but with regard to countless other events as well.

In all fairness it should be mentioned that the Stoics are not alone in maintaining that the mental and the physical do not interact. In philosophic history this view, labeled *occasionalism,* was maintained in various forms by René Descartes (1596 – 1650), Benedict de Spinoza (1632 – 1677), and Nicholas Malebranche (1638 – 1715).[5] Furthermore, not all Stoics see a total split between volition and action. Epictetus, for example, said he would not betray a friend, which suggests that at least his lips were under his control, and discussed the discipline needed to become an athlete, the need to eliminate fancy food, drink, clothing, and other luxuries, and the virtue of risking one's life for friends or country — all of which imply some degree of physical power. But to whatever extent the separation is made the problem is present. In our ordinary way of thinking we tend to ascribe far more control over our lives than the Stoic will allow and to see a much closer connection between our choices and what in fact occurs.

4. All of the preceding points stem from the Stoic belief in destiny, which raises the question as to whether this belief is justified. Do the Stoics really offer convincing arguments to show that destiny rules the universe and all events were

meant to be? Their main proof for the claim that all events are unchangeable is that some events cannot be changed. They cite specifically those in the past and certain ones in the future such as the succession of night and day and the inevitability of each person's death. From this they conclude that every event occurs by necessity and that past, present, and future are a bloc unity.

The logic here is obviously faulty. Although some particular events are fixed and frozen that does not imply the entire universe of events has this character. Much more evidence needs to be provided in order to call this generalization highly probable—and it could never be regarded as certain. Technically the argument could also be classified as a "fallacy of composition"; that is, arguing from the features of some members of the group to the character of the group altogether. For example, we commit this fallacy if we argue that because a feather is light, a ton of feathers will be light. What holds true for the parts does not necessarily hold true for the whole, and this insight seems to have been missed by the Stoics when they argued that all events are fixed.

In addition, the "inevitable" future events mentioned by the Stoics might not be inevitable at all. At some astronomically distant point in the future, when our sun ceases to give off light, day will not follow night any longer. What's more, human beings could develop to the point where man is no longer mortal. For no one ever dies of old age but only as a result of some disease or body failure, which means that in principle there is no reason why all terminal illnesses could not be eliminated and death no longer occur. And even though John Dryden (and the tragic poet Agathon) said that heaven itself cannot change the past, we do have Samuel Butler's remark in *Erewhon* (Chapter 14) that "although God cannot alter the past, historians can." Butler's comment was meant ironically, but it points up the logician's contention that only syllogisms carry the quality of necessity; events could always be different and viewed differently.

Apart from specific problems with regard to fatalism, the lazy argument, and so forth, in general the Stoic presents a melancholy philosophy of resignation, even bitterness and disillusion toward a world that to his mind has not delivered its requisite lot of satisfactions. If you expect nothing you are invulnerable, he tells himself, and this fear of disappointment works to cripple him. In his outlook on life the Stoic seems too impressed with the events that are beyond his control and not confident enough to try to change his surroundings, to form a world that is closer to his heart's desires. He lacks hope and a commitment to action, settling instead for the inner peace of apatheia and the motto *abstine et sustine* (abstain and endure).

On the positive side, however, the Stoic approach to life can be very appealing during turbulent periods of history, such as the decline and fall of Rome between c. 180–476 A.D. or even our own era of economic uncertainty and political violence. At times like these it is extremely comforting to think that nothing outside ourselves can truly harm us, that if we are rationally controlled we render ourselves impervious to disaster. If the outside world provides few rewards we might decide to turn inward for the primary sources of our fulfillment and reduce stress in our lives by minimizing fruitless worry and anxiety. Our prosperity and safety may be beyond our control but rational tranquility is not, and that according to Stoicism is what makes life worthwhile. A tincture of the Stoic mentality, then, might be a very good thing.

Platonism: The Righteous Rule of Reason

The other ancient philosophy that places reason at its core is the system developed by the Greek philosopher Plato (c. 427–347 B.C.). Plato has probably exerted a greater influence on philosophy than any other single philosopher except perhaps Aristotle, but he never wrote a systematic treatise on ethics per se; his ethical views are contained mainly in *The Republic* in conjunction with his discussion of the ideal state. Studies in metaphysics and epistemology were his main concern, and his mind was so outstanding that, in the famous phrase, all of philosophy is merely "a footnote to Plato."

Although his interests and aristocratic background would normally have led Plato to a career in politics, he grew disenchanted with the Athenian society because of the insincerity and selfishness rampant at the time. Instead, he became a disciple of the philosopher Socrates (469–399 B.C.), who impressed him by his personal integrity and philosophic skill, especially his dialectic method of inquiry by means of question and answer; in subsequent years he became his most famous pupil. (The line then went to Aristotle who was Plato's student and to Alexander the Great who studied with Aristotle, but without much effect.) When Socrates was unjustly put to death for allegedly "corrupting the young men and not believing in the gods of the city," Plato left Athens in horror and traveled throughout the Greek colonies of Sicily and southern Italy for about fifteen years. Upon his return he founded the celebrated Academy, which has been called the world's first university. It was dedicated to the establishment of decent government and to philosophic understanding. Above all, the Academy was modeled on the ideal of reason as exemplified by Socrates, the man who had lived his philosophy and become its first martyr. Socrates had tried to follow the demands of reason in both thought and action, to gain self-understanding, including the limits of one's knowledge ("know thyself"), to openly consider criticism and carry arguments to their logical conclusion. It was this type of rational dedication that Plato tried to emulate, and although he departed from some of Socrates' ideas he never abandoned his spirit of rational inquiry.

Plato guided the work of the Academy for some forty years and wrote a series of works in dialogue form in which Socrates appears as chief spokesman. It is unclear to what extent Plato reported the thoughts of Socrates and to what extent he used Socrates as a vehicle for the expression of his own ideas, but scholars generally consider the works to be more Platonic than Socratic in nature.[6] Typically, the dialogues attempt to define some key concept such as virtue, justice, or piety, and to draw out the implications of the definitions that are offered, testing for coherence and consistency throughout. In addition to being models of philosophic thinking (and perhaps illustrating the dynamic character of truth), the dialogues are also excellent pieces of dramatic literature, showing Plato's artistry as well as the subtlety of his mind.

As a cutting edge into Plato's thought we should first consider his views on the nature of man. To his mind, human nature contains three aspects or as he conceives it the soul posesses three elements. *Appetite* is the first element and it is associated with the desires of the lower half of the body for objects such as food, drink, and sexual gratification. *Spirit* (or volition, the active impulse) is the second element and it naturally seeks honor and glory, the excitement of conflict and competition; residing in the chest, the high-spirited person is "great-hearted." Third is *Reason,* which springs from the mind and is the faculty by which we choose; knowledge is its natural aim.

Corresponding to each of these elements is a particular virtue or mode of excellence: for the appetites it is temperance or self-control; for the spirit, courage; and for reason the goal is wisdom. As might be expected, reason occupies the most significant position, but it does not function to the exclusion of the rest. For besides seeking knowledge in its own right it rules over the "lower" aspects of the soul, functioning to reconcile the disparate parts into a harmonious whole. And once the three elements exist in proper relation, then *justice* or righteousness is achieved for the human being. In the last analysis, that is the final goal, for goodness is simply the just functioning of the balanced person under the governance of reason.

These cardinal virtues of temperance, courage, wisdom, and justice make up the ideal of the good person. Notice that Plato does not say the spirit should be stifled but rather properly directed so that we are ambitious in the right ways and mobilize ourselves to fight for the right causes. The man of courage retains "the commands of reason about what he ought and ought not to fear." And we should not repress the appetites as evil but satisfy them in moderation and with self-restraint; "the ordering or controlling of certain pleasures and desires" is virtuous. Intelligence must be exercised throughout every part of the soul, producing a rule of the passions not rule by them, a disciplined courage, and a mind used for understanding not mere practical success. In addition, the intellect is used to balance the three forces so that, in just combination, each contributes to the good of the whole.

Plato went on to say that justice and the good for the individual is incomplete unless there is a corresponding organization of the city-state. Like Aristotle who once said, "Men form societies in order to live, states in order to live well," he believed that the person and the political society are inseparable, that the state is only the individual "writ large."[7] Therefore the state contains the same tripartite division, and should make use of citizens of each type in discharging its functions.

Specifically, those individuals who are primarily appetitive by nature should function to supply the basic economic needs of the state; in that way they can become prosperous, satisfying their own physical desires and meeting each other's bodily wants. Man's first need is food, his second a house, and third a coat. So farmers and herdsmen will be required initially, followed by builders then weavers and cobblers. As the economy of the state expands and develops the need will arise for smiths, cooks, and barbers, merchants and tradesmen, poets, actors, and dancers. Plato referred to this class as *artisans,* sometimes as traders and believed that their natural desires will induce them to work hard and build the material foundation of the state. They will have enough rational restraint however to keep their wants and ambitions from becoming excessive.

A second class of citizens, those of a predominantly spirited nature, should be used to defend the state from external attack. For the economic expansion of the various states will inevitably lead to conflict among them. "A slice of our neighbors' land will be wanted by us for pasture and tillage, and they will want a slice of ours." Those people with a natural aptitude for fighting should therefore be trained for military combat and also for maintaining order among citizens within the state's boundaries. Plato designates these individuals as *warriors* or auxiliaries. Their aggressive disposition suits them for the role of soldiers and police, and through disciplined training they will develop courage and the ability to use their courage wisely.

Lastly, the state requires a government to direct its affairs, and those in whom reason is uppermost are best qualified to be the political leaders. For it is the rational individuals, those possessing superior intelligence and wisdom, who can grasp the underlying principles of good policy and devote themselves to securing the welfare of all. They are the intellectual elite whom Plato called the *guardians,* viewing them as the natural rulers of the state.

The guardians understand that in the just society, as in the just individual, each of the parts must harmonize under the influence of reason. And they are the only ones able to act on that knowledge because in them the reasonable element is supreme. They know that each person must keep to his proper place, doing the task that he is best able to do, and that then alone will the republic become a utopia. Plato wrote:

> when the cobbler or any other man whom nature designed to be a trader, having his heart lifted up by wealth or strength or the number of his followers, or any like advantage, attempts to force his way into the class of warriors, or a warrior into that of legislators and guardians, for which he is unfitted, and either to take the implements or the duties of the other; or when one is trader, legislator, and warrior all in one, [this] is the ruin of the state. . . . On the other hand, when the trader, the auxiliary, and the guardian each do their own business, that is justice, and will make the city just.[8]

In terms of our political tradition of free choice, we might think Plato was being high-handed in advocating that each person be placed in a category based upon his principal ability, but his reasoning was that both the individual and the society will be better off under this scheme. For the person is very likely to be content if he expresses the major part of himself, and the society will be benefited most when each citizen contributes what he is best able to give. Conversely, by insisting on the freedom to choose we can damage both ourselves and the state. If an individual refuses to be an artisan or warrior or guardian when he is ideally suited to it, he is being unjust both to himself and his neighbors. We should act reasonably then not impulsively, and consent to the role cast for us by our nature.

The guardians, therefore, should be obeyed because they are capable of judging the strengths and weaknesses of people and assigning them to their proper place. They have the overall wisdom needed to ensure justice for all. Plato further stated that these highly rational guardians, who hold the greatest promise of ruling the state justly, are the philosophers. In a famous passage in *The Republic* Plato has Socrates say

> *Until philosophers are kings, or the kings and princes of this world have the spirit and power of philosophy, and political greatness and wisdom meet in one, and those commoner natures who pursue either to the exclusion of the other are compelled to stand aside, cities will never have rest from their evils,—no, nor the human race, as I believe,—and then only will this our State have a possibility of life and behold the light of day.* (V, 473)

In saying this Plato was not simply giving the highest status and position to his own group. The philosophers are simply seen as the most rational and therefore the best qualified for political governance. The guardians, in fact, have an arduous life not a plush one; they fulfill their natures and serve the state not through indulging their active impulses or their appetite for comfort but through the austere life of reason.

With regard to education, for example, for the first seventeen years everyone in the society is given physical and military training and instructed in art, music, and literature — "gymnastics for the body and music for the soul." Following that however, those who pass the moral and academic tests for guardians receive a rigorous ten year period of training in science and mathematics to teach them clear reasoning. Finally, the guardians are given five years of instruction in philosophy (starting at age thirty and not before) and then serve a fifteen-year apprenticeship in military and government service before becoming full-fledged rulers.

More important, their lives are thoroughly Spartan throughout, without wives or children and virtually no personal possessions. Plato specified that

> none of them shall have any property of his own beyond what is absolutely neces- sary; neither should they own a private house; their provisions should be only such as are required by trained warriors, who are men of temperance and courage; they should agree to receive from the citizens a fixed rate of pay, enough to meet the expenses of the year and no more, and they will go to mess and live together like soldiers in a camp. . . . And they alone of all the citizens may not handle silver or gold, or be under the same roof with them, or wear them, or drink from them. And this will be their salvation, and the salvation of the state. (III, 416D)

By being forced to have only meager possessions corruption will be eliminated, and by holding wives and children in common the guardians will not have divided loyalties, wanting more for their own family than the society receives as a whole.

It is worth noting that Plato maintained in *The Republic* that women should be given the same opportunities as men. Contrary to the beliefs of his day, he thought that women should advance as far as their abilities carried them. They could be educated in gymnastics and the humanities along with men, enter the various business fields or serve in the military depending upon their disposition, and even become rulers of the state. He was not entirely immune from the prejudices of his society for he believed that men generally excel over women in all fields, however he did say that "many women are in many things superior to many men." His overall attitude toward women was remarkably enlightened for the time, making him perhaps one of the earliest feminists.

As was mentioned, the guardians, whether male or female, are chosen pri- marily for their rational capabilities. But this rationality is not just necessary for integrating the parts of the state into a coherent whole. Plato had something even more profound in mind. The guardian's intellectual powers enable him to rule the state justly because he can grasp the universal "form" of the good. That is, through his mind the rational person can go beyond the transitory world of appearances to the eternal realm of essences, especially to an understanding of the idea of goodness and justice itself.

To elaborate this theory, Plato maintained as a cornerstone of his ethics, politics, and theory of knowledge that there are two worlds: that of *Sense,* which is the physical world of objects perceived by the senses, and that of *Ideas* or Forms, which consists of the concepts or classes of those objects. For example, a concrete thing such as a horse exists in the physical world but there is also the idea of horse in general that is not the same as any specific example of one. This horse or that horse is very different than the concept of a horse. Furthermore, physical horses that we see or remember are always inferior to the idea or form of horse; they are approximations, more or less distorted, of the abstract ideal that is their model. The same is true of every other material object that has ever existed, whether flowers or trees, shoes, ships, or sealing wax. They all have some idea corresponding to them, an idea that is separate and perfect in relation to the tangible object that represents it.

The aggregate of sense objects make up a world of Sense, and the sum of their ideas constitute a veritable world of Ideas. Both are real, but of the two levels Plato awarded greater reality to the Ideas, treating them at times as if they were the only true reality. For physical things are fleeting and imperfect; they come into being and pass out of being, and always have defects relative to the pure idea of them. A horse, to use the earlier example, is born and dies and can always be faulted for not being ideally proportioned, for having legs too short for its body, perhaps a swayback, bony "splints," or a short stride. The Idea of horse, on the other hand, is eternal, changeless, and perfect, and the same is true of every other Form.

This means that, contrary to conventional opinion, the invisible ideas of things are more real than the things themselves because they contain the time-less ideal. As the medieval thinkers would phrase it "spirit" or "universals" stand higher in the scale of reality than objects in the physical world, which is why Plato has been referred to as "a Christian four hundred years before Christ." In the more precise language of logic, the concept is prior to its denotation, the class is more real than its members. The world of Ideas explains the visible world, giving to it whatever degree of reality it possesses, and to devote oneself to comprehending the eternal Ideas is to be a philosopher, a "lover of wisdom."

The mind, then, has access to the absolute reality while the senses disclose the lesser reality of the experiential world. What we perceive in the everyday world is a poor copy of the transcendental Ideas but by means of rational reflection we know that another and greater reality exists beyond this veil of appearances. In Plato's famous Allegory of the Cave he compared the human situation to that of prisoners chained in a cave in such a way that they can see only shadows on a wall, cast by a light shining on actual objects behind them. Like these prisoners we should reason that the things we perceive must be mere shadowy representations of the true reality beyond our sight and strive to apprehend these essential forms and live in the light of their truth.

The state is just therefore insofar as it approximates the Idea of the Good, and the guardians rule through their understanding of this ideal and their devotion to its realization in the political structure. In this way they bring justice to earth, going beyond error and illusion to the higher realm of goodness itself.

It is impossible in this short sketch to convey the breadth and loftiness of Plato's vision, the "white Platonic dreams." However, the following excerpt from *The Republic* will at least illustrate some of the reasons why it is considered the grandest and most elegant system of rational thought ever devised. (Plato's philosophy is also developed in such works as the *Theaetetus, Parmenides, Sophist,* and *Timaeus.*)

Our selection begins at the point where Socrates has just described the cardinal virtues of temperance, courage, and wisdom.

The Citizen and the Republic*

And so, after much tossing, we have reached land, and are fairly agreed that the same principles which exist in the State exist also in the individual, and that they are three in number.

Exactly.

Must we not then infer that the individual is wise in the same way, and in virtue of the same quality which makes the State wise?

Certainly.

Also that the same quality which constitutes courage in the State constitutes courage in the individual, and that both the State and the individual bear the same relation to all the other virtues?

Assuredly.

And the individual will be acknowledged by us to be just in the same way in which the State is just?

That follows of course.

We cannot but remember that the justice of the State consisted in each of the three classes doing the work of its own class?

We are not very likely to have forgotten, he said.

We must recollect that the individual in whom the several qualities of his nature do their own work will be just, and will do his own work?

Yes, he said, we must remember that too.

And ought not the rational principle, which is wise, and has the care of the whole soul, to rule, and the passionate or spirited principle to be the subject and ally?

Certainly.

And, as we were saying, the united influence of music and gymnastic will bring them into accord, nerving and sustaining the reason with noble words and lessons, and moderating and soothing and civilizing the wildness of passion by harmony and rhythm?

Quite true, he said.

And these two, thus nurtured and educated, and having learned truly to know their own functions, will rule over the concupiscent, which in each of us is the largest part of the soul and by nature most insatiable of gain; over this they will keep guard, lest, waxing great and strong with the fulness of bodily pleasures, as they are termed, the concupiscent soul, no longer confined to her own sphere, should attempt to enslave and rule those who are not her natural-born subjects, and overturn the whole life of man?

Very true, he said.

Both together will they not be the best defenders of the whole soul and the

*Reprinted from Plato, *The Republic,* in *The Dialogues of Plato,* trans. B. Jowett (Oxford: Oxford University Press, 1924), vol. 3: 134–37, 207–10, 214–16 (Books IV, VI, and VII).

whole body against attacks from without; the one counselling, and the other fighting under his leader, and courageously executing his commands and counsels?

True.

And he is to be deemed courageous whose spirit retains in pleasure and in pain the commands of reason about what he ought or ought not to fear?

Right, he replied.

And him we call wise who has in him that little part which rules, and which proclaims these commands; that part too being supposed to have a knowledge of what is for the interest of each of the three parts and of the whole?

Assuredly.

And would you not say that he is temperate who has these same elements in friendly harmony, in whom the one ruling principle of reason, and the two subject ones of spirit and desire are equally agreed that reason ought to rule, and do not rebel?

Certainly, he said, that is the true account of temperance whether in the State or individual.

And surely, I said, we have explained again and again how and by virtue of what quality a man will be just.

That is very certain.

And is justice dimmer in the individual, and is her form different, or is she the same which we found her to be in the State?

There is no difference in my opinion, he said.

Because, if any doubt is still lingering in our minds, a few commonplace instances will satisfy us of the truth of what I am saying.

What sort of instances do you mean?

If the case is put to us, must we not admit that the just State, or the man who is trained in the principles of such a State, will be less likely than the unjust to make away with a deposit of gold or silver? Would any one deny this?

No one, he replied.

Will the just man or citizen ever be guilty of sacrilege or theft, or treachery either to his friends or to his country?

Never.

Neither will he ever break faith where there have been oaths or agreements?

Impossible.

No one will be less likely to commit adultery, or to dishonour his father and mother, or to fail in his religious duties?

No one.

And the reason is that each part of him is doing its own business, whether in ruling or being ruled?

Exactly so.

Are you satisfied then that the quality which makes such men and such states is justice, or do you hope to discover some other?

Not I, indeed.

Then our dream has been realized; and the suspicion which we entertained at the beginning of our work of construction, that some divine power must have conducted us to a primary form of justice, has now been verified?

Yes, certainly.

And the division of labour which required the carpenter and the shoemaker and the rest of the citizens to be doing each his own business, and not another's, was a shadow of justice, and for that reason it was of use?

Clearly.

But in reality justice was such as we were describing, being concerned however, not with the outward man, but with the inward, which is the true self and concernment of man: for the just man does not permit the several elements within him to interfere with one another, or any of them to do the work of others,—he sets in order his own inner life, and is his own master and his own law, and at peace with himself; and when he has bound together the three principles within him, which may be compared to the higher, lower, and middle notes of the scale, and the intermediate intervals—when he has bound all these together, and is no longer many, but has become one entirely temperate and perfectly adjusted nature, then he proceeds to act, if he has to act, whether in a matter of property, or in the treatment of the body, or in some affair of politics or private business; always thinking and calling that which preserves and co-operates with this harmonious condition, just and good action, and the knowledge which presides over it, wisdom, and that which at any time impairs this condition, he will call unjust action, and the opinion which presides over it ignorance.

You have said the exact truth, Socrates.

Very good; and if we were to affirm that we had discovered the just man and the just State, and the nature of justice in each of them, we should not be telling a flasehood?

Most certainly not.

May we say so, then?

Let us say so.

And now, I said, injustice has to be considered.

Clearly.

Must not injustice be a strife which arises among the three principles—a meddlesomeness, and interference, and rising up of a part of the soul against the whole, an assertion of unlawful authority, which is made by a rebellious subject against a true prince, of whom he is the natural vassal,—what is all this confusion and delusion but injustice, and intemperance and cowardice and ignorance, and every form of vice?

• • •

Still, I must implore you, Socrates, said Glaucon, not to turn away just as you are reaching the goal; if you will only give such an explanation of the good as you have already given of justice and temperance and the other virtues, we shall be satisfied.

Yes, my friend, and I shall be at least equally satisfied, but I cannot help fearing that I shall fail, and that my indiscreet zeal will bring ridicule upon me. No, sweet sirs, let us not at present ask what is the actual nature of the good, for to reach what is now in my thoughts would be an effort too great for me. But of the child of the good who is likest him, I would fain speak, if I could be sure that you wished to hear—otherwise, not.

By all means, he said, tell us about the child, and you shall remain in our debt for the account of the parent.

I do indeed wish, I replied, that I could pay, and you receive, the account of the parent, and not, as now, of the offspring only; take, however, this latter by way of interest, and at the same time have a care that I do not render a false account, although I have no intention of deceiving you.

Yes, we will take all the care that we can: proceed.

Yes, I said, but I must first come to an understanding with you, and remind you of what I have mentioned in the course of this discussion, and at many other times.

What?

The old story, that there is a many beautiful and a many good, and so of other things which we describe and define; to all of them the term 'many' is applied.

True, he said.

And there is an absolute beauty and an absolute good, and of other things to which the term 'many' is applied there is an absolute; for they may be brought under a single idea, which is called the essence of each.

Very true.

The many, as we say, are seen but not known, and the ideas are known but not seen.

Exactly.

And what is the organ with which we see the visible things?

The sight, he said.

And with the hearing, I said, we hear, and with the other senses perceive the other objects of sense?

True.

But have you remarked that sight is by far the most costly and complex piece of workmanship which the artificer of the senses ever contrived?

No, I never have, he said.

Then reflect: has the ear or voice need of any third or additional nature in order that the one may be able to hear and the other to be heard?

Nothing of the sort.

No, indeed, I replied; and the same is true of most, if not all, the other senses — you would not say that any of them requires such an addition?

Certainly not.

But you see that without the addition of some other nature there is no seeing or being seen?

How do you mean?

Sight being, as I conceive, in the eyes, and he who has eyes wanting to see; colour being also present in them, still unless there be a third nature specially adapted to the purpose, the owner of the eyes will see nothing and the colours will be invisible.

Of what nature are you speaking?

Of that which you term light, I replied.

True, he said.

Noble, then, is the bond which links together sight and visibility, and great beyond other bonds by no small difference of nature; for light is their bond, and light is no ignoble thing?

Nay, he said, the reverse of ignoble.

And which, I said, of the gods in heaven would you say was the lord of this element? Whose is that light which makes the eye to see perfectly and the visible to appear?

You mean the sun, as you and all mankind say.

May not the relation of sight to this deity be described as follows?

How?

Neither sight nor the eye in which sight resides is the sun?

No.

Yet of all the organs of sense the eye is the most like the sun?

By far the most like.

And the power which the eye possesses is a sort of effluence which is dispensed from the sun?

Exactly.

Then the sun is not sight, but the author of sight who is recognised by sight?

True, he said.

And this is he whom I call the child of the good, whom the good begat in his own likeness, to be in the visible world, in relation to sight and the things of sight, what the good is in the intellectual world in relation to mind and the things of mind:

Will you be a little more explicit? he said.

Why, you know, I said, that the eyes, when a person directs them towards objects on which the light of day is no longer shining, but the moon and stars only, see dimly, and are nearly blind; they seem to have no clearness of vision in them?

Very true.

But when they are directed towards objects on which the sun shines, they see clearly and there is sight in them?

Certainly.

And the soul is like the eye: when resting upon that on which truth and being shine, the soul perceives and understands, and is radiant with intelligence; but when turned towards the twilight of becoming and perishing, then she has opinion only, and goes blinking about, and is first of one opinion and then of another, and seems to have no intelligence?

Just so.

Now, that which imparts truth to the known and the power of knowing to the knower is what I would have you term the idea of good, and this you will deem to be the cause of science, and of truth in so far as the latter becomes the subject of knowledge; beautiful too, as are both truth and knowledge, you will be right in esteeming this other nature as more beautiful than either; and, as in the previous instance, light and sight may be truly said to be like the sun, and yet not to be the sun, so in this other sphere, science and truth may be deemed to be like the good, but not the good; the good has a place of honour yet higher.

· · ·

And now, I said, let me show in a figure how far our nature is enlightened or unenlightened: — Behold! human beings living in an underground den, which has a mouth open towards the light and reaching all along the den; here they have been from their childhood, and have their legs and necks chained so that they cannot move, and can only see before them, being prevented by the chains from turning round their heads. Above and behind them a fire is blazing at a distance, and between the fire and the prisoners there is a raised way; and you will see, if you look, a low wall built along the way, like the screen which marionette players have in front of them, over which they show the puppets.

I see.

And do you see, I said, men passing along the wall carrying all sorts of vessels, and statues and figures of animals made of wood and stone and various materials, which appear over the wall? Some of them are talking, others silent.

You have shown me a strange image, and they are strange prisoners.

Like ourselves, I replied; and they see only their own shadows, or the shadows of one another, which the fire throws on the opposite wall of the cave?

True, he said; how could they see anything but the shadows if they were never allowed to move their heads?

And of the objects which are being carried in like manner they would only see the shadows?

Yes, he said.

And if they were able to converse with one another, would they not suppose that they were naming what was actually before them?

Very true.

And suppose further that the prison had an echo which came from the other side, would they not be sure to fancy when one of the passers-by spoke that the voice which they heard came from the passing shadow?

No question, he replied.

To them, I said, the truth would be literally nothing but the shadows of the images.

That is certain.

And now look again, and see what will naturally follow if the prisoners are released and disabused of their error. At first, when any of them is liberated and compelled suddenly to stand up and turn his neck round and walk and look towards the light, he will suffer sharp pains; the glare will distress him, and he will be unable to see the realities of which in his former state he had seen the shadows; and then conceive some one saying to him, that what he saw before was an illusion, but that now, when he is approaching nearer to being and his eye is turned towards more real existence, he has a clearer vision, — what will be his reply? And you may further imagine that his instructor is pointing to the objects as they pass and requiring him to name them, — will he not be perplexed? Will he not fancy that the shadows which he formerly saw are truer than the objects which are now shown to him?

Far truer.

And if he is compelled to look straight at the light, will he not have a pain in his eyes which will make him turn away to take refuge in the objects of vision which he can see, and which he will conceive to be in reality clearer than the things which are now being shown to him?

True, he said.

And suppose once more, that he is reluctantly dragged up a steep and rugged ascent, and held fast until he is forced into the presence of the sun

himself, is he not likely to be pained and irritated? When he approaches the
light his eyes will be dazzled, and he will not be able to see anything at all of
what are now called realities.

Not all in a moment, he said.

He will require to grow accustomed to the sight of the upper world. And
first he will see the shadows best, next the reflections of men and other
objects in the water, and then the objects themselves; then he will gaze upon
the light of the moon and the stars and the spangled heaven; and he will see
the sky and the stars by night better than the sun or the light of the sun by day?

Certainly.

Last of all he will be able to see the sun, and not mere reflections of him in
the water, but he will see him in his own proper place, and not in another;
and he will contemplate him as he is.

Certainly.

He will then proceed to argue that this is he who gives the season and the
years, and is the guardian of all that is in the visible world, and in a certain
way the cause of all things which he and his fellows have been accustomed to
behold?

Clearly, he said, he would first see the sun and then reason about him.

And when he remembered his old habitation, and the wisdom of the den
and his fellow-prisoners, do you not suppose that he would felicitate himself
on the change, and pity them?

Certainly, he would.

And if they were in the habit of conferring honours among themselves on
those who were quickest to observe the passing shadows and to remark which
of them went before, and which followed after, and which were together;
and who were therefore best able to draw conclusions as to the future, do you
think that he would care for such honours and glories, or envy the possessors
of them? Would he not say with Homer,

‘Better to be the poor servant of a poor master,’

and to endure anything, rather than think as they do and live after their manner?

Yes, he said, I think that he would rather suffer anything than entertain these
false notions and live in this miserable manner.

Imagine once more, I said, such an one coming suddenly out of the sun to be
replaced in his old situation; would he not be certain to have his eyes full of
darkness?

To be sure, he said.

And if there were a contest, and he had to compete in measuring the shadows
with the prisoners who had never moved out of the den, while his sight was still
weak, and before his eyes had become steady (and the time which would be
needed to acquire this new habit of sight might be very considerable), would he
not be ridiculous? Men would say of him that up he went and down he came
without his eyes; and that it was better not even to think of ascending; and if
anyone tried to loose another and lead him up to the light, let them only catch
the offender, and they would put him to death.

No question, he said.

This entire allegory, I said, you may now append, dear Glaucon, to the previous argument; the prison-house is the world of sight, the light of the fire is the sun, and you will not misapprehend me if you interpret the journey upwards to be the ascent of the soul into the intellectual world according to my poor belief, which, at your desire, I have expressed—whether rightly or wrongly God knows. But, whether true or false, my opinion is that in the world of knowledge the idea of good appears last of all, and is seen only with an effort; and, when seen, is also inferred to be the universal author of all things beautiful and right, parent of light and of the lord of light in this visible world, and the immediate source of reason and truth in the intellectual; and that this is the power upon which he who would act rationally either in public or private life must have his eye fixed.

Evaluation

1. As in the case of Stoicism, we wonder whether the ideal of reasonable thinking and behavior isn't being over emphasized to the detriment of the full human being. The love of Forms is a cold love of abstractions and essences, of metaphysical structures that have the rightness but also the remoteness of mathematics. The self-mastery Plato respected so highly leaves no room for endearing weaknesses, indulgence in natural desires, acting on whims and impulses. He wanted us to temper our energy, express our desires moderately, and lead a rational life of grace and decorum. Our vision must be directed inward to the idea of the good impressed on our souls, not outward to the flesh and blood life surrounding us. In Plato's scheme the will and feelings are not neglected but they are emasculated, and comfort and sensuality are relegated to the lowest level. The intellectual elite who rule the state have an ascetic existence in barracks so that they are not distracted from the contemplation of the pure Ideas. All of this seems unduly demanding and severe, depriving life of color.

In addition, the world of enjoyment is treated with contempt by Plato except for the charms of theoretical debate; when someone suggests the good might be pleasure Socrates exclaims, "Heaven forbid." In the same way, art, poetry, and drama are banned or censored if they interfere with moral development and modes of music are only allowed if they are uplifting. Even the beautiful Homeric myths are criticized because the gods are sometimes pictured as quarreling among themselves or philandering with mortals; they even laugh uproariously. Plato considered this behavior undignified and a bad example for the young.

However, such an astringent life of reason, so completely disciplined and virtuous, neglects the basic joy in living. To feel contempt for the physical world and the body and the gratifications of the senses seems to exclude too much that is fulfilling and important. Although Socrates described the rational ideal in a lyrical and charming way it is still a frozen world of pure ideas not a fully embodied existence, and the guardians who deal with the administration of justice touch life only at its driest point. Even though Plato spoke of harmony and balance in the individual, it is the mind that was crucial to him not the heart or will. And because of this we come away from his system wanting the human, immediate experience of living—some warmth rather than metaphysical light. We may not go as far as David Hume, who once said "reason is, and ought to be, the slave of the passions," but neither do we want man to be a disembodied intellect.

2. A second point of criticism has to do with Plato's authoritarian politics that places the guardians in a position of absolute power. He was antidemocratic and actually endorsed a dictatorial system of government, not headed by fascist leaders or a politburo but by an intellectual elite. This position is the logical outcome of his belief that the bulk of the people are appetitive, fluctuating erratically from one desire to another without any guiding purpose. Just as the children should not govern the family, the people cannot be put in charge of the state. Democracy, to Plato's mind, is mob rule. The guardians, on the other hand, are qualified to govern the state by virtue of their superior rationality that above all enables them to understand the universal idea of justice.

It is his theory of the world of Ideas that led Plato to construct an authoritarian system of government, with only those who know the truth fit to rule. Obviously this is a highly dangerous doctrine, for all dictators claim to know what is best for the people and treat the citizenry as rabble—only interested, as Juvenal said of plebeians, in *panem et circenses*, bread and circuses. For this reason Plato has been called "the father of totalitarianism." He favors autocratic rule of the gifted few, and historically this has meant the entrenched minority using their position for personal power and advantage. Prior to the Reformation the Catholic Church became corrupt in this way and we have a modern example in Soviet Russia, where a dictatorship of the proletariat, ruling on behalf of the people, now grants special priveleges to the communist hierarchy. In Baron Acton's famous phrase, "power tends to corrupt and absolute power corrupts absolutely."

In a democratic system we assume that we are much safer entrusting ourselves to the general populace, especially an educated citizenry, and that a broad base of political authority is more reliable than a narrow one. It is also assumed that citizens have sufficient intelligence, good will, and rationality to be self-governing. Even if we assume the reality of a world of Ideas we are not committed to the view that only the few can discern it; perhaps the people at large are sufficiently capable of knowing what is essentially good.

We can deal only briefly with this vast subject of Plato's political philosophy but some of the standard criticisms should also be mentioned: that he translates justice as inequality whereas the usual definition of justice includes equality; that he champions a collectivism in which the individual is sacrificed to the good of the state; and that he minimizes the freedom of citizens by demanding that each person do what he does best not what he wants to do. But it is his overall principle—that "the wise shall lead and rule, and the ignorant shall follow"— that is most disturbing, for it offers a rationale for undemocratic, authoritarian government.[9]

3. An equally vast subject is Plato's metaphysical notion of two worlds. To begin with, it is not convincing for him to argue that Ideas are the essential reality because they are imperishable and ideal, for physical things existing in space and time could be more real even though they are imperfect and decay. Permanence is not necessarily an index of reality, and the essential Form of physical objects could be an imaginative construct not the unchanging truth.

Sometimes Plato argued that we could not identify an object as being of a particular kind unless there already existed a mental category into which it could be placed. For example, we would be unable to recognize something as a tree unless there were already the idea of tree. Furthermore, he claimed that these categories exist not just prior to the objects but subsequent to them, for they would persist even if the particular examples were no longer in existence. If trees became extinct we would still have the concept of a tree.

But through our perceptual abilities we could recognize similarities between objects that would enable us to place them in a common category; we need not begin with the category or move from Idea to Sense object in order to build knowledge. And all remembrance of a class could vanish if its members disappeared a long time before (assuming, of course, that the class or idea is not indelibly printed on all human souls). Even if the idea did precede and succeed its physical representation that still would not make it eternal but only temporally longer.

Perhaps then the world of sense objects contains the greater reality with ideas as mere shadows; the forms may function as reflections of actual, concrete things. And perhaps we should not withdraw to the realm of thought, which may be an imaginary world to inhabit, but remain in touch with our senses, experiencing this transitory but vital life instead of rationally contemplating its forms.

At the same time there is something elevating and sublime about Plato's world of objective ideas, the perfect models of all earthly objects from horses and trees to beauty, truth, and goodness. And for society and the individual to be governed by rational intelligence does hold a great deal of appeal. Certainly a worthwhile life cannot be achieved without rationality, but how great a part it should play is an ongoing question. The more we concentrate on our reason the more we differentiate ourselves from animals—and the closer we move to machines.

Notes

1. The label was also given because the Cynics met in a gymnasium called the Cynosarges and was actually a pun referring both to their meeting place and doglike appearance.
2. Antisthenes supposedly derived his views from Socrates' contempt for material goods. On one occasion, for example, Socrates said, "You, Antiphon, would seem to suggest that happiness consists in luxury and extravagance; I hold a different creed. To have no wants at all is, to my mind, an attribute of godhead; to have as few wants as possible the nearest approach to godhead." Xenophon, *Memorabilia*, i, 6.
3. Socrates is celebrated by the Stoics for his calmness at the time of his death (which has a counterpart in Seneca), and for his poise, rationality, and devotion to philosophy. Not only was it considered virtuous to control one's reaction to death, but suicide was strongly endorsed by the Stoics as an honorable act.
4. Burton F. Porter, *The Good Life: Alternatives in Ethics* (New York: Macmillan, 1980), 159. See also Everett S. Millard, *Ideals of Life* (New York: Wiley, 1954), 107–108.
5. Compare, for example, Spinoza's theory that thought and "extension" have

"nothing in common with one another" (*Ethics,* Part I, Axiom 5); for Spinoza, mental events simply parallel physical events.

6. The dialogues are generally divided into early, middle, and late, with the early dialogues assumed to express Socrates ideas and the middle and late, those of Plato. Others attribute the metaphysical and epistemological dialogues as Platonic and those dealing with individual ethics as Socratic. The entire issue, called *the Socratic problem,* remains in doubt.

7. The citizen and the state were probably too closely identified in Greek thought and by not differentiating sufficiently between the person and the collective they confused ethics and politics.

8. *The Dialogues of Plato,* trans. B. Jowett (Oxford: Oxford University Press, 1924), vol. 3: 25. In addition to Jowett, a number of excellent translations can be recommended including those of F. M. Cornford, G. M. Grube, A. D. Lindsay, and R. Sterling and William Scott.

9. For a notable (albeit controversial) analysis of Plato's utopian state see Karl R. Popper, *The Open Society and Its Enemies* (Princeton, N.J.: Princeton University Press, 1950), vol. 1.

Bibliography

AARON, R. I. *The Theory of Universals.* Oxford: Oxford University Press, 1952.

ANNAS, JULIA. *An Introduction to Plato's Republic.* Oxford: Oxford University Press, 1981.

ARNOLD, E. V. *Roman Stoicism.* Cambridge: Cambridge University Press, 1911.

AYER, A. J. "Particulars and Universals." *Proceedings of the Aristotelian Society* 34 (1933–34): 51–62.

BARKER, ERNEST. *Greek Political Theory.* London: Methuen, 1925.

BENN, S. I., and R. S. PETERS. *Social Principles and the Democratic State.* New York: Free Press, 1964.

BEVAN, E. *Stoics and Sceptics.* Oxford: Oxford University Press, 1913.

BLANSHARD, B. *Reason and Goodness.* London: Allen and Unwin, 1961.

————. *Four Reasonable Men.* New York: Harper & Row, 1984.

BRUMBAUGH, ROBERT S. *The Philosophers of Greece.* Albany: State University of New York Press, 1981.

CORNFORD, FRANCIS. *Before and After Socrates.* Cambridge: University Press, 1954.

CROSS, R. C., and A. D. WOOZLEY. *Plato's Republic: A Philosophical Commentary.* London: St. Martin's Press, 1979.

CROSSMAN, R. H. S. *Plato Today.* Oxford: Oxford University Press, 1939.

DAVIDSON, WILLIAM. *The Stoic Creed.* Edinburgh: T. and T. Clark, 1907.

DE VOGEL, C. J. "The Present State of the Socratic Problem." *Phronesis* 1 (1955): 2ff.

DIOGENES LAERTIUS. *Lives of the Eminent Philosophers,* trans. R. D. Hicks. Cambridge: Harvard University Press, 1950.

DUDLEY, D. R. *History of Cynicism.* London: Methuen, 1937.

EDELSTEIN, L. *The Meaning of Stoicism.* Cambridge: Harvard University Press, 1966.

EPICTETUS. *Works,* trans. A. Oldfather. London: Heinemann; and Cambridge: Harvard University Press, 1925–28.

FIELD, G. C. *Plato and His Contemporaries.* New York: E. P. Dutton, 1930.

FINDLAY, J. N. *Plato: The Written and Unwritten Doctrines.* New York: Humanities Press, 1974.

FULLER, B. A. G. *History of Greek Philosophy,* vol. 2. New York: Holt, 1931.

GOMPERZ, T. *The Greek Thinkers,* trans. L. Magnus and G. G. Berry. New York: Humanities Press, 1901–12.

GOULD, J. *The Development of Plato's Ethics.* London: Cambridge University Press, 1955.

GRUBE, G. M. *Plato's Thought.* Indianapolis: Hackett, 1980.

HARE, R.M. *Plato.* Oxford: Oxford University Press, 1982.

HICKS, R. D. *Stoic and Epicurean.* New York: Charles Scribner, 1910.

HOBHOUSE, L. T. *The Metaphysical Theory of the State.* New York: Macmillan, 1915.

HUBY, P. *Plato and Modern Morality.* London: Macmillan, 1972.

IRWIN, T. *Plato's Moral Theory.* Oxford: Clarendon Press, 1977.

LEVINSON, R. B. *In Defense of Plato.* Cambridge: Harvard University Press, 1953.

MARCUS AURELIUS. *Meditations,* trans. J. Collier. New York: F. M. Lupton, 1916. [Cf. trans. of A. S. L. Farquharson and of G. Long.]

MURPHY, ARTHUR E. *The Uses of Reason.* New York: Macmillan, 1943.

NETTLESHIP, R. C. *Lectures on the Republic of Plato.* New York: Macmillan, 1898.

OAKELEY, H. D. *Greek Ethical Thought.* Boston: Beacon Press, 1950.

OATES, W. J. *The Stoic and Epicurean Philosophers.* New York: Random House, 1940.

OVERSTREET, H. B. *The Mature Mind.* New York: Norton, 1949.

PEARS, D. F. "Universals." *Philosophical Quarterly* (1950–51): 218–27.

POPPER, KARL R. *The Open Society and Its Enemies.* Princeton, N.J.: Princeton University Press, 1950.

RIST, J. M. *Stoic Philosophy.* Cambridge: Cambridge University Press, 1969.

———. (ED.). *The Stoics.* Berkeley: University of California Press, 1978.

ROGERS, A. K. *The Socratic Problem.* New Haven: Yale University Press, 1933.

SAYRE, F. *The Greek Cynics.* Baltimore: J. H. Furst, 1948.

SENECA. *Moral Essays,* trans. J. W. Basore. London: Heinemann; and Cambridge: Harvard University Press, 1935.

SESONSKE, A., ED. *Plato's Republic.* Belmont, Calif.: Wadsworth, 1966.

SHOREY, PAUL. *What Plato Said.* Chicago: University of Chicago Press, 1933.

SPITZ, D. *Patterns of Antidemocratic Thought.* New York: Free Press, 1949.

STACE, W. T. *A Critical History of Greek Philosophy.* New York: Macmillan, 1920.

TAYLOR, A. E. *Plato, The Man and His Work.* London: Methuen and New York: Humanities Press, 1926.

———. *Socrates.* New York: Appleton-Century-Crofts, 1933.

TOULMIN, S. *The Place of Reason in Ethics.* Cambridge: Cambridge University Press, 1950.

VLASTOS, G., ED. *The Philosophy of Socrates.* Garden City, N.Y.: Doubleday, 1971.

———. *Platonic Studies.* Princeton, N.J.: Princeton University Press, 1981.

WHITE, N. P. A. *A Companion to Plato's Republic.* Indianapolis: Hackett, 1979.

WENLEY, R. M. *Stoicism and Its Influence.* New York: Cooper Square, 1963.

WILD, JOHN. *Plato's Modern Enemies and the Theory of Natural Law.* Chicago: University of Chicago Press, 1953.

WOODBRIDGE, F. J. E. *The Son of Apollo.* Boston: Houghton Mifflin, 1929.

XENAKIS, I. *Epictetus.* The Hague, Holland: Martinus Nijhoff, 1969.

XENOPHON. *Memorabilia.* Cambridge: Harvard University Press, 1923.

ZELLER, E. *Socrates and the Socratic Schools,* trans. O. J. Reichel. London: Longmans, 1885.

———. *Stoics, Epicureans and Sceptics,* trans. O. J. Reichel. London: Longmans, 1892.

CHAPTER 9

Formalism

It is one thing to perform an act because it is reasonable but another to do something because it is right. That is, apart from rationality as an end or a means, a worthwhile life could be thought to consist in following correct principles of behavior. These principles might be determined through rational reflection or intuitive apprehension but, regardless of the method, a good life might be regarded as one in which we do what is right.

Such a view is called *formalism* or deontologism, which can be defined as the theory that we should live in accordance with principles of right conduct. The rightness or wrongness of actions is thought to lie outside ourselves and not in any subjective attitude we might take. Certain acts are right to do, others are wrong, and we are obliged to pursue the one and avoid the other. According to the formalist prescription, we ought to meet our ethical obligations, do our duty, live in terms of our understanding of the moral responsibilities binding upon us.

Kantianism: Willing Universal Principles

The most outstanding representative of the formalist approach to ethics is Immanuel Kant (1724–1804). Kant was a German philosopher best known for his work in epistemology and metaphysics but who also contributed one of the most profound theories of ethics ever devised. In a famous quote he said "Two things fill the mind with ever new and increasing admiration and awe, the oftener and more steadily they are reflected on: the starry heavens above me and the moral law within me."

His philosophic reputation is based on three major works: *The Critique of Pure Reason, The Critique of Practical Reason,* and *The Critique of Judgment.* The first book is his magnum opus, but his ethical views are contained in the second critique and in a shorter work preceding it that can be translated as *The Metaphysical Foundations of Morals.*[1] According to Kant's own statement, his "sole aim" in this book was "to seek out and establish *the supreme principle of morality,*" and it stands as the clearest, most compact statement of his ethical position.

Kant exerted a profound influence on philosophic thinking throughout the nineteenth century and well into the twentieth. His ideas were revolutionary, which is peculiarly at variance with the ordinariness of his personal life. He lived a precise, methodical existence as professor of logic and metaphysics at the University of Königsberg, never marrying, never traveling more than forty miles from his native city, and never varying his daily routine. He arose at five every morning, was in bed by ten every night, and the townspeople used to set their watches by his three o'clock walk. From a safe distance he admired Rousseau and the French revolution, and when the Prussian king asked him not to publish any more of his "alarming" thoughts on religion he dutifully obeyed. As one writer phrased it, "Kant's life passed like the most regular of verbs." Nevertheless, the system of ideas that he produced is one of the great monuments of philosophy, and in the profundity of his thought he is often compared to Plato and Aristotle.

Intentionalism, Teleologism, and Formalism

In order to understand Kant's ethics we must recall a distinction made between three different criteria for judging the moral quality of actions (see page 170 ff.). According to the standard of *intentionalism* an act is praiseworthy when it is performed with good intentions, that is, with proper motives or reasons. Wanting what is best is the most important element in assessing conduct, regardless of the way things turn out. A good-hearted person who tries earnestly to do what is right can do no wrong, even if his actions produce negligible or harmful results. Conversely, someone with bad intentions can never be praised for what he does; his evil mindedness contaminates any benefits his actions might bring. As Blake writes, "A truth that's told with bad intent/ Beats all the lies you can invent."[2] If you want to kill them with kindness, or if mother love is meant as "smother love," then the virtues become vices.

This is the criteria we use when we say "they meant well" in approving an action, because it seems that having a good will makes up for a great deal of harm. If we receive a present that we dislike we qualify our reaction by saying "It's the thought that counts." In the same way, if a Boy Scout helps an old woman across the street we think he has done something generous, and this judgment would not change even if the old woman were struck by some falling bricks on the other side. In evaluating conduct we decide whether the motives at work were basically high or low. If the intentions were honorable, if the person's heart was in the right place, then his action is morally praiseworthy.

But isn't the road to hell paved with good intentions? The intentionalist does not mean that weak willed people, who are full of noble wishes but never translate their feelings into actions, deserve praise for what they would like to see happen. Rather, those people who exercise their will and try to the best of their ability to do what is right should be applauded for their efforts.

Teleologism or consequentialism, on the other hand, maintains that the outcome or results of an action determines its moral quality. Regardless of the agent's intention the significant factor involved in weighing conduct is the harm or good that is produced. If a person, with the best will in the world, acts in such a way that many people are seriously hurt, that action cannot be praised. As William James states in another context, "By their fruits ye shall know them not by their roots." Other philosophers have spoken of the "fallacy of origins," or the "biographical fallacy," when criticizing the view that the source of an object, idea, or action defines its value.

According to the teleological view only the effect matters, the benefit or injury that results as a consequence of an act being performed. For example, we can sympathize with a person who says "I didn't know the gun was loaded; I never meant to kill him," but we cannot excuse the person or say he acted rightly. The hard reality is that someone has been shot. The person may be sorry and may not have acted "with malice aforethought" or "mens rea" (an evil mind) but that does not change the facts.

A third approach is to celebrate neither the intention behind an act nor the consequences of it but the nature of the act itself. Such a position is called *formalism* or deontologism and it holds that actions should be judged in terms of their intrinsic worth. If we do the right thing, which might mean keeping a promise, saving a life, telling the truth, and so forth, then the reason or result does not matter. At least it counts far less because the main consideration is the inherent value of the act. To use our earlier examples, we should not keep a promise in order to be regarded as a conscientious, dependable person but because we recognize an obligation to keep promises. And if we can save a life we should do so, not because the person might then contribute enormously to society but because we have a responsibility to preserve human life. For the same reason, we ought to tell the truth, not in the hope that people will reciprocate and refrain from lying to us but simply out of a sense that truth telling is right.

Obviously the formalistic theory assumes the objectivity of values rather than believing that everything is relative. One man's meat should be every man's meat, according to the formalist, and action must be based on our awareness that certain acts are right in themselves and therefore ought to be done.

Immanuel Kant accepted two of these criteria in combination and excluded the third. He held that genuine moral judgments should take into account both the intention of the person and the character of the act, but the consequences to oneself or to others are irrelevant. Consequences should not be considered, Kant argued, because they may be out of our hands; external circumstances can always affect the outcome of an act, so it would not be fair to praise or blame a person for what is beyond his power. For example, if someone with "a heart of gold" gave all of his savings to alleviate starvation in a third world country, his money could be diverted to a terrorist organization and result in death not life for the people. What the person intended to do, on the other hand, was up to him and that benevolent attitude is what should be judged. Individuals are morally responsible only for their motives not the ramifications of their actions, which are external to them and often beyond their control.

This is why Kant began *The Metaphysical Principles of Morals* by saying that nothing "can be taken as a good without qualification except a *good will*" and "A good will is good not because of what it effects or accomplishes — because of its fitness for attaining some proposed end; it is good through its willing alone — that is, good in itself."

But when, exactly, is the will good? Here Kant introduces his formalistic viewpoint by saying that a good will is one that performs an action out of a sense of its rightness. If a person recognizes his duty to follow the objective "moral law" binding upon him, and tailors his actions to the principles of that law, then his will is being used in a moral way.

This means that a good will is not prompted by fine feelings of compassion, benevolence, and so forth but must be based solely on moral principles or maxims. For example, saving a drowning child because of a sudden tender impulse has no moral merit; neither does giving money to a beggar on a whim or out of sympathy. Even though such actions seem humane, they are actually valueless from a moral point of view. But if someone rescues a child because he recognizes an obligation to do so then the act has moral worth, and if the beggar is given money on the principle that "people who are in need should be helped" then it becomes something commendable. It is only when actions are performed "not from inclination, but from duty," Kant wrote, that they have any "moral content."

Even if our natural inclinations coincide with moral principles, so that the same action is done from impulse as from a sense of duty, we receive no credit unless our motivation is to obey the moral law. Only the rational will is reliable, for it operates in terms of external obligations; inclination, by contrast, is a subjective matter, changing with the person's mood.

Kant's formalism also means that if our motivation is to obtain our own advantage or even the well being of others, then our will is not good and our actions are not ethical. Utilitarianism is morally deficient to Kant for precisely this reason, that it justifies any action so long as it generates happiness. Honesty, for instance, is only a virtue if it provides the greatest happiness for the greatest number, but if dishonesty had greater utility in certain circumstances then the utilitarian would advocate dishonesty. The same holds true for all values in a utilitarian system, which means that there are no values at all. The ends justify the means, the situation dictates the type of action that is called for, and the will operates in the service of expediency rather than in the light of moral standards. For Kant, virtues such as honesty are not justified by their instrumental value, that is by their usefulness in attaining some purpose, but only by being the appropriate way to behave.

Moral principles, Kant argued, should take the form of *categorical* not *hypothetical* imperatives. A hypothetical imperative always comes freighted with conditions; it carries ifs and buts and depends upon the situation. If you want to lose weight then you should avoid fattening foods or If you want to be natural then you should live in the country. Categorical imperatives, on the other hand, state absolute rules — actions that are correct categorically, without exception or qualification. Be open and honest, Respect people's rights, or Support freedom and justice could be candidates for imperatives of a categorical kind. Such commands of duty are absolute; they are not justified by their context but by their nature. We *pursue* goals but we *follow* moral principles because they are recognized as obligations independent of any consequences.

The Categorical and Practical Imperatives

The next question that arises is how one can decide where one's duty lies. What determines whether a principle is truly moral and should be done? If the will is to be a good will, which actions should it intend to perform?

Kant's answer takes the form of what can be called the ultimate *Categorical Imperative*. In one of the most celebrated formulas in ethics he writes "I ought never to act except in such a way *that I can also will that my maxim should become a universal law.*" In other words, the Categorical Imperative states that we can establish which principles should be followed by asking ourselves whether they would be moral for anyone to do in similar circumstances. If it is wrong for my neighbor to steal my property then it is wrong for me to steal his; in fact, stealing another person's property is wrong for all people, at all times, in all places. Too often we use a double standard in our behavior and make an exception for ourselves, saying that it is all right if *we* do something questionable but we would not want anyone else to behave in the same way. When we do this, Kant said, we are only rationalizing our own immorality. An act that is truly right is capable of being subsumed under a universal principle, that is, the rule under which it falls should be applicable to everyone.

One example Kant uses to illustrate the functioning of the Categorical Imperative is that of borrowing money. If we do not intend to pay back a loan should we nevertheless promise to repay it in order to obtain the money? To reach a moral decision on this question we must ask ourselves whether we could will that everyone do likewise. Could we maintain that whenever anyone wants to borrow money he is justified in making an insincere promise to repay it? Obviously not, Kant said, for if everyone behaved in the same way then no one would ever lend money. Once we apply the categorical imperative we see that it cannot be universalized and, for that reason, cannot be right. If everyone practiced it then no one could practice it; the action would become impossible to do, which shows that it is basically immoral.[3]

Kant is actually asserting that whatever is objectively right is absolutely right and holds true universally. Just as $9 + 6 = 15$ is true for everyone, or the euclidean axiom that a whole is equal to the sum of its parts must be accepted by reasonable people as true, in the same way genuinely moral principles apply to all people without exception. Whatever is really right is right for everyone.

It is our rationality that tells us which principles are actually correct as we apply the Categorical Imperative (reason's primary tool) to moral issues. Wrong actions are also identified by reason, for if an action cannot be universalized without self-contradiction then we know it is not right. As was mentioned in Chapter 1, the primary axiom of logic is the Law of Noncontradiction, that no object can be said to possess and not possess the same characteristic, no statement can be both true and false. We cannot logically assert, for example, that a swan is white and not white at the same time. By the same token, we cannot recommend any action that contradicts itself when applied to everyone. This is why it is wrong to make a false promise, not because of the Golden Rule that we should do unto others as we would have them do unto us but because such action becomes logically impossible once we attempt to universalize it.

To further identify the realm of moral actions Kant added a second principle called the *Practical Imperative*, which he described as follows: "*Act in such a way that you always treat humanity, whether in your own person or in the person of any other, never simply as a means, but always at the same time as an end.*"

He arrived at this imperative by considering that reason determines the will to act "*in accordance with the idea of certain laws,*" which suggests to him that self-determined rational beings must be worthwhile in themselves. The rational person, who is the "ground" for the will to seek objective principles, must possess absolute value. Therefore, human beings, insofar as they are rational creatures, should be regarded as ends in themselves and not mere means.

Notice that Kant regarded people as having absolute worth because of their rationality. Any rational being in the universe deserves the same respect, and if man were not a rational animal he would not have intrinsic worth. In a Utilitarian system people are morally relevant because they feel pleasure and pain, in a Kantian system because they are autonomous and rational.

Notice also that he did not say human beings should never be treated as a means but never as a means only. He recognized that, to some extent, we cannot avoid using one another. Doctors are used for curing illness, policemen to protect us, teachers for acquiring knowledge, and so forth. But his plea was that we also regard one another as ends, that we should not behave as if people were just instruments or objects. As a governing principle we should act for other people not just on them.

The Practical Imperative, then, would prohibit racism and sexism, slavery and rape, the invasion of privacy and child abuse, manipulation and exploitation, all of which fail to allow people the dignity they deserve. For this reason it occupies an important position as a standard for moral behavior.

To summarize Kant's formalism, he maintains that having a good will is crucial to correct conduct, and the will is good when it acts not out of natural inclination or to accomplish some end but in accord with the rightness of an action. We should respond to our moral obligation to do what is right, which means obeying categorical not hypothetical imperatives. These right actions can be identified by rationally understanding that the overall form of morality lies in *the* Categorical Imperative. That is, we should recognize that moral behavior is universalizable behavior. As a second governing principle the Practical Imperative states that human beings, by virtue of their rationality, should be treated as ends not just as means.

Kant's broad ideal for a worthwhile life, then, is to discover universal moral principles and to fulfill our moral duty by acting in obedience to them. It is a severe and uncompromising theory but one that he thinks we are obliged to live. In the following excerpt from *The Metaphysical Foundations of Morals* Kant gives us the essential outlines of this very pure ethic.

The Foundations of Morality*

The Good Will

It is impossible to conceive anything at all in the world, or even out of it, which can be taken as good without qualification, except a *good will*. Intelligence, wit, judgement, and any other *talents* of the mind we may care to name, or courage, resolution, and constancy of purpose, as qualities of *temperament,* are without doubt good and desirable in many respects; but they can also be extremely bad and hurtful when the will is not good which has to make use of these gifts of nature, and which for this reason has the term *'character'* applied to its peculiar quality. It is exactly the same with *gifts of fortune.* Power, wealth, honour, even health and that complete well-being and

*Reprinted with permission from Immanuel Kant, *Groundwork of the Metaphysic of Morals,* trans. H. J. Paton (New York: Harper & Row, 1964), 61–71, 95–97.

contentment with one's state which goes by the name of *'happiness'*, produce boldness, and as a consequence often overboldness as well, unless a good will is present by which their influence on the mind—and so too the whole principle of action—may be corrected and adjusted to universal ends; not to mention that a rational and impartial spectator can never feel approval in contemplating the uninterrupted prosperity of a being graced by no touch of a pure and good will, and that consequently a good will seems to constitute the indispensable condition of our very worthiness to be happy.

Some qualities are even helpful to this good will itself and can make its task very much easier. They have none the less no inner unconditioned worth, but rather presuppose a good will which sets a limit to the esteem in which they are rightly held and does not permit us to regard them as absolutely good. Moderation in affections and passions, self-control, and sober reflexion are not only good in many respects: they may even seem to constitute part of the *inner* worth of a person. Yet they are far from being properly described as good without qualification (however unconditionally they have been commended by the ancients). For without the principles of a good will they may become exceedingly bad; and the very coolness of a scoundrel makes him, not merely more dangerous, but also immediately more abominable in our eyes than we should have taken him to be without it.

The Good Will and Its Results

A good will is not good because of what it effects or accomplishes—because of its fitness for attaining some proposed end: it is good through its willing alone—that is, good in itself. Considered in itself it is to be esteemed beyond comparison as far higher than anything it could ever bring about merely in order to favour some inclination or, if you like, the sum total of inclinations. Even if, by some special disfavour of destiny or by the niggardly endowment of step-motherly nature, this will is entirely lacking in power to carry out its intentions; if by its utmost effort it still accomplishes nothing, and only good will is left (not, admittedly, as a mere wish, but as the straining of every means so far as they are in our control); even then it would still shine like a jewel for its own sake as something which has its full value in itself. Its usefulness or fruitfulness can neither add to, nor subtract from, this value. Its usefulness would be merely, as it were, the setting which enables us to handle it better in our ordinary dealings or to attract the attention of those not yet sufficiently expert, but not to commend it to experts or to determine its value.

The Function of Reason

Yet in this Idea of the absolute value of a mere will, all useful results being left out of account in its assessment, there is something so strange that, in spite of all the agreement it receives even from ordinary reason, there must arise the suspicion that perhaps its secret basis is merely some high-flown fantasticality, and that we may have misunderstood the purpose of nature in attaching reason to our will as its governor. We will therefore submit our Idea to an examination from this point of view.

In the natural constitution of an organic being—that is, of one contrived for the purpose of life—let us take it as a principle that in it no organ is to be found for any end unless it is also the most appropriate to that end and the best fitted for it. Suppose now that for a being possessed of reason and a will the real purpose of nature were his *preservation,* his *welfare,* or in a word his *happiness.* In that case nature would have hit on a very bad arrangement by choosing reason in the creature to carry out this purpose. For all the actions he has to perform with this end in view, and the whole rule of his behaviour, would have been mapped out for him far more accurately by instinct; and the end in question could have been maintained far more surely by instinct than it ever can be by reason. If reason should have been imparted to this favoured creature as well, it would have had to serve him only for contemplating the happy disposition of his nature, for admiring it, for enjoying it, and for being grateful to its beneficent Cause—not for subjecting his power of appetition to such feeble and defective guidance or for meddling incompetently with the purposes of nature. In a word, nature would have prevented reason from striking out into a *practical use* and from presuming, with its feeble vision, to think out for itself a plan for happiness and for the means to its attainment. Nature would herself have taken over the choice, not only of ends, but also of means, and would with wise precaution have entrusted both to instinct alone.

In actual fact too we find that the more cultivated reason concerns itself with the aim of enjoying life and happiness, the farther does man get away from true contentment. This is why there arises in many, and that too in those who have made most trial of this use of reason, if they are only candid enough to admit it, a certain degree of *misology*—that is, a hatred of reason; for when they balance all the advantage they draw, I will not say from thinking out all the arts of ordinary indulgence, but even from science (which in the last resort seems to them to be also an indulgence of the mind), they discover that they have in fact only brought more trouble on their heads than they have gained in the way of happiness. On this account they come to envy, rather than to despise, the more common run of men, who are closer to the guidance of mere natural instinct, and who do not allow their reason to have much influence on their conduct. So far we must admit that the judgement of those who seek to moderate—and even to reduce below zero—the conceited glorification of such advantages as reason is supposed to provide in the way of happiness and contentment with life is in no way soured or ungrateful to the goodness with which the world is governed. These judgements rather have as their hidden ground the Idea of another and much more worthy purpose of existence, for which, and not for happiness, reason is quite properly designed, and to which, therefore, as a supreme condition the private purposes of man must for the most part be subordinated.

For since reason is not sufficiently serviceable for guiding the will safely as regards its objects and the satisfaction of all our needs (which it in part even multiplies)—a purpose for which an implanted natural instinct would have led us much more surely; and since none the less reason has been imparted to us as a practical power—that is, as one which is to have influence on the *will;* its true function must be to produce a *will* which is *good,* not as a *means* to some further end, but *in itself;* and for this function reason was absolutely necessary in a world where nature, in distributing her aptitudes, has everywhere else gone to work in a purposive manner. Such a will need not on this account be the sole and complete good, but it must be the highest good and the condition of all the rest, even of all our demands for happiness. In that case we can easily reconcile with the wisdom of nature our observation that the cultivation of reason which is required for the first and unconditioned purpose may in many ways, at least in this life, restrict the attainment of the second purpose—namely, happiness—which is always conditioned; and indeed that it can even reduce happiness to less than zero without nature proceeding contrary to its purpose; for reason, which recognises as its highest practical function the establishment of a good will, in attaining this end is capable only of its own peculiar kind of contentment—contentment in fulfilling a purpose which in turn is determined by reason alone, even if this fulfilment should often involve interference with the purposes of inclination.

The Good Will and Duty

We have now to elucidate the concept of a will estimable in itself and good apart from any further end. This concept, which is already present in a sound natural understanding and requires not so much to be taught as merely to be clarified, always holds the highest place in estimating the total worth of our actions and constitutes the condition of all the rest. We will therefore take up the concept of *duty,* which includes that of a good will, exposed, however, to certain subjective limitations and obstacles. These, so far from hiding a good will or disguising it, rather bring it out by contrast and make it shine forth more brightly.

The Motive of Duty

I will here pass over all actions already recognised as contrary to duty, however useful they may be with a view to this or that end; for about these the question does not even arise whether they could have been done *for the sake of duty* inasmuch as they are directly opposed to it. I will also set aside actions which in fact accord with duty, yet for which men have *no immediate inclination,* but perform them because impelled to do so by some other inclination. For there it is easy to decide whether the action which accords with duty has been done *from duty* or from some purpose of self-interest. This distinction is far more difficult to perceive when the action accords with duty and the subject has in addition an *immediate* inclination to the action. For example, it certainly accords with duty that a grocer should not overcharge his inexperienced customer; and where there is much competition a sensible shopkeeper refrains from so doing and keeps to a fixed and general price for everybody so that a child can buy from him just as well as anyone else. Thus people are served *honestly;* but this is not nearly enough to justify us in believing that the shopkeeper has acted in this way from duty or from principles of fair dealing; his interest required him to do so. We cannot assume him to have in addition an immediate inclination towards his customers, leading him, as it were out of love, to give no man preference over another in the matter of price. Thus the action was done neither from duty nor from immediate inclination, but solely from purposes of self-interest.

On the other hand, to preserve one's life is a duty, and besides this every one has also an immediate inclination to do so. But on account of this the often anxious precautions taken by the greater part of mankind for this purpose have no inner worth, and the maxim of their action is without moral content. They do protect their lives *in conformity with duty,* but not *from the motive of duty.* When on the contrary, disappointments and hopeless misery have quite taken away the taste for life; when a wretched man, strong in soul and more angered at his fate than faint-hearted or cast down, longs for death and still preserves his life without loving it — not from inclination or fear but from duty; then indeed his maxim has a moral content.

To help others where one can is a duty, and besides this there are many spirits of so sympathetic a temper that, without any further motive of vanity or self-interest, they find an inner pleasure in spreading happiness around them and take delight in the contentment of others as their own work. Yet I maintain that in such a case an action of this kind, however right and however amiable it may be, has still no genuinely moral worth. It stands on the same footing as other inclinations — for example, the inclination for honour, which if fortunate enough to hit on something beneficial and right and consequently honourable, deserves praise and encouragement, but not esteem; for its maxim lacks moral content, namely, the performance of such actions, not from inclination, but *from duty.* Suppose then that the mind of this friend of man were overclouded by sorrows of his own which extinguished all sympathy with the fate of others, but that he still had power to help those in distress, though no longer stirred by the need of others because sufficiently occupied with his own; and suppose that, when no longer moved by any inclination, he tears himself out of this deadly insensibility and does the action without any inclination for the sake of duty alone; then for the first time his action has its genuine moral worth. Still further: if nature had implanted little sympathy in this or that man's heart; if (being in other respects an honest fellow) he were cold in temperament and indifferent to the sufferings of others — perhaps because, being endowed with the special gift of patience and robust endurance in his own sufferings, he assumed the like in others or even demanded it; if such a man (who would in truth not be the worst product of nature) were not exactly fashioned by her to be a philanthropist, would he not still find in himself a source from which he might draw a worth far higher than any that a good-natured temperament can have? Assuredly he would. It is precisely in this that the worth of character begins to show — a moral worth and beyond all comparison the highest — namely, that he does good, not from inclination, but from duty.

To assure one's own happiness is a duty (at least indirectly); for discontent with one's state, in a press of cares and amidst unsatisfied wants, might easily become a great *temptation to the transgression of duty.* But here also, apart from regard to duty, all men have already of themselves the strongest and deepest inclination towards happiness, because precisely in this Idea of happiness all inclinations are combined into a sum total. The prescription for happiness is, however, often so constituted as greatly to interfere with some inclinations, and yet men cannot form under the name of 'happiness' any determinate and assured conception of the satisfaction of all inclinations as a sum. Hence it is not to be wondered at that a single inclination which is determinate as to what it promises and as to the time of its satisfaction may outweigh a wavering Idea; and that a man, for example, a sufferer from gout, may choose to enjoy what he fancies and put up with what he can — on the ground that on balance he has here at least not killed the enjoyment of the present moment because of some possibly groundless expectations of the good fortune supposed to attach to soundness of health. But in this case also, when the universal inclination towards happiness has failed to determine his will, when good health, at least for him, has not entered into his calculations as so necessary, what remains over, here as in other cases, is a law — the law of furthering his happiness, not from inclination, but from duty; and in this for the first time his conduct has a real moral worth.

It is doubtless in this sense that we should understand too the passages from Scripture in which we are commanded to love our neighbour and even our enemy. For love out of inclination cannot be commanded; but kindness done from duty — although no inclination impels us, and even although natural and unconquerable disinclination stands in our way — is *practical*, and not *pathological*, love, residing in the will and not in the propensions of feeling, in principles of action and not of melting compassion; and it is this practical love alone which can be an object of command.

The Formal Principle of Duty

Our second proposition is this: An action done from duty has its moral worth, *not in the purpose* to be attained by it, but in the maxim according with which it is decided upon; it depends therefore, not on the realisation of the object of the action, but solely on the *principle* of *volition* in accordance with which, irrespective of all objects of the faculty of desire, the action has been performed. That the purposes we may have in our actions, and also their effects considered as ends and motives of the will, can give to actions no unconditioned and moral worth is clear from what has gone before. Where then can this worth be found if we are not to find it in the will's relation to the effect hoped for from the action? It can be found nowhere but *in the principle of the will*, irrespective of the ends which can be brought about by such an action; for between its *a priori* principle, which is formal, and its *a posteriori* motive, which is material, the will stands, so to speak, at a parting of the ways; and since it must be determined by some principle, it will have to be determined by the formal principle of volition when an action is done from duty, where, as we have seen, every material principle is taken away from it.

Reverence for the Law

Our third proposition, as an inference from the two preceding, I would express thus: *Duty is the necessity to act out of reverence for the law.* For an object as the effect of my proposed action I can have an *inclination*, but *never reverence,* precisely because it is merely the effect, and not the activity, of a will. Similarly for inclination as such, whether my own or that of another, I cannot have reverence: I can at most in the first case approve, and in the second case sometimes even love — that is, regard it as favourable to my own advantage. Only something which is conjoined with my will solely as a ground and never as an effect — something which does not serve my inclination, but outweighs it or at least leaves it entirely out of account in my choice — and therefore only bare law for its own sake, can be an object of reverence and therewith a command. Now an action done from duty has to set aside altogether the influence of inclination, and along with inclination every object of the will; so there is nothing left able to determine the will except objectively the *law* and subjectively *pure reverence* for this practical law, and therefore the maxim of obeying this law even to the detriment of all my inclinations.

Thus the moral worth of an action does not depend on the result expected from it, and so too does not depend on any principle of action that needs to borrow its motive from this expected result. For all these results (agreeable states and even the promotion of happiness in others) could have been brought about by other causes as well, and consequently their production did not require the will of a rational being, in which, however, the highest and unconditioned good can alone be found. Therefore nothing but the *idea of the law* in itself, *which admittedly is present only in a rational being* — so far as it, and not an expected result, is the ground determining the will — can constitute that pre-eminent good which we call moral, a good which is already present in the person acting on this idea and has not to be awaited merely from the result.

The Categorical Imperative

But what kind of law can this be the thought of which, even without regard to the results expected from it, has to determine the will if this is to be called good absolutely and without qualification? Since I have robbed the will of every inducement that might arise for it as a consequence of obeying any particular law, nothing is left but the conformity of actions to universal law as such, and this alone must serve the will as its principle. That is to say, I ought never to act except in such a way *that I can also will that my maxim should become a universal law.* Here bare conformity to universal law as such (without having as its base any law prescribing particular actions) is what serves the will as its principle, and must so serve it if duty is not to be everywhere an empty delusion and a chimerical concept. The ordinary reason of mankind also agrees with this completely in its practical judgements and always has the aforesaid principle before its eyes.

Take this question, for example. May I not, when I am hard pressed, make a promise with the intention of not keeping it? Here I readily distinguish the two senses which the question can have — Is it prudent, or is it right, to make a false promise? The first no doubt can often be the case. I do indeed see that it is not enough for me to extricate myself from present embarrassment by this subterfuge: I have to consider whether from this lie there may not subsequently accrue to me much greater inconvenience than that from which

I now escape, and also — since, with all my supposed *astuteness*, to foresee the consequences is not so easy that I can be sure there is no chance, once confidence in me is lost, of this proving far more disadvantageous than all the ills I now think to avoid — whether it may not be a *more prudent* action to proceed here on a general maxim and make it my habit not to give a promise except with the intention of keeping it. Yet it becomes clear to me at once that such a maxim is always founded solely on fear of consequences. To tell the truth for the sake of duty is something entirely different from doing so out of concern for inconvenient results; for in the first case the concept of the action already contains in itself a law for me, while in the second case I have first of all to look around elsewhere in order to see what effects may be bound up with it for me. When I deviate from the principle of duty, this is quite certainly bad; but if I desert my prudential maxim, this can often be greatly to my advantage, though it is admittedly safer to stick to it. Suppose I seek, however, to learn in the quickest way and yet unerringly how to solve the problem 'Does a lying promise accord with my duty?' I have then to ask myself 'Should I really be content that my maxim (the maxim of getting out of a difficulty by a false promise) should hold as a universal law (one valid both for myself and others)? And could I really say to myself that every one may make a false promise if he finds himself in a difficulty from which he can extricate himself in no other way?' I then become aware at once that I can indeed will to lie, but I can by no means will a universal law of lying; for by such a law there could properly be no promises at all, since it would be futile to profess a will for future action to others who would not believe my profession or who, if they did so over-hastily, would pay me back in like coin; and consequently my maxim, as soon as it was made a universal law, would be bound to annul itself.

Thus I need no far-reaching ingenuity to find out what I have to do in order to possess a good will. Inexperienced in the course of world affairs and incapable of being prepared for all the chances that happen in it, I ask myself only 'Can you also will that your maxim should become a universal law?' Where you cannot, it is to be rejected, and that not because of a prospective loss to you or even to others, but because it cannot fit as a principle into a possible enactment of universal law. For such an enactment reason compels my immediate reverence, into whose grounds (which the philosopher may investigate) I have as yet no *insight*, although I do at least understand this much: reverence is the assessment of a worth which far outweighs all the worth of what is commended by inclination, and the necessity for me to act out of *pure* reverence for the practical law is what constitutes duty, to which every other motive must give way because it is the condition of a will good *in itself*, whose value is above all else.

. . .

The Formula of the End in Itself

The will is conceived as a power of determining oneself to action *in accordance with the idea of certain laws*. And such a power can be found only in rational beings. Now what serves the will as a subjective ground of its self-determination is an *end;* and this, if it is given by reason alone, must be equally valid for all rational beings. What, on the other hand, contains merely the ground of the possibility of an action whose effect is an end is called a *means.* The subjective ground of a desire is an *impulsion (Triebfeder);* the objective ground of a volition is a *motive* —*(Bewegungsgrund).* Hence the difference between subjective ends, which are based on impulsions, and objective ends, which depend on motives valid for every rational being. Practical principles are *formal* if they abstract from all subjective ends; they are *material,* on the other hand, if they are based on such ends and consequently on certain impulsions. Ends that a rational being adopts arbitrarily as *effects* of his action (material ends) are in every case only relative; for it is solely their relation to special characteristics in the subject's power of appetition which gives them their value. Hence this value can provide no universal principles, no principles valid and necessary for all rational beings and also for every volition — that is, no practical laws. Consequently all these relative ends can be the ground only of hypothetical imperatives.

Suppose, however, there were something *whose existence* has in itself an absolute value, something which as *an end in itself* could be a ground of determinate laws; then in it, and in it alone, would there be the ground of a possible categorical imperative — that is, of a practical law.

Now I say that man, and in general every rational being, *exists* as an end in himself, *not merely as a means* for arbitrary use by this or that will: he must in all his actions, whether they are directed to himself or to other rational beings, always be viewed *at the same time as an end.* All the objects of inclination have only a conditioned value; for if there were not these inclinations and the needs grounded on them, their object would be valueless. Inclinations themselves, as sources of needs, are so far from having an absolute value to make them desirable for their own sake that it must rather be the universal wish of every rational being to be wholly free from them. Thus the value of all objects that can *be produced* by our action is always conditioned. Beings whose existence depends, not on our will, but on nature, have none the less, if they are non-rational beings, only a relative value as means and are consequently called *things.* Rational beings, on the other hand, are called *persons* because their nature already marks them out as ends in themselves — that is, as something which ought not to be used merely as a means — and consequently imposes to that extent a limit on all arbitrary treatment for them (and is an object of reverence). Persons, therefore, are not merely subjective ends whose existence as an object of our actions has a value *for us:* they are *objective ends* — that is, things whose existence is in itself an end, and indeed an end such that in its place we can put no other end to which they should serve *simply* as means; for unless this is so, nothing at all of *absolute* value would be found anywhere. But if all value were conditioned — that is, contingent — then no supreme principle could be found for reason at all.

If then there is to be a supreme practical principle and — so far as the human will is concerned — a categorical imperative, it must be such that from the idea of something which is necessarily an end for every one because it is an *end in itself* it forms *objective* principle of the will and consequently can serve as a practical law. The ground of this principle is: *Rational nature exists as an end in itself.* This is the way in which a man necessarily conceives his own existence: it is therefore so far a *subjective* principle of human actions. But it is also the way in which every other rational being conceives his existence on the same rational ground which is valid also for me; hence it is at the same time an *objective* principle, from which, as a supreme practical ground, it must be possible to derive all laws for the will. The practical imperative will therefore be as follows: *Act in such a way that you always treat humanity, whether in your own person or in the person of any other, never simply as a means, but always at the same time as an end.* We will now consider whether this can be carried out in practice.

Illustrations

First, as regards the concept of necessary duty to oneself, the man who contemplates suicide will ask 'Can my action be compatible with the Idea of humanity *as an end in itself?*' If he does away with himself in order to escape from a painful situation, he is making use of a person merely as *a means* to maintain a tolerable state of affairs till the end of his life. But man is not a thing—not something to be used *merely* as a means: he must always in all his actions be regarded as an end in himself. Hence I cannot dispose of man in my person by maiming, spoiling, or killing. (A more precise determination of this principle in order to avoid all misunderstanding—for example, about having limbs amputated to save myself or about exposing my life to danger in order to preserve it, and so —I must here forego: this question belongs to morals proper.)

Secondly, so far as necessary or strict duty to others is concerned, the man who has a mind to make a false promise to others will see at once that he is intending to make use of another man *merely as a means* to an end he does not share. For the man whom I seek to use for my own purposes by such a promise cannot possibly agree with my way of behaving to him, and so cannot himself share the end of the action. This incompatibility with the principle of duty to others leaps to the eye more obviously when we bring in examples of attempts on the freedom and property of others. For then it is manifest that a violator of the rights of man intends to use the person of others merely as a means without taking into consideration that, as rational beings, they ought always at the same time to be rated as ends—that is, only as beings who must themselves be able to share in the end of the very same action.

Before we go on to evaluate the Kantian ethic an important distinction must be made between two types of formalism or, as the theory is usually called for purposes of this distinction, *deontologism.* The term *deontologism* is derived from the Greek *deon* (meaning obligatory or binding) and can be treated as synonymous with the formalistic theory—that we are obliged to perform morally correct actions.

Act deontologism holds that judgments regarding these obligations apply only to particular actions in specific circumstances. We can never generalize but must treat each case as unique and individual. For example, if someone is found cheating at cards we cannot apply any broad principle, such as Cheating is

reprehensible, and judge the action in those terms. Neither can we use a consequentialist criterion and decide the matter by assessing the amount of good the
winnings will do—the food it will buy for his starving children, perhaps.
Rather, we must study the facts and see whether cheating is right or wrong in
that particular situation. The decisive factor should be what we think or feel is
right under the circumstances.[4]

On the other side of the coin, *rule deontologism* maintains that we should
appeal to moral rules in judging the rightness or wrongness of conduct. Our
feelings or thoughts at the moment prove much too unreliable a guide, too
individual and prone to abuse. What's more, each action is not entirely different, it is argued, but falls into a category because of the features it holds in
common with other actions. This allows broad principles to be applied, perhaps
with certain distinctions and qualifications to allow for subgroups of cases, but
still holding fast to basic rules of behavior. For example, we can condemn
stealing in general while differentiating between shoplifting and armed
robbery.

Obviously, Immanuel Kant holds an extreme position of rule deontologism
because he believes not only that adherence to principles is fundamental to
moral conduct but that these principles are absolute and without exception.
Whether this position is tenable remains to be seen.[5]

It should also be obvious that act and rule deontologism run parallel to act and
rule utilitarianism discussed in Chapter 5, the chief difference being that deontologism is formalistic and utilitarianism is consequentialist. But to contrast each
with the other, the act deontologist tries to determine the right conduct for the
particular circumstances, the rule deontologist looks for the moral law governing all cases of that type; the act utilitarian endorses whatever action will maximize human happiness, and the rule utilitarian accepts those principles that
produce the greatest amount of happiness for the greatest number of people. It
is a searching question to ask which theory seems the most insightful and
convincing.

Evaluation

1. In the first place, Kant seems oblivious to the fact that consequences can
matter a great deal and ought to be considered in deciding on action. If by
telling the truth to someone with a weak heart we would precipitate a heart
attack, then we should not tell the truth. If following the dictum One should not
destroy human life means that we refrain from killing a homicidal maniac who is
threatening our family, then we should suspend that rule. If by keeping a
promise to love, honor, and cherish our spouse as long as we both shall live we
create an atmosphere that is destructive to our children, then we should seriously reconsider that promise. And in all these cases, incidentally, the consequences are within our control, which contrary to Kant's contention, seems very
typical.

With regard to the issue of truth telling, a contemporary philosopher Sissela
Bok has stressed the circumstances and effects that can justify lying while maintaining that Truthful statements are preferable in the absence of special considerations. In her book *Lying: Moral Choice in Public and Private Life* she discusses
lying in wartime, to children, to protect confidentiality, to conduct research,

and especially lying to medical patients about the severity of their illness. She concludes that in at least *some* of these cases lying is justified, it depends upon the beneficiality of the result.

Kant however regarded teleological thinking as the enemy of morality, mainly out of fear that it would erode principles altogether. This is certainly a real danger and it has led to doctrines of "expediency" and today's "cost-benefit" analysis. However, ignoring the consequences of action is not a corrective but the opposite defect. The ends do not justify the means but neither do the means justify the ends; both must be considered in the moral equation.

Kant's myopia can be seen in his example of the condemned man. He stated that if a man had been sentenced to hang today, that sentence should be carried out even if we knew the world was to end tomorrow. This seems absurd because no social good could possibly come of it. In the same way, George Herbert's (1593–1633) statement "Dare to be true: nothing can need a lie" is good poetry but bad philosophy.

Another way of putting this criticism is to say that the *good* achieved by action should be weighed along with principles that are *right.* It is certainly important to honor commitments, respect human life, pay one's debts, and so forth, and we might even prize the seven classic virtues of prudence, fortitude, temperance, justice, faith, hope, and charity, but overriding considerations can prevent our practicing these values. If widespread misery or destruction would occur as a result of our acting on some principle then we should give priority to the overall good instead. That is not to say that Mill was correct when he wrote "only the dry and hard consideration of the consequences of actions" really matters, but we should not go to the Kantian extreme of blindly following moral rules regardless of the harm they cause. This kind of high-mindedness can produce a dry, hard attitude in itself, a preference for principles over people that can be extremely cruel.[6]

As a psychological point, Kant's approach can lead people to feel smug and self-righteous, blaming the world when their noble actions do no good. Such individuals can feel virtuous even though they are ineffectual and actually set up situations where their actions are sure to fail, thereby confirming a high view of themselves and a low opinion of mankind.

2. Kant also can be faulted for his claim that acts have merit not when they are done from inclination but only when they are performed out of a sense of duty. For instance, refraining from killing someone is praiseworthy to Kant only if done out of a recognition that we have an obligation to preserve human life. But surely a person who does not harm someone else because he has no desire to do so deserves some kind of praise. In fact, numerous moral philosophers have held that behaving morally because it is our duty is an early stage in moral development, and that a higher level is reached when we have no inclination to do wrong. If a constant struggle takes place between our desires and our conscience then we have not arrived at moral maturity, but once the thought of hurting someone else is not even a temptation to be overcome then we are truly moral beings. And wouldn't it be far better if a person helped others because he wanted to rather than because he believed he had to and loved humanity by disposition rather than on principle? Wouldn't we prefer living next to someone with a generous disposition rather than someone who felt obliged to be kind?

3. Most of the problems encountered in Kant, however, have to do with his Categorical Imperative—the assumption that morality equals universalizability. For one thing, some principles appear to be moral even though they cannot be universalized. For example, self-sacrifice seems right in various circumstances, as in the case of a captured soldier who dies under torture rather than disclose information that would jeopardize his company. But as a principle it cannot be universalized, for if everyone were self-sacrificing there would be no one left to accept the sacrifice. Everyone would be trying to give and no one would be willing to take. Self-sacrifice then could not be considered moral in Kant's system since it entails an endless "after you Alphonse" dialogue. This clearly points up something wrong with the universalizability criterion.

Not only are some moral principles impossible to universalize but some immoral principles can be universalized without inconsistency. For instance, the rule that you should hate your neighbor rather than love your neighbor would not make for very pleasant relationships if everyone practiced it, but there is nothing logically impossible about universalizing that rule. As long as you are willing to tolerate a social environment of hatred there is nothing inconsistent in willing it for all. The same applies to the robber or murderer who accepts a society based on his own harsh code, confident that he could survive even if his actions were adopted by everyone. He may not be acting morally but there is nothing illogical in his willing that all people do likewise.

Here again we can detect something lacking in Kant's moral standard. If the Categorical Imperative can permit actions that are wrong then it cannot be the criterion for what is right. Kant held that if a rule could not be universalized it was wrong and if a rule could be universalized it was right, but neither seems to hold true.

4. Further difficulties with the Categorical Imperative begin to emerge when one tries apply it. Suppose that you believe in the principles of truth telling and preserving human life, which means in Kantian terms that your actions should always be governed by these rules. But one day a man with a smoking gun and a wild gleam in his eye asks you which way his wife went. If you know, should you tell him? Presumably if you tell the truth you will be contributing to a murder, but in order to preserve life you must lie—and lie as well as you can. In this situation you cannot follow both principles simultaneously and yet if they are genuine moral principles they must be carried out at all times without exception.

This reveals another basic flaw in Kant's system, that two universalized principles can conflict. A physician faces this dilemma in cases of euthanasia, for according to the Hippocratic Oath he should both save life and alleviate suffering. But if someone is dying an excruciating death he can end his life and release him from pain or keep him alive and perpetuate his pain. One principle or the other can be honored but not both, yet if each one is absolute neither can be broken.

This problem has bedeviled Kantianism from the outset and seems irreconcilable, for the Categorical Imperative offers no basis for deciding between conflicting duties. And if a decision could be made, only one principle would eventually emerge as moral—a supreme duty that would take precedence over all others. It would be the one that should always be done while all the rest would give way to it, thereby disqualifying them from being moral because of that exception. Assuming we could even determine such a rule, a moral system with only one rule is certainly inadequate as well as being rather odd.

5. This leads us to the most damaging criticism of Kant, which is that we cannot find a principle of conduct that would satisfy the standard of the Categorical Imperative. Nothing it seems should always be done without exception. If we claim one should never kill, we immediately find extenuating circumstances: cases of self-defense, the protection of innocent people, the safety of our country, "mercy killing" perhaps, or even the death penalty. If we propose that people should never deceive one another we can think of situations where deception is justified: cases of "white lies" intended to save someone's feelings, to reassure a panicky crowd and prevent a riot, to protect a secret important to national security, and so forth. The same holds true for each one of the rules listed in the Ten Commandments, the Sermon on the Mount, the Code of Hammurabi, the Eightfold Path, and every other compendium of moral laws. Even Kant's own Practical Imperative could be violated, for if a person must be sacrificed in order to save thousands of people we should do so even though that person would be used entirely as a means.

Kant therefore produced a very rarefied and noble standard in the Categorical Imperative, so rarefied that no principles seem to qualify as moral. An ethic such as hedonism seems cheap and vulgar by comparison and yet Kant's system, while infinitely finer, seems wholly empty.

One reason for this state of affairs is that Kant failed to distinguish between an *exception* to a rule and the *qualification* of a rule. He recognized that we tend to exclude ourselves from compliance with general rules, claiming far too often that we form a special case, and to eliminate that personal exception he opposes all exceptions. But a rule could be qualified to allow for certain types of cases where the rule does not hold, and the qualified rule could then be universalized. For example, Never take a human life unless it is in self-defense would be much more defensible as a moral principle than Never take a human life.

However, although this distinction would certainly help it does not solve the problem entirely. What about the cases cited of euthanasia or killing someone expendable in time of war? These are not cases of self-defense and yet they might be allowable. Once we start qualifying rules we might be able to include all the types of permissible cases or we might never come to the end of them; the rule could die the death of endless qualifications.

In an attempt to solve the problem twentieth century British philosopher W. D. Ross (1877–1971) introduced a novel modification of the Kantian doctrine. According to Ross certain kinds of situations create prima facie obligations, that is, duties incumbent upon us, all things being equal. Every actual rule has a qualification, Ross feels, but there can be unqualified prima facie rules. For example, we ought to keep promises; that is a rule we are obliged to fulfill. However, there may be intervening conditions that make it undesirable to do so at certain times.

In other words, what is objectively right is not absolutely or universally right; the fact that we always have a duty to perform an action does not mean that it ought always to be done. Since promise keeping is right in itself we can expect that by and large we would be obliged to keep promises in concrete situations but, for example, if keeping a promise meant contributing to a murder then we would have a higher obligation to fulfill the prima facie duty of preserving life.

In *The Right and the Good* W. D. Ross wrote:

> It is necessary to say something by way of clearing up the relation between *prima facie* duties and the actual or absolute duty to do one particular act in particular circumstances. If, as almost all moralists except Kant are agreed, and as most plain men think, it is sometimes right to tell a lie or break a promise, it must be maintained that there is a difference between *prima facie* duty and actual or absolute duty. When we think ourselves justified in breaking, and indeed morally obliged to break, a promise in order to relieve some one's distress, we do not for a moment cease to recognize a *prima facie* duty to keep our promise, and this leads us to feel, not indeed shame or repentance, but certain compunction, for behaving as we do . . .

This position is certainly "softer" than that of Kant since Ross does not claim that if something is right it should always be done, while at the same time he does not adopt a teleological view which uses good consequences as its criterion of morality. "When a plain man fulfills a promise because he thinks he ought to do so," Ross stated "it seems clear that he does so with no thought of its total consequences. . . . What makes him think it right to act in a certain way is the fact that he has promised to do so — that and, usually, nothing more. That his act will produce the best possible consequences is not his reason for calling it right."

Acts should be done then because we recognize a duty to do them regardless of their utility, but we should refrain from acting on that duty in circumstances where another prima facie obligation takes precedence. Under those conditions, we should suspend our obedience, not in terms of the superior consequences of following another principle but because that other principle is of superior importance.

Although this is a more promising approach, Ross was faced with the problem of determining which obligations are prima facie. He believed there are many duties of this kind — such as not telling lies, not injuring others, expressing gratitude, paying our debts, and so forth — and said that our "moral understanding" or "moral sense" makes us aware of them. Each principles is "self-evident," Ross claimed, "in the sense that when we have reached sufficient mental maturity, and have given sufficient attention to the proposition it is evident without any need of proof, or of evidence beyond itself. . . . The moral order expressed in these propositions is just as much part of the fundamental nature of the universe as is the spatial or numerical structure expressed in the axioms of geometry or arithmetic."[7]

Unfortunately, not all people or cultures would agree with Ross' list, not even "the plain man" he assumed would always understand. A self-evident principle too often means evident to oneself, and Ross is left with a set of moral rules that he would want followed but that cannot be proven as prima facie obligations for everyone.

In addition to the various criticisms that have been described, Kant has also been charged with (1) failing to realize that the rules that pass the test of universalizability may not be *moral* types of rules (for example, one could consistently will that everyone salute their cat when they got up in the morning or eat their peas with a knife but these are hardly moral obligations); (2) treating the individual as a means for realizing principles, thus creating tension between the practical and categorical imperatives; and (3) never showing how a rational understanding of what is right could be an inducement to do what is right. As the Scottish philosopher David Hume once pointed out "reason alone can never be a motive to any action of the will." Kant is certainly in good company, for Plato made the same mistake when he said "Virtue is knowledge," meaning that once people know what is good they will act in accordance with the good. But it is a mistake nonetheless (see Endnote).

Having said all this, however, Kant's system stands as a major contribution to our moral understanding. His Practical Imperative concerning the respect that should be accorded to persons is widely employed in judging contemporary moral issues and his Categorical Imperative with suitable modifications can function as a reliable guide to conduct; to ask whether you would be willing for anyone and everyone in the same situation to do as you are doing is a significant moral question.

Above all, Kant gave human conduct a cosmic dimension, linking moral principles with the natural order of the universe, "the moral law within" with "the starry heavens above." As the Quaker leader Rufus Jones summarized it, moral obligation for Kant

> is significant not so much for the specific deeds it leads to as for the fact that it reveals a deeper universe to which moral man belongs. Through the forms of reason which are native capacities in us we cooperate in building up the world of science but as moral beings, obedient to the commands of duty, we discover a world of a wholly different order, which rests for its stability and for its ultimate triumph on a permanent and unvarying good will grounded in the deepest nature of the universe itself.[8]

Christianity: Obeying Divine Commands

A major problem in formalistic ethical systems is finding a reason for declaring an action right and obligatory. Kant tried to base all ethical requirements squarely on logic, arguing that moral principles can be universalized with consistency while immoral ones are self-contradictory. However, another foundation for a dutiful life lies in religion. The theist, that is, the person who believes in the existence of god, maintains we should do what is right because that is god's will. Kant conceives his moral obligations through the use of reason but the religious believer obtains his through an act of faith.

Religion is, in fact, the principal source for the view that we should live righteous lives, fulfilling the moral responsibilities layed upon us. Sometimes referred to as the *divine command* theory, it maintains that god issues edicts that must be honored precisely because they issue from god. These commands may be in keeping with the moral laws discovered by reason or they may appear unreasonable and arbitrary. God may be thought of as rational by nature or a being who transcends the rules of logic. But whatever the case might be, his commandments must be obeyed; we live worthwhile lives by following the divine will. "For the true believer the author of the moral law is God. What pleases God, what God commands — that is the definition of right. What displeases God, what he forbids — that is the definition of wrong."[9]

Christianity is quite typical of this divine command approach to ethics and can be taken as a prototype for our discussion. It is not only useful as a paradigm of religious ethics but stands as the foundation of much of our Western morality. Christians may differ as to how they believe god's will is transmitted, Catholics trusting the authority of the church and the clergy, Protestants accepting the bible and "the still small voice of conscience," but all are united in believing that god's will can be known and should be done "on earth as it is in heaven."

The Christian who maintains this view does not say we should obey god for the sake of some heavenly reward or in order to avoid damnation. That would be prudential behavior, done in return for god's favor. Rather, we should obey god for his sake not ours, doing what he wills because of a creature's obligation to his creator. In Christian terms, it would be unacceptable to god if we followed his rules out of self-interest, as a type of bargain or reciprocity, but only if we behave unselfishly for the greater glory of god. One hand washes the other can operate in a business negotiation but not in man's relation to his heavenly father.

Also, the Christian does not believe that god merely reveals the moral principles inherent in the universe. He does not claim that absolute moral laws are written in the sky, and god interprets these objectively existing laws so man will understand and act morally. Rather, he maintains that an action is right simply because god commands it. The performance of our Christian duty lies in obedience to god's will not in acting on our understanding that god's laws are right in themselves.

Of course, most theologians argue that what god wills and what is right necessarily coincide, and in the eighteenth century, during the heyday of deism, it was believed that god's revelation and the dictates of conscience point to the same moral principles. The deists assert that god made the universe but does not interfere with the laws he promulgated and that he placed a rational conscience in every human breast. By following its urgings, that is by employing "the clear light of natural reason," we can arrive at each one of the principles contained in scripture. Our moral sense is an echo of god's word and corroborates the rightness of his judgments.

But regardless of whether god's commands are right and regardless of whether we can know them to be right through our conscience, Christianity claims we have a duty to obey these commands simply because they emanate from god.

Basic Christian Principles

Christianity is based upon the bible, which is a notoriously difficult document to interpret, not because it is impenetrable but because it lends itself to diverse readings. Many of the schisms within Christianity are due to differing interpretations of holy scripture, including the division between Eastern Orthodoxy and Roman Catholicism, Catholicism and Protestantism, and among the numerous denominations of Protestantism, such as Episcopalianism, Methodism, Lutheranism, Presbyterianism, and so forth. The bible may be infallible but people do not interpret it infallibly and disputes have raged for centuries over the true meaning of key passages. Whether the words were inspired by the spirit of god or whether the writing was automatically produced by god "pushing the pen," errors are bound to occur in transcribing and comprehending the message. It has often been pointed out that the earliest gospels, Matthew and Mark, were written about 75 A.D., some forty-five years after the death of Christ, and the latest, that of John, around 95 A.D. A gap of time of this magnitude would necessarily produce inaccuracies in the text.

In addition, the extra-biblical literature built up by theologians has not helped to clarify the situation but has served largely to perpetuate doctrinal disputes. And to make matters worse, when Gandhi asked "Why aren't you Christians more like your Christ," the reply was that a religion should not be judged by its representatives, but when parts of scripture are criticized some theologians claim "By their fruits ye shall know them."

To try to extract the basic Christian ethic from the welter of conflicting interpretations and positions is certainly a risky business, however a certain consensus does seem to emerge on a few basic principles. Primary among these is the notion of Christian love.

In order to understand the Christian view, a distinction must be made between two types of love described by the Greeks: eros and agape. *Eros* is a type of love that centers on a desire to possess the object beloved. One loves the person, place, or thing so much that one wants to own it, to have that object belong to oneself. Rather than viewing it from afar there is a strong need to appropriate the object one loves, so that its possession will expand one's own being. In fact, part of what causes our emotion of love is the desirability of the object to us; we are attracted by something that we want for ourselves, and the desire to incorporate what we long for or lust after generates feelings of love.

The attraction between men and women of course is the prototypical example. When erotic feelings are stimulated, each wants to "have" the other sexually, but their desires go beyond that. They also want the other to be theirs, to be available and accountable to them for their time, to form an "attachment" and be dependent upon them altogether. The woman fears abandonment, the man fears entrapment, but each is willing to run the risk of a relationship because having someone committed to you is so desirable. If the relationship should lead to marriage, the "bonds of matrimony" will further ensure the connection as the two become one. Then the legal contract and the spiritual sacrament impose rules that deny access to either of the partners by any outsiders; they belong to each other exclusively, "to have and to hold" from that day forth.

However, erotic feelings can even extend to something inanimate such as a house one loves. It will not be enough to pass by or to be a visitor inside; if you genuinely love the house you want to be the owner, to say "This is my property." If you should purchase it, you then experience an enlargement of your being, for the limits of the house are now the dimensions of your self, the boundaries of the land are the degree to which your reach has been extended. You are *more* because of what you own; you are greater to that extent. And if the house should burn to the ground you feel lessened, diminished inside, as though a part of you had been destroyed. You no longer have what you loved, and the loss is to your own person.

To a lesser extent, the same is true of buying clothing, a car, furniture, a pet, paintings, and so forth. If you feel erotically drawn to these objects you want them to become your possessions, part of your array of acquisitions. You have to buy that jacket, that sports car, that dog; you think they are wonderful and therefore must have them for yourself. You want to show them off because they reflect favorably on your taste and enhance you as a person.

In all these cases a causal link is felt between love and the desire to possess what one loves. The individual is essentially self-centered and absorbs whatever he loves for the sake of increasing his being. He wants to own without being owned by anyone, thereby adding to himself without subtracting anything. As the epigram by George Meredith puts it "[In] the book of Egoism, it is written, Possession without obligation to the object possessed approaches felicity."[10]

In sharp contrast to erotic love, *agape* (or *caritas*) stands for a love that wants what is best for the object beloved. This is the love that constitutes the heart of Christian virtue. The Christian who functions agapeistically never desires to own the person, place, or thing that is loved unless that would be beneficial for it. If he possesses he will not be possessive since his motive is only to serve. Instead of trying to obtain the thing he loves as his property and to enrich himself by its acquisition, he dedicates himself to the welfare of the object beloved in a selfless way. His love is so honest and pure that giving to the other not taking from the other is his sole aim.

The epitome of agape, of course, lies not in our relations with things but with other human beings. If we truly love one another in the brotherhood that God intends, we will be altruistic not egoistic in our outlook. We are here on earth to help our fellow man and we should do so without thought of what we will receive in return. As T. S. Eliot said, "A philosophy of life which involves no sacrifice turns out in the end to be merely an excuse for being the sort of person one is." Love of an agape type should typify all of our personal relations, replacing the seven deadly sins — pride, covetousness, lust, anger, gluttony, envy, and sloth — all of which spring from selfishness. Our individualism and self-love should give way to brotherhood as expressed in pity, caring, and kindness, especially toward the poor and lowly. All souls are equally precious in the sight of god, and the humble people in particular should elicit our greatest compassion. Charity, as St. Thomas Aquinas said, is "the mother and root of all the virtues" *(caritas est mater omnium virtutum, et radix).*

This agape attitude should even permeate the romantic relation between the sexes. For it means loving the other above ourselves, wanting their well being even if it conflicts with our own, and this would apply to interaction between men and women no less than with mankind at large. To follow the agapeistic principle, therefore, we should establish and maintain a relationship just so long as we believe the person is benefited by having us there. But if we discover that they are good for us but we are not good for them we would sever the relationship at once.

The depth of our love for the other would make us unwilling to possess them if that worked to their detriment. And if they then found a fulfilling life with someone else we would not be consumed with jealousy and resentment but would be happy for them because their well being had always been our primary concern. To begrudge the fact that they are better off with someone else than they were with us shows that our egos had been involved, that the relationship had served our pride. It shows self-love at work, and that our conceit had been central all along. Authentic Christian love is always for the other's sake not for our own, and would want whatever the other person requires — even if it is not ourselves. When a parent gives away a child in marriage he is evincing agape.

The same approach could be taken toward objects such as houses, clothing, and pets, although most Christians would not go this far. We would be adopting an agapeistic attitude if we regarded ourselves as caretakers of a house we love, responsible for its preservation until the keys were transferred to the next generation of "stewards." If we passed up that article of clothing because we felt we could not show it off to best advantage, do it justice or did not buy that sheepdog because it would be unfair to keep a large animal in a city apartment, then we are putting the object before ourselves.[11]

However, regardless of whether some Christians might take this view (perhaps with regard to our ecological stewardship of the planet), the primary application of the agape principle is in our conduct toward one another. Here the supreme model for agape is God's sacrifice in Christ, which was not offered with the expectation of a return but because "God so loved the world. . . ." His love for humanity was not awarded because of any special merit on man's part but in order to redeem us from sin and draw us into the realm of divine grace. Such love is of an unqualified character, an unreserved giving that is not predicated on receiving. God loves humanity for its own sake and man should love god in the same way, not for the blessings he can bestow, the prayers he will answer, or any guarantee of heaven to come but only because he is god. And our concern for our fellow man should be prompted by a sense of our common relationship to god in agape love. In scripture we read "This is my commandment, that you love one another as I have loved you" (John 15:12), and "Let no man seek his own but each his neighbor's good" (1 Corinthians 10:24).

To be truly loving we must not only refrain from harmful deeds but from evil desires, not just help one another but feel love in our hearts. The thought is as important as the act, so if we covet our neighbor's mate it is tantamount to committing the sin of adultery. In this and in the agape principle, there is a strong parallel to the intentionalism and formalism of Kant.

A second major principle in Christian ethics has to do with the concept of justice. *Human justice* usually means giving people what they deserve. The punishment (or reward) should fit the nature of the act and be neither more nor less severe than it merits. If a fair correlation exists between crime and punishment, sin and suffering, then we feel that justice has been done; if the punishment is too heavy or too light for the severity of the crime then we consider it unjust. For example, if a death sentence were handed down for a case of petty larceny, or a mass murderer were jailed for only one week, we would think there had been a gross miscarriage of justice.

To conceive of justice this way is to adopt a retributive position that stems from the Old Testament. Specifically, the Old Testament contains a belief in the Law of Talion *(lex talionis),* according to which a person could expect to have done to him the equivalent of the wrong he has done. Vengeance was visited on sinners by the god Yahweh according to this law, so that fire from heaven rained down on Sodom and Gomorrah "because of their carnal wickedness" (Genesis 19:16–28), and the flood drowned all of sinful humanity except for the faithful Noah and his wife (Genesis 6:5–7:10). Adam and Eve were expelled from the Garden of Eden as punishment for their disobedience, and the entire human race bears the stigma of their Original Sin. They were told "Ye shall not eat . . . of the fruit of the tree which is in the midst of the garden," but they yielded to the temptations of the devil (in the form of a snake) and for that reason they and their descendents had to inhabit a world of natural evil—disasters and disease, suffering and death (Genesis 3:3–6).[12]

The idea of giving people their just desserts, the quid pro quo model, was carried into legal justice, not so much in the vengeful form of An eye for an eye and a tooth for a tooth but more in the notion that a person should be punished in accordance with what he deserves, get his due, what he has coming. If a person's conduct merits a jail sentence then it would be just for him to receive one—a sentence in proportion to the severity of the crime. A fittingness is sought not just by evening out accounts on earth but by establishing a kind of cosmic equilibrium. The criminal not only pays his debt to society but the metaphysical scales of justice are balanced once more when reparation has taken place. It is as though the universe had cried out for satisfaction and the natural order needs to be returned to equipoise.

In opposition to this retributive idea the Christian endorses a theory of *divine justice,* according to which people should receive what they need not what they deserve. Rather than conceiving of justice in terms of retaliation or a "measure for measure" mentality, the New Testament stresses concern for the individual's well being, even though he may have committed some terrible offense. God hates the sin but loves the sinner and we should adopt the same attitude, taking a person's mistakes as an index of his need for help and care. No thought should be given to paying a person back for his crime or having the punishment fit the crime; our only concern should be to provide the support needed for improvement in the future. The Christian wants to make the person better not to make him pay, to extend a hand not point a finger. He tries to maintain a Christlike pity, compassion, and love for all mankind, giving people what they need regardless of their merit. A hungry man who steals food deserves punishment but what he needs is nourishment.

Another way of viewing this concept of justice is that the Christian looks forward not backward. He is concerned with changing a person's future conduct, refining his soul to a life of virtue, rather than dwelling on the vices of the past. And he is far more interested in the individual than the action, not distributing justice according to what has been done but in terms of what the person requires—those needs revealed by his behavior.

To illustrate the difference between human and divine justice, suppose a parent is informed that his young child has been caught shoplifting in a drug store. If the parent uses a standard of human justice the child will get what he deserves. That could mean a spanking, the withdrawal of love, ostracism from the family (Go to your room), deprivation of some privilege (television, dessert, that trip to the zoo), and so forth. However, if the parent operates with divine love he will try to determine what need impelled the child to steal. Perhaps it was the thrill of risk and danger, a cry for recognition and attention, the need to prove his cleverness or identity, the desire for proof of affection which the physical object represented. If these possibilities exist, then the parent would try to make the child feel more secure and loved, spend more time with him and show him respect as a worthwhile and separate individual. A response of this kind, based on the child's needs, would not show approval of stealing but would be mainly concerned to offer personal support to the child, while at the same time making it unlikely that he would want to steal again.

It is interesting to note in this example that human justice would dictate the withdrawal of love while divine justice would indicate a greater expression of it; whether the child is punished or hugged then depends upon the parent's theory of justice. It seems a general truth that children need love most when they deserve it least.

An example of a much more serious sort would be that of the murderer who faces justice in court. If he is to receive what he deserves then he should be given an extremely heavy sentence, perhaps life imprisonment or even capital punishment. Our primal "gut" reaction would be to avenge the victim by punishing the murderer to the full extent of the law. However, the Christian response, even in the case of a heinous crime, is to base the sentence on the needs involved. Are there extenuating circumstances such as the desperation of the murderer, the fact that he had been unable to find work for a year and was finally driven to armed robbery with disastrous results? Was his family hungry and homeless, suffering from illness and malnutrition? If this is the case then he should imprisoned only for the length of time needed to reform him so he will not turn to crime again and to rehabilitate him so that he acquires employable skills. The sentence should be determined by society's need to deter others from committing similar crimes. Meanwhile, his family requires health care services and low-income housing, some financial assistance until they are self-sufficient or he is released from prison and can find steady employment.

Again the response is radically different depending upon whether a human or divine theory of justice is applied. If the notion of just desserts is used then the murderer has a heavy debt to pay to society and a severe sentence is meted out. But if the idea of needs is uppermost then in the circumstances described the murderer would be helped to become a law-abiding person and lead a productive, fulfilling life. In Christian terms, no one is incorrigible and if there is sincere repentence anyone can be saved.

Obviously, the case of the child and the murderer are at two extremes but they illustrate the golden thread of Christian justice running throughout, that the needs of human beings are the most significant factor to be judged. Although society as it functions follows more of an Old Testament, retributive notion, Christians regard it as a virtue to overcome their natural desire for retaliation and to serve the needs of everyone. The New Testament states that all human beings are our brothers and we are our brother's keeper; whether they are worthy of our ministry and devotion is irrelevant. To the Christian the supreme example of such conduct is, of course, Christ who came to earth not because man deserved him but because humanity needed his sacrifice for its redemption.

Two other principles should be mentioned that are a logical outgrowth of agapeistic love and divine justice, the principles of forgiveness and pacifism. As the message of the gospels have come down to us, if we are struck on one cheek we are to turn the other one, if our coat is taken away we are to offer our cloak also, and if someone forces us to walk a mile we are to go two. That is, instead of returning evil for evil we should return good for evil, responding not in a reciprocal or vindictive way but with exemplary kindness and understanding. Christ preached a gospel of forgiveness and caring, pity, brotherhood, and peace, and the renunciation of aggression even against those who assault us. "Love your enemies, bless them that curse you, do good to them that hate you, and pray for them which despitefully use you, and persecute you." God has ordained that harming others is wrong, therefore it should not be done even to return an injury for the injuries one has sustained. "Forgive them for they know not what they do" was Christ's cry from the cross. To rise above the cruelty of others and not become a party to it, to feel love even in the face of hate is to do god's work on earth.

Christians hope that by the example of their strength and faithfulness to god's commands and through preaching the gospel of salvation, the world will come to accept Christian values. By example and by precept, the Christian believes that people can be led away from selfishness, vengeance, malice, and violence to a humane existence of love in Christ.

The excerpt that follows is Christ's "Sermon on the Mount" recorded in the Gospel according to St. Matthew. It contains the heart of the Christian message and is arguably the best known writing in Western history. The second selection is taken from St. Paul's "Epistle to the Romans" which is also a part of the New Testament canon. As one of the first disciples, Paul was extremely influential in spreading Christianity and in the development of its theological doctrines. The passage from his writings not only underscores points of ethical doctrine but affirms the central notion of Christianity, that faith in Christ brings redemption from sin and life everlasting. Also apparent in the selection is the Pauline emphasis on the depravity of the body as contrasted with the purity of the soul.

The Sermon on the Mount*

And seeing the multitudes, he went up into a mountain: And when he was set, his disciples came unto him: And he opened his mouth, and taught them, saying "Blessed are the poor in spirit: for theirs is the kingdom of heaven. Blessed are they that mourn: for they shall be comforted. Blessed are the meek: for they shall inherit the earth. Blessed are they which do hunger and thirst after righteousness: for they shall be filled. Blessed are the merciful: for they shall obtain mercy. Blessed are the pure in heart: for they shall see God. Blessed are the peacemakers: for they shall be called the children of God. Blessed are they which are persecuted for righteousness' sake: for theirs is the kingdom of heaven. Blessed are ye, when men shall revile you, and persecute you, and shall say all manner of evil against you falsely, for my sake. Rejoice, and be exceeding glad: for great is your reward in heaven: for so persecuted they the prophets which were before you.

"Ye are the salt of the earth: but if the salt have lost his savour, wherewith shall it be salted? It is thenceforth good for nothing, but to be cast out, and to be trodden under foot of men. Ye are the light of the world. A city that is set on a hill cannot be hid. Neither do men light a candle, and put it under a bushel, but on a candlestick; and it giveth light unto all that are in the house. Let your light so shine before men, that they may see your good works, and glorify your Father which is in heaven.

"Think not that I am come to destroy the law, or the prophets: I am not come to destroy, but to fulfill. For verily I say unto you, Till heaven and earth pass, one jot or one tittle shall in no wise pass from the law, till all be fulfilled. Whosoever therefore shall break one of these least commandments,

*Reprinted from Matthew, Chapters 5–7.

and shall teach men so, he shall be called the least in the kingdom of heaven: but whosoever shall do and teach them, the same shall be called great in the kingdom of heaven. For I say unto you, That except your righteousness shall exceed the righteousness of the scribes and Pharisees, ye shall in no case enter into the kingdom of heaven.

"Ye have heard that it was said by them of old time, Thou shalt not kill; and whosoever shall kill shall be in danger of the judgment. But I say unto you, That whosoever is angry with his brother without a cause shall be in danger of the judgment: and whosoever shall say to his brother, Raca, shall be in danger of the council: but whosoever shall say, Thou fool, shall be in danger of hell fire. Therefore if thou bring thy gift to the altar, and there rememberest that thy brother hath ought against thee; leave there thy gift before the altar, and go thy way, first be reconciled to thy brother, and then come and offer thy gift. Agree with thine adversary quickly, whilest thou art in the way with him; lest at any time the adversary deliver thee to the judge, and the judge deliver thee to the officer, and thou be cast into prison. Verily I say unto thee, Thou shalt by no means come out thence, till thou hast paid the uttermost farthing.

"Ye have heard that it was said by them of old time, Thou shalt not commit adultery. But I say unto you, That whosoever looketh on a woman to lust after her hath committed adultery with her already in his heart. And if thy right eye offend thee, pluck it out, and cast it from thee: for it is profitable for thee that one of thy members should perish, and not that thy whole body should be cast into hell. And if thy right hand offend thee, cut it off, and cast it from thee: for it is profitable for thee that one of thy members should perish, and not that thy whole body should be cast into hell. It hath been said, Whosoever shall put away his wife, let him give her a writing of divorcement. But I say unto you, That whosoever shall put away his wife, saving for the cause of fornication, causeth her to commit adultery: and whosoever shall marry her that is divorced committeth adultery.

"Again, ye have heard that it hath been said by them of old time, Thou shalt not forswear thyself, but shalt perform unto the Lord thine oaths. But I say unto you, Swear not at all; neither by heaven; for it is God's throne: nor by the earth; for it is his footstool: neither by Jerusalem; for it is the city of the great King. Neither shalt thou swear by thy head, because thou canst not make one hair white or black. But let your communication be, Yea, yea; Nay, nay: for whatsoever is more than these cometh of evil.

"Ye have heard that it hath been said, An eye for an eye, and a tooth for a tooth. But I say unto you, That ye resist not evil: but whosoever shall smite thee on thy right cheek, turn to him the other also. And if any man will sue thee at the law, and take away thy coat, let him have thy cloke also. And whosoever shall compel thee to go a mile, go with him twain. Give to him that asketh thee, and from him that would borrow of thee turn not thou away.

"Ye have heard that it hath been said, Thou shalt love thy neighbour, and hate thine enemy. But I say unto you, Love your enemies, bless them that curse you, do good to them that hate you, and pray for them which despitefully use you, and persecute you; that ye may be the children of your Father which is in heaven: for he maketh his sun to rise on the evil and on the good, and sendeth rain on the just and on the unjust. For if ye love them which love you, what reward have ye? Do not even the publicans the same? And if ye salute your brethren only, what do ye more than others? Do not even the publicans so? Be ye therefore perfect, even as your Father which is in heaven is perfect.

"Take heed that ye do not your alms before men, to be seen of them: otherwise ye have no reward of your Father which is in heaven. Therefore when thou doest thine alms; do not sound a trumpet before thee, as the hypocrites do in the synagogues and in the streets, that they may have glory of men. Verily I say unto you, They have their reward. But when thou doest alms, let not thy left hand know thy right hand doeth: That thine alms may be in secret: and thy Father which seeth in secret himself shall reward thee openly.

"And when thou prayest, thou shalt not be as the hypocrites are: for they love to pray standing in the synagogues and in the corners of the streets, that they may be seen of men. Verily I say unto you, They have their reward. But thou, when thou prayest, enter into thy closet, and when thou hast shut thy door, pray to thy Father which is in secret; and thy Father which seeth in secret shall reward thee openly. But when ye pray, use not vain repetitions, as the heathen do: for they think that they shall be heard for their much speaking. Be not ye therefore like unto them: for your Father knoweth what things ye have need of, before ye ask him. After this manner therefore pray ye: 'Our Father which art in heaven, hallowed be thy name. Thy kingdom come. Thy will be done in earth, as it is in heaven. Give us this day our daily bread. And forgive us our debts, as we forgive our debtors. And lead us not into temptation, but deliver us from evil: For thine is the kingdom, and the power, and the glory, for ever. A-men.'

"For if ye forgive men their trespasses, your heavenly Father will also forgive you: But if ye forgive not men their trespasses, neither will your father forgive your trespasses.

"Moreover when ye fast, be not, as the hypocrites, of a sad countenance: for they disfigure their faces, that they may appear unto men to fast. Verily I say unto you, They have their reward. But thou, when thou fastest, anoint thine head, and wash thy face; that thou appear not unto men to fast, but unto thy Father which is in secret: and thy Father, which seeth in secret, shall reward thee openly.

"Lay not up for yourselves treasures upon earth, where moth and rust doth corrupt, and where thieves break through and steal. But lay up for yourselves treasures in heaven, where neither moth nor rust doth corrupt, and where thieves do not break through nor steal: For where your treasure is, there will your heart be also. The light of the body is the eye: if therefore thine eye be single thy whole body shall be full of light. But if thine eye be evil, thy whole body shall be full of darkness. If therefore the light that is in thee be darkness, how great is that darkness!

"No man can serve two masters: for either he will hate the one, and love the other; or else he will hold to the one, and despise the other. Ye cannot serve God and mammon. Therefore I say unto you, Take no thought for your life, what ye shall eat, or what ye shall drink; nor yet for your body, what ye shall put on. Is not the life more than meat, and the body than raiment? Behold the fowls of the air: for they sow not, neither do they reap, nor gather into barns; yet your heavenly Father feedeth them. Are ye not much better than they? Which of you by taking thought can add one cubit unto his stature? And why take ye thought for raiment? Consider the lilies of the field, how they grow; they toil not, neither do they spin: And yet I say unto you, That even Solomon in all his glory was not arrayed like one of these. Wherefore, if God so clothe the grass of the field, which to day is, and to morrow is cast into the oven, shall he not much more clothe you, O ye of little faith? Therefore take no thought saying, What shall we eat? or, What shall we drink? or, Wherewithal shall we be clothed? (For after all these things do the Gentiles seek:) for your heavenly Father knoweth that ye have need of all these things. But seek ye first the kingdom of God, and his righteousness; and all these things shall be added unto you. Take therefore no thought for the morrow: for the morrow shall take thought for the things of itself. Sufficient unto the day is the evil thereof.

"Judge not, that ye be not judged. For with what judgment ye judge, ye shall be judged: and with what measure ye mete, it shall be measured to you again. And why beholdest thou the mote that is in thy brother's eye, but considerest not the beam that is in thine own eye? Or how wilt thou say to thy brother, Let me pull out the mote out of thine eye; and, behold, a beam is in thine own eye? Thou hypocrite, first cast out the beam out of thine own eye; and then shalt thou see clearly to cast out the mote out of thy brother's eye.

"Give not that which is holy unto the dogs, neither cast ye your pearls before swine, lest they trample them under their feet, and turn again and rend you.

"Ask, and it shall be given you; seek, and ye shall find; knock, and it shall be opened unto you: For every one that asketh receiveth; and he that seeketh findeth; and to him that knocketh it shall be opened. Or what man is there of you, whom if his son ask bread, will he give him a stone? Or if he ask a fish, will he give him a serpent? If ye then, being evil, know how to give good gifts unto your children, how much more shall your Father which is in heaven give good things to them that ask him? Therefore all things whatsoever ye would that men should do to you, do ye even so to them: for this is the law and the prophets.

"Enter ye in at the strait gate: for wide is the gate, and broad is the way, that leadeth to destruction, and many there be which go in thereat: Because strait is the gate, and narrow is the way, which leadeth unto life, and few there be that find it.

"Beware of false prophets, which come to you in sheep's clothing, but inwardly they are ravening wolves. Ye shall know them by their fruits. Do men gather grapes of thorns, or figs of thistles? Even so every good tree bringeth forth good fruit; but a corrupt tree bringeth forth evil fruit. A good tree cannot bring forth evil fruit, neither can a corrupt tree bring forth good fruit. Every tree that bringeth not forth good fruit is hewn down, and cast into the fire. Wherefore by their fruits ye shall know them.

"Not every one that saith unto me, Lord, Lord, shall enter into the kingdom of heaven; but he that doeth the will of my Father which is in heaven. Many will say to me in that day, Lord, Lord, have we not prophesied in thy name? And in thy name have cast out devils? and in thy name done many wonderful works? And then will I profess unto them, I never knew you; depart from me, ye that work iniquity.

"Therefore whosoever heareth these sayings of mine, and doeth them, I will liken him unto a wise man, which built his house upon a rock: and the rain descended, and the floods came, and the winds blew, and beat upon that house and it fell not: for it was founded upon a rock. And every one that heareth these sayings of mine, and doeth them not, shall be likened unto a foolish man, which built his house upon the sand: and the rain descended, and the floods came, and the winds blew, and beat upon that house; and it fell: and great was the fall of it.''

Epistle to the Romans*

. . . Being justified by faith, we have peace with God through our Lord Jesus Christ: By whom also we have access by faith into this grace wherein we stand, and rejoice in hope of the glory of God. And not only so, but we glory in tribulations also: Knowing that tribulation worketh patience; and patience, experience; and experience, hope: And hope maketh not ashamed: Because the love of God is shed abroad in our hearts by the Holy Ghost which is given unto us.

For when we were yet without strength, in due time Christ died for the ungodly. For scarcely for a righteous man will one die: Yet peradventure for a good man some would even dare to die. But God commendeth his love toward us, in that, while we were yet sinners, Christ died for us. Much more then, being now justified by his blood, we shall be saved from wrath through him. For if, when we were enemies, we were reconciled to God by the death of his Son, much more, being reconciled, we shall be saved by his life. And not only so, but we also joy in God through our Lord Jesus Christ, by whom we have now received the atonement. Wherefore, as by one man sin entered into the world, and death by sin; and so death passed upon all men, for that all have sinned: (For until the law sin was in the world: but sin is not imputed when there is no law. Nevertheless death reigned from Adam to Moses, even over them that had not sinned after the similitude of Adam's transgression, who is the figure of him that was to come. But not as the offence, so also is the free gift. For if through the offence of one many be dead, much more the grace of God, and the gift by grace, which is by one man, Jesus Christ, hath abounded unto many. And not as it was by one that sinned, so is the gift: For the judgment was by one to condemnation, but the free gift is of many offences unto justification. For if by one man's offence death reigned by one; much more they which receive abundance of grace and of the gift of righteousness shall reign in life by one, Jesus Christ.) Therefore as by the offence of one judgment came upon all men to condemnation; even so by the righteousness of one the free gift came upon all men unto justification of life. For as by one man's disobedience many were made sinners, so by the obedience of one shall many be made righteous. Moreover the law entered, that the offence might abound. But where sin abounded, grace did much more abound: That as sin hath reigned unto death, even so might grace reign through righteousness unto eternal life by Jesus Christ our Lord.

What shall we say then? Shall we continue in sin, that grace may abound?

*Reprinted from Paul, *Epistles*.

God forbid. How shall we, that are dead to sin, live any longer therein? Know ye not, that so many of us as were baptized into Jesus Christ were baptized into his death? Therefore we are buried with him by baptism into death: That like as Christ was raised up from the dead by the glory of the Father, even so we also should walk in newness of life. For if we have been planted together in the likeness of his death, we shall be also in the likeness of his resurrection: Knowing this, that our old man is crucified with him, that the body of sin might be destroyed, that henceforth we should not serve sin. For he that is dead is freed from sin. Now if we be dead with Christ, we believe that we shall also live with him: Knowing that Christ being raised from the dead dieth no more; death hath no more dominion over him. For in that he died, he died unto sin once; but in that he liveth, he liveth unto God. Likewise reckon ye also yourselves to be dead indeed unto sin, but alive unto God through Jesus Christ our Lord.

Let not sin therefore reign in your mortal body; that ye should obey it in the lusts thereof. Neither yield ye your members as instruments of unrighteousness unto sin: But yield yourselves unto God, as those that are alive from the dead, and your members as instruments of righteousness unto God. For sin shall not have dominion over you: For ye are not under the law, but under grace.

· · ·

I beseech you therefore, brethren, by the mercies of God, that ye present your bodies a living sacrifice, holy, acceptable unto God, which is your reasonable service. And be not conformed to this world: But be ye transformed by the renewing of your mind, that ye may prove what is that good, and acceptable, and perfect, will of God. For I say, through the grace given unto me, to every man that is among you, not to think of himself more highly than he ought to think; but to think soberly, according as God hath dealt to every man the measure of faith. For as we have many members in one body, and all members have not the same office: So we being many, are one body in Christ, and every one members one of another.

Having then gifts differing according to the grace that is given to us, whether prophesy, let us prophesy according to the proportion of faith; or ministry, let us wait on our ministering: or he that teacheth, on teaching; or he that exhorteth, on exhortation. He that giveth, let him do it with simplicity; he that ruleth, with diligence; he that sheweth mercy, with cheerfulness.

Let love be without dissimulation. Abhor that which is evil; cleave to that which is good. 'Be kindly affectioned one to another with brotherly love; in honour preferring one another; not slothful in business; fervent in spirit; serving the Lord; rejoicing in hope; patient in tribulation; continuing instant in prayer; distributing to the necessity of saints; given to hospitality. Bless them which persecute you: Bless, and curse not. Rejoice with them that do rejoice, and weep with them that weep. Be of the same mind one toward another. Mind not high things, but condescend to men of low estate. Be not wise in your own conceits. Recompense to no man evil for evil. Provide things honest in the sight of all men. If it be possible, as much as lieth in you, live peaceably with all men. Dearly beloved, avenge not yourselves, but rather give place unto wrath: For it is written, Vengeance is mine; I will repay, saith the Lord. Therefore if thine enemy hunger, feed him, if he thirst, give him drink: For in so doing thou shalt heap coals of fire on his head. Be not overcome of evil, but overcome evil with good.

Evaluation

1. One question that has been raised regarding all religion-based ethics since the time of the ancient Greeks is whether the rightness of a moral principle is derived from its having been commanded by god or whether the rightness is inherent in the principle itself. For example, does loving one's neighbor (or one's enemy) become right when god declares it so or was it always right? Are moral values invented by god or discovered by him, created or revealed as correct? Does god will that human beings perform an action purely in obedience to his commands or is there a moral reason why certain acts are required of man? In short, is an act right because god wills it or does god will it because it is right?

Most religious systems, including Christianity, adopt the first position, arguing that what makes something right is that it is commanded by god. Such a view is technically referred to as *theological voluntarism*. However, if this position were correct then god could make hating one's neighbor right or revenging oneself on an enemy right by willing it, and that does not seem possible. Obviously, the god of the Judao-Christian tradition would never will such values, but the point is that he *could not* do so even if he wanted to. God could not make right wrong or wrong right by an act of will. Therefore, we have to conclude that god commands various actions because he recognizes them to be right in and of themselves.

This point was first made in Plato's *Euthyphro* in connection with a discussion on the nature of holiness. In response to Socrates' attempt to educe the essential meaning of the holy, Euthyphro proposes that "holiness is what the gods all love, and its opposite is what the gods all hate, unholiness." Socrates then asks the key question "Is something holy because the gods love it, or do they love it because it is holy?" He forces Euthyphro to conclude that the gods love and approve of actions that are holy by their very nature, those which are "of a sort to be loved" because of their holiness. Otherwise, what is holy becomes a capricious and arbitrary matter, depending on the personal whims of the gods.

The implication of this conclusion is extremely important, because it means that a moral principle is right in itself and not because it issued from god. And it would remain right even if there were no god to point it out. A secular ethic then becomes possible, for the rightness of actions does not depend upon divine pronouncements. God is not the basis for moral principles; ethics is not founded on religion.[13] Therefore it is meaningful to believe in ethical principles even if one doesn't believe in god.

2. If the Christian ethic does not rest on the authority of god but must stand on its own philosophic feet then one of the frequent criticisms made against it is that it is highly impractical. A bank manager cannot operate according to the dictum "Give to him that asketh thee, and from him that would borrow of thee

turn not thou away"; the bank would soon close its doors. A business person cannot adopt an agape attitude toward his competitors, doing what is in their best interests, or he would soon be out of business. By the same token, in international relations one nation cannot put the welfare of a rival nation first. If the United States had served Germany's needs in the first part of the twentieth century or Russia's needs in the latter half the results would have been disasterous.

In the same way, if we rely on Christ's dictum of taking "no thought for the morrow," making no provision for food or clothing in the future, we will most likely find ourselves in a desperate state of poverty when we are old. Man may not live by bread alone but he needs at least that. We certainly cannot rely on human charity and the dictum "Ask, and it shall be given you" and "every one that asketh receiveth." It seems as if we should lay up some treasures upon earth or we will live to regret it, ending up destitute, homeless, and starving.

Practical wisdom also tells us that if when a person asks for our coat we give him our cloak also, he will soon have the shirt off our backs. And if when we are struck on one cheek we turn the other one we might be asking to be hit again. In other words, we could be encouraging violence by default, by not opposing it.

In brief, unless everyone operates in terms of agape principles, divine justice, forgiveness, charity, and pacifism, we will find ourselves casualties and victims when we try to lead a Christian life. What's more, little good will be accomplished by our sacrifice, for unscrupulous people will welcome generosity and nonresistance. (At least part of the reason for the low pay of teachers and nurses is that their dedication is not matched by generosity on the other side.) Even Christian theologians have acknowledged the practical difficulties involved in employing the ideals of Christ and have made various concessions to realpolitik and our business economy. These compromises are more or less successful, for instance, the permissibility of fighting a just war or revolutions of liberation for oppressed peoples, but they depart substantially from the pure Christian ethic.

The American Protestant theologian Reinhold Niebuhr (1892–1971), for example, concluded that we should abandon the law of love and engage in aggressive political action if we are to improve conditions in the world. The individual person may behave in just and loving ways toward other persons but "All human groups tend to be more predatory than the individuals which compose them . . . they take for themselves whatever their power can command." Therefore we cannot hope to make wide-scale moral progress through love or pacifism but only by employing the immoral tactics of racial, economic, and national groups. We have to get our hands dirty and, if we repent, Christ will forgive and receive us: he will understand and wash us clean.[14]

Niebuhr may have been correct in his assessment but his theology points up the impracticality of using Christian ethics in real social contexts. Only in a utopia of like-minded people could it operate effectively, not in the actual world of rampant selfishness and competition. The violence and crime that exists, the corruption and polluted environments, malnutrition and starvation of thousands, the terrorism and omnipresent threat of nuclear destruction shows how far we are from altruistic attitudes toward our fellow man.

3. Another defect within the Christian ethic is the uncertainty over whether our actions should be motivated by the basic principles of love, divine justice,

and so forth or by the particular commandments presented in scripture. This is usually described as a conflict between the spirit and the letter, especially the spirit of universal love and the letter of the moral laws.

For example, there have been incidents in which people were so badly burned that they have asked to be killed. They were liable to die at any moment but the pain was so intense that they begged to have their lives ended at once. In these circumstances humane love dictates that they be given what they need, but one of the Ten Commandments states Thou shalt not kill. Which standard, then, should take precedence? There is nothing in the ethical system to help resolve such dilemmas, and we wonder whether the rules against killing, stealing, adultery, and so forth should be honored or set aside in favor of some more encompassing Christian ethic.

In recent years certain theologians have addressed this issue and concluded that the spirit of love is the highest Christian virtue and should take priority over any and all rules. Theologians such as Rudolf Bultmann, John A. T. Robinson, and Joseph Fletcher, for example, have argued for the primacy of agape as the guiding principle for action. These theologians share numerous ideas with the God Is Dead movement, associated with the names J. J. Altizer and William Hamilton, which maintains that the biblical concept of god has become outmoded and is no longer applicable to our contemporary experience. God must be redefined, they say, and his living spirit resurrected as a real option for modern consciousness.

However, the primary concern of these theologians lies with the ethics not the metaphysics of Christian thought, and even if religious belief entirely disappeared they would want to salvage the ethic of love and not throw out the gold with the dross. To them this means "situation ethics," in which the context determines whether or not a rule should be applied. Contrary to Kant and other absolutists, situation ethics does not condemn out of hand such acts as killing or lying since the circumstances may mandate them; likewise, values such as faithfulness, loyalty, respect for property, and so forth might need to be sacrificed to some larger good. No moral laws can be practiced universally but each gains its sanction from the specific situation. As Joseph Fletcher wrote, we must "tailor our ethical cloth to fit the back of each occasion."[15]

The only norm of conduct that the situationist accepts is the spirit of agapeistic caring that looks toward the well being of others in all circumstances. Instead of being governed by specific commands the Christian should take the ideal of love as the sole criterion for action. To the situationist, it does not matter which value is chosen provided that our choice is motivated by feelings of love for humanity. In some contexts we should strike back against violence, in others we should return good for evil, and either one can be correct provided that the welfare of humanity is augmented. This is why Christians can justify the crusades of the twelfth and thirteenth centuries at the same time that St. Francis of Assisi was celebrating gentleness by preaching sermons to birds, for it all depends on what is needed at the time and place. Violence may be called for or pacifism, submission or revolt, honesty or deceit—all according to love's demands. There are no universal principles, only a Christian attitude which can even legitimize awful actions if they are required for human good.

The situationist goes so far as to say that traditional Christian rules and commands can be disregarded, that the ends justify the means and nothing else can. Legalism must give way to "agapeistic expediency" in which we adopt any means that will ensure the good for man. St. Paul is quoted with approval when he said that lawfulness does not make an act worthwhile but whether it is expedient, constructive, and edifying. In modern terms this implies that if divorce, abortion, euthanasia, contraceptives, artificial insemination or surrogate motherhood would effect some beneficial end then agapeistic love would approve of their practice. Genuine Christian ethics, according to the situationist, is not "living according to a code but a continuous effort to relate love to a world of relativities . . . its constant task is to work out the strategy and tactics of love, for Christ's sake."[16]

Paul Tillich, one of the most prominent theologians of the twentieth century, has expressed a similar position, trying to extract the pure gold from the Christian ethic. In *Morality and Beyond* Tillich wrote

love is both absolute and relative by its very nature. An unchanging principle, it nevertheless always changes in its concrete application. It "listens" to the particular situation. Abstract justice cannot do this; but justice taken into love and becoming "creative justice" or *agape* can do so. *Agape* acts in relation to the concrete demands of the situation — its conditions, its possible consequences, the inner status of the people involved, their hidden motives, their limiting complexes, and their unconscious desires and anxieties. Love perceives all these — and more deeply the stronger the *agape* element is.

• • •

Tables of laws can never wholly apply to the unique situation. This is true of the Ten Commandments as well as of the demands of the Sermon on the Mount and the moral prescriptions in the Epistles of Paul. "The letter kills" not only because it suppresses the creative potentialities of the unique moment which never was before and never will come again. The Spirit, on the contrary, opens the mind to these potentialities and determines the decisions of love in a particular situation. In this way the problem of the absolute and the relative character of the moral demands is solved in principle.[17]

This approach certainly resolves the dilemma but the price may be too high. We would be left without any firm moral rules and with too great a burden placed upon our conscience to decide which action best expressed the Christian spirit of love. Almost any act could be reconciled with someone's conscience, especially when the ends are said to justify the means, including the preaching of apartheid in South African churches, the incitements to violence in Northern Ireland, and the mass suicides of the Jim Jones cult in Guyana. The situation ethicist moves between an act deontologism and a consequentialist theory, neither of which provides a strong ethical foundation. If we are willing to violate any rule in the name of love we will soon find ourselves violating every rule — and without being sure that love is our motive.

The tension therefore remains between love and law. The legalism of the Old

Testament sins to the right while the individualism of situation ethics sins to the left, and the conflict appears to reflect a contradiction within the Christian ethic itself.

As relatively minor points, Christianity has also been charged with a "Platonic" contempt for the physical aspect of man, as when St. Paul talks about mortal lusts and presenting our bodies as a living sacrifice to god. The whole notion of man being inherently depraved, tainted with original sin, refers to our earthly sensuous desires. This emphasis has led to a sense of the human body as evil and its needs shameful, even to the ascetic notion of the mortification of the flesh for the purification of the soul.

Also, the Christian notion of sin consisting in thought as well as in deed is difficult to accept. Christ says that "whosoever is angry with his brother" is "in danger of the judgment" (of murder?) and whosoever looks at a woman with lust has already committed a sin (most notably adultery). However, feelings are notoriously difficult to control, including what we find repulsive or attractive; our will is simply not involved. We can avoid acting on our desires and can be held accountable for what we do but we cannot help what we feel. In fact, the more we are told not to feel something the more the feeling tends to persist because we have to remember the thing we are supposed to forget; we must keep in mind what we are supposed to put out of our minds. This is why the "hell fire and brimstone" sermons against lust so often backfire.

However, despite these problems and the more serious ones previously discussed, the Christian ethic stands as an extraordinary monument, dominating the ethics of our Western civilization. It has done more to shape our moral consciousness than any other theory and, whether divinely inspired or not, has colored the fabric of our thinking for nearly 2,000 years. Regardless of any philosophic difficulties, belief in the Christian ethic has inspired generations of people to lead better lives, modifying their selfishness and hatreds and exerting an influence for peace, caring, and brotherhood on earth. For these reasons alone it deserves to be taken very seriously as an ideal.

Notes

1. The title of this book has been variously translated as *Metaphysical Principles of the Metaphysic of Morals* (T. K. Abott), *Foundations of the Metaphysic of Morals* (L. W. Beck), and so forth. We will refer to the work as *The Metaphysical Foundations of Morals;* although a certain precision is lost by this rendering, greater readability and clarity is gained.
2. William Blake, "Auguries of Innocence." Sometimes a distinction is made between motive (e.g., jealousy) and intent (e.g., to get revenge).
3. In using the Categorical Imperative Kant has sometimes been accused of being a consequentialist and abandoning his formalistic position. But Kant is not arguing that disasterous consequences show a principle is wrong but that they point up the fact that the will would be involved in a self-contradiction. A person would be willing an action and at the same time willing the cessation of that action. For a good discussion of formalistic virtues see Philippa Foot, *Virtues and Vices and Other Essays in Moral Philosophy* (Berkeley: University of California Press, 1978), esp. 156–74.

4. Among the act deontologists are numbered E. F. Carritt, H. A. Pritchard, and Joseph Butler. See especially Carritt's *Theory of Morals*.
5. In this category is not only Immanuel Kant but W. D. Ross, Samuel Clarke, Richard Price, and Thomas Reid.
6. For an excellent example of a clash between a formalistic and consequentialist approach to ethics cf. the play *Antigone* by Jean Anouilh.
7. W. D. Ross, *The Right and the Good* (Oxford: Clarendon Press, 1930), Chapter 1.
8. Rufus Jones, *Fundamental Ends of Life* (New York: Macmillan, 1924), p. 74.
9. W. T. Stace, *The Concept of Morals* (New York: Macmillan, 1937), 6.
10. George Meredith, *Beauchamp's Career* (New York: Scribner's, 1915), Chapter 14.
11. By and large the bible speaks of the earth as belonging to man, which has justified some developers to exploit it for human purposes. Most ecologists, however, think it more Christian to regard man as a steward of the earth, charged by god to safeguard the planet.
12. Interpretations abound as to what the forbidden fruit might symbolize: knowledge (perhaps of good and evil), sexual experience, genuine choice (the precondition for humanness), private property (a Marxist view), and so forth. And it makes a difference whether one thinks of Eve as being tempted by the snake or by the apple and whether Adam was tempted by the Devil or by Eve (Woman, the Seductress). In any case, we wonder whether anything the fruit might symbolize should be forbidden to man, whether forbidden fruit should be dangled, and why subsequent generations should suffer for the sins of their forebears.
13. For a sound discussion of this point see Kai Nielsen, "Some Remarks on the Independence of Morality from Religion," *Mind* 52, no. 278 (April 1961). See also Ralph Cudworth's position in *The British Moralists,* ed. D. D. Raphael (Oxford: Clarendon Press, 1969), 1:105.
14. Reinhold Niebuhr, *Moral Man and Immoral Society* (New York: C. Scribner's Sons, 1953). See also Roland Bainton, *Christian Attitudes Toward War and Peace* (Nashville, Tenn.: Abingdon, 1960), Paul Ramsey, *The Just War* (New York: University of America Press, 1983), and *The Catholic Bishop and Nuclear War,* ed. J. Dwyer (Washington, D.C.: Georgetown University Press, 1984).
15. Joseph Fletcher, "Six Propositions: The New Look in Christian Ethics," *Harvard Divinity Bulletin* (October 1959): 17.
16. Joseph Fletcher, *Situation Ethics: The New Morality* (Philadelphia: Westminster Press, 1964), 158.
17. Paul Tillich, *Morality and Beyond* (New York: Harper & Row, 1963), 42–43. See also *Dynamics of Faith* (New York: Harper & Row, 1957).

Bibliography

ACTON, H. B. *Kant's Moral Philosophy.* London: Macmillan, 1970.
ALTIZER, THOMAS, J. J. *The Gospel of Christian Atheism.* Philadelphia: Westminster Press, 1966.
AQUINAS, ST. THOMAS. *Basic Writings of St. Thomas Aquinas.* New York: Random House, 1945.
AUGUSTINE, ST. *The City of God,* trans. Marcus Dods. New York: Random House, 1950.
AUNE, BRUCE. *Kant's Theory of Morals.* Princeton, N.J.: Princeton University Press, 1979.
BAIER, KURT. *The Moral Point of View.* Ithaca, N.Y.: Cornell University Press, 1958.
BARTH, KARL. *The Knowledge of God and the Service of God,* trans. J. L. M. Haire and I. Henderson. New York: Charles Scribner's Sons, 1939.
BEACH, WALDO, and H. R. NIEBUHR. *Christian Ethics.* New York: Ronald Press, 1955.

BENETT, JOHN C. *Christianity and Our World.* New York: Association Press, 1943.

BOK, SISSELA. *Lying: Moral Choice in Public and Private Life.* New York: Pantheon Books, 1978.

BONHOEFFER, DIETRICH. *Ethics.* New York, Macmillan, 1955.

BRUNNER, EMILE. *The Divine Imperative,* trans. Olive Wyon. Philadelphia: Westminster Press, 1947.

BURTT, EDWIN A. *Types of Religious Philosophy.* New York: Harper, 1951.

CARRITT, E. F. *The Theory of Morals.* London: Oxford University Press, 1928.

CAVE, SIDNEY. *The Christian Way.* New York: Philosophical Library, 1951.

DEAN, HERBERT A. *The Political and Social Ideas of St. Augustine.* New York: Columbia University Press, 1963.

DONAGAN, ALAN. *The Theory of Morality.* Chicago: University of Chicago Press, 1979.

FEUERBACH, L. *The Essence of Christianity.* New York: Frederick Ungar, 1957.

FUCHS, JOSEF. *Christian Ethics in a Secular Arena.* Washington, D.C.: Georgetown University Press, 1984.

GERT, BERNARD. *The Moral Rules: A New Rational Foundation for Morality.* New York: Harper & Row, 1970.

GEWIRTH, ALAN. *Reason and Morality.* Chicago: University of Chicago Press, 1979.

HAMILTON, WILLIAM. *Christian Man.* Philadelphia: Westminster Press, 1956.

HARE, R. M. *Freedom and Reason.* London: Oxford University Press, 1963.

HARRISON, JONATHAN. *Our Knowledge of Right and Wrong.* London: Allen and Unwin, 1971.

HELM, PAUL. *The Divine Commandment Theory of Ethics.* Oxford: Oxford University Press, 1979.

HOLLENBACH, DAVID. *Nuclear Ethics: A Christian Moral Argument.* New York Paulist Press, 1983.

JONES, WILLIAM T. *Morality and Freedom in the Philosophy of Immanuel Kant.* Oxford: Oxford University Press, 1940.

KANT, I. *Lectures on Ethics,* trans. L. Infield. New York: Harper & Row, 1963.

KENNY, ANTHONY. *The Five Ways: St. Thomas Aquinas' Proofs of God's Existence.* London: Routledge and Kegan Paul, 1969.

KORNER, S. *Kant.* Baltimore: Penguin Books, 1955.

KROPF, RICHARD W. *Evil and Evolution: A Theodicy.* Rutherford, N.J.: Fairleigh Dickinson Press, 1984.

LINDSAY, A. D. *Kant.* London: Oxford University Press, 1934.

MACINTOSH, D. C. *Social Religion.* New York: Charles Scribner, 1939.

MEIKLEJOHN, ALEXANDER. *Inclinations and Obligations.* Berkeley: University of California Press, 1948.

MORTIMER, R. C. *Christian Ethics.* New York: Rinehart, 1950.

NIEBUHR, REINHOLD. *An Interpretation of Christian Ethics.* New York: Harper and Brothers, 1935.

———. *The Nature and Destiny of Man.* New York: Charles Scribner's Sons, 1943.

NOVAK. V. M. *Christianity Today.* New York: Holt, Rinehart and Winston, 1966.

PATON, H. J. *The Categorical Imperative: A Study in Kant's Moral Philosophy.* Chicago: University of Chicago Press, 1948.

PRICHARD, H. A. *Duty and Interest.* Oxford: Clarendon Press, 1928.

RAHNER, KARL. *Christianity and the World.* New York: Kenedy, 1965.

RAMSEY, PAUL. *Basic Christian Ethics.* New York: Charles Scribner, 1951.

ROBINSON, JOHN A. T. *Honest to God.* London: S.C.M. Press, 1963.

ROSS, W. D. *Foundations of Ethics.* Oxford: Clarendon Press, 1939.

———. *Kant's Ethical Theory.* New York: Oxford University Press, 1954.

SCHILPP, PAUL. *Kant's Pre-Critical Ethics.* Evanston, Ill.: Northwestern University Press, 1938.

SCOTT, JOHN W. *Kant on the Moral Life*. New York: Macmillan, 1924.

SHWAYDER, D. S. "The Sense of Duty." *The Philosophical Quarterly* 7 (1957): 116–25.

SILBER, JOHN R. "The Contents of Kant's Ethical Thought." *Philosophical Quarterly* 9 (1959): 193–207, 309–18.

SINGER, MARCUS. *Generalization in Ethics*. New York: Random House, 1961.

STRANG, COLIN. "What If Everyone Did That." *Durham University Journal* 53 (1960).

TAYLOR, RICHARD. *Good and Evil*. Buffalo, N.Y.: Prometheus Books, 1984.

TEALE, A. E. *Kantian Ethics*. Oxford: Oxford University Press, 1951.

TILLICH, PAUL. *The Courage to Be*. New Haven: Yale University Press.

TORRANCE, THOMAS F. *God and Rationality*. New York: Oxford University Press, 1971.

VAHANIAN, GABRIEL. *The Death of God*. New York: George Braziller, 1961.

WHITNEY, G. T., and D. F. BOWERS, eds. *The Heritage of Kant*. Princeton, N.J.: Princeton University Press, 1939.

WOLFF, ROBERT PAUL. *The Autonomy of Reason*. New York: Harper & Row, 1973.

WOOD, ALLEN. *Kant's Moral Religion*. Ithaca, N.Y.: Cornell University Press, 1970.

CHAPTER 10

Humanism

Scientific Humanism: The Well Being of Mankind

When ethical ideals are based upon religion they carry authority because of belief in the religion. There may not be a logical connection between the two (as the *Euthyphro* clearly shows) but a strong psychological connection does exist. By the same token, when people lose their faith they tend to reject the values associated with that faith. Perhaps the baby should not be thrown out with the holy water, the ethics along with the metaphysics, but it is a common tendency and since many people do not accept religion or believe in a personal god, a different foundation is needed for their values.

The ethic of humanism proposes to fill that void and to substitute other goals and standards for the values that have been displaced. Humanism explicitly rejects all traditional religion and aims at the promotion of human welfare in man's actual, concrete existence. It may be described as a philosophy that asserts the dignity and worth of man, rejects supernaturalism, and advocates the maximum welfare of all human beings here on earth. Philosophers such as John Dewey (1859–1952) and Bertrand Russell (1872–1970) have endorsed this type of humanism, but more mainstream representatives include Sidney Hook, Paul Kurtz, Corliss Lamont, H. J. Blackham, and Edwin Wilson.

Other meanings of humanism are sometimes confused with this philosophic one, for example, the historical movement of humanism during the Renaissance that revived the study of classical literature and ideals. Although this movement differed in several respects from the scientific humanism of the twentieth century (especially in its retention of belief in god), there are strong parallels as well. The humanism of the Renaissance tried to recover some of the cultural ideals of ancient Greece and Rome, which contemporary humanism also prizes. Another common feature is an insistence on the value of autonomy, rationality, and independence and the worth of human personality. In addition, Renaissance humanism proclaimed the worth of man, his self-respect and pride, and refused to accept the notion of human depravity and sinfulness. This also became extremely important to contemporary humanism, and stands as a critical difference between humanism and most types of theism, especially Christianity.

For the humanist takes pride in man's accomplishments and will not practice humility before a transcendent god. He will not abase himself, bend his knee or bow his bead before a power greater than himself. He affirms the intrinsic value of human life, and resents having his self-esteem called vanity and rebellion. To the humanist, man should be elevated not degraded, whereas most types of theism teach people to think of themselves as having little merit or importance relative to god.

In *Humanism versus Theism* J. A. C. Fagginger Auer and Julian Hartt wrote that religion is always asserting

"Man, being man, is bound to do evil." The "General Confession of Sins," found in the Book of Common Prayer, states positively "that there is no health in us," nor do we find any limiting clause. True, the "Confession" is an ancient statement which no one is expected to take too literally, which is just as well, since few do so take it. But, the church has not changed it; and even those who repeat the Confession with certain mental reservations would be greatly surprised if their minister should ask the congregation to repeat in unison, "We are filled with health."

We have been told so often that we are sinners that we have come to believe it; and so infrequently have we been assured that there is good in us that we hesitate to accept this. To admit one's sins, frequently and sincerely, is counted a Christian virtue; to point to the fact that one is capable of doing good is called self-adoration.

John Calvin, for example, wrote that we should be "utterly despising [of] everything that may be supposed an excellence in us. This humility is unfeigned submission of a mind overwhelmed with a weighty sense of its own misery and poverty."[1] Similarly, in "God Glorified in Man's Dependence," Jonathan Edwards declared we are "without any true excellency, but are full of, and wholly defiled with, that which is infinitely odious. . . . By the creature being thus wholly and universally dependent on God, it appears that the creature is nothing, and that God is all."[2]

Rather than accepting the littleness of man and greatness of god, humanists insist that the human being is centrally important and should be the locus of all moral effort. "Humanism" by its very name implies that the main concern should be man in his earthly existence not any spiritual or other-worldly matters. It advocates a commitment to the welfare of all people and sees a moral obligation in being humanitarian and striving to improve the conditions of human life.

To most humanists this means engaging in practical actions that create the conditions for a just and equitable society, and working to solve the social problems of one's age. For example, contemporary humanists are concerned about urban decay and rural poverty, street crime and global warfare, about overpopulation and mass starvation in third-world countries, attitudes toward minorities and the aging, abortion and euthanasia (the right to life and the right to death), women's rights, human rights, civil rights, and so forth. There is no unanimity among humanists with regard to the methods for achieving social justice and equality but most humanists support a democratic program in which the individual is accorded maximum power and dignity, and change occurs through peaceful means, that is, through rational discussion not military confrontation.

In keeping with their humanitarian concerns, most humanists also stress that all moral values are derived from human experience rather than some divine laws of right and wrong. The worth of these values is measured by their contribution to the enhancement of human life. Humanists, in fact, reject belief in a personal god or a supernatural realm stretching beyond the natural one. They refuse to base man's life on the authoritarian commandments of religion or an alleged cosmic purpose that must be fulfilled. Man is thought to be alone in the universe, without divine protection or comfort, and all values are the product of human beings as they try to fulfill their needs (without infringing on the needs of others). There is no pity, justice, or love inherent in the cosmos, no warmth or personality, but people can affirm values that support their own welfare, individually and collectively.

Rather than being distressed then at the prospect of an empty, purposeless universe, indifferent to human aspirations and suffering, the humanists see this as immensely liberating. For man is no longer inconsequential in relation to an ideal father in heaven. He does not have to feel like an abject sinner, weak, dependent and inherently corrupt, ashamed of his natural desires and constantly acting under the eye of a judgmental god. He is finally free to develop his life fully. He can call his impulses wholesome, his body beautiful, and pleasure and comfort desirable. For the first time, human beings can claim the status of adults, responsible to themselves alone for what they do. They can believe in their own will power and the ability to solve their own problems and can focus on securing the well being of the human race, without the distraction of a hell to avoid or a heaven to hope for. Salvation no longer has to mean life after death or immortal bliss in the presence of god but an ennobling and enriching existence for humanity this side of the grave. The only criterion for good is what is good for man [A typical humanist passage states]:

> Only man himself can determine the criterion for virtue and sin, and not an authority transcending him. Humanistic ethics is anthropocentric; not, of course, in the sense that man is the center of the universe but in the sense that his value judgments, like all other judgments and even perceptions, are rooted in the peculiarities of his existence and are meaningful only with reference to it; man, indeed, is "the measure of all things." The humanistic position is that there is nothing higher than man and nothing more dignified than human existence.[3]

Humanists therefore are essentially optimistic in their attitudes. The earth need not be filled with suffering, a realm of punishment for original sin or a testing ground for the life to come, and man is not insignificant or depraved. Through reason and intelligence, especially the employment of science and technology, genuine progress can be made to better our condition. Reason is capable of forming ethical standards, unaided by any divine revelation, so that life is improved for the family of man.

The humanists are not ashamed to include in this betterment a higher and more just standard of living for all mankind. Poverty is not an honorable thing to their minds but crushing and demeaning; people are far better off when they are properly clothed, housed, and fed. An adequate amount of earthly goods (if not affluence) is essential to the spirit of man and being in want is not a purifying discipline. Humanists decry, for example, the type of Christian attitude toward poverty expressed by the following encyclical. It was issued in 1932, at the height of the Great Depression, and advised the poor that they should

> Suffer with great resignation the privations imposed upon them by these hard times and state of society, which Divine Providence in an ever-loving but inscrutable plan has assigned them. Let them accept with a humble and trustful heart from the hand of God the effects of poverty, rendered harder by the distress in which mankind now is struggling. . . . Let them take comfort in the certainty that their sacrifices and troubles borne in a Christian spirit will concur efficaciously to hasten the hour of mercy and peace.[4]

It is far better, the humanist argues, to improve our physical circumstances rather than resign ourselves to hardships that in some mystical way win rewards in an afterlife.

The humanist rejects belief in immortality altogether; he calls it an illusion and maintains "This life is all and it is enough." Those who believe that the end is not the tomb, who have faith in a life to come, are regarded as weak and emotionally immature. Such faith is cowardice, a type of wishful thinking and intellectual dishonesty. Some humanists agree with Freud that religion is an "infantile neurosis" and that the belief in life after death only functions to reduce deep-seated anxieties. According to Freud, the neurotic person needs to believe that his heavenly father will reward him with eternal life in return for being a good and faithful child; it is the ultimate proof of the parent's power and love. The person has been deprived of the assurance he desperately needs from his earthly father so he must substitute a father in heaven who loves him so much he will let him live forever. Not all humanists accept this explanation but they all agree that immortality is an illusion springing from psychological need; it in no way reflects the reality. The present, physical, embodied life is all we can rely upon. The humanist Corliss Lamont summarized the position this way:

> Humanism is the viewpoint that man has but one life to lead and should make the most of it in terms of creative work and happiness; that human happiness is its own justification and requires no sanction or support from supernatural sources; that in any case the supernatural, usually conceived of in the form of heavenly gods or immortal heavens, does not exist; and that human beings, using their own intelligence and cooperating liberally with one another, can build an enduring citadel of peace and beauty upon this earth.
> It is true that no people has yet come near to establishing the ideal society. Yet humanism asserts that man's own reason and efforts are man's best and, indeed, only hope; and that man's refusal to recognize this point is one of the chief causes of his failures throughout history. In times of confusion and disintegration like the present, men face the temptation of fleeing to some compensatory realm of make-believe or supernatural solace. Humanism stands uncompromisingly against this tendency, which both expresses and encourages defeatism. The Humanistic philosophy persistently strives to remind men that their only home is in the mundane world. There is no use of our searching elsewhere for happiness and fulfillment, for there is no place else to go. We human beings must find our destiny and our promised land in the here and now, or not at all.[5]

In place of religion and the promise of immortality, humanists would like to substitute other spurs to moral living. Instead of helping one another in order to win personal rewards in heaven, the humanist calls upon people's highest feelings of mutual benevolence and concern. We should respond to each other's needs because we are all human beings together on this planet, a planet that is more like a space ship than a cornucopia, and the character of this self-contained space is determined by the ethics we practice. If we are cruel the whole is made worse; if we are kind then everyone is better off. Quite simply, the humanists enjoin us to take care of one another.

In order to substitute this humane foundation for the supernatural one, the humanist relies upon people's good sense and good-heartedness, as well as the social and legal penalties imposed for injuring others. Above all they pin their hopes on education to rid people of their superstitions and dependencies and bring about a new commitment to the well being of man on earth.

Science and technology is the method selected for improving the human condition, and humanists encourage the application of scientific knowledge to all areas of life. There is no such thing as "forbidden knowledge," the tasting of forbidden fruit, but only open inquiry and the use of scientific method to understand and control our environment. Ignorance is not bliss but slavery to groundless fears and the more we know the greater our ability to transform nature into an ideal home for man. The social sciences are considered especially important in this program, for psychological, social, political, and economic forces affect us very strongly and personally, but the physical sciences must also be developed and utilized for better products, homes, energy sources, health, and general ease in living.

In short, the humanists declare that man unaided, using his reason and the tools of science, can improve life on earth, that religion is an illusion and a distraction, preaching a transcendent god and a teleological universe that mature human beings can no longer accept. A new consciousness must be achieved as to man's place in the scheme of things and a realization that human beings do not find their values in the cosmos but create them out of the humane requirements of concrete situations. The entire world community must now come of age and join together in a movement of brotherhood and unity, promoting a higher standard of living for all mankind as well as the democratic virtues of justice, freedom, and equality.

In 1933 a *Humanist Manifesto* was published that expressed the main points of the doctrine. Some forty years later Paul Kurtz and Edwin Wilson presented a *Humanist Manifesto II*, which updated the previous document and offered "a positive declaration for times of uncertainty." It was intended as a synthesis of contemporary humanist views, and was signed by hundreds of prominent philosophers, scientists, and intellectuals of every description. The list included figures such as Isaac Asimov, H. J. Blackham, Brand Blanshard, Francis Crick, Arthur Danto, Paul Edwards, Albert Ellis, Raymond Firth, Anthony Flew, Sidney Hook, Mary Mothersill, Kai Nielsen, P. H. Nowell-Smith, John Herman Randall, Jr., Andre Sakharov, Roy Wood Sellars, and B. F. Skinner.

The following pages contain the complete text of this manifesto, which is considered the most definitive statement of the humanist position to date.

The Humanist Manifesto*

The next century can be and should be the humanistic century. Dramatic scientific, technological, and ever-accelerating social and political changes crowd our awareness. We have virtually conquered the planet, explored the moon, overcome the natural limits of travel and communication; we stand at the dawn of a new age, ready to move farther into space and perhaps inhabit other planets. Using technology wisely, we can control our environment, conquer poverty, markedly reduce disease, extend our life-span, significantly modify our behavior, alter the course of human evolution and cultural development, unlock vast new powers, and provide humankind with unparalleled opportunity for achieving an abundant and meaningful life.

The future is, however, filled with dangers. In learning to apply the scientific method to nature and human life, we have opened the door to ecological damage, overpopulation, dehumanizing institutions, totalitarian repression, and nuclear and biochemical disaster. Faced with apocalyptic prophesies and doomsday scenarios, many flee in despair from reason and embrace irrational cults and theologies of withdrawal and retreat.

Traditional moral codes and newer irrational cults both fail to meet the pressing needs of today and tomorrow. False "theologies of hope" and messianic ideologies, substituting new dogmas for old, cannot cope with existing world realities. They separate rather than unite peoples.

Humanity, to survive, requires bold and daring measures. We need to extend the uses of scientific method, not renounce them, to fuse reason with compassion in order to build constructive social and moral values. Confronted by many possible futures, we must decide which to pursue. The ultimate goal should be the fulfillment of the potential for growth in each human personality — not for the favored few, but for all of humankind. Only a shared world and global measures will suffice.

A humanist outlook will tap the creativity of each human being and provide the vision and courage for us to work together. This outlook emphasizes the role human beings can play in their own spheres of action. The decades ahead call for dedicated, clear-minded men and women able to marshal the will, intelligence, and cooperative skills for shaping a desirable future. Humanism can provide the purpose and inspiration that so many seek; it can give personal meaning and significance to human life.

Many kinds of humanism exist in the contemporary world. The varieties and emphases of naturalistic humanism include "scientific," "ethical," "democratic," "religious," and "Marxist" humanism. Free thought, atheism, agnosticism, skepticism, deism, rationalism, ethical culture, and liberal religion all claim to be heir to the humanist tradition. Humanism traces its roots from ancient China, classical Greece and Rome, through the Renaissance and the Enlightenment, to the scientific revolution of the modern world. But views that merely reject theism are not equivalent to humanism. They lack commitment to the positive belief in the possibilities of

*Reprinted with permission from Paul Kurtz, ed., *Humanist Manifesto II* (Buffalo, N.Y.: Prometheus Books, 1985; first edition 1973), 14–23.

human progress and to the values central to it. Many within religious groups, believing in the future of humanism, now claim humanist credentials. Humanism is an ethical process through which we all can move, above and beyond the divisive particulars, heroic personalities, dogmatic creeds, and ritual customs of past religions or their mere negation.

We affirm a set of common principles that can serve as a basis for united action—positive principles relevant to the present human condition. They are a design for a secular society on a planetary scale.

For these reasons, we submit this new *Humanist Manifesto* for the future of humankind; for us, it is a vision of hope, a direction for satisfying survival.

Religion

First: In the best sense, religion may inspire dedication to the highest ethical ideals. The cultivation of moral devotion and creative imagination is an expression of genuine "spiritual" experience and aspiration.

We believe, however, that traditional dogmatic or authoritarian religions that place revelation, God, ritual, or creed above human needs and experience do a disservice to the human species. Any account of nature should pass the tests of scientific evidence; in our judgment, the dogmas and myths of traditional religions do not do so. Even at this late date in human history, certain elementary facts based upon the critical use of scientific reason have to be restated. We find insufficient evidence for belief in the existence of a supernatural, it is either meaningless or irrelevant to the question of the survival and fulfillment of the human race. As nontheists, we begin with humans not God, nature not deity. Nature may indeed be broader and deeper than we now know; any new discoveries, however, will but enlarge our knowledge of the natural.

Some humanists believe we should reinterpret traditional religions and reinvest them with meanings appropriate to the current situation. Such redefinitions, however, often perpetuate old dependencies and escapisms; they easily become obscurantist, impeding the free use of the intellect. We need, instead, radically new human purposes and goals.

We appreciate the need to preserve the best ethical teachings in the religious traditions of humankind, many of which we share in common. But we reject those features of traditional religious morality that deny humans a full appreciation of their own potentialities and responsibilities. Traditional religions often offer solace to humans, but, as often, they inhibit humans from helping themselves or experiencing their full potentialities. Such institutions, creeds, and rituals often impede the will to serve others. Too often traditional faiths encourage dependence rather than independence, obedience rather than affirmation, fear rather than courage. More recently they have generated concerned social action, with many signs of relevance appearing in the wake of the "God Is Dead" theologies. But we can discover no divine purpose or providence for the human species. While there is much that we do not know, humans are responsible for what we are or will become. No deity will save us; we must save ourselves.

Second: Promises of immortal salvation or fear of eternal damnation are both illusory and harmful. They distract humans from present concerns, from self-actualization, and from rectifying social injustices. Modern science discredits such historic concepts as the "ghost in the machine" and the "separable soul." Rather, science affirms that the human species is an emergence from natural evolutionary forces. As far as we know, the total personality is a function of the biological organism transacting in a social and cultural context. There is no credible evidence that life survives the death of the body. We continue to exist in our progeny and in the way that our lives have influenced others in our culture.

Traditional religions are surely not the only obstacles to human progress. Other ideologies also impede human advance. Some forms of political doctrine, for instance, function religiously, reflecting the worst features of orthodoxy and authoritarianism, especially when they sacrifice individuals on the altar of Utopian promises. Purely economic and political viewpoints, whether capitalist or communist, often function as religious and ideological dogma. Although humans undoubtedly need economic and political goals, they also need creative values by which to live.

Ethics

Third: We affirm that moral values derive their source from human experience. Ethics is *autonomous* and *situational*, needing no theological or ideological sanction. Ethics stems from human need and interest. To deny this distorts the whole basis of life. Human life has meaning because we create and develop our futures. Happiness and the creative realization of human needs and desires, individually and in shared enjoyment, are continuous themes of humanism. We strive for the good life, here and now. The goal is to pursue life's enrichment despite debasing forces of vulgarization, commercialization, bureaucratization, and dehumanization.

Fourth: Reason and intelligence are the most effective instruments that humankind possesses. There is no substitute: neither faith nor passion suffices in itself. The controlled use of scientific methods, which have transformed the natural and social sciences since the Renaissance, must be extended further in the solution of human problems. But reason must be tempered by humility, since no group has a monopoly of wisdom or virtue. Nor is there any guarantee that all problems can be solved or all questions answered. Yet critical intelligence, infused by a sense of human caring, is the best method that humanity has for resolving problems. Reason should be balanced with compassion and empathy and the whole person fulfilled. Thus, we are not advocating the use of scientific intelligence independent of or in opposition to emotion, for we believe in the cultivation of feeling and love. As science pushes back the boundary of the known, one's sense of wonder is continually renewed, and art, poetry, and music find their places, along with religion and ethics.

The Individual

Fifth: The preciousness and dignity of the individual person is a central humanist value. Individuals should be encouraged to realize their own creative talents and desires. We reject all religious, ideological, or moral codes that denigrate the individual, suppress freedom, dull intellect, dehumanize personality. We believe in maximum individual autonomy consonant with social responsibility. Although science can account for the causes of behavior, the possibilities of individual *freedom of choice* exist in human life and should be increased.

Sixth: In the area of sexuality, we believe that intolerant attitudes, often cultivated by orthodox religions and puritanical cultures, unduly repress sexual conduct. The right to birth control, abortion, and divorce should be recognized. While we do not approve of exploitive, denigrating forms of sexual expression, neither do we wish to prohibit, by law or social sanction, sexual behavior between consenting adults. The many varieties of sexual exploration should not in themselves be considered "evil." Without countenancing mindless permissiveness or unbridled promiscuity, a civilized society should be a *tolerant* one. Short of harming others or compelling them to do likewise, individuals should be permitted to express their sexual proclivities and pursue their life-styles as they desire. We wish to cultivate the development of a responsible attitude toward sexuality, in which humans are not exploited as sexual objects, and in which intimacy, sensitivity, respect, and honesty in interpersonal relations are encouraged. Moral education for children and adults is an important way of developing awareness and sexual maturity.

Democratic Society

Seventh: To enhance freedom and dignity the individual must experience a full range of *civil liberties* in all societies. This includes freedom of speech and the press, political democracy, the legal right of opposition to governmental policies, fair judicial process, religious liberty, freedom of association, and artistic, scientific, and cultural freedom. It also includes a recognition of an individual's right to die with dignity, euthanasia, and the right to suicide. We oppose the increasing invasion of privacy, by whatever means, in both totalitarian and democratic societies. We would safeguard, extend, and implement the principles of human freedom evolved from the *Magna Carta* to the *Bill of Rights*, the *Rights of Man*, and the *Universal Declaration of Human Rights*.

Eighth: We are committed to an open and democratic society. We must extend *participatory democracy* in its true sense to the economy, the school, the family, the workplace, and voluntary associations. Decision-making must be decentralized to include widespread involvement of people at all levels—social, political, and economic. All persons should have a voice in developing the values and goals that determine their lives. Institutions should be responsive to expressed desires and needs. The conditions of work, education, devotion, and play should be humanized. Alienating forces should be modified or eradicated and bureaucratic structures should be held to a minimum. People are more important than decalogues, rules, proscriptions, or regulations.

Ninth: The separation of church and state and the separation of ideology and state are imperatives. The state should encourage maximum freedom for different moral, political, religious, and social values in society. It should not favor any particular religious bodies through the use of public monies, nor espouse a single ideology and function thereby as an instrument of propaganda or oppression, particularly against dissenters.

Tenth: Humane societies should evaluate economic systems not by rhetoric or ideology, but by whether or not they *increase economic well-being* for all individuals and groups, minimize poverty and hardship, increase the sum of human satisfaction, and enhance the quality of life. Hence the door is open to alternative economic systems. We need to democratize the economy and judge it by its responsiveness to human needs, testing results in terms of the common good.

Eleventh: The principle of moral equality must be furthered through elimination of all discrimination based upon race, religion, sex, age, or national origin. This means equality of opportunity and recognition of talent and merit. Individuals should be encouraged to contribute to their own betterment. If unable, the society should provide means to satisfy their basic economic, health, and cultural needs, including, wherever resources make possible, a minimum guaranteed annual income. We are concerned for the welfare of the aged, the infirm, the disadvantaged, and also for the outcasts—the mentally retarded, abandoned or abused children, the handicapped, prisoners, and addicts—for *all* who are neglected or ignored by society. Practicing humanists should make it their vocation to humanize personal relations.

We believe in the *right to universal education.* Everyone has a right to the cultural opportunity to fulfill his or her unique capacities and talents. The schools should foster satisfying and productive living. They should be open at all levels to any and all; the achievement of excellence should be encouraged. Innovative and experimental forms of education are to be welcomed. The energy and idealism of the young deserve to be appreciated and channeled to constructive purposes.

We deplore racial, religious, ethnic, or class antagonisms. Although we believe in cultural diversity and encourage racial and ethnic pride, we reject separations which promote alienation and set people and groups against each other; we envision an *integrated* community where people have a maximum opportunity for free and voluntary association.

We are *critical of sexism or sexual chauvinism*—male or female. We believe in equal rights for both women and men to fulfill their unique careers and potentialities as they see fit, free of invidious discrimination.

World Community

Twelfth: We deplore the division of humankind on nationalistic grounds. We have reached a turning point in human history where the best option is to *transcend the limits of national sovereignty* and to move toward the building of a world community in which all sectors of the human family can participate. Thus we look to the development of a system of world law and a world order based upon transnational federal government. This would appreciate cultural pluralism and diversity. It would not exclude pride in national origins and accomplishments nor the handling of regional problems on a regional basis. Human progress, however, can no longer be achieved by focusing on one section of the world, Western or Eastern, developed or underdeveloped. For the first time in human history, no part of humankind can be isolated from any other. Each person's future is in some way linked to all. We thus reaffirm a commitment to the building of world community, at the same time recognizing that this commits us to some hard choices.

Thirteenth: This world community must *renounce the resort to violence and force* as a method of solving international disputes. We believe in the peaceful adjudication of differences by international courts and by the development of the arts of negotiation and compromise. War is obsolete. So is the use of nuclear, biological, and chemical weapons. It is a planetary imperative to reduce the level of military expenditures and turn these savings to peaceful and people-oriented uses.

Fourteenth: The world community must engage in *cooperative planning* concerning the use of rapidly depleting resources. The planet earth must be considered a single *ecosystem*. Ecological damage, resource depletion, and excessive population growth must be checked by international concord. The cultivation and conservation of nature is a moral value; we should perceive ourselves as integral to the sources of our being in nature. We must free our world from needless pollution and waste, responsibly guarding and creating wealth, both natural and human. Exploitation of natural resources, uncurbed by social conscience, must end.

Fifteenth: The problems of *economic growth and development* can no longer be resolved by one nation alone; they are worldwide in scope. It is the moral obligation of the developed nations to provide — through an international authority that safeguards human rights — massive technical, agricultural, medical, and economic assistance, including birth control techniques, to the developing portions of the globe. World poverty must cease. Hence extreme disproportions in wealth, income, and economic growth should be reduced on a worldwide basis.

Sixteenth: Technology is a vital key to human progress and development. We deplore any neo-romantic efforts to condemn indiscriminately all technology and science or to counsel retreat from its further extension and use for the good of humankind. We would resist any moves to censor basic scientific research on moral, political, or social grounds. Technology must, however, be carefully judged by the consequences of its use; harmful and destructive changes should be avoided. We are particularly disturbed when technology and bureaucracy control, manipulate, or modify human beings without their consent. Technological feasibility does not imply social or cultural desirability.

Seventeenth: We must expand communication and transportation across frontiers. Travel restrictions must cease. The world must be open to diverse political, ideological, and moral viewpoints and evolve a worldwide system of television and radio for information and education. We thus call for full international cooperation in culture, science, the arts, and technology *across ideological borders*. We must learn to live openly together or we shall perish together.

Humanity as a Whole

In closing: The world cannot wait for a reconciliation of competing political or economic systems to solve its problems. These are the times for men and women of good will to further the building of a peaceful and prosperous world. We urge that parochial loyalties and inflexible moral and religious ideologies be transcended. We urge recognition of the common humanity of all people. We further urge the use of reason and compassion to produce the kind of world we want—a world in which peace, prosperity, freedom, and happiness are widely shared. Let us not abandon that vision in despair or cowardice. We are responsible for what we are or will be. Let us work together for a humane world by means commensurate with humane ends. Destructive ideological differences among communism, capitalism, socialism, conservatism, liberalism, and radicalism should be overcome. Let us call for an end to terror and hatred. We will survive and prosper only in a world of shared humane values. We can initiate new directions for humankind; ancient rivalries can be superseded by broad-based cooperative efforts. The commitment to tolerance, understanding, and peaceful negotiation does not necessitate acquiescence to the status quo nor the damming up of dynamic and revolutionary forces. The true revolution is occurring and can continue in countless non-violent adjustments. But this entails the willingness to step forward onto new and expanding plateaus. At the present juncture of history, commitment to all humankind is the highest commitment of which we are capable; it transcends the narrow allegiances of church, state, party, class, or race in moving toward a wider vision of human potentiality. What more daring a goal for humankind than for each person to become, in ideal as well as practice, a citizen of a world community. It is a classical vision, we can now give it new vitality. Humanism thus interpreted is a moral force that has time on its side. We believe that humankind has the potential intelligence, good will, and cooperative skill to implement this commitment in the decades ahead.

Evaluation

1. In one sense it is refreshing to have an ethic that liberates itself from the confining aspects of religion, breathes freely and looks hopefully toward the future of the human race. However, humanism may not be rejecting god at all but making a god of man. According to some critics, man is being substituted for god in the humanist system and belief is not abandoned as an outmoded, childish relic but reinstituted with a new object.

It is further charged that human beings are hardly fit objects of worship. The history of man on earth is not one of continual progress and benevolent interaction but repeated warfare and atrocities down to the present day. In our century alone we have witnessed the massacre of 6 million Jews in Nazi Germany and 10 million of Stalin's opponents in Russia, as well as untold millions of Chinese by Mao's Red Guards and Cambodians by the Khymer Rouge. World Wars I and II resulted in the deaths of 1.5 million American military men, and hundreds of thousands have been killed in wars and revolutions in Africa, Asia, and the Middle East in the past forty years. In the light of man's inhumanity to man it is a rather macabre and bitter joke to celebrate the glory of humanity.

2. A related criticism has to do with the optimistic attitude toward the future of the human race that humanism seems to hold. James Freeman Clark's statement of faith "I believe in salvation by character and the progress of mankind onward and upward forever" now seems very naive. Serious questions are being raised today about the "perfectibility of man" and building "an enduring citadel of peace and beauty upon this earth." Not only are we threatened in the twentieth century with nuclear destruction on a global scale but a pervasive scepticism now exists as to whether science, technology, and the rational mind are sufficient to solve human problems. The former belief, that man could exploit nature as he pleased and engineer his own future, has given way to feelings of futility in the face of pollution, toxic waste, chronic starvation, chemical warfare, electronic surveillance, carcinogenic food, intractable diseases, and so forth. We now wonder about the limits of science and whether some problems might not be insoluble, about the extent of man's intellectual ability and of his reasonableness. We question whether our creations have become too complex for us to control, and whether our advanced, industrial culture can be considered genuine progress. Not only might science and technology not be helping us to a brave new world but they could be part of the problem itself, worsening man's condition as well as threatening his survival.

To regard the creations of science as Frankenstein's monster is not new, but the ambivalent attitude toward science on the part of educated people is a unique development. Perfectly intelligent individuals today are seriously troubled over the prospects for humanity and wonder whether man can manage the powers he has unleashed. Numerous books have appeared asking whether we can recork the genii, close Pandora's box before Hope, too, is allowed to escape.[6]

3. It is also charged that humanism's situation ethics, derived not from recognized rights of man but "human need and interest," only makes matters worse. Values cannot be built from consensus or cooperative accord since that would make prevailing opinion right—including intolerance or imperialism if that were in vogue. A monstrous set of values could then emerge based, for example, on the need for torturing and killing people on a vast scale, and if no higher source of values were thought to exist there would be no foundation for criticizing such desires as wrong.

In short, by claiming that what people want is what they should have, the humanist has no basis for rejecting unhealthy desires. He cannot say there is a "general will" different than people's expressed will, the truly good as opposed to what people seek, since to his mind whatever is desired is desirable. This is blatant nonsense, derived from too high an estimate of man's nature. As was pointed out in Chapter 1, people can desire that which is not "desirable," that is, not worthy of being desired. Having a need and interest does not justify an action ipso facto. The humanist rejects any objective moral standard (which he labels as a creed, dogma, or ideology), but that is precisely what is required to separate those needs that should be fulfilled from those that should be suppressed.

The humanist actually contradicts himself because he champions certain values as important while at the same time maintaining that the importance of values is a function of circumstance and free choice. He believes in tolerance, creativity, dignity, participatory democracy, reason, freedom, equality of opportunity, peace, conservation of resources, cooperation, world unity, and so forth. But as a situationist he cannot endorse such a battery of values, and if they should conflict, which one would take precedence?

4. Not only does a defect exist in this respect but many critics charge that humanism is weak overall. It lacks the rigor, consistency, and thoroughness that characterize the major ethical theories, being more concerned with what it denies (authoritarian religion) than developing what it affirms. And the values that are affirmed often seem to be little more than a string of liberal platitudes, difficult to argue with but somewhat shallow and clichéd.

For example, phrases such as "the dignity of the individual person" and "the building of a world community" should be explained more thoroughly, because individualism and the common good could be diametrically opposed.[7] In the same way, terms such as *freedom* and *equality* need to be defined more precisely if they are to have any significance or application to actual affairs. For instance, capitalists and communists each claim that their system promotes freedom and equality and the other does not, and each claims to be the more democratic. We find in fact that the free-enterprise system in capitalism tends to produce inequalities in the distribution of wealth and that the economic equality prized in communist countries leads to limitations on the freedom of its citizens. What, exactly, do humanists mean by these key terms, and where would they draw the lines?

Humanists admit that many of their moral concepts are vague, but that this allows the individual sufficient latitude to interpret matters for himself. However, as one commentator stated, "the risk of reasonably precise definitions of moral terms is one that moral philosophy is obliged to run. Our common moral experience itself reveals definite cleavages between good and evil, and right and wrong; and a theory which is not prepared to furnish a rational foundation for at least equally clear distinctions is not worth very much." We need "much more precise definitions of right and value than the Humanists are prepared to furnish."[8]

However, although humanism exaggerates the worth of man, places too much faith in reason and science to improve the world, and fails to ground or properly define its ethical concepts, it does provide a positive moral force at a time of widespread social problems. The values listed in the *Humanist Manifesto* may be somewhat hackneyed but in a larger sense such clichés cannot be repeated too often. Above all, humanism offers people moral direction in a secular age and urges people to work together for their common welfare. Whatever imperfections humanism might have, this is certainly a worthwhile aim and an ideal that cannot be dismissed lightly.

Existentialism: Investing Life with Meaning

Scientific humanism is usually identified as humanism per se, but existentialism is another modern movement often classified as a humanistic philosophy. To label existentialism as a humanism may mean fitting it to a procrustean bed in order to contain figures such as Friedrich Nietzsche, who oppose "the slaves" that are the bulk of mankind and celebrate "the masters" that are individuals of outstanding strength, nobility, and courage. Nevertheless, existentialism is a homocentric doctrine, concentrating on man's uniqueness, freedom, and responsibility in a universe devoid of divine direction, and the concepts are central to humanism.

Although existentialism is considered a twentieth century phenomenon its roots go back to the nineteenth century in the writings of Friedrich Nietzsche (1844–1900) and Soren Kierkegaard (1813–1855), the founders of the atheistic and theistic branches, respectively. Jean-Paul Sartre (1905–1980) was the acknowledged leader of the contemporary existential movement, and he carried forward the atheistic strain that has become the dominant form.[9] Other prominent figures include Martin Heidegger (1899–1976), Karl Jaspers (1883–1969), Gabriel Marcel (1889–1973), Simone de Beauvoir (1908–1983) and the phenomenologist Edmund Husserl (1859–1938), who contributed a basic methodology. On the fringes of existentialism are two Spanish writers, Miguel de Unamuno (1864–1936) and Ortega y Gasset (1883–1955), and two Russians, Nikolai Berdyaev (1874–1948) and Leon Shestov (1868–1938). A number of literary figures are also identified with the existential perspective including Fedor Dostoevsky (1821–1881), Franz Kafka (1883–1924), André Gide (1869–1951), Jean Gênet (1910–1983), and most notably Albert Camus (1913–1960).

As mentioned, Jean-Paul Sartre may be taken as the prime representative of the existential position. Like Gabriel Marcel, he presented his ideas in literary as well as treatise form; in fact, he was awarded the Nobel prize for literature in 1964. *Being and Nothingness* is his magnum opus but many of his themes are sounded in novels and plays such as *No Exit, The Flies, The Age of Reason*, and *Nausea*. In the last mentioned work, Sartre illustrated his theory of two modes of being, and this could serve as a cutting edge into his thought.

> "I was in the park just now," [a character named Roquentin declares.] "The roots of the chestnut tree were sunk in the ground just under my bench. I couldn't remember it was a root any more. The words had vanished and with them the significance of things, their methods of use, and the feeble points of reference which men have traced on their surface. I was sitting, stooping forward, head bowed, alone in front of this black, knotty mass, entirely beastly. . . . Existence had suddenly unveiled itself. It had lost the harmless look of an abstract category: it was the very paste of things, this root was kneaded into existence. Or rather the root, the park gates, the bench, the sparse grass, all that had vanished: the diversity of things, their individuality, were only an appearance, a veneer. . . . Absurdity was not an idea in my head, or the sound of a voice, only this long serpent dead at my feet, this wooden serpent. . . . below all explanation."[10]

What Roquentin comprehends is the kind of being that things possess, the burgeoning, oozing, proliferation of matter that is unending yet entirely meaningless. Sartre calls it *being-in-itself* (*être-en-soi*) and views the objects in this phenomenal realm as characterized by absolute "plenitude" coupled with total absurdity. They exist without any gaps or defects, in complete fullness, while at the same time their being is absurd and pointless. Being-in-itself is *de trop*, excessive, superfluous, and unwanted, but it spreads and swells, enlarges and distends itself until its bulk induces nausea.

At the same time Roquentin becomes aware that he, too, is *de trop*, that his existence is as accidental and senseless as any other natural object, but he also understands that he differs from objects insofar as he is a *being-for-itself* (*être-pour-soi*). As a human being he possesses consciousness, and that enables him to create meaning within the meaninglessness, to decide the terms of his existence, investing his life with value even though the universe itself contains none at all.

In a sense, the being-for-itself of man is inferior to the being-in-itself of objects because people are forever incomplete, always lacking in terms of the ideal selves they can imagine, whereas objects can never be faulted as deficient. One cannot expect an artichoke or a frog to be anything more than it is, but every person is less than he could be. And as we know some people make a mess of their lives, which is something one can never say about the roots of a chestnut tree.

Man is also inferior to the being of objects because of an internal gap produced by his consciousness. That is, human beings are separated from themselves by their self-awareness. They are both the "I" that is the knower and the "me" that is known, both the subject and the object of understanding. Man is therefore a discordant being, divided from himself by "nothing," as Sartre said, but it is an eternal nothing that leaves him incomplete. Once consciousness evolved in man, a schism opened up within each conscious being, a wound that nonconscious objects do not have. And this division only multiplies with an increase in consciousness. For there is the self, and the self contemplating the self, and the self that is aware of the self contemplating the self, and so on ad infinitum. The only way that the separations can be eliminated would be through loss of consciousness, but since that is the main constituent of humanness a person can only be complete by becoming less than human. Therefore man will always have gaps within his being unless he consents to be an unconscious object; *qua* man, he will remain perpetually divided.

At the same time human beings enjoy a superior mode of being, because the possibilities that always lie before us and our consciousness of acting in the world give us a command over existence that objects lack. We deplore our disadvantage in relation to the absolute plenitude and completeness of objects, but man's compensation lies in is his power of choice. As a result of our ontological inferiority, Sartre says, we are free to choose the kind of people we want to become.

Ideally we would like to be the in-itself-for-itself (*l'en-soi-pour-soi*), but that is logically impossible. If we possessed the completeness of objects we would loose our consciousness, thus our unity and wholeness would have no value since we could not be aware of it. If, on the other hand, we retain our consciousness as human beings then we cannot be complete and undivided but continually separated from ourselves.

The endless chase after this impossible goal makes man a "futile passion" (*une passion inutile*), but we cannot help wanting full being and full consciousness. And the logical contradiction within the *en-soi-pour-soi*, incidentally, also means that god cannot exist, for this is the only adequate concept of god yet it is impossible.[11]

Man is therefore stymied and frustrated by his situation, nevertheless his awareness is more of a blessing than a curse. Human beings are "condemned to be free," Sartre declared, but that means we are able to decide the contours of our individual lives.

Existence and Essence

Sartre reached the same conclusion via another distinction that has become basic to the existential philosophy. He stated that in the case of objects "essence precedes existence," which means that the essential nature of an object is already present at the time it comes into being. However, in the case of human beings *existence precedes essence*, that is, man first exists then he develops his essential character by the decisions and commitments he makes.

There is no given human nature that all people must fulfill by virtue of being a member of the species, no inherent potential that should be realized during our tenure on earth. The classic view, that man has an essential nature, present from birth and altered very little by the environment, must be rejected. "Man in general" does not exist; there are only individuals who build their identities subsequent to existence. We create ourselves from an infinity of possibilities, amassing a personal history that forms a unique character.

This means that each person is totally responsible for the kind of human being he becomes and cannot claim any inherent depravity because of original sin. He cannot escape blame by maintaining that "bad blood" or a brutal upbringing made him selfish or cruel. There are no excuses; man is free to be what he chooses. Responsibility for our past actions cannot be evaded with a "just so" story and we cannot avoid the decision as to what we want to become in the future by living for today.

However, although human beings are free to choose their actions, that is, themselves, they are not free to refrain from choosing; they cannot *not* choose. Since existence precedes essence we are forced to make decisions in our lives, otherwise we will never develop an essence as individuals. To use Sartre's example, a paper knife already possesses its basic characteristics from the time it is brought into existence (it has a definite form, material, color, etc.) but people must build their individual identities through their choices subsequent to existence, otherwise they are empty and anonymous. Our actions do not follow from our character but our character from our actions; therefore we have to act and commit ourselves to ideals and goals. We do not have the luxury of withdrawing from life or enjoying the role of spectator. What we do is what we are and to do nothing is to be nothing. This is why Sartre characterized existentialism as a philosophy of action and the very opposite of quietism with which it is charged.

The next question that arises of course is If we are nothing but the ensemble of our actions, what actions exactly should we perform, what decisions ought people to make? What guidelines are there to give us direction in making the best choices?

Unfortunately, most existentialists feel there is no external source to turn to in deciding our lives. If we are honest with ourselves and operate in good faith, we have to admit that god does not exist and the universe is without a purpose we could serve. It makes us feel forlorn to know that there is no vital place for us in some grand plan, no cosmic backdrop against which we act out our existence. We are alone in an indifferent universe, a speck of matter with just enough consciousness to realize the absurdity of our condition.

We want a universe that cares about us, with values written indelibly in the sky, some objective principles that would provide the grounds for our conduct. We need a system of cosmic rewards and punishments, an afterlife, a divine being who offers comfort and hope. In short, we need a purposeful universe governed by a loving god, but the reality contradicts our longings. As Albert Camus said, the universe itself is not absurd but the disparity between our need for meaning and the utter meaninglessness of the universe makes the human condition absurd.

Nevertheless, even though the world is not all we want, it is enough. We have no touchstone for values but we can create values through our choices, acting on our *feelings* and investing life with meaning. Although god is absent and we are left with "total responsibility in total solitude," we can still act passionately to create the type of person and existence we desire. The universe is senseless and nothing can tell us which acts to choose, but the experience of living can be exquisite nonetheless.

Camus is the most brilliant of the existentialists in describing the celebration of life in the face of its absurdity, especially in his philosophic essay *The Myth of Sisyphus*.

The Myth of Sisyphus*

The gods had condemned Sisyphus to ceaselessly rolling a rock to the top of a mountain, whence the stone would fall back of its own weight. They had though with some reason that there is no more dreadful punishment than futile and hopeless labor.

. . .

You have already grasped that Sisyphus is the absurd hero. He *is*, as much through his passions as through his torture. His scorn of the gods, his hatred of death, and his passion for life won him that unspeakable penalty in which the whole being is exerted toward accomplishing nothing. This is the price that must be paid for the passions of this earth. Nothing is told us about Sisyphus in the underworld. Myths are made for the imagination to breathe life into them. As for this myth, one sees merely the whole effort of a body straining to raise the huge stone, to roll it and push it up a slope a hundred times over; one sees the face screwed up, the cheek tight against the stone, the shoulder bracing the clay-covered mass, the foot wedging it, the fresh start with arms outstretched, the wholly human security of two earth-clotted hands. At the very end of his long effort measured by skyless space and time without depth, the purpose is achieved. Then Sisyphus watches the stone

* Reprinted with permission from Albert Camus, *The Myth of Sisyphus and Other Essays*, trans. Justin O'Brien (New York: Alfred Knopf, 1975), 119, 120–21, 123.

rush down in a few moments toward that lower world whence he will have to push it up again toward the summit. He goes back down to the plain.

It is during that return, that pause, that Sisyphus interests me. A face that toils so close to stones is already stone itself! I see that man going back down with a heavy yet measured step toward the torment of which he will never know the end. That hour like a breathing-space which returns as surely as his suffering, that is the hour of consciousness. At each of those moments when he leaves the heights and gradually sinks toward the lairs of the gods, he is superior to his fate. He is stronger than his rock.

If this myth is tragic, that is because its hero is conscious. Where would his torture be, indeed, if at every step the hope of succeeding upheld him? The workman of today works every day in his life at the same tasks, and this fate is no less absurd. But it is tragic only at the rare moments when it becomes conscious. Sisyphus, proletarian of the gods, powerless and rebellious, knows the whole extent of his wretched condition: it is what he thinks of during his descent. The lucidity that was to constitute his torture at the same time crowns his victory. There is no fate that cannot be surmounted by scorn.

· · ·

All Sisyphus' silent joy is contained therein. His fate belongs to him. His rock is his thing. Likewise, the absurd man, when he contemplates his torment, silences all the idols. In the universe suddenly restored to its silence, the myriad wondering little voices of the earth rise up. Unconscious, secret calls, invitations from all the faces, they are the necessary reverse and price of victory. There is no sun without shadow, and it is essential to know the night. The absurd man says yes and his effort will henceforth be unceasing. If there is a personal fate, there is no higher destiny, or at least there is but one which he concludes is inevitable and despicable. For the rest, he knows himself to be the master of his days. At that subtle moment when man glances backward over his life, Sisyphus returning toward his rock, in that slight pivoting he contemplates that series of unrelated actions which becomes his fate, created by him, combined under his memory's eye and soon sealed by his death. Thus, convinced of the wholly human origin of all that is human, a blind man eager to see who knows that the night has no end, he is still on the go. The rock is still rolling.

I leave Sisyphus at the foot of the mountain! One always finds one's burden again. But Sisyphus teaches the higher fidelity that negates the gods and raises rocks. He too concludes that all is well. This universe henceforth without a master seems to him neither sterile not futile. Each atom of that stone, each mineral flake of that night-filled mountain, in itself forms a world. The struggle itself toward the heights is enough to fill a man's heart. One must imagine Sisyphus happy.

Seriousness, Anguish, and Sharing Freedom

A decided joy and purpose then can be projected into life, but in order to live an authentic existence certain steps must be taken. According to Sartre we must first renounce the *spirit of seriousness* (*l'esprit de sérieux*). Seriousness is the tendency to seek a frame of reference in the world rather than accepting the freedom to construct our lives. He referred to Karl Marx as *"le prince des gens serieux"* because he is the epitome of the person who looks for a point of departure in "matter." Marx wanted to root himself in the reason for things and, by finding a justifiable cause, to belong in the world. But there is no external justification for our commitments and it is "bad faith" to behave as though there were. We are "doomed to ultimate failure" if we pretend that certain ways of living are superior or certain values are really worthwhile. In point of fact "it makes little difference whether a man is a drunkard or a leader of nations."[12]

In addition we must accept the *anguish* that free choice entails, which means the full weight of responsibility for choosing a model for others to follow as well as ourselves. For we never act in a vacuum but always in the sight of other people almost as though we were spotlighted on stage, and our audience is always affected by our behavior. Although we choose in the void, arbitrarily and without any objective standard, yet our choice has repercussions for all mankind. "In creating the man that we want to be," Sartre writes we "create an image of man as we think he ought to be . . . nothing can be good for us without being good for all." This realization, that we are responsible to others as well as ourselves for our choices, causes us acute anguish in our freedom.

Finally, we must be prepared to *share our freedom* with our fellow man, for human life is terrible enough without our obstructing one another. As part of the human condition, we live with the chilling sense of our own mortality, an underlying anxiety at our eventual annihilation, and this should induce a comradship among all human beings. Everyone wants to live as fully as possible in the brief time allowed by the biological clock and each person's efforts to absorb experience and express emotions should be eased and respected. Soon enough our consciousness will be extinguished, and we will slip into a state of nonbeing in which freedom will cease altogether.

Aside from these qualifications, we should strive to maximize our existence, to commit ourselves to our projects and interests so that our lives gain meaning. Without expecting to find acts that are valuable to choose, we should make acts valuable by choosing them, thereby increasing and defining our essence throughout our existence. The more we become engaged with life (*un homme engagée*) the more fully we exist and as we make these free commitments we create ourselves like veritable gods.

The following selection from Sartre's famous essay *The Humanism of Existentialism*, is often considered to be a definitive, concise account of the existential philosophy. In addition to *Being and Nothingness* previously mentioned, Sartre's philosophical works include *Existentialism and Human Emotions, The Imagination*, and *Critique of Dialectical Reasonings*.

The Humanism of Existentialism*

I should like on this occasion to defend existentialism against some charges which have been brought against it.

First, it has been charged with inviting people to remain in a kind of

*Reprinted with permission from Jean-Paul Sartre, *The Humanism of Existentialism*, trans. Bernard Frechtman (New York: Philosophical Library, 1947), 31–49.

desperate quietism because, since no solutions are possible, we should have to consider action in this world as quite impossible. We should then end up in a philosophy of contemplation; and since contemplation is a luxury, we come in the end to a bourgeois philosophy. The communists in particular have made these charges.

On the other hand, we have been charged with dwelling on human degradation with pointing up everywhere the sordid, shady, and slimy, and neglecting the gracious and beautiful, the bright side of human nature; for example, according to Mlle. Mercier, a Catholic critic, with forgetting the smile of the child. Both sides charge us with having ignored human solidarity, with considering man as an isolated being. The communists say that the main reason for this is that we take pure subjectivity, the Cartesian *I think*, as our starting point; in other words, the moment in which man becomes fully aware of what it means to him to be an isolated being; as a result, we are unable to return to a state of solidarity with the men who are not ourselves, a state which we can never reach in the *cogito*.

From the Christian standpoint, we are charged with denying the reality and seriousness of human undertakings, since, if we reject God's commandments and the eternal verities, there no longer remains anything but pure caprice, with everyone permitted to do as he pleases and incapable, from his own point of view, of condemning the points of view and acts of others.

I shall today try to answer these different charges. Many people are going to be surprised at what is said here about humanism. We shall try to see in what sense it is to be understood. In any case, what can be said from the very beginning is that by existentialism we mean a doctrine which makes human life possible and, in addition, declares that every truth and every action implies a human setting and a human subjectivity.

As is generally known, the basic charge against us is that we put the emphasis on the dark side of human life. Someone recently told me of a lady who, when she let slip a vulgar word in a moment of irritation, excused herself by saying, "I guess I'm becoming an existentialist." Consequently, existentialism is regarded as something ugly; that is why we are said to be naturalists; and if we are, it is rather surprising that in this day and age we cause so much more alarm and scandal than does naturalism, properly so called. The kind of person who can take in his stride such a novel as Zola's *The Earth* is disgusted as soon as he starts reading an existentialist novel; the kind of person who is resigned to the wisdom of the ages — which is pretty sad — finds us even sadder. Yet, what can be more disillusioning than saying "true charity begins at home" or "a scoundrel will always return evil for good"?

We know the commonplace remarks made when this subject comes up, remarks which always add up to the same thing: we shouldn't struggle against the powers-that-be; we shouldn't resist authority; we shouldn't try to rise above our station; any action which doesn't conform to authority is romantic; any effort not based on past experience is doomed to failure; experience shows that man's bent is always toward trouble, that there must be a strong hand to hold him in check, if not, there will be anarchy. There are still people who go on mumbling these melancholy old saws, the people who say, "It's only human!" whenever a more or less repugnant act is pointed out to them, the people who glut themselves on *chansons realistes*; these are the people who accuse existentialism of being too gloomy, and to such an extent that I wonder whether they are complaining about it, not for its pessimism, but much rather its optimism. Can it be that what really scares them in the doctrine I shall try to present here is that it leaves to man a possibility of choice? To answer this question, we must re-examine it on a strictly philosophical plane. What is meant by the term *existentialism?*

Most people who use the word would be rather embarrassed if they had to explain it, since, now that the word is all the rage, even the work of a musician or painter is being called existentialist. A gossip columnist in *Clartés* signs himself *The Existentialist*, so that by this time the word has been so stretched and has taken on so broad a meaning, that it no longer means anything at all. It seems that for want of an advanced-guard doctrine analogous to surrealism, the kind of people who are eager for scandal and flurry turn to this philosophy which in other respects does not at all serve their purposes in this sphere.

Actually, it is the least scandalous, the most austere of doctrines. It is intended strictly for specialists and philosophers. Yet it can be defined easily. What complicates matters is that there are two kinds of existentialists; first, those who are Christian, among whom I would include Jaspers and Gabriel Marcel, both Catholic; and on the other hand the atheistic existentialists among whom I class Heidegger, and then the French existentialists and myself. What they have in common is that they think that existence precedes essence, or, if you prefer, that subjectivity must be the starting point.

Just what does that mean? Let us consider some object that is manufactured, for example, a book or a paper-cutter: here is an object which has been made by an artisan whose inspiration came from a concept. He referred to the concept of what a paper-cutter is and likewise to a known method of production, which is part of the concept, something which is, by and large, a routine. Thus, the paper-cutter is at once an object produced in a certain way and, on the other hand, one having a specific use; and one can not postulate a man who produces a paper-cutter but does not know what it is used for. Therefore, let us say that, for the paper-cutter, essence — that is, the ensemble of both the production routines and the properties which enable it to be both produced and defined — precedes existence. Thus, the presence of the paper-cutter or book in front of me is determined. Therefore, we have here a technical view of the world whereby it can be said that production precedes existence.

When we conceive God as the Creator, He is generally thought of as a superior sort of artisan. Whatever doctrine we may be considering, whether one like that of Descartes or that of Leibniz, we always grant that will more or less follows understanding or, at the very least, accompanies it, and that when God creates He knows exactly what He is creating. Thus, the concept of man in the mind of God is comparable to the concept of a paper-cutter in the mind of the manufacturer, and, following certain techniques and a conception, God produces man, just as the artisan, following a definition and a technique, makes a paper-cutter. Thus, the individual man is the realization of a certain concept in the divine intelligence.

In the eighteenth century, the atheism of the *philosophers* discarded the idea of God, but not so much for the notion that essence precedes existence. To a certain extent, this idea is found everywhere; we find it in Diderot, in

Voltaire, and even in Kant. Man has a human nature; this human nature, which is the concept of the human, is found in all men, which means that each man is a particular example of a universal concept, man. In Kant, the result of this universality is that the wild-man, the natural man, as well as the bourgeois, are circumscribed by the same definition and have the same basic qualities. Thus, here too the essence of man precedes the historical existence that we find in nature.

Atheistic existentialism, which I represent, is more coherent. It states that if God does not exist, there is at least one being in whom existence precedes essence, a being who exists before he can be defined by any concept, and that this being is man, or, as Heidegger says, human reality. What is meant here by saying that existence precedes essence? It means that, first of all, man exists, turns up, appears on the scene, and, only afterwards, defines himself. If man, as the existentialist conceives him, is indefinable, it is because at first he is nothing. Only afterward will he be something, and he himself will have made what he will be. Thus, there is no human nature, since there is no God to conceive it. Not only is man what he conceives himself to be, but he is also only what he wills himself to be after this thrust toward existence.

Man is nothing else but what he makes of himself. Such is the first principle of existentialism. It is also what is called subjectivity, the name we are labeled with when charges are brought against us. But what do we mean by this, if not that man has a greater dignity than a stone or table? For we mean that man first exists, that is, that man first of all is the being who hurls himself toward a future and who is conscious of imagining himself as being in the future. Man is at the start a plan which is aware of itself, rather than a patch of moss, a piece of garbage, or a cauliflower; nothing exists prior to this plan; there is nothing in heaven; man will be what he will have planned to be. Not what he will want to be. Because by the word "will" we generally mean a conscious decision, which is subsequent to what we have already made of ourselves. I may want to belong to a political party, write a book, get married; but all that is only a manifestation of an earlier, more spontaneous choice that is called "will." But if existence really does precede essence, man is responsible for what he is. Thus, existentialism's first move is to make every man aware of what he is and to make the full responsibility of his existence rest on him. And when we say that a man is responsible for himself, we do not only mean that he is responsible for his own individuality, but that he is responsible for all men.

The word subjectivism has two meanings, and our opponents play on the two. Subjectivism means, on the one hand, that an individual chooses and makes himself; and, on the other, that it is impossible for man to transcend human subjectivity. The second of these is the essential meaning of existentialism. When we say that man chooses his own self, we mean that every one of us does likewise; but we also mean by that in making this choice he also chooses all men. In fact, in creating the man that we want to be, there is not a single one of our acts which does not at the same time create an image of man as we think he ought to be. To choose to be this or that is to affirm at the same time the value of what we choose, because we can never choose evil. We always choose the good, and nothing can be good for us without being good for all.

If, on the other hand, existence precedes essence, and if we grant that we exist and fashion our image at one and the same time, the image is valid for everybody and for our whole age. Thus, our responsibility is much greater than we might have supposed, because it involves all mankind. If I am a workingman and choose to join a Christian trade-union rather than be a communist, and if by being a member I want to show that the best thing for man is resignation, that the kingdom of man is not of this world, I am not only involving my own case—I want to be resigned for everyone. As a result, my action has involved all humanity. To take a more individual matter, if I want to marry, to have children; even if this marriage depends solely on my own circumstances or passion or wish, I am involving all humanity in monogamy and not merely myself. Therefore, I am responsible for myself and for everyone else. I am creating a certain image of man of my own choosing. In choosing myself, I choose man.

This helps us understand what the actual content is of such rather grandiloquent words as anguish, forlornness, despair. As you will see, it's all quite simple.

First, what is meant by anguish? The existentialists say at once that man is anguish. What that means is this: the man who involves himself and who realizes that he is not only the person he chooses to be, but also a lawmaker who is, at the same time, choosing all mankind as well as himself, can not help escape the feeling of his total and deep responsibility. Of course, there are many people who are not anxious; but we claim that they are hiding their anxiety, that they are fleeing from it. Certainly, many people believe that when they do something, they themselves are the only ones involved, and when someone says to them, "What if everyone acted that way?" they shrug their shoulders and answer, "Everyone doesn't act that way." But really, one should always ask himself, "What would happen if everybody looked at things that way?" There is no escaping this disturbing thought except by a kind of double-dealing. A man who lies and makes excuses for himself by saying "Not everybody does that," is someone with an uneasy conscience, because the act of lying implies that a universal value is conferred upon the lie.

Anguish is evident even when it conceals itself. This is the anguish that Kierkegaard called the anguish of Abraham. You know the story: an angel has ordered Abraham to sacrifice his son; if it really were an angel who has come and said, "You are Abraham, you shall sacrifice your son," everything would be all right. But everyone might first wonder, "Is it really an angel, and am I really Abraham? What proof do I have?"

There was a madwoman who had hallucinations; someone used to speak to her on the telephone and give her orders. Her doctor asked her, "Who is it who talks to you?" She answered, "He says it's God." What proof did she really have that it was God? If an angel comes to me, what proof is there that it's an angel? And if I hear voices, what proof is there that they come from heaven and not from hell, or from the subconscious, or a pathological condition? What proves that they are addressed to me? What proof is there that I have been appointed to impose my choice and my conception of man on humanity? I'll never find any proof or sign to convince me of that. If a voice addresses me, it is always for me to decide that this is the angel's voice; if I consider that such an act is a good one, it is I who will choose to say that it is good rather than bad.

Now, I'm not being singled out as an Abraham, and yet at every moment I'm obliged to perform exemplary acts. For every man, everything happens as if all mankind had its eyes fixed on him and were guiding itself by what he does. And every man ought to say to himself, "Am I really the kind of man who has the right to act in such a way that humanity might guide itself by my actions?" And if he does not say that to himself, he is masking his anguish.

There is no question here of the kind of anguish which would lead to quietism, to inaction. It is a matter of a simple sort of anguish that anybody who has had responsibilities is familiar with. For example, when a military officer takes the responsibility for an attack and sends a certain number of men to death, he chooses to do so, and in the main he alone makes the choice. Doubtless, orders come from above, but they are too broad; he interprets them, and on this interpretation depend the lives of ten or fourteen or twenty men. In making a decision he can not help having a certain anguish. All leaders know this anguish. That doesn't keep them from acting; on the contrary, it is the very condition of their action. For it implies that they envisage a number of possibilities, and when they choose one, they realize that it has value only because it is chosen. We shall see that this kind of anguish, which is the kind that existentialism describes, is explained, in addition, by a direct responsibility to the other men whom it involves. It is not a curtain separating us from action, but is part of action itself.

When we speak of forlornness, a term Heidegger was fond of, we mean only that God does not exist and that we have to face all the consequences of this. The existentialist is strongly opposed to a certain kind of secular ethics which would like to abolish God with the least possible expense. About 1880, some French teachers tried to set up a secular ethics which went something like this: God is a useless and costly hypothesis; we are discarding it; but, meanwhile, in order for there to be an ethics, a society, a civilization, it is essential that certain values be taken seriously and that they be considered as having an *a priori* existence. It must be obligatory, *a priori*, to be honest, not to lie, not to beat your wife, to have children, etc., etc. So we're going to try a little device which will make it possible to show that values exist all the same, inscribed in a heaven of ideas, though otherwise God does not exist. In other words — and this, I believe, is the tendency of everything called reformism in France — nothing will be changed if God does not exist. We shall find ourselves with the same norms of honesty, progress, and humanism, and we shall have made of God an outdated hypothesis which will peacefully die off by itself.

The existentialist, on the contrary, thinks it very distressing that God does not exist, because all possibility of finding values in a heaven of ideas disappears along with Him; there can no longer be an *a priori* Good, since there is no infinite and perfect consciousness to think it. Nowhere is it written that the Good exists, that we must be honest, that we must not lie; because the fact is we are on a plane where there are only men. Dostoevsky said, "If God didn't exist, everything would be possible." That is the very starting point of existentialism. Indeed, everything is permissible if God does not exist, and as a result man is forlorn, because neither within him nor without does he find anything to cling to. He can't start making excuses for himself.

If existence really does precede essence, there is no explaining things away by reference to a fixed and given human nature. In other words, there is no determinism, man is free, man is freedom. On the other hand, if God does not exist, we find no values or commands to turn to which legitimize our conduct. So, in the bright realm of values, we have no excuse behind us, not justification before us. We are alone, with no excuses.

That is the idea I shall try to convey when I say that man is condemned to be free. Condemned, because he did not create himself, yet, in other respects is free; because, once thrown into the world, he is responsible for everything he does. The existentialist does not believe in the power of passion. He will never agree that a sweeping passion is a ravaging torrent which fatally leads a man to certain acts and is therefore an excuse. He thinks that man is responsible for his passion.

The existentialist does not think that man is going to help himself by finding in the world some omen by which to orient himself. Because he thinks that man will interpret the omen to suit himself. Therefore, he thinks that man, with no support and no aid, is condemned every moment to invent man. Ponge, in a very fine article, has said, "Man is the future of man." That's exactly it. But if it is taken to mean that this future is recorded in heaven, that God sees it, then it is false, because it would really no longer be a future. If it is taken to mean that, whatever a man may be, there is a future to be forged, a virgin future before him, then this remark is sound. But then we are forlorn.

To give you an example which will enable you to understand forlornness better, I shall cite the case of one of my students who came to see me under the following circumstances: his father was on bad terms with his mother, and, moreover, was inclined to be a collaborationist; his older brother had been killed in the German offensive of 1940, and the young man, with somewhat immature but generous feelings, wanted to avenge him. His mother lived alone with him, very much upset by the half-treason of her husband and the death of her older son; the boy was her only consolation.

The boy was faced with the choice of leaving for England and joining the Free French Forces — that is, leaving his mother behind — or remaining with his mother and helping her to carry on. He was fully aware that the woman lived only for him and that his going-off — and perhaps his death — would plunge her into despair. He was also aware the every act that he did for his mother's sake was a sure thing, in the sense that it was helping her to carry on, whereas every effort he made toward going off and fighting was an uncertain move which might run aground and prove completely useless; for example, on his way to England he might, while passing through Spain, be detained indefinitely in a Spanish camp; he might reach England or Algiers and be stuck in an office at a desk job. As a result, he was faced with two very different kinds of action: one, concrete, immediate, but concerning only one individual; the other concerned an incomparably vaster group, a national collectivity, but for that very reason was dubious, and might be interrupted en route. And, at the same time, he was wavering between two kinds of ethics. On the one hand, an ethics of sympathy, of personal devotion; on the other, a broader ethics, but one whose efficacy was more dubious. He had to choose between the two.

Who could help him choose? Christian doctrine? No. Christian doctrine says, "Be charitable, love your neighbor, take the more rugged path, etc., etc." But which is the more rugged path? Whom should he love as a brother? The fighting man or his mother? Which does the greater good, the vague act of fighting in a group, or the concrete one of helping a particular human being to go on living? Who can decide *a priori*? Nobody. No book of ethics can tell him. The Kantian ethics says, "Never treat any person as a means, but as an end." Very well, if I stay with mother, I'll treat her as an end and not as a means; but by virtue of this very fact, I'm running the risk of treating the people around me who are fighting, as means; and, conversely, if I go to join those who are fighting, I'll be treating them as an end, and, by doing that, I run the risk of treating my mother as a means.

If values are vague, and if they are always too broad for the concrete and specific case that we are considering, the only thing left for us is to trust our instincts. That's what this young man tried to do; and when I saw him, he said, "In the end, feeling is what counts. I ought to choose whichever pushes me in one direction. If I feel that I love my mother enough to sacrifice everything else for her—my desire for vengeance, for action, for adventure—then I'll stay with her. If, on the contrary, I feel that my love for my mother isn't enough, I'll leave."

But how is the value of a feeling determined? What gives his feeling for his mother value? Precisely the fact that he remained with her. I may say that I like so-and-so well enough to sacrifice a certain amount of money for him, but I may say so only if I've done it. I may say "I love my mother well enough to remain with her" if I have remained with her. The only way to determine the value of this affection is, precisely, to perform an act which confirms and defines it. But, since I require this affection to justify my act, I fine myself caught in a vicious circle.

On the other hand, Gide has well said that a mock feeling and a true feeling are almost indistinguishable; to decide that I love my mother and will remain with her, or to remain with her by putting on an act, amount somewhat to the same thing. In other words, the feeling is formed by the acts one performs; so, I can not refer to it in order to act upon it. Which means that I can neither seek within myself the true condition which will impel me to act, nor apply to a system of ethics for concepts which will permit me to act. You will say, "At least, he did go to a teacher for advice." But if you seek advice from a priest, for example, you have chosen this priest; you already knew, more or less, just about what advice he was going to give you. In other words, choosing your adviser is involving yourself. The proof of this is that if you are a Christian, you will say, "Consult a priest." But some priests are collaborating, some are just marking time, some are resisting. Which to choose? If the young man chooses a priest who is resisting or collaborating, he has already decided on the kind of advice he's going to get. Therefore, in coming to see me he knew the answer I was going to give him, and I had only one answer to give: "You're free, choose, that is, invent." No general ethics can show you what is to be done; there are no omens in the world. The Catholics will reply, "But there are." Granted—but, in any case, I myself choose the meaning they have.

When I was a prisoner, I knew a rather remarkable young man who was a Jesuit. He had entered the Jesuit order in the following way: he had had a number of very bad breaks; in childhood, his father died, leaving him in poverty, and he was a scholarship student at a religious institution where he was constantly made to feel that he was being kept out of charity; then, he failed to get any of the honors and distinctions that children like; later on, at about eighteen, he bungled a love affair; finally, at twenty-two he failed in military training, a childish enough matter, but it was the last straw.

This young fellow might well have felt that he had botched everything. It was a sign of something, but of what? He might have taken refuge in bitterness or despair. But he very wisely looked upon all this as a sign that he was not made for secular triumphs, and that only the triumphs of religion, holiness, and faith were open to him. He saw the hand of God in all this, and so he entered the order. Who can help seeing that he alone decided what the sign meant?

Some other interpretation might have been drawn from this series of setbacks; for example, that he might have done better to turn carpenter or revolutionist. Therefore, he is fully responsible for the interpretation. Forlornness implies that we ourselves choose our being. Forlornness and anguish go together.

As for despair, the term has a very simple meaning. It means that we shall confine ourselves to reckoning only with what depends upon our will, or on the ensemble of probabilities which make our action possible. When we want something, we always have to reckon with probabilities. I may be counting on the arrival of a friend. The friend is coming by rail or street-car; this supposes that the train will arrive on schedule, or that the street-car will not jump the track. I am left in the realm of possibility; but possibilities are to be reckoned with only to the point where my action comports with the ensemble of these possibilities, and no further. The moment the possibilities I am considering are not rigorously involved by my action, I ought to disengage myself from them, because no God, no scheme, can adapt the world and its possibilities to my will. When Descartes said, "Conquer yourself rather than the world," he meant essentially the same thing.

The Marxists to whom I have spoken reply, "You can rely on the support of others in your action, which obviously has certain limits because you're not going to live forever. That means: rely on both what others are doing elsewhere to help you, in China, in Russia, and what they will do later on, after your death, to carry on the action and lead it to its fulfillment, which will be the revolution. You even *have* to rely upon that, otherwise you're immoral." I reply at once that I will always rely on fellow-fighters insofar as these comrades are involved with me in a common struggle, in the unity of a party or a group in which I can more or less make my weight felt; that is, one whose ranks I am in as a fighter and whose movements I am aware of at every moment. In such a situation, relying on the unity and will of the party is exactly like counting on the fact that the train will arrive on time or that the car won't jump the track. But, given that man is free and that there is no human nature for me to depend on, I can not count on men whom I do not know by relying on human goodness or man's concern for the good of society. I don't know what will become of the Russian revolution; I may make an example of it to the extent that at the present time it is apparent that the proletariat plays a part in Russia that it plays in no other nation. But

I can't swear that this will inevitably lead to a triumph of the proletariat. I've got to limit myself to what I see.

Given that men are free and that tomorrow they will freely decide what man will be, I can not be sure that, after my death, fellow-fighters will carry on my work to bring it to its maximum perfection. Tomorrow, after my death, some men may decide to set up Fascism, and the others may be cowardly and muddled enough to let them do it. Fascism will then be the human reality, so much the worse for us.

Actually, things will be as man will have decided they are to be. Does that mean that I should abandon myself to quietism? No. First, I should involve myself; then, act on the old saw, "Nothing ventured, nothing gained." Nor does it mean that I shouldn't belong to a party, but rather that I shall have no illusions and shall do what I can. For example, suppose I ask myself, "Will socialization, as such, ever come about?" I know nothing about it. All I know is that I'm going to do everything in my power to bring it about. Beyond that, I can't count on anything. Quietism is the attitude of people who say, "Let others do what I can't do." The doctrine I am presenting is the very opposite of quietism, since it declares, "There is no reality except in action." Moreover, it goes further, since it adds, "Man is nothing else than his plan; he exists only to the extent that he fulfills himself; he is therefore nothing else than the ensemble of his acts, nothing else than his life."

According to this, we can understand why our doctrine horrifies certain people. Because often the only way they can bear their wretchedness is to think, "Circumstances have been against me. What I've been and done doesn't show my true worth. To be sure, I've had no great love, no great friendship, but that's because I haven't met a man or woman who was worthy. The books I've written haven't been very good because I haven't had the proper leisure. I haven't had children to devote myself to because I didn't find a man with whom I could have spent my life. So there remains within me, unused and quite viable, a host of propensities, inclinations, possibilities, that one wouldn't guess from the mere series of things I've done."

Now, for the existentialist there is really no love other than one which manifests itself in a person's being in love. There is no genius other than one which is expressed in works of art; the genius of Proust is the sum of Proust's works; the genius of Racine is his series of tragedies. Outside of that, there is nothing. Why say that Racine could have written another tragedy, when he didn't write it? A man is involved in life, leaves his impress on it, and outside of that there is nothing. To be sure, this may seem a harsh thought to someone whose life hasn't been a success. But, on the other hand, it prompts people to understand that reality alone is what counts, that dreams, expectations, and hopes warrant no more than to define a man as a disappointed dream, as miscarried hopes, as vain expectations. In other words, to define him negatively and not positively. However, when we say, "You are nothing else than your life," that does not imply that the artist will be judged solely on the basis of his works of art; a thousand other things will contribute toward summing him up. What we mean is that a man is nothing else than a series of undertakings, that he is the sum, the organization, the ensemble of the relationships which make up these undertakings.

Evaluation

Existentialism is an extraordinarily honest philosophy, frightening in its honesty perhaps, but what we do not like to hear may still be true. It certainly deserves praise for affirming the worth of human life in a universe described as wholly unconcerned and devoid of justice or pity. (Pascal wrote "What am I? Unto the universe, nothing; unto myself, everything!") And existentialism deserves credit for showing us how responsible we are for the values we elect and embody despite our rationalizations that we could not do otherwise. Its insights into such psychological states as forlornness, anguish, and despair are also commendable and it is especially renowned for its analysis of the human condition and the distinction between objects and human beings.

1. However, despite these achievements and its appealing colorfulness, many critics think that the existentialist position is extreme and not well founded. To begin with, Sartre and other existentialists claimed that human beings are *entirely* responsible for their choices, their character, and their lives. This seems to be an exaggeration at best, for we cannot ignore the effect of a person's biological inheritance and environmental circumstances. Perhaps these factors are not "determinants" but surely they limit the range of our choices. The person living at a starvation level in a backward village in sub-Sahara Africa does not have the same chance in his "project toward self" that the affluent Frenchman would have; neither does the physically handicapped child in the ghetto. Even with regard to the development of character traits such as courage or cowardice there can be what the law calls "diminished responsibility" because of the surrounding conditions.

It is all well and good to say that man is totally free and accountable for what he becomes but in actual terms that seems overly severe and unrealistic. Human beings may not have their essence fully formed at birth, so that they merely express their innate qualities during their lifetime, but neither do people choose themselves entirely, "invent man" at every instant of existence.

2. As a related point, existentialists are also criticized for contradicting themselves with regard to human nature. On the one hand, they maintain there is no such thing as human nature, and on the other, they describe various characteristics of humanness. A purely formal aspect of this criticism is that if man has no essence then not having an essence must be essential to him, but the main objection centers round the notion of freedom and consciousness. These capabilities are ascribed to man as necessary elements, without which he would not be human. But then they are part of the essence of the human being and man, in fact, has a nature.

The existentialist tries to defend himself by claiming that freedom and consciousness are the given foundation on which the person's essence is built, but this may be a distinction without a difference; it does seem as though they are thought necessary to being human. For didn't Sartre say that we cannot refrain from the exercise of our freedom and that if we relinquish consciousness to achieve the plenitude of objects then we lose our humanness?

To make matters worse, the existentialists Gabriel Marcel and Karl Jaspers refer to man's basic need to establish social communication, and the theologian Soren Kierkegaard affirms man's essentially sinful nature. In fact, Kierkegaard believes that man is doomed to despair because of the forces within him and that the only way out of fear and trembling is through commitment to god.

All of this suggests that the idea of human nature is very much alive in existential thought while at the same time the existentialists are busy denying it. Perhaps the idea of innate tendencies or dispositions is considered an intolerable encumberance to man's development, and yet in elaborating their philosophy the existentialists are forced to admit that certain features are present in man.

3. The very strong emphasis given to freedom of action in existential thinking is another cause for concern. Not all the existentialists tell us to share our freedom with others as Sartre (and Camus) did, but there is a pervasive sense that since god is dead everything is permissible. Friedrich Nietzsche's hard code of the superman (the *Übermensch*) has already been mentioned, and Nietzsche explicitly rejected the values of democratic equality and Christian compassion; only the courageous, free, willful act matters. In *The Joyful Wisdom* Nietzsche wrote "The greatest fruitfulness and the greatest enjoyment of existence is: to live dangerously" and "make war." Similarly, in *Crime and Punishment* Dostoevsky had the principal character, Raskolnikov, kill a pawnbroker woman with an axe, mainly to prove to himself that he is an extraordinary person, above society's arbitrary rules.

Andre Gide, in *The Vatican Cellars*, had one man throw another out of a train as a spontaneous, unpremeditated act, the truest expression of the individual's real self. Jean Gênet's books, such as *The Thief's Journal* and *Our Lady of the Flowers*, are full of brutal homosexuality and criminal actions (for which Gênet himself was jailed repeatedly). And on an even more sinister note, Martin Heidegger endorsed the Nazi cause, welcoming it as the fulfillment of his ideal.

Such ininhibited freedom is closer to license than responsible action, giving us a vicious world of moral anarchy. It is freedom gone wild, extolling the individual at the expense of humanity.

4. Finally, implied in the above criticism is the existentialist rejection of any objective moral standards. It holds that values are created not discovered, that an action gains its worth by virtue of the fact that we choose it. But that would mean that murdering people with an axe or throwing them out of trains would be valuable if it were authentically chosen. Surely such a position is morally repulsive and carries subjectivism to the point of absurdity.

The same objection therefore applies to existentialism as to scientific humanism, that it fails to recognize the possibility of having an objective, secular morality without the existence of a deity. As we have seen, objectivism in ethics has a great deal to recommend it and subjectivism can lead to the nonsensical point where worthless actions are judged worthwhile. An action is not right because we choose it but rather we should choose an action because it is right.

On the positive side we can appreciate existentialism mainly for stressing that each individual must assume responsibility for his own life, deciding in the void (with no assurances from the cosmos) what character he wants to have. "Total responsibility in total solitude" is a hard saying but it can be viewed as strong and invigorating. If we are alone then we should have the courage to make those choices that will maximize our existence.

Notes

1. John Calvin, *Institutes of the Christian Religion* (Philadelphia: Presbyterian Board, 1928), 681.
2. Jonathan Edwards, "God Glorified in Man's Dependence," in *The Development of American Philosophy*, eds. Walter Muelder and Laurence Sears (Boston: Houghton Mifflin, 1940), 19, 22.
3. Erich Fromm, *Man for Himself* (New York: Holt Rinehart and Winston, 1947), 78. Fromm has been variously classified as a self-realizationist, humanistic psychologist, and existentialist.
4. The encyclical was issued by Pope Pius XI. I owe this example to Corliss Lamont in his *The Philosophy of Humanism*.
5. Corliss Lamont, *Humanism as a Philosophy* (New York: Philosophical Library, 1949), 21 ff.
6. See David Ehrenfeld, *The Arrogance of Humanism* (New York: Oxford University Press, 1978) and William Barrett, *The Illusion of Technique* (Garden City, N. Y.: Anchor Books, 1978).
7. Compare John Dewey's *Human Nature and Conduct* and Warner Fite's *Individualism* (Lecture III).
8. T. E. Hill, *Contemporary Ethical Theories* (New York: Macmillan, 1957), 187–88.
9. Although existentialism is largely an atheistic movement it has strongly influenced theologians such as Martin Buber (1878–1965) in his celebrated *I and Thou* and Paul Tillich (1886–1965) in *The Courage to Be*. Karl Barth, Emile Brunner, and Rudolf Bultmann also are strongly indebted to existentialism, especially to Kierkegaard. Sometimes St. Augustine's *Confessions* and Pascal's *Pensées* are classified as existential in outlook.
10. Jean-Paul Sartre, *Nausea*, trans. Lloyd Alexander (New York: New Directions, 1964), 126–29.
11. Jean-Paul Sartre, *Being and Nothingness*, trans. Stuart Gilbert (New York: Philosophical Library, 1965), 708 ff.
12. Jean-Paul Sartre, ibid., 722.

Bibliography

ARON, RAYMOND. *Marxism and the Existentialists*. New York: Harper & Row, 1965.
AUER, J. A. C. FAGGINGER. *Humanism States Its Case*. Boston: Beacon Press, 1933.
————. *Humanism and Theism*. Ames: Iowa State University Press, 1981.
BARNES, HAZEL E. *An Existentialist Ethics*. New York: Alfred Knopf, 1967.
BARRETT, WILLIAM. *Irrational Man*. Garden City, N.Y.: Anchor, 1958.
————. *What Is Existentialism?* New York: Grove Press, 1964.
BLACKHAM, H. J., ED. *Objection To Humanism*. London: Constable, 1963.
————. *Humanism*. Hammondsworth, England: Penguin, 1968.
BRÉE, GERMAINE. *Camus and Sartre: Crisis and Commitment*. New York: Delacorte Press, 1972.
BREISACH, ERNST. *Introduction to Modern Existentialism*. New York: Grove Press, 1962.
CAMUS, ALBERT. *The Myth of Sisyphus and Other Essays*, trans. Justin O'Brien. New York: Alfred Knopf, 1975.
DOSTOEVSKY, FEODOR. *Notes From Underground*, trans. Constance Garnett. New York: Macmillan, 1957.
DAKIN, ARTHUS H. *Man the Measure: Essay on Humanism as Religion*. Princeton, N.J.: Princeton University Press, 1939.

DEWEY, JOHN. *A Common Faith*. New Haven: Yale University Press, 1934.

FRANKEL, CHARLES. *The Case for Modern Man*. New York: Harper's, 1956.

FROMM, ERICH. *Man for Himself*. New York: Rinehart, 1947.

——. *Socialist Humanism*. Garden City, N.Y.: Doubleday, 1966.

GILMORE, MYRON PIPER. *The World of Humanism, 1453–1517*. New York: Harper, 1952.

HARTSHORNE, CHARLES. *Beyond Humanism*. Chicago: Willett, Clark, 1937.

HAWTON, HECTOR. *The Humanist Revolution*. London: Barrie and Rockliff, 1963.

HEIDEGGER, MARTIN. *An Introduction to Metaphysics*, trans. Ralph Mannheim. Garden City, N.Y.: Doubleday, 1957.

HEINEMANN, FREDERICK. *Existentialism and the Modern Predicament*. New York: Harper & Row, 1958.

HUXLEY, JULIAN. *Religion Without Revelation*. New York: Harper's, 1957.

——, ED. *The Humanist Frame*. New York: Harper & Row, 1962.

JAEGER, WERNER. *Humanism and Theology*. Milwaukee: Marquette University Press, 1967.

JASPERS, KARL. *The Perennial Scope of Philosophy*, trans. Ralph Mannheim. New York: Philosophical Library, 1949.

——. *Man in the Modern Age*, trans. Eden Paul and Cedar Paul. New York: Doubleday, 1957.

KAUFMANN, WALTER, ED. *Existentialism from Dostoevsky to Sartre*. Cleveland: Meridian Books, 1956.

KEYSER, C. J. *Humanism and Science*. New York: Columbia University Press, 1931.

KIERKEGAARD, SOREN. *Fear and Trembling and The Sickness Unto Death*, trans. Walter Lowrie. New York: Doubleday, 1954.

KINGSTON, FREDRICH TEMPLE. *French Existentialism: A Christian Critique*. Toronto: University of Toronto Press, 1968.

KNIGHT, MARGARET, ED. *Humanist Anthology: From Confucius to Bertrand Russell*. London: Barrie and Rockliff, 1963.

KOESTENBAUM, PETER. *The Vitality of Death: Essays in Existential Philosophy and Psychology*. Westport, Conn.: Greenwood Publishing, 1971.

KURTZ, PAUL, ED. *The Humanist Alternative*. Buffalo, N.Y.: Prometheus Books, 1973.

——. *Moral Problems in Contemporary Society*. Buffalo, N.Y.: Prometheus Books, 1973.

——. *In Defense of Secular Humanism*. Buffalo, N.Y.: Prometheus Books, 1983.

LAMONT, CORLISS. *Humanism as a Philosophy*. New York: Philosophical Library, 1949.

MARCEL, GABRIEL. *Man Against Mass Society*, trans. G. S. Fraser. Chicago: Gateway, 1962.

——. *Being and Having*, trans. Katherine Farrer. New York: Harper & Row, 1965.

MOLINA, FERNANDO. *Existentialism as Philosophy*. Englewood Cliffs, N.J.: Prentice-Hall, 1962.

NIETZSCHE, FRIEDRICH. *Beyond Good and Evil*, trans. Walter Kaufmann. New York: Vintage Books, 1966.

OLSON, ROBERT. *An Introduction to Existentialism*. New York: Dover Publications, 1962.

POTTER, CHARLES FRANCIS. *Humanism: A New Religion*. New York: Simon and Schuster, 1930.

REESE, CURTIS. *The Meaning of Humanism*. Boston: Beacon Press, 1945.

RUSSELL, BERTRAND. "A Free Man's Worship." In *Mysticism and Logic*. London: Longmans, Green, 1919.

——. *Why I Am Not a Christian*. New York: Simon and Schuster, 1957.

SANBORN, PATRICIA F. *Existentialism*. New York: Pegasus, 1968.

SARTRE, JEAN-PAUL. *Being and Nothingness*, trans. Hazel Barnes. New York: Philosophical Library, 1956.

STORER, MORRIS B., ED. *Humanist Ethics*. Buffalo, N.Y.: Prometheus Books, 1980.

PART III

Endnote

Deciding Between Life Purposes

Having examined numerous theories as to what constitutes a worthwhile reason for living we may feel more confused than enlightened. There are many more options that we might have imagined and each appears to have appealing parts as well as serious defects. How is one to decide among the welter of possibilities which should be taken as the ideal life?

We began our study with the problem of relativism and our inclination at this point might be to return to square one and declare "everything is relative." Out of confusion or frustration we might feel that knowledge (including judgments of value) is whatever our culture decides is true at the time, and whatever we think of as good *is* good because we think so.

A number of contemporary philosophers have taken this position, reaffirming the point of view of Greek thinkers such as Gorgias and Thrasymachus. They have clothed their relativism in modern dress, finding new reasons for ancient ideas. For example, the continental "textualist" Michel Foucault argued that the interpretation of texts, whether literary or social, is not a matter of understanding their true meaning. Rather, different interpretations are made at different times according to the phenomenon of "power."

Foucault did not mean necessarily the military power of the state but something far more subtle and pervasive. He claimed, for example, that in the modern age the very structure of our thinking has been determined by the power mode of the human sciences. By continually monitoring, categorizing, and grading human behavior, science constructs a particular type of interpretive mesh through which texts are viewed. All interpretation is arbitrary, the consequence of power modes, and in the twentieth century power manifests itself through a structure of "permissions and exclusions" that cause us to judge behavior as normal or abnormal. We lay this grid over our interpretation of texts but the power framework functions in an even wider sense: it permeates the mental outlook of the interpreter, structuring his very self and determining his judgment of social systems.[1]

From a different direction Richard Rorty dismissed claims of achieving genuine truth by arguing that objectivity is only "a property of theories which, having been thoroughly discussed, are chosen by a consensus of rational discussants" and "never anything more than an expression of the presence of, or the hope for, agreement among inquirers."[2] He believed that philosophy should give up notions such as "truth," "seeing rightly," and "correspondence to reality" and recognize that we can have no confidence in the idea of knowledge. Truth is not "contact with reality" but "social practice" and that "which is good for us to believe." This is a clear return to the Sophists.

In his philosophical "hermeneutics" Hans-Georg Gadamer reached the same sceptical conclusions from still another vantage point. To his mind, language determines our theory of the world and "all thinking is confined to language, as a limit as well as a possibility." He did not think that our understanding of experience is expressed in language but "what is said [that is, language] constitutes the common world in which we live."[3] Genuine knowledge of external reality cannot be achieved; we are confined to the web of symbols in our understanding.

A great many other voices could be added to the chorus but we can only refer to some of these contemporary thinkers here and touch on their claims. In any case they do not help our problem but only exacerbate it, and we are looking for a solution so that we do not throw up our hands in despair. These ancient ghosts have come back to haunt us but the basic foundation of all ethical inquiry is that genuine moral knowledge is in fact possible.

One criterion that has traditionally been used by philosophers to decide between alternative theories is the *standard of reasonableness*. According to this approach a theory is considered sound if it (1) is consistent within itself and with regard to its implications, (2) takes the relevant facts into account and does not contradict those facts, and (3) provides the most probable interpretation of human experience. Examples of cases where each of these points was violated will help illustrate and explain them.

1. It would be inconsistent to claim, for instance, that all events occur according to inevitable laws of fate *and* at the same time to maintain that people can be held responsible for what they do. Such a position has been taken at various points in intellectual history by theologians such as St. Augustine, Martin Luther, and Soren Kierkegaard. All of them claimed that divine providence governed all occurrences in the universe yet human beings were still accountable for their behavior and deserved to be rewarded or punished for their actions. To explain the inexplicable they declared it to be a mystery.[4]

However, it makes no sense to claim that man is responsible for his actions if everything he does is predestined. In the chapter on determinism we discussed the problem of whether man is free if god is thought to foresee all choices, and that may be an arguable issue. But if a person's actions are foreordained then he has no freedom of choice and cannot be held responsible for what happens. "I could not help it" is a complete excuse, for no one is liable for what is beyond his control.

The position is therefore inconsistent and for that reason should be rejected as unreasonable.

2. As an illustration of the way in which the second point can been violated, we will take Plato's assertion that "virtue is knowledge." Presumably Plato meant that virtuous behavior is an automatic consequence of moral knowledge and immorality is the result of ignorance concerning morality. It was his view that no one who knows what is right would deliberately do what is wrong. All wrongdoing is due to people mistaking what is right, rather like a child who eats

too much dessert not realizing that it will give him a stomache ache. With understanding, one naturally performs correct actions. Moral education, Plato thought, will ensure a moral society, for whoever has knowledge of virtue will act in accordance with it.

However, Plato did not seem to have taken the relevant facts into account. In actual life, human beings will do what is wrong with full knowledge of its wrongness. Out of a desire for personal advantage or through moral weakness people will not listen to their "conscience"; they will act as they want not as they ought. Even if the action is wrong only for themselves, in the sense of being personally harmful, they will sometimes do it anyway, for as Freud has shown us, our need to punish ourselves for breaking social rules can lead to self-destructive behavior. Whenever we are hurt there is a certain relief at having atoned for so much.

Plato cannot be blamed for not having read Freud but he can be criticized for failing to notice that people do harm others with full awareness of their wrong-doing. By ignoring this obvious truth he neglected something highly relevant and perhaps contradicted these facts of human behavior altogether. In that respect therefore his position is not reasonable.

3. An example of a theory that violates the third point can be found in the doctrine of a retributive universe. This is the belief that a system of retribution operates in the world so that we are naturally rewarded for our good deeds and automatically punished when we do wrong.

People who endorse this view experience the weight of their guilt very strongly and feel that their wrongdoings will be punished by lawful powers that govern the universe. Usually this power is identified as god but it need not be; a general moral force or a mechanical system of rewards and punishments could be thought responsible for all joy and suffering. Whatever force the moral system is attributed to, these people believe that one reaps what one sows, and when disaster strikes it is due to some transgression on their part. What have I done to deserve this? is a familiar reaction when sickness strikes or when people find themselves caught up in some natural catastrophe. It is the cry of Job in the bible, an upright and god-fearing man who suffered a series of disasters appar-ently through no fault of his own, and it is the response of Everyman who experiences tragedy and searches for his personal sins that brought the punish-ment down upon his head.

But if we examine this retributive doctrine it does not seem an accurate explanation as to why good or bad events occur. For there does not seem to be any correlation between people's sinfulness and the amount of suffering they undergo or their virtuousness and their blessings. Some people who are essen-tially good will experience one accident or illness after another while some awful people have amazing luck, getting through life virtually unscathed.

In short, the universe is not necessarily fair; there is no evidence to support the idea that bad people suffer and good people prosper. The rain seems to fall on the just and the unjust alike. There may be justice in a heaven and hell, and we strive for justice in our human institutions, but in the natural world people do not necessarily get what they deserve.

A more probable reason as to why someone was the victim of an earthquake or volcanic eruption is that they happened to be at the wrong place at the wrong time, at that point on the earth where the catastrophe occurred. This explanation is more likely than that they were terrible sinners. Similarly, the reason people become ill with poliomyelitis or leukemia, for example, has to do with microrganisms that happen to be present in their bodies; it is not an indication of their moral character.

The retributive theory therefore does not offer the most probable interpretation of human experience and cannot be regarded as plausible.

Using the standard of reasonableness then, we have an effective instrument for examining the various theories of a worthwhile life to see which is most defensible, and it does not seem as if this standard is the product of "power," "consensus of discussants," or mere "language." As we have seen throughout our study, not all theories are equally valid in terms of the strength of their support. We can argue about which is truly best but at least we have a standard against which to measure their worth; we do not have to conclude that one person's opinion is as good as another's. Not everyone will be in agreement as to which idea is finest but there can be a common reference point for resolving disagreements, namely, the reasonableness of the position that is advanced. We can then engage in a dialogue and think our ideas through, testing our beliefs according to canons of consistency, factual basis, and interpretive power. In this way we can arrive at a respectable conclusion, something we can trust because it is reasonable and therefore justifiable.

This is the approach that has been used throughout the book in evaluating the various life ideals from the Cyrenaics to the Existentialists, and as a result we are not left empty handed. Rather, we are now equipped to judge the major reasons for living with a certain logical skill and an awareness of the various alternatives that exist. We know the considerations that apply in building and criticizing a theory, and the coherent and systematic reasoning it must exhibit. Therefore, we have not gone round in circles, passing through "the same door wherein we went," as Omar Khayyam said, but in upward spirals, and at this point we have the capability of reaching an intelligent decision with regard to our own lives.

In reaching this decision we cannot expect certainty; the world is not like that, especially the world of moral ideals. However it is possible to reach a defensible and worthwhile conclusion by the rational methods that have been described. As Bertrand Russell said, "We must act vigorously without absolute certainty," and knowing our options and how to judge them can give us that foundation for action, our basic reason for living.

Notes

1. See Michel Foucault, *Power/Knowledge: Selected Interviews and Other Writings 1972–77*, ed. and trans. Colin Gordon (New York: Pantheon Books, 1980). Jurgen Habermas expresses a parallel notion in his *Legitimation Crisis* when he describes modernization as the "colonization of the lifeworld" by administrative-political and economic subsystems.
2. Richard Rorty, *Philosophy and the Mirror of Nature* (Princeton, N.J.: Princeton University Press, 1979), 338 and 335.

3. Hans-Georg Gadamer, *Philosophical Hermeneutics*, ed. and trans. David Linge (Berkeley: University of California Press, 1977), 127 and 65.

4. See St. Augustine, *The City of God*, trans. M. Dods (Buffalo, 1887), vol. 1: 39; Martin Luther, *The Bondage of the Will*, trans. H. Cole (Grand Rapids, Mich.: William Erdmans, 1931), sec. 25: 72–74, and Sec. 26: 76–79; and Soren Kierkegaard, *Fear and Trembling and The Sickness Unto Death*, trans. W. Lowrie (New York: Doubleday, 1954), passim.

Index